economic growth

ECONOMIC GROWTH

HENRY Y. WAN, JR.   Cornell University

HARCOURT BRACE JOVANOVICH, INC.
New York   Chicago   San Francisco   Atlanta

ISBN: 0–15–518793–7
Library of Congress Catalog Card Number: 71–141611

Printed in the United States of America

to Simone

preface

This volume has developed from my lecture notes of the past few years for my course on economic growth. Used in its entirety, it may serve as the main text for a half-year course within a graduate macroeconomics sequence. By concentrating on the key chapters and sections, the instructor can easily adapt the material to a ten-week lecture series. Since the exposition is relatively nontechnical and the coverage encompasses divergent theories, the book is also suitable as a reference for advanced undergraduate students. For the same reasons it can be useful as supplementary reading for the general economist who desires a bird's-eye view of the field of economic growth. The essential background for the reader is two years of undergraduate economics plus one year of calculus.

For those specializing in growth theory, this book should prove to be a valuable road map for their own expeditions into the original articles and books. For such students, no textbook, however perfect, can be substituted for their own spadework. But since the present growth literature is voluminous, technical, and variegated—while at the same time rather vague on the motivations of the model building, the justification of various assumptions, and the policy implications of the final conclusion—this textbook will help to develop an overview of the forest rather than a delineation of the trees.

When I first embarked on this writing, nothing suitable existed as either a textbook for the graduate student or a handbook for the nonspecialist. In recent years, some excellent surveys, readings, monographs, and textbooks have appeared, each excelling in its own area. However, none serves the same purpose as the present volume—to convey those deep issues underlying (and dividing) the full spectrum of theories to the broadest audience in the simplest possible terms.

The theory of growth is an expanding field. It thrives on controversy; it matures on constant innovation; its ultimate success or failure rests on its pragmatic utility and relevance. It defies synthesis; it is given perspective only when all the contending views are reported. Elegant model formulation and brilliant mathematical manipulations are assets to a book on growth theory, but they are secondary to the economic content embodied therein. On this content alone we focus our full attention.

To maximize the expository power of my material, I have resorted to certain expediencies. Whenever graphic depictions can convey the subject matter, algebraic derivations are relegated to footnotes and appendixes. I have even omitted lengthy and highly technical proofs of certain propositions, after referring to the original sources. The essence of the text is accessible to students who have taken one year of calculus. However, a mathematical appendix summarizes analytical tools which will lead to a deeper understanding of the subject by those whose mathematical training is somewhat more advanced.

Where the latest developments were not included in the main text, end-of-chapter problems have been constructed to cover them.

For those who want to skip and scan the text material, this volume offers a built-in flexibility. The Introduction and Chapters 1 and 2 (with the exception of the final section of Chapter 2) are necessary preliminary reading for the remainder of the book. Chapter 9 (again minus the last section) should be read before Chapters 10 and 11. Those interested in the core matter of growth (or in a short ten-week course) should read the Introduction and Chapter 1 in their entirety and may then conclude with Chapters 2, 4, and 8 through 11 minus their respective final sections.

Space does not permit the inclusion of the following subjects: (1) dynamic input-output analysis; (2) optimal growth models of the dynamic programming type; and (3) economic growth under uncertainty. The first two areas have been analyzed by Morishima, Radner, and others. The third promises to be the most important in the future. Work has been done in this area by Phelps, Srinivasan-Levhari, Hahn, Stigum, and, most recently, Mirman.

I wish to acknowledge the help I have received from many quarters. W. J. Baumol, E. D. Domar, J. Robinson, E. S. Phelps, K. Shell, and R. M. Solow kindly read and commented upon the manuscript at various stages. L. Wegge made many valuable suggestions in reading the galley proof. Mrs. Flora Ayres, Mrs. Shirley Kelly, and Mrs. Arlene Martin provided expert typing services in preparing the text. Dr. Simone Clemhout, my wife, spent hundreds of hours improving the exposition and discussing its contents. Needless to say, the author has the unique responsibility for all shortcomings of the final product.

Henry Y. Wan, Jr.

contents

economic growth

introduction

GENERAL REMARKS

The theory of economic growth has been one of the fastest growing branches of economics over the past dozen years. Large sections of our profession, as well as most of the current graduate students, find it increasingly difficult to keep abreast of the snowballing literature. This is due partly to the subject matter: deep micro theorems are often involved in an essentially macro area, while challenging mathematics and a fast-growing body of prerequisite concepts, along with a proliferation of contending assumptions and nonuniform symbols, exact their tolls from the readers of the more recent articles. Partly, this is also a result of the current state of the profession. Many of the most creative and productive economists write only articles, and the scarcity of space in professional journals encourages the terse crystallization of highly analytical results—at the expense of the free expression of the authors' motivations, points of view, and conjectures. What is assumed to be obvious and is therefore left unsaid among the experts is often highly important to the understanding of the novice. The existing survey articles, such as those by Matthews and Hahn [1], are no substitute for the original source material, whereas such books as those by Meade [2] and Hicks [3] are designed to be vehicles to transmit the personal approaches of their respective authors rather than to be compendia of accepted doctrines. This leaves the beginners (who are the least able to skip and scan) the unpalatable choice between depth and breadth. Sometimes they may attain neither.[1] To bridge the gap is the aim of this book.

WHAT IS GROWTH THEORY?

The theory of economic growth, like the theories of trade cycles and inflation, deals with the dynamic (time) paths of macroeconomic variables. Unlike cycle theory, growth theory concentrates only on long-run trends. Unlike inflation theory, growth theory does not concentrate exclusively on price phenomena. The distinction between growth theory and cycle theory should not be over-

---

[1]The appearance of *Readings in the Modern Theory of Economic Growth* [4], edited by Stiglitz and Uzawa, is a great help to the students. However, any "selected readings" has to limit itself to a restrictive choice of the literature. Moreover, readers must still reconcile the different symbols and assumptions to obtain an integrated picture.

emphasized. Certain economists, with reason, maintain that growth is possible only by intermittent spurts, when one bottleneck is broken through and the next has not yet become restrictive. Others, with equally convincing argument, contend that the principal cause of cycles is growth.

This still leaves the difference between growth theory and development theory unmentioned. Basically, developing economies operate under different "regimes" than already developed economies, just as ordinary physics and cryogenics are directed to different sets of environments.

Growth theory, in the most widely used sense, is focused toward the "regime" of developed economies. *Development theory* aims at both the workings of a developing economy and the critical transformation process that may metamorphose a developing economy into a developed economy.

From the above discussions, we may synthesize a working definition: *The theory of economic growth studies the trend of the time paths for macroeconomic variables in developed economies.*

TYPES OF GROWTH THEORY

Like other areas of economics, the field of growth can be subdivided into the "positive" and the "normative" branches. Positive growth theory studies how the world *will* grow. Normative growth theory studies how the world *should* grow. The former is usually called "growth theory" in the narrow sense, and the greater part of the latter is usually called "optimal growth theory." The former describes a forecast growth pattern, given specific parametric values and functional forms contained in the formulation. The latter prescribes an optimal growth pattern, given similar data.

The growth pattern for an economy includes the movement of the whole system of prices, quantities, stocks, and flows throughout time. In order to gain insight into the problem, usually we concentrate on one or more aspects of the growth process at a time.

1. Momentary equilibrium. In standard economic parlance, an *equilibrium* is a position capable of repeating itself, provided perhaps that certain data are conceptually held as given. Like a single frame in a documentary film, a *momentary* equilibrium can be understood only by recognizing the impetus of certain movements over time. A snapshot showing an athlete clearing the hurdle does not indicate zero gravitation on earth; it reveals the cumulate momentum of the athlete's movement at the instant the photograph was taken. Similarly, the momentary equilibrium of a growing economy is basically different from a stationary state in a stagnating economy. Kinematic forces play a dominant role at each and every instant. That the concept of equilibrium is relevant here is shown by the snapshot example: the athlete can duplicate the feat, given the same data—his momentum, the wind velocity, etc.

2. The dynamic paths. The evolution of an economy also may be traced throughout its hypothetical history. The time paths of certain key variables or functions thereof (ratio, difference, sum, etc.) are placed under meticulous scrutiny. This is like the referee examining the photofinish of a close race. Attention is zeroed in on the time sequence of one or two objects at a time.

3. The dynamic equilibrium. A dynamic equilibrium is a dynamic path in which no variable (e.g., factor supplies) is arbitrarily held constant, yet certain economic variables (e.g., commodity and service prices) and the ratios or limiting ratio between other economic variables (e.g., capital/output ratio, the marginal product of capital) take self-perpetuating values. This is more general than either the concept of *stationarity*, in which all variables (output and capital and labor inputs) assume constant values, or the concept of *balanced* growth, in which outputs, capital, and labor grow at identical rates. An example is the *golden-age equilibrium*, in which every quantity other than labor grows at a rate faster than labor, although the qualitative improvement of the labor force always makes up such a difference. The *existence*, the *uniqueness*, and the *stability* (i.e., the tendency of the system to return to a path when sidetracked) of a dynamic equilibrium often attract the attention of growth economists.

4. Asymptotic and catenary properties. Let the term *horizon* stand for that time interval with which one is concerned. Growth problems can be of either the finite-horizon or the infinite-horizon variety.

(a) Asymptotic behavior for infinite-horizon problems. In the infinite-horizon case, if, starting from a given position, the further one proceeds (back-tracks) in time the closer a dynamic path approaches a dynamic equi-librium, then such an equilibrium is the asymptote of the said path.

(b) Catenary behavior of finite-horizon problems. In the finite-horizon case, suppose that whenever the horizon is of sufficient length, the sojourn time over which the dynamic path passes within any given distance of certain dynamic equilibrium approaches 100% of the whole horizon; then the dynamic path is said to exhibit a catenary behavior with respect to the dynamic equilibrium.

5. Comparative dynamics. By varying systematically either the starting points (the so-called initial condition) of the economy or the functional relationships involved in the dynamic system or certain parameters, one can generate a family of dynamic paths together with the corresponding family of asymptotes, etc. The study of the relationships between the perturbations (i.e., variations) and the responses is called *comparative dynamics*.

Each of these five categories may be illustrated by empirical problems:

The momentary equilibrium: What is the effect of a high growth rate on the wage level? on the profit share? on per capita consumption?

The dynamic path: Will the chronic rise of the capital/labor ratio lead to capital saturation, or will it taper off into a sustainable growth equilibrium? Is the slowing down of the Soviet growth rate an approach to the long-run dynamic equilibrium, or is it a switch to a different path (due to, say, increased resource allocations to consumption sectors)? What are the theoretical con-sequences of aging industrial plants (as emphasized by Lamfalussy years ago)?

The dynamic equilibrium path: Are the constancies of the capital/output ratio and the wage/profit shares unverified myths, statistical coincidences, or theoretical necessities?

The asymptotic/catenary properties: Is the development of heavy industry sectors an optimal strategy to attain the greatest increase of living standards in the long run?

Comparative dynamics: What are the most effective means to induce speedy technical progress? What accounts for the wide country-to-country variations in observed growth rates? What are the consequences of the automation movement?

So far we have discussed the precise growth patterns predicted by the "positive" theories or prescribed by the "normative" theories. There also exist dynamic efficiency criteria which are normative in nature yet stop short of recommending any one specific growth pattern. Without defining precisely what constitutes social welfare, these criteria state that as long as the social welfare is positively associated with such and such magnitudes (e.g., per capita consumption), then certain categories of growth patterns must not be allowed to exist. For example, the Phelps-Koopmans theorem shows the inadvisability of excessive capital accumulation (i.e., when marginal product of capital is reduced to levels forever lower than the population growth rate by at least some constant margin).

A BROAD HISTORICAL SKETCH

The subject of economic growth has attracted the attention of economists since classical times. Adam Smith, D. Ricardo, T. R. Malthus, and many others have discussed this topic. However, their treatments are, at least in the light of present-day knowledge, frequently incomplete in scope, oversimplified in formulation, and defective in reasoning. Also, the informal, literal form of their arguments and their reliance on implicit assumptions make the interpretation of their writings a difficult and controversial undertaking. The mainstream of classical growth theory culminated in the writing of J. S. Mill. The work of Karl Marx bears some family resemblance to the classical school, yet it has not received general acceptance in its central theme—the absolute impoverishment of the workers together with a falling profit rate.

From 1870 to 1920, economists generally refrained from offering ambitious explanations for the entire span of economic history. Detailed microanalysis increased at the expense of the sweeping theories of the "magnificent dynamics" of the earlier age. During this period both the partial equilibrium approach of Marshall and the general equilibrium approach of Walras came into full blossom. The theories of capital and interest also made great advances in the hands of Bohm-Bawerk, Clark, Wicksell, Fisher, and others. Capital accumulation does enter into the economic fluctuation models of Aftalion, Hayek, and Kalecki, but in such models the emphasis is not on the long-run trend. All in all, few tried to develop a theory that could explain the growth of the whole national economy and yet be tested and evaluated with available statistics.

The revival of interest in macroeconomic growth theories is due mainly to the macroaggregate analysis of Keynes and the "Keynesians." While Keynesian economics emphasizes the short-run problems of depression or stagnation, the rehabilitation of the honor of "heroic aggregation" encouraged the studies of Harrod and Domar. Long-run growth problems were reinvestigated in forms both more rigorous and more statistically testable than the classical works.

However, such works are crucially dependent upon the essential constancy of the capital/output and capital/labor ratios. This drawback was remedied by Solow. Like Tobin and Swan, Solow built a model of economic growth without assuming fixed proportions between capital and labor inputs and output. But unlike them, his theoretical model is aimed, to a large degree, at statistical testing. In fact, it is the combination of the aggregate growth theory (as revived by Harrod and Domar) and the statistical estimation of the aggregate production function (initiated by Paul Douglas) that distinguishes his work and conditions his approach.

The use of an aggregate production function in growth theory has met with strong objections from a number of British economists, such as Mrs. Robinson and Kaldor, who point out the treacherous nature of the concepts of both the aggregate production function and the quantity of capital. Solow agrees with their criticism on theoretical grounds, but they do not seem to be able either to offer a rigorous substitute which can be statistically estimated or to explain the general trend of an economy in simple and unequivocal terms.

Starting from the micro theory of capital and interest, Samuelson points out that under certain conditions a surrogate capital can be computed so that the Solovian aggregate production function can be rigorously justified. Starting from the macro theory side, Solow and others have constructed a series of models which either successively approximate reality or can be econometrically estimated or numerically simulated. However, if growth theories are to be useful in quantitative policy making, some degree of aggregation cannot be avoided. The crucial question is not whether misleading results can theoretically arise or not. The answer is always affirmative to such a query. Such aggregate models stand or fall only on their empirical goodness of fit, for which no amount of analytical discussion can be substituted. A good analogy is the Keynesian assumption of a linear aggregate consumption function. Its validity defies theoretical justification under convincingly realistic assumptions, but it has been vindicated statistically as an operationally fruitful approximation to reality.

Optimal growth theory is so far a rather heterogeneous field. In his trail-blazing paper of 1927, Ramsey, established the first utility-maximizing optimal growth model. Von Neumann offered his model on maximal rate of balanced growth in 1935. The adaptation of this model to the efficient capital accumulation model was first proposed by Dorfman, Samuelson, and Solow (DOSSO for short) as the "turnpike theorem". Gale, Radner, Morishima, and McKenzie ruled out certain exceptions to that theorem in the early 1960s. About the same time, Phelps and Swan independently discovered the so-called golden rule of growth, where among all the exponential growth paths (at the same rate) the one with the highest per capita consumption is chosen. Subsequently, the golden rule path was found to be an asymptotic path to certain Ramsey problems. The plethora of optimal growth models offer a range of possible policies, each pertaining to a type of specific policy goal. However, there exist much milder welfare criteria which should be satisfied by all types of optimal growth paths. These are the DOSSO conditions for capital accumulation and the Malinvaud and the Phelps-Koopmans conditions for utility maximization.

THE ESSENCE OF GROWTH THEORY

We may now pause to consider a few questions that presumably intrigue many nonspecialists, and venture to offer some tentative answers.

1. What is the impact of growth theory on other fields? From the earliest days, many writers on economic matters were interested in general, dynamic changes of an enduring nature. Static analysis and comparative static studies are partial answers to long-run dynamic problems that are dear to the hearts of most economists. Growth theory is neither a passing fancy nor a special, albeit precocious, field. It may be considered as an approach or viewpoint which is bound to revolutionize diverse areas of economics in a manner comparable to the role played by quantum theory or the theory of relativity in physics. To cite a few examples, the works of Samuelson, Diamond, and Cass and Yaari have clarified the significant roles played by money in intergenerational allocation; the studies of Tobin, Patinkin, and others cast monetary policy in an entirely new light. The model of Oniki and Uzawa constitutes the first satisfactory treatment of the interactions between trade and investment. The work by Malinvaud and the Phelps-Koopmans theorem indicate that static welfare analysis can be relevant in the dynamic context only after major modifications. Growth theory not only introduces new results into each of the fields mentioned, it also invalidates old results due to the dynamic aspects of its scope.

2. Which types of growth theory are most relevant for nonspecialists? The various types of growth models that have arisen in the past dozen years represent neither a duplication of effort nor an obsolescence of the older models. The refinement and precision of more recent, disaggregate models complement the power and sweep of earlier, simpler versions. The relevance of a model depends upon the specific purpose at hand. Analogously, moon-trained telescopes continue to play their role even though astronauts have brought back the first moon rock for the microscope.

3. Why are growth models so involved and mathematical? Any growth path involves levels of a given quantity at infinitely many points of time. A growth model involves a price–quantity configuration (outputs, wages, etc.) which evolves throughout the time dimension. Hence, the inherent complexity of the problem requires considerable mathematical tools for its resolution. It may be noted that growth economists such as Solow and Tobin usually take great

ECONOMIC GROWTH

Sent at the request of:

Date **3-24-77**

R . SAVOIE

THE COLLEGE DEPARTMENT

SB

ECONOMIC GROWTH

by

Henry Y. Wan, Jr.

ERRATA

Exercise	Page and line		
1.1	p. 31, line 3	For	$Q < q < 1$
		read	$0 < q < 1$
3.1	p. 93, line 2	For	if v is
		read	if C' is
5.1	p. 183	For	$\hat{Q} = \dfrac{LF_L}{Q} \hat{L} = sF_k$
		read	$\hat{Q} - \dfrac{LF_L}{Q} \hat{L} = sF_k$
7.1	p. 242, line 18	For	Q
		read	Q_i
9.2	p. 293, line 6	For	$Q = nK + \dfrac{KL}{k + L}$
		read	$Q = nK + \dfrac{KL}{K + L}$
10.1	p. 343, line 16	For	$f(c) = k$
		read	$f(k) = k$
A.3	p. 424, line 21	For	solution of (a)-(i)
		read	solution of (a)-(ii)
A.4	p. 424, line 11 from bottom	For	e^t in the denominator of $$P(t) = \dfrac{1}{1+(1/P(0)-1)e^t}$$
		read	e^{-t}

pains to reduce a rigorous, technical argument to plain, intuitive English. The end product may still not be easy reading, reflecting, perhaps, that simple tools do not exist for discussing a not very simple topic.

4. What will growth theory lead to in the long run? At this moment, the evolution of business cycle theory into a more general theory of fluctuation and the development of both short-run and long-run growth models are tending to unify the entire field of macroeconomics. Eventually, the long view and the short, trend theory and fluctuation theory, will undoubtedly merge.

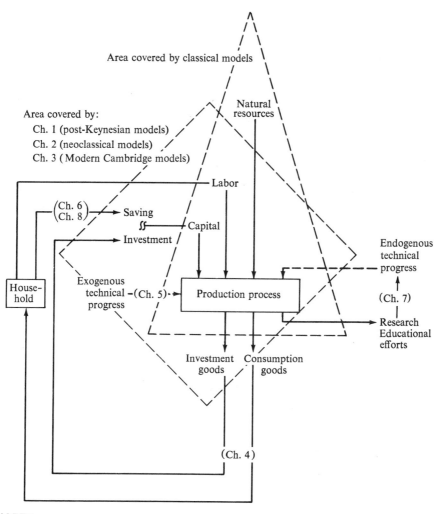

CHART 1

THE PLAN OF THE BOOK

Chart 1 is a schematic diagram of the relationships among the various aspects of macroeconomic theory, indicating the chapters in which these topics are discussed. In this diagram, the production process utilizes natural resources as well as the capital and labor inputs to produce various outputs according to the prevailing technology. Both labor and capital are supplied by the household. The outputs include consumption goods, investment goods, and research and education efforts. Technology may be affected by either exogenous or endogenous technical progress. Exogenous progress accrues at a rate unaffected by any factor within the economic system, whereas endogenous progress is influenced by the allocation of resources. The saving decision of the household, supported by the investment goods produced, decides capital accumulation.

The classical models emphasized the limitational role of land input upon production. The post-Keynesians (Harrod and Domar) shift emphasis to the interplay of saving decisions and production technology, as well as exogenous technical progress. That is the subject of Chapter 1. The neoclassical and modern Cambridge models in Chapters 2 and 3 also include all these elements. Chapter 4 covers disaggregation of outputs and capital goods. Chapter 5 concentrates on vintage capital goods, which result from exogenous technical progress, and Chapter 7 deals with endogenous technical progress, Chapters 6 and 8 investigate the saving decisions. Chapter 9 considers optimal growth in general. Chapters 10 and 11, respectively, deal with utility maximization (via consumption) and efficient capital accumulation.

REFERENCES

[1] Hahn, F. H., and R. C. O. Matthews, "The Theory of Economic Growth: A Survey," *Economic Journal*, vol. LXXIV, Dec. 1964, pp. 779–902.

[2] Meade, J. E., *A Neo-Classical Theory of Economic Growth*, Allen and Unwin, London, 1961.

[3] Hicks, John, *Capital and Growth*, Oxford University Press, Oxford, 1965.

[4] Stiglitz, Joseph E., and Hirofumi Uzawa, Eds., *Reading in the Modern Theory of Economic Growth*, M.I.T. Press, Cambridge, Mass., 1969.

1

the revival of growth theory: Post-Keynesian models

1.1 INTRODUCTION

The best way to appreciate the Harrod-Domar models is to consider their positions in the evolution of economic thought. The following observations are somewhat oversimplified and overdramatized. But by and large, they portray the Harrod-Domar models in their historical perspective.

Classical macrodynamics is like a Greek tragedy. The heroically aggregated model is preordained for the gloomy stationary state, which men foresee, may temporarily postpone, but can never permanently escape. As two centuries of continuous technical progress push the limits of natural resources ever backward, the Malthusian demon appears more and more like a scarecrow. Out of vogue, exit the classical theme. The Harrod-Domar theories also brought forth a cautious if not pessimistic message couched in macrodynamic terms. However, here the similarity ends. What haunted the Harrod-Domar world was not an inevitable and unkind fate lurking at some future date, but the potential revisitation of the traumatic, immediate past—the worst crisis in the entire history of capitalism, terminated only by six years of world-wide holocaust. Not through prodigal fecundity might the world come to grief, but because of excessive parsimony when the impetus of growth ricochets against the bounds of labor supply! So the virtue hailed by Adam Smith and the vice abhorred by Malthus interchanged their roles in the post-Keynesian days.

Although Harrod nursed the bud of dynamic theory [1] before the appearance of Keynes' *General Theory*, both Harrod and Domar developed their theories in reaction to Keynes. According to Harrod, Keynes neglected the reason for saving: to provide for the continuous growth of output. According to Domar, Keynes realized that accumulation of capital may depress its marginal efficiency, but he ignored the immediate effect of investment—the accumulation of physical capital goods.[1] Both Harrod and Domar carried over from Keynes the emphasis

[1] Keynes emphasized the "deepening" aspect: Each worker has more mechanized equipment to work with. Domar emphasized the "widening" aspect: Each worker is faced with more pieces of equipment of the same type.

on full employment, the break from marginalism, and the utilization of heroic aggregation to the highest degree. In fact, Harrod and Domar dispensed with the "marginal efficiency schedule" of Keynes—the last heritage of marginalism. Also, like Keynes, Harrod and Domar conducted their analysis solely in terms of national aggregates. This contrasts with the classical writings, where, now and then, more than one type of output invariably though parenthetically intrudes into the picture. Methodologically, Harrod and Domar reached the high water mark of aggregation. In pre-Keynesian days, the microeconomic analyses of Marshall, Walras, and others crowded macro variables into "departmental" economics (in the parlance of Harrod [2]), such as monetary economics and trade cycles. The arrival of aggregate national income accounting and the needs for policy making in depression and in war elevated macroeconomics (or "income theory") into a coequal of microeconomics (or "price theory").

The postwar prosperity eroded the awe economists held for depressions. The sources, the consequences, and the trend of growth in general became the objects of study of later growth theory, and the preoccupation with full employment receded to the background. The natural desire for generality and disaggregation led to the development of the neoclassical and the neo-Cambridge growth models. Pessimism and reserve are absent in these models, and both marginalism and certain degrees of disaggregation are back. However, one should never overlook the roles played by the works of Harrod and Domar and their similarities to the later models. Historically, Solow's first paper on growth grew out of a critique of Harrod and Domar. Moreover, aggregation had been the bench mark for growth models. A full-fledged *return* to the generalities of Walras would "leave the ordinary working economist . . . [to] flounder in the maze of $n \times r \times s$, etc., equations" (Harrod [2]).

We might venture to say that the works of Harrod and Domar and the earlier models of the neoclassical school (including the works of Solow) share the common feature of pragmatism. (This is also true regarding a model by Tinbergen [3].) The measurability of structural parameters and the applicability to policy issues dictate the forms their models take. Their efforts were never meant to be spent on purely intellectual exercises. The trend of growth theory in more recent years does not assure us that most participants still maintain this utilitarian *Weltanschauung*. Among the newer models, a smaller and smaller proportion have been tested or are designed to be testable. Of course, the round-about approach may still yield handsome fruits in the long run. But the prima-facie shift of emphasis appears to be food for thought.

To summarize the above observations, we may refer to Table 1.1.

Since both the Harrod model and the Domar model utilize the "income theory" approach which grew out of the Keynesian revolution, we shall call them post-Keynesian models. We will follow Hicks [4] in our review of such an approach. The general features of this method are as follows:

(1) The price system is fixed. This may be justified as follows:
(a) First there are the observations of Keynes. Money wage is downward

TABLE 1.1   EMPHASES

	Macro or micro	Dynamic or static	Pessimistic or optimistic	Pragmatical or theoretical
Classical growth models (–1850)	{Micro {Macro	{Static {Dynamic	Pessimistic	Pragmatical
{Neoclassical period (1850–1935) {Keynesian period	Micro Macro	Static Static	Optimistic Pessimistic	Theoretical }[a] Pragmatical }
Current growth models Post-Keynesian	Macro	Dynamic	Pessimistic	Pragmatical
Modern Cambridge	Macro	Dynamic	Optimistic	{Pragmatical {Theoretical
Neoclassical Early	Macro	Dynamic	Optimistic	Pragmatical
Recent	Macro	Dynamic	Optimistic	Theoretical

[a]Growth theory deemphasized.

inflexible over the entire underemployment range. The labor supply curve assumes the shape of a reversed letter L with the horizontal branch forming the relevant section (see Harrod [2]).

(b) Since the Anglo-Saxon countries have not been ravaged by runaway inflation in recent decades, a fixed price system serves as a good first approximation.

(2) At the existing prices, markets need not be cleared. The divergence between supply and demand is accommodated through the adjustment of buffer stocks. This assumption is highly realistic, and it is common in trade cycle models. Each period, the difference between the actual and desired stocks (however the latter is defined) is adjusted according to a certain decision rule. However, the specification of both the desired stock and the decision rule for adjustment plays a key role in the model. Yet there is scarcely any consensus about what constitutes a correct specification.

(3) Aggregation is carried to a high degree. As a result of a fixed system of relative prices, value weights are used to calculate aggregate output, aggregate labor, and aggregate capital.

(4) Fixed proportions are assumed between outputs and desired inputs. By postulating constant returns to scale and a fixed relative price system, a scale expansion (contraction) of the aggregate output can always be produced from input dosages scaled up (down) by the same factor.

(5) Some amount of unemployed resources is assumed to exist at all times. This is the companion assumption to perfectly elastic factor supplies, which underlie a constant price system.

Under such an approach, miscalculation is allowed and perfect foresight is not presumed. Expectation also enters into play in the specification of both the desired goals and the adjustment processes. Of necessity, such a formulation lacks the elegance and definiteness of the "price theory" approach used in most neoclassical growth models. Nonetheless, it is by no means inferior to its alternative from the methodological point of view. It is highly realistic.

The next two sections are devoted to the works of Harrod and Domar. Although the models of Harrod and Domar are usually regarded as equivalent, we shall see that this is far from the truth. Each has its own distinctive features.

1.2 HARROD

1.2.1. General remarks

Any economist attempting to summarize Harrod's work faces a twofold difficulty. First, his presentation is deliberately informal, as may be seen from the following quotations:

> These omissions were not accidental, but deliberate and the result of careful thought . . . . The omissions were due to the desire to achieve great *generality* . . . . ([5], p. 453)

> We must start with some generality however imperfect. We shall never go ahead if we remain in a world of trivialities and fine points ([6], pp. 80–81).

Most students today are used to precise models based upon assumptions not descriptively realistic. Harrod prefers "flexible" formulations to "achieve generality."

Then there is the protean structure of his writings. According to Harrod, the genesis of his dynamic concept occurred in 1934 [1] and it began to crystallize in 1936 [7]. Even if we start with his 1939 paper [8], its successive developments toward his 1963 view [9] span a twenty-four-year period and encompass one book [6] (in 1948), five articles (1939 [2], 1952 [12], 1959 [5], 1960 [11], 1963 [9]), and two notes (1951 [10], 1960 [11]). Symbols change and explanations vary. A plethora of variant equations becloud the fundamentals. Short of compiling a variorum version, the reader is likely to miss one subtle point or another.

These two difficulties complicate our understanding of two key components of the Harrod theory: the constancy of the capital/output ratio, and the adjustments initiated by the departure of actual investment from its desired levels. Harrod appears to offer too many reasons for the first and too little detail about the latter.

As it stands, we shall first state Harrod's conclusions and then search for conditions (consistent with Harrod's incomplete specification) under which they remain valid.

1.2.2. Harrod's conclusion

Synthesizing from the 1939 and 1948 versions of Harrod, we may state his main conclusions as follows:

(1) Through each initial position there exists a unique "equilibrium output path" (corresponding to any given saving/income ratio) along which output increases at a definite "warranted growth rate" (which equals the ratio of the saving propensity to unit capital requirement) such that:
  (a) Let alone, the entrepreneurs will be satisfied with this path, once they are on it.
  (b) The optimal capital/output ratio is uniquely determined along this path, given the interest rate and *labor-augmenting technical progress* (i.e., technical progress which has only one effect: one worker now can do the same job as $1 + \lambda$ workers one period ago, other things being equal).

(2) Any departure from the aforementioned path leads to even greater departures in the same direction.

(3) There exists an output ceiling itself growing at the "natural growth rate," i.e., the sum of the population growth rate and the labor-augmenting technical progress rate. If the warranted growth rate is higher than the natural growth rate, the economy can never move indefinitely along any "equilibrium path." Sooner or later a downward departure from the equilibrium path would lead to further departures according to conclusion (2).

(4) Supposing that the interest rate can be sufficiently reduced to affect an adequate increase of the capital/output ratio, then the excess of the warranted growth rate over the natural growth rate can be temporarily bridged so that the economy may conceivably continue to follow an equilibrium path. Once capital deepening (i.e., the increase of capital/output ratio) proceeds far enough, the warranted rate may become identical with the natural rate and the chronic Keynesian unemployment can be avoided. However, Harrod does not believe that the interest rate can decrease sufficiently to be of much help.

Points (1) and (3) represent Harrod's long-run view, while point (2) is his short-run analysis. Point (4) is an afterthought attached to his main theme. Summing up both the long run and short run, Harrod believes that if the economic system is left to itself, the long-run outlook is bleak, save for the fairy-tale chance of steady growth at full employment. The short-run mechanism is turbulent and disheartening: a chance downward displacement from the "warranted path" leads directly to a tailspin dive; a chance upward displacement leads to a foredoomed frantic upsurge head on into the insuperable output ceiling, only to be followed by a deflected crash. Harrod also stated that at the downswing the accelerator would not operate. Furthermore, replacement demand would eventually usher in the revival. But this is business-cycle theory on which we shall not elaborate. Suffice it to say that the economy is likely to suffer recurrent breakdowns.

Solow subsequently set up a version of the "Harrod-Domar model" under slightly different ground rules. This Solow version does not produce the diverging short-run adjustments arising from differences between the actual and the warranted growth rates. Nonetheless, the contrast between the warranted and natural growth rates was succinctly and definitively analyzed in a short subsection. Implications not included in the Harrod analysis were elucidated. For instance, Harrod regarded the excess of the natural rate over the warranted rate as conducive to "recurrent tendencies to develop boom conditions" except that too wide a difference of this type may "be of an inflationary and unhealthy character" ([6], p. 88). While this may follow from his short-run analysis, we know now, thanks to Solow, that this is the condition for a *labor surplus economy*! Point (4) above anticipated part of Solow's analysis, though Solow's treatment is more lucid. All these will be reviewed in the next chapter, when Solow's model is discussed.

1.2.3. Assumptions and proofs

A. ASSUMPTIONS

From Harrod's writings, we may distill five assumptions underlying the main theme:

(1) The level of *ex ante* aggregate saving is a constant proportion of aggregate income.

(2) The *overall* effect of technical progress is labor augmenting, or "neutral" in the Harrod sense. Suppose that the factor of increase of labor force is $1+n$ per period; then we may say that the increase of "efficiency labor" (i.e., the labor force in efficiency units) is at the rate of

$$
\begin{aligned}
n' &= (1+n)(1+\lambda)-1 \\
&= n+\lambda+n\lambda, \quad \text{where } \lambda \text{ is the labor-augmenting rate} \\
&\simeq n+\lambda, \quad \text{for small values of } n \text{ and } \lambda
\end{aligned}
$$

(3) The requirements for capital and (efficiency) labor per unit of (sustainable) output are constant. There exist alternative assumptions under which this assumption can be exactly or approximately justified. We shall return to this later.

(4) Constant returns to scale holds. This is only implied in the writings of Harrod.

(5) If investment *ex post* is justified in any period, the representative entrepreneur will (unless prevented by physical limitations) in the succeeding period increase the production in the same proportion as it has just been increased. If in one period investment *ex post* is less than the justified investment, entrepreneurs will in the next period increase the rate of growth of investment, and vice versa. (These constitute the so-called postulate A on p. 284 of *Economic Essays* [15]).

Assumptions (3) and (5) are most crucial, yet they were originally not spelled out in detail by Harrod. Note that assumption (3) implies assumption (4).

B. SYMBOLS AND EQUATIONS

Let:

$Q(t)$	be the aggregate output in period t
$Q^*(t)$	be the output along an equilibrium path
$K(t)$	be the aggregate capital input in period t
$L^D(t)$	be the aggregate labor input in period t
$L^S(t)$	be the aggregate labor supply
a	be the desired unit capital requirement
b	be the desired unit labor requirement
s	be the saving/income ratio
$S(t)$	be the aggregate saving at period t
$I(t)$	be the aggregate actual investment at t
$I^*(t)$	be the aggregate justified investment at t, which is the product of the actual increase in output and the desired unit capital requirement

Note that both L^D and L^S are measured in *efficiency units* (cf. assumption (2)).

We can now introduce several concepts which play key roles in the Harrod model:

	Our notation	Harrod's notation
The warranted rate of growth	s/a	G_w
The natural rate of growth	$n' = n + \lambda$	G_n
The actual rate of growth[2]	$[Q(t) - Q(t-1)]/Q(t)$	G
The equilibrium capital requirement	a	C (1939); C_r (1948)
The actual capital requirement	$s/\{[Q(t) - Q(t-1)]/Q(t)\}$	C_p (1939); C (1948)

To clarify these concepts, we shall refer to the isoquant diagram in Figure 1.1*a*. To begin with, note that the ordinary isoquant maps have input flows on their axes. An isoquant represents the pairs of least-input rates capable of yielding a given level of output rate. For the Harrod model, we borrow the production function concept of Vernon Smith, where labor input is a flow and capital input is a stock. An isoquant is the pairs of least (labor) flow–(capital) stock combinations that can produce a *sustained* output rate at a given level. Temporarily, by *running down* the stock of inventories, it may be possible to attain a certain instantaneous output rate with a labor flow–capital stock pair lower than that prescribed by the isoquant map. But such a production program can never be indefinitely repeated.

In Figure 1.1*a*, for the isoquant $Q = 1$, the desired capital (stock) and labor (flow) requirements are a and b, respectively. Suppose that the initial output is

---

[2]The definition of the growth rate here follows the usage in his 1952 footnote on p. 259 of *Economic Essays* [8]. It differs from the common usage: growth rate = $[Q(t) - Q(t-1)]/Q(t-1)$, which he himself adopted earlier. He regarded the difference as negligible in view of the shortness of the period. This facilitates his adoption of the instantaneous multiplier (see the same footnote) so that $S(t) = sQ(t)$.

$Q^*(0)$ and that the actual output has been growing at the rate s/a; a growth of output in the next period to[3]

$$Q^*(1) = \frac{Q^*(0)}{1-(s/a)}$$

is a warranted growth in the following sense:
   (a) Saving under such a program is $sQ^*(1) = [as/(a-s)]Q^*(0)$.
   (b) The desired investment needed to support the increased output is $a[Q^*(1)-Q^*(0)] = [as/(a-s)]Q^*(0)$.
Hence, saving matches investment and there is no tendency to depart from such a path.

The aforementioned quantity $a[Q^*(1)-Q^*(0)]$ is the *ex ante* investment, as shown in Figure 1.1a. However, this concept plays no role in Harrod's model. (See [12], pp. 278–279.)

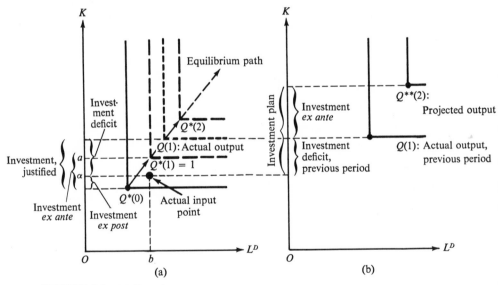

FIGURE 1.1   (a) Departure
α = actual capital/output ratio.
(b) Perpetuation of deviation.
Projected output = (Previous actual output) $\times(1+$warranted rate).

Suppose that for one reason or another actual output in period 1, $Q(1)$, is greater than the warranted output $Q^*(1)$. Hence, the "justified investment" becomes $I^* = a[Q(1)-Q^*(0)]$, which is higher than the *ex ante* investment. However, the exertion of producing such a large output is likely to deplete the stock of inventory (inventory is a part of the capital), so much so that the

---

[3]For simplicity, we set $Q^*(1)$ equal to 1 in Figure 1.1a.

net result is an *ex post* investment I that is even smaller than the *ex ante* investment, $a[Q^*(1)-Q^*(0)]$. I^*-I is the resultant "investment deficit."

C. DERIVATION OF RESULTS

We shall now prove conclusions (1), (2), and (3) of Section 1.2.2. Point (4) will be discussed in Section 1.2.4.

Proof of conclusion (1a).   Harrod's first conclusion concerns the existence of the warranted growth rate:

$$G_w C_r = s \qquad \text{(1948 notations)}$$

In our terms, this is

$$\frac{Q^*(t)-Q^*(t-1)}{Q^*(t)}\, a = s$$

Let us consider the growth path:

$$Q^*(t) = \frac{1}{1-(s/a)}\, Q^*(t-1) \tag{1.2.1}$$

$$= \left(\frac{1}{1-(s/a)}\right)^{(t-\tau)} Q^*(\tau)$$

Supposing such a path has been followed since time immemorial, then

$$K(t) = K(t-1)+I(t) \qquad \text{(by definition)} \tag{1.2.2}$$

$$= K(-\infty)+ \sum_{-\infty}^{t} I(\tau)$$

$$= 0+s \sum_{-\infty}^{t} Q^*(\tau) \qquad \text{(from assumption 1)}$$

$$= sQ^*(t) \sum_{-\infty}^{t} \left(\frac{1}{1-(s/a)}\right)^{(\tau-t)} \qquad \text{(using (1.2.1))}$$

$$= sQ^*(t) \sum_{0}^{\infty} [1-(s/a)]^{\tau}$$

$$= sQ^*(t)\frac{1}{1-[1-(s/a)]}$$

$$= aQ^*(t) \qquad \text{for all } t \text{ varying from} \\ -\infty \text{ to } \infty$$

which confirms that the actual capital/output ratio agrees with the desired ratio for all times. Entrepreneurs do not have to make any adjustment, because *ex ante* investment is always realized and justified. They can feel content about this path of "steady advance" [first part of assumption (5)]. Since s and a are unique, the warranted rate must also be unique.

log K, log L, log Q

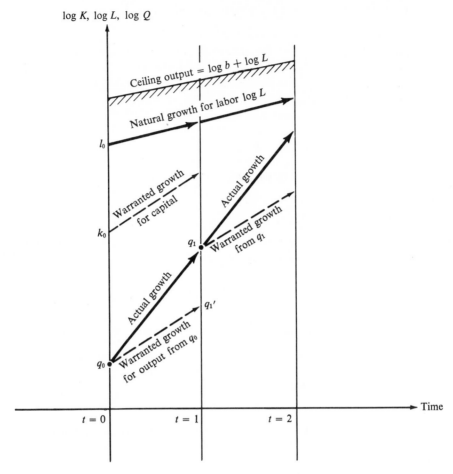

FIGURE 1.2   Illustration of various growth paths.

This proves conclusion (1a). Conclusion (1b) will be discussed in Section 1.2.4.
  Graphically, this is shown in Figure 1.2, the parallel arrows in the semi log diagram showing the consistent growth patterns between capital and output.
  Proof of conclusion (3). Since technical progress is solely of the labor-augmenting type, we can regard labor force as increasing at the rate n' and measure labor in "efficiency units." From assumption (3), we have the condition

$$Q(t) = bL^D(t)$$

$$\leq bL^S(t)$$

$$= bL^S(0)\,(1+n')^t$$

(1.2.3)

Obviously, if

$$n' < \frac{s/a}{1-(s/a)} = \frac{s}{a-s},$$

the equilibrium path cannot go on indefinitely. This is seen in Figure 1.2. Because the arrow from l_0 is less steep than the dotted arrow from k_0, the output ceiling ($\log b + \log L$) is bound to block the advance of $\log Q$ along the $q_0 q_1$ line.

Proof of conclusion (2). Before we proceed we must clarify saving behavior under disequilibrium. Harrod declined to specify whether *ex ante* saving is identical to *ex post* saving in his model ([8], p. 262). Both Baumol [16] and R. G. D. Allen [15] said it was. By postulating that the saving plan is always realized, they successfully formalized Harrod's result as long as the actual output growth is at the warranted rate. Both versions become unserviceable in explaining how the actual output path can *begin* to depart from a warranted path.[4] We shall make an eclectic modification (which appears to be the simplest way out):

Ex post saving agrees with ex ante saving for all periods except that period where for the first time the actual growth rate of output differs from the warranted rate.

In the example of Figure 1.1a, *ex post* saving is less than *ex ante* saving for period 1 due to the depletion of stocks.

We also recognize that assumption (5) (Harrod's Postulate A) is still not sufficiently precise. We follow R. G. D. Allen [15] and assume that "The increase of actual output in each period is the sum of two terms: (i) the increase over the output of the previous period according to the warranted growth rate, and (ii) the 'investment deficit' of the previous period."

We can now develop the following proof. First we note that

$$Q(t) = \frac{a}{a-s} Q(t-1) + I^*(t-1) - I(t-1) \tag{1.2.4}$$

Since

$$I^*(\tau) = a[Q(\tau) - Q(\tau-1)] \qquad \text{for } \tau = 2, 3, \ldots, t-1, \text{ where } I^*(1) \neq I(1) \tag{1.2.5}$$

and

$$I(\tau) = sQ(\tau) \tag{1.2.6}$$

[4]Baumol stated, "In order to make the assumption reasonable, we must assume that actual and intended saving are equal and that actual and expected income are equal" ([16], p. 38). R. G. D. Allen also wrote, "The main assumption made by Harrod is that saving plans ... are realized. This becomes a reasonable assumption once a lag is introduced" ([15], p. 75).

Consider now a counterexample illustrated by Figure 1.1a. Starting from $Q^*(0)$, two alternative evolutions are possible: (a) growing according to the warranted rate, one reaches $[Q^*(1), I^*(1)]$ one period later; (b) growing faster than the warranted rate and running down stocks in the process, one reaches $[Q(1), I(1)]$ one period later. In the example, $Q^*(1) < Q(1)$ and $I^*(1) > I(1)$. Since *ex post* saving is equal to *ex post* investment, the assumptions of Baumol and Allen equate *ex ante* saving to *ex post* investment. Hence, *ex ante* saving can be either $I^*(1)$ or $I(1)$. In Allen's version of a lagged multiplier, this requires $I^*(1) = sQ^*(0) = I(1)$, which is an impossibility, because $I^*(1) > I(1)$. In Baumol's version of an instantaneous multiplier, it requires that $I^*(1) = sQ^*(1)$ and $I(1) = sQ(1)$, i.e., $I^*(1)/Q^*(1) = s = I(1)/Q(1)$; this is also an impossibility, because $Q^*(1) < Q(1)$ and $I^*(1) > I(1)$.

we have

$$Q(t) - \frac{a}{a-s} Q(t-1) = I^*(t-1) - I(t-1) \qquad (1.2.7)$$

$$= a[Q(t-1) - Q(t-2)] - sQ(t-1)$$

$$= (a-s)\left[Q(t-1) - \frac{a}{a-s} Q(t-2)\right]$$

$$= (a-s)^{t-2}\left[Q(2) - \frac{a}{a-s} Q(1)\right]$$

$$= (a-s)^{t-2}[I^*(1) - I(1)]$$

This is a first-order, constant-coefficient, nonhomogenous difference equation and has the following solution:

$$Q(t) = \left(\frac{a}{a-s}\right)^{t-1} Q(1) + (a-s)^{t-2}\left\{\frac{1 - [a/(a-s)^2]^{t-1}}{1 - a/(a-s)^2}\right\}[I^*(1) - I(1)] \qquad (1.2.7')$$

$$= A\left(\frac{a}{a-s}\right)^t + B(a-s)^t$$

where A and B are constants.

As long as $(a-s)^2 > a$, the deviation term (the second term in the solution) dominates the equilibrium term (the first term). In technical terms, the system is *relatively unstable* with respect to the equilibrium path. This proves that Harrod's second conclusion *may be* valid.

This shows, in the 1948 notations of Harrod, that if $G < G_w$ in any period (e.g., $Q(1) < Q^*(1)$), the cumulative downward departure from the equilibrium path may occur. Moreover, if $G_w > G_n$ when the actual output path reaches its ceiling, then even the highest feasible growth ("crawling along the ceiling") means a downward departure from the equilibrium path.

1.2.4. Discussions

A. THE FIXED COEFFICIENT ASSUMPTION

In his short-run analysis, Harrod talked about a definite warranted rate of growth. In his long-run analysis, he discussed cases where the natural rate of growth is higher (lower) than the warranted rate. Since the warranted rate is the ratio of the propensity to save to the capital/output coefficient, any meaningful interpretation of Harrod's statements requires that the capital/output coefficient be fixed in the short run and have at most a limited range of variability in the long run. It should never be freely variable, as in the case of a Cobb-Douglas production function.

In "advocating" the Harrod model, four different approaches are possible.

(1) The input coefficients are technically fixed. This is a strong assumption used by Solow. Its merit rests in its strength. In Figure 1.3, the isoquant is represented by the dashed rectangular locus.

(2) The inputs are substitutable, yet due to the inflexibility of the ratio of input prices, the actual unit requirements are fixed. This was the position taken by Harrod in 1948 [6]. In his critique of Solow, Eisner also maintains this view.

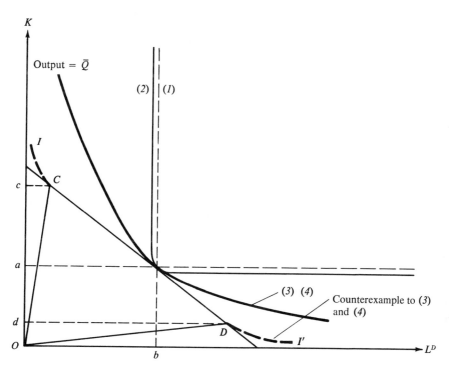

FIGURE 1.3   Alternate justifications for fixed (or "viscous") coefficients.
(1) Solow version: fixed coefficients.
(2) Harrod explanation (1960): limited substitution.
(3) Harrod explanation (1948): fixed interest rate.
(4) Harrod explanation (1968): "optimal" interest rate.

The question now becomes threefold:

(a) Is it realistic to assume fixed input prices? Harrod followed Keynes and argued that the interest rate is hard to reduce. But, as Hahn and Matthews ([17], p. 790) pointed out, the short-run causes behind the liquidity trap need not hold in the long period of Harrod.

(b) Is the system of input prices absolutely fixed? If not, then the fact that input prices have *very limited* variability does not imply *nearly fixed* input coefficients. The elasticity of substitution must be considered.

(c) Does an absolutely fixed input price system imply an absolutely fixed capital/output ratio? Figure 1.3 shows a counterexample, where the dashed curvilinear isoquant II' coincides with the isocost line over the whole segment CD. The same input price ratio is compatible with a capital/output ratio anywhere between $\overline{Oc}/\bar{Q}$ and $\overline{Od}/\bar{Q}$.[5]

[5]$\overline{Oc}$ and $\overline{Od}$ stand for the distances between O and c and between O and d, respectively.

(3) There is limited elasticity of input substitution. This is the line of defense Harrod entertained earlier. He said in 1960 [13] that due to imperfections of the capital market, interest rate may be quite influential, because higher interest rates are concomitant with "credit contractions" of the banking system. Hence, he retracted his early views based upon empirical studies of Hall and Hitch.

(4) Welfare considerations determine the interest rate. In 1960, Harrod conceded to the criticism of the neoclassical school and expanded his specification of the equilibrium path into the following:

$$\left\{ \begin{array}{ll} G_w C_r = s & \text{("First Dynamic Law")} \\[2mm] r_n = \dfrac{{}_{pc}G_n}{e} & \text{("Second Dynamic Law")} \\[2mm] C_r = f(r_n), \; f' < 0 & \end{array} \right.$$

where r_n is the "natural interest rate", ${}_{pc}G_n$ is the "natural" growth rate of per capita income, and e is the inverse of the elasticity of the marginal utility functions.

The third condition states that the higher the interest rate, the lower the capital/output ratio must be.

The second condition is derived from the works of Ramsey,[6] which we shall study in Chapter 10.

[6]Briefly stated, the underlying argument is as follows: Along the equilibrium growth path, per capita income grows at the rate of labor-augmenting technical progress, $\lambda = {}_{pc}G_n$. Assuming constancy of s, consumption per capita must grow at the same rate, i.e., $\dot{c}/c = \lambda$, where c stands for per capita consumption and $\dot{c}$ is its rate of increase. Let $u(c)$ be the instantaneous utility defined over per capita consumption, and (following Ramsey) let welfare be represented as the time integral of $u(c)$. The marginal instantaneous utility is u' and its elasticity is

$$\frac{1}{e} = -\frac{c}{u'}\frac{du'}{dc} = -\frac{\dot{u}'/u'}{\dot{c}/c},$$

i.e., a 1% increase in per capita consumption leads to a $(1/e)$% decrease of marginal utility. Hence, if per capita consumption increases at the rate λ each period, the marginal utility must decrease at the rate λ/e. Now the equilibrium interest rate r_n must be such that a person who lends one unit of consumption goods now and gets repaid with $1 + r_n$ one period later will break even in utility terms. Letting the marginal utility at the present be x, the above condition requires

$$(-1)x + (1 + r_n)\frac{x}{1 + (\lambda/e)} = 0$$

which reduces to Harrod's Second Dynamic Law.

This approach has been questioned by de Graaff [18] because of the nonmeasurability of e and the exclusion of the disutility of work, and because Harrod identified the growth rate of per capita income with the growth rate of per capita consumption. Harrod answered [10] that the labor supply is inelastic, so "disutility of work" is a constant and can hence be ignored. Also, he said that e might be conjectured if not observed. De Graaff's objection concerning growth rates turned out to be the most potent of the three. Harrod grafted the constant saving/income ratio assumption of Keynes onto the optimal saving model of Ramsey. But under what conditions will the optimal saving ratio be constant over time? We can now offer a definite answer to this. In an optimal saving model with constant capital/output ratio, constant elasticity of marginal utility, etc., the optimal output path should grow at the same rate as the optimal consumption path only when $e = 1$ (i.e., $u = \log c$ as in Cass and Yaari's model; see Section 6.1), a most restrictive case. See Phelps ([19], p. 95, Eq. (51)). Harrod eventually abandoned the fixed capital/output ratio in 1963 [9].

B. THE RELATIVE INSTABILITY

Ever since Harrod's *Toward a Dynamic Economics* came off the press, the relative instability property has been the subject of continuous debate. The problems that have arisen are of three types:

(1) Reasonableness of the behavioral assumption.

(a) On specific behavior rules: S. Alexander [20] argued that an entrepreneur satisfied with business conditions would more likely repeat the previous output than increase that output according to the warranted rate. This led Harrod to propose another assumption [15] rather than Postulate A [our assumption (5)].

(b) On general behavioral patterns: Baumol ([16], pp. 53-4) argued that if entrepreneurs are not so myopic but instead gear their operations to the long-run growth trend, the equilibrium growth path need not be unstable. Harrod agreed to this view [5], yet he does not consider that real-life entrepreneurs have such foresight.

(2) Divergence of the adjustment process. Hugh Rose [21] and Dale Jorgenson [22] showed that under rather reasonable assumptions the equilibrium path may remain stable. Jorgenson pointed out that even if the absolute magnitude of the divergence increases over time (say, growing at 1% per period), it may become proportionally less and less important if the equilibrium path increases much faster (say, growing at 10% per period). Economists are interested in *relative instability*, i.e., when the deviation outgrows the equilibrium path.

(3) Limits of divergence. Hicks pointed out that certain mechanisms must exist to generate recovery after an actual downturn [14]. (As we noted before, Harrod is aware of this fact.)

The survey article of Hahn and Matthews [17] includes an excellent discussion of this problem. We can conclude that there exist alternative assumptions about the adjustment processes, some implying the equilibrium path to be unstable, some stable, and that the comparative realism of these assumptions is not easy to determine by casual observation. Empirical studies are needed in this area.

C. IMPACT

The impact of Harrod's work has been threefold, each part of considerable importance in the development of separate realms of inquiry:

(1) As a critique of Harrod's 1948 volume, Hicks evolved a trade-cycle model [14] that parallels the earlier studies of Hansen and Samuelson.

(2) As a critique of the models of Harrod and Domar, Solow developed his trailblazing paper of 1956, which ushered in the neoclassical theories. Mrs. Robinson and Kaldor, on their part, also developed growth models that show the influence of Harrod's work.

(3) Perhaps the most elusive, albeit the most rewarding, element in Harrod's model is the "disequilibrium analysis" associated with his relative instability

problem. The allowance for entrepreneurial miscalculation is certainly a key to the next stage of development in macrodynamics. So far, Hahn [23] has done certain pioneering work in this area. Solow also recently devoted attention to such short-run adjustment mechanisms [24, 25]. Harrod certainly rekindled economists' interest in growth problems. Whether he initiated modern dynamic economics is harder to determine. As Samuelson pointed out ([26], Vol. II, p. 1123), the acceleration principle had a long history before Harrod's *Trade Cycle* arrived. What is regarded by Harrod as dynamics (the inclusion of time derivatives in a model) was surely present in the area of trade cycles since the days of Aftalion.

1.3 DOMAR

The main growth models of Domar published in 1946 [27] and 1947 [28] bear a certain family resemblance to the works of Harrod. In fact, Harrod himself appears to regard Domar's formulation as a rediscovery of his own version with a seven-year lag! Apart from the unfairness to Domar, such views tend to slur over the distinctive features of the Domar model, a theory which still has much to offer in its own right.

Domar criticized the Keynesian theory on two counts:

(1) Investment has two effects: (a) an income-generating effect through the multiplier, and (b) a productive capacity effect, by increasing the capacity for producing output. The short-run analysis of Keynes usually ignores the second point.

(2) Unemployment of labor elicits sympathy for the jobless, but the unemployment of capital attracts little attention. Yet the premature demise of equipment inhibits investment and hence reduces income. With income falling, labor tends to be unemployed. Thus, the Keynesian concept of labor unemployment misses the source of the ailment.

We shall first state the Domar system in our own symbols and develop its conclusions, and then compare it with Harrod's model. Commentaries will be summarized as a final note.

1.3.1. The formulation

To facilitate comparison, we shall introduce our own symbols for the Domar model. His symbols are put in parentheses. Let

$\bar{Q}$ be productive capacity for output (P)
Q be output (Y)
I be actual investment
I^0 be ideal investment
K be capital
L be labor

N be employment
d be the ratio of capital "junked"
s be saving/income ratio (α)
a be actual marginal capital/output ratio ($1/\sigma$)
a' be "virtual" marginal capital/output ratio ($1/s$)

Domar's model is based upon the following assumptions:

(1) Income is determined by investment via an instantaneous multiplier. For simplicity, constant saving propensity is assumed ([25], p. 76). This implies:

$$Q(t) = I(t)/s \tag{1.3.1}$$

(2) Productive capacity is created by investment according to the "potential social average investment productivity" ([27], p. 74). For simplicity, this is assumed to be constant ([27], p. 76). In our notations,

$$\bar{Q}(t) - \bar{Q}(t-1) = I(t)/a \tag{1.3.2}$$

(a is the reciprocal of "potential social average investment productivity")

(3) Investment is induced by output growth and modified by entrepreneurial confidence. The latter is adversely affected by "junking," i.e., the *untimely* loss of capital value due to the unprofitable operations of older facilities. This may come as a result of the shortage of (a certain class of) labor or the loss of market to new products.[7] For, Domar says, "unemployment of capital . . . inhibits investment" ([27], p. 79). We may supply an equation for this hypothesis:

$$\frac{I(t)}{I(t-1)} = G\left[\frac{Q(t-1)-Q(t-2)}{Q(t-2)-Q(t-3)}, d(t)\right] \tag{1.3.3}$$

where G is an increasing function of the rate of output acceleration but also a decreasing function of the "junking ratio" $d(t)$ to be defined below.

Moreover, without junking, investment increases at the same rate as output; i.e.,

$$G(x, 0) = x \qquad \text{for any } x \tag{1.3.3'}$$

(4) Employment depends upon the "utilization ratio," i.e., the ratio between actual output and productive capacity ([28], p. 87). We may formulate this as

$$\frac{N(t)}{L(t)} = H\left[\frac{Q(t)}{\bar{Q}(t)}, \ldots\right] \qquad H' > 0 \tag{1.3.4}$$

The dots are left there to indicate that Domar was fully aware of the existence of other determinants for the employment ratio. Moreover, we assume that $H = 1$ implies $Q(t) = \bar{Q}(t)$.

---

[7]In fact, with downward rigidity of wages, even with unemployment present, the appearance of labor-saving inventions can make older machines suddenly uneconomic. This is another possible cause for junking. Capital-saving inventions may also occur in reality, but this is in conflict with the constancy of K/Q.

We now come to Domar's central theme:

(5) Investment, past as well as present, can generate productive capacity at a given ratio ([27], p. 73). Due to past managerial miscalculation, the appearance of new investment projects will cause the *untimely* demise of certain old plants. If "junking" exists, it will pull down the incremental capacity of investment to the "potential social average investment productivity" ([27], p. 77). In our notations,

$$I(t)/a < I(t)/a' \qquad \text{or } a' < a \tag{1.3.5}$$

The accounting identity informs us that

$$K(t) - K(t-1) = I(t) - [d(t)K(t)] \tag{1.3.6}$$

where $d(t)K(t)$ is the amount of capital junked and $d(t)$ is the junking ratio.

For simplicity, Domar ([25], p. 76) assumes that

$$\frac{K(\tau)}{\bar{Q}(\tau)} = a' \qquad \text{for all } \tau \tag{1.3.7}$$

Hence, from (1.3.2), (1.3.6), and (1.3.7), we have

$$\frac{I(t) - d(t)K(t)}{a'} = \frac{I(t)}{a}$$

or

$$d(t) = \frac{I(t)}{K(t)} \left(\frac{a - a'}{a} \right) \tag{1.3.8}$$

Also, using (1.3.1) and (1.3.7),

$$d(t) = \left(\frac{s}{a'} \right) \left(\frac{Q(t)}{\bar{Q}(t)} \right) \left(\frac{a - a'}{a} \right) \tag{1.3.8'}$$

Our model is now complete. We have converted Domar's differential equation system to a difference equation system solely for the sake of deriving (1.3.3). From the casual point of view, current investment is geared to *observed* output increments. Hence, the time lag is essential for entrepreneurs to make such observations. Exercise 1.1 demonstrates that if this time lag is ignored, the mathematical solution leads to an entirely different type of time path from what we wanted.

1.3.2. The conclusions

Despite the fact that Domar's model is well known, some of the implications have never been fully worked out, to our knowledge. In the following, we shall assume that the G function has a very simple form:

$$G(x, y) = \begin{cases} x & \text{for } y = 0 \\ qx & \text{for } y > 0 \qquad 0 < q < 1 \end{cases} \tag{1.3.9}$$

The rationale for this specification is: (1) With full confidence, entrepreneurs will collectively increase investment by 1% for each percent of increased output increment. $[x(t)/x(t-1)$ is $(1+$ the growth rate of $x)$ for any $x.]$ (2) With the shaken confidence that results from the existence of scrapping of whatever magnitude, every 1% of increased output increment can induce only a $q\%$ increase of investment, where $q < 1$.

Let us assume that from time immemorial up to a period 0 there has been full utilization of capital, i.e., $Q(t) = \bar{Q}(t)$. Also, output, investment, etc. have been growing at the rate $(s/a')/[1-(s/a')]$. We can now verify the Domar conclusions.

Conclusion 1. Without unintended scrapping, i.e., $d = 0$ and $a = a'$, the investment, income, productive capacity, and capital will all grow at the same rate, $(s/a')/(1-s/a')$. Also, full employment is possible.

Proof. With zero scrapping (1.3.9) and (1.3.3) together imply that investment should grow at the same rate as before; i.e.,

$$\frac{I(t)}{I(t+1)} = \frac{Q(t)\left[(1-s/a')-(1-s/a')^2\right]}{Q(t)\left[(1-s/a')^2-(1-s/a')^3\right]}$$

$$= \frac{1}{1-s/a'} \qquad \text{for all } t > 0$$

From (1.3.1), income is proportional to investment, so it grows at the same rate.

For any period t, the incremental capacity is

$$\bar{Q}(t) - \bar{Q}(t-1) = \frac{I(t)}{a} = \frac{I(t)}{a'}$$

and the incremental output is

$$\frac{I(t)}{s} - \frac{I(t-1)}{s} = \frac{I(t)(s/a)}{s} = \frac{I(t)}{a}$$

Hence, the increments of both $Q(t)$ and $\bar{Q}(t)$ balance out, and $\bar{Q}$ grows at the same rate, $(s/a)/[1-(s/a)]$. Capital, being the accumulation of $I(t)$ (because there is no scrapping) since period $-\infty$, increases also at the same rate.

Finally, from (1.3.4), full employment of labor is possible.

Conclusion 2. If unintended scrapping occurs all the time after period 1, the economy is heading for an impasse.

Proof. (1.3.8) shows that as long as $a > a'$, scrapping exists. From equations (1.3.3) and (1.3.9) we can easily deduce the behavior of the system. Since $Q(t) = I(t)/s$ and $I(t)/I(t-1) = Q(t)/Q(t-1)$, (1.3.3) and (1.3.9) can be rewritten as

$$Z(t) = q\,\frac{Z(t-1)-1}{Z(t-2)-1}\,Z(t-2) \qquad \text{where } Z(t) = \frac{Q(t)}{Q(t-1)} \qquad (1.3.10)$$

with $Z(t) = 1/[1-(s/a')]$ for all $t \leq 0$ as the initial condition.

The behavior of this second-order nonlinear difference equation can be deduced as follows:

(1) If $Z(t-2) > 1 \geq Z(t-1)$, then (1.3.10) implies that $Z(t) \leq 0$, i.e., $Q(t) \leq 0 < Q(t-1)$. Since nonpositive output is economically nonviable, this symbolically signals the total breakdown of an economy. This occurs when income depends on investment and investment depends on the output increment which turns negative.

(2) If $Z(-1) \geq Z(0) > 0$ (which is true here), and $Z(s) > 0$ for $0 \leq s \leq t$, then

$$Z(t) \leq q^t Z(0) \qquad (1.3.1$$

This is because $Z(s-2) \geq Z(s-1) > 1$ implies

$$\frac{Z(s-1)-1}{Z(s-2)-1} \leq \frac{Z(s-1)}{Z(s-2)},$$

and, hence,

$$Z(s) = q \frac{Z(s-1)-1}{Z(s-2)-1} Z(s-2)$$

$$\leq q \frac{Z(s-1)}{Z(s-2)} Z(s-2)$$

$$= q Z(s-1)$$

Iteration on s yields (1.3.11).

Hence, there exists

$$T \geq \frac{\ln\left[1-(s/a')\right]}{\ln q}$$

such that for some $t \leq T$, output ceases to grow, investment stops, and economic collapse becomes inevitable (as shown in (1)).

1.3.3. Comparison with Harrod

The Domar and Harrod theories are similar in many ways:
   (1) Against Keynes, both feel that a dynamic element should be introduced.
   (2) In contrast with the neoclassical models, both are concerned with Keynesian difficulties, allow entrepreneurial mistakes, and postulate certain fixity of the capital/output ratio.
   (3) Both have obtained an exponential equilibrium path.
   (4) Both depict a "road to disaster" ever diverging from the equilibrium path.

Their dissimilarities can most easily be presented in tabular form.

	Domar	Harrod
1. Long-run difficulty	"Underinvestment" sapping growth	Labor shortage deflecting growth
2. Position of labor input	Shortage of certain labor may trigger scrapping and the inhibition of investment; optional element	Determinant of natural rate of growth; key element
3. Centrifugal force from equilibrium	Continuously undermined investment incentive	Unstable adjustment process
4. Reason for fixed capital/ output ratio	Assumed for convenience	Due to fixed interest rate, low substitutability, etc.
5. State of economy	Idle-capacity prevalent	Labor unemployment commonplace

1.3.4. Commentary

Domar's model contains quite a number of elements eventually included in later neoclassical models. These include (1) embodied technical progress,[8] (2) obsolescence of equipment, and (3) the presence of Keynesian unemployment (effective demand geared to the investment function). Point (1) was examined by Solow as well as other economists; points (2) and (3) were considered by Solow, Tobin, Weizsäcker, and Yaari. All these later studies will be discussed in Chapter 5. By training much heavier mathematical artillery to various aspects, these neoclassical models eventually obtained much more specific results; however, there are other essential elements of Domar not yet formalized in recent works. For instance, the investment function (as we represented it in (1.3.3)) appeared in various recent papers of Jorgenson and Solow, but it is treated either as a separate entity or as part of a short-run adjustment model, not in the context of growth. The junking process initiated by the appearance of new products has not yet been synthesized into any mathematical model.

In comparison with the "neoclassical" authors, Domar assumed fallible entrepreneurs who may be deterred from investment by unforeseen junking, whereas Solow et al. postulated perfect foresight, and hence no scrapping could affect investment action.

Domar never found it necessary to formalize his analysis of how an economy may break down. Our mathematical formulation of his model presents a process (stated in (1.3.10)) which is both relatively and absolutely unstable for $q < 1$. We have not built in, though, those stabilizing forces (population growth, the type of technical progress that spurs investment, etc.) mentioned by Domar to explain economic recoveries.

[8]"Labor productivity is . . . technological progress embodied in capital goods" ([27] p. 72).

In passing, we note that Domar subsequently considered his early view as overcautious ([29], p. 5) and his distinction between a and a' ($1/\sigma$ and $1/s$ in his notation) unsatisfactory ([29], p. 7). In his subsequent work (e.g., [30]) the former line was not followed. Later works on Harrod-Domar models, such as those of Shinkai [31] and Lucas [32], also laid more emphasis on the Harrod version. It seems that the Domar version of investment function so far has not received the attention it deserves.

REFERENCES

[1] Harrod, R. F., *Economic Essays*, Macmillan, London, 1952, Essay 11.

[2] *Ibid.*, Essay 12.

[3] Tinbergen, Jan, "Zur Theorie der Langfristigen Wirtschaftenwicklung," *Weltwirtschaftliches Archiv*, vol. 55, May 1942, pp. 511–49.

[4] Hicks, John, *Capital and Growth*, Oxford University Press, Oxford, 1965.

[5] Harrod, R. F., "Domar and Dynamic Economics," *Economic Journal*, vol. LXIX, Sept. 1959, pp. 451–64.

[6] Harrod, R. F., *Toward a Dynamic Economics*, Macmillan, London, 1948.

[7] Harrod, R. F., *The Trade Cycle*, Oxford University Press, Oxford, 1936.

[8] Harrod, R. F., *Economic Essays*, Macmillan, London, 1952, Essay 13.

[9] Harrod, R. F., "Themes in Dynamic Theory," *Economic Journal*, vol. LXXIII, Sept. 1963, pp. 401–21.

[10] Harrod, R. F., "Notes on Trade-Cycle Theory," *Economic Journal*, vol. LXI, June 1951, pp. 261–75.

[11] Harrod, R. F., "Comment" (to J. de V. Graaff), *Economic Journal*, vol. LXIXI, Dec. 1960, p. 851.

[12] Harrod, R. F., *Economic Essays*, Macmillan, London, 1952, Essay 14.

[13] Harrod, R. F., "Second Essay in Dynamic Theory," *Economic Journal*, vol. LXIXI, June 1960, pp. 277–93.

[14] Hicks, J. R., "Mr. Harrod's Dynamic Theory," *Economica*, N.S. vol. 16, May 1949, pp. 106–21.

[15] Allen, R. G. D., *Mathematical Economics*, Macmillan, London, 1957.

[16] Baumol, W. J., *Economic Dynamics*, 2nd ed., Macmillan, London, 1959.

[17] Hahn, F. H., and R. C. O. Matthews, "The Theory of Economic Growth: A Survey," *Economic Journal*, vol. LXXIV, Dec. 1964, pp. 779–902.

[18] Graaff, J. de V., "Sir Roy Harrod's 2nd Essay," *Economic Journal*, vol. LXIXI, Dec. 1960, pp. 849–51.

[19] Phelps, Edmund S., *Golden Rules of Economic Growth*, Norton, New York, 1966.

[20] Alexander, S. S., "Mr. Harrod's Dynamic Model," *Economic Journal*, vol. LX, Dec. 1950, pp. 724–39.

[21] Rose, Hugh, "The Possibility of Warranted Growth," *Economic Journal*, vol. LXIX, June 1959, pp. 313–32.

[22] Jorgenson, Dale, "On Stability in the Sense of Harrod," *Economica*, N.S. vol. 27, Aug. 1960, pp. 243–48.

[23] Hahn, F. H., "The Stability of Growth Equilibrium," *Quarterly Journal of Economics*, vol. LXXIV, May 1960, pp. 206–26.

[24] Solow, R. M., and J. E. Stiglitz, "Output, Employment and Wages in the Short-Run," *Quarterly Journal of Economics*, vol. LXXXII, Nov. 1968, pp. 537–60.

[25] Solow, R. M., "Short-Run Adjustment of Employment to Output," in *Papers in Honor of Sir John Hicks: Value, Capital and Growth*, J. N. Wolfe, Ed., Aldine, Chicago, 1968.

[26] Samuelson, P. A., *Collected Scientific Papers*, M.I.T. Press, Cambridge, Mass., 1966.

[27] Domar, E. D., *Essays in the Theory of Economic Growth*, Oxford University Press, Oxford, 1957, Chapter III.

[28] *Ibid.*, Chapter IV.

[29] *Ibid.*, Foreword.

[30] *Ibid.*, Chapter V.

[31] Shinkai, Yoichi, "An Effect of Price Changes in the Harrod-Domar Model," *Quarterly Journal of Economics*, vol. LXXVII, 1963, pp. 459–69.

[32] Lucas, Jr., R. E., "Optimum Investment Policy and the Flexible Accelerator," *International Economic Review*, vol. 8, Feb. 1967, pp. 78–85.

EXERCISES

1.1. Consider the Domar model. If we assume that $Q = I/s$ and $\dot{I}/I = q(\ddot{Q}/\dot{Q})$, where $Q < q < 1$:
   (a) What mathematical properties does this system possess?
   (b) What economic reason can you find to explain such a phenomenon?

1.2. (a) Does the relative stability of the Harrod system imply absolute stability?
   (b) If the saving/income ratio is negative, what conclusions can you reach? Analyze.

2

the rise of "neoclassical" models:
Solow and Swan

Of the growth models that dominate macroeconomic theory today, the majority are extensions and generalizations of the pioneering papers of Solow [1] and Swan [2]. Since Solow's article appeared earlier and exhibits a much broader scope than Swan's, it will receive our main attention in this chapter. In Sections 2.1–2.4 we shall discuss, in turn, the formulation, the properties, the extension, and the criticisms pertaining to the Solovian model. Swan's model will be reviewed in Section 2.5.

2.1 THE SOLOW MODEL—ASSUMPTIONS AND FORMULATION

In contrast with the Cassandra-like view of Harrod, Solow took a stand of guarded optimism. He admitted that the Keynesian difficulties were deliberately assumed away when he investigated the neoclassical side of the coin. But on the other hand, since he believed that Keynesian theory applies only in the short run whereas the neoclassical theory is suitable for the long run, the neoclassical side is at least equally (if not much more) relevant to the theory of growth.

The basic assumptions of Solow include perfect foresight for all individuals, and smooth adjustment in goods, labor, and capital markets. These imply that both saving and investment plans are simultaneously fulfilled, and that neither miscalculated output nor misdirected investment can ever arise. Market clearance is usually achieved, while Keynesian unemployment is hardly possible. These are the main differences that distinguish the Solow-Swan theory from the theories of Harrod and Domar.

In other aspects, the two schools are not that distinct. In particular, Solow explicitly assumed a linear homogeneous aggregate production function. This is also implicitly postulated by Harrod. If there were no functional relationships between the aggregate output and the aggregate capital and labor inputs, one

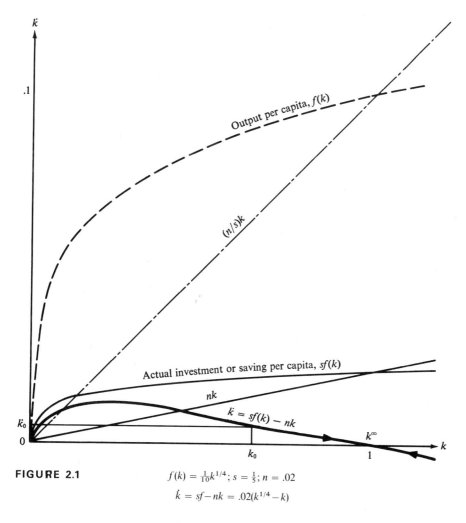

FIGURE 2.1

$$f(k) = \tfrac{1}{10}k^{1/4}; \; s = \tfrac{1}{5}; \; n = .02$$

$$\dot{k} = sf - nk = .02(k^{1/4} - k)$$

could hardly comprehend Harrod's model.[1] Solow also explicitly assumed the substitutability between capital and labor. Harrod held similar views; his analysis of "capital deepening" parallels Solow's treatment. Harrod thought that a fixed interest rate could lead to fixed proportions between inputs and output; however, in Chapter 1 we have shown that this is not so.

Solow explicitly introduced the "composite good." Domar postulated the measurability of capital, while most of Harrod's arguments make sense only with heroic aggregation. Finally Solow assumed that the saving/income ratio

---

[1] For example, Harrod assumed a ceiling for *aggregate* output in terms of *aggregate* labor supply. He also calculated required *aggregate* capital formation according to the growth of *aggregate* output.

is a macroeconomic constant, just as Harrod and Domar did. This, in fact, is a Keynesian vestige in an otherwise neoclassical model.

Growing out of a critique of Harrod and Domar, the Solow article paved the way for an entire decade of growth models.

Like Harrod, Solow assumed the following:

(1) The labor force grows at the constant rate n; i.e.,

$$L(t) = L_0 e^{nt} \tag{2.1.1}$$

(2) Output is produced from capital and labor through a linear homogeneous production function:[2]

$$Q(t) = F[K(t), L(t)] \tag{2.1.2}$$

$$= L(t)F\left[\frac{K(t)}{L(t)}, 1\right] \qquad \text{(linear homogeneity of } F\text{)}$$

$$= L(t)F[k(t), 1] \qquad \text{(setting } k = K/L\text{)}$$

$$= L(t)f(k) \qquad \text{(defining } f(k) = F(k, 1)\text{)}$$

Like Domar, Solow assumed an instantaneous multiplier:

$$\dot{K}(t) = I(t) \tag{2.1.3}$$

$$= S(t) \qquad \text{(investment–saving identity)}$$

$$= sQ(t) \qquad \text{(constant saving propensity)}$$

By differentiating $k(t)$ logarithmically, he obtained:[3]

$$\dot{k} = sf(k) - nk \qquad \text{(after multiplying both sides by } k\text{)} \tag{2.1.4}$$

---

[2]That is, if all inputs are multiplied by a common multiple, the resultant output will be multiplied by the same multiple. Hence, $Q = F(K, L)$ implies $F(\lambda K, \lambda L) = \lambda Q$. In (2.1.2), λ is set equal to $1/L$.

[3]The step-by-step derivation is as follows (given $\hat{x} = \dfrac{\dot{x}}{x} = \dfrac{d}{dt} \ln x$):

$$\hat{k} = \hat{K} - \hat{L} \qquad \left(\text{since } \frac{d}{dt} \ln k = \frac{d}{dt} \ln (K/L) = \frac{d}{dt} (\ln K - \ln L)\right.$$

$$= \frac{d}{dt} \ln K - \frac{d}{dt} \ln L\Big)$$

$$= \frac{sQ}{K} - n \qquad \text{(since } \hat{K} = \dot{K}/K \text{ and } \dot{K} = sQ \text{ from (2.1.3);}$$

$$\text{also, } \hat{L} = n \text{ from (2.1.1))}$$

$$= \frac{sQ/L}{k} - n \qquad \text{(since } K = kL\text{)}$$

$$= \frac{sf(k)}{k} - n \qquad \text{(from (2.1.2), } Q/L = f(k)\text{)}$$

Multiplying both sides by k, one obtains (2.1.4).

Illuminating insights into the behavior of this differential equation can be obtained from the phase diagram of Figure 2.1.

The curve $f(k)$ is actually the "total product of the capital input curve" from elementary price theory, with the labor input held constant at unity. Under the assumption of constant returns, this shows the dependence of the output per capita upon the capital per capita. Since investment equals saving and saving equals a constant fraction of income (or output), $sf(k)$ shows the actual investment per capita. Since labor increases at the exponential rate n, capital must grow at an identical exponential rate to keep each worker equipped with the same amount of capital. This calls for an aggregate investment level nK, or, on a per capita investment level, $nK/L = nk$, to keep the capital/labor ratio k constant. Both the actual and the required investments per capita are functions of k. The difference of the two, represented by the heavy line in Figure 2.1, indicates the rate of change of k as a function of k. Its intercept with the k axis, k^∞, denotes the equilibrium capital per capita ratio.[4]

If initially $k = k_0 < k^\infty$, the heavy line shows that the corresponding value of $\dot{k}$ is $\dot{k}_0 > 0$ and k will increase. This holds true for all k, with $0 < k < k^\infty$; hence, $k(t)$ asymptotically approaches k^∞, as shown by the arrow on the heavy line. Similar analysis applies for an initial k greater than k^∞.

Since the movement of k can be gauged by the relative positions of the $sf(k)$ and nk curves for any particular k, the heavy line in Figure 2.1 is rarely drawn. Moreover, since

$$nk \begin{Bmatrix} > \\ = \\ < \end{Bmatrix} sf(k) \text{ if and only if } \left(\frac{n}{s}\right) k \begin{Bmatrix} > \\ = \\ < \end{Bmatrix} f(k)$$

the $f(k)$ and $(n/s)k$ curves give us the information we need, and we shall use them from now on.

2.2 THE SOLOW MODEL—THE DYNAMIC EQUILIBRIUM (BALANCED GROWTH) PATH

We shall discuss the existence, the uniqueness, the stability, and the employment implications of the balanced growth path under three subheadings: the general case, the Inada case, and the Harrod-Domar case.

2.2.1. The general case

Under the general case, anything can happen.

1. There may not exist any balanced growth path or any nontrivial (i.e., $k^\infty > 0$) balanced growth path. However, these are rather rare cases, requiring very high or low marginal productivity of capital (slope of $f(k)$) throughout the

---

[4]As we mentioned in Chapter 1, in growth theory *balanced growth* is defined as the proportional increase of output and all inputs. Hence, at k^∞ there is a balanced growth equilibrium.

entire range of capital/labor ratios. These exceptional cases are shown in Figure 2.2 as $f^1(k)$ and $f^2(k)$, respectively.

2. There may be more than one balanced growth path. Some of these paths may be *unstable*, such that any minor displacement may send the economy into some alternative balanced growth paths. Again, this is rather rare. If the marginal productivity of capital is decreasing over the entire range of k, then any balanced growth path that exists must be both unique and stable. The exceptional case is shown when $f(k)$ takes the form $f^3(k)$ of Figure 2.2.[5]

3. Departure from the balanced growth path or the lack of such a path does not usually imply the unemployment of either capital or labor. For instance, if

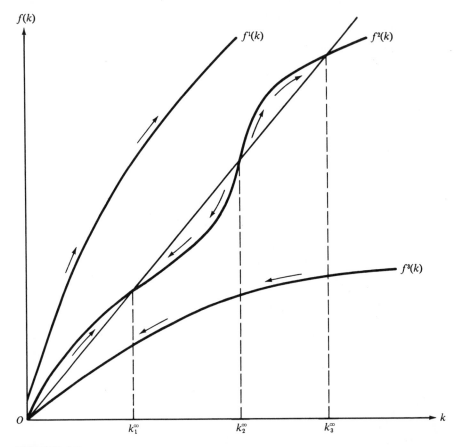

FIGURE 2.2

[5] This case (which originally appeared in Solow's paper [1]) is possible only when the production technology is nonconvex. It requires that, in Figure 2.2, $F[\frac{1}{2}(k_1{}^\infty + k_2{}^\infty), 1] < \frac{1}{2}[F(k_1{}^\infty, 1) + F(k_2{}^\infty, 1)]$ be possible for $k_1{}^\infty$ and $k_2{}^\infty$. Note that from advanced micro theory (e.g., Debreu's *Theory of Value*) we know that *convexity* and *constant returns* (i.e., the production set is a "cone") do not imply each other.

the production isoquants meet or approach asymptotically the two input axes, then any pair of given inputs can be fully employed, given that there is effective demand for the output.[6]

2.2.2. The Inada case

Inada [3] specified a set of conditions (his "derivative conditions") that guarantee the *existence*, *uniqueness*, and *stability* of the balanced growth capital/labor ratio, k^∞. These conditions are:

(1) $f'(k) > 0$; i.e., the marginal productivity of capital is always positive.
(2) $f''(k) < 0$; i.e., the marginal productivity of capital is always diminishing as capital per capita k increases.
(3) $f'(0) = \infty$; i.e., the marginal productivity of capital is infinite when the capital/labor ratio approaches zero.

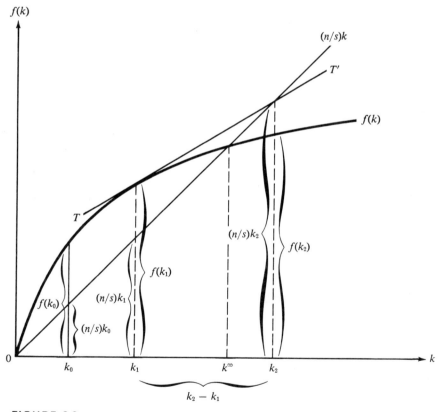

FIGURE 2.3

[6]In a Solovian model the effective demand is always present.

(4) $f'(\infty) = 0$; i.e., the marginal productivity of capital always falls asymptotically to zero when the capital/labor ratio increases indefinitely.

(5) $f(0) = 0$; i.e., no output can be produced without capital.

(6) $f(\infty) = \infty$; i.e., output per worker increases indefinitely with capital per worker.

Figure 2.3 illustrates an $f(k)$ curve that satisfies all six conditions.

From the first five conditions we can deduce the following.

The existence of $k^\infty > 0$.   Condition (3) asserts that $f'(k)$ has a "vertical takeoff" at $k = 0$. Since the $(n/s)k$ ray has only a *finite* positive slope, at some k_0 (nearing 0), $f(k_0) > (n/s)k_0$. This rules out the case $f^2(k)$ in Figure 2.2, where $f(k)$ lies entirely under $(n/s)k$, for all $k > 0$.

Next, conditions (2) and (4) guarantee that for some $k_1, f'(k_1) < (n/s)$, because $f'(k)$ decreases continuously toward zero. One may now assert that there exists k_2 such that $f(k_2) \leq (n/s)k_2$. In fact, if $f(k_1) \leq (n/s)k_1$, then k_1 itself fulfills the qualification (i.e., $k_2 = k_1$ will do). Otherwise, if $f(k_1) > (n/s)k_1$, one can construct the tangent line TT' to $f(k)$ at $k = k_1$ (Figure 2.3). Since the slope of $TT' = f'(k_1) < n/s$, TT' must intersect $(n/s)k$ at k_2, say. Now, we can prove graphically that $f(k_2) < (n/s)k_2$. This rules out the case $f^1(k)$ in Figure 2.2, where $f(k) > (n/s)k$ for all k.[7]

The continuity of $f(k)$ then assures us that there must be one intersection between $f(k)$ and $(n/s)k$ at k^∞, say, with $k^\infty > 0$.

The uniqueness of k^∞.   Choose k^∞ as the smallest k, where $f(k)$ cuts $(n/s)k$. At k^∞, $f(k)$ cuts $(n/s)k$ from above; i.e., $f'(k^\infty) < (n/s)$. Any further intersection requires that at the second intersection $f(k)$ cut $(n/s)k$ from below; i.e., $f'(k^+) > n/s > f'(k^\infty)$ for some $k^+ > k^\infty$. This contradicts condition (2). The choice of k^∞ has also ruled out the possibility that f cuts $(n/s)k$ from below somewhere between 0 and k^∞. This proves there can be only one balanced growth value of k.

The stability property of k^∞.   Applying the Mean Value Theorem of calculus:

$$(n/s)k^\infty = f(k^\infty)$$

$$= k^\infty f'(\theta k^\infty) \qquad \text{for some } \theta, 0 < \theta < 1$$

$$> k^\infty f'(k^\infty) \qquad \text{[from condition (2)]}$$

---

[7]The algebraic proof is as follows:

$$f(k_2) = f(k_1) + \int_{k_1}^{k_2} f'(k)\, dk$$

$$< f(k_1) + \int_{k_1}^{k_2} f'(k_1)\, dk \qquad \text{(since } f'' < 0, f'(k_1) > f'(k) \text{ for } k > k_1)$$

$$= f(k_1) + (k_2 - k_1) f'(k_1)$$

$$= \left(\frac{n}{s}\right) k_2 \qquad \text{(by the choice of } k_2)$$

Hence, $f'(k^\infty) < n/s$, assuring us that $f(k)$ cuts $(n/s)k$ from above and that the equilibrium is stable (compare Figure 2.1).

The full-employment property of k^∞.   Condition (1) guarantees that $f'(k^\infty) > 0$. Hence, the marginal product of capital is positive, so capital cannot be redundant. The marginal product of labor at k^∞ is

$$\frac{\partial}{\partial L}\left\{ Lf\left(\frac{K}{L}\right)\right\} = f(k^\infty) - k^\infty f'(k^\infty)$$

$$> 0 \qquad \text{(from the proof of the stability property)}$$

So labor is not redundant either. Note that we do not need all six conditions to prove each result.

Although the above conditions are highly plausible, it must be noted that they are not fulfilled by a broad class of production functions. For instance, out of the CES (constant elasticity of substitution) production function family [4], where

$$Q(t) = [\delta K^{-\beta} + (1-\delta)L^{-\beta}]^{-1/\beta} \qquad \beta \geq -1$$

the only member that fulfils the Inada conditions is the case $\beta = 0$, i.e., the Cobb-Douglas form. If $\beta > 0$, then $f'(0) < \infty$, violating Inada's condition (3), and there may exist no positive balanced growth capital/labor ratio (cf. f^2 in Figure 2.2). If $\beta < 0$, then $f(0) > 0$, violating Inada's condition (5), and there

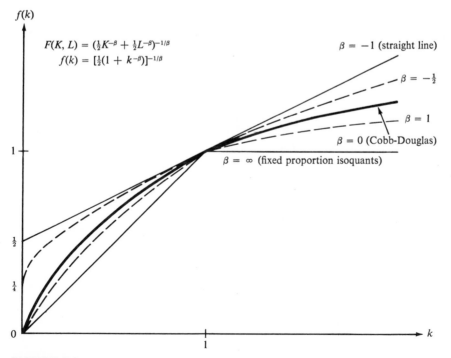

FIGURE 2.4

may be no balanced growth capital/labor ratio at all (cf. f^1 in Figure 2.2). In particular, if the isoquants are all parallel straight lines ($\beta \equiv -1$) or "nested" rectangular loci (i.e., fixed proportions case with $\beta = \infty$), the Inada conditions will not be fulfilled. The $f(k)$ curves for five members of the CES family are plotted in Figure 2.4 (for further graphical analysis of the CES function see [5, 6]) and the form of $f(k)$ and the values of $f(0)$ and $f'(0)$ for each of those five specimens are given in Table 2.1.

TABLE 2.1[a]

β	$f(k)$	$f(0)$	$f'(0)$	
-1	$\frac{1}{2}(1+k)$	$\frac{1}{2}$	$\frac{1}{2}$	Fail to meet condition (5)
$-\frac{1}{2}$	$\frac{1}{4}(1+\sqrt{k})^2$	$\frac{1}{4}$	∞	
0	$\sqrt{k}$	0	∞	
1	$2k/(1+k)$	0	2	Fail to meet condition (3)
∞	Min $[1, k]$	0	1	

[a]The evaluation of $f(k)$ for $\beta = 0$ and $\beta = \infty$ requires limiting processes. See [4].

2.2.3. The "Harrod-Domar" case

Basing our discussion on that of Solow, we can analyze the "Harrod-Domar" case as follows. Suppose the aggregate production function is the fixed proportion type; then

$$F(K, L) = \text{Min} \begin{Bmatrix} K/a \\ L/b \end{Bmatrix}$$

Unless capital and labor inputs bear the proportion $a:b$ to each other, the relatively scarcer input forms the bottleneck and the other input becomes redundant at the margin. We can derive the per capita output function:

$$f(k) = \text{Min} \begin{Bmatrix} K/aL \\ 1/b \end{Bmatrix} = \text{Min} \begin{Bmatrix} k/a \\ 1/b \end{Bmatrix}$$

This is shown in Figure 2.5. We can obtain three subcases depending upon whether $n/s - 1/a$ is positive, zero, or negative.

Subcase 1: $\dfrac{n_1}{s_1} > \dfrac{1}{a}$, or $n_1 > \dfrac{s_1}{a}$ (natural rate > warranted rate)

Subcase 2: $\dfrac{n_2}{s_2} = \dfrac{1}{a}$, or $n_2 = \dfrac{s_2}{a}$ (natural rate = warranted rate)

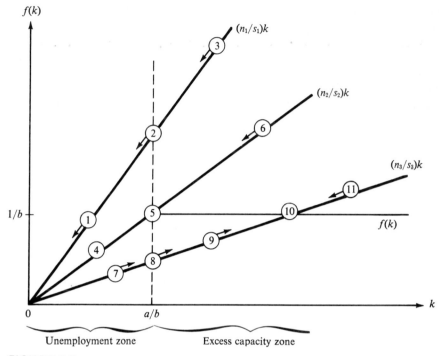

FIGURE 2.5

Subcase 3: $\dfrac{n_3}{s_3} < \dfrac{1}{a}$, or $n_3 < \dfrac{s_3}{a}$ (natural rate < warranted rate)

For each subcase, different growth patterns may emerge because the initial capital/labor ratio may take various values. By plotting the pairs of $[k(0), (n/s)k(0)]$, we can obtain eleven different positions in Figure 2.5, each represented by a numbered circle. Certain positions generate motions toward other positions. These motions are indicated by arrows. We first partition initial positions into three types:

(1) Initial (labor) unemployment, i.e., $k(0) < a/b$
(2) Initial full employment and full capacity, i.e., $k(0) = a/b$
(3) Initial excess capacity, i.e., $k(0) > a/b$

In the subcase where the natural rate is less than the warranted rate and with initial excess capacity, we again subdivide the initial position into three types:

(a) $(n/s)k(0) < 1/b$
(b) $(n/s)k(0) = 1/b$
(c) $(n/s)k(0) > 1/b$

because these three situations have different growth patterns.

These eleven cases can be analyzed via the phase diagram approach, as shown in Figure 2.1. The results are summarized in Table 2.2.

TABLE 2.2 CLASSIFICATION OF POSITIONS

		Natural rate higher than warranted rate $\dfrac{n}{s} > \dfrac{1}{a}$	Natural rate equal to warranted rate $\dfrac{n}{s} = \dfrac{1}{a}$	Natural rate lower than warranted rate $\dfrac{n}{s} < \dfrac{1}{a}$
Initial unemployment $k(0) < \dfrac{a}{b}$		(1) Unstable position; capital/labor ratio falling, unemployment rising more than exponentially	(4) Neutral position; capital/labor ratio remaining the same, unemployment rising exponentially	(7) Unstable position; capital/labor ratio rising, unemployment falling
Initial full employment without excess capacity $k(0) = \dfrac{a}{b}$		(2) Unstable position; capital/labor ratio falling, unemployment tending to rise	(5) Neutral-stable position; capital/labor ratio remaining the same, full employment without excess capacity	(8) Unstable position; capital/labor ratio rising, excess capacity tending to rise
Initial excess capacity $k(0) > \dfrac{a}{b}$	$\left(\dfrac{n}{s}\right)k < \dfrac{1}{b}$			(9) Unstable position; capital/labor ratio rising, excess capacity rising more than exponentially
	$\left(\dfrac{n}{s}\right)k = \dfrac{1}{b}$			(10) Stable position; capital/labor ratio remaining the same, excess capacity rising exponentially
	$\left(\dfrac{n}{s}\right)k > \dfrac{1}{b}$	(3) Unstable position; capital/labor ratio falling, excess capacity falling	(6) Unstable position; capital/labor ratio falling, excess capacity falling	(11) Unstable position; capital/labor ratio falling, excess capacity falling or rising less than exponentially

We shall analyze position (1) as an example. Since $f(k(0)) - (n/s)k(0) = \dot{k}(0) < 0$, the position is unstable and the capital/labor ratio tends to fall. Initially, the total working population $L(0)$ requires a capital level of $L(0)(a/b)$ to keep employed. Actual available capital is $L(0)k(0) < L(0)(a/b)$, resulting in an initial unemployment of $L(0)[a/b - k(0)]$. $L(t)$ grows at rate n. But $[a/b - k(0)]$ increases as k decreases. Hence, unemployment, $L(t)[a/b - k(0)]$, grows at a rate faster than n. The analyses of the other ten positions are similar to this.

We note that position (4) is a *neutral equilibrium,* meaning that the position is self-perpetuating if left alone but it has no tendency to return to any status quo after a small perturbation. Position (5) is a neutral-stable equilibrium in the sense that the position is self-perpetuating and any upward perturbation of $k(0)$ leads to an eventual return of the status quo. For position (11), a decreasing proportion of productive capacity remains idle although total labor L is always rising and the aggregate capital $K = Lk$ may or may not be rising. Hence, it is not clear whether the absolute volume of excess capacity, $K - L(a/b) = L(k - a/b)$, is rising or not.

Summing up, in this "Harrod-Domar" case,

(1) A balanced growth path does not always exist. It exists only when $n \leq s/a$.
(2) If there is a balanced growth path, it either lacks full stability (as when $n = s/a$) or implies that the unemployment of one or another input will grow exponentially or more than exponentially.

After reviewing the above results, Solow concluded that:

(1) The assumption of a fixed proportion production function is responsible for the Harrod-Domar view that the capitalistic system can hardly achieve a balanced growth path with full employment (of both factors).
(2) The relaxation of this crucial assumption invalidates their conclusions.
(3) The real-life situation hardly justifies such a crucial but extremely restrictive assumption.

Although Solow's model contains neither the scrapping mechanism of Domar nor the short-run unstable adjustment of Harrod, it does capture the essence of Harrod's long-run analysis. In fact, it improves upon Harrod in pointing out the following facts:

(1) Full-employment balanced growth is neutral-stable. Any perturbation of the system toward excess capacity can be self-adjusted, yet any displacement toward unemployment of labor will lead to exponentially growing unemployment.
(2) If the natural rate is lower than the warranted rate, then there exists a stable equilibrium with growing excess capacity.

2.3 THE SOLOW MODEL—COMPARATIVE BALANCED GROWTH, UNBALANCED GROWTH, AND EXTENSIONS

Besides providing a critical appraisal and generalization of the Harrod-Domar long-run analysis, Solow also dealt with growth problems concerning dynamic equilibrium as well as the dynamic path. He further showed how various modifications can be made to his main theme. We shall examine these topics in turn.

Consider the following two problems:

(1) If two economies grow along balanced growth paths, how can we predict

or explain the divergent growth patterns pertaining to these two countries?
(2) If a given economy is growing according to an unbalanced path, what can
be predicted about the long-run tendencies of such an economy?

That the Solow model can answer the first problem is recognized by most if
not all economists. Its ability to answer the second problem is somewhat more
controversial. Although its approximate validity may be accepted by Samuelson,
English economists such as Mrs. Robinson and Hicks have strong reservations
about such claims; much will be said on this topic in the next two chapters.

2.3.1. Comparative balanced growth and unbalanced growth

Before analyzing the comparative dynamic problems, we shall make a brief
digression into the production theory. Under perfect competition and constant
returns to scale, one can deduce at any point on a differentiable arc of the $f(k)$
curve seven types of magnitudes, three on production relations and four on
income distributions. We shall first tabulate the results in Table 2.3 and then
discuss their derivations.

TABLE 2.3

	Algebraic representation in terms of k and f	Geometrical representation Figure 2.6
Input-output relations:		
1. Capital/labor ratio, K/L	k	Length $\overline{OB}$
2. Output/labor ratio, Q/L	$f(k)$	Length $\overline{OC}$
3. Output/capital ratio, Q/K	$f(k)/k$	Slope of OA
Income distribution magnitudes:		
4. Rent rate,[a] r	$f'(k)$	Slope of DA
5. Wage rate, w	$f(k) - kf'(k)$	Length $\overline{OD}$
6. Wage/rent ratio, $\omega = w/r$	$[f(k)/f'(k)] - k$	Length $\overline{EO}$
7. Wage and rent shares		
a. Wage share, wL/Q	$1 - [kf'(k)/f(k)]$	Length $\overline{OD}$/length $\overline{OC}$
b. Rent share, rK/Q	$kf'(k)/f(k)$	Length $\overline{CD}$/length $\overline{OC}$

[a]The term "rent rate" used here and in subsequent chapters is a "shorthand" for the
return of capital.

The algebraic representations for items 1, 2, and 3 in Table 2.3 follow from the
definitions of k and $f(k)$. Remembering that $f(k) = F[(K/L), 1]$, we can derive
the expression in item 4; i.e.,

$$\frac{\partial Q}{\partial K} = \frac{\partial (Lf)}{\partial K} \qquad \text{(since } Q = LF[(K/L), 1] \text{ from (2.1.2))}$$

$$= L \frac{df}{dk} \frac{\partial k}{\partial K} = f'(k) \qquad \text{("chain rule" of differentiation)}$$

The results for items 3 and 4 yield the algebraic representation of item 7b. Item 7a follows, since wage share and capital share add to unity. Items 2 and 7a then imply item 5, while items 4 and 5 combined lead to item 6.

In Figure 2.6, the curve representing the $f(k)$ function passes through A and A'. If k is represented by $\overline{OB}$, we can draw the vertical line AB to intersect the $f(k)$ curve at A, linking O and A and obtaining the ray[8] OA.[9] The tangent to $f(k)$ at A cuts the $f(k)$ axis at D and its extension reaches the horizontal axis at E. The line AC is the horizontal line from A reaching the $f(k)$ axis. The identification of $k, f(k)$, and $f(k)/k$ with lengths $\overline{OB}$ and $\overline{OC}$ and the slope of OA is immediate. So is the representation of f' by the slope of $DA = \overline{CD}/\overline{AC} = \overline{OD}/\overline{OE}$. Since $\overline{OB} = \overline{AC}$ stands for capital per capita and $\overline{CD}/\overline{AC}$ is the rent rate, we see that $\overline{CD}$ is the rental expenditure per capita. Dividing this amount by output per capita, we obtain the rent share, $\overline{CD}/\overline{OC}$, and subtracting this amount from output per capita, we obtain the "wage expenditure per capita," which is the wage rate, $\overline{OD}$. The derivations of the wage/rent ratio and the wage share are left for the interested reader.

The above preliminary analysis supplies the tools for the following discussions.

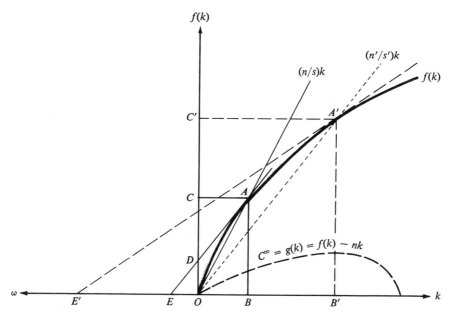

FIGURE 2.6

A. COMPARATIVE BALANCED GROWTH

1. In the Solow model, if there exists a stable balanced growth path, then the long-run growth rate is not affected either by the saving/income ratio or by the

---

[8]A ray is a line through the origin.

[9]So far, A may be any point on $f(k)$.

form of the production function. This follows from the definition of balanced growth under which output must grow at the same rate as labor, i.e., at the rate n.

2. Under the same conditions, the long-run output/capital ratio is also independent of the particular form of the production function. This ratio must be equal to n/s, as can be seen from Figure 2.6, where A is now assumed to be the intersection between the $(n/s)k$ line and the $f(k)$ curve.

3. In general, as long as the marginal product of capital is nonincreasing (i.e., $f''(k) < 0$), the comparative analysis for balanced growth paths can be summarized as in Table 2.4.

TABLE 2.4

Sign of the corresponding change of	An increase of		Graphic derivation from Fig. 2.6
	s	n	
1. K/L	+	−	$\overline{OB'} > \overline{OB}$
2. Q/L	+	−	$\overline{OC'} > \overline{OC}$
3. Q/K	−	+	Slope of $OA' <$ slope of OA
4. r	−	+	Slope of $DA' <$ slope of DA
5. w	+	−	$\overline{OD'} > \overline{OD}$
6. $\omega = w/r$	+	−	$\overline{OE'} > \overline{OE}$
7a. wL/Q	$\left\{\begin{matrix} - \\ 0 \\ + \end{matrix}\right\}$	$\left\{\begin{matrix} + \\ 0 \\ - \end{matrix}\right\}$ if $\sigma \left\{\begin{matrix} > \\ = \\ < \end{matrix}\right\} 1^a$	
7b. rK/Q	$\left\{\begin{matrix} + \\ 0 \\ - \end{matrix}\right\}$	$\left\{\begin{matrix} - \\ 0 \\ + \end{matrix}\right\}$ if $\sigma \left\{\begin{matrix} > \\ = \\ < \end{matrix}\right\} 1^a$	

$^a \sigma = \dfrac{w/r}{K/L} \dfrac{d(K/L)}{d(w/r)}$ is the elasticity of factor substitution, i.e., $\sigma = (d \ln k)/(d \ln \omega)$, the percent response in capital per capita k for 1% change of the input price ratio ω.

In Figure 2.6, the dotted line $(n'/s')k$ is flatter than $(n/s)k$. This can occur with various combinations of the values n, n', s, and s'. However, two special cases are especially illuminating:

(a) $s = s'$, $n > n'$, i.e., a variation of n alone.
(b) $s' > s$, $n' = n$, i.e., a variation of s alone.

Reading off the relative magnitudes of $\overline{OB}$, $\overline{OB'}$, etc., from Figure 2.6, we obtain the entries in the last column of Table 2.4. Comparing the last column of Table 2.3, where capital/labor ratio has the geometric representation $\overline{OB}$, etc., we can deduce the results in the first six rows of Table 2.4..

For results in rows 7a and 7b, we observe that:

(a) Since wage share and rent share add up to unity, the wage share increases (rent share decreases) if and only if the ratio of wage share to rent share increases.

(b) The ratio of wage share to rent share is equal to the wage/rent ratio divided by the capital/labor ratio. If the wage/rent ratio increases by 1%, the capital/labor ratio increases by $\sigma\%$, and hence the ratio of wage share to rent share rises by approximately

$$\frac{1+1\%}{1+\sigma\%} - 1 = \frac{(1-\sigma)\%}{1+\sigma\%}$$

(c) Hence, the directions of change of wage rate and wage share are the same or opposite depending upon whether $\sigma < 1$ or $\sigma > 1$. Futhermore, for $\sigma = 1$, the wage and rent shares will be unaffected by changes of n or s. (If $\sigma = 1$ for all values of ω, then the production function is Cobb-Douglas.)

The above analysis can be made rigorous with the help of elementary calculus.[10]

4. If for two countries with identical production functions the saving ratio and the population growth rate in one country are higher than those in the other by the same proportion, then both countries will have the same set of long-run values of K/L, Q/L, Q/K, w, r, and w/r, even though one economy grows faster than the other.

5. If two countries have the same production function with nonincreasing marginal product of capital (i.e., $f''(k) \leq 0$) and the same population growth rate, then different saving ratios imply different levels of consumption per capita. This topic will be discussed in full detail in Chapter 9 under the name "golden rule programs." We shall simply state the result that

$$\frac{\partial c^{\infty}}{\partial s} \begin{Bmatrix} > \\ = \\ < \end{Bmatrix} 0 \quad \text{if} \quad f'(k) \begin{Bmatrix} > \\ = \\ < \end{Bmatrix} n$$

where c^{∞} is the per capita consumption at the balanced growth equilibrium with $c^{\infty} = f(k) - nK = g(k)$. The $g(k)$ curve is shown as a broken line in Figure 2.6.

6. Comparisons between balanced growth paths involving different production functions can also be carried out by means of the phase diagram. The only requirement is that we know the specific shapes of the $f(k)$ curves.

The major objections to the method of comparative balanced growth are leveled against its practical relevancy. The results mentioned above are useful in comparing two economies under balanced growth that share the same technological know-how. These two economies may pertain to two contemporaneous societies or to two hypothetical historical courses an economy could conceivably take. The question now becomes: How realistic is it to assume

---

[10]Setting $rK/Q = \alpha$, $wL/rK = (1/\alpha) - 1$ and $(d/d\alpha)[(1/\alpha) - 1] = -\alpha^{-2} < 0$. Now $wL/rK = \omega/k$. Taking the logarithmic derivative with respect to ω,

$$\frac{d \ln (wL/rK)}{d\omega} = \frac{1}{\omega} - \frac{\sigma}{\omega} = \frac{1-\sigma}{\omega}$$

Combining all these results, $d\alpha/d\omega = -\alpha(1-\alpha)(1-\sigma)/\omega$ and $d(1-\alpha)/d\omega = \alpha(1-\alpha)(1-\sigma)/\omega$.

(a) that economies undertake balanced growth and (b) that the economies under comparison share the same technology? The answer seems to depend upon the specific problem one is dealing with and how accurate or how broad a picture one is aiming at.

B. UNBALANCED GROWTH

It is generally recognized that capital per worker has been increasing over time for most of the advanced economies. Hence, unbalanced growth models appear to have much more immediate relevance than balanced growth studies. The main problem for the Solow model, in this aspect, is the realism of the simplifying assumptions. For reasons we shall see in later chapters, under balanced growth some of these assumptions (e.g., perfect foresight) are much more plausible than under unbalanced growth; other assumptions (e.g., the existence of a homogeneous, all-purpose capital good) are much more defensible as useful "surrogates."[11] These will be discussed in Chapters 3 and 4. However, granted that those assumptions are accepted, then rigorous logical deductions can provide various results.

1. Quantitatively, if we are given the algebraic form of $F(K, L)$ or $f(k)$, the parametric values of n and s, and the initial values for k and L, we can solve for the exact time paths of all the economic variables.

Example. The production function is of the Cobb-Douglas form:

$$Q = K^{\alpha}L^{1-\alpha}$$

(2.1.3) then becomes:

$$\dot{K}(t) = sK^{\alpha}(t)\,L^{1-\alpha}(t)$$

$$= (sL_0^{1-\alpha})K^{\alpha}(t)e^{(1-\alpha)nt} \qquad \text{(from (2.1.1))}$$

This differential equation yields the solution

$$K(t) = \left[K^{1-\alpha}(0)+(sL_0^{1-\alpha}/n)\,(e^{n(1-\alpha)t}-1)\right]^{1/(1-\alpha)}$$

which can be verified by differentiating with respect to t and checking for $t = 0$.[12]

It is possible to deduce other time paths such as

$$Q(t) = \left[K^{1-\alpha}(0)+(sL_0^{1-\alpha}/n)\,(e^{n(1-\alpha)t}-1)\right]^{\alpha/(1-\alpha)}L_0^{1-\alpha}e^{n(1-\alpha)t}$$

$$k(t) = \left[K^{1-\alpha}(0)e^{-n(1-\alpha)t}+(sL_0^{1-\alpha}/n)\,(1-e^{-n(1-\alpha)t})\right]^{1/(1-\alpha)}/L_0$$

$$w(t) = (1-\alpha)\left[K^{1-\alpha}(0)e^{-n(1-\alpha)t}+(sL_0^{1-\alpha}/n)\,(1-e^{-n(1-\alpha)t})\right]^{\alpha/(1-\alpha)}/L_0^{\alpha}$$

[11]That is, as useful fables to generate accurate predictions of real events.

[12]
$$\frac{dK}{dt} = \frac{1}{1-\alpha}[\;]^{\{1/(1-\alpha)\}-1}(sL_0^{1-\alpha}/n)\{n(1-\alpha)e^{n(1-\alpha)t}\}$$
$$= ([\;]^{1/(1-\alpha)})^{\alpha}s(L_0e^{nt})^{1-\alpha}$$
$$= sK^{\alpha}L^{1-\alpha}, \text{ which satisfies the differential equation}$$

$K(t)|_{t=0} = \left[K^{1-\alpha}(0)+0\right]^{1/(1-\alpha)} = K(0)$, which satisfies the initial condition

The method of solving this type of differential equation is discussed in the Mathematical Appendix.

2. Qualitatively, the long-run trend for all the relevant magnitudes can be deduced either algebraically or geometrically.

(a) *The algebraic approach.* After obtaining the dynamic paths, one can analyze their long-run trends. Using the same example appearing above in item 1, we have, as $t \to \infty$:

$$K(t) = [\{K^{1-\alpha}(0) - (sL_0^{1-\alpha}/n)\}e^{-n(1-\alpha)t} + (sL_0^{1-\alpha}/n)]^{1/(1-\alpha)}e^{nt}$$
$$\sim (s/n)^{1/(1-\alpha)}L_0 e^{nt}$$

$$Q(t) = [\{K^{1-\alpha}(0) - (sL_0^{1-\alpha}/n)\}e^{-n(1-\alpha)t} + (sL_0^{1-\alpha}/n)]^{\alpha/(1-\alpha)}L_0^{1-\alpha}e^{nt}$$
$$\sim (s/n)^{\alpha/(1-\alpha)}L_0 e^{nt}$$

where the $\sim$ sign means the ratio of the two magnitudes separated by it approaches unity.

$$k(t) = [\{K^{1-\alpha}(0) - (sL_0^{1-\alpha}/n)\}e^{-n(1-\alpha)t} + (sL_0^{1-\alpha}/n)]^{1/(1-\alpha)}/L_0$$
$$\to (s/n)^{1/(1-\alpha)}$$

$$w(t) = (1-\alpha)[\{K^{1-\alpha}(0) - (sL_0^{1-\alpha}/n)\}e^{-n(1-\alpha)t} + (sL_0^{1-\alpha}/n)]^{\alpha/(1-\alpha)}/L_0^{\alpha}$$
$$\to (1-\alpha)(s/n)^{\alpha/(1-\alpha)}$$

Moreover, $k(t)$ and $w(t)$ approach their asymptotic values monotonically from below (above) if $[K(0)/L_0] - (s/n)^{1/(1-\alpha)}$ is negative (positive).

(b) *The geometric approach.* Suppose we know the general form of $f(k)$ as well as the initial capital/labor ratio $k(0)$; using a phase diagram (such as the one in Figure 2.1), we can deduce that $k(t)$ approaches 0, ∞, or some stable equilibrium value k^{∞} in a monotonic manner or, in the rare case, stays at some stable or unstable equilibrium value of k. The point $\{k(t), f[k(t)]\}$ also moves along a certain section of the $f(k)$ locus. At each of these points, Table 2.3 provides the graphical determination of eight economic magnitudes: output per capita, wage rate, etc. Therefore, the time trends of these eight magnitudes can be graphically ascertained in a manner similar to the derivation of Table 2.4.

2.3.2. Simple extensions

The Solow model discussed above can be easily extended in various directions.

A. HARROD-NEUTRAL TECHNICAL PROGRESS

Under the assumption of Harrod-neutral technical progress[13] (i.e., labor-augmenting technical progress), the efficiency of labor input alone increases over time so that each person today can handle more than one worker's job of

---

[13]Such technical progress does not affect the capital/output ratio, other things being equal. Hence, Harrod called it neutral.

last year. We discussed this concept in Chapter 1 under fixed coefficient production functions. The general definition is as follows:

$$Q = F(K, L; t) \qquad \text{(this shows the production surface shifts over time)}$$

$$= \bar{F}[K, A(t)L] \qquad \text{(this specifies that the shifts reflect that there is "more working force per worker" as time goes on)}$$

where $\bar{F}$ is linear homogeneous.

We shall approach the problem from two different angles:

(1) We may redefine labor in "efficiency units"; i.e., we may set $L'(t) = A(t)L(t)$. Likewise, we introduce the "primed" variable and parameter:

$$k'(t) = K(t)/L'(t)$$

$$n' = n + \dot{A}(t)/A(t)$$

where $\lambda = \dot{A}(t)/A(t)$ is conventionally assumed to be a constant.

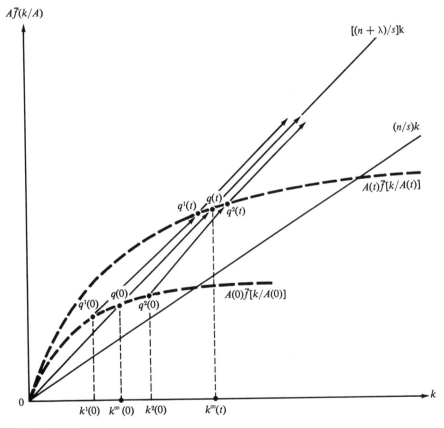

FIGURE 2.7

Also, we set

$$\bar{f}(k') = \bar{F}[(K/AL), 1]$$

We can obtain the dynamic equation,

$$\dot{k}' = s\bar{f}(k') - n'k'$$

The earlier analysis can be paraphrased word by word. The growth path under which

$$\dot{k}' \equiv 0 \equiv s\bar{f}(k') - n'k'$$

is called the "golden age" path. We may regard the balanced growth path as a special case of the golden age path with $\lambda = 0$. In terms of natural units, however, we may note that in a golden age growth path,

(a) The output/labor ratio, the capital/labor ratio, the wage rate, and the wage/rent ratio will increase exponentially at rate λ.
(b) The capital/output ratio, the rent rate, the wage share, and the rent share will remain the same.

The derivations of these results can be sketched below. If K/L' and Q/L' are constant, K/L and Q/L must increase at rate λ. $K/Q = (K/L')/(Q/L')$ remains constant. The constancy of wage and rent shares can be seen graphically by relabeling Figure 2.6 so that k becomes k' and $f(k)$ becomes $\bar{f}(k')$. Since the wage share is the ratio between the wage rate and Q/L, constant wage share requires the wage to grow also at the rate λ. By the same token, the rent rate is constant. Hence, w/r grows at the rate λ.

(2) We may use natural units for labor. We note that output per capita at time t is

$$F[K(t), L(t); t]/L(t) = \bar{F}[K(t), A(t)L(t)]/L(t)$$

$$= A(t)\bar{F}[K(t)/A(t)L(t); 1]$$

or, dividing both sides by $A(t)$ and setting q equal to $Q(t)/L(t)$,

$$\frac{q}{A(t)} = \bar{f}\left[\frac{k}{A(t)}\right]$$

Plotting q against k for various values of $A(t)$, we obtain a family of "homothetic curves" such as the dotted loci in Figure 2.7. Each curve is similar to every other curve, differing only in scale.

The golden age path is represented by the ray $Oq(0)q(t)$. This ray lies above the $(n/s)k$ ray, indicating the continuing rise of the capital/labor ratio. The fact that $Oq(0)q(t)$ is a ray shows that the output/capital ratio is constant. The homotheticity of the $A\bar{f}(k/A)$ family shows that the tangent line to $A(0)\bar{f}[k/A(0)]$ at $q(0)$ is parallel to the tangent line to $A(t)\bar{f}[k/A(t)]$ at $q(t)$. Hence, the rent rate is constant. Dividing the rent rate by the output/capital ratio, we obtain the rent share. Hence, the rent share is also constant. *Ipso facto*, so is the wage share. The rise of the capital/labor ratio k and output per worker, $A\bar{f}(k/A)$, can be read off the diagram. Drawing tangents to the dotted $A\bar{f}(k/A)$ curves from $q(0)$ and $q(t)$ (not shown), one can also note that the vertical intercepts of such tangents (i.e., the wage rate; cf. Table 2.3) rise over time in proportion to the rise in output per worker. Moreover, the stability property of the golden age output/capital ratio (i.e., the slope of $Oq(t)$) can also be determined from Figure 2.7. Suppose at time 0 the economy is at $q^1(0)$, having less capital per worker as well as less output per worker than at position $q(0)$. But the output/capital ratio is higher at $q^1(0)$ than at $q(0)$. To keep capital growing at the rate of labor growth plus the rate of technical progress, we need an investment of $(n+\lambda)k^1(0)L(0)$. Under the given saving propensities, we need only an output level of $[(n+\lambda)/s]k^1(0)L(0)$, or per capita output of $[(n+\lambda)k^1(0)/s]$. Since $A(0)f[k^1(0)/A(0)]$ (i.e., the length of $q^1(0)k^1(0)$) is higher than the latter level because $q^1(0)$ is above the $[(n+\lambda)/s]k$ ray, capital grows at a rate faster than $(n+\lambda)$ and the relative shortage of labor supply will make the output grow more slowly than capital. Hence, the output/capital ratio at t, i.e., the slope of the line $Oq^1(t)$ (not drawn) is flatter than the slope of $Oq^1(0)$ (not drawn either). A similar analysis in $q^2(0)$ and $q^2(t)$ can be conducted. Hence, the Q/K ratio approaches $[(n+\lambda)/s]$ as $t \to \infty$.

B.   VARIABLE POPULATION GROWTH RATE AND/OR SAVING PROPENSITY

One may assume that either n or s or both are functions of k. Two possible justifications are:

(1) The higher the capital/labor ratio, the lower the rent rate, and the smaller the saving propensity:

$$\frac{ds}{dk} < 0$$

(2) The lower the capital/labor ratio, the lower the wage rate, and the smaller the population growth rate:

$$\frac{dn}{dk} > 0$$

If these reasonings hold, the $(n/s)k$ ray must be curvilinear, as shown in Figure 2.8. The existence and implications of the balanced growth path can be analyzed as before.

C.   HICKS-NEUTRAL TECHNICAL PROGRESS

Under the assumption of Hicks-neutral technical progress[14] (i.e., output-augmenting technical progress), the production surface shifts in such a way that the isoquant map remains invariant except that the output level associated with any given isoquant increases over time according to the technical progress index $A(t)$, which is usually assumed to be $e^{\lambda t}$. Formally, we can write

$$Q(t) = A(t)F[K(t), L(t)]$$

---

[14]Such technical progress does not affect the capital/labor ratio, other things being equal. Hence, Hicks called it neutral.

where F is linear homogeneous in K and L as before, and $A(t) = e^{\lambda t}$. It can be shown that the Hicks-neutral technical progress is incompatible with:

(1) The golden age growth path, unless the production function is Cobb-Douglas. That is,

$$Q(t) = e^{\lambda t} K^{\alpha}(t) L^{1-\alpha}(t) \quad \text{where } L(t) = L_0 e^{nt}$$

In this special case, it is no different from the Harrod-neutral technical progress case with labor efficiency rising at the rate $\lambda/(1-\alpha)$. This result was first obtained by Uzawa [7]. An alternative graphical proof is provided in Appendix 2.1.

(2) The balanced growth path. In fact, under the Inada conditions stated earlier, it can be shown[15] that except for a possible initial phase the capital/labor ratio, the output/labor ratio, the wage rate, and the wage/rent rate must increase monotonically toward infinity.

---

[15](2.1.4) can now be modified into:

$$\dot{k} = sf(k)e^{\lambda t} - nk$$

This is equivalent to the integral equation:

$$k(t) = k(0) \exp \int_0^t (\{sf[k(u)]e^{\lambda u}/k(u)\} - n)\, du$$

One may differentiate the latter by t to obtain the former, and when $t = 0$, the latter becomes an identity. Suppose there exists an upper bound $\bar{k}$ for all $k(t)$. Since

$$\frac{d}{dk}\left[\frac{f(k)}{k}\right] = \frac{1}{k^2}[kf'(k) - f(k)] < 0$$

due to $f''(k) < 0$ (see proof of the stability property of k^{∞} in Section 2.2.2), we have

$$sf[k(u)]/k(u) > sf(\bar{k})/\bar{k} = m$$

where $m > 0$ is some constant, for all u between 0 and t. Thus,

$$k(t) > k(0) \exp \int_0^t (me^{\lambda u} - n)\, du$$

$$= k(0) \exp\{[m(e^{\lambda t} - 1)/\lambda] - nt\}$$

$> \bar{k}$ for all $t > \bar{t}$, where $\bar{t}$ is some large value which is a contradiction. Hence, $k(t)$ is unbounded from above.

Differentiating the above differential equation by t, we obtain

$$\dot{k}(t) = [f'(k)\dot{k} + \lambda f(k)]se^{\lambda t} - n\dot{k}$$

which takes the positive sign whenever $\dot{k} = 0$. Now consider $\dot{k}(t)$ as a function of t. This function can cross the horizontal axis at most once at a positive angle; let this point be called T. Obviously, $\dot{k} > 0$ for all $t > T$.

Using Inada's conditions (1) and (6) (Section 2.2.2), one can conclude that $f(k)$ also increases steadily toward positive infinity beyond T. The same holds for per capita output: $e^{\lambda t}f(k)$.

Now $w(t) = e^{\lambda t}\{f[k(t)] - k(t)f'[k(t)]\}$, where $(d/dk)\{\ \} = -k(t)f''[k(t)] > 0$ and $k(t) \geq k(T)$ for all $t > T$. Since $\{\ \} \geq f[k(T)] - k(T)f'[k(T)] > 0$, $e^{\lambda t}$ grows monotonically to positive infinity and $w(t)$ eventually approaches infinity. Moreover, for $t > T$, $w(t)$ increases all the time.

The analysis of $\omega(t) = e^{\lambda t}\{f[k(t)]/f'[k(t)] - k(t)\}$ is similar to this.

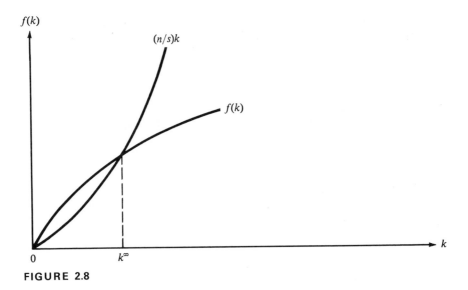

FIGURE 2.8

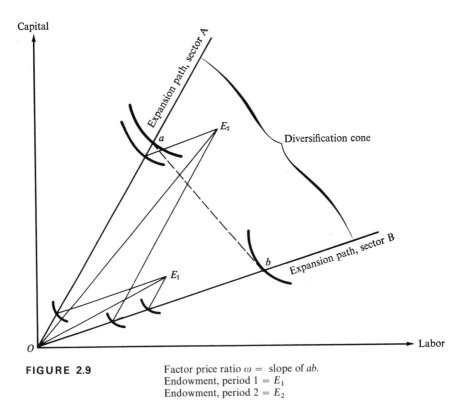

FIGURE 2.9   Factor price ratio $\omega =$ slope of ab.
Endowment, period 1 $= E_1$
Endowment, period 2 $= E_2$

D. MISCELLANEOUS

Actually, the versatility of the simple Solovian model is limited only by the imagination and ingenuity of its potential users. Without going into details, we may cite as an example the fruitful application of the Solovian model to the economics of developing countries by S. C. Tsiang [8].

2.4 THE SOLOW MODEL—DISSENTIONS AND CRITICISMS

The objections raised to the Solow model over the past dozen years can be classified into three categories typified by the Modern Cambridge School, Ryuzo Sato, and Robert Eisner.

1. The Modern Cambridge School, notably Mrs. Robinson, Kaldor, and Pasinetti. Their attacks concentrate upon the realism of the Solovian assumptions. These are fundamental issues. We shall discuss these in the next two chapters.

2. Ryuzo Sato [9, 10]. His contention is that the variations of the capital/labor ratio in reality cannot possibly be very large. Hence, the Harrod-Domar rigidity in factor proportions is essentially correct. In view of the successive disaggregations in "latter-day" growth models, such arguments become relatively unimportant. In fact, the Rybcynski theorem in international trade shows that significant changes of overall factor proportions can be accommodated by intersectoral shifting of resources, without changing the sectoral factor proportions.[16] See Figure 2.9. Hence, it is hard to justify the Harrodian pessimism about capital deepening by the empirical observation that sectoral factor intensities are slow to alter. Certain studies by students of Arrow and Kuh also indicate that Sato's result follows certain very special assumptions (see Stiglitz and Uzawa [11], p. 7, footnote 4).

3. Robert Eisner [12]. The objections raised by Eisner include two different points:

(a) Harrod never assumed fixed proportion production functions. Instead he postulated rigidity in interest rate, which then leads to fixity of factor proportions. Hence, in Eisner's view, Solow attributed to Harrod a position Harrod never maintained.

(b) Solow did not pay adequate attention to the Keynesian difficulties, e.g., liquidity trap, downward inflexibility of wage rate, etc. Moreover, the marginal product of capital may become zero at some finite capital/labor ratio.

In his reply [13], Solow pointed out that he already indicated in his paper that:

(i) The Keynesian difficulties may be introduced as side constraints, i.e.:
$f'(k) \geq$ Liquidity trap rate of interest $= f'(k^2)$
$f(k) - kf'(k) \geq$ Minimum acceptable rate of wage $= f(k^1) - k^1 f'(k^1)$

---

[16]In the context of growth, the important issue is whether an economy can be induced to consume more of the product produced by the relatively abundant factor.

The effect is to introduce the side condition, $k^1 \leq k \leq k^2$, which is reflected in Figure 2.10.

(ii) The Keynesian difficulties presumably are short run in character (for a supporting view, see Matthews and Hahn [14]). Long-run adjustments (in both institutional and expectational aspects) may change the values k^1 and k^2. This is reflected by the essentially steady (though somewhat zigzag) trend of growth experienced by capitalistic economies. Ultimate barriers (zero marginal product of capital) may eventually come into play, but this is not of current concern.

(iii) The Keynesian difficulties may occupy their legitimate places in a supermodel of the future. For the time being, investigations into the neoclassical side of the coin will be fruitful both in their own right and as a preparation for future synthesis.

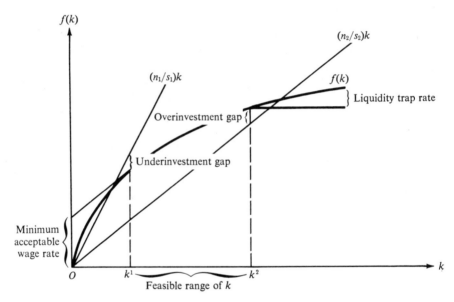

FIGURE 2.10   Case 1: $(n_1/s_1)k$, ever-worsening unemployment
Case 2: $(n_2/s_2)k$, ever-worsening excess capacity

In addition to these Solovian points, we may include the Samuelsonian view [15] that proper monetary and fiscal policies can assuage the Keynesian rigidities in such a way that the resulting economic system may behave in a neoclassical fashion. However, this approach of "neoclassical synthesis" has not yet gained universal support among economists. Recently, Arrow [16] lamented that the government-controlled economy may not behave in neoclassical fashion, yet there exists no better synthesis. This reflects some of the dissenters' stand.

Finally, we may note that Solow could have taken a much stronger view on point (a), above. Eisner was formally correct to assert that the basic Harrodian assumption is a fixed interest rate, rather than a fixed capital/labor ratio. But as we have shown in Chapter 1, Harrod cannot legitimately deduce that fixed interest rate implies fixed factor proportions. Hence, only the "Solow version" of the Harrod theory is logically valid.

In retrospect, the 1956 Solow model is one of the earliest attempts to reconcile neoclassical traditions with the macroaggregate analysis of the Keynesians. Due to subsequent studies, some of them by Solow, such a synthesis appears to be nearer to us today than before. We would like to discuss here why such a synthesis is hard to come by:

(a) The Keynesian "side conditions" in Figure 2.10 only suggest how Keynesian difficulties may occur. A full-fledged model incorporating Keynesian elements must include the formation of effective demand and hence the inducement to invest as well as a full-fledged monetary sector. In these areas it is rather difficult to construct a theory that is simple enough to manipulate yet realistic enough to be relevant.

(b) It is reasonable to assign short-run problems to the Keynesian approach and to gauge the long-run broad trends with neoclassical growth theory. But the long run is the congregation of a sequence of short runs. There is yet no integrated theory to explain why the Keynesian difficulties are likely to develop in any short intervals (say, for one or two years) but are unlikely to persist over longer periods (say, for five or ten years).

(c) The Keynesian analysis and the neoclassical growth theory are based upon quite different behavioral-institutional assumptions. Knowing well the two sides of the coin does not imply that one can easily synthesize the two separate parts into a whole.

The paper by Solow and Stiglitz [17] appears to be an important step toward eventual synthesis.

2.5 THE SWAN MODEL

In 1956, Trevor Swan also published his model of growth [2]. The phase diagram he used differs from that of Solow. Otherwise, the two models are approximately parallel to each other, although differing in certain features, which we will review briefly.

1. The production function is the Cobb-Douglas type. Thus, Swan's model is much less general than Solow's. However, the strength of the Cobb-Douglas function enables him to tackle the problems to be discussed below.

2. Swan discusses an "Adam Smith" case of increasing return and a "Ricardo" case of fixed land supply. We shall now consider these two cases in turn:

(a) The "Adam Smith" case:

$$Q = K^{\alpha}L^{\beta} \qquad \alpha+\beta > 1 > \alpha$$

Suppose we define:

$$L' = L^{\beta/(1-\alpha)}$$
$$= L_0 e^{n[\beta/(1-\alpha)]t}$$
$$= L_0 e^{n't}$$

Then,

$$Q = K^\alpha L'^{(1-\alpha)}$$

This is a case we can easily handle in a manner similar to the analysis in Section 2.3.2-A.

(b) The "Ricardo" case:

$$Q = K^\alpha L^\beta T^{1-\alpha-\beta} \qquad \alpha+\beta < 1$$

where T represents land in fixed supply. By completely analogous methods, we can obtain an equivalent form:

$$Q = AK^\beta L'^{(1-\alpha)} \text{ with } L' = L^{\beta/(1-\alpha)} = L_0 e^{n[\beta/(1-\alpha)]t}$$

where $A = T^{1-\alpha-\beta}$ is a constant.

3. A Hicks-neutral technical progress case is also discussed. As Uzawa [7] later showed, the Cobb-Douglas case is the only case under which Hicks-neutral technical progress is equivalent to Harrod-neutral progress. Hence, another equivalent transformation can be used. In particular, if λ is the technical progress rate, then

$$Q = e^{\lambda t} K^\alpha L^{1-\alpha}$$

By defining:

$$L' = L(t) e^{[\lambda/(1-\alpha)]t}$$
$$= L_0 e^{[n+\lambda/(1-\alpha)]t}$$
$$= L_0 e^{n't}$$

we again obtain the case:

$$Q = K^\alpha L'^{(1-\alpha)}$$

APPENDIX 2.1.

Golden age growth and neutral technical progress in the Harrodian and Hicksian senses

Proposition 1. If a simple Solow model is capable of golden age growth at the rate $g > n$ for all values of s, then the technical progress must be Harrod-neutral: i.e., $F(K, L, t) = \bar{F}[K, A(t)L] = F[K, Le^{(g-n)t}, 0]$.

Proof. Let K_0, L_0, and Q_0 be the initial values of K, L, and Q.

$$Q(t) = F[K(t), L(t), t]$$
$$= F[K_0 e^{gt}, L_0 e^{nt}, t]$$
$$= K_0 e^{gt} F[1, \frac{L_0}{K_0} e^{-(g-n)t}, t]$$

Also,

$$Q(t) = Q_0 e^{gt}$$
$$= e^{gt} F[K_0, L_0, 0]$$
$$= K_0 e^{gt} F[1, \frac{L_0}{K_0}, 0]$$

Hence,

$$F[1, \mu, t] = F[1, \mu e^{(g-n)t}, 0] \quad \text{where } \mu = \frac{L_0}{K_0} e^{-(g-n)t} \quad \text{and} \quad \mu e^{(g-n)t} = \frac{L_0}{K_0}$$

Since this holds for all s, it must hold for all μ because

$$\frac{g}{s} = \frac{\dot{Q}/Q}{\dot{K}/Q} = \frac{Q}{K} = F[1, \mu, t]$$

Now setting $\mu = L/K$ and applying the linear homogeneity of both $F(\cdot, \cdot, t)$ and $\bar{F}(\cdot, \cdot)$ by multiplying both inputs by K, we obtain

$$F(K, L, t) = F[K, Le^{(g-n)t}, 0]$$
$$= \bar{F}[K, A(t)L]$$

where $A = e^{(g-n)t}$

Proposition 2. If technical progress is neutral in both the Hicksian and Harrodian senses, i.e.,

$$F(K, L, t) = F[K, A(t)L, 0]$$
$$= B(t)F[K, L, 0]$$

then $F[K, L, 0] = CK^\alpha L^{1-\alpha}$, with $B(t) = A^{1-\alpha}(t)$. That is, the production function has to be Cobb-Douglas.

Proof. A graphical yet rigorous proof proceeds as follows: In Figure 2.11 the isoquant AB represents the factor requirement for unit output at the base period (time 0); the isoquant ab represents the same at the current period (time t). The reduction of input requirement may be regarded as a Hicks-neutral technical process, which maps point P_1 into P_2, shrinking both inputs by a factor B. Alternatively, it can be represented as Harrod-neutral technical progress, which shrinks the unit labor requirement by a factor A. The latter maps the point P_1 to P_3. At P_2, both the capital/labor ratio k and the marginal rate of factor substitution ω are identical to what they are at P_1. At P_3 both k and ω have increased their values by a factor A compared to P_1. But P_2 and P_3 lie on the same isoquant, showing that the percent increase of k is exactly matched by an identical percent change in ω. This holds true irrespective of the base period we use. Hence, the elasticity of factor substitution must be

$$\sigma = \frac{d \ln k}{d \ln \omega} = 1$$

Therefore, the production function must be of the unit elasticity of substitution (Cobb-Douglas) type: $Q = BK^\alpha L^{1-\alpha} = K^\alpha(AL)^{1-\alpha}$. The relation $B = A^{1-\alpha}$ follows immediately.

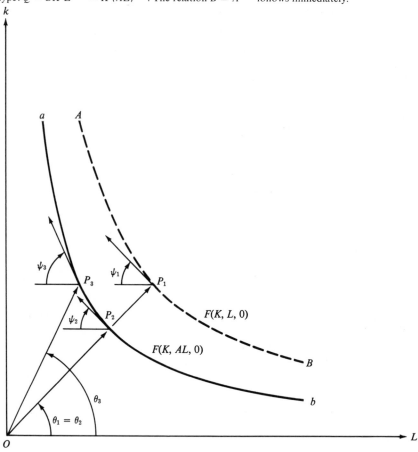

FIGURE 2.11

$$k_1 = k_2 = \tan \theta_1 = \tan \theta_2$$

$$= \tfrac{1}{2} \tan \theta_3 = k_3$$

$$\omega_1 = \omega_2 = \tan \psi_1 = \tan \psi_2$$

$$= \tfrac{1}{2} \tan \psi_3 = \omega_3$$

$$F(K, L, 0) = K^{1/4}L^{3/4}$$

$$F(K, AL, 0) = F(K, L, t) = BF(K, L, 0)$$

$$A(t) = 2; \; B(t) = 2^{3/4}$$

Note. Readers not at home with the limiting process

$$\lim_{\beta \to 0} [\delta K^{-\beta} + (1-\delta)L^{-\beta}]^{-1/\beta} = K^{\delta}L^{1-\delta}$$

can follow the alternative approach: since all the CES functions imply

$$\ln(Q/L) = \sigma \ln(w) + \text{constant} \quad \text{where } w = \partial Q/\partial L$$

for $\sigma = 1$, the integration of this partial differential equation ends up with

$$Q = G(k)L^{c_1} \quad \text{for some function } G \text{ and constant } c_1$$

Symmetrically, we can obtain

$$Q = H(L)K^{c_2}$$

Using the fact of constant returns to scale, we get a Cobb-Douglas function (see [4]) with $c_2 = \delta$, $c_1 = 1-\delta$.

REFERENCES

[1] Solow, Robert M., "A Contribution to the Theory of Economic Growth," *Quarterly Journal of Economics*, vol. LXX, Feb. 1956, pp. 65–94.

[2] Swan, Trevor, "Economic Growth and Capital Accumulation," *Economic Record*, vol. XXXII, Nov. 1956, pp. 334–61.

[3] Inada, K., "On a Two-Sector Model of Economic Growth: Comments and a Generalization," *Review of Economic Studies*, vol. XXX, June 1963, pp. 119–27.

[4] Arrow, K. J., H. Chennery, B. Minhas, and R. M. Solow, "Capital-Labor Substitution and Economic Efficiency," *Review of Economics and Statistics*, vol. XLIII, Aug. 1961, pp. 225–50.

[5] Chipman, J. S., "A Survey of the Theory International Trade, Part 3," *Econometrica*, vol. 34, Jan. 1966, pp. 18–76.

[6] Clemhout, Simone, "A Class of Homothetic Isoquant Production Functions," *Review of Economic Studies*, vol. XXXV, Jan. 1968, pp. 91–104.

[7] Uzawa, Hirofumi, "Neutral Inventions and the Stability of the Growth Equilibrium," *Review of Economic Studies*, vol. XXVIII, Feb. 1961, pp. 117–24.

[8] Tsiang, S. C., "A Model of Economic Growth in Rostovian Stages," *Econometrica*, vol. 32, Oct. 1964, pp. 619–48.

[9] Sato, Ryuzo, "Fiscal Policy in a Neoclassical Growth Model: An Analysis of Time Required for Equilibrating Adjustment," *Review of Economic Studies*, vol. XXX, Feb. 1963, pp. 16–23.

[10] Sato, Ryuzo, "The Harrod-Domar Model vs. the Neo-classical Growth Model," *Economic Journal*, vol. LXXIV, June 1964, pp. 380–87.

[11] Stiglitz, Joseph, and Hirofumi Uzawa, eds., *Readings in the Modern Theory of Economic Growth*, M.I.T. Press, Cambridge, Mass., 1969.

[12] Eisner, Robert, "On Growth Models and the Neo-Classical Resurgence," *Economic Journal*, vol. LXVIII, Dec. 1958, pp. 707–21.

[13] Solow, R. M., "Is Factor Substitution a Crime, If So, How Bad? Reply to Professor Eisner," *Economic Journal*, vol. LXIX, Sept. 1959, pp. 597–99.

[14] Hahn, Frank, and R. C. O. Matthews, "The Theory of Economic Growth: A Survey," *Economic Journal*, vol. LXXIV, Dec. 1964, pp. 779–902.

[15] Samuelson, P. A., *Economics. An Introductory Analysis*, 7th ed., McGraw-Hill, New York, 1967.

[16] Arrow, K. J., "Samuelson Collected," *Journal of Political Economy*, vol. LXXV, Oct. 1967, pp. 730–3.

[17] Solow, R. M., and Joseph Stiglitz, "Output, Employment and Wages in the Short-Run," *Quarterly Journal of Economics*, vol. LXXXII, Nov. 1968, pp. 537–60.

EXERCISES

2.1. Two economies A and B share the same technology for production which can be summarized in an aggregate production function fulfilling all the Inada conditions. The population growth rate is 2% per annum in A and 3% in B. The saving/income ratio is 10% in A and 12% in B. Compare (a) the long-run growth rate, (b) the long-run wage rate, and (c) the long-run consumption per capita for the two economies, assuming there is no technological progress.

2.2. An economy has an aggregate production function which is linear homogeneous and exhibits positive, diminishing marginal products of capital. There is no technological progress. With population growth rate standing at $2\frac{1}{2}\%$ per annum and the saving/income ratio at 25%, it is possible to attain long-run balanced growth. The observed capital/output ratio is about $3:1$ plus or minus a 20% error margin. The elasticity of factor substitution varies from 0.5 to 0.7 depending upon the capital/labor ratio. Derive the long-run trends for (a) the capital/labor ratio, (b) the rent rate, and (c) the rent share.

2.3. Suppose the world comes to a technological standstill and every economy shares the same aggregate production function which satisfies all the Inada conditions. Also suppose that the saving/income ratio and the population growth rates become uniform throughout the world, but that the "Leontief phenomenon" persists so that the U.S. labor is exactly three times as productive as the labor force in the rest of the world. Compare the rent rate, the wage rate, the factor shares, and the capital/labor ratio in the U.S. and the rest of the world in the long run.

3

the principal critics of the neoclassical models: the Modern Cambridge school

3.1 GENERAL REMARKS

If the frequency of publication reflects the relative importance of schools of thought, neoclassical models certainly dominate the arena of growth theory. Perhaps such superficial "relevance indices" do reflect the intrinsic worth of these models, yet it is our view that any true admirer of the neoclassical school should read with care the works of their severest critics: Mrs. Robinson and Kaldor[1]. The reasons are twofold:

First, journal articles concentrate on principal conclusions and their derivations. Methodological foundations of the approach and common-sensical justification of the assumptions are sketched briefly at best. "Serious" readers supposedly already have the appropriate background. Only in controversies and in debates do the novice and the outsider have opportunities to examine the foundations of theories in due detail.

Second, cross-fertilization is the most fruitful channel for scientific progress. The neoclassical writers, being bountifully endowed with analytical capability, usually study their problems with exhaustive generality. The successive incorporations of components of theories outside their school have been an important means to enrich the neoclassical literature. Sections 6.2 and 7.1 will provide good examples of this "absorption" process.

However, readers familiar with the neoclassical works may find the reading of Mrs. Robinson's and Kaldor's works hard going. Like Harrod, both Mrs. Robinson and Kaldor developed their theories over decades, and both eschew the practice of the "neoclassicals" (like Solow) of conducting their argument entirely in symbolic terms. Whereas verbal argument, in principle, can carry through any reasoning conveyed in analytic terms, it is much harder to make sure that certain hidden assumptions or even errors in logic have not crept in

[1] Perhaps also the writings of Sraffa.

at some stage of the discussion.[2] We shall not trace the evolution of Mrs. Robinson's and Kaldor's theories stage by stage; instead, a synopsis will be attempted in both cases.

Although both Mrs. Robinson and Kaldor developed their models in the Keynesian strain, Kaldor's emphasis is more on the macroeconomic aspects, while Mrs. Robinson stresses the micro relationships. The initial development of their theory was stimulated by Harrod's theory as well as Rothbarth's postwar study of Anglo-American comparative productivity. They were also significantly influenced by the work of P. Sraffa. We insert the present chapter between the early Solow-Swan models and the later neoclassical chapters because in this way we can discuss the critiques of Mrs. Robinson and Kaldor (against the neoclassicals) with the most facility.

In passing, we may note that Harrod, Mrs. Robinson, Kaldor and Bliss are the only British economists whose works we shall report separately. Meade's work on two-sector models is indirectly reported through its later development by Uzawa, Inada, Drandakis and others. His life-cycle saving theory is by-passed in favor of a similar work of Cass and Yaari. Hahn's discovery in heterogeneous goods, Kennedy's theory of induced technical progress, and Pasinetti's model on differential saving propensities are introduced indirectly through the work of Samuelson, Shell and Stiglitz, and of Samuelson and Modigliani. This avoids repetition and prevents the present volume from growing into encyclopedic proportions.

3.2 MRS. ROBINSON

We shall try to synthesize the contents of the two dozen or so publications of Mrs. Robinson on economic growth, under two categories: the "negative part" and the "constructive part" (in her own parlance). The first is at least as important as the second. But before delving into details, we shall present some introductory discussions as a background.

3.2.1. An intellectual genealogy

One can understand Mrs. Robinson's view better by considering the sources of her theory. From Marx she obtained the schema of "expanded reproduction" which may be traced all the way to Quesnay. Marx has a two-sector (two-department) model complete with the resource flows in the economy. Following Marx, Mrs. Robinson's theory also takes account of the incentive to invest. Marx regards the impulse to accumulate as inherent in the capitalist system. From Keynes, Mrs. Robinson inherited the "income theory" approach, including concepts such as "effective demand," "inflationary gap," "hoarding," etc.; the "animal spirit" explanation of investment which regards the readiness for risk-taking as more important than profit calculations in investment

---

[2]On the other hand, Mrs. Robinson and Kaldor both define exactly the terms they use, while Harrod sometimes declines to do so (see Section 1.2).

decisions; and what later became known as the Kalecki saving function: capitalists save all and workers spend all. To Keynes, this latter feature justified capitalism as a means of speedy accumulation. From Harrod she received the concepts of balanced growth and Harrod-neutral technical progress. Besides these, the long-run/short-run dichotomy of Marshall, the capital theory of Wicksell, and the heterogeneous capital goods model of Sraffa all contribute to the panoramic vista of the Robinsonian world.

3.2.2. The methodological preference

After carefully listing her assumptions, Mrs. Robinson usually presents a literal model with numerical examples and diagrams demonstrating her point. The practice of using symbols and equations very sparsely makes her intricate models even harder to grasp. The particular features of her approach are:

(1) The *puritanic insistence on descriptive realism* in her model. Wage bargaining, degree of monopoly, imperfection of capital market, as well as a "book of who's who" of blueprints, all have their places in her model.
(2) The *persistent aversion to postulation of a closed-end model.*
   (a) In a 1959 postscript to the article "The Model of an Expanding Economy" [1], she wrote: "I do not rely on any fixed relationship, for the long run, between the inducement to invest and the rate of profit. . . . There is no point to postulate a long run inducement to invest function. . . . A loose-jointed model of this kind seems to me to be more . . . useful. . . . "
   (b) In her paper "Normal Prices," she concluded [2], "There is no way to close the model that is both neat and plausible. We must be content to leave it open."

The combination of these two features makes it extremely difficult to check *inter alia* the consistency of her theory. The neoclassical growth literature emphasizes tight logical deductions but allows assumptions that are not all descriptively accurate. Mrs. Robinson appears to prefer the opposite.

3.2.3. The critiques

Mrs. Robinson made extensive comments on various types of theories relating to growth. The most important ones from our point of view are addressed to the neoclassical growth models. In the following, we shall consider briefly her remarks on "classicals," Marx, Keynes, and Harrod, while concentrating on her controversies with the neoclassical school.

A. CRITICISM OF THEORIES OTHER THAN NEOCLASSICAL MODELS

1. Against the laissez faire view.   Mrs. Robinson considers that:

(a) Classical models are unsuitable for modern monetary economies [3].
(b) Without governmental measures, capitalism may develop Keynesian

malaise. Saving without matching investment becomes a vice rather than a virtue, contrary to the laissez faire view [4].

2. Against Marx and Marxians. Mrs. Robinson maintains [4–7] that the Marxian predictions of growing misery for the workers, falling profit rates, and worsening economic crises are neither vindicated by history nor sustained by theoretical studies.

3. Against Keynesian theory. Mrs. Robinson believes that:

(a) Long-run problems were not adequately dealt with by Keynes [8].
(b) Once Keynesian policies are adopted against unemployment, a large portion of the pre-Keynesian tradition again becomes relevant [9, 10].
(c) The marginal efficiency theory of investment determination fails to explain the existence of risk premiums [3].
(d) Keynes emphasizes the volume of employment, not its content. It is precisely the overconsumption, underinvestment pattern of British full employment that causes the sluggish growth of her productivity, the chronic inflationary pressure, and the endemic balance-of-payments difficulties [10].

On points (b) and (c), she further quoted Keynes to show that the latter also shared such views. Point (b) coincides with the "neoclassical synthesis" concept of Samuelson, while point (c) is derived from the "animal spirit" view of Keynes.

4. Against Harrod. Mrs. Robinson complains that

(a) the Harrod model operates on too high a level of abstraction. Specifically [8]:
    (i) The differential saving propensities between profit and wage shares are ignored by Harrod.
    (ii) Technical progress need neither be Harrod-neutral (purely labor-augmenting) nor exogenous to the economy.
    (iii) Relative prices tend to vary in the real world. Therefore, index number problems would affect the validity of the aggregation carried out by Harrod.
    (iv) The term "capital" represents different concepts in Harrod's usage, sometimes as productive capacity, sometimes as cumulative foregone consumption (investment).
(b) Capitalistic growth is intermittent. It is difficult to separate the trend from fluctuations [3].
(c) Harrod has no theory to determine the profit rate. Profit affects savings due to the high saving propensity out of the capital share (in Mrs. Robinson's view, investment determines profit) [11, 15].

The above summary provides the background for understanding Mrs. Robinson's own model as well as her intense objections to the neoclassical models.

B. CRITICISM OF NEOCLASSICAL GROWTH MODELS

The running debate between Mrs. Robinson and the neoclassical school goes back to her exchange with Solow in 1953–1954 [12] and spreads over various articles, comments, etc. We shall first summarize her points and then present a commentary.

1. Mrs. Robinson's objections to the neoclassical models fall into four main categories. In her view, the neoclassical models are (a) obsolete in theory, (b) unrealistic in postulates, (c) erroneous in methodology, and (d) faulty in empirical testing. We shall consider these charges in turn.

(a) Theoretical obsolescence.   Keynes had already shown that:

(i) Thriftiness does not guarantee accumulation. Investment decisions depend upon entrepreneurial experiences of the recent past, governmental policies at present, and sociocultural influences upon the willingness to bear risk. All these are subsumed under the code name *animal spirit*. Investment need not match full-employment savings.

(ii) There is no convincing adjustment mechanism under the laissez faire policy that assures perpetual full employment.

Hence, neoclassical models today are pre-Keynesian anachronisms in the post-Keynesian era.

Since Keynesian views are valid in the short run, there is no reason why they should become false in the long run [13, 14].

(b) Postulatory unrealism.

(i) Nonexistence of "ectoplasm" or "leets" (the latter is a satire on Meades' representation of capital goods by "chameleonesque steel") [14]. Neoclassical writers of microeconomic orientation such as Swan and Meade would assume an all-purpose capital good that can be efficiently used over a broad range of capital/labor ratios. Such models are of little use, because real-life capital goods, once made, can never alter their form, use, or specifications.

(ii) The unrealism of the marginal productivity theory of distribution. In real life, income shares are determined by investment levels and saving propensities [2, 15], while modern firms equate marginal product of labor not with the wage rate but with wage rate plus a gross margin ([16], postscript). The marginal productivity theory does not correspond to reality.

(c) Methodological errors.   Some neoclassical economists such as Solow would not assume any contrivance such as ectoplasm. Instead, an aggregate capital input is inserted into an aggregate production function. This is erroneous, because (see [12–14, 17]):

(i) In general, value-weighted aggregation is permissible only when relative prices are constant. Except for balanced growth paths (and golden age paths), economic growth implies changing relative prices and hence varying value-weights. Therefore, neoclassical comparisons of positions along the same path are misleading (although comparisons of alternative balanced growth paths can be justified). In fact, the change of the list of available goods further weakens the comparability.

(ii) The aggregation of capital presents even more serious problems than the aggregation of outputs. Capital can be measured by its opportunity cost: past consumption foregone for its accumulation. It can also be measured by its future earning potential, discounted with appropriate interest rates. Or else it can be measured by its labor cost, because capital is "congealed labor," directly or indirectly applied in constructing the means of production. Yet when relative prices change, these three measures do not move in unison.

(iii) The present-value measure of capital is even more objectionable. An interest rate has to be assumed in order to arrive at any capital value. Yet the interest rate is supposedly the marginal product of capital from the aggregate production function. This causes circular reasoning. (This was the main point made by Sraffa [18].)

(iv) At any rate, the aggregate production function cannot provide information for marginal products. A given level or a given increment of aggregate capital can represent quite different ensembles of physical equipment. Hence, corresponding to a given incremental capital dosage over a given capital level, there exists no unique output increment.

In Chapter 4 we shall review these aggregation problems with numerical examples.

(d) Empirical faults.   Solow used certain procedures in his empirical work which are controversial:

(i) The separation of technical progress from capital deepening with observed data (this was attacked also by Pasinetti). See [18].

(ii) The imputation of observed growth rates to contributing factors; i.e., out of an $x\%$ growth rate, $y\%$ is due to deepening, $(x-y)\%$ to technical progress [16].

(iii) The employment of concepts such as "effective capital stock," i.e., weighting capital with a capital-augmenting technical progress index [16].

We shall not go into such matters of statistical procedures in this volume.

2. Mrs. Robinson's charges can best be appraised by classifying her differences with the neoclassicals.

(a) Differences in judgment.   Mrs. Robinson is by no means entirely averse to aggregation. At times she is willing to take index number problems in stride. We may quote her:

On aggregation: "A model which took account of all the variegation of reality would be of no more use than a map at a scale of one to one" ([3],

p. 33). Later she explained that she doubted that useful aggregation could be made in the context of growth.

On index number problems: "When large changes are taking place . . . over . . . short periods, the indications given . . . describe what is happening.

And even over the long run such indications are not entirely hopeless." ([20], p. 24)

Turning to the neoclassical camp, the statistical expediencies opted by Solow are necessitated by the dearth of reliable, disaggregated data as well as the prohibitive calculation required for a study with heterogeneous capital and output. Latter-day theoretical models of the neoclassical brand can handle multisector, nonmalleable capital goods and endogenous technical progress cases as well as differential saving propensities. These we shall see in Chapters 4–7. The marginal productivity need not be defined in some of these models (see Section 5.3). As we shall see in Chapter 4, Solow is well aware of the lack of theoretical rigor in the aggregate production function approach. Hence, in spite of the protracted debates, a large portion of the differences between Mrs. Robinson and Solow (if not the entire neoclassical school) lies in the judgment of whether useful empirical results can be obtained by following the Solovian procedures.

(b) Differences of substance. The main difference between Mrs. Robinson and the neoclassical school, in our view, is not in capital theory or distribution or aggregation, but in the attainment of full employment. Mrs. Robinson's emphasis is that under laissez faire, effective demand may not sustain full employment. Solow (in 1956), while acknowledging that his theory depicts only the neoclassical side of the coin, argues that historically, vigorous growth with high levels of employment has been the rule rather than the exception even before counterunemployment measures came into vogue. Hence, his theory more or less reflects the long-run picture.

Independent of either position, we may cite the Samuelsonian concept of *neoclassical synthesis*, which states that under proper public control, perpetual full employment is within reach. The post–World War II experience in industrial nations appears to substantiate this view. Such a position is consistent with observations in Mrs. Robinson's policy writings [20, 21] and is not contradicted by her theoretical writings. In fact, she wrote, "As soon as Keynes' views . . . become orthodox . . ., a large part of them ceases to be relevant. . . . All this sounds much like pre-Keynesian . . . . But we cannot return to the pre-Keynesian view that saving governs investment" ([9], pp. 91–2). With governmental policy, her last proviso becomes purely academic. Hence, what she termed pre-Keynesian models may actually correspond to post-Keynesian reality better than her own work. However, it is still true that the administration of counterunemployment measures is not reflected in the neoclassical models.

On the other hand, Mrs. Robinson's criticism does suggest certain possible improvements for the neoclassical framework. Supposing there may be unemployment under a laissez faire policy, there may also be various policy combinations that can achieve full employment. Some measures will stimulate investment incentive, others will increase consumption propensity, and still others will operate on both in such a way as to achieve full employment. The explicit introduction of both an investment function (i.e., demand for new capital goods) and employment policies has two advantages: (1) On the pragmatic level, one can test Mrs. Robinson's hypothesis that in the "political cycle" (i.e., controlled business cycle), "restriction . . . falls mainly upon investment while the relaxation . . . goes mainly to consumption," causing the poor showing of her country. (2) On the theoretical side, causal determinacy may be restored to certain neoclassical growth models (two-sector or heterogeneous capital goods models), depending upon the additional assumptions in each case.

3.2.4. Open models

Mrs. Robinson constructed a sequence of models, which may be categorized as "open" or "closed." In "open" models she analyzed both the effects of investment decisions and the constraints on the investment level. The determination of the precise level of investment is left as an open question. Such models do not generate determinate growth paths. They only delineate the possible directions of movement at each instant of time. Within this category of open models, successive degrees of complexities were introduced into a basic theme. The emphasis of these writings is on the key role of investment.

We shall concentrate on certain main themes of her models and comment on other highlights; closed models will be discussed in the following section.

Our discussion mainly follows Mrs. Robinson's Chapter 8 in *The Accumulation of Capital* [20] and her exchanges with Findlay [15, 23, 24]. Graphic analysis is emphasized.

A. ASSUMPTIONS

Mrs. Robinson's basic assumptions are:

(1) There are three goods in the economy:

Capital goods for producing capital goods, K_1 ⎫

Capital goods for producing consumption goods, K_2 ⎬ both capital goods depreciate at rate δ

Consumption goods, C ⎭

and there is one nonproducible input: labor L

(2) Both consumption goods C and gross investment $G = (\delta K_1 + \Delta K_1) + (\delta K_2 + \Delta K_2)$ are produced according to fixed-coefficient technology, with $\Delta K_i = K_i(t) - K_i(t-1)$ as the net capital formation for good i, $i = 1, 2$. The production lag is one unit in either case. Let the labor input for the capital good and consumption good sectors be L_1 and L_2; then,

$$G(t) = \delta[K_1(t-1) + K_2(t-1)] + [K_1(t) - K_1(t-1)] + [K_2(t) - K_2(t-1)]$$

$$= \text{Min}\left[\frac{K_1(t-1)}{a_1}, \frac{L_1(t-1)}{b_1}\right] \geq 0 \tag{3.2.1}$$

$$C(t) = \text{Min}\left[\frac{K_2(t-1)}{a_2}, \frac{L_2(t-1)}{b_2}\right] \geq 0 \tag{3.2.2}$$

where a_i and b_i are unit capital and labor requirements for sector i.

The labor supply condition takes the form

$$L_1(t) + L_2(t) \leq L(t) \tag{3.2.3}$$

Choosing appropriate units, we can normalize L, b_1, and b_2 to unity. The subsistence level of consumption is C^1, i.e.,

$$C(t) \geq C^1 \tag{3.2.4}$$

There are also certain behavioral assumptions:

(1) Wage earners cannot tolerate any real wage rate below v, say; otherwise a cost–price spiral will emerge; i.e.,

$$w(t)/p(t) \geq v \tag{3.2.5}$$

where w is the money wage rate and p is the price of consumption good (wage-good).

(2) Capitalists sell the consumption good at price p according to a certain markup formula. Let us assume this formula takes the form

$$p(t) = w(t)[1 + \pi(t)]$$

$$\pi(t) = \frac{1-v}{v-C_0}[1 - \frac{C_0}{C}] \tag{3.2.6}$$

where $\pi(t)$ is the markup ratio, $C_0 > 0$ such that $v \geq C_0 \geq C^1$.[3] This special assumption implies that:

(a) The markup ratio π is positively associated with the actual consumption output C (shown in Fig. 3.1a).

(b) The actual consumption level C is an increasing linear function of the gross investment level G, as we shall see below. This agrees with the popular diagram version of Keynesian economics in elementary texts.

(c) There exists a positive consumption level, C_0, at zero investment level, also to be seen below.

(3) Workers consume all of their wage income, capitalists consume nothing.[4] (One may suppose that all entrepreneurs live on their salaries but plow back

---

[3] Exercise 3.1 gives the motivation for this pair of inequalities.

[4] This simplifying assumption has been relaxed in more recent works of Mrs. Robinson.

any dividends received.) Hence,

$$p(t)C(t) = w(t)[L_1(t-1)+L_2(t-1)] \qquad \text{(workers bought all consumption good)} \quad (3.2.7)$$

$$= w(t)[C(t)+G(t)]$$

(Since $b_1 = b_2 = 1$, (3.2.1) and (3.2.2) imply that $L_1(t-1) = G(t)$, $L_2(t-1) = C(t)$.)

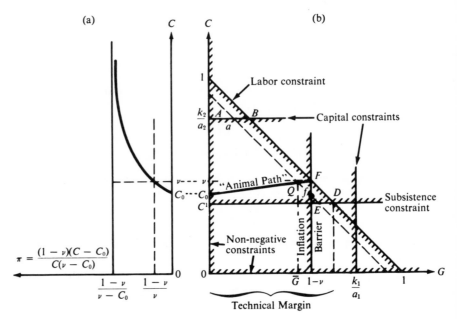

FIGURE 3.1

B.   GRAPHICAL ANALYSIS

From (3.2.1)–(3.2.3) we can obtain the equivalent constraints:

$$\left.\begin{array}{l} K_1/a_1 \geq G \geq 0 \\ K_2/a_2 \geq C \geq 0 \end{array}\right\} \quad \text{capital constraints} \qquad \begin{array}{l}(3.2.1') \\ (3.2.2')\end{array}$$

$$1 \geq G+C \qquad \text{(since } L = b_1 = b_2 = 1) \quad \text{labor constraints} \qquad (3.2.3')$$

Depending upon the values of K_i/a_i, $i = 1, 2$, we can have surplus-labor $[1 > (K_1/a_1)+(K_2/a_2)]$ or scarce-labor $[1 < (K_1/a_1)+(K_2/a_2)]$ regimes. We shall depict the former case in Figure 3.1b, with (3.2.1'), (3.2.2'), (3.2.3'), and (3.2.4) shown as linear constraints. Hence, the "output point" (G, C) must be between EF and the C axis from (3.2.1'), between AB and the G axis from (3.2.2'), below and to the left of BD (from 3.2.3'), and above C^1D (from 3.2.4).

Combining (3.2.6) and (3.2.7), we can deduce the linear relation:

$$G = \frac{1-v}{v-C_0}(C-C_0) \qquad (3.2.8)$$

which leads from $(0, C_0)$ to $(1-v, v)$ (labeled the "animal path" in Figure 3.1b.)

According to Mrs. Robinson's analysis:

(1) An economy under total planning can select any output point in the trapezoid $ABDC^1$. The limit for the accumulation rate is the *technical margin*.

(2) An economy with all production plans controlled by the state but with a working class capable of demanding and obtaining wage raises will be restricted to the area of $ABFEC^1$. Accumulation rate beyond the FE line (*inflationary barrier*) would reduce the total consumption good producible below v, along the labor constraint BFD. With full employment (hence $L_1 + L_2 = 1$), labor's demand for higher real wage would lead to inflation.

(3) An economy operating along strict laissez faire lines would be restricted on the linear segment C_0F, in view of the *effective demand* equation (3.2.7) and the *cost–price* function (3.2.6). Without assuming downward inflexibility of money wage, we still can obtain the deficient effective demand phenomenon. The precise position of the economy is now seen as determined by the investment level. Since the latter is decided by "animal spirit," we shall call the C_0F interval the "animal path" for short. We note that:

(a) From (3.2.7) we may subtract wC from both sides, and divide by w; hence,

$$\frac{p-w}{w} C = \pi C = G \tag{3.2.9}$$

The "surplus value" (or the "labor value of profit margin") in the consumption sector is shown to be identical to G. For capitalists, the more willing they are to invest, the higher is their "surplus value."

(b) Suppose the actual investment is $\bar{G}$; hence, the output is at Q on C_0F. Draw af through Q parallel to BFD. af can be regarded as a member of the family of iso-unemployment loci, all parallel to BFD. Hence, the higher $\bar{G}$ is, the lower unemployment is.

(c) Real wage is

$$\frac{w}{p} = \frac{1}{1+\pi} \tag{3.2.10}$$

Hence, along the C_0F path

$$\frac{\partial(w/p)}{\partial G} = \left(\frac{\partial(w/p)}{\partial \pi}\right)\left(\frac{\partial \pi}{\partial C}\right)\left(\frac{\partial C}{\partial G}\right)$$

$$< 0 \qquad \text{(from Figure 3.1}a, b)$$

showing the higher the investment, the lower the real wage. This corroborates the observation that in deep depression, real wage rate may rise, although unemployment also goes up and the total wage bill (i.e., C) goes down.

Equation (3.2.6) is admittedly our own concoction based upon Mrs. Robinson's remarks (postscript to [16]). But we believe that this is consistent with her main line and explains the Keynesian unemployment (of all factors) in the clearest way. This assumption of administered prices (or "price-fixing" power) sidesteps the question of how much capital cost (i.e., G) should be assigned to each unit of output when excess capacity is present.

This completes our summary of Mrs. Robinson's main conclusions: the comparative efficacy of a totalitarian regime in resource mobilization, and the likelihood that laissez faire policy results in either unemployment or inflation (if the animal spirit breaks through the inflation barrier); the key role played by gross investment in the economy; and the relative independence of investment level from the wage rate (unless the animal spirit is affected, the real wage temporarily ruling on the market will be modified, once the investment decision is made). Investment also affects the future values of K_i, $i = 1, 2$. But Mrs. Robinson did not consider it in detail in open models.

C. COMMENTS

1. Although the above Keynesian analysis appears to be satisfactory, Mrs. Robinson declines to define the determinants of the animal spirit. She regards it as involving sociopsychology, but we believe that a makeshift contrivance such as the investment function we constructed for the Domar model will serve some purpose. Nor did she comment upon the real-life experience in the last two decades, where perpetual full employment has been the rule rather than the exception. She explained that her purpose is to concentrate on the system without control [3]. Here, the neoclassical school is equally reticent. The best clue is still the neoclassical synthesis concept of Samuelson, showing that governmental policy will push the economy to somewhere along the BF frontier. Where, we do not know, unless we consider the effects of alternative public policies.

2. Although Figure 3.1b depicts the various possibilities of accumulation under various political systems, we must note that a fundamental assumption has been made that the aggregate production set of an economy is not affected by the degree of centralized control in that economy. The advent of Liebermannism in Soviet Russia and in Eastern European countries suggests otherwise. These states seem to believe that decentralization improves efficiency (and hence enlarges the production set).

3. Some readers have probably already noticed that investment makes little sense in an economy depicted in Figure 3.1b: both capital constraints are nonbinding and hence both types of equipment are superfluous. We drew the diagram in such a way in order to simplify our analysis. Alternatively, we could shift K_1/a_1 to the left so that it lies on or to the left of the FE curve. However, we shall not go into these matters here.

4. Mrs. Robinson also considered variations of the open models.

(a) Consumption out of profit. The effect of this is to reduce further the capacity to invest.

(b) Technical progress, spectrum of technique, etc. These will be considered in a closed model.

3.2.5. Closed models

In "closed" models Mrs. Robinson imposed the assumption that full employment is *somehow* attained without any governmental intervention. She then considered the conditions under which continuous full employment can be maintained as well as the alternative growth patterns. The "golden age" case (wherein capital and output grow at a rate equal to the population growth rate plus the rate of labor-augmenting technical progress) and the perpetual capital-deepening model are examined. She maintained, however, that the basic assumption (continued full employment under laissez faire) is not plausible in reality.

The closed models resemble the open models in structure. Rather than discussing everything afresh each time, we shall consider a sequence of topics concerning these models.

A. ANALYSIS OF "ANIMAL SPIRIT"

An open model can be closed by specifying the determinants of the propensity to accumulate $[G/(C+G)]$. These, according to Mrs. Robinson, can be divided into profit expectations (which depend upon economic forces) and risk preferences (which depend upon sociopsychological factors). To steer away from the quagmire of sociopsychology, two alternatives are possible, the assumption of perfect foresight or of perfect "tranquility."

Perfect foresight.   This is a self-validating expectation, provided that every household and entrepreneur acts under its presumptive validity. Every individual acts with perfect confidence in his predictions, which is reinforced by the continuous fulfillment of his forecasts. (Example: If every depositor believes a bank is going bankrupt, the stampede for withdrawal will bankrupt the bank.) Mrs. Robinson used this in her perpetual capital-deepening model [17]. Obviously it is a very strong assumption.

Perfect tranquility.   This means that all relative prices, profit rate, etc., with the possible exception of wage, have stayed constant for a sufficiently long period. Wage increases at a constant relative rate (which may be zero). The sufficiently long period is assumed so that the pretranquility history cannot affect the economy at present or during any future period through existing equipment, lagged demand or supply responses, etc. For all practical purposes, we may assume that tranquility exists from the beginning of the universe. This assumption is still rather strong, yet it is more palatable than the perfect foresight assumption. It is more likely that people expect that tomorrow everything will be the same as today than that they have total confidence in their detailed foreknowledge of future markets. This is the assumption Mrs. Robinson used in her "golden age" models in *The Accumulation of Capital* [20].

B. GOLDEN AGE, PLATINUM AGE, AND TECHNICAL PROGRESS

In considering the conditions under which golden age can exist, Mrs. Robinson studies the twin relations [3]. Under perfect tranquility, the supply for savings implies

$$s = s_r\beta(r) \tag{3.2.1}$$

and the demand for investment implies

$$s = g(r) \tag{3.2.1:}$$

where s is the gross saving ratio $[G/(G+C)]$ at equilibrium
s_r is the saving ratio out of profit share
$\beta(r)$ is the profit share as a function of the profit rate
$g(r)$ is the investment function showing the dependence of the gross saving ratio on the profit rate.

Solving (3.2.11) and (3.2.12) simultaneously, one obtains s^* and r^*, say. The "warranted rate" of growth is simply:

$$\frac{s^*}{a} = \frac{r^*s^*}{\beta(r^*)} \qquad \left(\beta = \frac{K}{Q} \quad r = ra\right)$$

$r^*s^*/\beta(r^*)$ can then be compared with the labor growth rate, n. There are three possibilities:

$r^*s^*/\beta(r^*) = n$ This is the knife-edge case, where there is balanced growth in the economy.

$r^*s^*/\beta(r^*) < n$ There cannot be any balanced growth. The system will lose its "tranquil" state due to increased population pressure. The analysis is similar to what we have seen in the last two chapters.

$r^*s^*/\beta(r^*) > n$ Mrs. Robinson believes that if the difference is not large, the scarcity of labor may lead to labor-augmenting technical progress to make up the difference. In that case, all capital inputs, outputs, and "efficiency labor" (i.e., labor in efficiency units) would increase at the same constant rate.

The latter case together with full or near-full employment constitutes the "golden age" growth. The adjective "golden age" is used to show the unlikely prospect of steady growth with near-full employment. If an economy does not have suitable initial conditions (i.e., composition of equipment) for golden age growth, yet over time it approaches such a state while near-full employment is maintained at all times, this remarkable and rather improbable feat is called "platinum age growth." We may note that:

(1) Capital and labor are symmetrical in the neoclassical production function, but asymmetrical in a growth model. Labor grows exogenously; capital is produced inside the economic system. Hence, the scarce-labor case is amenable to golden age growth, given labor-augmenting technical

progress. The surplus-labor case cannot be coaxed into a golden-agelike path through capital-augmenting technical progress. It takes "labor-*wasting*" technical *retrogression* to achieve a symmetrical case of "anti-golden age." But, of course, entrepreneurs would never adopt retro-gressive technical changes.

(2) Mrs. Robinson's argument about induced technical progress is definitely influenced by the controversy over the Anglo-American productivity study of Rothbarth. Later, Kennedy formulated a model on this topic which we shall consider in Chapter 7.

(3) The introduction of the investment function makes her model closer to Harrod's than to the neoclassical models.

C. THE SPECTRUM OF TECHNIQUES

Mrs. Robinson's analysis of the existence of golden age paths is akin to Harrod's. However, the capital/output ratio a and the investment function $g(r)$ in (3.2.12) are deceptively simple façades for deep microeconomic mechanisms underneath. To brush them aside, in Mrs. Robinson's view, would be simple deception. Her heterogeneous capital goods model ([20], Section II, Book II) is a perceptive, literal tour de force on comparative golden age paths. She noted that if golden age is a rarity in real life, a study of two economies undergoing golden age growth while sharing the same technology but facing different factor price ratios must have severely limited applicability. Her aim is to show how a disaggregated capital model can be constructed (cf. Samuelson's work discussed in Section 4.1). We shall consider the basic structure of her model here and the technical details in Appendix 3.1. Such technical analysis indicates that only under the assumed conditions does the theoretical construction remain valid. We shall first consider the assumptions, then set up a model, and finally analyze the results. The model is somewhat more general than Mrs. Robinson's original version and closer to a later version (her Model III in "Capital, Technique and Relative Shares" [19]).

1. Assumptions.   (a) There is one composite consumption good, producible with any one of a whole set of techniques. Each technique prescribes a given outfit of capital equipment, which takes a definite gestation period and a definite flow of labor input to construct, and functions over a definite operational life, producing a specific product outflow with the aid of a specific labor inflow manning the equipment. The same outfit of physical equipment produced with a different time-profile of labor input over the gestation period will count as a different technique. Similarly, the same equipment manned by a crew of different size or operated at a different speed or abandoned after a different length of operational life will count as a different technique. Let $T = \{\alpha, \beta, \gamma, \ldots\}$ be the set of all these techniques, all of which exhibit constant returns to scale and no externality. T may be finite or infinite. There is no technical progress.

(b) Labor grows exponentially at rate n.

(c) Capitalists select techniques that maximize their profit rate. Prices are determined competitively.

(d) Capitalists save s_r of their profit and workers consume all their wage income.

(e) Full employment is continuously maintained under balanced growth.

These assumptions differ from those underlying the simple open model in the presence of alternative techniques, the attainment of full employment of inputs, the practice of competitive pricing, and the consumption out of profits.

2. Basic concepts. Since the production techniques exhibit constant returns to scale, balanced growth is consistent with constant relative prices, and hence perfect "tranquility" à la Robinson. Now balanced growth is possible only if the age distribution of the equipment is of an appropriate form. For instance, if the population grows at 2% per year, the number of two-year-old automobiles per capita next year can be the same as this year if and only if there are 2% more one-year-old automobiles than two-year-olds this year (assuming all automobiles last more than two years). This introduces the concept of a *"balanced stock."* Assuming that all equipment is scrapped at the same age (there is no random destruction), then a balanced stock means the age distribution of equipment is exponential, with the size of each age-class increasing at the same rate as population.

Each technique i can be associated with a balanced stock corresponding to any particular population growth rate n.

Define:

$K_{i,n}$ = an ensemble of balanced stock of technique i and growth rate n ($K_{i,n}$ is not a number)

(w, r) = a pair of wage-interest rates

$C(K_{i,n}; w, r)$ = the *cost valuation* of $K_{i,n}$ corresponding to (w, r).

Specifically, this comprises three parts: (i) cost of equipment in process, (ii) cost of equipment, new, and (iii) cost of equipment, depreciated. Depreciation should be so calculated so that the depreciated cost will be proportional to the remaining earning power

$L_1(K_{i,n})$ = the labor force engaged in *making* new equipment for $K_{i,n}$

$L_2(K_{i,n})$ = the labor force engaged in *manning* $K_{i,n}$

$Q(K_{i,n})$ = the consumption good produced from $K_{i,n}$

$q(K_{i,n}) = Q(K_{i,n})/L_2(K_{i,n})$ = the output per worker in consumption sector for $K_{i,n}$

$k(K_{i,n}; w, r) = C(K_{i,n}; w, r)/wL_2(K_{i,n})$ = the "real capital/labor" ratio, i.e., the value of investment per worker in the consumption sector, where (C/w) is the "real value" of capital (i.e., value of capital using labor as the numeraire[5]). In the literature, such a valuation is given in "J.R. units" [22].

$\mu(K_{i,n}) = L_1(K_{i,n})/L_2(K_{i,n})$

---

[5]For those readers not already acquainted with the term, a numeraire is a unit of value chosen by the writer for convenience in the discussion of a given problem. It need not coincide with either the medium of exchange, if any, or the unit of account. English-speaking economists have adopted the word from the writings of Leon Walras.

We note that $C(K_{i,n}; w, r)$, $L_2(K_{i,n})$, and $Q(K_{i,n})$ grow over time at rate n; under balanced growth, however, the ratios $q(K_{i,n})$, $k(K_{i,n}; w, r)$, and $\mu(K_{i,n})$ are constant over time. $k(K_{i,n}; w, r)$ depends upon the interest rate r. This is easily seen, because a new machine made by one unit of labor over one unit of time has the "real value" $[(e^r - 1)/r]$ units, which is an increasing function of r. What is less obvious is that $k(K_{i,n}; w, r)$ depends upon the wage rate w as well. This is because in calculating the depriciated value of an old machine in the balanced stock, the yet realized present value of quasi-rent is used as a basis of allocation. As the wage rate varies, this depreciation basis also changes in response.

3. Graphical analysis.   Now for a given (w, r) pair, we can plot $q(K_{i,n})$ against $k(K_{i,n}; w, r)$ for each i in T. We can now construct its "northwestern envelope" and this becomes a "technical frontier." For the same w, say, $\bar{w}$, each chosen r corresponds to a different frontier, as shown in Figure 3.2a. The higher the interest rate used, the more to the right is the frontier, since the cost valuation $C(K_{i,n}; \bar{w}, r)$ is an increasing function of r for any $K_{i,n}$ and $\bar{w}$ being given. We shall let

$$q = \phi(k; \bar{w}, r)$$

represent such a frontier. Three members of such loci are shown in Figure 3.2a. Now consider the profit per worker in a given consumption sector, say Π:

$$\Pi(k; \bar{w}, r) = q - \bar{w}(1 + rk)$$

$$= \phi(k; \bar{w}, r) - \bar{w}(1 + rk)$$

(3.2.13)

where q is the product per worker in the consumption sector
$\quad \bar{w}$ is the labor cost per worker in the consumption sector
$\quad \bar{w}k$ is the capital value per worker in the consumption sector in *product* units (k is in J.R. units)
$\quad r\bar{w}k$ is the capital cost per worker in the consumption sector

Corresponding to given $\bar{w}$, a very high r would entail negative Π for all k. This shows that no matter what k value one has—*ipso facto*, no matter what technique i one selects—loss is inevitable. Hence, no balanced growth is possible at such a high interest rate, the wage rate being what it is. At the other extreme, for that same $\bar{w}$, a particularly low r would entail positive values of Π. Under competitive conditions, any entrepreneur who can borrow will make a profit. Hence, the market force will bid up the interest rate above such a level. In Figure 3.2a we see that rate r_1 is too high and r_2 is too low with respect to $\bar{w}$. If we reduce r from r_1 downward, then under normal assumptions upon the technology set T (something similar to the mathematical concept of "closure" is needed here) there exists an interest rate $\bar{r}$ such that:

$$\Pi(k; \bar{w}, \bar{r}) = 0 \quad \text{for some } k \text{ inside an interval } (k^1, k^2),$$
$$\text{say (possibly } k^1 = k^2)$$

$$\Pi(k; \bar{w}, \bar{r}) \leq 0 \quad \text{for all } k$$

(3.2.14)

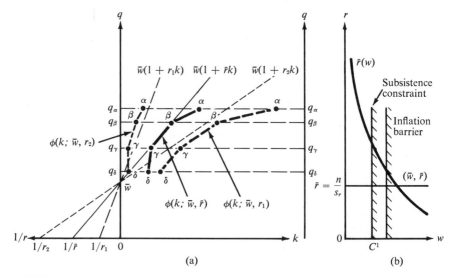

FIGURE 3.2

In other words, there exists a subset of technology, say, $T(\overline{w})$, within which all techniques break even while all other techniques involve some loss. In Figure 3.2a $T(\overline{w})$ includes techniques β and γ.

In this way, one can set up a schedule: for any wage rate $\overline{w}$ there exists an associated interest rate $\bar{r}(\overline{w})$ and a class of appropriate techniques $T(\overline{w})$.

We note the family resemblance between Figure 3.2a and the diagram used by Solow that we discussed in Chapter 2. Both trace their lineage back to Wicksell.

We now inquire wnat relation exists between the population growth rate n and the interest rate r.

Considering first the demand and supply for consumption goods, we have:

$$\{L_1 + L_2[1 + (1 - s_r)\bar{r}k]\}\overline{w} = pL_2q$$

where the workers' consumption is $(L_1 + L_2)\overline{w}$ and the capitalists' profit is $L_2\bar{r}k\overline{w}$. Out of the latter a portion $(1 - s_r)$ is consumed. Consider then the cost–revenue equality for the consumption sector,

$$pL_2q = \overline{w}L_2(1 + \bar{r}k)$$

Combining the above two equations to eliminate pL_2q, and dividing through the result by $\overline{w}L_2$, we have

$$\mu + 1 + (1 - s_r)\bar{r}k = 1 + \bar{r}k$$

which readily reduces to

$$\mu = s_r\bar{r}k = s_r\left(\frac{\bar{r}}{\overline{w}}\right)\left(\frac{C}{L_2}\right) \qquad (3.2.15$$

The economic implication is that the labor allocation ratio for the appropriate technique must be equal to the product of the saving ratio out of profit, the interest wage ratio, and the value of capital (in product terms) per worker for the consumption sector. If capital goods are perfectly durable and the labor input and consumption output are constant over the equipment life, then labor force in the investment sector is geared to expansionary demand (to equip the incremental labor force) only. In that case, $nC = wL_1$. Dividing by wL_2 on both sides,

$$\mu = nk$$

Therefore, substituting into (3.2.15)

$$n = s_r \bar{r}$$

If capitalists save all and hence invest all (since full employment is presumed), we have

$$n = \bar{r}$$

By using the curve $\bar{r}(\bar{w})$ and assuming $n = s_r r$, we can summarize the above discussion in Figure 3.2b. The $\bar{r}(\bar{w})$ curve (factor price frontier à la Samuelson) reflects the technical possibility of an economy. The subsistence wage marks the technical margin. The inflation barrier further narrows the range of alternative balanced growth paths. It is the ratio n/s_r, however, that decides the precise $[\bar{w}, \bar{r}(\bar{w})]$ pair that rules in the economy. Granted that accumulation is desirable, then the more "virtuous" (parsimonious) are the capitalists and hence the larger the value of s_r the better. Mrs. Robinson would even draw the conclusion that state ownership of productive means would be the best for developing nations desirous of fast accumulation (of course, the State sometimes can also waste resources). Also, we can see that as s_r increases, $\bar{r}$ increases and $\bar{w}$ decreases, showing that parsimonious capitalists implies poorly paid workers.

A comparison between her balanced growth model and the neoclassical balanced growth models may be simply tabulated:

	Neoclassical model	Mrs. Robinson's model
Output/capital ratio	n/s	Determined by technology
Marginal product of capital	Determined by technology	n/s_r
Saving/investment	Saving determines investment	Investment determines saving

4. Comments. (a) Mrs. Robinson attempted to relate the wage rate to "degrees of mechanization" by ranking techniques according to their "real capital ratios." It was thought that at higher wage rates, techniques with higher real capital ratios would be used. This was pointed out as an impossibility by Ruth Cohen, although for a time Mrs. Robinson continued to regard such a case as a curiosum. Subsequent research work on the reswitching phenomenon (see Section 4.1 and also her joint paper with Naqri [25]) shows that theoretically such phenomena can arise on various occasions. Whether they are empirically irrelevant or whether we can postulate certain easily verifiable sufficient conditions to exclude them remains to be seen.

(b) The J.R. units can be properly used only in Mrs. Robinson's context: as a steppingstone to deduce the wage/interest locus. Champernowne [26], Solow [27], and Samuelson [28] all point out that paradoxical results can arise if this concept is used otherwise; e.g., the same ensemble of physical equipment may be represented by different numbers of J.R. units (under different interest rates), or the same number of J.R. units may represent totally different equipment.

(c) Equation (3.2.15) shows the difficulty of relating the "thriftiness condition" s_r and the population growth rate n to the ruling interest rate. Behind the symbols k and C lies the technology of the entire economy.

(d) The main advantage of the above exercise is perhaps to gain insight into how things work out in a rather complicated model. Figure 3.2a and equations (3.2.13) and (3.2.14) serve as the key elements in this analysis. The shifting of the ϕ curve under different interest rates suggests the difficulty in analyzing rigorously an actual growth path that has a changing interest rate.

(e) Mrs. Robinson's perpetual capital-deepening model [17] relaxes the tranquility condition. It deals with a case rarely emphasized in neoclassical literature these days. It is assumed that population growth is zero but saving exceeds investment needs for replacement. She stated that it is possible though unlikely that full employment can continue due to perfect foresight. The "degree of mechanization" increases most of the time and the interest rate eventually decreases to its minimum level.

3.3 KALDOR

There exists a broad area of similarity between the growth theories of Mrs. Robinson and Kaldor: their affinity to Keynesian economics, their mistrust of the marginal productivity theory of distribution, and their emphasis on the divergent saving propensities out of profit and wage income. However, certain differences in orientation set their theories apart. Kaldor first contributed to the areas of capital theory and growth in 1937–1938 [29, 30], defending the approximate relevance of an aggregate concept of capital intensity in the world of heterogeneous equipment. This position was eventually modified, and a series of six papers [31–36] between 1954 and 1962 propounded his later theories of growth. These later papers again indicate gradual evolution of his position. We shall divide our discussion into two parts: his viewpoint and a single specimen model. Kaldor's theory is not only important in its own right but also has had significant influence on the development of later neoclassical growth models.

3.3.1. Outlook and viewpoints

A. EXCHANGES WITH THE NEOCLASSICAL SCHOOL

The most revealing source of Kaldor's view (as well as the stands of Samuelson and Solow) on record is the "summary record of the debate" in the Corfu Conference of the International Economic Association [37]. We can synthesize Kaldor's views as follows:

(1) He shares Mrs. Robinson's misgivings about the use of aggregate capital and the aggregate production function on logical grounds, but he realizes that only a model with a small number of variables can be handled at ease (both points, [37], p. 371). This rationale for aggregation is shared by Solow ([37], p. 382).

(2) His main objection to the earlier neoclassical models concerns their empirical validity ([37], p. 372). Specifically:
   (a) There is no investment function (which depends upon profit rates) in such models ([37], p. 392).
   (b) There is no theory explaining the pace and direction of technical progress. The latter can be studied in his model through a technical progress function without a production function ([37], p. 372).
   (c) The marginal productivity theory of distribution is "all nonsense" ([37], pp. 294–5). For one thing, capital/labor ratios are often fixed by technology; eleven men can hardly share ten spades ([37], p. 295). For another, it does not provide an empirically testable hypothesis. Over the long run, when it is vaguely testable, it is refuted by facts ([37], p. 398). It should be replaced by "a Keynesian theory of distribution."
   (d) The separation of technical progress and capital deepening as done by Solow is rather tenuous, since the two are interdependent [35].

To these views Solow would agree that:

(1) An investment behavior function is desirable. Yet his own model excludes such an element, since a satisfactory treatment requires the solution of some extremely challenging problems of behavior under uncertainty ([33], p. 393; also [38], p. 13).

(2) Technical progress is not entirely exogenous, but its dependence upon economic forces is so far not clearly known to him ([37], p. 393).

On the other hand, Solow shows that:

(1) The marginal product is not crucial to neoclassical theory (see Section 5.3).

(2) The fact that the capital/labor ratio is fixed *ex post* would not affect the neoclassical theory either ([37], p. 297 and Section 5.2 below).

(3) Fruitful empirical measurement of technical progress and the production

function can be made even in the "embodied" case (see Section 5.1).

(4) Kaldor's technical progress function is not stable, in general. It will shift all the time, except for the Cobb-Douglas case (we shall see this later; see also [37], p. 372).

Both the concepts of differential saving propensities and the technical progress function eventually played their roles in the development of growth theory. The former led to the work of Pasinetti and the exhaustive analysis of Samuelson and Modigliani (Section 6.2). The latter led to the Kennedy model of induced investment, which eventually was studied in depth by Phelps and Drandakis, Samuelson, and others (Section 7.1). Arrow's work on "learning by doing" is also related in some sense to Kaldor's technical progress function (Section 7.1). On its own merits, as we shall see, the Kaldor theory leaves many questions unanswered. But the various components of his theory, imperfectly integrated as they are, do stimulate the growth of growth literature.

B.   COMPARISON WITH MRS. ROBINSON

It is informative to compare the stands of Mrs. Robinson with Kaldor's.

(1) While Mrs. Robinson is most wary about any measurement of capital-in-general, Kaldor is willing to use any of these measures. Regarding the constancy of the capital/output ratio he said, "In terms of any reasonable index that we may choose, we should get substantially the same answer."

(2) While Mrs. Robinson is unwilling to specify any precise relation between technical progress and the degree of mechanization, Kaldor is contented to postulate a technical progress function of his own or to use Arrow's model if it can be slightly modified (see [35]).

(3) While Mrs. Robinson prefers a loose-jointed investment theory ([1], pp. 86–87), Kaldor assumes a definite relationship between investment and profit.

All these emphasize Kaldor's preference for and faith in a macroeconomic approach which makes use of "some overriding conditions operating on the markets which restricted the individuals." Hence, aggregates are not "merely a summation of individual decisions" ([37], p. 299).

3.3.2. A specimen model

Rather than trace the evolution of Kaldor's theory over time, we shall attempt to synthesize a model out of his writings with the main emphasis on his 1959 *Economica* paper [35]. We shall first consider Kaldor's purpose of study. Next, we shall examine the main components of his theory. Finally, there will be a short commentary.

A.   PURPOSE

Kaldor claimed that the history of capitalistic development bears evidence of the following six "stylized facts" (i.e., essentially valid observations) [34]:

(1) Output and per capita output grow exponentially.
(2) Capital per capita increases all the time.
(3) Interest rate does not change appreciably.
(4) The capital/output ratio is constant.
(5) Profit share and investment/income ratio are highly correlated.
(6) The growth rate of output and output per capita vary widely among various economies.

The existing theories, he maintained, cannot explain such facts. Important causal determinants of the growth pattern, such as the saving/income ratio, technical progress, and population growth, are relegated as exogenous to the economic system [33]. It is the purpose of his model to explain historical developments in terms of simple macro relationships among aggregate variables.

We may note that some of the stylized facts, such as (4) and (5), are subject to controversy, but this lies outside the scope of this volume.

B. COMPONENTS OF THE KALDOR THEORY

1. The saving function.   Define:

Q as output
r as the interest (profit rate)
$\dot{K}$ as investment and K as capital
s_r and s_w as saving ratios out of profit and wage shares, respectively;
$\quad s_r > s_w$

Kaldor writes the saving–investment identity as:

$$\dot{K} = s_r(rK) + s_w(Q - rK)$$

$$= s_w Q + (s_r - s_w) rK$$

Hence,

$$\frac{rK}{Q} = \frac{1}{s_r - s_w}\left[\frac{\dot{K}}{Q} - s_w\right] \tag{3.3.1}$$

showing the dependence of the profit share upon the level of investment.

Kaldor believes that (3.3.1) constitutes a Keynesian distribution theory to supplant the marginal productivity theory of distribution.

Assuming that s_w is near zero and hence negligible, and that balanced growth takes place with labor growing at rate n, (3.3.1) becomes

$$r = n/s_r \tag{3.3.1'}$$

which we have already mentioned in Mrs. Robinson's theory in the last section. This is an area where the discussions between Mrs. Robinson and Kaldor developed a theory adopted by both.

2. The "Keynesian theory" for full employment.   Kaldor assumed that the economy consists of many firms with price-making power. The cost structure and pricing decisions can best be shown by Figure 3.3a.

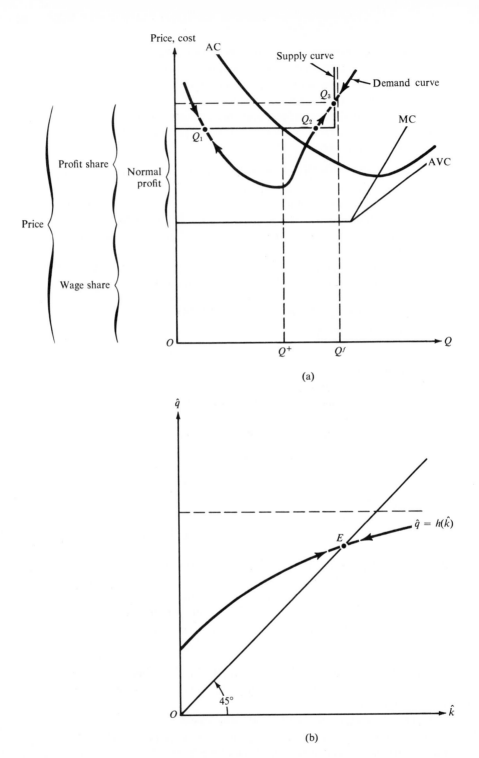

FIGURE 3.3

The average variable cost is constant up to a certain point before it goes up due to the limited capacity of existing plants. Superimposed on that there is the full-employment barrier due to labor availability. Firms fix prices by adding a "normal profit" margin upon their *variable costs*, up to the full-employment barrier. Hence, the aggregate supply curve takes the form of a reversed letter L.

We then come to the aggregate demand curve of Kaldor. It indicates the maximum price at which a given volume of output can be sold. Rewriting the expression for profit share on the left-hand side of (3.3.1) as $1 - (c/P_D)$, where c stands for average cost and P_D for price, we can deduce from that equation:[6]

$$P_D = \frac{(s_r - s_w)c}{s_r - \dot{K}/Q}$$

(3.3.2)

where $\dot{K}/Q$ is a constant when the supply curve is below AC (i.e., $Q < Q^+$), and a sharply increasing function of Q when the supply curve is above AC (i.e., $Q > Q^+$). This is based upon the fact that above-normal profit stimulates *induced* investment above and beyond the constant flow of *autonomous* investment.

In this fashion, Kaldor obtains a U-shaped demand function, intersecting the supply curve at $Q_1, Q_2,$ and Q_3. By applying the Marshallian criterion of stability (shown by arrows), Q_1 and Q_3 are stable equilibria, whereas Q_2 is unstable.

From this "Keynesian demand curve," Kaldor stated that Keynesian economics is able to explain the near-full-employment growth (represented by Q_3) that dominated British economic history up to 1920. It also explains that where Keynesian unemployment occurs (represented by Q_1) balanced growth is impossible, since there is no induced investment.

3. Technical progress function.   Kaldor believes that the rate of growth of per capita output is an increasing function of the rate of growth of per capita capital. Such a function shows diminishing returns, and it crosses the 45° ray from above, as shown in Figure 3.3*b*. In algebraic terms

$$\hat{q} = h(\hat{k})$$

(3.3.3)

where $\hat{q} = \dot{q}/q$ is the rate of growth of per capita output q and $\hat{k} = \dot{k}/k$ is the rate of growth of per capita capital k. The shape of this function is dictated by the following facts:

(a) Some technical progress is possible even if the capital/labor ratio is fixed. Therefore, the h curve cuts the $\hat{q}$ axis.

(b) Technical progress rises when the capital/labor ratio rises because new inventions must be embodied in the physical stock of capital. But as more profitable innovations are exhausted, h must taper off. Therefore, $h' > 0 > h''$.

[6] After transposition and cancellation, we obtain

$$c/P_D = (s_r - \dot{K}/Q)/(s_r - s_w)$$

Taking reciprocals, we get (3.3.2).

(c) There is a speed limit beyond which the growth rate of output per worker cannot rise no matter how fast the capital/worker ratio grows. Therefore, h is bounded above by the dotted line in Figure 3.3b.

It is held that for different countries the h function can have very different shapes. This is a matter of "technical dynamism," which leads to different growth rates.

Kaldor introduced various ways to ensure that the economic system will converge toward E, the intersection of the h function and the 45° line. For instance, if $\hat{q} > \hat{k}$ (i.e., above the OE ray), expected profit rate rises above actual profit rate such that $\hat{k}$ will increase. The arrows on the h function reflect such movements. At E, both the capital/labor ratio and output/labor ratio would grow at an exponential rate, while the capital/output ratio remained constant, proving his stylized facts (1), (2), and (4) (see Section 3.3.2-A). Now with a fixed capital/output ratio, and his Keynesian demand function, etc., an equilibrium at Q_3 means a constant profit share, as well as a constant investment/income ratio. This proves his stylized fact (5). Dividing the constant profit share rK/Q by the constant capital/output ratio K/Q proves stylized fact (3).

The varying h functions for each country prove that each country can have a different growth rate, proving stylized fact (6).

C. COMMENTS

Kaldor's theory is inspiring in its sweep and audacity. But usually, due to its rough-hewn nature, it only provides prototypes for more sophisticated development. First, the Kaleckian saving function (i.e., $s_r > s_w$) does not constitute a distribution theory in its own right. It can be incorporated into the neoclassical framework while the marginal productivity theory of distribution remains intact (see Section 6.2). As Kaldor pointed out [31], the main question is whether investment is independently determined. In Mrs. Robinson's context where underemployment is highly likely, the key role of investment is more justified. Under the Kaldorian emphasis on perennial full employment, aggregate investment level does not appear to have much independence to speak of. Second, the technical progress function is a rather bizarre contraption. Solow [37], Black [40], and others pointed out that if this function coexists side by side with a neoclassical production function, then either that production function has to be of the Cobb-Douglas form or the technical progress function will shift all the time. But more than that, if Kaldor wanted to discard the neoclassical production function altogether, then investment in capital goods serves the sole function of stimulating labor-augmenting technical progress. Unless all investment takes the form of time and motion studies, obviously such an assumption is unrealistic. As we noted before, the modified versions of both the above-mentioned ideas have been "swallowed up" by neoclassical models. The third element in Kaldor's theory concerns growth under administered prices, complete with induced investment functions, etc. This pioneering piece deserves much of our attention.

On the methodological plane, Kaldor's view that macroeconomic forces override microeconomic factors is also an intriguing angle worthy of much closer analysis. Present-day macroeconomics is predominantly a matter of aggregation carried to heroic heights. Interfirm interactions on expectations, etc., presumably affect investment decisions of most, though not all, entrepreneurs. The contagious spread of pessimism or optimism so far defies systematic theorizing, but doubtless such elements shape the business environment through channels other than the price mechanism. Applying the same principle in the intertemporal context, one may even turn the table on the "Keynesian" stands. The 1956 Solow model may be a good description of the long-run capitalistic growth precisely because there exist overriding forces that prevent Keynesian difficulties from arresting secular growth for any length of time. This, of course, is pure conjecture. Current research on short-run macroeconomics, such as the work of Solow and Stiglitz [41], presumably serves as building blocks for such eventual syntheses.

APPENDIX 3.1

The calculation of "real capital ratio," etc.

Consider a balanced stock associated with technique i and growing at an exponential rate n. The wage and interest rates are w and r, respectively. For simplicity, let new capital stock produced at the present be unity and the consumption good be the numeraire.

For any particular technique i, define:

$f(t)$ as the labor input requirement for an equipment at age t during its gestation period
$g(t)$ as the consumption good output for an equipment at age t during its operational life
$h(t)$ as the labor input requirement for an equipment at age t during its operational life

The gestation period is the interval $[-F, 0]$ (age in gestation period is regarded as negative) and the operational life is the interval $[0, H]$. Also let

$D(t)$ be the discounted, future quasi-rent of a *completed* equipment of age t, $0 \leq t \leq H$

$$D(t) = \int_t^H [g(s) - wh(s)]e^{-r(s-t)} \, ds$$

$D(0)$ be the present worth of an equipment, new
$d(t)$ be the "undepreciated proportion" of an equipment of age t, $0 \leq t \leq H$
$\quad d(t) = D(t)/D(0)$
$J(0)$ be the full cost of new equipment
$J(t)$ be (i) the cumulate cost of an in-process equipment of age t, $-F \leq t < 0$

$$J(t) = \int_{-F}^t f(s)e^{-r(s-t)} \, ds$$

$J(t)$ be (ii) the unamortized cost of a used equipment of age t, $0 \leq t \leq H$

$$J(t) = J(0)d(t)$$

$N(t)$ be the class size of equipment of age t,

$$N(t) = e^{-nt}$$

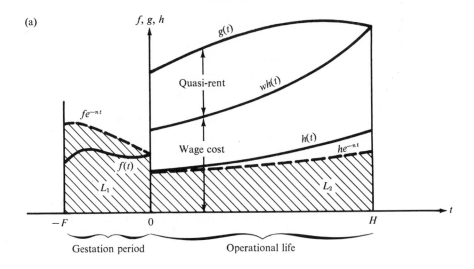

(a)

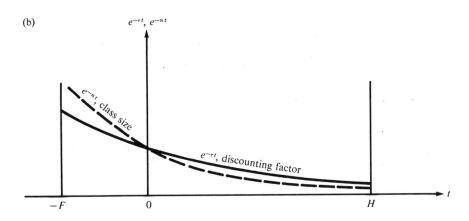

(b)

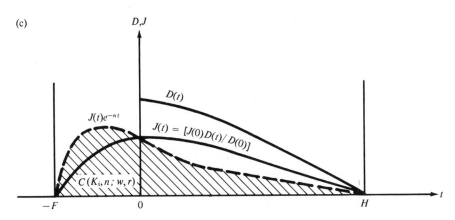

(c)

FIGURE 3.4

From the above definitions,

$$L_1 = \int_{-F}^{0} e^{-nt} f(t)\, dt$$

$$L_2 = \int_{0}^{H} e^{-nt} h(t)\, dt$$

$$Q = \int_{0}^{H} e^{-nt} g(t)\, dt$$

$$C = \int_{-F}^{H} e^{-nt} J(t)\, dt$$

These calculations are illustrated in Figure 3.4. The time flows f, g, and h are shown in Figure 3.4a. The equipment population size e^{-nt} for age t is shown in Figure 3.4b. Since we assumed that the current machine output is $1 = e^0$, current labor input for all age t machines (either to make them during their gestation period or to man them during their operational span) is indicated by the dotted lines in Figure 3.4a. The area under fe^{-nt} is L_1, and the area under he^{-nt} is L_2.

Back in Figure 3.4.a, the line $wh(t)$ is a scaling up of $h(t)$ to show labor cost (in product terms) for one age t machine. The vertical distance between $g(t)$ and $wh(t)$ is the quasi-rent. Figure 3.4b shows e^{-rt}, the discounting factor. The convolution integrals

$$\int_{-F}^{t} f(s) e^{-r(s-t)}\, ds \quad \text{and} \quad \int_{t}^{H} [g(s) - wh(s)] e^{-r(s-t)}\, ds$$

represent, respectively, the cumulate cost on in-process equipment $J(t)$, $t < 0$, and the yet realized present value of quasi-rent, $D(t)$. They are plotted in Figure 3.4c. The depreciated value $J(t)$, $t \geq 0$, is also shown in the same diagram. The dotted line $J(t)e^{-nt}$ represents cost-value of all equipment at age t. The area under the curve is C, the cost valuation of the entire balanced stock. In this example $D(0) > J(0)$, showing that the interest rate r is too low to be compatible with the wage rate w. When $D(0) = J(0)$, r is the Keynesian marginal efficiency of capital (or the internal rate of return).

REFERENCES

[1] Robinson, J., "The Model of an Expanding Economy," in *Collected Essays*, vol. 2, Oxford University Press, Oxford, 1960, pp. 74–83.

[2] Robinson, J., "Normal Prices," in *Essays in The Theory of Economic Growth*, Macmillan, London, 1962, pp. 1–21.

[3] Robinson, J., "A Model of Accumulation," in *Essays in the Theory of Economic Growth*, Macmillan, London, 1962, pp. 22–87.

[4] Robinson, J., "Marx and Keynes," in *Collected Economic Essays*, vol. 1, Oxford University Press, Oxford, 1960, pp. 133–45.

[5] Robinson, J., *An Essay on Marxian Economics*, Macmillan, London, 1949.

[6] Robinson, J., "Marx, Marshall and Keynes," in *Collected Economic Essays*, vol. 2, Oxford University Press, Oxford, 1960, pp. 1–17.

[7] Robinson, J., "What Remains of Marxism?" in *Collected Economic Essays*, vol. 3, Oxford University Press, Oxford, 1965, pp. 158–66.

[8] Robinson, J., "Mr. Harrod's Dynamics," in *Collected Economic Essays*, vol. 1, Oxford University Press, Oxford, 1960, pp. 155–74.

[9] Robinson, J., "Notes on the Theory of Economic Development," in *Collected Economic Essays*, vol. 2, Oxford University Press, Oxford, 1960, pp. 88–106.

[10] Robinson, J., "Beyond Full Employment," in *Collected Economic Essays*, vol. 3, Oxford University Press, Oxford, 1965, pp. 103–12.

[11] Robinson, J., "Harrod's Knife-Edge," in *Collected Economic Essays*, vol. 3, Oxford University Press, Oxford, 1965, pp. 52–55.

[12] Robinson, J., "The Production Function

and the Theory of Capital," in *Collected Economic Essays*, vol. 2, Oxford University Press, Oxford, 1960, pp. 132–44.

[13] Robinson, J., "Pre-Keynesian Theory After Keynes," in *Collected Economic Essays*, vol. 3, Oxford University Press, Oxford, 1965, pp. 56–69.

[14] Robinson, J., "Equilibrium Growth Models," in *Collected Economic Essays*, vol. 3, Oxford University Press, Oxford, 1965, pp. 15–29.

[15] Robinson, J., "Robinson on Findlay on Robinson," in *Collected Economic Essays*, vol. 3, Oxford University Press, Oxford, 1965, pp. 48–51.

[16] Robinson, J., "Solow on the Rate of Return," in *Collected Economic Essays*, vol. 3, Oxford University Press, Oxford, 1965, pp. 36–47.

[17] Robinson, J., "Accumulation and the Production Function," in *Collected Economic Essays*, vol. 2, Oxford University Press, Oxford, 1960, pp. 132–44.

[18] Sraffa, P., *Production of Commodities by Means of Commodities*, Cambridge University Press, Cambridge, 1960.

[19] Robinson, J., "Capital, Technique and Relative Shares," in *Collected Economic Essays*, vol. 2, Oxford University Press, Oxford, 1960, pp. 159–84.

[20] Robinson, J., *The Accumulation of Capital*, Irwin, Homewood, Ill., 1956.

[21] Robinson, J., "Latter-Day Capitalism," in *Collected Economic Essays*, vol. 3, Oxford University Press, Oxford, 1965, pp. 113–24.

[22] Robinson, J., *Economics, An Awkward Corner*, Allen and Unwin, London, 1966.

[23] Findlay, Ronald, "A Robinsonian Model of Accumulation," *Economica*, vol. N.S. 30, Feb. 1963, pp. 1–12.

[24] Findlay, Ronald, "A Reply," *Economica*, vol. N.S. 30, Nov. 1963, pp. 411–2.

[25] Robinson, Joan, and K. A. Naqri, "The Badly Behaved Production Function," *Quarterly Journal of Economics*, vol. LXXXI, Nov. 1967, pp. 579–91.

[26] Champernowne, D., "The Production Function and Theory of Capital," *Review of Economic Studies*, vol. XXI, 1954, pp. 112–35.

[27] Solow, R. M., "The Production Function and the Theory of Capital," *Review of Economic Studies*, vol. XXIII, no. 2, 1956, pp. 101–08.

[28] Samuelson, P. A., "Parable and Realism in Capital Theory," *Review of Economic Studies*, vol. XXX, June 1962, pp. 193–206.

[29] Kaldor, N., "The Recent Controversy on the Theory of Capital," *Econometrica*, vol. 5, July 1937, pp. 201–33.

[30] Kaldor, N., "Addendum: A Rejoinder to Professor Knight," *Econometrica*, vol. 6, April 1938, pp. 163–76.

[31] Kaldor, N., "Alternative Theories of Distribution," *Review of Economic Studies*, vol. XXIII, no. 2, 1956, pp. 83–100.

[32] Kaldor, N., "Capitalistic Evolution in the Light of Keynesian Economics," *Sankhyā*, vol. 18, May 1957, pp. 173–82.

[33] Kaldor, N., "A Model of Economic Growth, *Economic Journal*, vol. LXVIII, 1957, pp. 591–624.

[34] Kaldor, N., "Capital Accumulation and Economic Growth," in *The Theory of Capital*, F. A. Lutz and D. C. Hague, Eds., Macmillan, London, 1961.

[35] Kaldor, N., "Economic Growth and the Problem of Inflation," *Economica*, vol. E.S. 26, Aug. and Nov. 1959, pp. 212–26, 287–98.

[36] Kaldor, N., and J. A. Mirlees, "A New Model of Economic Growth," *Review of Economic Studies*, vol. XXIX, June 1962, pp. 174–92.

[37] Hague, D. C., "Summary Record of the Debate," in *The Theory of Capital*, F. A. Lutz and D. C. Hague, Eds., Macmillan, London, 1961.

[38] Solow, R. M., *Capital Theory and the Rate of Return*, Rand McNally, Chicago, 1963.

[39] Kaldor, N., "Comment," *Review of Economic Studies*, vol. XXIX, June 1962, pp. 249–50.

[40] Black, John, "The Technical Progress Function and the Production Function," *Economica*, vol. N.S. 29, May 1962, pp. 166–70.

[41] Solow, R. M., and J. E. Stiglitz, "Output, Employment and Wages in the Short-Run," *Quarterly Journal of Economics*, vol. LXXXII, Nov. 1968, pp. 537–60.

EXERCISES

3.1. Explain the significance of the condition $v \geq C_0 \geq C'$, with reference to Figure 3.1b. Show that if v is greater than C_0, then the physical survival of the working class during a deep depression is in doubt.

3.2. Why did Mrs. Robinson and Kaldor pay more attention to the pricing policies of firms in their models than Solow did in his? Can Solow handle the same considerations within his 1956 framework?

4

extensions of the neoclassical models:
aggregation and disaggregation

4.1 GENERAL REVIEW: SOLOW ON AGGREGATION AND GROWTH

For the past 12 years, the theory of growth has been dominated by the models of
the neoclassical school. The *locus classicus* of this theory rests with the works of
Solow and Swan, introduced in Chapter 2. These first-generation models are
open to certain objections and criticisms. The views of their critics have been
presented in detail in Chapters 2 and 3. The subsequent development of the
growth theory can be viewed as a series of attempts to rectify the limitations of
the early models. Before presenting the later developments, we shall review the
limitations of the early models, the view of the "neoclassicals" on such issues,
and the subsequent extensions of the neoclassical models.

4.1.1. Limitations of the first-generation models

The simple Solovian model presented in Chapter 2 rests upon a series of
simplifying hypotheses. For economists who disagree with these assumptions,
the model suffers from various types of conceptual and empirical shortcomings.
There are three main conceptual disagreements:

(1) Labor, capital, and output are all treated as homogeneous commodities.
The lack of realism of this hypothesis is self-evident.[1]

(2) The usefulness of such simple models presumably lies in their adaptability
for empirical studies. In that context, capital input is likely to be measured in
value terms. However, as seen in Chapter 3, the value of capital is a function of
the interest rate (which, in turn, is determined by the marginal product of
capital). Hence, as interest rate varies, the same physical assemblage of capital
goods assumes different values. Although there exists a functional relationship
between outputs and the *physical* quantities of the various heterogeneous inputs

---

[1]Usually the critics concentrate on the difficulties of aggregating capital. Recent studies by Franklin
Fisher [1, 2] discovered that the difficulties in aggregating labor and output are only slightly less.

(including diverse types of capital), no systematic relation can be posited between outputs on one side and labor and the *value* of capital on the other. The nonexistence of the aggregate production function rules out the explanation of an unbalanced growth path (where interest rate varies over time) by means of a neoclassical model.

(3) Capital is a *produced* input. Its opportunity cost in terms of consumption goods may vary over time. In the one-sector Solovian model, consumption and capital goods are assumed to be identical. This means that the Wicksell effect[2] is postulated to be always neutral. However, history has shown that such price variability plays an important role in economic development.

Added to these three are the empirical limitations:

(4) In the real world, the owner of a physical capital good can hardly vary the capital/labor ratio in its operation. Such nonmalleability of specific capital goods was overlooked in the early growth models.

(5) As a rule, technical progress can be incorporated into the production process only by the adoption of new capital goods. The disembodied technical progress in early growth models is unrealistic.

(6) Technical progress is frequently the fruit of experience, education, and/or research work. It may be conditioned by current production and price patterns. The early growth models treat technical progress as entirely exogenous in nature.

(7) Investment is not passive in nature. Therefore, we cannot assume (as in early neoclassical models) that the saving plan is always realized so that *ex post* investment and saving are identical to *ex ante* saving.

(8) Saving behavior of capitalists is quite different from that of workers. This is especially so when "capitalists" stands for modern corporations whose reinvestment motive differs widely from the saving urges of the wage-earner. This aspect again is not emphasized by early growth models.

(9) Perfect foresight is an unrealistic assumption. It is justifiable only under golden age growth. Neoclassical models apply the technique of comparative balanced growth (or golden age growth) to analyze unbalanced growth paths (cf. Section 2.3). Since relative prices are changing along an unbalanced path, it is most doubtful that entrepreneurs will have the perfect foresight needed to exclude errors in output and investment decisions. Therefore, the neoclassical analysis of unbalanced growth is based upon an unrealistic assumption.

(10) Various Keynesian rigidities should have been given heavier weights.

All the above criticisms have been raised by one economist or another on various occasions. In particular, points (1)–(3), (7), and (9) have been noted by Mrs. Robinson [4]; points (5)–(8) by Kaldor [5]; point (4) by Sato [6]; and point (10) by Eisner [7]. In fact, both Samuelson [8] and Hicks [9] expressed some misgivings about the neoclassical growth models.

---

[2] *Wicksell effect* is defined as the divergence of the current value of cumulate capital from the time integral of the value of investments, where "value" denotes opportunity cost. *Neutrality* means no divergence. (See Swan [3], pp. 352–361.)

We may note that points (1), (2), (7), and (9) are more basic criticisms. It is hard to modify the existing theory to meet fully such objections. The other points are more easily accommodated.

4.1.2. The neoclassical stand

We shall cite the views of Solow here. Solow is certainly the founder of the neoclassical theory of growth. Also, he showed an awareness of its shortcomings as keen as any of his critics. Moreover, in each and every aspect of the extension of growth theory, he has made his contributions. We shall quote Samuelson and Solow on the Solovian view of the growth theory: its motivation, its approaches, and its perspective.

1. On motivation. Samuelson said:

Solow, in the interest of empirical measurements and approximation, has been occasionally willing to drop his rigorous insistence upon a heterogeneous capital programming model; instead of heroic abstraction, he has carried forward the seminal work of Paul H. Douglas on estimating a single production function for society. [8]

Solow himself stated:

I have never thought of the macroeconomic production function as a rigorously justifiable concept. . . . It is either an illuminating parable, or else a mere device for handling data, to be used so long as it gives good empirical results, and to be abandoned as soon as it doesn't, or as soon as something better comes along. [10]

2. On approaches. Solow remarked in his comment on Pasinetti,

General equilibrium is fundamentally microeconomic. It runs in terms of the prices and outputs of individual goods and services. . . . However, to make the theory usable, some amount of aggregation is indispensable. . . . Two tacks are possible. . . . One is try to preserve the rigor . . . by making special assumptions. . . . The other is to give up the rigor and . . . construct macro-systems . . . by analogy with microeconomics. Whether this device works can be discovered only by trying it out. But it seems to me to be a mistake to ask deep philosophical questions of such loose concepts. [11]

3. On perspective. On two different occasions Solow pointed out:

The theory is incomplete, but there is still point in following out the logical implications. . . . They will still have a role to play in a more complete theory. . . . The Walrasian synthesis will come by bits and pieces. [12]

Capital theory seems . . . to consist of a catalog of models. [13]

From these we can surmise that Solow is content with the imperfect and incomplete models of growth only because either they are empirically testable or they serve as necessary links for the successive approximation to reality. Solow disagrees with Mrs. Robinson mainly because in his view she is against some useful (though inexact) constructions without providing a better substitute.

4.1.3. A summary of the alternative types of models

In all the criticism raised against the neoclassical theory, the most fundamental point concerns the aggregation difficulties. Therefore, the handling of the aggregation problem forms a natural classification scheme for all neoclassical models.

   1. Heroic aggregation.   This is the basic approach of Solow's path-breaking paper [14]. In its defense, one may argue that the functional relation between Q and K, L is an "empirical law" in its own right. In the methodological parlance of Samuelson, this is an operationally meaningful law, since it can be empirically refuted. It is entirely irrelevant to criticize such models because the macro relations are not derived from micro relations via aggregation. After all, few would criticize the Keynesian aggregate consumption function, Consumption $= a + b$(Income), on the grounds that it cannot be deduced from utility and profit maximization behavior of individual households and firms under generally acceptable conditions.

   2. Rigorous aggregation.   In this approach, certain special assumptions are postulated so that one can rigorously prove that the multi-capital-goods world we live in can be satisfactorily represented by a model with a single aggregate capital index. One can predict the behavior of the real world by analyzing the aggregate model alone. The model fulfills the "sufficiency criterion" of Fisherian statistics, since nothing of interest is lost in the aggregation process. It is "isomorphic" to reality in the mathematical sense, since every phenomenon in the heterogeneous capital goods world corresponds in a one-to-one fashion to the simple model with a single capital good index. There are two different types of aggregation of this type: the Solow aggregation [15], which will be treated at the end of the present section, and the Samuelson aggregation [8], which will be considered in Section 4.2.

   3. Analytically oriented disaggregation.   By making a series of special assumptions, one may also set up a disaggregated model. The golden mean of such model building is both to capture enough realism to remain relevant and to preserve a sufficient measure of simplicity to facilitate analytical scrutiny. The elaboration of certain focal aspects is balanced by the abstraction in other aspects. Otherwise, a global disaggregation will make the model mathematically unmanageable. Most of the current models belong to this category, and the area of disaggregation provides a subclassification schemata:
   (a) Disaggregation by sector
   (b) Disaggregation by types of capital goods
   (c) Disaggregation by vintages of capital goods
   (d) Disaggregation by sources and forms of saving

The last two sections of this chapter are devoted to two-sector and multi-capital-goods models. Chapter 5 deals with vintage capital models and Chapters 6 and 8 with behavior of saving and monetary models, respectively.

4. Simulation-oriented disaggregation. Even more realistic assumptions can be made. The resultant model is then so intricate that purely analytical tools can no longer disentangle its complexity. The last resort is numerical simulation. This approach has been followed by very few economists. A prominent example is Solow's model on vintage goods [16].

There are other extensions of the basic Solovian model that defy the aggregation–disaggregation classification. A case in mind is endogenous technical progress. Such features can be introduced in both the aggregate and the disaggregate models. Usually, special assumptions are adopted here to approximate reality as in analytically oriented disaggregation.

One may now contrast the early models (heroic aggregation) against the later versions (the rest). The successor models may claim to be superior, since they represent higher orders of approximation to the truth. Nonetheless, from the methodological point of view, the early models propose empirical laws of a more aggregate type. Hence, they are equally respectable. The relative validity is not proved short of a statistical test. Even then it is conceivable that, due to mechanisms akin to the central limit theorem of probability, the aggregate models may possess predictive prowess surpassing that of the disaggregated models (analogy: it is easier to predict the consumption/income ratio for the entire American economy than for Mr. John Doe next door). Nothing about their relative merits can be said *a priori*.

For the rest of this section, we hasten to introduce a special model: the Solovian aggregation.

Solow set forth [15] an existence criterion for an aggregate capital index that can be used to replace a whole set of heterogeneous capital goods. His reasons for doing so are presumably the following:

(1) There exists a powerful arsenal of theorems for a two-input production function. If one can legitimately compress the *n* capital goods into a single-capital index, one can avail himself of this fabulous inheritance.

(2) Capital data available to the applied economist are notoriously poor. Separate series for various physical capital goods is a seldom-realized ideal. In most circumstances, when a single capital series is available it is imperative to know whether the series at hand can serve as the "surrogate" index appropriate in theory. The available index may not bear the necessary relation to the represented capital goods to qualify as a "surrogate," or a legitimate surrogate may not exist. We shall introduce the Solovian criterion without proof. Examples will be used to clarify its significance.

The work of Solow is based upon earlier works of Leontief [17, 18] and has since led to the work of Franklin Fisher [19]. Solow showed that:

(1) For a production function $Q = Q(K_1, K_2, \ldots, K_n, L)$ to possess a "collapsed" form $Q = F(K, L)$ with $K = \phi(K_1, K_2, \ldots, K_n)$, it is necessary

and sufficient that the marginal rates of factor substitution between any pair K_i and K_j be independent of the labor L; i.e.,

$$\frac{d}{dL}\left(\frac{\partial Q/\partial K_j}{\partial Q/\partial K_i}\right) = 0 \qquad \text{for all } i, j; i \neq j$$

For convenience, we shall refer to this condition as "capital goods form an independence set."

(2) If the function Q exhibits the properties of constant returns, or the law of variable proportions, so will the function F whenever it exists.

Example. The actual production function is

$$Q = Q(K_1, K_2, \ldots K_n, L)$$

$$= \left[\frac{1}{2n}\sum_{i=1}^{n}(K_i^{-\beta}) + \frac{1}{2}L^{-\beta}\right]^{-1/\beta} \tag{4.1.1}$$

where K_i is the ith capital input, L is the labor input, and $\beta \geq -1$ is a constant. A simple check can readily verify that

$$K = \left[\frac{1}{n}\sum_{i=1}^{n}(K_i^{-\beta})\right]^{-1/\beta} \tag{4.1.2}$$

serves well as a surrogate capital index: we can transform (4.1.1) into its equivalent form:

$$Q = F(K, L)$$

$$= \left[\frac{1}{2}K^{-\beta} + \frac{1}{2}L^{-\beta}\right]^{-1/\beta} \tag{4.1.3}$$

This reveals that a legitimate surrogate can exist. However, if the actually available capital index takes the form

$$\bar{K} = \frac{1}{n}\sum_{i=1}^{n}K_i \tag{4.1.4}$$

then we cannot replace (4.1.1) by some function $\bar{F}(\bar{K}, L)$. This observation does limit somewhat the empirical value of this aggregation procedure (can we hope that the compiler of the United States capital series chose that particular form of a generalized mean?).

The cutting edge of the Solovian results rests more with the other half of the theorem. Suppose we have a production function

$$Q = (K_1^{1/3}L^{2/3}) + (K_2^{2/3}L^{1/3}) \tag{4.1.5}$$

Since

$$\frac{d}{dL}\left[\frac{\partial Q/\partial K_2}{\partial Q/\partial K_1}\right] = -\frac{2}{3}K_1^{2/3}K_2^{-1/3}L^{-4/3} < 0$$

no legitimate surrogate K can ever exist. Hence, any aggregate capital series cannot be of much value to the applied economist.

4.2 FOUNDATIONS OF CAPITAL THEORY: SAMUELSON ON AGGREGATION AND GROWTH

In contrast to Solow, Samuelson is much more deeply committed to the maintenance of microeconomic rigor. His view [8] can be summarized as follows:

(1) The correct formulation of capital theory must be Walrasian. Millions of equations and unknowns are needed to depict the wealth and preference of each household and the techniques available to each firm. In general, one cannot depict the working of the production system with a single aggregate production function containing a single "abstract" capital input.

(2) Under very restrictive conditions, one can postulate a surrogate capital index and derive a surrogate production function for the whole economy. In comparing different economies, each enjoying balanced growth and all sharing the same set of techniques (as summarized by the surrogate production function), one can pretend that they all share one single aggregate production function with labor and the surrogate capital index as inputs. Therefore, under ideal conditions, the Solovian models conceivably can be an exact description of reality.

(3) What Solow actually has done is to use an "approximately valid" method for obtaining *empirical measurements* of the economy. The results of such a model are highly useful.

In deriving a set of sufficiency conditions for the existence of a useful surrogate indicator, Samuelson has introduced the concept of a factor price frontier. This shows the maximum rent rate an economy can afford while paying a certain wage rate, with a given available technology. Such a frontier exists under fairly general conditions and its properties are very interesting in their own right. However, unless special assumptions are adopted, the existence of this frontier does not guarantee the existence of a surrogate capital index, to say nothing of a useful surrogate production function. Studies of the conditions under which such a useful surrogate indicator fails to exist have yielded extremely fruitful insights. In fact, by now these studies have revolutionized capital theory from its very roots. The issue is not quite closed as yet.

Our discussion will be divided into three parts: the derivation of the factor price frontier, the derivation of a useful surrogate production function, and a survey of the pathological cases where no useful surrogate production function exists. Section 4.2.1 examines a model much more general than Samuelson's canonical formulation. Section 4.2.2 pinpoints the crucial roles played by each of Samuelson's special assumptions. The derivation of the surrogate production function is examined against the general duality relation between cost and production functions and is illustrated with an example. Section 4.2.3 synthesizes the more recent developments.

4.2.1. Derivation of the factor price frontier

We shall first state a very general model and then derive a factor price frontier from it.

A. ASSUMPTIONS FOR A GENERAL MODEL

(1) There is only one primary input, labor L, and one final output, C, which serves as the numeraire. There are n different capital goods.

(2) There is a set of technologies $A = \{\alpha\}$, where each α is an index of the production technique specifying how each of the goods existing in the economy is produced. Under each technique, there are $n_\alpha \leq n$ capital goods existing side by side. Under any given technique, the production of any one capital good requires fixed amounts of either labor or the *services* of some capital goods or of both. Production takes place either instantaneously or over a gestation period. The same holds true for the production of the final good, C.

(3) Under a given technique, the output flow of *capital service* from a unit of any capital good follows a known time profile.

(4) There exist perfect competition and constant returns.

B. THE WORKING OF THE ECONOMY

Consider technique α_0, under which $m = n_{\alpha_0}$ capital goods in conjunction with labor are used to produce the same m capital goods as well as the consumption good. These $m+1$ production processes may either be instantaneous or require a given gestation period. There exist m prices for the m capital goods, the consumption goods being the numeraire. Each capital good commands a rent. Adding the wage rate w and the interest rate r, there are $2m+2$ "price variables."[3] The production of the $m+1$ goods give rise to $m+1$ activities; the holding and operating of the capital goods, another m activities. So there are $2m+1$ activities all told.

Lemma 1. *Balanced growth is possible.* Constant returns imply that if a list of inputs is adequate to produce a list of outputs, multiplying the input list throughout by the common factor e^{nt} (i.e., the population growth factor over a period of length t) will enable us to produce a list of outputs e^{nt} times larger than the original output list, item by item. But this is precisely balanced growth.

Lemma 2. *Constant equilibrium prices are compatible with balanced growth.* Under constant returns, an equilibrium price system is one that allows every activity in use to break even but none to make any positive profit.[4] If a set of constant equilibrium prices allows all $2m+1$ activities commencing at instant 0 to break even, constant returns imply that under balanced growth these $2m+1$ activities also break even at instant t, for all t.

Therefore, we now have $2m+1$ equations with $2(m+1)$ price variables, each

---

[3]The symbol r is used here as interest (i.e., time preference) rate, which may be said to be the price for waiting.

[4]Hence, no party has any inducement to alter his action in a conceptual replay. Thus the appelation *equilibrium prices* is justified.

indicating the breaking even of a given activity. (The algebraic form is shown in Appendix 4.1.) Barring pathological cases,[5] one can eliminate the $2m$ prices and rents for all the capital goods, leaving one equation between wage and interest, say,

$$C_{\alpha_0}(r, w) = 0 \qquad \text{(See Figure 4.1.)} \qquad (4.2.1)$$

In an economy undergoing balanced growth, if the wage rate (rent rate) is $\overline{w}(\overline{r})$ and (4.2.1) is satisfied by $(\overline{r}, \overline{w})$, then (a) the national product will be exactly exhausted after interest and wage payments and (b) the production and operation of all the m capital goods and the production of the final good exactly break even.

C. THE DERIVATION OF THE FACTOR PRICE FRONTIER

Consider the whole family of factor price curves in the form (4.2.1) with α ranging over all elements in the technology set. Construct then the "northeastern side envelope"[6] (cf. DD in Figure 4.1). This is the factor price frontier with the following interpretation:

(1) For each wage rate w, r is the maximum interest the economy can afford under the available technology.
(2) For each interest rate r, w is the maximum wage rate the economy can afford under the available technology.

Under perfect competition, inputs can be bid away from any firm that offers a less-than-maximum remuneration. Therefore, all the possible balanced growth states must exhibit a wage–interest combination belonging to the factor price frontier. If we can further identify the technique α_0 under which a specific wage–interest pair is realized, we have gained all the information about the alternative (balanced growth) states attainable by the economy in question.

However, the concept of a factor price frontier falls short of what both Samuelson and Solow desired, on the following grounds:

(1) In deriving the factor price frontier, constant wage and interest rates have been assumed. This rules out the possibility of studying most of the unbalanced growth models (in which wage and interest change over time). This reveals why the Solovian aggregation is more suitable for general growth models than the Samuelsonian aggregation. Under the former, changes of relative factor prices present no problem.

(2) Most economists aim at general, qualitative conclusions, the validity of which does not depend upon the specific details of the production techniques. They wish to obtain statements such as, "At higher wage levels, the appropriate techniques are those associated with higher output/worker ratios." The concept of a factor price frontier (as derived so far) offers no such answers.

---

[5] Inconsistency and/or degeneracy among the $2m + 1$ equations.
[6] Mathematical definition: $\{(r, w) | w = \text{Max } w' \text{ with } C_\alpha(r, w') = 0 \text{ for some } \alpha, r \text{ given or } r = \text{Max } r' \text{ with } C_\alpha(r', w) = 0 \text{ for some } \alpha, w \text{ given}\}$.

(3) Samuelson intended to construct a *useful* capital stock index that can justify the aggregate capital concept in the Solovian models. This has not yet been achieved in the above derivations.

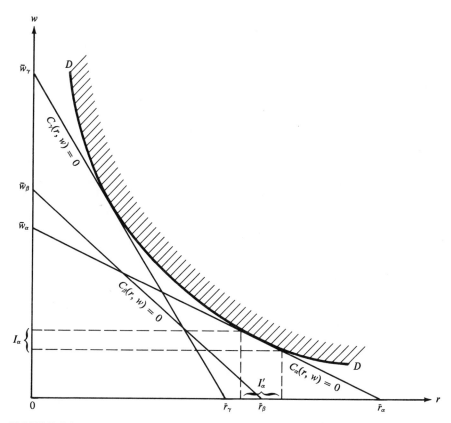

FIGURE 4.1

4.2.2. Derivation of the surrogate production function

After deriving the factor price frontier for the *actual economy* with heterogeneous capital goods, Samuelson considers a parable: Perhaps there can be a certain hypothetical economy in which two inputs, labor L and "capital jelly" J, combine to produce the universal output according to a linear homogeneous production function $F(J, L)$. Since the marginal products of both inputs are functions of the jelly/labor ratio J/L, plotting one against the other parametrically, the resulting factor price frontier in the parable coincides with the actual factor price frontier. For each actual economy, one would attempt to concoct a corresponding parable. The miraculous attributes of the capital jelly are: (1) durability—there is no problem in comparing old assets with new ones;

(2) malleability—like the "meccano set" of Swan or "leets" of Meade, it can be used in all proportions with labor; (3) instant producibility—no gestation period is needed; and (4) consumability—since it is made of the same "universal good" as consumption goods, the Wicksell effect never arises.

Like the simple Solovian economy, every technique in the hypothetical economy can be unidirectionally ranked according to the jelly/labor ratio, the output/labor ratio, and/or the connected interval of wage rates over which this technique affords the highest interest rate[7] (we shall call this interval the "efficient wage interval"). In the ranking of hypothetical techniques, any one of these three criteria implies the same ranking. The remaining question is whether techniques in the actual economy can be partitioned into classes, each of which is associated with one and only one hypothetical technique. An affirmative answer would allow us (1) to analyze the choice of *actual* techniques (among alternative balanced growth paths) by means of a simple Solovian model with the *surrogate* production function serving in lieu of the aggregate production function, and (2) to evaluate the alternative "balanced stocks" (see Section 3.2) of heterogeneous capital with a useful surrogate capital index, namely, the quantity of capital jelly for the associated hypothetical techniques. This would remove the last two limitations listed at the end of Section 4.2.1.

Two problems remain: (1) the derivability of the surrogate production function and the surrogate capital index and (2) the associability of a class of *actual techniques* to one specific *hypothetical technique*. If one actual technique is associated with two hypothetical techniques and one ensemble of capital stock can be represented by two alternative surrogate capital indices, then neither the surrogate production function nor the surrogate capital index is of much use in justifying the simple Solow model.

We shall first sketch the derivability problem and then discuss the Samuelsonian special assumptions under which both the derivability and the associability problems are solved. The uses of these concepts are discussed and an example is constructed to illustrate Samuelson's point.

A. THE SURROGATE PRODUCTION FUNCTION AND THE SURROGATE CAPITAL INDEX

The derivation of these concepts is related to Shephard's results [20] on the duality relationship between the production function and the "minimal unit cost function" (where cost is expressed in terms of output). The latter function describes the lowest unit cost one can attain as a function of the input prices and the scale of output; the available alternative techniques of production are assumed given. The constant returns assumption leaves the minimal unit cost unaffected by the scale of output. Minimal unit cost can then be plotted as a surface over the $r–w$ plane. The contour line of this surface where minimal unit cost is unity (i.e., producers breaking even) is the factor price frontier sought after.

---

[7]There may be only one element in this interval; i.e., the technique is efficient at a unique wage rate.

The elegant conclusions of Shephard indicate that:

(1) If the minimum unit cost function is convex,[8] one can derive from it a production function that is concave.[9] The reverse is also true.
(2) If the factor price frontier is convex,[10] one can derive a unit output isoquant that is also convex. The reverse is also true.
(3) Let (r_0, w_0) be the point on the factor price frontier that corresponds to the point (J_0, L_0) on the unit output isoquant; then:
(a) Along the factor price frontier at (r_0, w_0) the slope is $dw/dr = -J_0/L_0$.
(b) Along the unit output isoquant at (J_0, L_0), the slope is $dJ/dL = -w_0/r_0$.

If one is provided with the observed factor prices (r_0, w_0), the slope of the factor price curve $M(r, w) = 1$ near (r_0, w_0), and the size of labor force L_0, then from (3a) above, we can deduce the surrogate capital index (cf. Figure 4.12, Appendix 4.2).

$$J_0 = -L_0 \frac{dw}{dr}\bigg|_{(r_0,\, w_0)} \tag{4.2.2}$$

The actual graphical construction is discussed in Appendix 4.2.

B. THE SPECIAL MODEL OF SAMUELSON

To meet both the derivability and associability problems, Samuelson postulated four special assumptions:

(1) Under any technique α, there is one and only one capital good in use, say, K_α.
(2) The capital service produced by K_α forms an exponential time pattern:

$$g_\alpha(t) = \exp\{-\delta_\alpha t\} \qquad t \geq 0$$

(3) Both the capital and the final goods are produced instantaneously.
(4) The production of either output requires the same amounts of input, *viz*:
Unit requirement for capital service: a_α
Unit requirement for labor service: b_α

The working of the system.   Under the special assumptions, the breaking even of the productive activities for both K_α and C implies the following twin equalities between costs and revenues:

$$wb_\alpha + v_\alpha a_\alpha = p_\alpha$$
$$wb_\alpha + v_\alpha a_\alpha = 1 \tag{4.2.3}$$

where v_α and p_α are the rental rate and unit price for equipment K_α and C is the numeraire.

[8]That is, the minimum unit cost *surface* is "cuplike" over the wage–interest plane.
[9]That is, the production surface is "caplike" over the capital–labor plane.
[10]That is, if under the interest rates $x_1\%$ and $x_2\%$ the maximum wage rates sustainable by the economy are $\$y_1$ and $\$y_2$, respectively, then there is no technique the economy can use and pay a wage higher than $\$(y_1+y_2)/2$ under an interest rate greater than $[(x_1+x_2)/2]\%$.

Under assumption (2), the breaking even of holding and operating activity for equipment K_α implies equality between the price of equipment, new, and the present worth of its rental stream:

$$p_\alpha = v_\alpha \int_0^\infty e^{-rt} g_\alpha(t)\, dt \qquad\qquad (4.2.4)$$

where e^{-rt} is the discounting factor per dollar t periods hence, or, equivalently,

$$1 = v_\alpha \int_0^\infty \exp\left[-(r+\delta_\alpha)t\right] dt \qquad \text{(from (4.2.3), } p_\alpha = 1\text{)}$$

$$= v_\alpha/(r+\delta_\alpha) \qquad\qquad \text{(by integration)}$$

$$(4.2.4)$$

i.e.,

$$v_\alpha = r+\delta_\alpha$$

Substituting back into the second equation of (4.2.3), one obtains:

$$C_\alpha(r, w) = a_\alpha r + b_\alpha w - (1 - a_\alpha \delta_\alpha) = 0 \qquad\qquad (4.2.5)$$

which is a straight line with a negative slope.

The derivation of the factor price frontier from (4.2.5) proceeds as in Section 4.2.1-C. These are depicted in Figure 4.1. It is evident from the figure that technique β is inefficient. Under any wage rate w, one can afford a higher interest rate by using either technique α or technique γ than by using technique β. As long as a technique is "jointly dominated" by a set of other techniques, it will never be utilized. Graphically, the factor price curve C_β never has any common point with the factor price frontier DD.

The properties of the factor price frontier.   From the construction of the factor price frontier, we can easily deduce the following:

(1) The factor price frontier has a *negative slope*. The economic implication is that, given the available techniques, a higher wage rate can be brought about only at the expense of the interest rate. Mathematically, one can characterize the factor price frontier by the equation

$$w = w(r) \qquad \text{with } \frac{dw}{dr} < 0 \qquad\qquad (4.2.5a)$$

(2) The factor price frontier is *convex* toward the origin,[11] i.e., $d^2w/dr^2 \le 0$. The economic implication is that each technique α (which corresponds to a certain slope of its factor price curve, $-a_\alpha/b_\alpha$) is most efficient over at most one connected interval of wages rates, such as I_α in Figure 4.1. This interval may consist of only one point. Alternatively, a technique can also be associated with an interval of interest rates, such as I_α' in Figure 4.1. Mathematically, this

---

[11] A set-theoretical proof of convexity can be sketched here. DD is the lower boundary of the shaded set in Fig. 4.1. The shaded region is the "intersection" of convex half-spaces, $\{(r, w) | C_\alpha(r, w) \ge 0\}$. Thus, the shaded set is convex, and its lower boundary DD will also be convex.

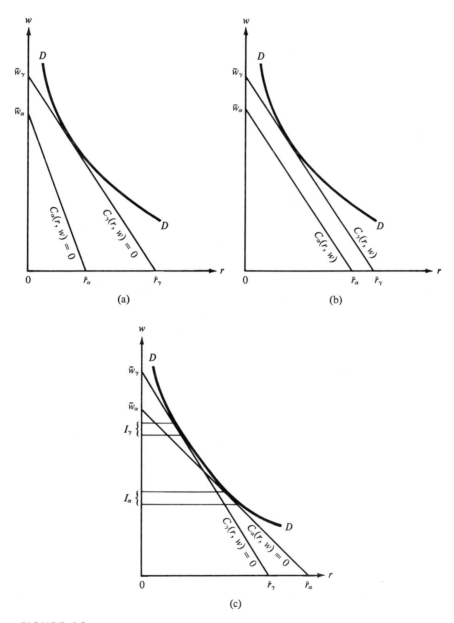

FIGURE 4.2

establishes *the unidirectional rankability of all techniques*: namely, according to the corresponding *efficient wage intervals*.

(3) Among all the efficient techniques, the higher the corresponding net product per worker, the higher its efficient wage interval. This remarkable

result can be derived as follows. Let

$\bar{w}_i = (1 - a_i\delta_i)/b_i$ be the maximum attainable wage under technique i; $i = \alpha, \gamma$

$\bar{r}_i = (1 - a_i\delta_i)/a_i$ be the maximum attainable interest rate under technique i

Both techniques α and γ are efficient so that both $C_\alpha = 0$ and $C_\gamma = 0$ contact $M(r, w) = 1$ at some points.

We shall show that if $\bar{w}_\alpha < \bar{w}_\gamma$, then $a_\alpha/b_\alpha < a_\gamma/b_\gamma$.

Figure 4.2 indicates that since both $C_\alpha = 0$ and $C_\gamma = 0$ are linear and C_α starts with a lower vertical intercept, unless $C_\alpha = 0$ is less steep than $C_\gamma = 0$ it will never meet $C_\gamma = 0$ in the nonnegative quadrant. Hence, it can never contact the frontier DD. But if $a_\alpha/b_\alpha < a_\gamma/b_\gamma$, the efficient wage interval I_α for technique α must be lower than the efficient wage interval for I_γ, as a result of the convexity of DD, the locus for $M(r, w) = 1$.

Since $\bar{w}_i$ is the net product per worker for technique i, we have proved the assertion.

The above results allow us to analyze the choice of techniques in capitalistic production without explicit reference to capital. We may note that Solow in his econometric work sometimes comes close to this. The constant elasticity production function is estimated by regressing loglinearly the output per worker on wage rates.[12]

The use of the surrogate capital index.   Results above imply that among the balanced growth states, the higher the wage rate w, the lower will be the interest rate r, the higher will be the wage/interest ratio w/r, and the higher will be the output/worker ratio Q/L. The only difference between this statement and the summary of results in Section 2.3 is that nothing is said here about the capital/labor ratio and the capital/output ratio.

Since $M(r, w) = 1$ is convex, we can derive the surrogate function F and the surrogate capital J (see Appendix 4.2). Since $C_\alpha = 0$ is linear for all α, we can associate with any actual technique one and only one hypothetical technique, i.e., $J/L = a_\alpha/b_\alpha$. Hence, a useful capital index exists and we can further conclude that the higher w is, the higher is $j = J/L$, due to the monotonicity of

$$w(j) = f(j) - jf'(j) \quad \text{as } dw/dj = -jf''(j) > 0 \text{ for all } j$$

and the higher is $J/Q = j/f(j)$, due to the fact that

$$\frac{d(J/Q)}{dw} = \frac{d(J/Q)/dj}{dw/dj}$$

$$= \frac{-(f - jf')}{jf^2f''}$$

$$= -\frac{w}{jf^2f''} > 0$$

---

[12]However, Samuelson's analysis only holds for comparative balanced growth studies. Solow usually deals with unbalanced growth paths where in (4.2.3) $p_\alpha \neq 1$ and in (4.2.4) v_α varies with time.

Once again we can talk about the capital/labor ratio or the capital/output ratio. Of course, since "capital" here is a hypothetical construction, one may question how much is gained by such an exercise. Whenever technique α has a lower J/L ratio than technique γ, it will necessarily have a lower Q/L ratio as well. Hence, one can unambiguously rank processes by their output/worker ratios, without introducing the capital jelly.

An example.   In order to demonstrate how the Samuelsonian aggregation works, the following example may be helpful.

In the special model of Samuelson, suppose that

$$\delta_\alpha = 0 \text{ for all } \alpha$$

$$\left. \begin{aligned} a_\alpha &= \alpha^\beta \\ b_\alpha &= \alpha^{\beta-1} \end{aligned} \right\} \quad 0 < \beta < 1$$

The factor price line for technique α now becomes

$$\alpha^\beta r + \alpha^{\beta-1} w = 1 \tag{4.2.6}$$

Taking the derivative of (4.2.6) with respect to α, we obtain

$$\beta \alpha^{\beta-1} r + (\beta - 1)\alpha^{\beta-2} w = 0 \tag{4.2.7}$$

or

$$\alpha = \left(\frac{1}{\beta} - 1 \right) \frac{w}{r} \tag{4.2.8}$$

Eliminating α from (4.2.6) with (4.2.8), we obtain the envelope locus:

$$w^\beta r^{1-\beta} = A \tag{4.2.9}$$

where $A = \beta^\beta (1-\beta)^{1-\beta}$.

It can be shown, however, that a surrogate production function,

$$Q = J^{1-\beta} L^\beta \tag{4.2.10}$$

yields exactly the same factor price frontier as in (4.2.9).[13] The reader can also check that

$$J = L\left(-\frac{dw}{dr} \right)$$

by evaluating dw/dr from (4.2.9) and substituting $\beta(J/L)^{1-\beta}$ and $(1-\beta)(J/L)^{-\beta}$ for w and r.

4.2.3. A survey of the "pathological" cases where no surrogate production function exists

During the five years subsequent to the publication of Samuelson's surrogate production function model, economists discovered that such a "useful" aggre-

---

[13] $r = (1-\beta)j^{-\beta}$, $w = \beta j^{(1-\beta)}$. Raising the former to the $1-\beta$ power and the latter to the β power and multiplying the two together, we obtain (4.2.9).

gation procedure is usually infeasible. Such studies brought to light the following:

(1) The aggregate production function should best be defended as a heroic aggregation. Its approximate validity should be judged on econometric grounds. To justify it through rigorous aggregation would involve conditions that are empirically false.
(2) Production techniques usually are not rankable according to their capital/labor ratios or capital/output ratios, since a surrogate capital index cannot be usefully defined, due to the "associability" problem discussed above.
(3) Contrary to our intuition, the wage rate and the output per worker do not always vary in the same direction.
(4) As a consequence, one cannot always rank techniques according to their corresponding wage intervals either. In fact, one technique may be appropriate over many wage ranges.

The upshot is that the "Ruth Cohen curiosum" (see Chapter 3) [4] is logically a rule rather than an exception. In fact, with all her objections to the aggregate production function, Mrs. Robinson originally was not pessimistic enough. She still maintained the hope that techniques can generally be ranked by their "real" capital/labor ratio.

We shall first examine a sufficient condition for the nonexistence of the surrogate production function and then examine the various causes that may give rise to such a condition.

A.   A SUFFICIENT CONDITION FOR NONSURROGABILITY

If there exists a surrogate production function, linear homogeneous in its inputs and possessing isoquants convex to the origin, then we can write

$$Q = Lf(j) \quad \text{with } w = f(j) - jf'(j) \quad \text{and} \frac{Q}{L} = f(j)$$

where

$$\frac{dw}{dj} > 0, \qquad \frac{d}{dj}\left(\frac{Q}{L}\right) > 0$$

This shows that if there exists a surrogate production function, wage w and output per head Q/L must move in the same direction. On the other hand, if the technical conditions of an actual economy are such that w and Q/L move in opposite directions, then no association can be made between an actual technique and a hypothetical technique. Hence, the Samuelsonian aggregation would not work.

We can now establish that the so-called process-reswitching phenomenon constitutes a sufficient condition for the nonexistence of a "useful" surrogate production function.

In Figure 4.3 the factor price lines $C_\alpha = 0$ and $C_\gamma = 0$ intersect twice. When wage moves from I_α^2 to I_γ, the production process is switched from α to γ. When wage moves further into interval I_α^1, the production process is switched back into α. This is the so-called reswitching phenomenon.

Technique α is seen to be superior to technique γ (affording higher interest rates) over the intervals I_α^1 and I_α^2, while technique γ is seen to be superior over the range I_γ. If technique α has a higher output/worker ratio, then the movement of the wage rate from I_α^2 to I_γ signifies opposite movements between w and Q/L. If technique γ has a higher output/worker ratio, then the movement of the wage rate from I_γ to I_α^1 again signifies opposite movement. One way or another, no surrogate production function can exist.

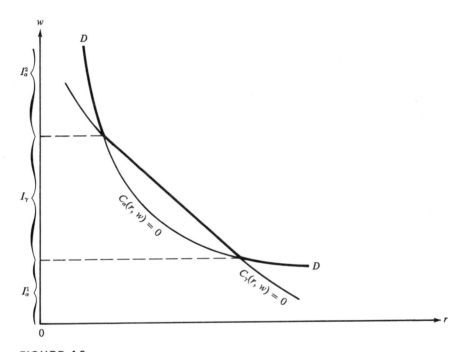

FIGURE 4.3

B. CIRCUMSTANCES THAT GIVE RISE TO THE RESWITCHING PHENOMENON

In the *Quarterly Journal of Economics* Symposium [21], a number of examples have been given for process reswitching. Summing up, we may conclude that:

(1) The reswitching phenomenon may arise either because of the alternative input flows during the gestation periods of the capital goods or because of the alternative (quasi) rent flows available for capital goods over their life spans. The latter emerge due to either the existence of more than one type of capital goods under a given technique or different input proportions in producing the capital goods and the consumption good.

(2) The reswitching phenomenon is sufficient but unnecessary for the non-existence of a "useful" surrogate capital or, for that matter, for an inverse association between the wage rate and the output/worker ratio.

(3) The possible inverse association between the wage rate and the output/worker ratio is a phenomenon with no concept of capital directly involved. Hence, it is somewhat misleading to attribute the "paradoxical" phenomena to the impossibility of defining the capital/labor ratio or the capital/output ratio. It is the existence of nonaggregable production processes that underlies the problem.

We now present two examples to indicate that reswitching can emerge due either to alternative time patterns of capital service or to alternative input distributions in the gestation period.

Example 1. In our economy there is one primary input, labor L; two outputs, capital K and consumable good C. The latter serves as the numeraire.

The production of K is instantaneous. It takes one unit of labor input and one unit of consumable good (used as raw material) to fabricate one unit of capital good. Thus, the production function is Min $\{L, C_K\}$, where C_K represents the C input used for producing K.

The production process for C is also instantaneous. Each unit of *capital service* alone can produce one unit of consumable good. However, by adopting alternative setups we can have the following two alternative time distributions of capital service from the same unit of capital good:

Method 1: $f_1(t) = e^{-1t}$, $0 \leq t \leq \infty$

Method 2:

$$f_2(t) = \begin{cases} 0.79087 & 0 \leq t \leq 10 \\ 0 & 10 < t \leq \infty \end{cases}$$

The zero-profit conditions under perfect competition entail the following factor price curves:

$$(w+1) = \int_0^\infty f_i(t)e^{-rt}\,dt \qquad i = 1, 2$$

where w and r are wage and interest rates, respectively. The left-hand side is the cost for one unit of K, and the right-hand side is its discounted rental stream.

After substituting f_1 and f_2 into this formula, we find that there exist two switching points:

$$r_1 = .1, w_1 = 4 \quad \text{and} \quad r_2 = 3.1, w_2 = 1.44$$

When the ruling interest rate is below r_1, method 1 is superior; when it is between r_1 and r_2, method 2 is superior; once the rate is above r_2, method 1 is again the preferred alternative.

Example 2. There are two goods in the economy, capital good K and consumption good C. The capital good is indestructible, providing one unit of capital service per unit of time. This alone can produce one unit of consumption good. Labor is the sole input required to produce the capital good over a gestation period, but there are two alternative input flows available:

Method 1:

$$f_1(t) = \begin{cases} 0 & -\infty < t < -10 \\ 10+t & -10 \le t \le 0 \end{cases}$$

Method 2:

$$f_2(t) = \begin{cases} 0 & -\infty < t < -9 \\ 5.5 & -9 \le t \le 0 \end{cases}$$

The factor price curves now take the algebraic form

$$w \int_{-\infty}^{0} f_i(t)e^{-rt}\, dt = \frac{1}{r} \qquad i = 1, 2$$

where the left-hand side stands for the production cost for the capital good and the right-hand side represents the present worth of the rent flow.

Observing that for any given r, w varies inversely with the "cost integral" $\int_{-\infty}^{0} f_i e^{-rt}\, dt$, we can establish the existence of the reswitching phenomenon graphically by scanning the $f_i(t)$'s in Figure 4.4. We note that

(1) For $r = 0$, w is undefined, but $\int_{-\infty}^{0} f_1\, dt = 50 > 49.5 = \int_{-\infty}^{0} f_2\, dt$. At small enough values of r, w is defined for both factor price curves. The inequality between the cost integrals remains valid as long as the term e^{-rt} is close enough to 1 (i.e., r small). Hence, method 2 can offer a higher wage than method 1.

(2) For extremely large r, again the cost integral $\int_{-\infty}^{0} f_1 e^{-rt}\, dt$ is larger than $\int_{-\infty}^{0} f_2 e^{-rt}$, since for $-10 \le t \le -9$, $f_1 > 0 = f_2$. At extremely large compound interest rates, this element dominates the comparison between the two cost integrals. Hence, method 2 is again the superior technique, attracting labor away from its rival by offering a higher wage.

(3) For medium ranges of r, say, $r = 1$, method 1 is superior. In fact, for $r = 1$, $\int_{0}^{-\infty} f_2 e^{-rt}\, dt = 44,562 > 22,015 = \int_{0}^{-\infty} f_1 e^{-rt}\, dt$,[14] allowing method 1 to pay a higher wage (1/22,015) than what can be afforded under method 2 (1/44,562).[15]

---

[14]
$$\int_{-\infty}^{0} f_1 e^{-rt}\, dt = \int_{-10}^{0} (t+10)e^{-rt}\, dt = e^{10} \int_{0}^{10} \tau e^{-\tau}\, d\tau \quad \text{(setting } \tau = t+10 \text{ and noting that } r = 1\text{)}$$

$$= e^{10}(-10e^{-10} - e^{-10} + 1) = 22,015 \quad \text{(integrating by parts)}$$

$$\int_{-\infty}^{0} f_2 e^{-rt}\, dt = \int_{-9}^{0} 5.5 e^{-rt}\, dt = e^{9} \int_{0}^{9} 5.5 e^{-\tau}\, d\tau \quad \text{(setting } \tau = t+9 \text{ and noting that } r = 1\text{)}$$

$$= 5.5(e^{9} - 1) = 44,561$$

[15]
$w = 1/r \int_{-\infty}^{0} f_i e^{-rt}\, dt$. With $r = 1$, we get the desired results.

Hence, the reswitching phenomenon is established.

The moral of these two examples is that capital goods are *economically heterogeneous* if they can either be built with alternative input flows or be used to produce alternative service outflows. The fact that they are *physically homogeneous* is totally irrelevant.

Moreover, the surrogate production function and the surrogate capital are of dubious use unless (a) the factor price curves are linear or (b) each factor price curve touches the factor price frontier at most once. Otherwise, even without reswitching, the same *actual technique* will be represented by different *hypothetical techniques* with different jelly/labor ratios, when the wage (interest) rate changes. This is due to the fact that the slope of the factor price curve varies unless the curve is a straight line and that same slope is equal to the negative of the jelly/labor ratio.

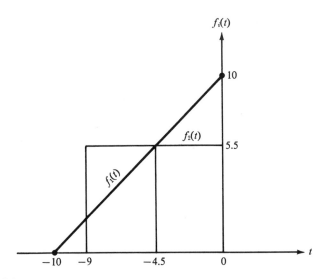

FIGURE 4.4

4.3 MULTISECTOR MODELS

4.3.1. Introduction

Among the various attempts to disaggregate a neoclassical growth model, multisector models rank high on the priority list. Presumably, such analyses may be relevant in answering the following questions:

(1) How do the allocation ratios of factors shift over the growth path?

(2) How do the relative product prices change as the economy grows?

(3) Different sectors may employ quite different capital intensities. How does the growth of the overall capital/labor ratio affect the growth pattern of various sectors?

(4) How does the rise of per capita income affect the demand for different products?

The list could be extended considerably, but the present literature does not offer much by way of answering such queries. Partly this is due to the lack of emphasis on certain empirically interesting questions (points (1) and (2) above); partly it is due to the dearth of observed data (point (3) above; we know little about sectoral differences in production functions); partly it is due to our limited analytical power (point (4) above; multiple consumption goods and multiple capital goods involve analytical complexities). All the same, there still exist many interesting but unresolved questions in multisectoral growth models. Moreover, before tackling the listed problems, one must be familiar with the existing works. If experience is a fair guide, satisfactory answers to more "interesting" empirical questions cannot come without careful specifications of assumptions and rigorous detection of their implications.

The existing multisector growth models shall be classified according to the number of consumable goods in the model.

(1) No consumable good. The von Neumann model of balanced growth belongs to this category. Consumption is regarded as a necessary input to produce labor. There is little discretion left to the consumer.

(2) One consumption good. This is the Meade case, with outputs divided into capital goods and consumption good. Most two-sector models belong to this type.

(3) More than one consumption good. So far, few models have fallen into this category. Among the exceptions are the Jorgenson model of a dual economy [22] and the Dhrymes model of N-sector balanced growth [23]. Both rely on the very special assumptions of a Cobb-Douglas production function.

Our present discussion is centered around Meade's type of model. Although these models originated in Meade's book *A Neoclassical Theory of Growth* [24], the main contributions came from the works of Uzawa [25, 26], Inada, [27, 28], and Drandakis [29]. The more literal versions of Solow [30] and Hahn [31] provide useful insights into the matter. Papers by Amano [32], Diamond [33], and Takayama [34, 35] throw further light on these models.

The Meadean two-sector model is basically a straightforward extension of Solow's model. However, the relevant literature is so technically challenging that the less mathematically oriented readers are often at a loss over the central issues involved.

Briefly speaking, most of the work done to date concentrates either on the sufficiency conditions that guarantee the existence, uniqueness, and stability of a balanced growth path or on the "causal determinacy" of the model. While problems concerning the balanced growth paths also face the one-sector Solow model, the Meadean models confront one curious but fundamental fact: The growth path itself may be entirely indeterminate.

In Solovian models, information about (a) the overall capital/labor ratio, (b) the production possibilities, (c) the labor growth rate, and (d) the saving behavior is sufficient for predicting the rate of change of the capital/labor ratio. Symbolically,

$$\dot{k}/k = \frac{sf(k)}{k} - n$$

where k is the capital/labor ratio, $f(k)$ is the output/labor ratio, s is the propensity to save, and n is the rate of labor growth.

This fact holds true even if the saving propensities for capitalists and workers are different. [16] However, in the Meade two-sector model, similar information is consistent with more than one rate of change for the overall capital/labor ratio.

In Section 4.3.2, we shall first list nine assumptions underlying the two-sector models and then briefly discuss each. In Section 4.3.3, a formal model is synthesized out of these assumptions culminating with both a graphic summary of the momentary equilibrium prevailing at any instant and a dynamic equation relating such an equilibrium with the past and the future. In Section 4.3.4, the dynamic equation is scrutinized to determine whether it can unambiguously specify the direction of movement (the causal determinacy problem) and whether it admits a stationary solution for the overall capital/labor ratio (the existence and uniqueness problems of balanced growth). The stability of the balanced growth path is also discussed. In Section 4.3.5, the time trends for overall and sectoral capital/labor ratios, the wage rate, the rent rate, the wage/rent ratio, and the relative prices are discussed. The Wicksell effect is also considered.

4.3.2. Assumptions

The usual assumptions of the Meadean models parallel those of the Solovian models. Perfect foresight, perfect competition, and constant returns to scale are postulated along with exponential population growth. Gross investment (rather than net investment in the Solow case) is equated to saving. Exponential depreciation is then prescribed for all capital goods. The saving propensities out of interest and wage shares are explicitly allowed to differ. Capital goods are produced in the first sector. They are perfectly malleable (as in Solovian models) and can be used with labor inputs according to any proportions and in either sector. Consumption goods are produced in the second sector. They also serve as the numeraire. Out of this set of assumptions, various possibilities can emerge:

(1) There may exist a unique, stable, balanced growth path.
(2) There may not be any balanced growth path or there may be more than one, with some of these unstable.
(3) There may be no determinate growth path at all.

---

[16]The net effect is to make s a function of k: $s = (ks_r + \omega s_w)/(\omega + k)$, where s_r and s_w are capitalists' and workers' saving ratios.

To help rule out the second possibility, the Inada derivative conditions can be imposed. This also holds true in Solovian models, as we noted in Chapter 2. To rule out the third possibility, three alternatives are possible: Either the equisaving-propensity hypothesis of Keynes or the "capital-intensity" assumption (capital goods less capital-intensive than consumption goods at all times) may help. Or else the elasticities of factor substitution for the two sectors can be assumed to be sufficiently high.

We shall now enumerate the various assumptions in algebraic terms.

Basic assumptions.   These are similar to those Solow adopted in 1956:

Assumption 1. Perfect foresight.

Assumption 2. Smooth adjustment under perfect competition.

Assumptions 1 and 2 together rule out any discrepancy between *ex ante* saving and investment. Nor is it possible to have any random disturbance in the model.

Assumption 3. There exist constant returns in both sectors; i.e., for both sectors, the production functions are linear homogenous in the two inputs, capital and labor:

$$F_i(K_i, L_i) = L_i f_i(k_i) \qquad i = 1, 2 \tag{4.3.1}$$

where K_i and L_i are capital and labor inputs for sector i, $k_i = K_i/L_i$ is the capital/labor ratio for sector i, and $f_i(k_i) = F(k_i, 1)$ is the output per worker for sector i.

Assumption 4. The total labor force grows exponentially:

$$L(t) = L_0 e^{nt}$$
$$= L_1(t) + L_2(t) \tag{4.3.2}$$

Assumption 5. The saving/income ratios for wage and interest shares of income are s_w and s_r, respectively, such that

$$0 \leq s_w \leq s_r \leq 1; \quad 0 < s_r; \quad s_w < 1 \tag{4.3.3}$$

This includes:

(a) The Keynesian special case: $s_w = s = s_r$. This was adopted by Harrod, Domar, Solow, and Swan.

(b) The Kaleckian special case: $s_w = 0 < 1 = s_r$. This was adopted by Mrs. Robinson and Kaldor in some of their models.

Sectoral assumptions

Assumption 6. The output of the first sector is a perfectly malleable capital good that is used in both sectors and depreciates exponentially over time [i.e., depreciation $= \delta$ (capital)]:

$$F_1 = (\dot{K}_1 + \dot{K}_2) + \delta(K_1 + K_2) \quad \text{(Gross investment = net investment}$$
$$= \dot{K} + \delta K \qquad\qquad\qquad \text{plus depreciation)} \tag{4.3.4}$$

where K is total capital.

The output of the second sector is the consumption good:

$$F_2 = C \tag{4.3.5}$$

This serves as the numeraire.

Assumption 7. Gross investment in "value terms" equals *ex ante* savings:

$$pF_1 = s_w(wL) + s_r(rK)$$
$$= rL(s_w \omega + s_r k) \tag{4.3.6}$$

where p is the price of the capital good, $\omega = w/r$ is the wage/rent ratio, and $k = K/L$ is the overall capital/labor ratio.

Note that saving equals *gross* rather than *net* investment here.

Special assumptions

Assumption 8. Inada "derivative conditions":
(a) $f_i'(k_i) > 0 > f_i''(k_i)$ for all values of k_i, $i = 1, 2$
(b) $f_i'(0) = \infty$ \qquad $f_i'(\infty) = 0$ \hfill (4.3.7)
(c) $f_i(0) = 0$ \qquad $f_i(\infty) = \infty$

As discussed in Chapter 2, these assumptions are highly restrictive.

In economic terms these assumptions imply, in turn, that:

(a) The marginal product of capital is always positive, yet it diminishes with higher and higher capital/labor ratios.
(b) As the capital/labor ratio decreases toward zero, the marginal product of capital approaches infinity. As capital per worker increases without limit, capital saturation leads to zero marginal product of capital.
(c) Without any capital good, output per worker is zero. When capital per worker increases without limit, any level of output per worker can be reached.

As noted before, these assumptions exclude a great number of interesting production functions from the analysis. Still, it helps to assure the existence, the stability, and the uniqueness of a balanced growth path. Hence, it has certain pedagogical value.

Assumption 9. "Capital-intensity condition":

$$k_1 < k_2 \tag{4.3.8}$$

i.e., the capital goods industry is always more labor-intensive than the consumption goods industry.

Assumption (9) is also very special in character, and, as Solow noted [30], it is not convincing without empirical evidence.

4.3.3. Formulation; momentary equilibrium

We can now introduce the two-sector model.

Preliminary results. These facilitate the derivation of the "fundamental dynamic equation" and the description of the momentary equilibrium.

(1) Accounting identities:[17]

$$k = K/L$$
$$= (L_1/L)k_1 + [1 - (L_1/L)]k_2 \qquad (4.3.9)$$

This shows that the overall capital/labor ratio is the weighted average of sectoral capital/labor ratios with labor allocation ratios, L_1/L and $L_2/L = 1 - (L_1/L)$, in either sector as weights.

$$L_1/L = (k_2 - k)/(k_2 - k_1) \qquad (4.3.10)$$

which is derived from (4.3.9).

(2) Market conditions:

$$pf_1' = r = f_2'$$
$$p(f_1 - k_1 f_1') = w = (f_2 - k_2 f_2') \qquad (4.3.11)$$

These equations show that rent and wage equal the value of marginal products for capital and labor in either sector.

$$\omega = (f_i/f_i') - k_i \qquad (4.3.12)$$

or

$$f_i/f_i' = k_i + \omega \qquad (4.3.12a)$$

Equations (4.3.12) and (4.3.12a) are obtained from (4.3.11) by dividing the second equation into the first equation.

(3) Mathematical identity:

$$\hat{k} = \hat{K} - \hat{L} \qquad \text{where } \hat{x} = \frac{\dot{x}}{x} = \frac{d}{dt}(\ln x), \, x = k, K, \text{ or } L \qquad (4.3.13)$$

The fundamental dynamic equation. As we shall see, the equations we stated above describe a momentary equilibrium. But the kinematic force that carries the whole system forward is the fundamental dynamic equation (an analog to (2.1.4) in the simple Solow model):

$$\dot{k} = \hat{k}k$$
$$= \{[(F_1 - \delta K)/K] - n\}k \qquad \text{(from (4.3.13), (4.3.2), and (4.3.4)}[18]) \qquad (4.3.14)$$
$$= (s_w \omega + s_r k)f_1' - (n + \delta)k \qquad \text{(from (4.3.6) and (4.3.11)}[19])$$

The momentary equilibrium. The model specified so far contains the key variables: the overall capital/labor ratio k and the wage/rent ratio ω. k is given historically whereas ω is determined by market forces. Once ω is determined,

---

[17] $K = K_1 + K_2 = L_1 k_1 + L_2 k_2$. Since $L_2 = L - L_1$, (4.3.9) is obtained by rearrangement.

[18] $\dot{K} = F_1 - \delta K$ and $\hat{L} = n$ as consequences of (4.3.4) and (4.3.2), respectively.

[19] From (4.3.6), $F_1 = (r/p)L(s_w \omega + s_r k)$. From (4.3.11), $r/p = f_1'$.

the sectoral capital/labor ratios k_1 and k_2 are determined from (4.3.12). Wage w, rent r, and the price p for K, are determined via (4.3.11). In conjunction with the historically given k, the labor allocation ratios L_1/L and $1-(L_1/L)$ are determined through (4.3.9) and the rate of change for k is determined in (4.3.14). The value assumed by ω cannot be totally arbitrary; it has to satisfy (4.3.6) in view of the given value of k. But here is the crux of the matter. For a given k, the choice of ω that satisfies (4.3.6) need not be unique. This implies that (4.3.14) may not be a differential equation. Knowing the initial value $k(0)$ does not allow us to predict the course of evolution for $k(t)$. This so-called causal determinacy problem will be discussed below. A schematic summary with elementary diagrammatic components is presented in Figure 4.5.

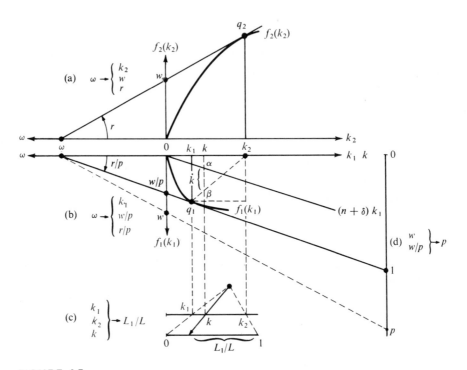

FIGURE 4.5

In Figure 4.5a and b, we construct tangent lines to $f_i(k_i)$ from any value of ω. In so doing, r, w, r/p, k_1, and k_2 are all simultaneously determined. In Figure 4.5c, the relative magnitudes of k_1, k_2, and k are projected onto the unit interval to determine L_1/L. We then mark the length of w (in Figure 4.5a) on the vertical axis of Figure 4.5b at point w. Again by projection, we determine the magnitude of p, the price for capital good, in Figure 4.5d. Suppose now that the value of ω chosen is compatible with the overall capital/labor ratio (more on this point later). Back in Figure 4.5b, construct $q_1 k_2$, the distance $\overline{k\beta} = (\overline{q_1 k_1})(k_2 - k)/(k_2 - k_1) = f_1 L_1/L = F_1/L$. Construct the line $(n+\delta)k$; the distance $\alpha\beta$ is then:

$$\dot{k} = F_1/L - (n+\delta)k$$

What is left out of the above graphic summary is the saving relation. For any given k, any ω leads to a per capita supply for new capital goods at the level of F_1/L. Will such supply be matched by an equal demand for new capital goods? Equation (4.3.6) states that the per capita demand for new capital goods is

$$(s_w\omega + s_r k)r/p = (s_w\omega + s_r k)f_1'[k_1(\omega)]$$

where k_1 is an increasing function of ω (Figure 4.5b). Hence, it is the clearance of the capital goods market that restricts the value of ω for given k.

4.3.4. Dynamic equilibrium and causal determinacy

A. A SUMMARY OF RESULTS

In analogy with the graphic analysis of the simple Solow model in Figures 2.1–2.3, we can plot (4.3.14) in Figure 4.6. The three representative cases are summarized in Table 4.1. We note that, in Figure 4.6, case c, whenever k is inside the indeterminate zone, $\dot{k}$ can take any one of three values. (On the boundaries of the zone, $\dot{k}$ can take either of two values.)

TABLE 4.1

Economic properties	Mathematical statement	Geometric representation	Is the property satisfied?		
			Case a	Case b	Case c
1. Existence of a unique nontrivial balanced growth	There is one and only one positive k for which $\dot{k} = 0$	$(n+\delta)k$ cuts $(s_w\omega + s_r k)f_1'$ once and only once	Yes	No	Yes
2. There is a causally determinant path for any initial capital/labor ratio	There is one and only one value of $\dot{k}$ for every value of k	Any vertical line $k = \text{const.}$ cuts the $(s_w\omega + s_r k)f_1'$ once and only once	Yes	Yes	No

Synthesizing the results in the literature, we note that:

(1) The Inada derivative conditions (assumption 8, Section 4.3.2) guarantee the *existence* of at least one nontrivial[20] balanced growth path consistent with the dynamic equation (4.3.14).[21]

---

[20] That is, the capital/labor ratio is positive.

[21] Even if $k(0) = k^\infty$ in Fig. 4.6, case c, the economy *can* but *need not* stay on the balanced growth path. $\dot{k}(0)$ may be positive, negative, or zero.

(2) Unlike the one-sector model, the Inada derivative conditions cannot assure the uniqueness of the balanced growth path. Additional assumptions are required to assure uniqueness; for example,
  (a) The capital good industry is labor-intensive under all factor prices, or
  (b) Elasticities of substitution are greater than unity for both sectors.
(3) Causal determinacy is assured if one assumes the Inada derivative conditions and one of the alternative sets of sufficiency conditions. The more interesting alternatives are:
  (a) Assumptions 1–4 and 6–8, while assumption 5 takes the Keynesian special form: workers and capitalists save the same portion of income.
  (b) Assumptions 1–8 together with assumption 9: the consumption good sector is more capital-intensive under all wage/rent ratios.
  (c) Assumptions 1–8 together with the Drandakis [29] assumption: the sum of the elasticities of substitution for the two sectors is not less than unity.
(4) A causally determined model satisfying the Inada derivative conditions is *globally stable as a system*. This means that, regardless of its initial value, the overall capital/labor ratio will approach one balanced growth path or another (cf. the middle curve in Figure 4.6 case *b*).
(5) A causally determined model with a unique, nontrivial balanced growth path is *globally stable with respect to that path*: The overall capital/labor ratio must approach that balanced growth ratio, regardless of its initial value.

The elementary but tedious mathematical derivation of these results is included in Appendix 4.3. In Section B we shall present a graphical interpretation of how causal indeterminacy can be ruled out through the equal saving ratio and capital-intensity assumptions. (For an alternative graphic analysis, see Findlay [36].) The Drandakis assumption (3c) appears to be empirically interesting, since the realism of the capital-intensity assumption is rather controversial.[22] However, this assumption defies easy graphical depiction. We shall comment on the problem of stability in Section C.

B.   A GRAPHIC INTERPRETATION OF CAUSAL DETERMINACY

1. Equation (4.3.14) is equivalent to

$$F_1 = [\dot{k} + (n+\delta)k]L$$

Given the historically inherited values of k and L, the multiplicity of $\dot{k}$ values implies the multiplicity of F_1 values.

2. From Figure 4.7, multiple levels of gross investment F_1, at $\overline{OA_1}$, $\overline{OA_2}$, and $\overline{OA_3}$ correspond to multiple output points a_1, a_2, and a_3, as well as multiple

---

[22]Strictly speaking, whenever we apply the results involving elasticities of substitution, the Inada derivative assumptions may be replaced by some weaker assumption to achieve more generality. One such assumption is roughly that the overall capital/labor ratio permits full employment of both factors and both sectors employ both factors. See Drandakis [29].

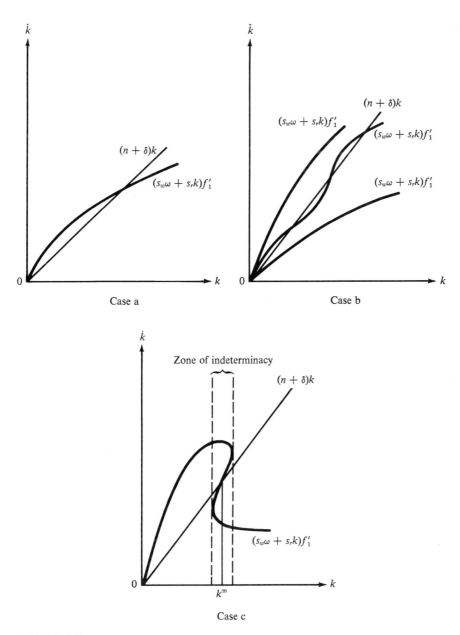

FIGURE 4.6

price lines $b_1 c_1$, $b_2 c_2$, and $b_3 c_3$. Since gross output values (in terms of K) are $\overline{Ob_1}$, $\overline{Ob_2}$, and $\overline{Ob_3}$, we observe the following inequality relation among the multiple gross saving ratios:

$$\overline{OA_1}/\overline{Ob_1} > \overline{OA_2}/\overline{Ob_2} > \overline{OA_3}/\overline{Ob_3}$$

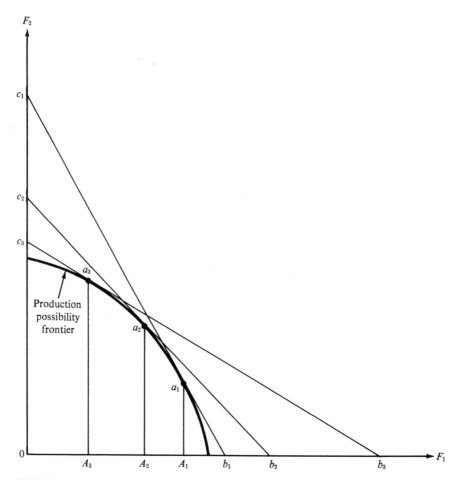

FIGURE 4.7

Hence, we conclude that:

(a) The multiplicity of F_1 implies the multiplicity of the gross saving ratios for the same k.

(b) Among the set of possible multiple values for gross investment F_1 (which satisfy (4.3.14)), the higher the specific value gross investment assumes, the higher is the associated gross saving ratio. (Figure 4.7 depicts the case where $k_1 \neq k_2$. If $k_1 = k_2$, the production frontier is linear, but both of the above conclusions stand.)

(c) The Keynesian saving assumption rules out indeterminacy, since under that assumption the gross saving ratio is unique and given, contrary to the requirement in (a).

3. The gross saving ratio is [23]

$$\frac{s_w(wL)+s_r(rK)}{wL+rK} = s_w + \frac{k}{\omega+k}(s_r-s_w) \qquad \text{with } s_r \geq s_w$$

which is graphically shown in Figure 4.8 as a hyperbola, $(d/d\omega)$(saving ratio) < 0. Hence, we conclude that indeterminacy implies multiple values for both F_1 and ω, with higher F_1 values associated with lower values of ω (using 2(a) and (b) above).

Overall saving ratio

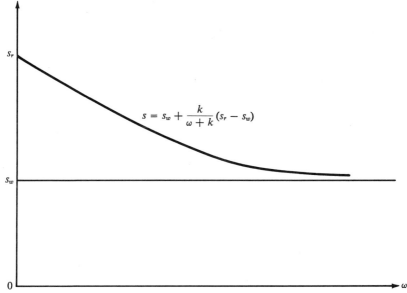

$$s = s_w + \frac{k}{\omega+k}(s_r - s_w)$$

FIGURE 4.8

4. In the Edgeworth-Bowley box diagrams in Figure 4.9, cases a, b, and c indicate, respectively, the cases where the capital good industry is more, equally, and less capital intensive compared with the consumption good industry. O_i is the origin for sector i. F_1 is larger at a_1 than at a_2. Hence, we conclude:

(a) Indeterminacy implies inverse association between F_1 and ω, but such

[23]
$$\frac{s_w(wL)+s_r(rK)}{wL+rK} = s_w + (s_r - s_w)\frac{rK}{wL+rK}$$

$$= s_w + (s_r - s_w)\frac{rK/rL}{(wL+rK)/rL}$$

$$= s_w + (s_r - s_w)\frac{k}{\omega+k} \qquad \text{(since } k = K/L \text{ and } \omega = w/r)$$

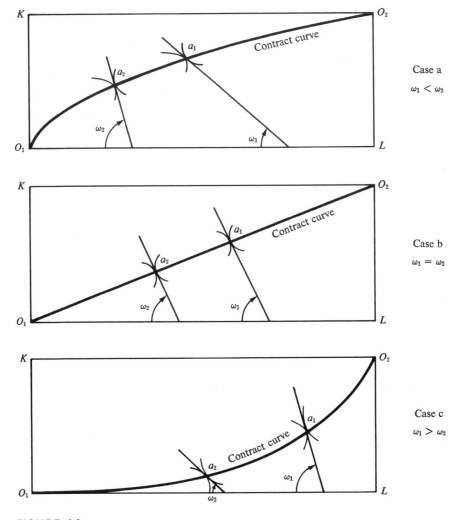

FIGURE 4.9

inverse association is possible only when the capital good industry is more capital-intensive than the consumption good industry (case a).

(b) The knife-edge case depicted in Figure 4.9, case b is, in substance, the one-sector Solow model in disguise. Therefore, the Kalecki assumption does not cause indeterminacy in a one-sector model.

In the theory of general equilibrium, if the competitive equilibrium is unique, then without redistribution of wealth, no public legislation or union tactics can raise the wage level and still maintain full employment. In a two-sector model with causal indeterminacy, the momentary equilibria are nonunique, such that *without changing the overall capital/labor ratio*, or relaxing either the full-employment assumption or the competitive market structure, one can still raise the wage/rent ratio. This feat is all the more astounding since as a consequence, the capital/labor ratios in both sectors would be increased. The only occasion in which *increased* capital/labor ratios in both sectors can coexist with a *constant* overall capital/labor ratio is a demand shift (and hence a labor reallocation) in favor of the less capital-intensive industry. Such a demand shift must be supported by a shift in the overall saving ratio, as a consequence of the change of relative factor prices. Therefore, the necessary conditions for causal indeterminacy include all the following:

(1) Unequal capital intensities: hence, one sector can be *less* capital-intensive than the other.

(2) Unequal saving ratios: hence, the overall saving ratio depends on factor prices.

(3) "Matching inequalities" between factor intensities and saving ratios: if a higher wage/rent ratio means a lower overall saving ratio (workers save less proportionately), the resulting demand shift favors the consumption sector; then that sector must be less capital-intensive for indeterminacy to exist.

(4) Adequate leverage: a higher wage/rent ratio (together with the full employment of given factor supplies) causes intrasector factor substitution as well as intersector factor substitution. The latter is the demand shift accompanying the induced fall of the overall gross saving ratio. Unless intrasector factor substitution is of very limited scope, the intersector factor substitution need not be adequate to reduce the value proportions between the outputs of the two sectors. The Drandakis result on elasticities of substitution plays its role here.

Discussions of causal determinacy illustrate the crucial role played by the uniqueness problem in general equilibrium in the context of growth models. On the other hand, the stability criterion in atemporal equilibrium theory offers no help in establishing causality. Samuelson noted that there may be multiple momentary equilibria, all of them "stable" according to the atemporal criterion (cf. case c, Figure 4.6, where the highest and lowest branches of $(s_w \omega + s_r k) f_1'$ represent stable positions). The attempts to rule out indeterminacy with empirically dubious assumptions (as Solow pointed out in [30] and Hahn in [37]) are of little consolation. Nor is it advisable to dismiss indeterminacy as a curiosum. There is a faulty plank in the foundation of disaggregated growth theory, which will become evident in the next section. Essentially, saving assumptions traditionally formulated may not be powerful enough to assure a determined growth pattern.

C. THE STABILITY OF BALANCED GROWTH PATH

Equation (4.3.14) can be rewritten as

$$\hat{k} = \phi - (n + \delta) \tag{4.3.14a}$$

where $\phi = (s_w \omega + s_r k) f_1'/k$, showing the ratio of gross investment to capital.

The causal determinacy of the system guarantees that $\omega = \omega(k)$, and hence we can concentrate on the properties of ϕ as a function of k. In Figure 4.6, $\phi(k)$ is the slope of the ray from the origin through any point on the curve $(s_w\omega + s_rk)f_1'$. It is possible to show that the Inada derivative conditions assure that $\phi(k)$ approaches zero for large k and infinity for k approaching zero (i.e., the $(s_w\omega + s_rk)f_1' = k\phi(k)$ curve has a vertical takeoff and eventually "flattens out"). Since ϕ is continuous, there must exist at least one k^∞ at which there is balanced growth (i.e., $\dot{k} = 0$). Moreover, at extremely low positive values of the overall capital/labor ratio, that ratio increases over time (i.e., $k\phi$ lies above $(n+\delta)k$). At extremely high overall capital/labor ratios, the reverse is true. Therefore, the overall capital/labor ratio must approach one long-run limit or another.

In a Solovian one-sector model, diminishing marginal product of capital $(f'' < 0)$ assures the uniqueness of the balanced growth path. In a two-sector model, one must assume either that the consumption good industry is the more capital-intensive or that the elasticity of factor substitution is not less than unity in both sectors to assure the monotonically decreasing property of the $(s_w\omega + s_rk)f_1'/k$ curve. (cf. Fig. 4.6, case a). This property rules out nonuniqueness of the balanced growth path. It also implies that starting from arbitrary overall capital/labor ratios, the balanced growth capital/labor ratio will be reached eventually.

4.3.5. The dynamic paths of the various variables in the system

In a causally determined two-sector model where there exists one unique, globally stable balanced growth path, we can conclude the following:

(1) The overall capital/labor ratio will approach asymptotically and monotonically its balanced growth value (from the phase diagram approach).
(2) A rising (falling) overall capital/labor ratio is always accompanied by a rising (falling) wage/rent ratio (proved in Appendix 4.3).
(3) A rising (falling) wage/rent ratio leads to:
   (a) rising (falling) capital/labor ratios in both sectors
   (b) a rising (falling) wage rate
   (c) a falling (rising) rent rate
   (d) a change in relative product prices in favor of (against) the good that is the more labor-intensive.

Items (a)–(c) can be graphically derived as in Figure 4.5. Item (d) can be proved as follows:

$$p = f_2'/f_1'$$

Taking the logarithmic derivative with respect to ω, we have:

$$\frac{dp/d\omega}{p} = -\frac{f_2'}{f_2} + \frac{f_1'}{f_1} \qquad \text{(using (4.A.3)[24] and (4.3.12a))}$$

$$= \frac{k_2 - k_1}{(k_1 + \omega)(k_2 + \omega)}$$

[24]See Appendix 4.3.

(4) The Wicksell effect is evidenced by

$$p(t)K(t) = p(t) \int_{-\infty}^{t} \dot{K}(\tau) \, d\tau < \int_{-\infty}^{t} p(\tau)\dot{K}(\tau) \, d\tau$$

This happens whenever $p(t)$ is falling over time. The negative Wicksell effect is similarly defined, *mutatis mutandis.*

4.4 MULTI-CAPITAL-GOODS MODELS

The most recent and perhaps most important modification of the Solovian model concerns the expectation *cum* market structure aspects of the model. The original contribution came from Hahn [37]. Works by Samuelson [38], Shell and Stiglitz [39], and Kurz [40] generalized such investigations in several directions. Some of these issues will be examined in Section 6.3, as well as in Chapter 9. Here we are concerned with the implications of many capital goods coexisting in a model. This was the starting point of Hahn's study; our discussion follows closely the Shell and Stiglitz analysis.

In Solovian and Meadean models, there is always only one capital good. In the works of Mrs. Robinson and Samuelson, discussed earlier, the potential existence of many capital goods does not alter the fact that at any one instant, only one composite equipment will actually be used. Direct generalization of the Solovian model leads to *underdeterminacy* of the momentary equilibrium, which is much more serious than the *indeterminacy* in two-sector models. Indeterminacy means that multiple solutions occur accidentally; underdeterminacy means that the number of unknowns outnumber the number of equations. One may, like Hahn, introduce an "equal rate of return" condition that takes account of the expected capital gain or loss. Prices in the growth model are now no longer derived from market-clearing conditions alone. Initial values of prices are listed as known data, and "price equations" generate their dynamics in conjunction with the quantity equations. The reformulated system still faces the possibility of nonunique momentary equilibria. However, this need not lead to causal indeterminacy if the nonuniqueness can happen only for an infinitesimal interval of time. The crucial questions now become: Is the growth path stable? and What is the implication of an unstable path?

In Section 4.4.1 we shall give a simple example to illustrate the problem. In Section 4.4.2 we shall report briefly the results of Shell and Stiglitz.

4.4.1. A simple example

We shall use an extremely simple example here

A. ASSUMPTIONS

1. Three outputs (the consumption good-numeraire and two capital goods) can be produced with three inputs (labor and the stocks of the two capital goods) according to the following constant-returns production function:

$$0 \geq C - [K_1^{2\alpha_1} K_2^{2\alpha_2} L^{2(1-\alpha_1-\alpha_2)} - \dot{K}_1^2 - \dot{K}_2^2]^{1/2}$$

$$= C - F(K_1, K_2, L, \dot{K}_1, \dot{K}_2)$$

(4.4.1)

where C, L, K_1, and K_2 stand for the consumption output, the labor input, and the two types of capital inputs, respectively. F represents the "capacity" to produce C. Also,

$$K_1^{2\alpha_1}(0)K_2^{2\alpha_2}(0)L^{2(1-\alpha_1-\alpha_2)}(0) = 1$$

2. Saving represents a constant proportion of output value[25]:

$$(1-s)(p_1\dot{K}_1 + p_2\dot{K}_2) = sC$$

(4.4.2)

where p_1 and p_2 are prices of the two capital goods.

3. Prices of capital goods are equal to their opportunity costs:

$$p_i = -\frac{\partial F}{\partial \dot{K}_i} = \frac{\dot{K}_i}{F}$$

(4.4.3)

4. Capital goods are permanently durable.

B.   ANALYSIS

At a momentary equilibrium, $C = F$, showing that all capacity is utilized. Using this equality and substituting (4.4.3) and (4.4.2) into (4.4.1) we obtain

$$sC = (1-s)(\dot{K}_1^2 + \dot{K}_2^2)/C$$

(4.4.4)

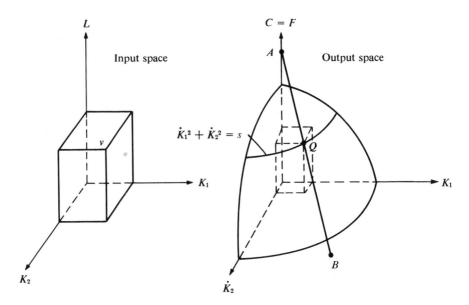

FIGURE 4.10

[25]Equation (4.4.2) comes from the equation $p_1\dot{K}_1 + p_2\dot{K}_2 = s(p_1\dot{K}_1 + p_2\dot{K}_2 + C)$.

Using the fact that $C^2 + \dot{K}_1^2 + \dot{K}_2^2 = 1$, we get

$$\dot{K}_1^2 + \dot{K}_2^2 = s \quad \text{at } t = 0 \tag{4.4.4'}$$

which shows a "one-dimensional infinity of indeterminacy"; i.e., there are as many multiple equilibria positions as the number of points on a line. This is shown in Figure 4.10.

Corresponding to each input triplet $v = (K_1, K_2, L)$ there exists in the output space a production surface. The increase of any one input, other things being equal, implies an expansion of the production surface. A typical output triplet $Q = (\dot{K}_1, \dot{K}_2, C)$ on the production surface is also shown. The increase of any investment rate $\dot{K}_i$, other things being equal, must result in a decrease in consumption output.

The $\dot{K}_1^2 + \dot{K}_2^2 = s$ locus satisfies the following relation: Construct a plane P passing through both the C axis and any point Q on that locus (the plane not shown). Construct then the tangent line lying in P and tangent to the surface at Q, say AB, where A is on the C axis and B in the $\dot{K}_1$–$\dot{K}_2$ plane; then $\overline{AQ}:\overline{BQ} = s:(1-s)$.

C. INTERPRETATION

In a general equilibrium system with dated commodities (cf. Hicks [41], or Debreu [42]), the period-by-period investment levels in various capital goods are determined by microeconomic decisions of the profit maximization or utility maximization types. Aggregate income and aggregate saving in each period may be derived from the system, but there can be no problem of allocating an (independently derived) aggregate saving for various purposes.

Similar situations exist in an optimal growth model, although here the decision of the central planner takes the position of the myriad microeconomic decision makers.

From Keynes to Harrod and Domar to Solow, the saving function has been used as a convenient short cut. It is only when people feel both dissatisfied with heroic aggregation and reluctant to scuttle the aggregate saving function that difficulties emerge. Trying still to retain the best of both the micro and macro worlds, Hahn invoked the concept of "short-run perfect foresight": Each individual is supposed to entertain the same expectation about the immediate rates of price changes, and such concensus leads to actions that validate that very expectation.[26] The consequence of this assumption is discussed below.

4.4.2. The price equations

A. INTRODUCTION

In view of what has been discussed above, the assumption of a historically given price system $(1, p_1(0), p_2(0))$ may solve the underdeterminacy problem in

---

[26]"Perfect foresight" pertains to a self-validating, unanimous expectation on $p(\tau)$, $t \leq \tau \leq \infty$. "Short-run perfect foresight" pertains to a self-validating, unanimous expectation on $\dot{p}(t)$, where t stands for the present.

our example. However, $p_1(0)$ and $p_2(0)$ cannot be entirely arbitrary, or the production point would not be located within the locus of $\dot{K}_1^2 + \dot{K}_2^2 = s$. This restriction can be shown as[27]

$$p_1^2 + p_2^2 = \frac{s}{1-s} \tag{4.4.5}$$

Now, the introduction of a historically given price system begs the question of what determines the history of the price system. Traditional capital theory prescribes that every type of investment actually undertaken at the same instant must command the same rate of return, i.e., the sum of rent and capital gain accrued on each dollar of investment. This implies

$$\frac{(\partial F/\partial K_1) + \dot{p}_1}{p_1} = \frac{(\partial F/\partial K_2) + \dot{p}_2}{p_2} \tag{4.4.6}$$

Equations (4.4.5) and (4.4.6) determine the price movement over time,[28] given initial values $p_1(0)$, $p_2(0)$ satisfying (4.4.5).

B.   EXISTENCE AND STABILITY OF BALANCED GROWTH
For convenience, let us define

$$Q = K_1^{\alpha_1} K_2^{\alpha_2} L^{1-\alpha_1-\alpha_2}$$

From (4.4.1) and (4.4.3) it can be shown that

$$\frac{\partial F/\partial K_i}{p_i} = \frac{\alpha_i Q^2}{K_i \dot{K}_i}$$

$$= \frac{\alpha_i(Q^2/K_i^2)}{\dot{K}_i} \tag{4.4.7}$$

We can now prove that there exists a unique balanced growth path in our example.

Proof.   Under balanced growth and constant returns, relative prices stay constant (cf. Section 4.2): $\dot{p}_1/p_1 = 0 = \dot{p}_2/p_2$.

Substituting this information into (4.4.6), and using both (4.4.7) and the balanced growth definition,

$$\hat{K}_1 = n = \hat{K}_2 \tag{4.4.8}$$

where n is the growth rate for labor, we obtain

$$
\begin{aligned}
K_2/K_1 &= \sqrt{\alpha_2/\alpha_1} \\
&= \dot{K}_2/\dot{K}_1 && \text{(from (4.4.8))} \\
&= p_2/p_1 && \text{(from (4.4.3))}
\end{aligned}
$$

---

[27] $s(1 + p_1^2 + p_2^2)C = p_1^2 C + p_2^2 C$ from (4.4.2) and (4.4.3). Cancelling C and rearranging, (4.4.5) is obtained.

[28] Strictly speaking, the price equations and quantity equations are simultaneously determined. $\partial F/\partial K_i$, $i = 1, 2$, must be determined from the quantity equations.

Using (4.4.5), we can prove that

$$p_i^* = \sqrt{s\alpha_i/(1-s)(\alpha_1 + \alpha_2)}$$

$$K_i^*(t) = \gamma\sqrt{\alpha_i}\,e^{nt}$$

where p_i^* is the balanced growth value for p_i, K_i^* is the balanced growth level of K_i, and, from (4.4.4a),

$$\gamma = \frac{1}{n}\sqrt{\frac{s}{\alpha_1 + \alpha_2}}$$

The uniqueness of the balanced growth is thus proved along with its existence.

We can also demonstrate that the balanced growth path is unstable, in the sense that for each pair of values $(K_1/L, K_2/L)$ there exists exactly one pair of initial prices (p_1, p_2) satisfying (4.4.5) that would induce an asymptotic approach to the balanced growth path. If the initial price pair and the capital per capita pair are "mismatched," then the actual growth path will diverge forevermore from the balanced growth path. Our purpose is to make a graphic demonstration of the situation rather than construct a proof of full rigor.

Demonstration.   In Figure 4.11a we plot K_2 against K_1. The heavy ray through the origin with slope $\sqrt{\alpha_2/\alpha_1}$ stands for the balanced growth path. The dashed ray with slope $[K_2(0)/K_1(0)]$ indicates the initial position of the "quantity system." In Fig. 4.11b, p_2 is plotted against p_1 and the graph of $p_1^2 + p_2^2 = s/(1-s)$ is represented by a quarter-circle.

Without loss of generality,[29] we can assume that $K_2(0)/K_1(0) \geq \sqrt{\alpha_2/\alpha_1}$.

Case a: $p_2(0)/p_1(0) \geq K_2(0)/K_1(0) \geq \sqrt{\alpha_2/\alpha_1}$ but $p_2(0)/p_1(0) > \sqrt{\alpha_2/\alpha_1}$. From (4.4.3), $K_2(0)/K_1(0) \leq p_2(0)/p_1(0) = K_2(0)/K_1(0)$, i.e., $K_2(0) \geq K_1(0)$. From (4.4.6) and (4.4.7),

$$\hat{p}_2(0) - \hat{p}_1(0) = \frac{\alpha_1 Q^2}{K_2 \dot{K}_2}\left[\left(\frac{K_2}{K_1}\right)\left(\frac{p_2}{p_1}\right) - \frac{\alpha_2}{\alpha_1}\right] > 0$$

Hence, both K_2/K_1 and $\dot{K}_2/\dot{K}_1 = p_2/p_1$ rise at $t = 0$. Thus, the trajectory described by the point (K_1, K_2) rises at an increasing angle of inclination that is already steeper than the ray with slope K_2/K_1 (and hence the ray with the slope $\sqrt{\alpha_2/\alpha_1}$. Graphical considerations indicate that at subsequent positions along the trajectory, the double inequalities characterizing case a remain valid. Hence, the departure from the balanced growth path grows forever.

Case b: $K_2(0)/K_1(0) > p_2(0)/p_1(0) \geq \sqrt{\alpha_2/\alpha_1}$. By a similar analysis, K_2/K_1 falls and p_2/p_1 rises. By the time both coincide at some value greater than $\sqrt{\alpha_2/\alpha_1}$, K_2/K_1 momentarily stays constant but p_2/p_1 keeps on rising and the case merges into case a.

---

[29] If $K_i(0)/\sqrt{\alpha_i} \geq K_j(0)/\sqrt{\alpha_j}$, then let $i = 2, j = 1$.

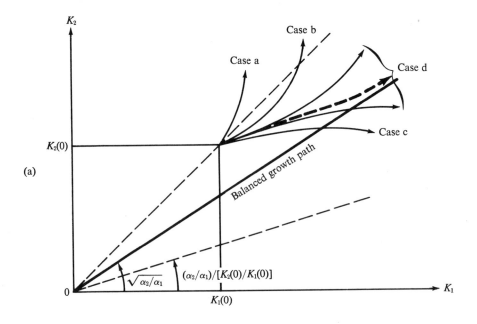

(a)

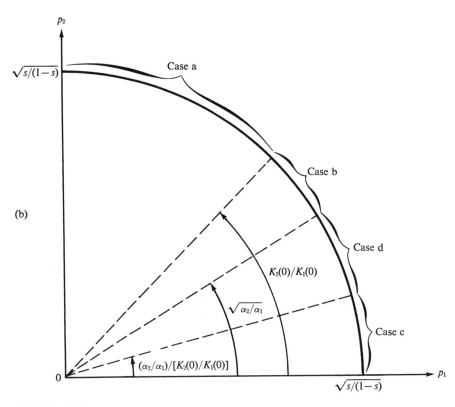

(b)

FIGURE 4.11

Case c: $K_2(0)/K_1(0) > \sqrt{\alpha_2/\alpha_1} > (\alpha_2/\alpha_1)/(K_2/K_1) \geq (p_2(0)/p_1(0))$. Analysis shows that both K_2/K_1 and p_2/p_1 fall continuously until $K_2/K_1 = \sqrt{\alpha_2/\alpha_1} > p_2/p_1$ and we have a case of continuously falling K_2/K_1, symmetrical to case a.

Case d: $K_2(0)/K_1(0) > \sqrt{\alpha_2/\alpha_1} > p_2(0)/p_1(0) > (\alpha_2/\alpha_1)/(K_2/K_1)$. In this case, K_2/K_1 falls and p_2/p_1 rises. But everything depends upon the initial value of $p_2(0)/p_1(0)$. There is a knife-edge subcase where K_2/K_1 approaches $\sqrt{\alpha_2/\alpha_1}$ asymptotically from above and p_2/p_1 approaches the same limit from below. This is the unique initial price pair corresponding to $K_2(0)$, $K_1(0)$ and permitting an asymptotic approach to balanced growth. A lower initial $p_2(0)/p_1(0)$ ratio causes K_2/K_1 to fall to $\sqrt{\alpha_2/\alpha_1}$ in finite time, and the case symmetrical to case a arises. A higher initial $p_2(0)/p_1(0)$ ratio causes p_2/p_1 to rise to $\sqrt{\alpha_2/\alpha_1}$ in finite time. Then case b arises and eventually case a emerges.

Note that once case a or its symmetrical case arises, prices will move along a path of no return, until one capital good becomes free[30] in a foreseeable future.

C. INTERPRETATIONS

The short-run perfect foresight assumption is a rather bizarre hypothesis. Initial prices are *fait accompli*; they are to be justified by "appropriate" price expectations. Since short-run foresight is assumed to be perfect, such expectations are postulated to be realized, and this leads to the next round of *fait accompli*. As in the Samuelsonian model of accelerator-multiplier interaction, where excess plant capacity is to be resolved by producing more new equipment, here, those existing prices that are too high relative to their values of use are supported by further increases in such prices. The unstable price paths invariably lead to an impasse. When a free capital good is disposable, no further price fall is possible. With a possible rent flow accruing to a free capital good, an infinite demand will occur on the competitive market. It is also easy to show that such centrifugal unbalanced paths are inefficient. All these indicate that such models at best can explain the South Sea Bubble, the tulip mania, and similar speculative extravaganzas. The added descriptive realism in disaggregating the Solow model brings about only empirical irrelevance.

In their penetrating study, Shell and Stiglitz not only pointed out the theoretical cul-de-sac along the above-mentioned lines, they also suggested several alternative realistic assumptions as remedies:

(1) All individuals expect that future prices will be identical to present prices (static expectation).
(2) No rental market or used equipment market exists; hence, (4.4.6) ceases to operate.
(3) There are no future markets; hence, the hypothesis of equal rate of return can be somewhat relaxed.

Their conclusion is that market imperfection leads to stability. Such an explanation seems plausible to any bicycle rider: Overreaction destabilizes the

---

[30]That is, reaching the point $(\sqrt{s/(1-s)}, 0)$ or $(0, \sqrt{s/(1-s)})$ in Figure 4.11b.

vehicle. Some readers may wonder why we cannot go back to the good old assumption of (long-run) perfect foresight of the traditional type. The reason is twofold. It staggers the imagination to postulate that all decision makers will automatically reach the consensus of some self-validating expectations at all times. Nor can we expect that the existence of future markets can equate future supply and demand along the Walrasian lines—it requires the meeting of minds for all individuals presently extant as well as those yet unborn! The key to the problem appears to lie in the allowance of errors in decision making, a theme seldom returned to since the models of Harrod and Domar. The postulation of static expectation appears to be a step in this direction. A further improvement perhaps can be made by explicitly assuming some adaptive mechanism by which decision makers strive to improve their forecasting power after gathering the evidence of past errors.

APPENDIX 4.1

Derivation of (4.2.1)

Under technique α_0, let:

K_j be the jth capital good, $j = 1, 2, \ldots, m = n_{a_0}$
p_j be the price of K_j
v_j be the rent of one unit of capital service of K_j, per unit of time
w be the wage rate
r be the interest rate
$g_j(t)$ be the output of a unit of a t-period-old equipment K_j, $0 \leq t \leq N_j \leq \infty$
N_j be the economic life for K_j, which can be finite or infinite
A_{ij} be the requirement for the ith input in producing one unit of the jth output if output j is produced instantaneously
$a_{ij}(t)$ be the requirement for the ith input by a unit of work in process of K_j that entered the production process t periods ago, $0 \leq t \leq M_j < \infty$, where M_j is the length of the gestation period
$i = 0$ stand for labor services
$i > 0$ stand for capital services of K_i
$j = 0$ represent the production of C
$j > 0$ represent the production of K_j

For instantaneous production, if the activity breaks even, we have:

$$wA_{0j} + \sum_{i=1}^{m} v_i A_{ij} = p_j \tag{4.A.1}$$

For production with gestation periods, if the activity breaks even we have

$$\int_0^{M_j} \left[wa_{0j}(t) + \sum_{i=1}^{m} v_i a_{ij}(t) \right] e^{-rt} \, dt = p_j e^{-rM_j} \tag{4.A.2}$$

Between (4.A.1) and (4.A.2), j takes all the values $0, 1, \ldots, m$ with $p_0 = 1$.

For the operation of capital goods, if the holding of capital goods breaks even we have

$$p_j = v_j \int_0^{N_j} g_j(t) e^{-rt} \, dt \qquad j = 1, 2, \ldots, m$$

Together there are $2m+1$ equations in $p_j, v_j, j = 1, \ldots, m, r$, and w. In principle, we may eliminate the $2m$ variables v_j and $p_j, j = 1, 2, \ldots, m$. We are left with one equation in r and w: (4.2.1).

APPENDIX 4.2

Graphical derivation of the production isoquant and the surrogate capital

In the present context, Shephard's *minimal unit cost function* takes the form

$$M(w, r) = \underset{L, J}{\text{Min}} \, (wL + rJ)$$

subject to:
$$F(J, L) = 1$$

The *factor price frontier* takes the form

$$M(r, w) = 1$$

Shephard showed that the unit output isoquant $F(J, L) = 1$ and the factor price frontier $M(r, w) = 1$ are so-called polar reciprocals of each other and are derivable graphically from one another. This will be illustrated below.

1. Derivation of $F(J, L) = 1$ from $M(r, w) = 1$

Consider $P_0 = (r_0, w_0)$ on $M(r, w) = 1$. We want to find (J_0, L_0) corresponding to it such that $\partial F/\partial L$ and $\partial F/\partial J$ evaluated at (J_0, L_0) equal (r_0, w_0).

(a) Algebraically, the linear homogeneity of the F-function implies that

$$\begin{aligned} F(J, L) &= LF(j, 1) \qquad j = J/L \\ &= Lf(j) \end{aligned}$$

where $f(j)$ is defined as $F(j, 1)$.

Results in Chapter 2 imply that

$$w = f(j) - jf'(j) \qquad r = f'(j)$$

The slope of the factor price frontier is then

$$\frac{dw}{dr} = \frac{dw/dj}{dr/dj} = -\frac{J_0}{L_0}$$

which substantiates (4.2.2).

(b) Graphically, the tangent line through P_0, i.e., TP_0, has the equation

$$\begin{aligned} (w - w_0) &= (dw/dr)(r - r_0) \\ &= -(J_0/L_0)(r - r_0) \end{aligned}$$

This tangent line is perpendicular to the ray through the origin $OT = \{(\gamma J_0, \gamma L_0) | \gamma \geq 0\}$. Hence (J_0, L_0) is on the OT ray; the question is, Where?

Point T is on the tangent line, and we can write $T = (r_1, w_1)$, with $w_1 L_0 + r_1 J_0 = w_0 L_0 + r_0 J_0$. The point T is also on the ray OT; hence, we can write $T = (\gamma_0 J_0, \gamma_0 L_0)$. Length $\overline{OT}$ is then

$$\begin{aligned} \sqrt{(\gamma_0 L_0)^2 + (\gamma_0 J_0)^2} &= \gamma_0 \sqrt{L_0^2 + J_0^2} \\ &= \sqrt{\gamma_0} \sqrt{w_1 L_0 + r_1 J_0} \qquad (w_1 = \gamma_0 L_0 \text{ and } r_1 = \gamma_0 J_0) \\ &= \sqrt{\gamma_0} \sqrt{w_0 L_0 + r_0 J_0} \qquad (T = (w_1, r_1) \text{ is on the same tangent line as } (w_0, r_0)) \\ &= \sqrt{\gamma_0} \qquad \begin{array}{l}\text{(The so-called adding-up theorem states: } w_0 L_0 + \\ r_0 J_0 = 1) \end{array} \end{aligned}$$

The point $(J_0, L_0) = (r_1, w_1)/\gamma_0$, whereby $\sqrt{L_0^2 + J_0^2} = 1/\sqrt{\gamma_0}$. In Figure 4.12, the point q is unit distance from the origin and located on the OT ray. Extend the $P_0 T$ line to cut the horizontal axis at a. Construct a parallel to $P_0 T$ through q, which cuts the horizontal axis at b. Link aq and construct bQ_0 parallel to aq to cut the OT ray at Q_0. Then $\overline{OQ_0}/\overline{Oq} = \overline{Ob}/\overline{Oa} = \overline{Oq}/\overline{OT} = 1/\sqrt{\gamma_0}$. Hence, $Q_0 = (J_0, L_0)$ is what we desired.

By choosing various (r_0, w_0) pairs as starting points, one obtains the unit output isoquant.

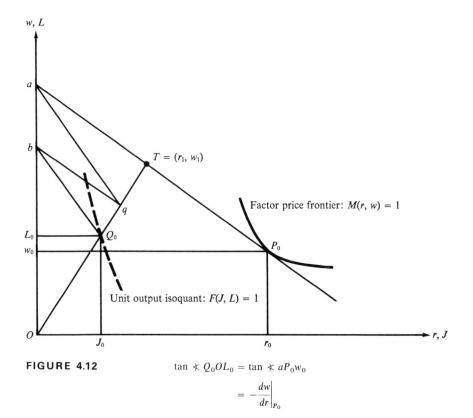

FIGURE 4.12

$$\tan \measuredangle\, Q_0OL_0 = \tan \measuredangle\, aP_0w_0$$

$$= -\frac{dw}{dr}\bigg|_{P_0}$$

2. Derivation of $M(r,\ w) = 1$ from $F(J,\ L) = 1$.

Consider $Q_0 = (J_0, L_0)$ on $F(J, L) = 1$ in Figure 4.13. Draw tangent line Q_0T' of $F(J, L) = 1$ at Q_0. Construct the OT' ray perpendicular to Q_0T'. Q_0T' is the isocost line under which Q_0 is most economical (the tangency condition implies that to produce the same output, alternative techniques cannot yield a lower unit cost). The OT' ray reflects the factor price ratio for Q_0T'. Determining points q', a', b', and P_0 as in Section 1, we can prove that P_0 is the desired (r_0, w_0) pair. By the same process, we can obtain other points on $M(r, w) = 1$.

APPENDIX 4.3

Sufficiency conditions for causal determinacy; existence and uniqueness of balanced growth paths

1. Causal determinacy

From (4.3.14a) we note that the system is determined if for every k there is a corresponding value of ϕ, the ratio of gross investment to capital.

The relationship between k and ϕ is shown schematically below:

$$k \longrightarrow \phi = (s_w \frac{\omega}{k} + s_r) f_1'(k_1)$$

Obviously, to each triplet (k, ω, k_1) there can be only one value for ϕ. We shall prove that k_1 corresponds in a one-to-one manner to ω under the derivative conditions. The only issue is whether the relationship between k and ω constitutes a one-to-one function relationship.

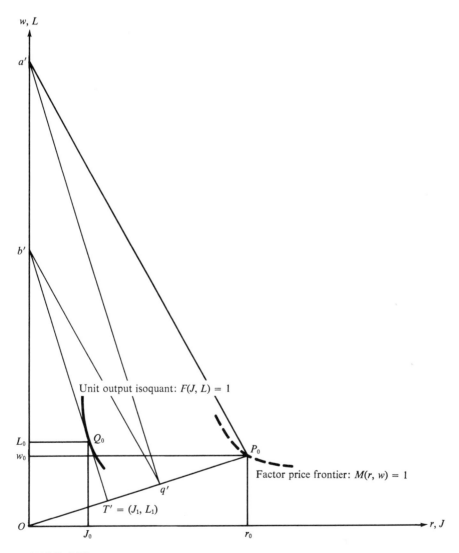

FIGURE 4.13

A.   PRELIMINARY RESULTS

1. Assuming the derivative conditions, then, between ω and k_i:

(a) $dk_i/d\omega > 0$

(b) $\underset{\omega \downarrow 0}{\text{Lim}}\, k_i = 0$

(c) $\underset{\omega \uparrow \infty}{\text{Lim}}\, k_i = \infty$

(d) k_i is an increasing function of ω, over $[0, \infty]$

Proof.   Differentiating (4.3.12) with respect to k_i, we find:

$$\frac{d[(f_i/f_i') - k_i]}{dk_i} = \frac{-f_i f_i''}{(f_i')^2} > 0 \tag{4.A.3}$$

This shows the rate of change of the marginal rate of substitution corresponding to a shift of the sectoral capital/labor ratio. Since the marginal rate of substitution can be equated to the wage/rent ratio, the reciprocal of (4.A.3) shows the rate of change of the sectoral capital/labor ratio corresponding to the changing factor prices; i.e.,

$$\frac{dk_i}{d\omega} = \frac{-(f_i')^2}{f_i f_i''} > 0$$

This proves 1(a).

Next, we note that

$$\underset{k_i \downarrow 0}{\text{Lim}} \left[\frac{f_i}{f_i'} - k_i \right] = \frac{0}{\infty} \cdot 0 = 0$$

This substantiates 1(b).

By symmetry,

$$\underset{(1/k_i) \downarrow 0}{\text{Lim}} \left[\frac{f_i'}{f_i - f_i' k_i} \right] = \underset{(1/k_i) \downarrow 0}{\text{Lim}}\, \frac{1}{\omega} = 0$$

But this is equivalent to

$$\underset{k_i \uparrow \infty}{\text{Lim}}\, \omega = \infty$$

which proves 1(c).

Combining all these results, we obtain 1(d).

2. Between k and ω,

(a) $k = \dfrac{k_1(\omega) \cdot k_2(\omega) + \omega s_w k_1(\omega) + \omega(1 - s_w) k_2(\omega)}{\omega + s_r k_2(\omega) + (1 - s_r) k_1(\omega)} = \psi(\omega)$

where ψ is a single-valued function of ω

(b) $\underset{\omega \downarrow 0}{\text{Lim}}\, \psi(\omega) \downarrow 0$

(c) $\underset{\omega \uparrow \infty}{\text{Lim}}\, \psi(\omega) \uparrow \infty$

(d) If $\psi'(\omega) > 0$ for all ω, then ω is an increasing function of k over $[0, \infty]$.

Proof.   Dividing (4.3.6) by pL and noting that from (4.3.1), (4.3.10), and (4.3.11) $F_1/L = (L_1/L)f_1 = [(k_2 - k)/(k_2 - k_1)]f_1$ and $r/p = f_1'$, we obtain, after rearrangement,

$$\left(\frac{k_2 - k}{k_2 - k_1} \right) \left(\frac{f_1}{f_1'} \right) = s_w \omega + s_r k$$

Using (4.3.12) to substitute $k_1 + \omega$ for f_1/f_1', we obtain

$$\left(s_r + \frac{k_1 + \omega}{k_2 - k_1}\right) k = \frac{(k_1 + \omega)k_2}{k_2 - k_1} - s_w \omega$$

Result 2(a) is obtained after regrouping.

Define

$$k_M(\omega) = \text{Max } (k_1, k_2) \qquad k_m(\omega) = \text{Min } (k_1, k_2)$$

Obviously,

$$k_m \leq [s_w k_1 + (1 - s_w)k_2], \quad [(1 - s_r)k_1 + s_r k_2] \leq k_M$$

$$k_m k_M = k_1 k_2$$

Hence,

$$k_m \equiv k_m(\omega + k_M)/(\omega + k_M)$$

$$\leq \frac{k_m k_M + \omega[s_w k_1 + (1 - s_w)k_2]}{\omega + [(1 - s_r)k_1 + s_r k_2]} \equiv \psi(\omega)$$

$$\leq k_M(\omega + k_m)/(\omega + k_m)$$

$$\equiv k_M$$

Results 1(b) and 1(c) imply that $\text{Lim}_{\omega \downarrow 0} k_m, k_M \downarrow 0$ and $\text{Lim}_{\omega \uparrow \infty} k_m, k_M \uparrow \infty$. Therefore,

$$\text{Lim } \psi = 0 \quad \text{and} \quad \text{Lim } \psi = \infty$$
$$\,_{\omega \downarrow 0} \qquad \qquad \,_{\omega \uparrow \infty}$$

proving results 2(b) and 2(c).

In 2(a), we showed that for each ω there corresponds one value of k; from 2(b) and 2(c) we know that ω and k approach zero or plus infinity together. Once we can show that $\psi'(\omega) > 0$, the Inverse Function Theorem of calculus can be invoked to establish that for each k there can only be one value of ω, proving 2(d).

B. MAIN RESULTS

1. If the relative capital intensity of the two sectors does not reverse itself over the whole range of non-negative wage/rent ratios ("unambiguous factor intensity" à la Samuelson), then we have the *first type* of sufficiency conditions for causal determinacy. This type is related to the saving ratios of the two income shares as well as the relative capital intensity between the two sectors as shown in Table 4.A.1.

TABLE 4.A.1

	$k_2 > k_1$	$k_2 = k_1$	$k_2 < k_1$
$s_r > s_w$	Determined	Determined	?
$s_r = s_w$	Determined	Determined	Determined
$s_r < s_w$	?	Determined	Determined

2. Alternatively, if the sum of elasticities for factor substitution is greater than unity, the model is again causally determined.

Proof. $\psi'(\omega) = (\alpha + \beta)/\psi_D^2$, where

$$\alpha = \{-(1 - s_r)\psi_N + (k_2 + s_w \omega)\psi_D\}k_1' + \{-s_r\psi_N + [k_1 + (1 - s_w)\omega]\psi_D\}k_2'$$

$$\beta = -\psi_N + [s_w k_1 + (1 - s_w)k_2]\psi_D$$

and ψ_N and ψ_D stand for the numerator and denominator of ψ, respectively.

After multiplying out the components of α and β and cancelling certain terms, we have:

$$\alpha = [s_w\omega + s_r k_2](k_2 + \omega)k_1' + [(1-s_w)\omega + (1-s_r)k_1](k_1 + \omega)k_2'$$

$$\beta = \{k_2[s_r(1-s_w)] - k_1[s_w(1-s_r)]\}(k_2 - k_1)$$

$$= s_r(1-s_w)(k_2 - k_1)^2 + k_1(s_r - s_w)(k_2 - k_1)$$

Since $\psi_D^2 > 0$ and $\alpha > 0$, if $\beta > 0$ then $\psi' > 0$. Now we note:

(i) If $s_r = s_w = s$, $\beta = s(1-s)(k_2 - k_1)^2 \geq 0$. This substantiates entries in the second row of Table 4.A.1.
(ii) If $k_1 = k_2$, $\beta = 0$. This substantiates entries in the second column of Table 4.A.1.
(iii) If $(k_2 - k_1)$ and $(s_r - s_w)$ are not of opposite sign, $\beta > 0$. This substantiates entries in the "principal diagonal" of Table 4.A.1.

Defining $\sigma_i = \omega k_i'/k_i$ as the elasticity of factor substitution for sector i, $i = 1, 2$, we can rewrite $(\alpha + \beta)\omega$ as

$$[s_w\omega + s_r k_2]k_1(k_2 + \omega)\sigma_1 + [(1-s_w)\omega + (1-s_r)k_1](k_1 + \omega)k_2\sigma_2$$
$$+ [s_w(1-s_r)k_1^2 + s_r(1-s_w)k_2^2]\omega + 2s_w s_r k_1 k_2\omega - (s_w + s_r)k_1 k_2\omega$$

$$= [s_w k_1\sigma_1 + (1-s_w)k_2\sigma_2]\omega^2 + [(1-s_r)k_2\sigma_2 + s_w(1-s_r)\omega]k_1^2 + [s_r k_1\sigma_1 + s_r(1-s_w)\omega]k_2^2$$
$$+ \omega k_1 k_2\{(s_w + s_r)\sigma_1 + (2-s_w - s_r)\sigma_2 - (s_w + s_r) + 2s_w s_r\}$$

$$> \omega k_1 k_2\{(s_w + s_r)\sigma_1 + (2-s_w - s_r)\sigma_2 - (s_w + s_r) + 2s_w s_r\} = \gamma$$

where γ represents the last expression.

We showed in 1(a) of Section 1-A that $k_i' > 0$; hence, $\sigma_i > 0$, $i = 1, 2$. Suppose that $\sigma_1 + \sigma_2 \geq 1$. Then we can prove that $\gamma \geq 0$ from the following table.

Cases	Inequalities	Remarks
$\sigma_1 \geq 1$	$\gamma \geq \omega k_1 k_2[(\sigma_1 - 1)(s_w + s_r) + 2s_w s_r] \geq 0$	By replacing σ_2 with 0
$\sigma_1 < 1$ $\quad(1 - s_w - s_r) \geq 0$	$\gamma \geq 2\omega k_1 k_2[(1 - s_w - s_r)(1 - \sigma_1) + s_w s_r] \geq 0$	By replacing σ_2 with $(1 - \sigma_1)$
$(1 - s_w - s_r) < 0$	$\gamma \geq 2\omega k_1 k_2[(1 - s_w - s_r)(1 - \sigma_1) + s_w s_r]$ $> 2\omega k_1 k_2[(1 - s_w)(1 - s_r)] \geq 0$	By replacing $(1 - \sigma_1)$ with 1

Therefore, $\psi' = (\alpha + \beta)/\psi_D^2 > 0$, substantiating result 2.

2. Balanced growth path

A.   EXISTENCE THEOREM

The Inada derivative conditions assure that there exists $(\omega^\infty, k^\infty)$ such that

$$k^\infty = \psi(\omega^\infty)$$

$$\phi = (s_w \frac{\omega^\infty}{k^\infty} + s_r)f_1'[k_1(\omega^\infty)] = n + \delta$$

Consequently, the time path $k(t) \equiv k^\infty$ is consistent with (4.3.14).

Proof.   We first assert that

(1) $\mathrm{Lim}_{\substack{\omega \downarrow 0}}\ \phi \uparrow \infty$

(2) $\mathrm{Lim}_{\substack{\omega \uparrow \infty}}\ \phi \downarrow 0$

Proof of the assertions.   Since $\omega/k \geq 0$,

$$\mathrm{Lim}_{\substack{\omega \downarrow 0}}\ \phi \geq \mathrm{Lim}_{\substack{\omega \downarrow 0}}\ s_r f_1'[k_1(\omega)]$$

$$= s_r \mathrm{Lim}_{\substack{k_1 \downarrow 0}}\ f_1'(k_1) \qquad \text{(result 1(b) of Section 1)}$$

$$= \infty \qquad \text{(Inada derivative condition)}$$

proving assertion (1).
   Next,

$$\phi = (s_w\omega + s_r k)f_1'/k$$

$$= \frac{(L_1/L)f_1}{k} \qquad \text{(from (4.3.6), (4.3.1), and (4.3.11))}$$

$$\leqq \frac{(L_1/L)f_1}{(L_1/L)k_1} \qquad \text{(from (4.3.9))}$$

$$= f_1/k_1$$

Hence,

$$\mathrm{Lim}_{\substack{\omega \uparrow \infty}}\ \phi \leq \mathrm{Lim}_{\substack{\omega \uparrow \infty}}\ \frac{f_1[k_1(\omega)]}{k_1(\omega)}$$

$$= \mathrm{Lim}_{\substack{k_1 \uparrow \infty}}\ \frac{f_1(k_1)}{k_1}$$

$$= \mathrm{Lim}_{\substack{k_1 \uparrow \infty}}\ f_1'(k_1) \qquad \text{(L'Hospital's rule)}$$

$$\mathrm{Lim}_{\substack{k \uparrow \infty}}\ = 0 \qquad \text{(Inada derivative condition)}$$

proving assertion (2).
   Due to the continuity of $\phi = [s_w\omega + s_r\psi(\omega)]f_1'[k_1(\omega)]/\psi(\omega)$ as a function of ω, there must be at least one ω^∞ such that the corresponding ϕ has the value $n+\delta$. Let $k^\infty = \psi(\omega^\infty)$; $(\omega^\infty, k^\infty)$ satisfies the requirement of the "existence theorem."

B.   UNIQUENESS THEOREMS

   1. If $d\phi/d\omega < 0$, then k^∞ is unique.
   Proof.   If $d\phi/d\omega < 0$, obviously there is only one root ω^∞ for $\phi = n+\delta$. Hence, $\psi(\omega^\infty)$ is the only balanced growth overall capital/labor ratio.
   2. The capital-intensity assumption guarantees that $d\phi/d\omega < 0$.
   Proof.   Under the capital-intensity assumption, $\psi(\omega)$ is invertible; hence, $\phi = \phi(k)$. Now, taking the logarithmic derivative,

$$\frac{d\phi}{dk} = \phi \left\{ \frac{(s_w/\psi') + s_r}{s_w\omega + s_r k} - \frac{1}{k} + \frac{f_1''}{f_1'} \left[-\frac{(f_1')^2}{f_1 f_1''} \right] \frac{1}{\psi'} \right\} \qquad \text{(using (4.A.3))}$$

$$= \phi \left\{ \left[\frac{1}{k + (s_w/s_r)\omega} - \frac{1}{k} \right] + \left[\frac{s_w/s_r}{k + (s_w/s_r)\omega} - \frac{1}{k_1 + \omega} \right] \frac{1}{\psi'} \right\} \qquad \text{(using (4.3.12a))}$$

In view of

$$
\frac{s_w/s_r}{k+(s_w/s_r)\omega} =
\begin{cases}
0 & < \dfrac{1}{k_1+\omega} \quad \text{for } s_w = 0 \\[3ex]
\dfrac{1}{(s_r/s_w)k+\omega} \leq \dfrac{1}{k+\omega} & \quad \text{for } s_w > 0
\end{cases}
$$

$$
\leq \frac{1}{k_1+\omega} \quad \text{(since } k_1 \leq k \leq k_2\text{)}
$$

$d\phi/dk < 0.$

This assures the uniqueness of the balanced growth path for the overall capital/labor ratio, thus proving (2).

Remark.   We shall not go into the elasticity of substitution criterion for proving uniqueness of k^∞. Nor shall we discuss the stability problem. The latter is not so hard to tackle through a phase diagram approach.

REFERENCES

[1] Fisher, Franklin, "Embodied Technology and Existence of Labor and Output Aggregates," *Review of Economic Studies*, vol. XXXV, Oct. 1968, pp. 397–412.

[2] Fisher, Franklin, "Embodied Technology and the Aggregation of Fixed and Movable Capital Goods," *Review of Economic Studies*, vol. XXXV, Oct. 1968, pp. 417–28.

[3] Swan, Trevor W., "Economic Growth and Capital Accumulation," *Economic Record*, vol. XXXII, Nov. 1956, pp. 334–61.

[4] Robinson, J., *Collected Economic Papers*, vols. II and III, Oxford University Press, Oxford, 1960 and 1965.

[5] Kaldor, N., "Record of Debates," in *The Theory of Capital*, Frederich A. Lutz and D. C. Hague, Eds., Proceedings of International Economic Association Conference, Macmillan, London, 1961.

[6] Sato, R., "The Harrod-Domar Model vs. the Neoclassical Growth Model," *Economic Journal*, vol. LXXIV, June 1964, pp. 380–87.

[7] Eisner, R., "On Growth Models and the Neoclassical Resurgence," *Economic Journal*, vol. LXVIII, Dec. 1958, pp. 707–21.

[8] Samuelson, P. A., "Parable and Realism in Capital Theory: The Surrogate Production Function," *Review of Economic Studies*, vol. XXIX, June 1962, pp. 193–206.

[9] Hicks, J. R., *Capital and Growth*, Oxford University Press, Oxford, 1965.

[10] Solow, R. M., "Review of Capital and Growth," *American Economic Review*, vol. LVI, Dec. 1966, pp. 1257–60.

[11] Solow, R. M., "Reply" (to Pasinetti), *Review of Economics and Statistics*, vol. XL, Nov. 1958, pp. 411–13.

[12] Solow, R. M., "Competitive Valuation in a Dynamic Input-Output System," *Econometrica*, vol. 27, Jan. 1959, pp. 30–53.

[13] Solow, R. M., J. Tobin, C. C. von Weiszäcker, and M. E. Yaari, "Neoclassical Growth with Fixed Factor Proportions," *Review of Economic Studies*, vol. XXXIII, April 1966, pp. 79–116.

[14] Solow, R. M., "A Contribution to the Theory of Economic Growth," *Quarterly Journal of Economics*, vol. LXX, Feb. 1956, pp. 65–94.

[15] Solow, R. M., "Investment and Technical Progress," in *Mathematical Methods in the Social Sciences, 1959*, K. J. Arrow, S. Karlin, and P. Suppes, Eds., Stanford University Press, Stanford, Calif., 1960.

[16] Solow, R. M., "Heterogeneous Capital and Smooth Production Functions: An Experimental Study," *Econometrica*, vol. 31, Oct. 1963, pp. 623–45.

[17] Leontief, W. W., "A Note on the Interrelation of Subsets of Independent Variables of a Continuous Function with Continuous Derivatives," *Bulletin of the American Mathematical Society*, vol. 53, 1947, pp. 343–50.

[18] Leontief, W. W., "Introduction to a Theory of the Internal Structure of Functional Relationships," *Econometrica*, vol. 15, Oct. 1947, pp. 361–73.

[19] Fisher, Franklin, "Embodied Technology and the Existence of an Aggregate Capital Stock," *Review of Economic Studies*, vol. XXXII, 1965, pp. 263–88.

[20] Shephard, R., *Cost and Production Functions*, Princeton University Press, Princeton, N.J., 1953.

[21] *Quarterly Journal of Economics*, vol. LXXX, Nov. 1966.

[22] Jorgenson, Dale, W., "The Development of a Dual Economy," *Economic Journal*, vol. LXXI, June 1961, pp. 309–34.

[23] Dhrymes, Phoebus, "A Multi-Sectoral Model of Growth," *Quarterly Journal of Economics*, vol. LXXVI, May 1962, pp. 264–78.

[24] Meade, J. E., *A Neoclassical Theory of Growth*, Allen and Unwin, London, 1961.

[25] Uzawa, H., "On a Two-Sector Model of Economic Growth, I," *Review of Economic Studies*, vol. XXIX, Oct. 1961, pp. 40–47.

[26] Uzawa, H., "On a Two-Sector Model of Economic Growth, II," *Review of Economic Studies*, vol. XXX, June 1963, pp. 105–18.

[27] Inada, Ken-ichi, "On a Two-Sector Model of Economic Growth: Comments and a Generalization," *Review of Economic Studies*, vol. XXX, June 1963, pp. 119–27.

[28] Inada, Ken-ichi, "On the Stability of Growth Equilibria in Two-Sector Models," *Review of Economic Studies*, vol. XXXI, April 1964, pp. 127–42.

[29] Drandakis, E. M., "Factor Substitution in the Two-Sector Growth Model," *Review of Economic Studies*, vol. XXX, Oct. 1963, pp. 217–28.

[30] Solow, R. M., "Note on Uzawa's Two-Sector Model of Economic Growth," *Review of Economic Studies*, vol. XXIX, Oct. 1961, pp. 48–50.

[31] Hahn, Frank H., "On Two-Sector Growth Models," *Review of Economic Studies*, vol. XXXII, Oct. 1965, pp. 339–46.

[32] Amano, A., "A Further Note on Professor Uzawa's Two-Sector Model of Economic Growth," *Review of Economic Studies*, vol. XXXI, April 1964, pp. 97–102.

[33] Diamond, Peter A., "Disembodied Technical Change in a Two-Sector Model," *Review of Economic Studies*, vol. XXXII, April 1965, pp. 161–68.

[34] Takayama, A., "On a Two-Sector Model of Economic Growth: A Comparative Static Analysis," *Review of Economic Studies*, vol. XXX, June 1963, pp. 95–104.

[35] Takayama, A., "On a Two-Sector Model of Economic Growth with Technical Progress: A Comparative Static Analysis," *Review of Economic Studies*, vol. XXXII, July 1965, pp. 251–62.

[36] Findlay, R., "Neutral Technical Progress and the Relative Stability of Two-Sector Models," *International Economic Review*, vol. 8, Feb. 1967, pp. 109–15.

[37] Hahn, Frank H., "Equilibrium Dynamics with Heterogeneous Capital Goods," *Quarterly Journal of Economics*, vol. LXXX, Nov. 1966, pp. 633–46.

[38] Samuelson, P. A., "Indeterminacy of Development in a Heterogeneous-Capital Model with Constant Saving Propensity," in *Essays on the Theory of Optimal Economic Growth*, K. Shell, Ed., M.I.T. Press, Cambridge, Mass., 1967.

[39] Shell, K., and J. E. Stiglitz, "The Allocation of Investment in a Two-Sector Economy," *Quarterly Journal of Economics*, vol. LXXXI, Nov. 1967, pp. 592–609.

[40] Kurz, M., "The General Instability of a Class of Competitive Growth Processes," *Review of Economic Studies*, vol. XXXV, April 1968, pp. 155–74.

[41] Hicks, J. R., *Value and Capital*, Oxford University Press, Oxford, 1939.

[42] Debreu, Gerard, *Theory of Value, An Axiomatic Analysis of Economic Equilibrium*, Wiley, New York, 1959.

EXERCISES

4.1. Consider a Meadean two-sector model satisfying the Inada conditions, the capital-intensity condition, and the Keynesian saving assumption.
(a) Show that the steady state solution must satisfy the following equations:

$$s(\omega + k)f_1'(k_1) = (n + \delta)k$$

$$k_1 = k_1(\omega); \quad k_2 = k_2(\omega); \quad \omega = \psi^{-1}(k)$$

(b) Suppose the production functions for both sectors are Cobb-Douglas where the output elasticity with respect to capital is $\frac{1}{3}$ for the capital-good sector and $\frac{2}{3}$ for the consumption-good sector, $s = \frac{1}{2}$, and $(n+\delta) = \sqrt[3]{\frac{4}{3}}$. Solve for ω, k_1, k_2, and k.

4.2. Consider a Meadean two-sector model satisfying the Inada conditions, the capital-intensity condition, and the Keynesian saving function. Empirical studies indicate that the saving ratio is 0.2, and the rent share is 20% of national income. The "gross" own rate of interest for capital is 12%, the population growth rate is 2%, and the depreciation rate is 8%. Without technical progress, will the wage rate rise? Discuss.

5

extensions of neoclassical models: vintage capital goods

5.1 INTRODUCTION: THE PUTTY–PUTTY MODEL

The neoclassical growth models comprise two principal components: the production potential and the thriftiness conditions. The thriftiness conditions will be considered in Chapters 6 and 8. The production potential is determined by (1) alternative productive activities along a given production surface and (2) systematic shifts of the production surface. Since most growth models presume constant returns to scale, any production surface can be characterized by a single isoquant. Alternative techniques along an isoquant are discussed under the topic "input substitutability." Shifts of isoquants are referred to as "technical progress."

We shall now discuss the alternative hypotheses concerning technical progress and input substitutability.

1. Technical progress implies an "inward" shifting of the entire isoquant map. It reflects the fact that for any given output, less input is required to produce it now than before. This may be due to the mere passage of time; if so, technical progress is said to be exogenous and disembodied. On the other hand, it may be due to the use of newer equipment, in which case the technical progress is said to be exogenous and embodied (in the capital input). Or it may be due to research, education, learning, etc.; then technical progress is an endogenous element of the economic system.

Because arbitrary shiftings of the isoquants are difficult to measure or to analyze, Hicks introduced the output-augmenting assumption that for any input vector, the attainable output increases by a uniform margin. This is termed "Hicks neutrality." Harrod and Solow, respectively, introduced the labor-augmenting and capital-augmenting assumptions that one unit of labor or capital now is equivalent to a given number (greater than unity) of units of the same input before (see J. Robinson [1] and Solow [2]). These have been termed "Harrod neutrality" and "Solow neutrality." To crystallize the above concepts, we shall introduce some symbols and summarize the formulations in Table 5.1.

TABLE 5.1

(a) Exogenous technical progress:

	Disembodied	Embodied
Output-augmenting (Hicks-neutral)	$Q(v, t) = A(t)F[K(v, t), L(v, t)]$	$Q(v, t) = A(v)F[K(v, t), L(v, t)]$
Labor-augmenting (Harrod-neutral)	$Q(v, t) = F[K(v, t), A(t)L(v, t)]$	$Q(v, t) = F[K(v, t), A(v)L(v, t)]$
Capital-augmenting (Solow-neutral)	$Q(v, t) = F[A(t)K(v, t), L(v, t)]$	$Q(v, t) = F[A(v)K(v, t), L(v, t)]$

where $A(\cdot)$ is the technical progress index with $A'(\cdot) \geq 0$

(b) Endogenous technical progress: $Q(v, t) = F[K(v, t), L(v, t); x(t)]$,[a]
where $x(\cdot)$ may reflect education, research efforts, learning, etc.

[a]In special cases, an input- or output-augmenting index can be introduced, with such an index equal to $A[x(t)]$.

Consider $K(v, t)$ as the amount of capital input at t that was constructed at v (i.e., of vintage v) and $L(v, t)$ as the amount of labor input at t working on such equipment. The resultant output $Q(v, t)$ is usually assumed to be dependent upon $K(v, t)$ and $L(v, t)$ according to one of the equations presented in Table 5.1.

The simplicity of the various neutrality assumptions is reflected by the preservation of essentially the same isoquant map throughout time. Hicks-neutral technical progress only requires that each isoquant locus represents growing output levels (with the rate of growth identical for all isoquant loci). Harrod (Solow) neutrality only requires that labor (capital) input for the isoquant map be measured in efficiency units; i.e., the natural units of labor (capital) input should be multiplied by a growing index, the technical progress indicator. Inplications of Hicks and Harrod neutralities have been discussed in Chapter 2. Embodied Solow-neutral technical progress will be discussed in this section; endogenous technical progress will be considered in Chapter 7.

TABLE 5.2

Ex post input substitution	Ex ante input substitution	
	Possible	Impossible
Possible	Putty–putty[a]	
Impossible	Putty–clay[a]	Clay–clay[a]

[a]These terms are due to Phelps [12]. "Putty" stands for capital in a "malleable" state, which can be made into equipment requiring capital/labor ratios of various magnitudes; "clay" stands for capital in a "hardened" state, its use requiring one unique capital/labor ratio.

2. Various assumptions on input substitutability can be classified according to Table 5.2. The earlier Solow models usually assume that input proportions can vary at any time. This is the putty–putty type. Johansen [3] first revived the Marshallian short-run, long-run distinction. He assumed that equipment can be designed to require various input proportions, yet once the equipment has been constructed, input proportions become immutable. This is the genesis of the putty–clay models. By postulating that at any point of time one technique will always be chosen irrespective of factor prices, one obtains the clay–clay model. These will be studied in turn in this and the following two sections.

The key issues involved in this chapter are the embodiment hypothesis and the nonmalleability of equipment. The former is related to the policy question of how best to stimulate the growth of output per head. The latter is an attempt to incorporate more realism into the neoclassical model, through both disaggregation and a better characterization of the process of technical progress.[1]

In this section we shall first consider a fundamental formula, decomposing growth rates of output per head into various causal factors. Next, the putty–putty model of Solow regarding the embodiment hypothesis will be considered. Finally, a brief summary will be presented of the policy implications of the works of Solow, Phelps, Matthews, and others.

5.1.1. The causal decomposition of growth

Consider the aggregate production function in the simple Solow model,

$$Q = F(K, L, t)$$

which is linear homogeneous in K and L. Total differentiation of this formula and division by Q yields

$$\hat{Q} = \frac{\partial \ln Q}{\partial \ln K} \hat{K} + \left[1 - \frac{\partial \ln Q}{\partial \ln K} \right] n + \frac{\partial Q / \partial t}{Q}$$

[because $(\partial \ln Q)/(\partial \ln K) + (\partial \ln Q)/(\partial \ln L) = 1$].
Subtracting n from both sides and regrouping, we have

$$\widehat{f(k)} = \frac{\partial \ln Q}{\partial \ln K} \hat{k} + \frac{\partial Q / \partial t}{Q} \tag{5.1.1}$$

It was on the basis of such a formula that Solow stated in 1957 [4] that capital deepening did not account for very much of the increase of output per capita in the current American economy. This, in fact, reflects the general view in that period: Increasing investment would not improve the growth rate of labor productivity to any extent (see Phelps [5]). The main significance of the 1959 Solow model is that investment occupies a much more strategic position than previously—it serves as the vehicle to carry through technical progress.

---

[1]Except for rare cases like time-and-motion studies, improvement of equipment layout, etc., the implementation of technical progress needs new equipment.

5.1.2. The putty–putty model and embodied technical progress

Both the 1956 and the 1959 Solow models assume not only that equipment can be designed to accommodate varying capital/labor proportions, but that once made it can still be combined with labor in various ratios.[2] While both models are of the "putty–putty" type, the main innovation Solow made in 1959 was to assume that technical progress can only benefit new equipment, an idea that appeared in Domar's and Kaldor's writings but was never explored fully. We shall first list Solow's assumptions, then synthesize a model out of them, and finally derive certain theoretical conclusions from the model.

A. ASSUMPTIONS

Solow's assumptions can be classified into three types:

(1) Retained assumptions: homogeneous labor and output, constant returns, law of variable proportions, smooth input substitutability, constant labor growth rate, and perfect competition with perfect foresight.
(2) Modified assumptions:
    (a) Technical progress is both embodied and Solow-neutral (cf. Table 5.1).
    (b) Capital depreciates according to its age.
    (c) The gross saving/gross output ratio is constant.
(3) Special assumptions:
    (a) Depreciation is exponential: Each period, equipment loses a constant portion of its remaining value.
    (b) Technical progress is exponential: The efficiency of capital of every vintage increases by a fixed percentage over the preceding vintage.
    (c) The production function is Cobb-Douglas.

Assumptions (1) and (2) imply a general, embodied, vintage capital model. For this model it is possible to construct an aggregate production function with a surrogate capital input. Under assumption (3a), we obtain a functional equation that implies a differential equation akin to (2.1.4) in the simple Solow model. Assumptions (3b) and (3c) further assure the existence of a golden-age path.

B. THE MODEL IN ACTION: DISAGGREGATED LEVEL

We shall now consider a disaggregated model, based upon the retained and modified assumptions stated above.

(1) Production relation:

$$Q(t) = \int_{-\infty}^{t} Q(v, t)\, dt$$

$$= \int_{-\infty}^{t} L(v, t) f[k^0(v, t)]\, dv \tag{5.1.2}$$

[2] For instance, a piece of equipment can be run one shift per day or three shifts.

where $k^0(v, t)$ is the ratio of the efficiency-weighted capital existing at t to the labor force assigned to it; i.e.,

$$k^0(v, t) = A(v)K(v, t)/L(v, t) \quad \text{with } A(0) = 1 \tag{5.1.3}$$

$f[k^0]$ is the output per worker with k^0 units of efficiency-weighted capital; i.e., $f[k^0] = F[k^0, 1]$, where F is the production function.

(2) Gross investment equal to gross saving:

$$K(t, t) = sQ(t) \tag{5.1.4}$$

(3) Depreciation of capital goods:

$$K(v, t) = K(v, v)D[(t - v)] \tag{5.1.5}$$

where $D[(t - v)]$ is the proportion of effectiveness left in equipment of age $t - v$. D is a nonincreasing function. $D(0) = 1$.

(4) Equal marginal productivity for the homogeneous labor:

$$f[k^0(v, t)] - k^0(v, t)f'[k^0(v, t)] = w(t) \tag{5.1.6}$$

where $w(t)$ stands for the wage rate and $(f - k^0 f')$ is the marginal product of labor.[3]

(5) Total supply of labor:

$$\int_{-\infty}^{t} L(v, t)\, dv = L(t) \tag{5.1.7}$$
$$= L(0)e^{nt}$$

We have now synthesized a model that is self-contained in its causal relations. Assuming that the assemblage of capital stock $K(v, t)$ is known for all v between $-\infty$ and t (early vintage may be nonexistent by now), then (5.1.7) gives the total labor supply and (5.1.6) decides the labor allocations. Equation (5.1.2) determines the total output from which (5.1.3) provides the size of the current vintage and (5.1.5) governs the portions of old vintages lost due to the passage of time.

C. SOME STOCK-TAKING

The above model leads to the following conclusions:

(1) There exists a fundamental functional equation that allows us to predict the future output path (and hence all other magnitudes) from the past history of outputs:

$$Q(t) = f\left\{ sL(0)^{-1}e^{-nt} \int_{-\infty}^{t} A(v)D[(t - v)]Q(v)\, dv \right\} L(0)e^{nt} \tag{5.1.8}$$

(2) There exists a surrogate capital jelly,

$$J(t) = s \int_{-\infty}^{t} A(v)D[(t - v)]Q(v)\, dv \tag{5.1.9}$$

---

[3] $\dfrac{d\{L(v, t)f[A(v)K(v, t)/L(v, t)]\}}{dL(v, t)} = f - k^0 f'$

such that

$$Q(t) = F[J(t), L(t)] \tag{5.1.10}$$

and at any instant t,

$$k^0(v, t) = J(t)/L(t) \quad \text{for all } v, \ -\infty \le v \le t \tag{5.1.11}$$

Proof of (2)

$$(d/dk^0)[f(k^0) - k^0 f'(k^0)] = -k^0 f''(k^0)$$

$$> 0$$

This means that the higher k^0 ("efficient capital" per worker) is, the higher the wage rate must be. Therefore, corresponding to the same marginal product of labor $w(t)$, the ratio of efficiency-weighted capital to labor $A(v)K(v, t)/L(v, t)$ must be the same over machines of all vintages. This common value, say, $j(t)$, can be used to define the capital jelly; i.e.,

$$J(t) = j(t)L(t)$$

Now, $A(v)K(v, t)/L(v, t) = j(t)$ is equivalent to $A(v)K(v, t) = j(t)L(v, t)$. Integrating both sides over v up to t and noting that $K(v, t) = sQ(t)D[(t-v)]$, we have verified (5.1.9) and (5.1.11). Constant returns imply that

$$F[J(t), L(t)] = L(t)f[j(t)]$$

$$= \int_{-\infty}^{t} L(v, t)f[j(t)]\, dv$$

$$= \int_{-\infty}^{t} Q(v, t)\, dv$$

$$= Q(t)$$

which proves (5.1.10).

D. THE EFFECTS OF SPECIAL ASSUMPTIONS

1. The exponential depreciation assumption.   In Section 4.2, exponential depreciation is shown as essential to the Samuelsonian aggregation; otherwise one can hardly convert an old machine into new machine equivalents. Here, the existence of the capital jelly J is independent of the form of $D[(t-v)]$, thanks to the postulation of Solow-neutral technical progress. However, Solow's assumption of exponential depreciation makes the dynamic system "Markovian"; the future depends only on the present stock of J, not on its entire past history. This facilitates the analysis. Differentiating (5.1.9) with respect to time, we get

$$\dot{J}(t) = A(t)[sQ(t)] + s\int_{-\infty}^{t} A(v)D'[(t-v)]Q(v)\, dv \tag{5.1.12}$$

which depends upon (i) the detailed age distribution of existing stocks, $sQ(v)D[(t-v)]$ (or, in efficiency terms, $s[A(v)Q(v)D(t-v)]$), and (ii) the detailed proportional rate of depreciation $D'[(t-v)]/D[(t-v)]$. However, if $D[(t-v)] = e^{-\delta(t-v)}$, (5.1.12) becomes a simple differential equation,

$$
\begin{aligned}
\dot{J}(t) &= A(t)[sQ(t)] - \delta J(t) \\
&= A(t)sF[J(t), L(t)] - \delta J(t)
\end{aligned}
$$
(5.1.12′)

if $D[(t-v)] = e^{-\delta(t-v)}$.

The exponential technical progress index and the Cobb-Douglas production function. Since we have the mathematical identity:

$$
\frac{\dot{j}}{L} = \frac{d(jL)/dt}{L} = \frac{dj}{dt} + nj
$$

if we divide (5.1.12′) by L, we obtain

$$
\frac{dj}{dt} = sA(t)f[j(t)] - (n+\delta)j(t)
$$
(5.1.13)

which is analytically similar to the Hicks-neutral technical progress case for the simple Solow model.[4] As discussed in Section 2.3, if $A(t)$ is exponential and f is Cobb-Douglas, then golden-age growth exists. It should be added that the existence of a golden-age path is neither crucial to the statistical estimation Solow engaged in nor verifiable from historical observations.[5] This special case led to considerable discussion due to its simplicity. We now turn to this argument.

5.1.3. Policy implications

Supposing that in the real world, technical progress is of the embodied type, what difference does this make regarding (1) the causal decomposition of the growth of output per worker and (2) the effect of increased savings both in the short run and in the long run? The answer is anything but simple. While Solow made certain general observations, a thoroughgoing analysis was carried out by Phelps [5] for the Cobb-Douglas production function and by Matthews [6], who introduced embodied Harrod-neutral technical progress in the place of Solow-neutral technical progress and relaxed the Cobb-Douglas production function assumption. Due to lack of space, we shall discuss only the results of Phelps.

Phelps considered a general model where both Solow-neutral and Hicks-neutral technical progress occurs. Assuming a Cobb-Douglas production function, exponential technical progress indices of both Hicks and Solow types, and an exponential depreciation rate, Phelps showed that a 1% Hicks-neutral

---

[4] There, the equation is $\dot{k} = sA(t)f(k) - nk$.

[5] On the other hand, if the production function is such that the lasticity of substitution is larger than 1 for all large capital/labor ratios, then Akerlof and Nordhaus [19] proved that the rate of increase of the jelly/labor ratio will approach infinity. If the elasticity of substitution is smaller than 1 for all large jelly/labor ratios, then the interest rate may become negative.

technical progress rate achieves the same long-run growth rate as a $(1/\alpha)\%$ Solow-neutral technical progress rate (where α is the capital share), yet under the embodiment hypothesis the output per worker approaches a lower long-run asymptotic path at a faster speed. Under his assumptions, (5.1.8) can be re-written as

$$Q(t) = \exp\left[\lambda_h t\right] L(t)^{-\alpha} \left\{\int_{-\infty}^{t} s(v) \exp\left[\lambda_s v\right] \exp\left[-\delta(t-v)\right] Q(v)\, dv\right\}^{\alpha} L(t)$$

$$= \left\{\int_{-\infty}^{t} s(v) Q(v) \exp\left[(\lambda_s + \delta)v\right] dv\right\}^{\alpha} L(0)^{1-\alpha} \exp\left\{\left[(1-\alpha)n + \lambda_h - \alpha\delta\right]t\right\}$$

(5.1.14)

where $\lambda_h \geq 0$ is the Hicks-neutral technical progress rate

$\lambda_s \geq 0$ is the Solow-neutral technical progress rate

α is the rent share

$s(t)$ is a variable saving/income ratio that reaches its maximum, constant value s for all $t \geq 0$

Taking the time derivative, one obtains a differential equation, the solution of which is reducible to the form[6]

$$1 - [Q(t)/\bar{Q}(t)]^{(1-\alpha)/\alpha} = \{1 - [Q(0)/\bar{Q}(0)]^{(1-\alpha)/\alpha}\} \exp\{-[\lambda_h + \lambda_s + (1-\alpha)(n+\delta)]t\} \quad (5.1.15)$$

where

$$\bar{Q}(t) = \bar{Q}(0) \exp\{[n + (\lambda_h + \alpha\lambda_s)/(1-\alpha)]t\} \quad (5.1.16)$$

---

[6] The differential equation has the form

$$\dot{Q} = [(1-\alpha)n + \lambda_h - \alpha\delta]Q + \alpha s L(0)^{(1-\alpha)/\alpha} Q^{2-(1/\alpha)} \exp\{[(1-\alpha)n + \lambda_h + \alpha\lambda_s]t/\alpha\}$$

Multiplying both sides by the integrating factor $[(1-\alpha)/\alpha]Q^{(1/\alpha)-2}$, we obtain

$$(d/dt)Q^{(1-\alpha)/\alpha} = \{(1-\alpha)[(1-\alpha)n + \lambda_h - \alpha\delta]/\alpha\}Q^{(1-\alpha)/\alpha} + (1-\alpha)sL(0)^{(1-\alpha)/\alpha} \exp[(1-\alpha)n + \lambda_h + \alpha\lambda_s]t/\alpha\}$$

Multiplying again by the integrating factor, $\exp\{[1-(1/\alpha)][(1-\alpha)n + \lambda_h - \alpha\delta]t\}$ and integrating, we obtain

$$Q(t)^{(1-\alpha)/\alpha} = \left\{Q(0)^{(1-\alpha)/\alpha} - \left[\frac{(1-\alpha)sL(0)^{(1-\alpha)/\alpha}}{(1-\alpha)(n+\delta) + \lambda_s + \lambda_h}\right]\right\} \exp\{(1-\alpha)[(1-\alpha)n + \lambda_h - \alpha\delta]t/\alpha\}$$

$$+ \left[\frac{(1-\alpha)sL(0)^{(1-\alpha)/\alpha}}{(1-\alpha)(n+\delta) + \lambda_s + \lambda_h}\right] \exp\{[(1-\alpha)n + \lambda_h + \alpha\lambda_s]t/\alpha\}$$

Setting

$$\bar{Q}(0) = L(0)\{s/[n+\delta + (\lambda_s + \lambda_h)/(1-\alpha)]\}^{\alpha/(1-\alpha)}$$

$$\bar{Q}(t) = \bar{Q}(0) \exp\{[n + (\lambda_h + \alpha\lambda_s)/(1-\alpha)]t\}$$

we observe (i) that if $Q(0) = \bar{Q}(0)$, then $Q(t) = \bar{Q}(t)$, and (ii) that $[\bar{Q}(t)^{c_1} - Q(t)^{c_1}] = [\bar{Q}(0)^{c_1} - Q(0)^{c_1}]e^{c_2 t}$, where $c_1 = (1-\alpha)/\alpha$ and $c_2 = (1-\alpha)[(1-\alpha)n + \lambda_h - \alpha\delta]/\alpha$.

Dividing the expression in (ii) by $\bar{Q}(t)^{c_1} = \bar{Q}(0)^{c_1} \exp\{c_1[n + (\lambda_h + \alpha\lambda_s)/(1-\alpha)]t\}$, we obtain (5.1.15).

with

$$\bar{Q}(0) = L(0)\{s/[n+\delta+(\lambda_h+\lambda_s)/(1-\alpha)]\}^{\alpha/(1-\alpha)} \tag{5.1.17}$$

The economic implications are:

(1) The long-run output path approaches, in the proportional sense, the $\bar{Q}(t)$ path. The growth rate of output per capita approaches $(\lambda_h + \alpha\lambda_s)/(1-\alpha)$. Given the capital coefficient α and the technical progress rates λ_h and λ_s, any variation of the saving/income ratio s cannot affect the long-run growth rate. But the higher the saving/income ratio, the higher is the long-run output per worker.[7] From (5.1.17),

$$\frac{d \ln [\bar{Q}(0)/L(0)]}{d \ln s} = \frac{\alpha}{1-\alpha}$$

(2) Given the capital coefficient α, (5.1.16) implies that 1% of Hicks-neutral technical progress is equivalent to $(1/\alpha)$% of Solow-neutral technical progress, so far as the long-run growth rate is concerned. But a 1% Hicks-neutral technical progress rate implies a higher long-run output per worker than is implied by $(1/\alpha)$% Solow-neutral technical progress. This is seen from (5.1.17). The reason is that under the embodiment hypothesis, older machines are obsolete in production and form a drag.

(3) The short-run situation is depicted in Figure 5.1 and in (5.1.15).

We are interested in the gradual elimination of the "proportional output deficiency" over time under the two alternative modes of technical progress, i.e., Hicks-neutral and Solow-neutral, assuming that the long-run growth rates of output per capita are the same, viz., $\lambda_s \equiv \lambda_h/\alpha > \lambda_h$. The proportional output deficiency is defined as $1 - [Q(t)/\bar{Q}(t)]$. However, for analytic convenience we shall use another index:

$$z(t) = 1 - [Q(t)/\bar{Q}(t)]^{(1-\alpha)/\alpha}$$

Due to the fact that α is a proper fraction, the proportional output deficiency is positive or zero if and only if $z(t)$ is positive or zero, respectively. In fact, $z(t)$ is a monotonically increasing function of the proportional output deficiency at t or, equivalently, a monotonically decreasing function of the ratio $Q(t)/\bar{Q}(t)$ as depicted in Figure 5.1a. The convenience of using $z(t)$ is due to the following formula:

$$z(t) = z(0)e^{-xt} \tag{5.1.15a}$$

where x now takes either the value $\lambda_s + (1-\alpha)(n+\delta)$ or the value $\lambda_h + (1-\alpha)(n+\delta)$. The potential courses of $z(t)$ under either case (pure Solow-neutral or pure Hicks-neutral) are shown in Figure 5.1b.

Starting from the point $Q(0)/\bar{Q}(0)$ on the horizontal axis of Figure 5.1a, we construct a vertical line to determine the value of $z(0)$. Carrying that value into Figure 5.1b, we obtain the common initial point of the two exponential curves.

---

[7]This does not imply that consumption per capita is always higher with higher s. See Chapter 9.

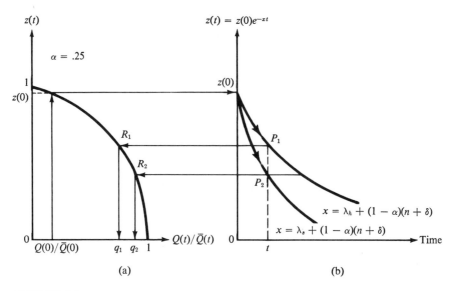

FIGURE 5.1

As the investments join the production process at an accelerating rate, $z(t)$ decreases under either assumption of technical progress to reach points P_1 and P_2 at time t. Carrying back horizontal lines to Figure 5.1a determines points R_1 and R_2, which in turn imply the respective points q_1 and q_2 on the axis for $Q(t)/\bar{Q}(t)$. Obviously, the Solow-neutral technical progress implies that the embodiment hypothesis leads to a faster approach to the respective long-run paths.[8]

In order to judge the implications of embodied technical progress, apart from the theoretical problems, statistical problems of measurability must also be considered. Fisher [7] discusses the assumptions needed for valid aggregations, and Jorgenson [8] questions the distinguishability between the embodied and disembodied hypotheses using the statistical procedures commonly followed. However, these are outside the scope of our book.

5.2 THE PUTTY–CLAY MODEL

5.2.1. Introduction

Leif Johansen [3] initiated a model in 1959 in which equipment can be designed with various capital/labor ratios, yet once machines are made, the capital/labor ratio remains constant. Salter [9] studied a model with similar properties. Soon afterwards, Solow [10–12], Phelps [13], Kurz [14], and Kemp and Thanh [15]

---

[8]Warning: The two hypotheses imply different potential output paths; see point (2) above. Hence, Phelps regards the embodiment hypothesis as implying a *more* flexible economy, while Solow considers the same hypothesis as *less* optimistic.

all contributed to the extension and perfection of such a type of model, where the *ex ante* factor substitutability and *ex post* nonsubstitutability were aptly called putty–clay by Phelps. The early studies concentrated on the Cobb-Douglas production function case, while Solow, Tobin, Weizsäcker, and Yaari [16] specialized in a clay–clay model in which the choice-of-technique problems are assumed away even in the *ex ante* stage. Our discussion in this section follows the work of Bliss [17], whose paper relaxes the Cobb-Douglas assumption and provides penetrating insight into the choice-of-technique problems in the context of comparative golden age paths. The clay–clay model will be considered in the next section.

The putty–clay model presents a highly complicated structure. To help readers gain a better grasp of the concepts involved, a set of diagrams is provided to depict the essence of the basic assumptions in Section 5.2.2. The formal model is synthesized and the golden age path characterized in Section 5.2.3. Comparative dynamic results are reported in Section 5.2.4, some without proof, due to the complexity of the derivations.

5.2.2. Assumptions

These can be classified into two groups: the retained assumptions, which are carryovers from the simple Solow model, and the modified assumptions, which determine the nature of the model. The retained assumptions are:

(1) Output and labor are homogeneous.
(2) Labor grows exponentially; capital is nondepreciable.[9]
(3) There is perfect competition and perfect foresight.
(4) The saving/income ratio is constant.

The assumption of perfect foresight deserves some comment. In the simple Solow model, perfect foresight means that there are no entreprenurial miscalculations as in the Harrod-Domar world. Here, perfect foresight means something much more definite and less likely: Firms share the same expectations about future wage and interest rates, whereas these expectations validate themselves on the strength of the common belief.

The modified assumptions are:

(5) The technology of production consists of a spectrum of "linear" production activities,[10] each of which can be realized by use of a special machine. The unit capital and labor requirements of any particular type of machine are independent of either the numbers of machines used or the age of these machines.[11] The pairs of unit capital-and-labor requirements form an isoquant-like locus in the input space, which is convex and smooth.

---

[9]Depreciation can be introduced if it is either the exponential type or "one-hoss shay" (sudden death) type. See [15].

[10]This implies (a) constant returns to scale and (b) no mutual interactions (externalities) between different activities carried out side by side.

[11]That is, "fixed coefficients" prevail once the machine is made.

(6) Entrepreneurs buy and operate machines to maximize the net worth of the investment, i.e., the difference between the present value of the quasi-rent stream and the initial cost of investment.

(7) Embodied Harrod-neutral technical progress prevails.

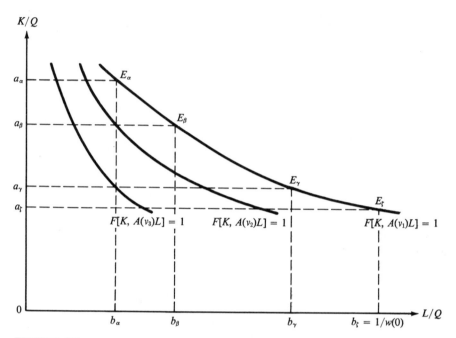

FIGURE 5.2

The significance of the last three assumptions can best be understood by examining Figures 5.2–5.8.

Let $a = K/Q$ be the unit capital requirement and $b = L/Q$ be the unit labor requirement. At instant v, all the available alternative production techniques can be depicted by the set of points (b, a) as in Figure 5.2. The points pertaining to any one instant form an isoquant-like locus. Three specimens are shown in Figure 5.2, for $v = v_1$, v_2, and v_3, where $0 = v_1 < v_2 < v_3$. The embodied Harrod-neutral technical progress makes the unit-output isoquant shrink, pro rata, horizontally to the left (assumption (7)). For any given technique, K/Q remains constant for all vintages, but L/Q falls lower and lower for newer and newer vintages.

Defining $k^0 = K(v, v)/A(v)L(v, v)$ as the effective capital/labor ratio, where $A(v)$ is the labor-augmenting technical progress index, each technique can be characterized by its associated k^0 value. Setting $f(k^0) = 1/b$, in Figure 5.2 we have

$$a = K/Q = k^0/f(k^0)$$

$$b = L/Q = 1/f(k^0)$$

The isoquant-like locus for $v_1 = 0$ is then

$$F[k^0/f(k^0), 1/f(k^0)] = 1 \qquad (5.2.1)$$

Using our results in Section 2.3, Harrod-neutral technical progress means that labor in efficiency units grows faster than labor in natural units. Using our results in Section 4.2, if output, capital, and labor *in efficiency units* increase at the same proportional rate (i.e., golden age growth), the constant returns assumption implies that the relative proportions between the output price, the interest rate, and "the reward per unit of efficiency-labor" ("efficiency-wage") remain the same. At each *feasible*[12] rate of "efficiency-wage" there exists a highest interest rate under which some activities break even, none reaps a profit. Hence, we have an interest and efficiency-wage frontier. Harrod-neutral technical progress implies that each natural unit of labor corresponds to an ever-rising number of efficiency-labor units and hence commands an ever-rising wage rate. The wage–interest frontier under golden age growth therefore shifts, pro rata, horizontally to the right, as depicted in Figure 5.3. A particular golden age wage–interest path is shown there by the line $p_1 p_2 p_3$, along which rent takes the constant value $\bar{r}$, while wage increases all the time. A non-golden-age path, $\pi_1 \pi_2 \pi_3$, may also occur. This indicates that wage first rises, then falls, and finally rises again. For the present, we shall assume that the economy follows the golden age path.

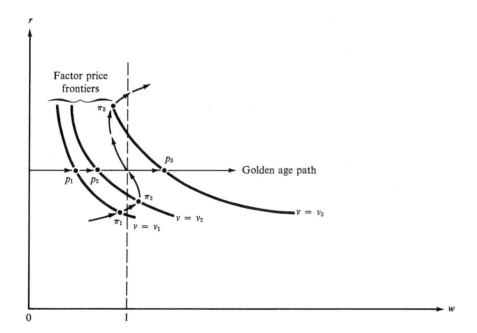

FIGURE 5.3

[12] Every sustainable efficiency-wage must be compatible with a non-negative interest rate.

We shall now turn to the dynamic cost–price relations under a given technique, say, k_α^0. Once the equipment is constructed, we have a short-run situation à la Marshall. Since the product is the numeraire, the average revenue is unity by definition. Since we have a fixed-proportion production relation and the investment in equipment constitutes sunk cost, the average variable cost is equal to the unit labor cost, which is the product of the unit labor requirement and the wage rate. At any given wage rate, the average variable cost curve is a horizontal line, up to the capacity of the existing machines. At that point, the average variable cost turns vertically upward. As a consequence of assumption (5), if there is only enough labor to man half the vintage v machines, according to the market forces, then output from such machines will be half of their capacities.[13] The difference between the average revenue curve and the average variable cost curve is the quasi-rent. As long as the quasi-rent is positive, the entrepreneur produces up to the maximum capacity, which is one unit of output in our model by definition. For each instant t there corresponds a wage rate $w(t)$ and, hence, an average variable cost curve, $b_\alpha \cdot w(t)$. In Figure 5.4, three specimen

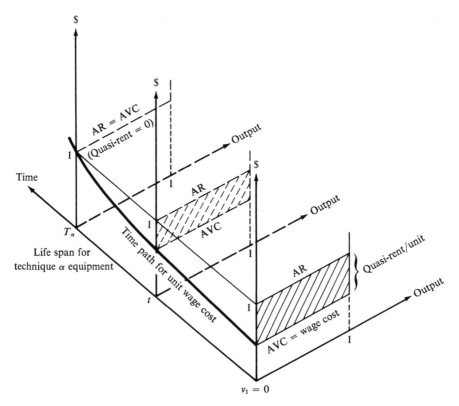

FIGURE 5.4

[13]For all practical purposes, we can and shall assume that either all vintage v machines are fully utilized or all of them are laid aside.

average-cost-and-revenue diagrams are presented, with time as the third axis. Along the time dimension, one can observe that unit labor cost (which is constant over all ranges of output rates) rises over time as wage increases. By time T_α, wage rises to such an extent that the quasi-rent is entirely eliminated and variable cost equals revenue. This is the terminal instant at which the equipment will be laid aside.

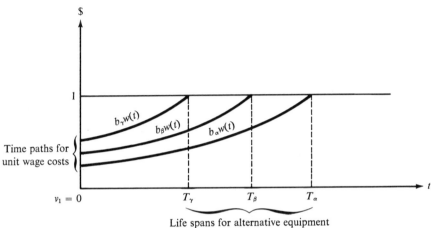

FIGURE 5.5

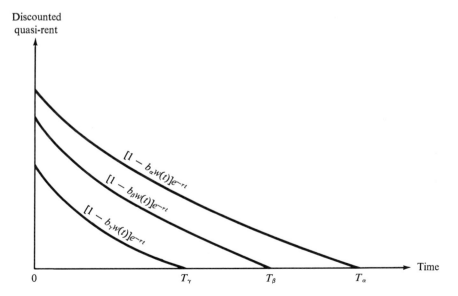

FIGURE 5.6

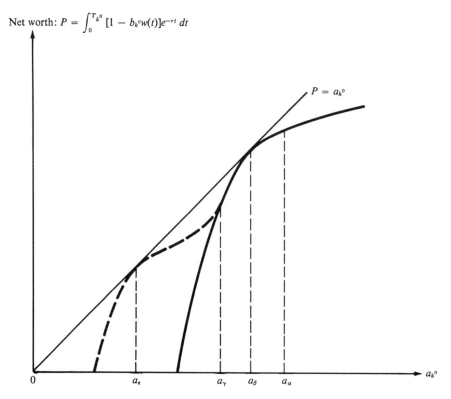

Net worth: $P = \int_0^{T_{k^0}} [1 - b_{k^0}w(t)]e^{-rt}\, dt$

$P = a_{k^0}$

0 a_ϵ a_γ a_β a_α a_{k^0}

FIGURE 5.7

Since perfect foresight is postulated (assumption (3)), entrepreneurs use dynamic cost–revenue data to select equipment types. Back in Figure 5.2, four techniques k_α^0, k_β^0, k_γ^0, and k_ζ^0 are singled out for further study. In Figure 5.4, we have examined the time path of the unit wage cost under technique k_α^0. In Figure 5.5, similar time paths of unit wage cost are plotted for techniques k_α^0, k_β^0, and k_γ^0. The economic life spans for the respective techniques are T_α, T_β, and T_γ, where the corresponding unit wage cost curves reach the unity line. Since b_ζ is assumed to be $1/w(0)$, the economic life of equipment under technique k_ζ^0 is zero. Also, we note that the higher the unit labor requirement, the shorter is the economic life span. The difference between output and labor cost, $1 - b_{k^0}w(t)$, is the quasi-rent flow for technique k^0. The discounted quasi-rent flow $[1 - b_{k^0}w(t)]e^{-rt}$ is depicted in Figure 5.6.[14] The areas under the discounted quasi-rent curves are the present values of the quasi-rent streams and they are plotted against the unit capital input in Figure 5.7. From the theory of competitive equilibrium, no technique should give rise to positive net worth, whereas the adopted technique (k^0) must result in zero net worth. These are shown in Figure 5.7, where technique k_β^0 is chosen at time $v_1 = 0$.

[14]We assume here a golden age path; hence, $r \equiv \bar{r}$.

Note that the shape of the wage–interest path in Figure 5.3 plays an interesting role. If $w(t)$ is nondecreasing over time, from Figure 5.5 we conclude that any equipment once disposed of will never be reinstated. However, if wage falls over some interval as the $\pi_1\pi_2\pi_3$ path in Figure 5.3 indicates, there may be a reinstatement, as shown in Figure 5.8.

Such potential reinstatement makes the analysis of non-golden-age paths highly intractable in the putty–clay model. Actually, even among golden age paths causal determinacy is by no means assured. In Figure 5.7, suppose that the net worth curve contacts the 45° ray at another point where $a_{k^0} = a_\varepsilon$ (as shown by the dotted lines); then even if the technique with unit capital requirement a_β has been used since time immemorial, sudden shifts to technique k_ε^0 may happen at any time. Moreover, the assumption of "linear" production activities allows the blending of techniques k_β^0 and k_ε^0. Such causal indeterminacy also leads to difficulties in comparative golden age studies.

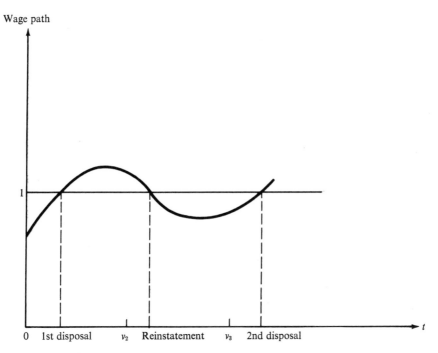

FIGURE 5.8

5.2.3. The formulation

A. THE GENERAL MODEL

The putty–clay model captures a high degree of realism only at the price of great analytical complexities. The broad outlines of the model are summarized in Table 5.3.

TABLE 5.3   THE WORKING OF THE MODEL

Individual level	Equation	Market level	Equation

Households
  Saving/consumption decisions
Firms
  Choice of technique decisions
  Labor allocation decisions
	(5.2.2)
	
	(5.2.3)
	(5.2.4)
		Labor market
		  Wage determination
		Capital market
		  Interest determination
			(5.2.5)
			
			(5.2.6)

1. Saving/consumption decisions

$$K(t, t) = sQ(t)$$
$$= s \int_{-\infty}^{t} f[k^0(v)]A(v)L(v, t)\, dv \tag{5.2.2}$$

where $k^0(v)$ is the effective capital/labor ratio for vintage v machines, $f(k^0)$ and $L(v, t)$ are the output per effective worker and the labor force associated with such machines, respectively, and $A(v)L(v, t)$ is their effective production force.

The expression $A f L$ is therefore the output produced with vintage v machines.

2. The choice of techniques decisions

$$\frac{P[k^0(v), v; w(\cdot), r(\cdot)]}{k^0(v)A(v)} \geq \frac{P[k^0, v; w(\cdot), r(\cdot)]}{k^0 A(v)} \quad \text{for all } k^0 \geq 0 \tag{5.2.3}$$

where

$$P[k^0, v; w(\cdot), r(\cdot)] = \underset{0 \leq \rho(t) \leq 1}{\text{Max}} \int_{v}^{\infty} \{[f(k^0)A(v) - w(t)]\rho(t)\} \exp\left[-\int_{v}^{t} r(\tau)\, d\tau\right] dt$$

is the present worth of investment per worker, which is (a "functional") dependent upon the time paths of wage and interest, the vintage, and capital intensity. Taking values between zero and unity, $\rho(t) = L(v, t)/L(v, v)$, is the "utilization ratio." $Af - w$ is the quasi-rent per worker. The present value factor between v and t is $\exp\left[-\int_{v}^{t} r(\tau)\, d\tau\right]$ with a variable and continuously compounding interest rate r.

This condition states that the net worth per invested dollar should be at the maximum when using the chosen technique.

3. The labor allocation decisions.
There exist $w_M(t)$, $w_m(t)$, such that $w_M(t) \geq w(t) \geq w_m(t)$, where

$$\text{If } f[k^0(v)]A(v) > w_M(t) \qquad \text{then } L(v, t)/L(v, v) = 1$$
$$\text{If } f[k^0(v)]A(v) < w_m(t) \qquad \text{then } L(v, t)/L(v, v) = 0 \tag{5.2.4}$$

w_M and w_m are the "left-hand" and "right-hand" marginal products of labor.[15]
The full meaning of (5.2.4) will be graphically depicted below.

[15]That is, the products of one "decremental" and "incremental" unit of labor.

4. The operation of the labor market.

$$\int_{-\infty}^{t} L(v,\,t)\,dv \le L(t)$$

$$= L_0 e^{nt} \qquad\qquad (5.2.5)$$

Equations (5.2.4) and (5.2.5) together decide the wage level as well as the allocation of the labor force. The excess of output per worker over the wage rate is the quasi-rent per worker. Only machines with non-negative quasi-rent will be utilized. Figure 5.9 presents the various cases that may emerge. We assume that there are only three discrete vintages of capital stock, and they are arranged in descending order of their output-per-worker levels, $A(v)f[k^0(v)]$. Each vintage is represented by a rectangle with $A(v)f[k^0(v)]$ as its height and $L(v,\,v)$ as its base. The ceiling of these blocks forms the (derived) demand for labor locus. The vertical line $L = L(t)$ stands for the fixed supply. If the labor supply line lies to the right of all the blocks (Figure 5.9a), wage is zero and there is surplus labor. If the vertical supply curve bisects a given block (Figure 5.9b), wage is determined and equipment of the vintage associated with the bisected block is partially utilized; i.e., $0 < [L(v,\,t)]/[L(v,\,v)] < 1$. If the vertical supply

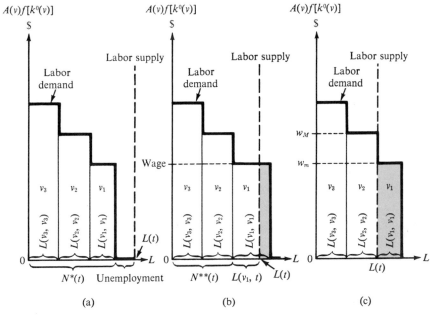

FIGURE 5.9   (a) Surplus labor, zero wage.

(b) Determined wage, partially utilized marginal vintage.

(c) Undetermined wage, no partial utilization.

Shaded areas represent overcapacity.

curve coincides with the side of a certain block (Figure 5.9c), wage rate is determined only up to the "twilight zone" between w_m and w_M, but every vintage will be either fully manned or totally laid aside.

In a model with a continuum of vintages, wage indeterminacy is rather unlikely. Since only a few vintages are partially utilized, one can usually assume that each vintage is either fully manned or completely laid aside. One may note that (5.2.4) allows a given vintage to be reinstated after its initial disposal.

5. Operation of the capital market.   For all v,

$$\frac{P[k^0(v), v; w(\cdot), r(\cdot)]}{k^0(v)A(v)} = 1 \tag{5.2.6}$$

This condition guarantees that the most profitable investment in every vintage barely breaks even. The combination of (5.2.3) and (5.2.6) is reflected in Figure 5.7, where the highest ray through both the origin and the $P(k^0)$ curve makes a 45° angle.

Equations (5.2.1) through (5.2.6) constitute a dynamic framework, yet this system need not be causally determined. The situation is akin to the difficulties encountered in Sections 4.3 and 4.4. The saving propensity determines the "volume of investment" in (5.2.2). The "form of investment" has to be chosen via (5.2.6). But as Bliss pointed out, the choice may not be unique. Once again our model specification is inadequate to describe the historical evolution of an economy. Until this gap is bridged, there is no point in discussing non-golden-age growth paths or, for that matter, the stability properties of the golden age paths. Solow [11, 12] conducted certain simulation studies but they are not quite in the same context and we shall not report them here.

B.   GOLDEN AGE PATHS

We shall consider those golden age growth paths where $\hat{A} = \lambda$ and

$$\hat{L} = \hat{L}(t, t) = n \geq 0$$
$$\hat{Q} = \hat{K}(t, t) = n + \lambda > n \tag{5.2.7}$$

(Balanced growth is thus ruled out.)

We can obtain the following results (the derivations are in Appendix 5.1):

(1) Under assumptions (1), (2), (3), (5), and (6) (Section 5.2.2), the golden age path implies the following:
   (a) The saving/income ratio is constant (assumption (4) is necessary for golden age growth).
   (b) Either all equipment will be in use or the equipment used is only of newer vintages.
   (c) Once equipment is laid aside, no reinstatement will ever occur.
   (d) The economic life span of equipment will be the same for all vintages.
(2) Golden age growth with Harrod-neutral technical progress implies the following:
   (a) The technique in use may be constant.

(b) The wage rate rises at the proportional rate λ and the interest rate remains constant.

(3) Full employment of labor force under golden age growth requires that

$$
(s) \sup_{k^0} \left[\frac{f(k^0)}{k^0} \right] > \frac{n + \lambda}{1 - \exp\left[-(n + \lambda)T \right]} \qquad \text{for some } T > 0 \qquad (5.2.8)
$$

5.2.4. Comparative golden age paths

Bliss found that the only comparative golden age result that has general validity is the following: Among two alternative golden age paths, the higher interest rate is associated with the lower wage per unit of effective labor force. This is a corollary of the result in Section 4.2, where the wage–interest frontier has a negative slope. Let (w_0, r_0), (w_1, r_1) be two points in such a frontier, $w_0 > w_1$. Those breaking-even activities under (w_0, r_0) would show profit under (w_1, r) for all $r \leq r_0$, since quasi-rent for every activity at every moment rises with the fall of the wage rate. But competitive conditions plus constant returns implies zero profit. Therefore, $r_1 > r_0$.

Difficulties in deriving other results are due to the nonuniqueness of optimal techniques under the same wage–interest pattern. Bliss found it hard to rule out such nonuniqueness in any simple criterion. Britto [20] concluded that if the elasticity of substitution is no greater than 1, then corresponding to each (w_0, r_0) pair there can be at most one optimal technique.

We shall summarize without derivation what Bliss has proved:

(1) If the elasticity of substitution is small enough that the present worth of investment per worker is concave in k^0, then there is no multiple optimal technique corresponding to any given r.
(2) If the above condition holds for all r, then
   (a) Higher interest rates are associated with lower effective capital/labor ratios.
   (b) Higher interest rates tend to lengthen equipment lives due to the corresponding lower wages and also to shorten equipment lives due to the corresponding lower initial investments. The force of the second effect is positively associated with the elasticity of substitution.

For intermediate values of the elasticity coefficient, interest rates may be positively associated with equipment life over one range and negatively associated over another range.

(3) Little can be said in relating the interest rate to the saving/income ratio.

5.2.5. Concluding remarks

The putty–clay model successfully combines the microeconomic investment theory on the one hand and the growth theory on the other. It shows certain family resemblances to the Cass-Yaari model to be discussed in Section 6.1.

The most important special feature consists of the strong requirements placed upon the perfect foresight assumption. Every person has to share the identical conviction about the future time patterns of $w(t)$ and $r(t)$. Further, these expected values must be such that they can materialize with the help of such unanimous expectations. Strictly speaking, we have a functional equation with $w(\cdot)$ and $r(\cdot)$ as unknown functions to be determined. No longer do we have a dynamic system in the conventional sense. In the latter case, in order to generate the future path we only need either some initial values at a given point (e.g., the simple Solow model) or the whole past history (e.g., the putty–putty model in Section 5.1). The putty–clay model begs the deep methodological question: Granted that an individual has perfect foresight, does he commit himself to an inflexible lifelong program during his first business transaction? As time goes by, is it likely that he may change his mind in the Strotzian manner [18]? It seems that more research work is needed in this area. (Goldman's work [19] is perhaps a starting point.)

One alternative to the perfect foresight assumption is the zero-foresight assumption (i.e., "stationary expectations") explored by Kemp and Thanh [15]. Wages keep on rising, yet entrepreneurs always believe that future wage rates will be the same as today's. They always make mistakes in one direction: building and using machines that require too much labor for long-run profit; they never learn. So the story goes. In a world where wage rates have risen by the same percentage since time immemorial, the zero-foresight assumption is no more realistic than the perfect-foresight assumption. Akerlof's study on the stability properties of the putty–clay model [23] assumes zero foresight, but since there is no technical progress in his model, static expectations seem to be more justified than under the assumption of technical progress.

5.3 THE CLAY–CLAY MODEL

Vintage capital models of the fixed proportions type were first investigated by Salter [9] and Bergström [21]. The most comprehensive work along this line is due to Solow, Tobin, von Weizsäcker, and Yaari [16]. Our present discussion shall be based on their study.

Among the three types of vintage capital models, the putty–putty model is perhaps the simplest. The putty–clay model presents the most challenging complexities, while the clay–clay model is a simplified version of the putty–clay formulation. Whereas there is a spectrum of techniques available for selection under the putty–clay case, there is only one "efficient" equipment design for any one vintage in the clay–clay formulation. Such drastic simplification is made in the hope that certain mathematically difficult or conceptually elusive problems can be analyzed in depth. These include (1) the consideration of general embodied technical progress, rather than the pure labor-augmenting type; (2) the "Keynesian" case where aggregate demand determines an output below the production potential of the economy; and (3) the working of the "neoclassical" theory of distribution, even where there is no factor substitutability, either *ex ante* or *ex post*. The full range of results attained by Solow et al. cannot be reported here with rigor. Instead we shall survey their conclusions and provide interpretive commentaries. The formulation of the general model is presented first, next comes the sequence of findings, and finally some concluding remarks.

5.3.1. Model formulation

Five of the seven assumptions of the putty–clay model in the last sections are retained in the clay–clay model. The two modifications are:

(1) For any vintage of equipment, there exists only one efficient technique under which the universal output can be produced under constant returns. (Compare assumption (5) in Section 5.2.2.)
(2) Technical progress may reduce either the unit capital requirement or the unit labor requirement or both. (Compare assumption (7) in Section 5.2.2.)

Using the symbols of the last section, we can quickly present the following model:

(1) The input–output relation:

$$Q(v, t) = \text{Min} \begin{Bmatrix} A_1(v)K(v, t)/a \\ A_2(v)L(v, t)/b \end{Bmatrix} \tag{5.3.1}$$

where a and b are the unit capital and labor requirements, which we shall assume to be unity after appropriate choice of units. $A_1(v)$ and $A_2(v)$ are positive numbers representing the technical progress indices for vintage v equipment, $A_1'(v), A_2'(v) \geq 0$.

(2) The saving/consumption decisions:

$$K(t, t) = s \int_{-\infty}^{t} Q(v, t) \, dv = s \int_{-\infty}^{t} A_2(v)L(v, t) \, dv \tag{5.3.2}$$

(3) The labor-allocating decisions: There exist $w_M(t)$, $w_m(t)$ such that $w_M(t) \geq w(t) \geq w_m(t)$

$$\begin{aligned} &\text{If } A_2(v) > w_M(t) &&\text{then } L(v, t)/L(v, v) = 1 \\ &\text{If } A_2(v) < w_m(t) &&\text{then } L(v, t)/L(v, v) = 0 \end{aligned} \tag{5.3.3}$$

(4) The operation of the labor market:

$$N(t) = \int_{-\infty}^{t} L(v, t) \, dv$$

$$\leq \text{Min} \left\{ L_0 e^{nt}, \int_{V(t)} K(v, v) \left[A_1(v)/A_2(v) \right] dv \right\} \tag{5.3.4}$$

where $N(t)$ stands for total employment. $V(t) = \{v | L(v, t) > 0\}$ represents the vintages in use.

Since there is a continuum of vintages, the influence of the partially utilized vintage can be ignored.

(5) The operation of the capital market:

$$A_1(v) \int_v^\infty \left[1 - \frac{w(t)}{A_2(v)} \right] \left[\frac{L(v, t)}{L(v, v)} \right] \exp\left[-\int_v^t r(u)\, du \right] dt = 1 \qquad (5.3.5)$$

Here, whenever $[1 - w(t)/A_2(v)]$ becomes negative, from (5.3.3), $L(v, t)/L(v, v) = 0$.

The left-hand side of (5.3.5) is the net worth of a vintage v machine. The right-hand side reflects the fact that the capital good is completely interchangeable with the consumption good-numeraire.

(6) The effect of effective demand:

$$\int_{-\infty}^t Q(v, t)\, dv = Q(t) \leq \bar{Q}(t) \qquad (5.3.6)$$

where $\bar{Q}(t)$ is the effective demand.

Equations (5.3.1) through (5.3.5) are comparable with (5.2.1) through (5.2.6), except that there is no need for a choice-of-technique relation (5.2.3) in a clay–clay model. The "distribution theory" is exhibited in (5.3.3)–(5.3.5). Wage is determined on the "extensive margin" of existing vintage machines. Interest is decided by an intertemporal arbitrage so that every investment operation undertaken reaps zero profit. The inequality sign in (5.3.4) allows effective demand to fall below the output ceilings implied by the supply of both labor and capital. The appearance of $A_1(v)$ alongside $A_2(v)$ allows all possible patterns of technical progress. If (5.3.4) takes the strict inequality form (when Keynesian unemployment exists), then (5.3.1)–(5.3.6) no longer form a closed model, since output $Q = \bar{Q}$ is undetermined in the system.

Since $A_2'(v) \geq 0$, in view of (5.3.3), one concludes that only older vintages need be laid aside,[16] although reinstatement of machines cannot be ruled out (e.g., as a result of fluctuating effective demand).

5.3.2. Preliminary results

A.   TYPES OF TECHNICAL PROGRESS AND THE DETERMINATION OF OPERATIONAL VINTAGES

Under the fixed proportions assumption, technical progress of various kinds can be identified as in Table 5.4.

It is apparent that the pattern of technical progress may have a profound effect on deciding which vintage should be operational. We shall concentrate on the following special cases.

(1) *The surplus-labor regime.* Due to a large initial labor force, a rapid

---

[16]Subject to a proviso discussed later.

TABLE 5.4

	Algebraic representation	Geometric representation
Solow-neutral	$A_1'(v) > 0 = A_2'(v)$	L-shaped isoquant shifts toward labor axis
Harrod-neutral	$A_1'(v) = 0 < A_2'(v)$	L-shaped isoquant shifts toward capital axis
Hicks-neutral	$A_1'(v)/A_1(v) = A_2'(v)/A_2(v) > 0$	L-shaped isoquant shifts proportionally toward origin
No progress	$A_1'(v) = 0 = A_2'(v)$	No shift

increase of population, or the fact that inadequate savings are cumulated from an inadequate national income, it is possible that even if equipment of *all* vintages were manned, it would only absorb a fraction of the available labor. In such a case, all vintages are operational and the wage rate falls to zero along with the marginal physical product. This was depicted in Figure 5.9a. In that diagram, $N^*(t) = \int_{-\infty}^{t} [K(v, v)A_1(v)/A_2(v)]\, dv$ is the amount of labor force needed at t to operate all the existing equipment. When the total labor force $L(t)$ exceeds the maximum employment $N^*(t)$, then surplus labor emerges and the output of the marginal laborer and the wage rate both become zero.

(2) *The full-employment regime and the Keynesian unemployment regime.* In the case of full employment, the available labor force $L(t)$ limits the volume of production (cf. Fig. 5.9c). In the Keynesian unemployment regime, the effective demand limits the maximum number employed. For this Keynesian case, the employment at t is

$$N^{**}(t) = \int_{h(t)}^{t} L(v, t)\, dv$$

where $h(t)$ is the oldest vintage in operation chosen such that

$$\int_{h(t)}^{t} A_2(v)L(v, t)\, dv = \bar{Q}$$

the effective demand $\bar{Q}$ being the aggregate area of all the bars of the operating vintages.[17] In Figure 5.9b

$$\bar{Q} = A_2(v_3)L(v_3, v_3) + A_2(v_2)L(v_2, v_2)$$

and

$$N^{**}(t) = L(v_2, v_2) + L(v_3, v_3)$$

In both cases, $N(t)$, the actual employment, is equal to the lesser of $L(t)$, supply of labor, and $N^{**}(t)$, the derived demand for labor. Furthermore, $N(t) < N^*(t)$, so an incremental unit of labor can produce some positive output. This, of course, determines the wage rate, just as the extensive marginal land determines the Ricardian rent.

[17] Again subject to the proviso discussed in subcase b.

Here we can consider two subcases:

Subcase a. Labor-augmenting technical progress has been going on for a sufficiently long period. Hence, by allocating $N(t)$ over the most efficient vintages, the newest vintages are selected for operation. There exists a vintage $v = h(t)$ such that the marginal unit of $N(t)$ operates on that vintage. Thus, $A_2[h(t)]$, which is the output per worker on that vintage, determines the wage. Since $A'_2(v) > 0$ near $h(t)$, we conclude: (i) The operating vintage $V(t)$ is simply $\{v|h(t) < v \leq t\}$. Hence, all vintages earlier than $h(t)$ will not be used and all later ones will be. (ii) Wage cost does not exhaust the product for newer vintages.

Subcase b. Labor-augmenting technical progress has been absent for a long enough period so that by allocating labor to the newest vintages the marginal unit of $N(t)$ is associated with the same output per worker as for those workers operating on the most modern equipment. There are again two consequences: (i) The set $V(t)$ of the vintages in operation at t is no longer uniquely determined. For example, if $A_2(v) = 1$, $\bar{Q}(t) = L(t, t) + L(t-1, t-1)$. But $L(t-1, t-1) = L(t-2, t-2)$. $V(t)$ can be $\{t, t-1\}$, as we have stated before, but $V(t)$ can also be $\{t, t-2\}$. (ii) Wage cost absorbs the total of output value. Hence, quasi-rent is identically zero.

Intermediate cases where $V(t)$ is indeterminate but $w(t) < A_2(t)$ (i.e., the most modern vintage earns quasi-rent) are also possible. The interested reader may depict these with a diagram.

B. PRODUCTION CONSTRAINTS AND ALTERNATIVE REGIMES

The production process transforms capital and labor services into outputs. The scale of production operations may be limited by any of the following conditions: (a) the supply of labor, (b) the supply of capital, or (c) the (effective) demand for output.

Remembering the definitions of $N^*(t)$ and $N^{**}(t)$, we have the following relations in terms of labor force:

$$N(t) = \mathrm{Min}\begin{Bmatrix} L(t) \\ N^*(t) \\ N^{**}(t) \end{Bmatrix} \qquad \text{where } L(t) = L_0 e^{nt}$$

If $N(t) = L(t)$, this is the full-employment regime, and labor limits production operations.

If $N(t) = N^*(t) < L(t)$, this is the surplus labor regime, and capital limits production operations.

If $N(t) = N^{**}(t) < L(t)$, this is the Keynesian unemployment regime, and effective demand limits production operations.

The surplus labor regime corresponds to that subcase of the "Harrod-Domar" special case of Section 2.2.3 where the natural rate outstrips the warranted rate. The full-employment regime covers those subcases of Section 2.2.3 where the natural rate is less than or exactly equal to the warranted rate. We said before that the Solovian analysis discussed in Section 2.2 is superior to the Harrodian analysis because it points out the existence of an excess capacity equilibrium.

Here we see that such excess capacity may take the form of obsolescence. This, of course, corresponds to the scrapping mechanism in the Domar theory. However, in a vintage model, the discarding of obsolete equipment is a normal, well-anticipated process, while in Domar's model it may impede the incentive to invest. Which view is more realistic is hard to judge *a priori*. Presumably, in an economy endowed with continuous technical dynamism, obsolescence is accepted as a fact of life. Hence, it engenders no destabilizing tendencies. However, if technical revolutions cause unexpected idling of equipment, then Domar's view remains relevant.

It is worthwhile to note that both of the above regimes are neoclassical in the sense that supply conditions determine the effective demand. Hence, factor substitution is not indispensable in neoclassical growth. The most interesting development here is the potential synthesis of the Keynesian and neoclassical types of macro theory outlined under the Keynesian unemployment regime. However, this is not fully developed by Solow et al. [16] because no money is included in this model. As they pointed out, both the downward inflexibility of the money wage and the phenomenon of hoarding can be dealt with only when money appears in the model. Then and only then can the effective demand be explained satisfactorily. For a discussion of the role of money in growth, see Chapter 8. We may note that there are five ways to juxtapose the Keynesian theory with the neoclassical theory:

(1) Keynesian theory explains the short-run disturbances; neoclassical theory explains the long-run trend.
(2) Keynesian theory explains the boundary cases of unacceptably low wage or interest rates; neoclassical theory explains the intermediate situations.
(3) Keynesian theory explains the uncontrolled tendencies; neoclassical theory explains the pattern under the guidance of optimal monetary and fiscal policies.
(4) Keynesian theory deals with a system containing a money sector; neoclassical theory deals with a "real" model.
(5) Keynesian theory deals with short-period dynamics. Just as a chain is made of separate links, growth theory can emerge from the joining up of the Keynesian dynamic mechanisms.

The first three views have been treated in Chapter 2. The fourth mentioned here seems the most fundamental approach to the problem. The last view was expressed by Solow and Stiglitz [24].

C. CAUSALITY UNDER VARIOUS REGIMES

Since the inputs are substitutable neither *ex ante* nor *ex post*, the causal determination of various variables is somewhat different from that of ordinary models. This will be illustrated by Table 5.5.

Note that (5.3.1) plays reversible roles under the various regimes and that the wage rate is used to derive the interest rate, while the interest rate is a sort of "end product" in the system.

TABLE 5.5

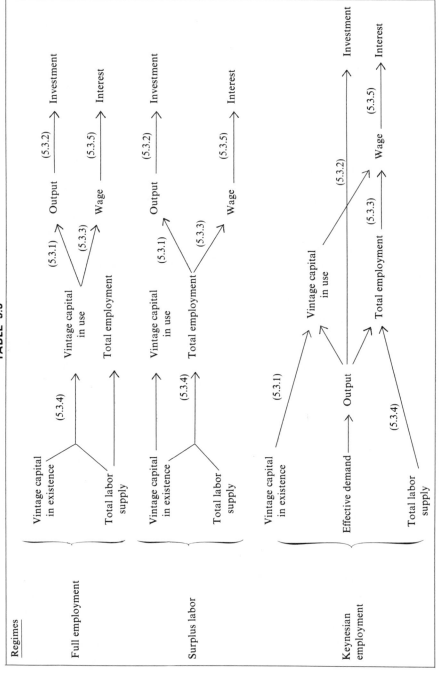

D. SOURCES OF GROWTH

In a simple Solow model where $Q = F(K, L)$, it can be shown that

$$\frac{\dot{Q}}{Q} = \frac{F_K \cdot \dot{K}}{Q} + \frac{F_L \cdot \dot{L}}{Q} = sF_K + \frac{LF_L}{Q} \cdot \frac{\dot{L}}{L}$$

This *decomposition* formula states that:

(Output growth rate) = (Saving/income ratio) (Marginal product of capital)
$\qquad\qquad\qquad\qquad\qquad$ + (Wage share) (Labor growth rate)

In the present model under the full-employment regime, we have a similar result. Note that

$$Q(t) = \int_{h(t)}^{t} Q(v, v)\, dv \qquad \text{(for } A_2' > 0,\ V(t) = \{v | h(t) \leq v \leq t\})$$

$\dot{Q}(t) = Q(t, t) - Q[h(t), h(t)]h'(t) \qquad$ (by differentiation)

$\quad = A_1(t)K(t, t) - w(t)L[h(t), h(t)]h'(t) \qquad$ (from (5.3.1) and the definition of $h(t)$)

$\quad = \left[A_1(t) - w(t)\frac{L(t, t)}{K(t, t)} \right] K(t, t) + w(t)\{L(t, t) - L[h(t), h(t)]h'(t)\}$

$\quad = \left[A_1(t) - w(t)\frac{L(t, t)}{K(t, t)} \right] K(t, t) + w(t)\dot{L}(t) \qquad$ (from differentiation of (5.3.4) and since $N \equiv L$)

Hence,

$$\frac{\dot{Q}}{Q} = s\left[A_1(t) - w(t)\frac{L(t, t)}{K(t, t)} \right] + \left(\frac{wL}{Q}\right)\frac{\dot{L}}{L} \quad \text{(from (5.2.2))} \tag{5.3.7}$$

where $[A_1(t) - w(t) L(t, t)/K(t, t)]$ is "the quasi-rent rate on the newest equipment."

We note that after substituting "the quasi-rent on newest equipment" for "the marginal product of capital" in the decomposition formula we also obtain (5.3.7).

5.3.3. Golden age growth, sensitivity analysis, and asymptotic paths

A. SUMMARY OF RESULTS

Solow et al. found the following results for the golden age paths:

(1) In a clay–clay model, if labor and output increase exponentially and unit capital and/or labor requirements decrease exponentially, full employment is possible only with Harrod-neutral technical progress. In other words, the growth mode must be the golden age type where output and new capital grow at the rate of increase of labor in efficiency units.

(2) Assuming Harrod-neutral technical progress, we can prove that (a) the economic life of equipment will be constant over time along the golden age path

and (b) it varies positively with the capital share and negatively with the saving/income ratio.

(3) There exists a given range of saving/income ratios that is consistent with golden age growth. Choosing the time unit such that the capital/output ratio is unity (see Section 5.3.1), the saving/income ratio must not be smaller than the rate of increase of labor in efficiency units (i.e., the warranted rate must not be less than the natural rate). Otherwise, the system passes under the labor surplus regime. On the other hand, the saving/income ratio certainly cannot exceed unity, since consumption can never be negative.

(4) Along the golden age path, (a) wage rises at the labor-augmenting technical progress rate and (b) interest can be proved to remain at a constant level.

(5) The higher the interest rate, the longer the equipment life.

(6) If the saving/income ratio is between unity and the growth rate of "efficiency labor force," then it has been proved that no matter what initial distributions the vintage capital goods may take, eventually the vintage distribution as well as other magnitudes will approach asymptotically a golden age path.

Some of the derivations involve mathematical proofs beyond the scope of the present volume. Interested readers may refer to the original article [16]. However, certain simpler developments as well as interpretive comments are sketched below.

Results (2a), (3), and (4) hold true in the general putty–clay model, as we saw in the last section. With the exception of (4b),[18] these results automatically hold in the clay–clay case where factor substitution is absent. The proofs of (4b) and (6) are too complicated to be included here; we comment only briefly on them. Bliss has stated that result (1) holds for the general putty–clay case. The comparative dynamic results in (2b) and (5) and the stability properties of the golden age path are obtainable in the clay–clay case. But as Bliss showed, there is no simple generalization of (2b) and (5) in the putty–clay framework.

B. DERIVATION AND COMMENTS

1. On result (1). In a clay–clay model, if full employment prevails and if output (hence gross investment), labor, and technical progress indices all grow exponentially, then output must grow at the same rate as "efficiency labor" and technical progress must be Harrod-neutral. The proof follows. Let

$$L(t) = L(0)e^{nt}; \; K(t, t) = K(0, 0)e^{gt}; \; A_1(v) = e^{\mu v}; \; A_2(v) = e^{\lambda v} \tag{5.3.8}$$

Under the full-employment regime,

$$
\begin{aligned}
L(0)e^{nt} &= \int_{h(t)}^{t} L(v, t) \, dv \\
&= \int_{h(t)}^{t} \frac{A_1(v)K(v, v)}{A_2(v)} \, dv \qquad [\text{since } A_1(v)K(v, v) = Q(v, t) = A_2(v)L(v, t)] \tag{5.3.9} \\
&= K(0, 0) (1 - \exp\{-(\mu+g-\lambda)[t-h(t)]\}) \exp[(\mu+g-\lambda)t]/(\mu+g-\lambda)
\end{aligned}
$$

---

[18]The proof of (4b) in the last section depends upon *ex ante* factor substitutability.

Again, from the instantaneous multiplier relation,

$K(0, 0)e^{gt}/s = Q(t)$

$$= \int_{h(t)}^{t} A_1(v)K(v, v)\, dv \tag{5.3.10}$$

$$= K(0, 0)\,(1 - \exp\{-(\mu+g)[t-h(t)]\})\, \exp\,[(\mu+g)t]/(\mu+g)$$

Hence, from (5.3.10) we have

$$[t - h(t)] = -\frac{1}{\mu+g} \ln\left[1 - \left(\frac{\mu+g}{s}\right)e^{-\mu t}\right] \tag{5.3.11}$$

Substituting back in (5.3.9) and rearranging,

$$(\mu+g-\lambda)L(0)\cdot\exp\,[(n+\lambda-\mu-g)t]/K(0, 0) = 1 - [1-(g+\mu)e^{-\mu t}/s]^{1-[\lambda/(\mu+g)]} \tag{5.3.12}$$

For $\mu \neq 0$, the right-hand side can never grow exponentially while the left-hand side must grow (or decay, exponentially. Hence, μ must equal zero, i.e., exponential growth is inconsistent with any capital-augmenting technical progress. But once μ is equated to zero, the right-hand side is a constant, which implies that the left-hand side must also be a constant, showing that $n+\lambda = g$. This means that the growth rate of new investment $K(t, t)$, and hence output $Q(t) = K(t, t)/s$, must be growing at the same rate as labor in efficiency units. In other words, all exponential growth paths satisfying (5.3.9) must be golden age paths. This completes the proof.

 2. Equipment life.   Substituting in (5.3.11) the relations $\mu = 0$ and $g = n+\lambda$, we get

$$t - h(t) = \frac{-\ln\,[1-(n+\lambda)/s]}{n+\lambda} = T$$

where T is a positive constant.

This proves that equipment life is constant under golden age growth. We now can analyze the effects of variations of s and the capital share α on T.

By direct differentiation,

$$\frac{\partial T}{\partial s} = \frac{(1/s)-\{1/[s-(n+\lambda)]\}}{n+\lambda}$$
$$< 0$$

Now,

$$\alpha = 1 - \frac{w(t)L(t)}{Q(t)}$$

From (5.3.3), $w(v+T) = A_2(v) = e^{\lambda v}$, and thus $w(t) = e^{\lambda(t-T)}$. From (5.3.9) and (5.3.10) and taking account of $t-h(t) = T$, $\mu = 0$ and $g = n+\lambda$, we obtain

$$\frac{Q(t)}{L(t)} = \left[\frac{n(1-e^{-gT})}{g(1-e^{-nT})}\right]e^{\lambda t}$$

Hence,

$$\alpha = 1 - \frac{w(t)L(t)}{Q(t)}$$

$$= 1 - \frac{g(e^{-\lambda T} - e^{-gT})}{n(1 - e^{-gT})}$$

$$= 1 - \frac{g\,(e^{nT} - 1)}{n\,(e^{gT} - 1)}$$

Differentiating $(1 - \alpha)$ logarithmically with respect to T, one finds

$$\frac{\partial \alpha}{\partial T} = (1 - \alpha)\left[\frac{g}{1 - e^{-gT}} - \frac{n}{1 - e^{-nT}}\right]$$

$$= (1 - \alpha)\left[\left(\int_0^T e^{-gt}dt\right)^{-1} - \left(\int_0^T e^{-nt}dt\right)^{-1}\right] > 0 \text{ for } g > n$$

This completes the derivation of assertion (2) of Section 5.3.3-A.

3. The range of the saving/income ratio.   By definition, $s \leq 1$. Should $s = 1$, $T = -\ln(1 - n - \lambda)/(n + \lambda)$. On the other hand, s must be greater than or equal to $n + \lambda$. Otherwise, from (5.3.11), T is undefined. For $s = n + \lambda$, according to (5.3.11), $T = -\ln 0 = \infty$. The economic meaning is that the warranted rate, $s/a = s/1 = s$, must not be less than the natural rate. Otherwise, part of the labor force rather than obsolete vintages of capital goods would be unemployed. This proves assertion (3).

4. Constant interest and rising wage.   The fact that wage increases according to the formula $e^{\lambda(t - T)}$ has been proved above. On the other hand, the condition for capital-market clearance is

$$\int_v^{v + T} [1 - w(t)]\exp\left\{-\int_v^t r(u)\,du\right\}dt = 1$$

$$= \int_0^T (1 - e^{\lambda(t - T)})\exp\left\{-\int_0^t r(v + u)\,du\right\}dt$$

(The final expression results from changing the variable of integration.)

Certainly this functional equation for $r(\cdot)$ admits a constant solution $r(t) = \bar{r}$ for all t. $\bar{r}$ is the internal rate of return for such an investment. The proof that the interest rate must be constant is too complicated to be shown here.

5. Equipment life rises with interest rate.   This is a case where definite results can be obtained under the clay–clay model but not under the putty–clay model. Rewriting the formula in 4 with constant r, we obtain

$$0 = \int_0^T [1 - e^{-\lambda(T - t)}]e^{-rt}\,dt - 1 = H, \text{ say}$$

Total differentiation of H yields

$$0 = \frac{\partial H}{\partial T} dT + \frac{\partial H}{\partial r} dr$$

$$= 0 + \left\{ \lambda \int_0^T [e^{-\lambda(T-t)}]e^{-rt} dt \right\} dT - \left\{ \int_0^T [1 - e^{-\lambda(T-t)}]te^{-rt} dt \right\} dr$$

Since both bracketed expressions are positive, $dT/dr > 0$. This proves assertion (5).

As we noted in the last section, one cannot obtain such a conclusion in the putty–clay model (Kemp and Thanh noted that for the Cobb-Douglas case, in fact, $\partial T/\partial r < 0$).

The interpretation of this paradoxical result is as follows. The Austrian model (or for that matter, the Wicksell model) deals with the point-input, point-output type of investment. Only under a low interest rate can entrepreneurs afford a more roundabout process (capital deepening). Here we face a point-input, flow-output model, where entrepreneurs will abandon their equipment quickly (capital quickening) in order to shift the labor force to equipment of newer vintages only under low interest (and given the technology, a high wage rate along the factor price frontier).

6. Asymptotic behavior. The derivation of the asymptotic behavior of the system is too intricate to be reported here. However, some heuristic analogy may help. In Chapter 2, Figure 2.5, we note that if the ratio n/s is larger than $1/a$ there is unemployment and no equilibrium, if n/s is smaller than $1/a$ there is a stable equilibrium with excess capacity, and if n/s is equal to $1/a$ both capital and labor will be completely employed. Here, the population growth rate n should be substituted by the growth rate of efficiency labor $n + \lambda$, and the unit capital requirement has been normalized to unity. Hence, for $(n + \lambda)/s > 1$ or $(n + \lambda) > s$, no equilibrium will be approached and a chronic surplus-labor regime will persist. Conversely, if $(n + \lambda)/s < 1$ or $(n + \lambda) < s$, excess capacity takes the form of finite equipment life as well as the abandoning of obsolete equipment. In fact, there is a stable equilibrium path. The knife-edge case of $(n + \lambda)/s = 1$ or $n + \lambda = s$ implies that all capital goods will be in operation forever and all labor force will be employed. In some sense, the disaggregation by vintages only under low interest (and given the technology, a high wage rate along the factor price frontier).

5.3.4. Other results

Solow et al. also considered some other aspects of the model, such as:

(1) The social rate of return. By reducing the consumption flow now, a society can increase investment and hence increase its future consumption flow. The measure of the productivity of such investment is called the *social rate of*

return. It is found that under competitive conditions the rate of interest is equal to the social rate of return.

(2) The competitive valuation of old equipment. It is found that the value of a piece of used equipment is the discounted stream of its future quasi-rent flow. The rate of depreciation of such valuation measures the excess of the current quasi-rent above the product of the interest rate and the current valuation of the equipment.

5.3.5. Concluding comments

The clay–clay model offers us certain definite results unattainable in a more general version of the putty–clay model. Moreover, it also focuses attention on the boundary conditions when labor outgrows the capacity to accumulate in an economy. There is no reason that a general putty–clay model cannot handle such eventualities by postulating ridge lines for the aggregate isoquant map. However, matters are much clearer in a clay–clay model.

The comparison with the "Harrod-Domar special case" in Section 5.2 is very illuminating. Harrod and Domar regard labor shortage or equipment scrapping as possible signals for recession or even depression. The clay–clay model shows, however, that "normal" layoff of obsolete equipment is a healthy sign for a competitive economy endowed with technical progress. It is the *lack of foresight* which may cause economic crises and depression. Short of a complete model incorporating expectations and business confidence, one can hardly explain how Harrod-Domar difficulties can emerge.

APPENDIX 5.1

The derivation of results in Section 5.2.3-B

From (5.2.2), $\hat{s} = \hat{K}(t, t) - \hat{Q} = 0$, in view of (5.2.7). This proves (1a). Since $\hat{K}(t, t) > \hat{L}(t, t)$, capital/labor ratio in natural units is rising for newly built machines. Even without technical progress, output per worker rises with capital deepening. The *progress* of technology can reinforce but can never offset such a trend. From Figure 5.9, only older vintages may be laid aside, proving (1b). From (5.2.5) and assuming that some older vintages are not in use, we have

$$L_0 e^{nt} = \int_{t-T(t)}^{t} L(v, t)\, dv$$

$$= \int_{t-T(t)}^{t} L(v, v)\, dv$$

(Since $0 < L(v, t) < L(v, v)$ for at most one value of v, the value of the integral is unaffected.)
Taking time derivatives of both sides,

$$\dot{L} = (nL_0)e^{nt}$$

$$= L(t, t) - L[t - T(t), t - T(t)] [1 - T'(t)]$$

$$= [nL(0, 0)]\{1 - e^{t - T(t)}[1 - T'(t)]\}e^{nt} \qquad \text{(from (5.2.7))}$$

This equality can hold either when $T'(t) = 1$ or when $T'(t) = 0$. The first possibility leads to a contradiction; if $T(0) = x > 0$, vintage $-(x+1)$ machines must have a negative life span, -1. Therefore, T is constant, proving (1d). But then vintage v machines will be in use only for $t - T < v \leq t$, i.e., over the period $v \leq t < v + T$, ruling out reinstatement. This proves (1c).

Equation (5.2.7) implies that $(Q/Le^{\lambda t})$ is constant. By definition this means $f(k^0)$ is constant and hence k^0 is constant, proving (2a). At the end of equipment life, zero quasi-rent implies that

$$f(k^0)e^{\lambda v} = w(v + T) \qquad \text{(in view of Fig. 5.4)}$$

or

$$w(t) = f(k^0)e^{\lambda(t - T)}$$

proving the first part of (2b).

Equation (5.2.3) can now be written as

$$\int_v^{v+T} \{f[k^0(v)] - w(0)e^{\lambda(t-v)}\} \exp\left[-\int_v^t r(\tau)\,d\tau\right] dt/k^0(v)$$

$$\geq \text{Max}_{k_0} \text{Max}_{T_1} \left[\int_v^{v+T_1} \{f(k^0) - w(0)e^{\lambda(t-v)}\} \exp\left[-\int_v^t r(\tau)\,d\tau\right] dt/k^0\right]$$

Therefore,

$$\int_v^{v+T} \{f[k^0(v)] - w(0)e^{\lambda(t-v)}\} \exp\left[-\int_v^t r(\tau)\,d\tau\right] dt/k^0(v)$$

$$\geq \text{Max}_{k^0} \left[\int_v^{v+T} \{f(k^0) - w(0)e^{\lambda(t-v)}\} \exp\left[-\int_v^t r(\tau)\,d\tau\right] dt/k^0\right]$$

$$= \text{Max}_{k^0} g(k^0)$$

where $g(k^0)$ depends only on k^0. Hence,

$$g'[k^0(v)] = 0$$

$$= \frac{d \ln g[k^0(v)]}{dk^0}$$

Using the fact that $g[k^0(v)] = 1$, we have, for all v,

$$f'[k^0(v)] \int_v^{v+T} \exp\left[-\int_v^t r(\tau)\,d\tau\right] dt = 1$$

Therefore,

$$g[k^0(v)] = \left\{\frac{f[k^0(v)]}{f'[k^0(v)]} - w(0) \int_v^{v+T} \exp\left[\int_v^t [\lambda - r(\tau)]d\tau\right]\right\}/k^0(v)$$

$$= 1$$

Now differentiating the condition

$$\int_v^{v+T} \{f[k^0(v)] - w(0)e^{\lambda(t-v)}\} \exp\left[-\int_v^t r(\tau)\,d\tau\right] dt = k^0(v)$$

with respect to v, we obtain

$$-\{f[k^0(v)] - w(0)\} + \lambda\left\{f[k^0(v)] \int_v^{v+T} \exp\left[-\int_v^t r(\tau)\,d\tau\right] dt - k^0(v)\right\} + r(v)k^0(v) = 0$$

or

$$r(v) = \frac{f[k^0(v)] - w(0)}{k^0(v)} + \lambda \left\{ 1 - \frac{d \ln k^0}{d \ln f(k^0)} \right\} \qquad \text{for all } v$$

This proves the second part of (2b).

In (5.2.8), the left-hand side is obviously the maximal "gross" growth rate for "capital." However, if the new investment grows at the rate $n + \lambda$, the vintage being retired will bear the proportion $e^{-(n+\lambda)T} : 1$ to the new investment. The "net" growth rate of "capital" is $[sf(k^0)/k^0] [1 - e^{-(n+\lambda)T}]$, which should not be less than the growth rate of "effective labor," $n + \lambda$, if full employment is to be maintained. Note that "capital" here measures the number of machines to be manned. This proves (3).

REFERENCES

[1] Robinson, Joan, "The Classification of Inventions," *Review of Economic Studies*, vol. V, Feb. 1938, pp. 138–42.

[2] Solow, R. M., "Investment and Technical Progress," in *Mathematical Methods in the Social Sciences, 1959*, K. J. Arrow, S. Karlin, and P. Suppes, Eds., Stanford University Press, Stanford, Calif., 1960.

[3] Johansen, Leif, "Substitution vs. Fixed Production Coefficients in the Theory of Economic Growth: A Synthesis," *Econometrica*, vol. 27, April 1959, pp. 157–75.

[4] Solow, R. M., "Technical Change and the Aggregate Production Function," *Review of Economics and Statistics*, vol. XXXIX, Aug. 1957, pp. 312–20.

[5] Phelps, Edmund S., "The New View of Investment: A Neoclassical Analysis," *Quarterly Journal of Economics*, vol. LXXVI, Nov. 1962, pp. 548–67.

[6] Matthews, R. C. O., "The New View of Investment: Comment," *Quarterly Journal of Economics*, vol. LXXVIII, Feb. 1964, pp. 164–76.

[6] Fisher, F. M., "Embodied Technical Change and the Existence of an Aggregate Capital Stock," *Review of Economic Studies*, vol. XXXII, Oct. 1965, pp. 263–88.

[8] Jorgenson, Dale, "The Embodiment Hypothesis," *Journal of Political Economy*, vol. LXXIV, Feb. 1966, pp. 1–17.

[9] Salter, W. E. G., *Productivity and Technical Change*, Cambridge University Press, Cambridge, 1960.

[10] Solow, R. M., "Substitution and Fixed Proportions in the Theory of Capital," *Review of Economic Studies*, vol. XXIX, June 1962, pp. 207–18.

[11] Solow, R. M., "Technical Progress, Capital Formation and Economic Growth," *American Economic Review*, Papers and Proceedings, vol. LII, May 1962, pp. 76–86.

[12] Solow, R. M., "Heterogeneous Capital and Smooth Production Functions: An Experimental Study," *Econometrica*, vol. XXXI, Oct. 1963, pp. 623–45.

[13] Phelps, Edmund S., "Substitution, Fixed Proportions, Growth and Distribution," *International Economic Review*, vol. 4, Sept. 1963, pp. 265–88.

[14] Kurz, Mordecai, "Substitution vs. Fixed Production Coefficients: A Comment," *Econometrica*, vol. XXXI, Jan.–April 1963, pp. 209–17.

[15] Kemp, M. C., and P. C. Thanh, "On a Class of Growth Models," *Econometrica*, vol. XXXIV, April 1966, pp. 257–82.

[16] Solow, R. M., James Tobin, C. C. von Weizsäcker, and M. Yarri, "Neoclassical Growth with Fixed Proportions," *Review of Economic Studies*, vol. XXXIII, April 1966, pp. 79–116.

[17] Bliss, Christopher, "On Putty–Clay," *Review of Economic Studies*, vol. XXXV, April 1968, pp. 105–32.

[18] Strotz, Robert, "Myopia and Inconsistency in Dynamic Utility Maximization," *Review of Economic Studies*, vol. XXIII, 1956, pp. 165–80.

[19] Goldman, Steven, "Optimal Growth and Continuous Plan Revisions," *Review of Economic Studies*, vol. XXXV, April 1968, pp. 145–54.

[20] Britto, R., "On Putty–Clay: A Comment," *Review of Economic Studies*, vol. XXXVI, July 1969, pp. 395–98.

[21] Bergström, A. R., "A Model of Technical Progress, The Production Function and Cyclical Growth," *Economica*, vol. N.S. 29, Nov. 1962, pp. 357–70.

[22] Akerlof, George A., "Stability, Marginal Products, Putty and Clay," in *Essays on the Theory of Optimal Economic Growth*, K. Shell, Ed., M.I.T. Press, Cambridge, Mass., 1967.

[23] Akerlof, George A., and W. D. Nordhaus, "Balanced Growth—A Razor's Edge?,"

International Economic Review, vol. 8, Oct. 1967, pp. 343–48.

[24] Solow, Robert M., and Joseph E. Stiglitz, "Output, Employment and Wages in the Short-Run," *Quarterly Journal of Economics*, vol. LXXXII, Nov. 1968, pp. 537–60.

EXERCISES

5.1. In a centrally planned economy, the production technique is of the putty–putty type, representable by a Cobb-Douglas production function. The population growth rate is 2%, and the labor-augmenting technical progress rate is 3%. The labor coefficient, LF_L/Q, is equal to 0.75. The planning bureau sets a *constant* output growth rate at 8%. It is stated that whenever necessary, saving will be stepped up to fulfill this policy goal. Analyze the feasibility of such a program. *Hint:* Rewrite the decomposition formula in Section 5.3.2-D as

$$\hat{Q} = \frac{LF_L}{Q} \hat{L} = sF_K$$

where L is measured in efficiency units. If the target is realized, Q/L increases exponentially and F_K falls toward zero. On the other hand, $s \leq 1$.

5.2. It was observed that both the wage rate and the output per worker have been higher in America than in England for a century or more. Moreover, early observers noted that American craftsmen wore out their machinery much faster than their British counterparts. Many explanations exist. However, if we assume that both countries enjoyed golden age growth and shared the same clay–clay technology at all times, we may explain all the observed differences on the strength of a single premise—the Puritan ethic makes New Englanders more parsimonious than the English. Discuss.

6

Extensions of the neoclassical models: saving behavior

The growth models discussed in Chapters 1 through 5 share a common feature: Aggregate saving is postulated as a constant fraction of aggregate income either for the whole economy or for each factor share. This feature of the Keynesian or Kaleckian saving functions may be justifiable on the grounds of both convenience and realism. It is not only one of the simplest possible formulations, statistically estimable with commonly available data, but it may be argued that real-life firms and households operate according to simple decision rules. Saving a constant portion out of each dollar earned is a plausible rule.

Over the years, attempts have been made either to modify the saving function into some equally simple but presumably more plausible formulas or to offer some entirely different alternative theories of saving.[1] Back in the early post-Keynesian era, such studies as those of Dusenberry, Friedman, Modigliani and Brumberg, and others appeared in the "static" macroeconomic field. The subsequent developments in growth theory parallel these early works. In the present chapter, we shall consider three types of extensions of the neoclassical models. The work of Cass and Yaari substitutes a life cycle theory of saving for the saving function. After all, if profit maximization considerations are assumed to guide entrepreneurial decisions in the choice of techniques, utility maximization motives may also regulate the saving behavior of households.[2] The approach of Pasinetti is motivated by the query: If a person receives both wage and rental incomes, why should he behave schizophrenically by saving different fractions out of different sources of income? Saving propensity should be identified with the "class" orientation of the income recipient rather than with

[1] Even these extensions and modifications still subscribe to the view that saving determines the (value of) investment. The causal indeterminacy problems arising in Sections 4.3, 4.4, and 5.2 throw doubt on this general approach. We shall not pursue it here.

[2] An "eclectic" model like Solow's may nevertheless be more realistic. Well-staffed large corporations may select techniques along "marginalist" approaches, whereas individual households have neither the information nor the capacity to decide levels of current saving by maximizing lifetime utility.

the source of income. The study of Shell, Sidrauski, and Stiglitz questions the definition of income. Capital gain, in their view, is as much a part of personal income as factor rewards. A modified saving function, therefore, should include capital revaluation gain in its argument.

In the ensuing sections, we shall consider these three types of theories in turn.

6.1 SAVING BY AGE GROUPS: CASS AND YAARI

6.1.1. Introduction

The post-Keynesian trend of macroeconomics is a step-by-step reconciliation with the much older micro theory. The Keynesian and Kaleckian saving functions are "empirical laws" between macroaggregates. Not until 1954 did Modigliani and Brumberg [1] make the first attempt to derive the macro saving behavior from micro household decisions. The 1956 paper of Solow explicitly introduced the production function into macroeconomics. Nonetheless, the Keynesian saving function was retained as a Harrod-Domar vestige. This approach served Solow's purpose well for two reasons. On the one hand, the Keynesian saving function is simpler and possibly more satisfactory than the Modigliani-Brumberg theory. The latter leaves out the important element of corporate saving. On the other hand, Solow proved unambiguously that the input-nonsubstitution assumption alone is responsible for the Harrod-Domar tightrope view. This was done by keeping all the other Harrod-Domar hypotheses intact.[3] The attempt by Cass and Yaari [2] to fuse the Modigliani-Brumberg saving theory into the Solovian growth theory is the logical final step to bringing the growth theory completely back to the micro fold.

As one would expect, the Cass-Yaari model involves mathematical analysis of considerable complexity. The end results can be divided into two groups:

(1) The "positive" aspects. Cass and Yaari covered the following features:

  (a) The individuals and the society: how the life-cycle saving patterns fit into the economy-wide growth trend.

  (b) Assets and savings: individuals save in order to acquire assets. Saving is the rate of change for assets, just as investment is the rate of change for the stock of capital. Hence, a basic equality between desired assets and existing capital underlies the Cass-Yaari model.

  (c) The role of perfect foresight. In the simple Solow model, "perfect" foresight is assumed to ensure that *ex ante* saving equals *ex ante* investment. But this does not necessarily imply detailed knowledge of future price patterns. Every individual in the Cass-Yaari model must possess that sort of foresight to plan correctly for the whole lifetime. This is altogether a much stronger hypothesis.

---

[3]Without explicitly going into micro decisions of households, Solow also sketched the possibility of the saving/income ratio being dependent upon the capital/labor ratio.

(d) The existence and uniqueness of balanced growth paths. Unlike the simple Solow model where the saving per capita is a constant fraction of the output per capita, more elaborate analysis is needed for the existence and uniqueness problems of the balanced growth paths.

(2) The "normative" aspects. These concern the "efficiency" of a competitive equilibrium path.[4] It can be shown that the existence of money and debt can move an economy from an inefficient path to an efficient path. Here, the Cass-Yaari study follows the footsteps of Samuelson and Diamond. We shall postpone such matters until a later chapter.

We shall first examine in Section 6.1.2 the assumptions of a simplified Cass-Yaari model. From these assumptions we shall graphically synthesize a model in Section 6.1.3. As a by-product of such a synthesis, points (1a)–(c) will be discussed in detail. A mathematical derivation of such a synthesis is relegated to Appendix 6.1. In Section 6.1.4, we examine various properties of the balanced growth paths. Some final comments are made in Section 6.1.5.

6.1.2. Assumptions

The Cass-Yaari model is based partially upon certain "conventional" assumptions that are identical with those in the simple Solow model:
(1) A universal output is produced with homogeneous capital and labor inputs under constant returns, constant technology, and competitive institutions.
(2) All individuals have perfect foresight. In the present context, asset holdings match existing capital and planned saving equals actual investment.
(3) Capital goods are nondepreciable and perfectly malleable.

In addition, there are three special assumptions:
(1) The labor force consists of a continuum of overlapping generations each with a unit length lifetime. The size of generations increases at a constant exponential rate.
(2) Each individual supplies a unit flow of labor throughout his lifetime.
(3) The discounted lifetime wage stream is spent to maximize each individual's own welfare. The discounting rate is identical with the marginal product of capital. There is no inheritance.

6.1.3. Formulation

There are two main features of the Cass-Yaari formulation. The first is the derivation of desired asset holdings at the micro level. The desired asset holdings at instant t by an individual are shown to depend on only two parameters: the individual's date of birth v and his age $t - v$. Aggregating over all individuals of age $t - v$, we get the aggregate desired asset holdings for age group v. Aggre-

---

[4]"Efficiency" here follows the Phelps-Koopmans definition to be discussed in Chapter 9.

gating again over all age groups present at instant t, we obtain the aggregate desired asset holdings for the whole economy.

Second, the equality between desired asset holdings and capital stock plays the central role in the Cass-Yaari model. Taking the derivatives, this equation implies the familiar saving–investment equality. However, the saving–investment equation does not imply the equality between desired assets and capital stock.[5]

Before we proceed to these matters, we shall first consider the individual consumption path.

A. THE DERIVATION OF THE OPTIMAL INDIVIDUAL CONSUMPTION PATH

Given wage and interest paths $w(\cdot)$ and $r(\cdot)$, the assumption of a unit flow of labor per individual lifetime implies that each individual of generation v faces the problem

$$\text{Max } U[c_v(\cdot)] = \int_v^{v+1} \ln c_v(t)\, dt \tag{6.1.1}$$

subject to the budgetary condition

$$\int_v^{v+1} c_v(t)P_v(t)\, dt = \int_v^{v+1} w(t)P_v(t)\, dt \tag{6.1.2}$$

where $c_v(\cdot)$ is the consumption path for an individual generation v

$U[\cdot]$ is a utility indicator defined over all feasible consumption paths

$P_v(t)$ is the discounting factor, $\exp\left[-\int_v^t r(\tau)\, d\tau\right]$

To attain simple results, we follow Cass and Yaari to assume that U takes the special form in (6.1.1), which implies a hyperbolic marginal utility curve.[6]

The left-hand and right-hand sides of (6.1.2) are, respectively, the present worth of the lifetime consumption and income streams. Equation (6.1.2) is the conventional budget constraint.

From micro theory, a rational consumer equates his marginal utilities per dollar for every object he buys; i.e.,

$$\frac{\text{Marginal utility of consumption good at } t}{\text{Unit discount value of consumption good at } t} = \frac{\dfrac{d}{dc_v(t)} \ln c_v(t)}{P_v(t)}$$

$$= \frac{1}{c_v(t)P_v(t)} = \gamma > 0$$

where γ is a constant.

[5]Suppose the initial stock of capital falls short of the initial desired levels of asset holdings. Then the equality between investment and saving from that instant on to eternity would only imply a persistent constant gap between the stock of capital and desired assets. Since saving is the derivative of asset holdings and investment is the derivative of capital stock, elementary calculus shows that even if the derivatives of two functions are equal, one may differ from the other by a constant.

[6]Marginal utility at any instant is $d \ln c_v/dc_v = 1/c_v$, which is a rectangular hyperbola.

This means that *the discounted consumption expenditure should be constant at all times*. This remarkable result comes from the special form of (6.1.1).

Substituting this result into the left-hand side of (6.1.2) and integrating, we have

$$\frac{1}{\gamma} = \int_v^{v+1} w(t)P_v(t)\,dt$$

Hence, after substituting back into the equation, $1/c_vP_v = \gamma$,

$$c_v(t) = \frac{1}{\gamma}\left[\frac{1}{P_v(t)}\right] \tag{6.1.3}$$

$$= \left[\int_v^{v+1} w(\tau)P_v(\tau)\,d\tau\right]\exp\left[\int_v^t r(u)\,du\right]$$

Equation (6.1.3) provides the following observations:
(1) The consumption stream rises at a rate equal to the interest rate.
(2) When lifetime income increases by a constant factor, consumption at any given point rises by the same factor. (This is Friedman's homogeneity postulate [3].)
(3) As long as the total present worth of wage income remains the same, variations in the time distribution of wage income will never affect the time pattern for consumption.

B. THE DERIVATION OF THE DESIRED ASSET HOLDINGS

The derivation of average per capita desired asset holdings is rather intricate. We shall outline the general procedure, followed by graphic depictions. An algebraic summary tying in the various steps is provided in Appendix 6.1.

To begin with, for given $w(\cdot)$ and $r(\cdot)$, the discounted wage income stream and discounted expenditure stream are, respectively,

$$w(t)P_v(t) \quad \text{and} \quad c_v(t)P_v(t) \equiv \int_v^{v+1} w(t)P_v(t)\,dt$$

These are "initial valuations" for wage and expenditure, evaluated at v, the instant when generation v first joined the economy. The difference is saving (or dis-saving) at initial valuation. Cumulating such a difference, one obtains the initial valuation of desired asset holdings. This can be calculated for an individual of generation v at instant t. However, to calculate the desired asset holdings for the whole economy at t, we must convert the initial valuations (evaluated at v) to current valuations (evaluated at t) by multiplying by $1/P_v(t)$. We then calculate the size of generation v for each surviving generation v. These values serve as weights when we calculate:

Total desired asset holdings

$$= \int_v (\text{Current value, desired asset holdings of generation } v)$$

$$\times (\text{Size of generation } v)$$

Dividing this magnitude by the size of population, i.e., $\int_v$ (size of generation v), we obtain the average desired asset holdings.

In Figure 6.1, we assume for simplicity that w and r are stationary. Figure 6.1a summarizes the discounted wage stream, the discounted expenditure stream (which is constant), and their difference, the discounted rate of saving (dis-saving) stream. It turns out that the individual saves a diminishing amount until some instant before the midpoint of his lifespan. From then on, he dis-saves at an increasing rate until the end of his life. The solid curve in Figure 6.1b represents desired assets, initial valuation. This represents the cumulative area between the discounted wage and the discounted expenditure streams in Figure 6.1a, from v to t (if the wage stream is less than the expenditure stream, then the area is counted as negative). This curve starts at zero and ends at zero, showing the nonexistence of inheritance. It reaches its peak exactly when the wage curve crosses the expenditure curve in Figure 6.1a. The conversion into current valuation is reflected by the dotted line, which lies above the solid curve by an increasing factor. The peak of the dotted curve therefore appears some-what later than the peak of the solid curve.

Figure 6.1b depicts the desired asset holding for a generation-v individual at age $t - v$, i.e., at instant t. Since w and r are assumed constant, each generation shares the same desired asset holding pattern. Suppose an individual of generation v desires an asset holding of x dollars at age y; then any person of generation $v = t - y$ must also desire asset holdings of x dollars. At t, the youngest generation is generation t, and the oldest is $t - 1$, the life span being unity. By "flipping over" the dotted curve in Figure 6.1b from left to right, we obtain the dotted curve of Figure 6.1c, showing how much asset holding per person is desired by each surviving generation.

Figure 6.1d plots the size of each generation against the generation parameter v. The shaded area under this curve between $t - 1$ and t indicates the total population size. Multiplying the generation size in Figure 6.1d by the individual desired asset holdings in Figure 6.1c, one obtains the holdings-by-generation curve in Figure 6.1e.[7] The total shaded area under the curve from $t - 1$ to t is the economy-wide desired holdings. This divided by the population size yields the desired asset holdings per capita.

C. THE FUNDAMENTAL EQUATION: DESIRED ASSETS AND STOCK OF CAPITAL

The above tortuous exercise in national accounting leads to the following equation:

$$k(t) = \frac{ne^{-nt}}{1 - e^{-n}} \int_{t-1}^{t} e^{nv} \left\{ \int_v^t \left[w(\tau) \exp \int_\tau^t r(u)\, du \right] d\tau - (t-v) \left[c_v(t) \right] \right\} dv \qquad (6.1.4)$$

(from (6.1.3))

where $k(t)$ is the capital per capita, while the right-hand side can be shown to be the average desired asset holdings per capita. (See Appendix 6.1 for derivations.)

---

[7]For example, $\overline{ab}$ (in Figure 6.1c) times $\overline{\alpha\beta}$ (in Figure 6.1d) equals $\overline{AB}$ (in Figure 6.1e).

Discounted value   (a)

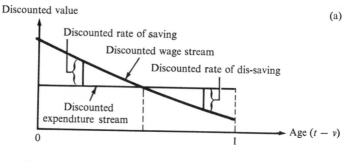

Discounted rate of saving

Discounted wage stream

Discounted rate of dis-saving

Discounted expenditure stream

0   1   Age $(t - v)$

Value   (b)

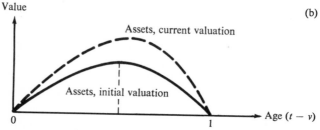

Assets, current valuation

Assets, initial valuation

0   1   Age $(t - v)$

Current valuation   (c)

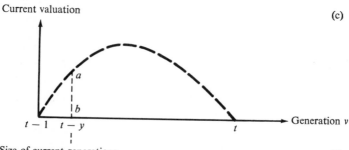

a

b

$t - 1$ $t - y$ t Generation v

Size of current generations   (d)

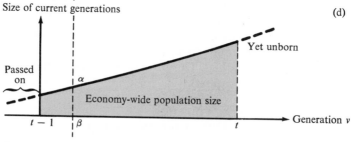

Yet unborn

Passed on

α

Economy-wide population size

$t - 1$ β t Generation v

Current valuation   (e)

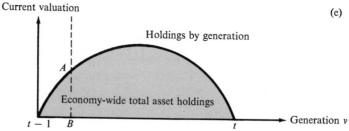

Holdings by generation

A

Economy-wide total asset holdings

$t - 1$ B t Generation v

The competitive market assumption in Section 6.1.2 implies that

$$r(t) = f'[k(t)]$$
$$w(t) = f[k(t)] - k(t)f'[k(t)]$$

(6.1.5)

Equations (6.1.4) and (6.1.5) yield a single fundamental functional equation involving one unknown function $k(\cdot)$ defined over the interval (half-line) $\{t | 0 \le t < \infty\}$ subject to the initial condition $k(0) = k_o$. This provides the basis for three types of studies:

(1) Numerically, one can explicitly solve for the $k(\cdot)$ path, once the form of f is known. $w(t)$, $r(t)$, and $c_v(t)$ can then be derived.
(2) Conceptually, one can compare such a model with the simple Solow model and note its similarities and dissimilarities.
(3) Experimentally, one may employ simplifying assumptions to explore the balanced growth behaviors of the model in certain selected examples.

The numerical approach is not pursued here. The comparison with the simple Solow model is examined below, leaving the balanced growth studies to Section 6.1.4.

D. COMPARISON WITH THE SIMPLE SOLOW MODEL

The Solow model is centered around the fundamental differential equation,

$$\dot{k} = sf(k) - nk$$

(2.1.4)

$$= f(k) - [(1-s)f(k)] - nk$$

where the [ ] term stands for per capita consumption. A close comparison with the Cass-Yaari model can be achieved by taking the time derivative of the fundamental equality (6.1.4).

Applying repeatedly the rule of differentiating an integral with both variable limits and integrand (see Appendix 6.1), we obtain

$$\dot{k}(t) = f[k(t)] - c(t) - nk(t)$$

(6.1.6)

where

$$c(t) = \int_{t-1}^{t} c_v(t) \left\{ \frac{ne^{-n(t-v)}}{1 - e^{-n}} \right\} dv$$

FIGURE 6.1

(a) Income and expenditure for an individual of generation v.
(b) Cumulate asset holding for the same person as in (a).
(c) Current-valuation holdings at t for individuals according to date of birth.
    (c) is (b) "flipped over."
(d) Size of population according to date of birth.
(e) Total current-valuation holdings according to date of birth.
    This figure represents the "product" of (c) and (d).

is the per capita consumption because $\{ne^{-n(t-v)}/(1-e^{-n})\}$ is the proportion of generation-v individuals in the total population and $c_v(t)$ is the per capita consumption of a generation-v individual (i.e., $c(t)$ is the weighted average of $c_v(t)$).

The close resemblance between (2.1.4) and (6.1.6) is remarkable. However, there are two subtle yet basic differences:

(1) The simple Solow model is adequately summarized by (2.1.4), while the Cass-Yaari model is not entirely reflected in (6.1.6). As we noted before, equality between investment flow and desired saving flow does not imply equality between capital stock and desired stock of asset holdings.

(2) The term $(1-s)f(k)$ in Solow's model depends only upon the current value of k. The term $c(t)$ in the Cass-Yaari model is a weighted average of $c_v(t)$ for all v between $t-1$ and t. $c_v(t)$, in turn, depends upon $w(\tau)$ and $r(\tau)$, for all τ between v and $v+1$, while $w(\tau)$ and $r(\tau)$ are dependent upon $k(\tau)$. Hence, $c(t)$ is a *functional* of that segment of the k path between $t-1$ and $t+1$.[8] The ubiquitous role of the perfect foresight assumption in the Cass-Yaari model is again obvious here.

6.1.4. Balanced growth paths

First we shall consider the necessary conditions for balanced growth. Its rate of change, $\dot{k}$, must be identically zero. From (6.1.6), the average per capita consumption c must also be constant. The first relation between the balanced growth values of k and c is thus

$$f(k^\infty) - nk^\infty = c^\infty$$

where the superscript denotes the balanced growth value.

By its definition, c is a weighted average of the age-group per capita consumption levels c_v. In (6.1.3), c_v depends upon wage and rent rates w and r, which are functions of the capital/labor ratio k. Hence, we have a second relation between c^∞ and k^∞, which we shall write as

$$c^\infty = G(k^\infty) \tag{6.1.7}$$

Combining the two relations, we obtain a single equation in terms of the balanced growth capital/labor ratio:

$$f(k^\infty) - G(k^\infty) = nk^\infty \tag{6.1.8}$$

Since $G(k^\infty)/f(k^\infty)$ is the propensity to consume, we can define

$$s^\infty = 1 - \frac{G(k^\infty)}{f(k^\infty)}$$

---

[8] Therefore, (6.1.6) is not a differential equation. Nor can it predict the future from the present state plus past history.

This allows us to rewrite (6.1.8) as

$$f(k^\infty) = (n/s^\infty)k^\infty$$
$$= H(k^\infty)k^\infty \qquad (6.1.8')$$

(where $H(k^\infty) = n/s^\infty$), which is similar to the case of variable s in the simple Solow model (cf. Section 2.3). This constitutes a necessary condition for balanced growth.

Next comes the sufficiency condition for balanced growth and the uniqueness problem for the solution of (6.1.8'). As in Chapter 2, we plot the two sides of (6.1.8') in the first quadrant of Figure 6.2 for an example with a Cobb-Douglas production function. The detailed derivation is contained in Appendix 6.1. It is seen that $H(k^\infty)k^\infty$ intersects the curve $f(k^\infty)$ at Q_1 and Q_2. However, the implication of multiple solutions for (6.1.8') is not the same as in a simple Solow model.

As has been shown by Cass and Yaari, the intersection of the $H(k^\infty)k^\infty$ and

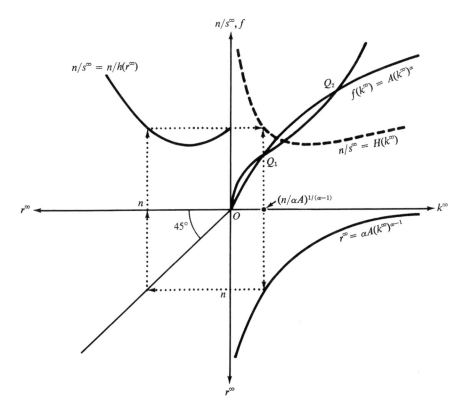

FIGURE 6.2

$f(k^\infty)$ curves is a necessary but insufficient condition for a balanced growth capital/labor ratio. The necessity is obvious. The insufficiency is again due to the fact that the equality between investment and saving in (6.1.8) (represented by Figure 6.2) does not imply the equality between desired asset holdings and stock of capital in (6.1.4). In fact, the intersection at $k^\infty = (n/\alpha A)^{1/(\alpha - 1)}$ can be proved not to be a balanced growth position.

Cass and Yaari also found that, in general, there may be more than one balanced growth path or there may not be any. However, the asymptotic behavior of the unbalanced growth paths is still largely unexplored at this date.

6.1.5. General remarks

The Cass-Yaari model represents a "limiting case" of the neoclassical growth theory. Not only does "marginalism" pervade every part of the model, the model also depicts in microeconomic detail how capital accumulation goes on in an economy where everybody is primarily a worker and no one bequeaths more than he inherits (in fact, inheritance is nil). This is in sharp contrast with Kalecki's position that capitalists play the key role in the evolution of the private enterprise society, since they *alone* save. The subscription to the Kaleckian view culminates in Mrs. Robinson's position that state centralism is most conducive to developing programs because the state can be more omnipotent and single-purposed than private capitalists in the role of "capital accumulator." The most eloquent formulation of such a "class" theory of growth is that of Pasinetti, which will be examined in the next section. Perhaps reality lies somewhere between these two positions, and an analysis of corporate saving behavior in the growth context should be an item high on the priority list.[9] The question of realism concerning the Cass-Yaari version of perfect foresight has already been discussed in Section 4.4.

The Cass-Yaari model also assumes away the intergenerational inter-dependence of utility, hence inheritance, of the type envisaged by Marglin [4], for instance. For a model including inheritance, one may refer to Meade [5].

From the technical point of view, Cass and Yaari asked much deeper questions on the thriftiness condition as compared to the simple Solow model. If two countries share the same population growth rate and technological know-how, why does one economy end up with a higher capital/output ratio than the other economy in the long run? The Solovian approach provides the simple reply: The first economy saves more. This would not be accepted as an answer in the Cass and Yaari case. In their model, differences in forms of household utility function or differences in wage–interest expectations pre-sumably are the ultimate causes. But an empirical study along those lines (e.g., a cross-country comparison) would also be a much more challenging (and less pragmatic) undertaking.

---

[9]For an empirical verification of the life-cycle hypothesis, see Tobin [15].

6.2 SAVING BY SOCIAL CLASSES: PASINETTI, SAMUELSON, AND MODIGLIANI

6.2.1. Introduction

The neoclassical growth model attributes the pattern of economic growth to three key elements: technology as characterized by the function $f(k)$, thriftiness as represented by the magnitude of s, and population growth as reflected by the value n. When the saving/income ratio varies according to income shares, the only modification one need introduce is to replace s with $(s_w\omega + s_r k)/(\omega + k)$, where s_w and s_r are saving ratios out of wage and rent shares and ω is the wage/rent ratio (cf. Section 4.2). But more fundamental modification is needed if saving ratios differ not according to sources of income but according to the "class" orientation of the income recipients. This forms the subject matter of the present section.

As shown in Chapter 3, both Mrs. Robinson and Kaldor pay much attention to the Kaleckian saving assumption, which was first discussed by Keynes in *The Economic Consequences of Peace*. It is believed that the neoclassical emphasis on the aggregate production function is neither realistic nor necessary. After criticizing all the drawbacks of the aggregate production function, the Modern Cambridge School entertains the hope that interesting issues such as the income distribution between workers and capitalists can be solved by concentrating on saving propensities.

Kaldor, in generalizing Kalecki, allowed workers as well as capitalists to save. Pasinetti [6] claimed that the resultant Kaldor model contains an oversight. He argued that if workers accumulate, they will receive interest form *their* own capital. Hence, part of the interest income belongs to the working class, whose saving/income ratio is lower than that of capitalists. It appears that Kaldor overestimated the saving volume. Table 6.1 compares the Kaldor and Pasinetti models. The difference between the two is seen to lie in the saving ratio applied to workers' rental income.

TABLE 6.1[a]

	Saving ratio applied to income	
Income, $Lf(k)$	Kaldor model	Pasinetti model
Rental income, $Kf'(k)$		
to capitalists, $K_c f'(k)$	High	High
to workers, $K_w f'(k)$	High	Low
Wage income, $Lf(k) - Kf'(k)$	Low	Low

[a]K_c and K_w are amounts of capital owned by capitalists and workers, respectively. $K_c + K_w = K$.

Kaldor ("comment" to Samuelson and Modigliani [7]) maintained that his model reflects the separation between corporate ownership and management in noncommunist economies. The size of retained earnings in corporations depends upon how much has been earned rather than on who (capitalists or workers) owns what proportion of the stock. In defense of Pasinetti, one can argue that heavy ploughing back of earnings leads to appreciation of corporate stocks. Worker-stockholders can consume their capital gains by selling some stocks. Hence, corporate management can hardly carry out a forced saving program against the will of the stockholders.[10] Only empirical studies of the workers' behavior can settle the issue.

Pasinetti's article led to his exchanges with Meade [8–10] as well as Kemp's generalization [11] where the saving/income ratio depends upon both the income source and the social class of the income recipient. Our discussion follows a paper by Samuelson and Modigliani [12]. Stiglitz [13] studied the same topic in a two-sector model.

In Section 6.2.2 we shall formulate a model depicting the evolution of capital ownership. Section 6.2.3 is devoted to the "duality theorem," where one of the two possible growth patterns will emerge. The asymptotic behavior of both systems will also be sketched.

6.2.2. Model formulation

Following Samuelson and Modigliani, we shall consider a modified simple Solow model. All assumptions in Section 2.1 except the last one (the sixth, concerning a constant saving/income ratio) are retained.

Let

s_w and s_c be the saving propensities of the "worker class" and the "capitalist class," respectively

$k_w = K_w/L$ be the workers' capital per worker

$k_c = K_c/L$ be the capitalists' capital divided by the number of workers

We tolerate the conceptual monstrosity of k_c because of its analytical convenience.

Starting from the results in Table 6.1, we tabulate in Table 6.2 the steps of operations that lead to the twin dynamic equations depicting the capitalistic evolutions in wealth distribution.

The twin dynamic equations

$$\dot{k}_c = [s_c f'(k) - n]k_c; \qquad \dot{k}_w = s_w[f(k) - k_c f'(k)] - nk_w \tag{6.2.1}$$

together with the accounting identity,

$$k = k_c + k_w \tag{6.2.2}$$

completely describe the system.

---

[10]In fact, in the next section we shall consider a model by Shell et al. that includes capital gain in calculating saving volume.

TABLE 6.2

	For capitalists	For workers
Income received	$K_c f'(k)$	$Lf(k) - K_c f'(k)$
×saving ratios = Rate of capital accumulation	$s_c K_c f'(k)$	$s_w[Lf(k) - K_c f'(k)] =$ $\qquad s_w L[f(k) - k_c f'(k)]$
÷ capital owned = Growth rate of capital owned	$\hat{K}_c = s_c f'(k)$	$\hat{K}_w = \dfrac{s_w[f(k) - k_c f'(k)]^a}{k_w}$
− growth rate of labor = Growth rate of capital owned per worker	$\hat{k}_c = s_c f'(k) - n$	$\hat{k}_w = \dfrac{s_w[f(k) - k_c f'(k)]}{k_w} - n$ [b]
× capital owned per worker = Rate of change of capital owned per worker	$\dot{k}_c$	$\dot{k}_w$

[a] Since $L/K_w = 1/k_w$.

[b] Growth rate of any quotient (e.g., $\hat{k}_i = (d \ln k_i)/dt$, $i = c, w$) is the growth rate of the numerator ($\hat{K}_i$) minus the growth rate of the denominator ($\hat{L} = n$).

We now ask what long-run wealth distributions will emerge when this model reaches its balanced growth state, namely:

$$\dot{k}_c = \dot{k}_w = 0 \tag{6.2.3}$$

$$k_c(t) = k_c^\infty \geq 0; \qquad k_w(t) = k_w^\infty \geq 0$$

We shall assume that both s_w and s_c are positive. Substituting (6.2.3) into (6.2.1) and dividing the two sides of the equations by s_c and s_w, respectively, we have

$$k_c^\infty f'(k^\infty) = \frac{n}{s_c} k_c^\infty \tag{6.2.4}$$

$$f(k^\infty) = k_c^\infty f'(k^\infty) + \frac{n}{s_w} k_w^\infty$$

$$= n\left(\frac{k_c^\infty}{s_c} + \frac{k_w^\infty}{s_w}\right)$$

This pair of innocent-looking equations contains deep and interesting implications.

6.2.3. The dual possibilities

It may be said that in Pasinetti's universe there are two types of possible worlds, each evolving toward its distinctive type of balanced growth path. These two balanced growth cases can be characterized as follows:

(1) The "Pasinetti case." There exist (pure) capitalists who provide no labor service: $k_c^\infty > 0$.

(2) The "dual case." There exist no pure capitalists. All capital owners are workers: $k_c^\infty = 0$.

We shall first discuss the analytical properties of each of these two types of balanced growth path. Next comes a graphic depiction of the situation, and finally criteria will be stated determining which balanced growth path will be approached in the long run.

A.   ANALYTICAL DESCRIPTIONS

1. The Pasinetti case.   We concentrate on (6.2.4). Dividing through the first equation by the positive quantity k_c^∞, we get $f'(k^\infty) = n/s_c$. It follows that:

(a) The capitalists' saving ratio s_c plays a dominant role. Since the first equation of (6.2.4) becomes

$$f'(k^\infty) = n/s_c$$

s_c (in conjunction with the population growth rate n) decides (i) the balanced capital/labor ratio k^∞, and consequently (ii) the rent rate $f'(k^\infty)$, (iii) the wage rate $f(k^\infty) - k^\infty f'(k^\infty)$, (iv) the output per worker $f(k^\infty)$, and (v) the capital/output ratio $k^\infty/f(k^\infty)$.

(b) The workers' saving ratio, s_w, apparently plays a limited role. Through the second equation in (6.2.4), s_w participates in the determination[11] of (i) workers' share in capital, k_w^∞/k^∞, and (ii) their share in income, $1 - [k_c^\infty f'(k^\infty)/f(k^\infty)]$. In fact, variations of s_w *within limits* would have no effect on items (i)–(v) in (a) above.

(c) The form of $f(\cdot)$ apparently has no effect on the rent rate n/s_c. These results lead to the twin conclusions of the Modern Cambridge School: (i) Capitalists' saving propensity alone plays the crucial role in growth. (ii) The precise technological profile $f(\cdot)$ does not affect the rent rate.

2. The dual case.   Since $k_c^\infty = 0$, two things happen. First, the first equation in (6.2.4) drops out, because it is now an identity: $0 \equiv 0$. Second, the overall capital/labor ratio is the same as workers' capital per worker, because $k^\infty = k_c^\infty + k_w^\infty = 0 + k_w^\infty$. The second equation in (6.2.4) becomes

$$f(k_w^\infty) = \frac{n}{s_w} k_w^\infty$$

Except that s_w plays the role of s, every economic magnitude is determined in the same way as in the simple Solow model of Chapter 2. Thus,

(a) The workers' saving ratio, s_w, determines all the important magnitudes in the economy.

---

[11]Specifically, (6.2.2) and the second equation of (6.2.4) form the simultaneous equation system, where k^∞ and $f(k^\infty)$ are already determined in the first equation of (6.2.4):

$$k_c^\infty \quad + \quad k_w^\infty \quad = k^\infty$$
$$(n/s_c)k_c^\infty + (n/s_w)k_w^\infty = f(k^\infty)$$

Therefore,

$$k_w^\infty = \frac{s_c s_w[f(k^\infty) - nk^\infty/s_c]}{n(s_c - s_w)}, \text{ and } k_c^\infty = \frac{s_c s_w[nk^\infty/s_w - f(k^\infty)]}{n(s_c - s_w)}$$

(b) The capitalists' saving ratio, s_c, plays no apparent role in the system. In fact, variations of s_c within limits would have no effect on the balanced growth path.

(c) The form of $f(\cdot)$ apparently has no effect on the output/capital ratio, n/s_w.

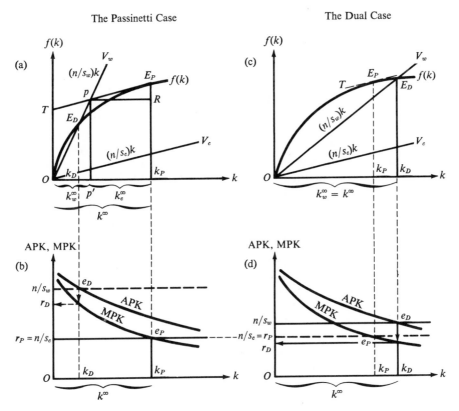

FIGURE 6.3

B. A GRAPHIC ANALYSIS

In Figure 6.3 we shall illustrate diagrammatically the above analysis and also clarify why, in the Pasinetti (dual) case, the effects of s_w (s_c) are only apparently limited (nil) and $f(\cdot)$ apparently has no effect on the rent rate (output/capital ratio), and what the limits of "inconsequential variations" for $s_w(s_r)$ are.

Figure 6.3 contains two types of diagrams: panels (a) and (c) depict the $f(k)$ curves, showing that the Pasinetti model can be an extension of the simple Solow model; panels (b) and (d) plot the average and marginal products of capital (APK and MPK in Samuelson and Modigliani's terms) against k, throwing further light on the dual nature of the two cases. As noted before, the $f(k)$ curve is the total product of capital (TPK) schedule in micro theory, labor input being held constant at the unit level.

To facilitate comparison, the Pasinetti case in Figure 6.3a and b and the dual case in Figure 6.3c and d are illustrated with the same f-function, the same n, and the same s_c. Only s_w (the supposedly "dormant" parameter in the modern Cambridge theories) is assumed to take different values in the two cases.

1. The Pasinetti Case. In Figure 6.3a, the balanced growth capital/labor ratio k_P corresponds to the point E_P, where the slope of the $f(k)$ curve is parallel to the OV_c ray, i.e., the line $(n/s_c)k$. This implies

$$f'(k) = n/s_c$$

satisfying the first equation of (6.2.4).

Construct the tangent line TE_P to $f(k)$ at E_p, cutting the OV_w ray, i.e., the line $(n/s_w)k$, at p. We shall show that the pp' line partitions the Ok_p interval into the ratio $k_w^\infty : k_c^\infty$. In other words, $k_w^\infty = \overline{Op'}$ and $k_c^\infty = \overline{p'k_P}$ satisfy (6.2.4). We first note that $f(k_p) = \overline{E_Pk_P} = \overline{E_PR} + \overline{Rk_P} = \overline{E_PR} + \overline{pp'}$. Now $\overline{E_PR} = \overline{pR}f'(k_P) = \overline{p'k_P}(n/s_c)$ and $\overline{pp'} = \overline{Op'}(n/s_w)$. Therefore, $f(k) = k_c^\infty(n/s_c) + k_w^\infty(n/s_w)$, as required in the second equation of (6.2.4).

2. The dual case. In Figure 6.3c, the OV_w ray, with the formula $(n/s_w)k$, cuts the $f(k)$ curve at E_D. As in the Solow model, all the interesting economic magnitudes, such as the capital/labor ratio k, the output/labor ratio $f(k)$, the output/capital ratio $f(k)/k$, the interest rate $f'(k)$, and the wage rate $f(k) - kf'(k)$, can be readily read from the diagram.

To determine under which circumstances each case will apply, one has to refer to the technology f, the population growth rate n, and the savings ratios of both capitalists and workers. This is why we said before that s_w is only *apparently* irrelevant in the Pasinetti case, s_c is only *apparently* irrelevant in the dual case and $f(\cdot)$ is only *apparently* irrelevant in the determination of rent rate or output/capital ratio for these two cases, respectively.

Consider the Pasinetti case in Figure 6.3a first. If s_w is somewhat larger than it used to be, OV_w must have a flatter slope. The value of k_w^∞ will increase at the expense of k_c^∞, leaving $k^\infty = k_w^\infty + k_c^\infty$ unchanged. But should s_w be so large that OV_w becomes flat enough to pass through E_P or to its right, then k_c^∞ becomes zero and we pass under the dual case.

Next, we can consider the dual case in Figure 6.3c. The OV_c curve is such that its parallel line TE_P is tangential to $f(k)$ at point E_P. This implies that for capitalists' capital to grow at the same rate as population (as in the Pasinetti case), the capital/labor ratio must be as low as k_P and the interest rate as high as n/s_c. At E_D the interest rate is not adequate to support such a growth rate for K_c. On the other hand, if s_c is larger than we have assumed, the OV_c ray will be flatter and the required interest for constant k_c (i.e., for $\hat{K}_c = n$) is hence smaller. Once s_c is large enough, n/s_c will be less than $f'(k_D)$ and the dotted tangent line for $f(k)$ will contact $f(k)$ to the right of E_D. This will prevent the economy from operating according to the dual case, and we are back under the Pasinetti case.

All these imply that the dormant saving ratio (s_w for the Pasinetti case and s_c for the dual case) must be within a certain range to allow the alternative saving ratio to decide the pattern for balanced growth.

C. CRITERIA FOR DETERMINING WHICH CASE PREVAILS

To gain further insight into the matter, we first observe that in Figures 6.3*a* and *c* there exist two alternative equilibria, E_P and E_D. In the Pasinetti case (Figure 6.3*a*), E_P is operative and E_D is dormant. In the dual case (Figure 6.3*c*), E_D is operative and E_P is dormant. To study the criteria for determining which equilibrium is operative, we shift to Figures 6.3*b* and *d*. We find that three sets of equivalent criteria are available.

To begin with, let $A(k) = f(k)/k$, the average product of capital. A^{-1} is its inverse function, assigning to each level of average product of capital the corresponding capital/labor ratio. Similarly, since $f'(k)$ is the marginal product of capital, its inverse, f'^{-1}, assigns the corresponding capital/labor ratio to each level of marginal product of capital. The magnitudes of n/s_c and n/s_w are shown as horizontal lines in Figures 6.3*b* and *d*. In the Pasinetti case, the MPK curve cuts n/s_c; hence, $k_P = f'^{-1}(n/s_c)$; in the dual case, the APK curve cuts n/s_w; hence, $k_D = A^{-1}(n/s_w)$. Defining r_P and r_D as the rent rate under the Pasinetti and dual cases, respectively, e_P and e_D are the equilibria under the two cases. From Figures 6.3*b* and *d*, we can illustrate the criteria as in Table 6.3.

TABLE 6.3

	Pasinetti regime (at e_P)	Dual regime (at e_D)	Criteria
I. Interest criterion	$r_P = n/s_c$	$r_D = f'[A^{-1}(n/s_w)]$	$r^\infty = \text{Min}\,[r_P, r_D]$
II. Capital/labor ratio criterion	$k_P = f'^{-1}(n/s_c)$	$k_D = A^{-1}(n/s_w)$	$k^\infty = \text{Max}\,[k_P, k_D]$
III. Ratio between saving propensities (a) Preliminary inequalities	$n/s_w > f(k^\infty)/k^\infty$ $f' = n/s_c$	$f(k^\infty)/k^\infty = n/s_w$ $n/s_c \geq f'$	
(b) Derived inequalities	$s_w/s_c < kf'/f$	$s_w/s_c \geq kf'/f$	$\dfrac{s_w}{s_c} < \dfrac{kf'}{f} \Rightarrow e_P$ $\dfrac{s_w}{s_c} \geq \dfrac{kf'}{f} \Rightarrow e_D$

The first two criteria state that the invisible hand selects the alternative regime that provides the higher capital/labor ratio and the lower rent rate. The third criterion compares the ratio of workers' saving propensity to that of the capitalists against the rent share of income. The Pasinetti case emerges if and only if the former is strictly smaller than the latter. The last result appears to be independent of the population growth rate n. But this is not the case. n enters the determination of k^∞ in either case.

6.2.4. The asymptotic properties, etc.

We shall report without proof the findings of Samuelson and Modigliani:
(1) The balanced growth paths of (k_c, k_w) in both the Pasinetti and the dual

cases are locally stable. Any small displacement from balanced growth will lead to an asymptotic return to the original path.

(2) The balanced growth path of (K_c, K_w, L), on the other hand, need not be locally stable. A displacement may lead to a divergence from the balanced growth path that increases over time in absolute terms. The rate of increase of such a divergence must be less than the population growth rate. Hence, as point (1) above stated, on a per capita basis, local stability exists.

The Kalecki and Pasinetti assumptions are generalizations of the Keynesian saving function. The history of the Pasinetti assumption is beclouded by two misconceptions.

(a) The Pasinetti assumption seems to provide a short cut to determine the interest rate from the macroeconomic parameters n and s_c. Neither the question-begging aggregate production function reflected by $f(\cdot)$ nor the workers' saving ratio s_w seems to be relevant.

(b) The Pasinetti assumption seems to bear some "special relationship" to the criticisms against the neoclassical models and the alternative theories of the Modern Cambridge School.

On both scores, Samuelson and Modigliani set the record straight. For one thing, n, s_c, s_w, and $f(\cdot)$ are all needed in deciding which case (Pasinetti or its dual) the economy belongs to. Hence, none of these data is irrelevant. The early elation discussed in (a) is thus overoptimistic. For another, the Pasinetti assumption can be superimposed upon a Modern Cambridge model as well as upon a simple Solow model, as Samuelson and Modigliani have done. In fact, all the analyses Samuelson and Modigliani made lead to results quite similar to those of Solow. Neither factor substitutability nor the "derivative conditions" of Inada (including the monotonicity of $f'(\cdot)$) nor the forms of income distribution determination (according to marginal products or not) are crucial to the neoclassical theory of growth. We have seen this to some extent in Section 5.3. Considered in its own right, the Pasinetti assumption is a desirable step toward realism via disaggregation. However, this implies permanent memberships among various social classes, each with a distinct saving ratio. Such an assumption appears to be not very realistic. Conceivably, other similar saving assumptions will prove more satisfactory in this respect. It may be noted here that neither the life-cycle saving theory nor the Pasinetti assumption has taken account of the essential imperfection of the capital market. More than the commodity and labor markets, uncertainty and institutional barriers make the capital market even more dissimilar to the textbook markets. Corporations save (ploughing back profits) in order to invest inside their own business circles. Institutional savers lend only to certain special types of investors. Banks take initiative in credit transactions rather than serve as passive intermediaries. All these aspects presumably should be taken into account in future generations of growth models.

We should add one more observation. In its present form, it is doubtful that the model in the present section can predict future wealth distributions in a real-life private enterprise economy, even if there were no technological change. Granted that social mobility is usually imperfect, saving ratios within the same "class" may still depend upon income levels. The model discussed above can admit no possibility of increasing wealth concentration only because workers are postulated to save a definite fixed portion of their income even under destitutely low wages! Of course, more realistic assumptions may be included if the necessary modifications can be made.

6.3 SAVING OUT OF CAPITAL GAIN:
SHELL, SIDRAUSKI, AND STIGLITZ

6.3.1. Introduction

The saving assumption in the neoclassical models suggests that households adopt a simple decision rule; i.e., a certain fraction is always saved. Consider an asset that has doubled its value. Obviously, its owner can sell half his asset without depleting the value of his holdings. Therefore, Shell et al. [14] propose that asset appreciation should be included in income. Only by applying the saving ratio to the redefined income do we attain the appropriate measure for the saving level. Inherent in such an approach is the problem of selecting the numeraire. A person in a two-goods world, where a consumption good is consumed and a capital good is conserved, has to make his choice. Should the capital good be the numeraire, no capital gain can ever occur and we are back to the neoclassical growth literature. Should the consumption good be the numeraire, capital gain or loss may then emerge. Shell et al. examined a one-sector model, a two-sector model, and a model with monetary assets. Here we shall consider their one-sector model.

6.3.2. The model

A. ASSUMPTIONS

Shell et al. retain all the assumptions of the simple Solow model, except the last one on saving. It is assumed that saving is proportional to the value of output plus (minus) capital gain (loss). On the other hand, the universal output of the Solow model can be "fashioned" into two forms: the consumption good numeraire and the capital good whose price is p.

Under competitive conditions, if the price at instant t, $p(t)$, is greater than unity, all output goes into investment. If $p(t)$ is less than unity, all output will be consumed. If $p(t) = 1$, the allocation between consumption and investment goods is indeterminate. This can be seen by drawing an isosceles right triangle as the production set and maximizing the value of output $(p\dot{K} + C)$ over that set. C and $\dot{K}$ stand for outputs allocated for consumption and investment purposes, depreciation rate having been assumed zero for simplicity. Plotting the invest-ment ratio, $\phi(p) = [\dot{K}/Lf(k)]$, against p, we obtain the graph in Figure 6.4a.

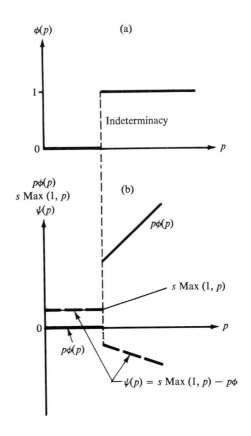

FIGURE 6.4

We note that

$$\phi(p) = \begin{cases} 1 & \text{if } p > 1 \\ \text{undetermined}^{12} & \text{if } p = 1 \\ 0 & \text{if } p < 1 \end{cases}$$

according to the above discussions.

B. THE TWIN DYNAMIC EQUATIONS

The saving assumption now takes the form

$$\frac{d}{dt}(pK) = s\left[K \frac{d}{dt}p + Lf(k) \text{ Max } (1, p)\right] \tag{6.3.}$$

$$\underbrace{\phantom{\frac{d}{dt}(pK)}}_{\text{Saving}} \quad \underbrace{\phantom{K \frac{d}{dt}p}}_{\substack{\text{Capital} \\ \text{gain}}} \quad \underbrace{\phantom{Lf(k) \text{ Max } (1, p)}}_{\text{Value of output}}$$

Noteworthy is the fact that saving includes both the value of incremental capital $p\dot{K}$ and the incremental value of capital $\dot{p}K$, i.e., capital gain.

---

[12] However, we know that $0 \leq \phi(p) \leq 1$.

Dividing by L and rearranging, the above equation is reducible to the form

$$\dot{p} = [s \operatorname{Max}(1, p)f(k) - p(\dot{K}/L)]/(1-s)k \qquad (6.3.2)$$

$$= [s \operatorname{Max}(1, p) - p\phi(p)]f(k)/(1-s)k$$

$$= \psi(p)A(k)/(1-s)$$

where $\psi(p)$ stands for the terms in the [ ] signs and $A(k)$ for $f(k)/k$. The locus of $s \operatorname{Max}(1, p)$, $p\phi(p)$, and their difference ψ is plotted in Figure 6.4b.

Equation (6.3.2) depicts the price movement. For each pair of p and k, the rate of change for price p can be determined.

Next, we have to determine the dynamic equation concerning the capital/labor ratio k. We note that

$$\hat{k} = \hat{K} - \hat{L} = \dot{K}/K - n$$

Multiplying by k, we have

$$\dot{k} = \phi(p)f(k) - nk \qquad (6.3.3)$$

Given initial values for the capital/labor ratio and the price for capital good $[k(0), p(0)]$, (6.3.2) and (6.3.3) essentially determine the dynamic behavior of the $[K(t), p(t)]$ path. When $p(t) = 1$, there may exist some momentary indeterminacy. However, over any interval of finite length, the time pattern of both variables can be shown to be determined.

In comparison with the simple Solow model, the dynamic process depicted here has two distinctive features.

(1) On the quantity side, the simple Solow model always allocates part of the current output to consumption, the rest to investment. In the Shell-Sidrauski-Stiglitz model, unless $p(t) = 1$, the entire output goes either to consumption or to investment. Such an all-or-none off-and-on output allocation is consistent with a constant saving ratio greater than zero and less than unity only because capital gain or loss enters income. A large capital loss may offset the value of the entire output and justify the diversion of all output to investment.[13] Or else a sufficiently large capital gain may satiate the desire for saving and release the entire current production for consumption.[14]

(2) On the price side, the simple Solow model requires that it be always equally profitable to allocate outputs partly for consumption and partly for investment. Hence, the price for a capital good must always be identical to its opportunity cost, viz., unity. In the model of Shell et al., price is historically inherited along with the capital/labor ratio. The perfect foresight assumption in their model implies that every market price is a justified price: justified by a price variation expectation always validated on its own strength, hence the price equation (6.3.2).

---

[13] If $\dot{p} = -f(k)/k$ and $p \geq 1$, then $\dot{K} = Lf(k)$ will cause (6.3.1) to become $0 = s(0) = 0$.

[14] If $\dot{p} = [s/(1-s)]f(k)/k$ and $p \leq 1$, then $\dot{K} = 0$ will satisfy (6.3.1).

C. THE EXISTENCE, UNIQUENESS, AND STABILITY
OF THE BALANCED GROWTH PATH

Let us assume that the Inada conditions are met, so that there exists a unique, stable balanced growth for the simple Solow model in question. What can be said for the reformulated model when capital gain is included in income?

(1) Since constant returns are assumed, balanced growth implies a constant price: $\dot{p} = 0$. Since labor grows at rate $n > 0$, capital accumulation must go on along the balanced growth path for a nontrivial economy (i.e., ruling out the case where $k = 0 = f(k) = \dot{k}$); hence, the price of capital good must not be lower than its opportunity cost, i.e., $p \geq 1$. Should the price of the capital good exceed its opportunity cost, i.e., $p > 1$, then, from (6.3.2), $\dot{p} = (s-1)pf(k)/(1-s)k < 0$ (since $\phi(p) = 1$ for $p > 1$), which is a contradiction. Therefore, $p = 1$. From the balanced growth solution for the Solow model, $\dot{k} = 0$ implies that $k^{\infty} = A^{-1}(n/s)$ (cf. the value of k_D in Table 6.3, Section 6.2). Therefore, back in (6.3.3), the indeterminate form $\phi(p) = \phi(1)$ must take the value s except for a "nonessential" collection[15] of isolated instants such that the value of $k(t) = k^{\infty}$ is unaffected by these "errant moments," if any.

Hence, the existence and uniqueness properties of the reformulated model coincide with those of the original Solow model.

(2) For the stability analysis, we shall consult the phase diagram in Figure 6.5a and b. We draw the usual $f(k)$ diagram in Figure 6.5b to determine the levels of $A^{-1}(n)$ and $A^{-1}(n/s)$, respectively. In the p–k space of Figure 6.5a we plot the following:

(a) The locus (p, k) over which $\dot{p}$ is undetermined, i.e., $p = 1$. This is because in (6.3.2), sgn $(\dot{p}) =$ sgn $\psi(p) =$ sgn $(1-p)$ for $p \neq 1$, as shown in Figure 6.4b.

(b) The locus (p, k) over which $\dot{k} = 0$, i.e.,

$$k = \begin{cases} A^{-1}(n) & \text{for } p > 1 \\ A^{-1}(n/s) & \text{for } p = 1 \\ 0 & \text{for } p < 1 \end{cases}$$

Together these two loci partition the non-negative quadrant of Figure 6.5a into three zones, I, II, and III, together with three linear segments: (i) the segment between the origin and (1, 0) along the p-axis, (ii) the half-line $p = 1$ and $k \geq 0$, and (iii) the half-line $k = A^{-1}(n)$ and $p > 1$.

Table 6.4 summarizes the behavior of p and k over these zones and linear segments, as deduced from (6.3.2) and (6.3.3).

Along $p = 1$, $\dot{p}$ may be of either sign; hence, p may assume a value different from 1 for some isolated instants. But even such isolated instants must not be too "frequent." There exist definite forces preventing p from wandering persistently off $p = 1$. So $\dot{p}$ almost always vanishes. From (6.3.2) and (6.3.3), almost always when $p = 1$, $\dot{k} = sf(k) - nk$.[16]

---

[15]Mathematically speaking, that collection must be of Lebesgue measure zero.

[16]For p "essentially" equal to unity, $\dot{p}$ is essentially equal to zero, and (6.3.2) implies that $\phi = s$ most of the time.

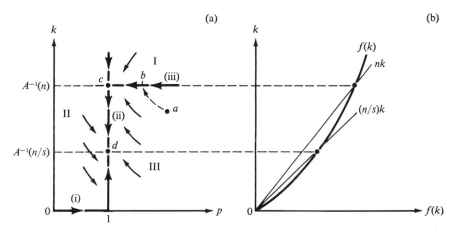

FIGURE 6.5

TABLE 6.4

	$\dot{p}$	$\dot{k}$
Zone I	$(-)$	$(-)$
Zone II	$(+)$	$(-)$
Zone III	$(-)$	$(+)$
Segment (i)	$(+)$	(0)
Segment (ii)	Essentially 0	$\mathrm{sgn}\,[A^{-1}(n/s)-k]$
Segment (iii)	(0)	$(-)$

Such information is depicted with arrows in Figure 6.5a. The global stability of the system at $p = 1$, $k = A^{-1}(n)$ is evident.

In comparison with the simple Solow model, the dynamic path here is quite different. The Solovian approach of the balanced growth path for k is monotonic, and $(\dot{k}+nk)/f(k) = s < 1$ for all t. In Figure 6.5a the *abcd* locus for the reformulated model shows two major differences: (1) the capital/labor ratio first rises and then falls and (2) up to point c, all outputs are devoted to investment goods. The simple Solow model only admits a time path similar to the *cd* arc.

6.3.3. Remarks

In reality, capital gain presumably affects consumption/saving decisions, yet the effect is not identical to an equal increment of factor income. Some weighting can be made before summing the two to obtain the basis for calculating savings. Such a general model is reduced to the simple Solow model if any of the following three conditions are met: (a) there is zero weight for capital gain, (b) the capital good is the numeraire, or (c) the initial price for capital good equals its opportunity cost: unity.

On the other hand, if equal weights are assigned to both income components, the consumption good is chosen as the numeraire, and the initial price differs from unity, then the general model becomes the case analyzed by Shell et al.

While the single-good case is pedagogically the simplest to discuss, the full measure of the contribution by Shell, Sidrauski, and Stiglitz emerges in their two-sector model and the case with a monetary asset. The choice-of-numeraire problem can no longer be sidetracked, once there exist two different assets.[17] The discussion of price variations becomes nonartificial if supply or demand conditions warrant price changes without the assumption of short-run perfect foresight. Thus, in a two-sector model where the opportunity cost of capital does vary over time, the introduction of capital gain is the more meaningful. In a one-sector model, the only ultimate cause for any capital gain is some mysterious divergence of the initial price for capital from its immutable opportunity cost. Hence, readers interested in the approach of Shell et al. should concentrate on the other two cases they analyzed, which are not reported here due to lack of space.

APPENDIX 6.1

1. Derivation of average desired asset holdings per capita

We start from the "equimarginal principle," *marginal utility per dollar should be equal to*

$$\frac{1}{c_v(t)P_v(t)} = \gamma$$

Using this result in the left-hand side of (6.1.2),

$$\frac{1}{\gamma} \int_v^{v+1} dt = \frac{1}{\gamma} = \int_v^{v+1} w(t)P_v(t)\, dt$$

Thus, (6.1.3) is obtained. The subsequent calculation is shown in Table 6.5.
According to (6.1.3), the term

$$\frac{t-v}{\gamma} \exp \int_v^t r(\tau)\, d\tau = \frac{t-v}{\gamma P_v(t)}$$

in the last line of Table 6.5 can be written as $(t-v)c_v(t)$. So we have (6.1.4).

2. Derivation of (6.1.6)

Differentiating (6.1.4) by applying the rule of differentiating parametrically an integral with variable limits and integrand, we have

$$\dot{k}(t) = -nk(t) + 0 - 0 + w(t)\frac{ne^{-nt}}{1-e^{-n}} \int_{t-1}^t e^{nv}\, dv - \int_{t-1}^t \left[\frac{ne^{-n(t-v)}}{1-e^{-n}}\right] c_v(t)\, dv + r(t)k(t)$$

---

[17] If there is only one nonperishable good, then the use of that good for numeraire eliminates capital gain. This is true for a Meade two-sector model as well as for the simple Solow model.

We may note that the two zero terms indicate that the per capita desired holding is unaffected by the fact that a different generation is just born and a different generation is about to die at each instant. This is due to the zero inheritance assumption. Since these generations have no desire for assets, their identity and size are of no account here.

$$\frac{ne^{-nt}}{1-e^{-n}} \int_{t-1}^{t} e^{nv} \, dv = 1$$

Therefore,

$$\dot{k}(t) = [w(t) + r(t)k(t)] - \int_{t-1}^{t} \left[\frac{ne^{-n(t-v)}}{1-e^{-n}} \right] c_v(t) \, dv - nk(t)$$

Under competitive conditions and constant returns,

$$f(k) = \frac{wL + rK}{L} = w + rk$$

This leads to (6.1.6).

3. Analysis of the example with a Cobb-Douglas production function

With balanced growth, $k(t) \equiv k^{\infty}$, say. Hence,

$$w^{\infty} = f(k^{\infty}) - k^{\infty} f'(k^{\infty})$$

$$r^{\infty} = f'(k^{\infty})$$

and, from (6.1.3) and the fact that $P_v(\tau) \exp[r^{\infty}(t-v)] = \exp[r^{\infty}(t-\tau)]$,

$$c_v(t) = w^{\infty} \int_{v}^{v+1} \exp[r^{\infty}(t-\tau)] \, d\tau$$

Therefore, from the definition of $c(t)$, we obtain

$$G(k^{\infty}) = \frac{ne^{-nt}}{1-e^{-n}} \int_{t-1}^{t} e^{nv} \left\{ \int_{v}^{v+1} w^{\infty} \exp[r^{\infty}(t-\tau)] d\tau \right\} dv \qquad (6.1.7')$$

$$= \frac{w^{\infty} I(r^{\infty}) I(n - r^{\infty})}{I(n)} \qquad \text{(after integration)}$$

where

$$I(x) = \frac{1 - e^{-x}}{x} \quad \text{for any real number } x$$

When the production function is Cobb-Douglas, so that

$$f(k) = Ak^{\alpha} \quad \text{where } A > 0 \text{ is a constant}$$

then,

$$\begin{cases} r = \alpha A k^{\alpha - 1} \\ w = (1-\alpha) A k^{\alpha} = (1-\alpha) f(k) \end{cases}$$

Substituting back into the definition of s^{∞}, we have

$$s^{\infty} = 1 - G(k^{\infty})/f(k^{\infty})$$

$$= 1 - (1-\alpha)I(r^{\infty})I(n - r^{\infty})/I(n) \qquad (6.A.1)$$

$$= h(r^{\infty})$$

where $h(r^{\infty})$ is a function of r^{∞}.

TABLE 6.5

I. Accounting for an individual of generation v, at instant t

Wage income, initial valuation	$w(t)P_v(t)$
Subtract: Consumption expenditure, initial valuation	$(-)1/\gamma$
Saving rate, initial valuation	$w(t)P_v(t) - 1/\gamma$
Integrating (cumulating) up to t	$(\int)$
Desired asset holdings, initial valuation	$\displaystyle\int_v^t w(\tau)P_v(\tau)\,d\tau - (t-v)/\gamma$
Multiply: Compound interest factor	$\displaystyle(\times)\exp\int_v^t r(\tau)\,d\tau$
Desired asset holdings, current valuation[a]	$\displaystyle\int_v^t \left[w(\tau)\exp\int_\tau^t r(u)\,du\right]d\tau - \left[(t-v)\exp\int_v^t r(\tau)\,d\tau\right]/\gamma$

II. Economy-wide averaging

Multiply: Size of generation v	$(\times)\Lambda_0 e^{nv}$
Desired asset holdings for generation v, current valuation	$\Lambda_0 e^{nv}\left\{\int_v^t \left[w(\tau)\exp\int_\tau^t r(u)\,du\right]d\tau - [(t-v)\exp\int_v^t r(\tau)\,d\tau]/\gamma\right\}$
Integrating over all generations	$\left(\int\right)$
Desired asset holdings for the economy, current valuation	$\Lambda_0\int_{t-1}^t e^{nv}\left\{\int_v^t \left[w(\tau)\exp\int_\tau^t r(u)\,du\right]d\tau - [(t-v)\exp\int_v^t r(\tau)\,d\tau]/\gamma\right\}dv$
Divide by: Total population[b]	$(\div)\Lambda_0(1-e^{-n})e^{nt}/n$
Average desired asset holding	$ne^{-nt}\int_{t-1}^t e^{nv}\left\{\int_v^t \left[w(\tau)\exp\int_\tau^t r(u)\,du\right]d\tau - [(t-v)\exp\int_v^t r(\tau)\,d\tau]/\gamma\right\}dv/(1-e^{-n})$

[a] $P_v(\tau)\exp\int_v^t r(\tau)\,d\tau = \exp\left[-\int_v^t r(u)\,du + \int_v^t r(u)\,du\right] = \exp\int_\tau^t r(u)\,du$

[b] $\Lambda_0\int_{t-1}^t e^{nv}\,dv = \Lambda_0(1-e^{-n})e^{nt}/n$

Equation (6.1.8') now becomes

$$f(k^\infty) = \frac{n}{s^\infty} k^\infty = \frac{n}{h(r^\infty)} k^\infty \tag{6.1.8}$$

$$= \frac{n}{h[\alpha A(k^\infty)^{\alpha-1}]} k^\infty = H(k^\infty)k^\infty$$

This is reminiscent of the Solow model with a variable saving/income ratio depicted in Figure 2.8 of Chapter 2. Our task now is to deduce the shape of $H(k^\infty)$, which is the radial slope of the $[H(k^\infty)k^\infty]$ curve in the k–f space. This is done in Figure 6.2.

We first note that $H(k^\infty)$ is a composite function of $H = n/h(r)$ and $r = \alpha Ak^{\alpha-1}$. Next, we establish a result:

Lemma. $h(r)$ is a symmetric, concave function with its peak at $r = n/2$. Hence, n/s^∞ is a symmetric, convex function of r with its trough at the same point.

Proof. $h'(r^\infty) = -\dfrac{d}{dr^\infty}[1 - h(r^\infty)]$

$$= -[1 - h(r^\infty)]\frac{d}{dr^\infty} \ln [1 - h(r^\infty)]$$

$$= -(1 - s^\infty)\frac{d}{dr^\infty} \ln \left[\frac{(1-\alpha)I(r^\infty)I(n-r^\infty)}{I(n)}\right]$$

$$= -(1 - s^\infty)\left[\frac{d}{dr^\infty} \ln I(r^\infty) + \frac{d}{dr^\infty} \ln I(n-r^\infty)\right]$$

$$= (1 - s^\infty)\left[\frac{d}{d(n-r^\infty)} \ln I(n-r^\infty) - \frac{d}{dr^\infty} \ln I(r^\infty)\right]$$

Consider now the expression

$$\frac{d^2}{dx^2} \ln I(x) = \frac{d}{dx}\left\{\frac{d}{dx}\left[\ln (1 - e^{-x}) - \ln x\right]\right\}$$

$$= \frac{d}{dx}\left[\frac{1}{e^x - 1} - \frac{1}{x}\right]$$

$$= \frac{1}{x^2(e^x + e^{-x} - 2)}\left[e^x + e^{-x} - 2 - x^2\right]$$

$$= \frac{1}{x^2(e^x + e^{-x} - 2)}\left[\sum_{i=2}^{\infty} \frac{2x^{(2i)}}{(2i)!}\right] \qquad \text{(by series expansion of } e^x \text{ and } e^{-x}\text{)}$$

$$> 0$$

This proves that $h'(r^\infty) \begin{Bmatrix} > \\ = \\ < \end{Bmatrix} 0$ if and only if $(n - r^\infty) \begin{Bmatrix} > \\ = \\ < \end{Bmatrix} r^\infty$ or $r^\infty \begin{Bmatrix} < \\ = \\ > \end{Bmatrix} n/2$.

The lemma is now verified.

We now plot n/s^∞ against r^∞ in the second quadrant of Figure 6.2 and draw the curve $r^\infty = \alpha A(k^\infty)^{\alpha-1}$ in the fourth quadrant in the same diagram and a 45° line in the third quadrant. Starting from any value of r^∞, we can obtain the associated n/s^∞ value in the second quadrant and the associated k^∞ in the fourth quadrant. This pair of values corresponds to a unique point in the first quadrant. By choosing various values of r^∞, we can plot parametrically the broken line $H(k^\infty)$ in the first quadrant of Figure 6.2. As an illustration, we start from $k^\infty = (n/\alpha A)^{1/(\alpha-1)}$. The downward dotted arrow line cuts the $r^\infty = \alpha A(k^\infty)^{\alpha-1}$ locus to determine $r^\infty = n$ on the vertical r^∞ axis. Using the 45° line, we obtain the corresponding point $r^\infty = n$ on the horizontal r^∞ axis. In the second quadrant, the dotted arrow line then cuts the $n/s^\infty = n/h(r^\infty)$ locus to yield the point $n/s^\infty = n/\alpha$ (since $h(n) = 1 - (1-\alpha)I(0) = 1 - (1-\alpha) = \alpha$ as $I(0) = 1$ by L'Hospital's rule). The resulting point $[(n/\alpha A)^{1/(1-\alpha)}, n/\alpha]$ located at the intersection of the dotted arrow lines is a point on the $H(k^\infty)$ locus.

With $H(k^\infty)$ determined, one can plot the curve $H(k^\infty)k^\infty$. This curve intersects the $f(k)$ locus twice.

REFERENCES

[1] Modigliani, F., and R. Brumberg, "Utility Analysis and the Consumption Function: An Interpretation of the Cross-Section Data," in *Post-Keynesian Economics*, K. K. Kurihara, Ed., Allen and Unwin, London, 1955.

[2] Cass, David, and Menahem E. Yaari, "Individual Saving, Aggregate Capital Accumulation and Efficient Growth," in *Essays on the Theory of Optimal Economic Growth*, K. Shell, Ed., M.I.T. Press, Cambridge, Mass., 1967.

[3] Friedmann, Milton, *A Theory of the Consumption Function*, Princeton University Press, Princeton, N.J., 1957.

[4] Marglin, Stephan, "The Social Rate of Discount and the Optimal Rate of Investment," *Quarterly Journal of Economics*, vol. LXXVII, Feb. 1963, pp.95–111.

[5] Meade, J. E., "Life-Cycle Savings, Inheritance and Economic Growth," *Review of Economic Studies*, vol. XXXIII, Jan. 1966, pp. 61–78.

[6] Pasinetti, L. L., "Rate of Profit and Income Distribution in Relation to the Rate of Economic Growth," *Review of Economic Studies*, vol. XXIX, Oct. 1962, pp. 267–79.

[7] Kaldor, N., "Marginal Productivity and Macro-economic Theories of Distribution," *Review of Economic Studies*, vol. XXXIII, Oct. 1966, pp. 309–26.

[8] Meade, J. E., "The Rate of Profit in a Growing Economy," *Economic Journal*, vol. LXXIII, Dec. 1963, pp. 665–74.

[9] Pasinetti, L. L., "A Comment on Professor Meade's 'Rate of Profit in a Growing Economy'", *Economic Journal*, vol. LXXIV, June 1964, pp. 488–89.

[10] Meade, J. E., and F. H. Hahn, "The Rate of Profit in a Growing Economy," *Economic Journal*, vol. LXXV, June 1965, pp. 445–48.

[11] Kemp, M. C., "An Extension of the Neo-Keynesian Theory of Distribution," *Economic Record*, vol. XXXIX, Dec. 1963, pp. 465–68.

[12] Samuelson, P. A., and F. Modigliani, "The Pasinetti Paradox in Neoclassical and More General Models," *Review of Economic Studies*, vol. XXXIII, Oct. 1966, pp. 269–302.

[13] Stiglitz, Joseph, "A Two-Sector, Two-Class Model of Economic Growth," *Review of Economic Studies*, vol XXXIV, April 1967, pp. 227–38.

[14] Shell, K., M. Sidrauski and J. Stiglitz, "Capital Gains, Income and Saving," *Review of Economic Studies*, vol. XXXVI, Jan. 1969, pp. 15–26.

[15] Tobin, James, "Life-Cycle Saving and Balanced Growth," in *Ten Economic Studies in the Tradition of Irving Fisher*, W. Fellner et. al., Wiley, New York, 1967.

[16] Stiglitz, J. E., "Distribution of Income and Wealth among Individuals," *Econometrica*, vol. 37, no. 3, July 1969, pp. 382–97.

[17] Uzawa, H., "Time Preference and the Penrose Effect in a Two Class Model of Economic Growth," *Journal of Political Economy*, vol. 77, no. 4, part II, July/August 1969, pp. 628–52.

EXERCISES

6.1. In a definitive paper, Stiglitz [16] analyzes the equalizing and disequalizing factors of per capita income and wealth. The following is a simplified variation of the Stiglitz theme. Assume
   (1) The one-sector aggregate production function satisfies the Inada conditions.
   (2) The population is divided into a continuum of inbreeding classes, each sharing the same population growth rate, n. The relative weight of class x is $m(x) \geq 0$, where $\int_0^1 m(x)\, dx = 1$. The per capita wealth of class x at time t is $a_x(t) \geq 0$ with $\int_0^1 m(x)a_x(t)\, dx = k(t)$.
   (3) The dynamic equation depicting the evolution of a_x is

$$\dot{a}_x(t) = s[f(k(t)) - k(t)f'(k(t))] + f'(k(t))a_x(t) - na_x(t)$$

   where $f - kf'$ and f' are the competitive wage and interest rates ruling in the economy.

   Prove that:
   (a) There exists a unique, stable balanced growth path for the aggregate capital/labor ratio, $k(t)$. *Hint:* Multiplying the differential equation for a_x by $m(x)$ and integrating over x one obtains (2.1.4).
   (b) If the per capita wealth of class x is higher (lower) than the aggregate capital/labor for the economy, then the per capita wealth of that class grows more slowly (faster) than the aggregate capital/labor ratio, and therefore wealth per capita tends to equalize in the very long run. *Hint:* $\hat{a}_x - \hat{k} = s(f - kf')(1/a_x - 1/k)$.
6.2. In a very comprehensive model, Uzawa [17] postulates that:
   (1) Households maximize intertemporal utility with reference to the ruling interest rate i, so that the saving propensity is $s(i)$.
   (2) Firms maximize net worth with reference to the interest rate and the marginal productivity of capital $f'(k)$, so that the ratio of the investment expenditure to the capital stock is a function $\phi(f', i)$.
   (3) Given k, the equality between saving and investment *expenditure* $sf = \phi k$ determines the interest rate i, hence also ϕ.
   (4) Due to the cost of adjustment, the growth rate of capital z is always less than ϕ (the Penrose effect). However, under net worth maximization, there is a functional relationship between z and ϕ, $z = z(\phi)$.
   (5) The dynamic equation for the economy is $\dot{k} = (z - n)k$

   Compare the Uzawa model with the models in Sections 6.1 and 6.2.

7

endogenous technical progress

7.1 INTRODUCTION

In Chapter 5 we mentioned that technical progress may be regarded either as a spontaneous boon or as something attained through the conscious or unconscious working of the economy. The latter varieties are endogenous to the economy and are treated in detail in the present chapter.

Endogenous technical progress can be classified according to the way in which it comes about.

(1) Through "inducement" by the factor prices. The provocative work of E. Rothbarth in comparing English and American efficiency [1] led to the Habbakuk hypothesis [2] that the higher capital intensity in America was the source of faster technical progress as compared to England. The persistent reports of observed constancy of factor shares among various countries also call for economic explanations based upon the broadest possible assumptions. These considerations ushered in the studies of Kennedy [3], Weizsäcker [4], and Samuelson [5]. Drandakis and Phelps [6] and Chang [7] extended this line of thought.

(2) Through "experience" in production. This may be a result of the cumulation of either output or gross investment. What originally arose from the empirical works of Alchian [8] and Verdoorn [9] became the basis of Arrow's ingenious model of economic growth [10]. For all practical purposes, Arrow's model has superseded the technical progress function of Kaldor that we discussed in Chapter 3.

(3) Through education. Investment in human capital has long been regarded as an important factor in the economy (see Schultz [11]). Uzawa [12] brought this element into the context of economic growth.

(4) Through research activities. A variation of the Uzawa education model can be applied to research, which also raises the productivity of the production sector. See Phelps [13].

While induced technical progress and learning may proceed without conscious recognition, research and education are definitely results of deliberate economic decisions. The presence of endogenous technical progress of any kind provides economic planners additional opportunities to improve economic performance. But in the case of research and education, additional special assumptions have to be introduced to explain at what levels a competitive system would conduct such activities. Otherwise, one would not obtain a self-contained causal model.

The four types of endogenous technical progress models will be reviewed in the next two sections. Their implications for optimal growth theory are summarized in Appendix 7.1, which, however, can be postponed until after Chapter 10 if the reader prefers.

7.2 "INDUCEMENT" AND "LEARNING"

As we stated above, neither "inducement" nor "learning" need involve conscious decisions about the amount of technical progress an economy should have.

7.2.1. Induced technical progress

Among the four alternative hypotheses to be discussed in this chapter, the induced technical progress model is perhaps the most ambitious. All four theories attempt to explain the pace of technical progress; the "inducement" hypothesis also endeavors to predict the types of innovation likely to emerge.

We shall first review the motivation of the model—as an explanation of the supposed constancy of wage shares. Each assumption underlying the model will then be scrutinized concerning its realism. A formal model is set up to allow convenient comparison with the simple Solow model. After deducing the economic conclusions derived from the model, we provide a final summary.

A. CONSTANT FACTOR SHARES: A REVIEW

The study of induced technical progress is motivated by the desire to explain (1) why economies with different factor intensities experience technical progress of different types and at different paces and (2) why wage income is apparently a constant fraction of the national product. While the first point may have deeper relevance to the patterns of growth, the latter appears to be particularly intriguing to macroeconomists in general. Historically, the wage-share issue looms larger in the development of the "induced technical progress" thesis. Hence, a brief review of that question appears necessary.

Economists may approach the alleged constancy of the wage share from the following viewpoints:

(1) Wage-share constancy is a myth. This view has been registered by Solow [14], among others.
(2) The wage share is constant due to production technology. This view is held by "true believers" of a loglinear world. The Cobb-Douglas pro-

duction function, in conjunction with competitive factor markets, produces constant factor shares, under all circumstances. For empirical evidence one may refer to Zarembka [15].

(3) The wage share is constant due to the golden-age equilibrium. The models of both Mrs. Robinson and the neoclassical school indicate that if technical progress (if any) is of the labor-augmenting type, then long-run equilibrium will imply a constant wage share. This has been discussed in Chapters 2 and 3.

(4) The wage share is constant due to the interplay between technical progress and market forces (profit rate, capital/output ratio, etc.).

  (a) The Kaldor approach postulates a technical progress function, which we reviewed in Chapter 3.

  (b) The Kennedy approach is to postulate a technical progress frontier; this will be considered here.

For those who consider wage shares as "significantly" constant (hence deserving of serious efforts at explanation), approaches (2) and (3) are unsatisfactory due to the special assumptions (Cobb-Douglas production function or Harrod-neutral technical progress). The Kaldor approach is unsatisfactory, due to both its inability to explain short-run equilibrium (see Kennedy [16]) and its loose structure. The work of Kennedy, as it is further fortified through the works of Samuelson [5, 17] and Drandakis and Phelps [6], is by far the most convincing alternative. In the following passages we shall first spell out its assumptions and deduce its implications and then present our general commentary.

B. THE ASSUMPTIONS

The Drandakis-Phelps-Samuelson version of the Kennedy model postulates all the basic Solovian assumptions discussed in Section 2.1: linear homogeneous production function, absence of aggregation problems, perfect foresight and smooth adjustments, constant saving/income ratio, and constant population growth rate. The only point at which the present model departs from the basic Solovian model is in the introduction of "induced" technical progress.

There are three basic assumptions on technical progress.

(1) *The production function shifts over time according to the factor-augmenting hypothesis.* In other words, technical progress takes the form of a pure labor-augmenting (Harrod-neutral) type or a pure capital-augmenting type or a mixture of the two (of which the Hicks-neutrality is a special case). While real-life technical progress may or may not agree with such an assumption, this appears to be the most general hypothesis utilized by economists. Also it contains considerable simplicity in analytical terms. Samuelson observed that in plotting the isoquants on log-log paper, technical progress causes a shift of the origin only.[1] Symbolically,

[1]Using the notations of (7.2.1) below, the isoquant has the form

$$F[\exp(\ln K + \ln A_1), \exp(\ln L + \ln A_2)]$$

$$Q(t) = F[K(t), L(t), t] = F[A_1(t)K(t), A_2(t)L(t)] \qquad (7.2.1$$

where $A_1(t)$ and $A_2(t)$ are efficiency indices for capital K and labor L.

The following is an example for non–factor-augmenting technical progress:

$$Q = (\tfrac{1}{2}K^{-\rho(A)} + \tfrac{1}{2}L^{-\rho(A)})^{-1/\rho(A)}$$

where $\rho = [1/\psi(A)] - 1$ with $\psi'(A) > 0$, $\psi(A) \geq 0$.

The effect of technical progress $(\dot{A} > 0)$ in the above example is the increase of factor substitutability in such a way that, except for $K = L$, less input will be required to produce a given output.

(2) *There is a constant technical progress frontier exhibiting differentiability, concavity, boundedness, and a negative slope.* This means:

(a) At every moment and under all circumstances, the economy faces the same range of choices: to increase the capital-augmenting and labor-augmenting technical progress indices by $x_1\%$ and $y_1\%$, respectively, or by $x_2\%$ and $y_2\%$, respectively, or other alternative combinations.

(b) There is a trade-off between the rates of the two types of input-augmenting technical progress an economy can achieve. To speed up more and more the rate of one type of technical progress, one has to forgo the alternative type of progress at an increasing rate.

(c) Whatever the course taken by the economy, the technical progress rate of either type must be finite. In other words, input efficiency never experiences sudden quantum jumps. Symbolically,

$$\hat{A}_2(t) = g[\hat{A}_1(t)] \qquad (7.2.2$$

where $\hat{A}_1(t) \leq \bar{A}_1$, $\hat{A}_2(t) \leq \bar{A}_2$ define the domain for the graph of g. $g'(\cdot) < 0$, $g''(\cdot) < 0$.

Assumption (2) is a simplifying assumption with flimsy empirical evidence for its support. In particular, it presumes that exponential increase of the efficiency indices is forever possible in all directions. It also postulates that there always exists a broad spectrum of innovative opportunities that the society can choose from. Although the latter can be defended as a "smoothing" procedure and a first approximation to reality, the first implication appears to be harder to justify. History is replete with examples showing that civilizations may stagnate at certain technological plateaus after periods of brilliant and spirited progress. It is quite possible that in a surplus-labor economy, capital-saving inventions may be the only type worthy of the inventive activity. Yet the possibilities for such innovations may become exhausted in due course. But again, assumption (2) can be defended as a thesis valid within proper temporal and spatial bounds.

One major objection to the innovation frontier concept is that it slurs over the nature of such a frontier as well as invention. The "trade-off" phenomenon presupposes the allocation of resources for inventive activity, yet the diversion of such resources never appears in the model. Moreover, the inventive activity is highly risky to the innovator alone, yet a successful invention is beneficial to all imitators as well as to the innovator. Without a thorough study of these elements, it is difficult to justify the restrictions specified for the innovation frontier. It is to this point that Tobin [18] registered his objections, and Shell [19, 20] proposed an alternative approach.

(3) *Technical progress follows the direction that maximizes the instantaneous rate of unit cost reduction.* This assumption implies that the entrepreneurs would regard a 1% incremental reduction of labor requirement as desirable as a 3% incremental reduction of capital requirement if wage cost per unit were three times as much as interest cost. Symbolically,

$$-[\alpha \hat{A}_1(t) + (1-\alpha)\hat{A}_2(t)] \le -[\alpha \hat{A}_1 + (1-\alpha)\hat{A}_2] \quad \text{for all } \hat{A}_2 = g(\hat{A}_1) \qquad (7.2.3)$$

where $\alpha = A_1 K F_K / Q$ is the unit capital cost, F_K being the marginal product of capital. $1 - \alpha$ is the unit labor cost. $\hat{A}_1(t)$ and $\hat{A}_2(t)$ are rates of efficiency improvements actually realized at t.

Assumption (3) is a behavioral assumption fraught with dubious premises. First, the technological frontier must be *ex ante* in character. If its shape differs with actual innovational possibilities, then two issues arise: (a) the single frontier in the model cannot serve as both the *ex ante* and the *ex post* frontiers,

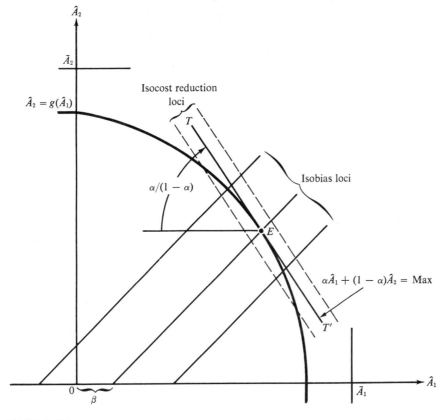

FIGURE 7.1

and (b) if expectations adapt to realized performances, then the *ex ante* frontier can never be a constant one. Second, would the entrepreneurial expectations about innovative opportunities be affected by factor shares or not? If the answer is affirmative, Samuelson showed that the results would be quite different from what Kennedy expected. Third, again as Samuelson pointed out, the entrepreneurs need not try to minimize instantaneous unit cost. One has to postulate instantaneous and total diffusion of innovations so that no firm has any prospect of monopolizing the fruit of invention for any duration of time. Hence, competitive firms behave myopically in the face of the external economy of innovation. Finally, the prospect of different firms holding divergent expectations also poses a difficult problem.

The joint implication of assumptions (2) and (3) is summarized in Figure 7.1. The g function is plotted in the $\hat{A}_1 - \hat{A}_2$ space. This graph may extend beyond the non-negative quadrant, since certain innovations may conceivably increase the efficiency of one input at the expense of the other. Each point along the technical progress frontier, $\hat{A}_2 = g(\hat{A}_1)$, is located on the intersection of two families of parallel lines. The first family has the form

$$\alpha\hat{A}_1 + (1-\alpha)\hat{A}_2 = \gamma$$

for some constant γ.

Points on the same line indicate equal rates of unit cost reduction, the input price ratio being given.[2]

The second family has the form

$$\hat{A}_1 - \hat{A}_2 = \beta \tag{7.2.4}$$

β being a constant which measures the differential rates of factor-augmenting technical progress, or bias of innovation.

Assumption (2) stipulates that $-\hat{\gamma}$ is to be maximized, showing that individual firms take factor prices as given and pursue the direction of "steepest descent" in unit cost reduction. Following the differentiability and strict concavity of g, Figure 7.1 implies that:

  (a) The marginal rate of substitution between two types of input-augmenting technical progress is equal to the ratio of factor shares (indicated by the

---

[2]Because, $\bar{r}$ and $\bar{w}$ being the market wage and rent,

unit cost $\gamma^0 = (\overline{rK} + \overline{wL})/Q$

$$= (\overline{rK} + \overline{wL})/(A_1\overline{KF}_K + A_2\overline{LF}_L)$$

Then,

$$\hat{\gamma}^0 = \frac{-(\dot{A}_1\overline{KF}_K + \dot{A}_2\overline{LF}_L)}{Q} = -\left[\frac{A_1\overline{KF}_K}{Q}\hat{A}_1 + \frac{A_2\overline{LF}_L}{Q}\hat{A}_2\right]$$

$$= -[\alpha\hat{A}_1 + (1-\alpha)\hat{A}_2]$$

tangency between TT' and the g curve), i.e.,

$$g'[\hat{A}_1(t)] = -\alpha/(1-\alpha) \tag{7.2.5}$$
$$= -A_1 K F_K/A_2 L F_L$$

(b) There is a monotonically increasing relation between the rate of capital-augmenting technical progress and capital share (due to the concavity of g); i.e.,[3]

$$\hat{A}_1(t) = h\left(\frac{\alpha}{1-\alpha}\right) \qquad h' > 0 \tag{7.2.6}$$

(c) The higher the rate of capital-augmenting technical progress, the higher the measure for capital bias in innovation (due to the fact that $g' < 0$ and $d\beta/d\hat{A}_1 = 1 - g'$); i.e.,

$$\beta = H[\hat{A}_1(t)] \qquad H' > 0 \tag{7.2.7}$$

Equations (7.2.2) and (7.2.5) determine the momentary equilibrium. For given values of $k(t)$, $A_1(t)$, and $A_2(t)$, we can find $\hat{A}_1$ and $\hat{A}_2$.

C. FORMULATION

We shall first introduce a few new variables to facilitate our discussion. Define

$$k' = A_1 K/A_2 L$$

as the "efficiency capital/labor" ratio, where $A_1 K$ and $A_2 L$ represent capital and labor measured in "efficiency units" rather than natural units.

$$f(k') = Q/A_2 L = F(k', 1)$$

Hence, we have the accounting relationship:

$$\hat{k}' = \hat{k} + \hat{A}_1 - \hat{A}_2$$

By analogy with the Solow model, we have a fundamental dynamic equation[4] like (2.1.4):

$$\dot{k}' = sA_1 f(k') + (\beta - n)k' \tag{7.2.8}$$

where (from (7.2.7), (7.2.6), and the definition of α)

$$\beta = H\left[h\left(\frac{k'f'}{f-k'f'}\right)\right] \tag{7.2.9}$$

[3](7.2.6) is obtained by inverting $g'(\cdot)$.

[4]The accounting identity and the definition for β lead to

$$\hat{k}' = \dot{K}/K - n + \beta$$

Since $\dot{K} = sA_2 Lf(k')$, invoking the definition of k' we have

$$\hat{k}' = [sA_1 f(k')/k'] + \beta - n$$

We now have a complete system between (7.2.8) and (7.2.9) easily comparable to the Solovian framework. This helps us to gain insight into what follows. By specifying $k'(0)$ and $A_1(0)$, this system can generate its own dynamic path.

We can next address ourselves to the twin questions of the existence and stability of the golden age path in the present model.

D. ANALYSIS OF THE EXISTENCE PROBLEM

Our early studies in Sections 2.3 and 5.3 indicate that unless technical progress is of the pure labor-augmenting variety (i.e., Harrod-neutral), golden age growth is possible only when the production function is Cobb-Douglas. Now in (7.2.8) we observe that a steady state requires $\dot{k}' = 0$. This necessitates the condition:

$$n - \beta = \frac{sA_1 f}{k'}$$

or

$$A_1 = \frac{(n - \beta)k'}{sf} \qquad (7.2.10)$$

With k' taking a constant value, f and hence also β (from (7.2.9)) are also constants. From (7.2.10), A_1 must also be a constant. Therefore, we have the steady-state values (indicated by the superscript ∞):

$$\hat{A}_1^\infty = 0$$

$$\hat{A}_2^\infty = g(0) = -\beta^\infty \qquad (7.2.11)$$

$$\alpha^\infty = \frac{g'(0)}{g'(0) - 1} \qquad \text{(from (7.2.5))}$$

By solving the equation

$$\frac{d \ln f}{d \ln k'} = \alpha^\infty \qquad (7.2.12)$$

we can also find a value of k' corresponding to α^∞. Hence, by substituting back into (7.2.10), A_1^∞ also may be determined.

The first equality in (7.2.11) tells us that *golden age equilibrium is compatible only with Harrod-neutral technical progress*. The solution of (7.2.12) and early discussion in Section 2.3 inform us that at the golden age equilibrium, the capital/labor ratio, the output/labor ratio, and the wage rate all increase at the rate $g(0)$. The capital/output ratio, the interest rate, and the factor shares stay constant. These correspond to Samuelson's results [16] for the present model.

We could have postulated, in the first place, that only labor-augmenting technical progress can occur. We may now inquire, if the resultant steady state is the Harrodian golden age, what have we gained? The answer is twofold:

(1) In the classical golden age case, steady state always exists under the Inada

conditions. In the present model, steady state fails to exist if the production function is Cobb-Douglas and the capital coefficient differs from $g'(0)/[g'(0)-1]$. (Incidentally, if $\alpha = g'(0)/[g'(0)-1]$, and k' qualifies as a steady-state value, so is the value associated with A_1 through (7.2.10)).

(2) In the classical golden age case, Harrodian technical progress must prevail at all times. In the present case, under certain conditions, the economic system premits non-Harrod-neutral technical progress at all times, yet its asymptotic state allows only Harrod-neutral technical progress. Such a limiting case emerges from the working of economic forces and not by postulation. Moreover, convergence toward golden age is likely to occur only when the elasticity of substitution is less than 1. This leads to our next topic.

E. ANALYSIS OF THE STABILITY CONDITIONS

For simplicity, a phase diagram in terms of k' and A_1 is used below to analyze the long-run behavior of the model. Drandakis and Phelps [6] used a different and somewhat more powerful phase diagram.

Rewriting (7.2.6) and (7.2.8), we have

$$\dot{A}_1(t) = h\left[\frac{k'f'}{f-k'f'}\right]A_1 \qquad \text{(from (7.2.6))} \qquad (7.2.13)$$

$$= \eta(k')A_1$$

for some function $\eta(\cdot)$.

$$\dot{k}'(t) = [sf(k')]A_1 - \{n - H[\eta(k')]\}k' \qquad \text{(from (7.2.8))} \qquad (7.2.14)$$

We can show that in the $k'-A_1$ diagram,[5]

$$\operatorname{sgn}(\dot{A}_1) = [\operatorname{sgn}(\sigma-1)][\operatorname{sgn}(k'-k)], \quad \text{near } k'^{\infty} \qquad (7.2.15)$$

where $\dot{k}'^{\infty} = 0$. We shall assume from now on that k'^{∞} is unique.[6] Then the above statement holds globally true for all $A_1 > 0$.

Again in the $k'-A_1$ diagram, we consider the points at which $\dot{k}' = 0$. From (7.2.14), if $\dot{k}' = 0$ for (k', A_1), then at any $(k', \tilde{A}_1)$ where $\tilde{A}_1 \neq A_1$ we have

$$\operatorname{sgn}(\dot{k}') = \operatorname{sgn}(\tilde{A}_1 - A_1) \qquad (7.2.16)$$

---

[5] $\operatorname{sgn}(d\eta/dk') = (\operatorname{sgn} h')\{\operatorname{sgn}\{(d/dk')[\alpha/(1-\alpha)]\}\}$

$\qquad = \operatorname{sgn}(d/dk')(k'/\omega) \qquad$ (since $h' > 0$ and since $\alpha/(1-\alpha) = k'(r/w) = (k'/\omega)$, where $\omega = (w/r)$)

$\qquad = \operatorname{sgn}\{(1/\omega)[1-(1/\sigma)]\} \qquad$ (where $\sigma = d \ln k'/d \ln \omega$)

$\qquad = \operatorname{sgn}(\sigma-1) \qquad (1/\sigma\omega > 0)$

Using Taylor expansion at k'^{∞} and noting $A_1 > 0$, we have verified (7.2.15).

[6] This is true whenever $\sigma-1$ is either positive over all values of k' or negative over all k', for then η is strictly monotonic. A special case is the class of constant elasticity of substitution production functions except for the Cobb-Douglas case.

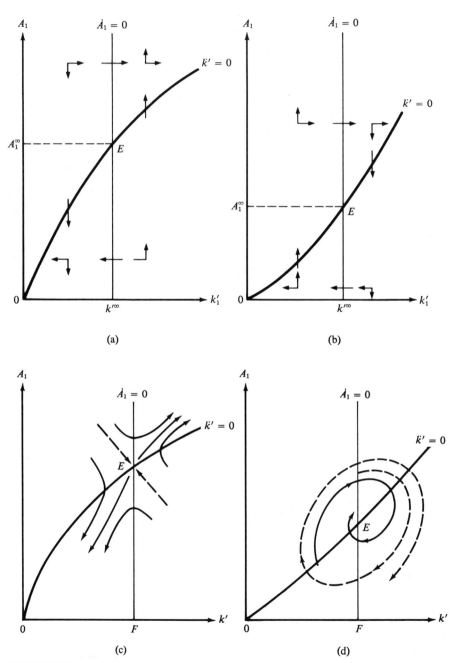

FIGURE 7.2

We can now plot the phase diagrams for the cases where either $\sigma > 1$ for all k' or $\sigma < 1$ for all k'. These are shown in Figure 7.2, parts (a) and (b), respectively.[7]

The arrow in Figure 7.2a and b indicate the motions of the system wherever it is located. These signs are constructed according to (7.2.15) and (7.2.16).

In Figure 7.2c it is shown that if $\sigma > 1$ for all k', then except for the coincidental cases where $[k'(0), A_1(0)]$ is located on the broken lines, the steady state is unstable. Eventually k' and A_1 will rise or fall together indefinitely. The case $\sigma < 1$ for all k' seems to allow for two steady-state equilibria, one at E and the other at F.[8] Hence, there appear to be three possibilities: spiral paths converging to E, spiral paths approaching F, and spiral paths converging to a limit circle. However, *logically* the system can never stay at F. If $A_1 = 0$, then $k' = A_1 K / A_2 L = 0$ by definition. The nonexistence of an equilibrium at F for the system rules out the dotted spiral. By a stability analysis through linearization, Samuelson [17] shows that in the neighborhood of E, the clockwise solid spiral represents the actual path, which converges to E. Drandakis and Phelps [6] establish global stability by means of a different type of phase diagram.

F.   A SUMMARY FOR THE "STYLIZED" WORLD

The general implication of this model is best summarized by Samuelson in [5]. If the elasticity of substitution is less than unity, then the "stylized facts" of the world can be schematically represented as in Figure 7.3.

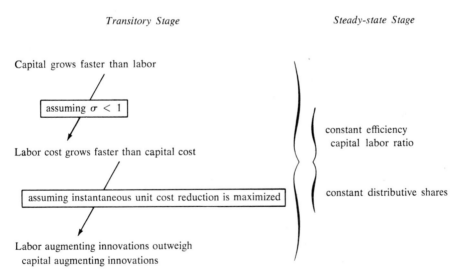

Transitory Stage   *Steady-state Stage*

Capital grows faster than labor

assuming $\sigma < 1$

Labor cost grows faster than capital cost

assuming instantaneous unit cost reduction is maximized

Labor augmenting innovations outweigh capital augmenting innovations

constant efficiency capital labor ratio

constant distributive shares

FIGURE 7.3

[7]The curvature and the slope of the $\dot{k}' = 0$ locus are derived by analyzing (7.2.14). However, the specific shapes of that locus do not affect the phase diagram analysis.

[8]Where (7.2.13) vanishes due to $A_1 = 0$.

The methodological upshot is that another Kaldorian insight is "swallowed up" by the aggregate production function approach with which Kaldor disagrees. The end product is superior to either the simpler neoclassical growth models or the makeshift formulation of a Kaldorian technical progress function.

We may also note that the myopic behavior of instantaneous unit cost reduction is not optimal. More shall be said on this point in Appendix 7.1.

The Kennedy formulation of the technical progress frontier is only one of the possible behavioral assumptions. An excellent analysis of alternative formulations is presented in Chang's work [7].

7.2.2. Learning by doing

We shall now discuss the work of Arrow, which was later extended by Levhari [21]. This model assumes vintage capital with a clay–clay technology, which in certain aspects anticipates the work of Solow, Tobin, Yaari, and Weizsäcker discussed in Section 5.3. In the parlance of that section, Arrow concentrates on the pure labor-augmenting technical progress case under the full-employment regime.

A. ASSUMPTIONS AND FORMULATION

Most of the assumptions made by Arrow are similar to those we discussed in Section 5.3. These include the fixed coefficient production function, embodied labor-augmenting technical progress, full employment for labor force which increases exponentially, and a constant saving/income ratio. Neoclassical assumptions such as perfect foresight and smooth adjustment are also postulated.

Arrow also assumed that the labor efficiency index $A(v)$ associated with workers tending machines of vintage v is a strictly increasing function of cumulate (gross) investment; i.e., of

$$G(t) = \int_{-\infty}^{t} K(v, t) \, dv$$

Specifically, Arrow assumed that

$$A(v) = G^m(v) \quad \text{where } m > 0 \tag{7.2.17}$$

$G(t)$ can be regarded as "capital," measured in terms of cumulate "opportunity cost" (consumption foregone). We refrain from using the symbol $K(t)$ because capital of different vintages is heterogeneous when used as an input.

For our discussion, we simplify Arrow's model by assuming that equipment lasts forever and machine disposal is due to economic obsolescence alone and not to physical breakdown. As in Section 5.3, we also choose units of time and commodities so that unit capital requirement and "initial" unit labor requirement (i.e., when $G = 1$) are unity.

Arrow's special assumption is somewhat at variance with empirical studies where unit labor requirement is shown as inversely related to the cumulative output in a loglinear equation. Moreover, such studies are conducted on a plant basis. Arrow argued that cumulate output *should* be less suitable than cumulate investment as an index of experience, since the appearance of new machines *should* provide more stimulation for innovation while the cumulation of outputs (say, at a constant rate per unit time) appears to be a rather uninspiring environment. One may take issue with Arrow on two counts: (a) repetitive operation leads to familiarity and expertise; hence, constant output rate is by no means an unfavorable situation for cost reduction; and (b) cumulate output as an index for experience is supported by observed evidence, whereas there is no empirical evidence of a similar dependency on cumulate investment.

From the above assumptions, we can now synthesize a complete model containing three equations.

(1) Saving–consumption decisions:

$$\dot{G}(t) = K(t, t) \qquad \text{(definition of } G\text{)} \tag{7.2.18}$$

$$= s \int_{h(t)}^{t} Q(v, t) \, dv \qquad \begin{array}{l}\text{(saving–investment identity;}\\ \text{aggregation of output)}\end{array}$$

$$= s \int_{h(t)}^{t} K(v, v) \, dv \qquad \begin{array}{l}\text{(capital/output ratio normalized}\\ \text{to unity; no depreciation)}\end{array}$$

where $t - h(t)$ is the equipment life for machines disposed of at t (cf. Section 5.2).

(2) Equipment-disposal decisions:

$$1 - w(t)/A[h(t)] = 1 - w(t)G^{-m}[h(t)] \tag{7.2.19}$$

$$= 0$$

(3) Operations of the labor market:

$$L_0 e^{nt} = \int_{h(t)}^{t} \frac{Q(v, t)}{A(v)} \, dv \qquad \begin{array}{l}\text{(unit labor requirement for}\\ \text{vintage } v \text{ is } 1/A(v))\end{array} \tag{7.2.20}$$

$$= \int_{h(t)}^{t} \frac{K(v, v)}{A(v)} \, dv \qquad \text{(from (7.2.18))}$$

$$= \int_{h(t)}^{t} G^{-m}(v)\dot{G}(v) \, dv$$

The above three equations are comparable to their counterparts in Section 5.3. The capital market condition in determining interest rate is not included here.

B. RESULTS

Computationally, the Arrow model is simpler than the clay–clay model we discussed in Section 5.3. There the speed of embodied technical progress is not related to the rate of investment. Here, the whole past history of investment is required as an initial condition. Here, we can derive a differential equation to serve as the fundamental dynamic equation.

Analytical convenience persuades us to derive the $G(\cdot)$ path first. From that information the time paths of output, equipment life, and wage can readily be derived.

Noting $K(v, v) = \dot{G}(v)$, (7.2.18) can be rewritten and integrated out on the right-hand side:

$$\dot{G}(t) = s\{G(t) - G[h(t)]\} \tag{7.2.21}$$

(Intuitively, $\{\ \}$ stands for equipment in use. Since the capital/output ratio is unity, $\{\ \}$ is also the output at t.)

Integrating (7.2.20) and using the result[9] to eliminate $G[h(t)]$ in (7.2.21), we obtain the fundamental differential equation:

$$\dot{G} = \begin{cases} sG\{1 - [1 - (1-m)G^{-1+m}L_0 e^{nt}]^{1/(1-m)}\} & \text{for } m \neq 1 \\ sG\{1 - \exp[-L_0 e^{nt}]\} & \text{for } m = 1 \end{cases} \tag{7.2.22}$$

From here we obtain

$$Q(t) = \dot{G}(t)/s \qquad \text{(instant multiplier relation)}$$

$$G[h(t)] = G(t) - Q(t) \qquad \text{(from (7.2.21) and the above)} \tag{7.2.23}$$

$$w(t) = [G(t) - Q(t)]^m \qquad \text{(from (7.2.19) and the above)}$$

The second equation can be used to study equipment life.

Given the initial condition, $G(t)$ can be numerically solved from (7.2.22) for $m \neq 1$. It can even be directly integrated, for $m = 1$, to obtain

$$G(t) = G(0) \exp\left\{ s \int_0^t [1 - \exp(-L_0 e^{nv})]\, dv \right\}$$

To most economists, the more interesting conclusions obtained by Arrow are his qualitative results: those on the welfare implications of learning, the comparative statics and the existence of a golden age path in his model. These will be considered in turn.

1. Welfare implications.   The presence of learning phenomena enables investment to influence production in three ways: It provides capital input; it embodies the latest technological advances; it stimulates the innovative process. Whereas the first two effects are rewarded under the market mechanism, the third is left uncompensated. The resultant divergence between social and private products causes inefficiency just as any external economy does. However, detailed discussions will be left for Appendix 7.1.

2. Comparative static results concerning the cumulative investment.   As we noted in Chapter 3, there are three different measures of capital: earning power, productive capacity, and opportunity cost (consumption foregone). In Arrow's model, capital goods are not only heterogeneous, but they cannot be rigorously

[9] $G^{1-m}(t) - G^{1-m}[h(t)] = (1-m)L_0 e^{nt}$ for $m \neq 1$

ln $\{G(t)/G[h(t)]\} = L_0 e^{nt}$ for $m = 1$

aggregated into one jelly input to measure productive capacity, since technical progress is not Solow-neutral (or capital augmenting).[10] However, the opportunity cost of the capital stock, as represented by the G measure, is always well defined. Arrow treated the G measure as if it were a veritable capital input and related aggregate output to both this G measure and the aggregate labor input. In so doing, he found that:

(a) Q/G increases if L and G increase by the same proportion.[11]

(b) A proportional increase of G and L allows for a more than proportional increase of Q,[12] Figure 7.4 depicts the isoquant maps of $Q = \phi(G, L)$ for $m = 1$ and $m = 2$. It is shown that doubling both inputs leads to more than double output.

(c) Wage share $1 - \alpha = wL/Q$ decreases with the ratio L/G^{1-m}. The laborious but mechanical proof is omitted here.

3. The existence and properties of a competitive golden age path. Owing to the fact that $\phi(G, L)$ exhibits "increasing returns" and learning generates external

---

[10]Compare Section 4.1.

[11]**Proof.** From (7.2.23) and (7.2.22),

$$Q/G = (\dot{G}/s)/G$$

$$= \begin{cases} \left\{ 1 - \left[1 - \dfrac{(1-m)L}{G^{1-m}} \right]^{1/(1-m)} \right\} & \text{for } m \neq 1 \\ 1 - e^{-L} & \text{for } m = 1 \end{cases}$$

Let $L/L_0 = \lambda = G/G_0$; then,

$$\frac{d}{d\lambda}(Q/G) = \begin{cases} \left[1 - \dfrac{(1-m)L}{G^{1-m}} \right]^{m/(1-m)} \dfrac{mL_0}{G^{1-m}} > 0 & \text{for } m \neq 1 \\ L_0 e^{-L} > 0 & \text{for } m = 1 \end{cases} \tag{7.2.24}$$

[12]**Proof.** From (7.2.22) and (7.2.23), one obtains the macroaggregate relationship:

$$Q = \begin{cases} G\left\{ 1 - \left[1 - \dfrac{(1-m)L}{G^{1-m}} \right]^{1/(1-m)} \right\} & \text{for } m \neq 1 \\ G(1 - e^{-L}) & \text{for } m = 1 \end{cases} = \phi(G, L), \text{ say}$$

which may be regarded as something like an aggregate production function (albeit G represents neither a homogeneous capital input nor a surrogate capital jelly fulfilling the conditions of Samuelson or Solow). If so, one can show that ϕ shows "increasing returns." Let

$$Q(\lambda) = \phi(\lambda G_0, \lambda L_0) = \phi(G \; L)$$

$$\frac{Q'(\lambda)}{Q(\lambda)} = \frac{dG/d\lambda}{G} + \frac{(d/d\lambda)(Q/G)}{Q/G} \qquad \text{(since } Q = G(Q/G)\text{)}$$

$$> \frac{dG/d\lambda}{G} \qquad \text{(from footnote 11)}$$

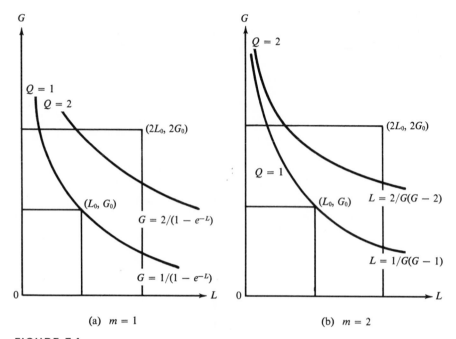

FIGURE 7.4

economy, it is not obvious that the Arrow model permits a golden age path. It may be shown that a golden age path can exist—but certain stringent conditions must be met. This is seen in the following.

By definition, golden age growth requires

$$\hat{Q} = \hat{L} + \hat{A} = \text{constant}$$

where A is the efficiency index for labor. For the present model, this means:

$$\frac{d\ln(\dot{G}/s)}{dt} = n + \frac{d\ln G^m}{dt}$$

$$= n'$$

or

$$\ddot{G}/\dot{G} = n + m(\dot{G}/G)$$

$$= n'$$

where n' is a number.

Since both $\dot{G}$ and G grow at constant relative rates, n' and $(n'-n)/m$, respectively, we deduce that $\hat{G} = \dot{G}$; i.e., $n' = (n'-n)/m$.[13] Thus, one can deduce, step by step, the following results:

(a) Output and investment must both grow at the rate $n' = n/(1-m)$.

(b) Whenever population grows, golden age growth requires that m be less than 1.

(c) For every saving/income ratio s within the full-employment range, $n < s < 1$,[14] there corresponds the ratio $Q/G = n/(1-m)s$, since:

$$\frac{n}{1-m} G = \dot{G} = sQ$$

(d) The ratio L/G^{1-m} takes the value:

$$L/G^{1-m} = \frac{1}{1-m}\left\{1 - \left[1 - \frac{n}{(1-m)s}\right]^{1-m}\right\}$$

from (7.2.22).

(e) The economic life of equipment equals:

$$-\frac{(1-m)/n}{\ln\left[1 - n/(1-m)s\right]}$$

(from (7.2.23).

Detailed derivation is left for the interested reader.

4. The competitive wage-interest patterns under golden age growth. Without going into details, one may summarize the following golden age results, which parallel those for the clay–clay case in Section 5.3:

(a) Wage share is constant.

(b) Wage increases at the rate $n' - n = mn/(1-m)$.

(c) It is possible to find a constant interest rate which can be used to discount the quasi-rent flow of an equipment to equal its initial investment.

7.3 EDUCATION AND RESEARCH

So far there has been no "positive" growth model incorporating the features of education and research. We shall report below the structural components of the models of Uzawa and Phelps. Without introducing behavioral assumptions of our own on how levels of research and education are determined in an economy without central planning, we shall leave these models open-ended. Later, in Appendix 7.1, we shall sketch the social utility functions of the Uzawa and Phelps models so that interested readers can visualize the working of the whole models mentioned above.

[13] $\hat{G} = (n'-n)/m$ implies $G(t) = G(0) \exp\left[(n'-n)t/m\right]$. Differentiating with respect to t,

$$\dot{G}(t) = (n'-n)G(0)/m \exp\left[(n'-n)t/m\right]$$
$$= \dot{G}(0) \exp\left[(n'-n)t/m\right]$$

[14] See Chapter 5.

7.3.1. Education

The work of T. W. Schultz [11] initiated the current interest in education. Uzawa included such studies under the context of neoclassical growth theory. We shall follow his general approach but simplify it by assuming that capital is nondepreciable. We shall first discuss the assumptions and then consider the model.

A. ASSUMPTIONS

The assumptions underlying the simple Solow model are accepted in toto. As in the case of the learning-by-doing model, technical progress takes the pure labor-augmenting form. Since education improves the skill of the labor force, it is somewhat justifiable to expect that, other things being equal, technical progress would not affect the capital/output ratio.[15] However, it may be argued that with better training, workers usually can utilize more sophisticated tools and either increase the capital/output ratio (more mechanized methods) or decrease it (productivity rises very fast). In that context, Harrod neutrality is only a first approximation to reality.

There are also two special assumptions underlying Uzawa's model:

(1) Labor can be divided into two types: productive, L_P, and educational, L_E. Only L_P is used as an input in production. This assumption does not differentiate between "teaching personnel," who are permanently withdrawn from the physical production process, and "personnel in training," who eventually will join the working force in producing commodities. Also worthy of note is that there is no reference to the allocation of material wealth to the education sector.

(2) The rate of increase for labor-augmenting technical progress is a concave, increasing function of $1-u$, where $u = L_P/L$ and $1-u = L_E/L$. In other words, the higher the proportion of the total labor force devoted to eductaion, the faster the increase in labor productivity, but such an increase is less than the increase of the education population/total population ratio. This assumption presumes that education increases productivity for material wealth (exceptions: Confucian studies, rabbinical training, etc.) and also that education benefits the whole labor force and not just those who receive the training.

On balance, one can regard Uzawa's model as a reasonable first approximation to reality, at the aggregate level. We may mention in passing that in an unpublished work, Park [22] generalized the Cass-Yaari model by permitting individuals to choose their optimal length of training, where training reduces a person's working life yet augments his instantaneous supply of efficiency labor. Since he assumed that labor forces of all grades of skill are perfect substitutes for each other (except for an efficiency weight), it turned out that *all individuals* would select the *same degree* of training. On the other hand, in the linear programming model of I. Adelman [23], labor force is cross-classified according

---

[15]That, of course, is the essence of the pure labor-augmenting technical progress.

to both its level of education and its end use. The marginal rate of substitution between a college graduate and a high school graduate varies according to the end use to which they are allocated. It seems Adelman's model is more satisfactory than Park's, and Park's is better than Uzawa's in this regard. However, for our purpose, the simplicity of the Uzawa formulation and its affinity to the growth context make it a suitable specimen study in this field.

B. FORMULATION

As in other neoclassical models, Uzawa postulated that the output per "efficiency worker" (working force in efficiency units) in the productive sector is an increasing, concave function of the "effective capital/labor ratio" (i.e., capital divided by the number of efficiency workers) in the productive sector.

Let

$$A(t)L_P(t) = A(t)u(t)L(t) \quad \text{represent productive, efficiency labor}$$

$$\frac{K(t)}{A(t)L_P(t)} = \frac{k(t)}{A(t)u(t)} \quad \text{represent the "effective capital/labor ratio"}$$

Then Uzawa's assumption can be symbolically represented as

$$\frac{Q(t)}{A(t)u(t)L(t)} = f\left[\frac{k(t)}{A(t)u(t)}\right] \qquad f' > 0 > f'' \tag{7.3.1}$$

Combining this equation with the special assumptions in Section A, above, we can obtain the twin dynamic equations:

$$\dot{k} = (\hat{K} - \hat{L})k \tag{7.3.2}$$

$$= \dot{K}/L - nk$$

$$= sAuf(k/Au) - nk \qquad \text{(using (7.3.1))}$$

$$\dot{A} = \phi(1-u)A \qquad \phi' > 0 > \phi'' \qquad \text{(from assumption (2))} \tag{7.3.3}$$

$k(0)$ and $A(0)$ being given.

These twin equations contain one discretionary parameter, u, the labor allocation ratio. In the original Uzawa model, the saving/income ratio s is also a variable function over time. By selecting optimal paths for both $u(t)$ and $s(t)$, we can maximize the social welfare function. On the other hand, if we introduce a "behavior assumption" explaining the level of the education effort an economy is likely to maintain, given that other circumstances (income per capita, etc.) are known, then we can also "close" the above system of (7.3.2) and (7.3.3) and obtain a positive model.

7.3.2. Research

The work of Phelps is essentially an effort to find a satisfactory "technological function" to incorporate into the simple Solow model. This function explains the source of the labor-augmenting technical progress endogenous to the economic system. We shall now consider the basic model of Phelps in terms of its assumptions and formulation.

A.   ASSUMPTIONS

1. Phelps postulated all the basic Solovian assumptions and the Uzawa assumption that labor input alone is needed to increase the efficiency of labor, A. In fact, his model differs from that of Uzawa only in the manner in which technical progress takes place. The labeling of the "nonproductive" sector either as education or as research does not make much analytical difference.

2. The "technological function" has to satisfy four properties:

(a) Diminishing returns with respect to current effort. This means that faster technical progress can be attained by intensified dosages of research labor forces, yet the law of diminishing returns applies to research efforts as well as to productive efforts.

(b) Diminishing (intertemporal) marginal rate of substitution of research efforts. This property is postulated to rule out the "bunching" of research efforts at any one instant.

(c) "Technical progress" in research. This reflects that as time goes on, research efforts can be more fruitful due to technical progress.

(d) Exponentially growing research efforts leading to an exponentially growing efficiency level. This property is assumed in order to allow for the existence of a golden age path.

One class of eligible functional forms Phelps selects is

$$\dot{A}(t) = A(t-\theta)\phi\left[\frac{L_R(t)}{A(t-\theta)}\right] \qquad \phi' > 0 > \phi'' \tag{7.3.4}$$

with θ as the time lag and L_R as the labor force devoted to research.

$\phi'' < 0$ implies property (a); hence, current research efforts tend to occupy only a portion of the available work force. Since (7.3.4) is equivalent to

$$A(t) = A(0) \exp\left\{\int_{-\infty}^{t} \frac{A(\tau-\theta)}{A(\tau)} \phi\left[\frac{L_R(\tau)}{A(\tau-\theta)}\right] d\tau\right\} \tag{7.3.5}$$

Phelps showed that the concavity of ϕ also discourages "bunching" of research efforts. Roughly speaking, with the same labor force devoted to research over a given period, bunching yields less technical progress over this period than a more even distribution. This corresponds to property (b). The appearance of $A(t-\theta)$ in (7.3.4) and the concavity of ϕ implies that $\dot{A}(t)$ is positively associated with the past achievement level $A(t-\theta)$, other things being equal. This satisfies property (c). Finally, if L_R and A increase at the same exponential rate, (7.3.4) can hold. This fulfills property (d). Properties (a) and (b) help to assure the existence of an efficient, smooth growth path. Property (d) permits balanced growth and property (c) adds realism to the formulation. As Phelps noted, while the first three properties appear reasonable, the fourth seems at least not to contradict our casual observations.

B.   FORMULATION

Based upon the above information, we can write the Phelps model as

$$\dot{k}(t) = sAuf(k/Au) - nk \tag{7.3.2}$$

and

$$\dot{A}(t) = A(t-\theta)\phi\left\{\frac{(1-u)L_0 e^{nt}}{A(t-\theta)}\right\} \tag{7.3.6}$$

We chose the same symbols used in the discussion of the Uzawa model to facilitate comparison.

Again, this model is not closed, because the parameter u is yet to be determined.

Phelps now deduces a surprising result:

[(7.3.2)–(7.3.6)] and golden-age growth together imply that the technical progress rate is exactly equal to the labor growth rate. In other words, output and capital grow twice as fast as labor (in natural units).

This is due to the fact that labor alone is required for research. His assumptions imply that if $A(t-\theta)$ grows at the same rate as L_R, then ϕ is constant and an exponential, balanced growth is assured. But this implies $\hat{A}(t) = \hat{A}(t-\theta) = \hat{L}_R(t) = \hat{L}(t)$. The first is a simple shifting relation. The last is implied by the constancy of u. But then:

$$\hat{Q} = \hat{K} = \hat{A} + \widehat{(uL)} \tag{7.3.7}$$
$$= \hat{A} + \hat{L}$$
$$= 2\hat{L}$$

This proves the assertion.

7.3.3.   Concluding remarks

Without going into the normative theory (which will be discussed briefly in Appendix 7.1), we shall note the following:

(1) In economies not under central planning, we need behavioral conditions to determine the levels of education and research for "closing" a model.
(2) The benefits of either education or research are long run in nature. Hence, individual decision makers must anticipate such gains in incurring the respective costs. Inasmuch as various decision makers have different and imperfect foresight, Pareto efficiency may be seldom achieved in reality. Moreover, due to the activity of imitators, the fruits of innovation often spread to firms not engaged in the initial research. In other words, external economy exists with respect to research.
(3) On the other hand, the nonexistence of an infallible central planner casts doubt about whether the apparent superiority of a planned economy

(as implied by optimal growth models) can be translated into actual gains for the society.

All these considerations point to the need for further studies of growth problems, especially under the context of uncertainty. So far this is still a virgin land.

APPENDIX 7.1

In this chapter we have deliberately sidestepped the implications of endogenous technical progress on optimal growth, a subject which we shall discuss in Chapters 9–11. However, the present appendix is devoted to reviewing the relevant literature in this area. For readers interested in such aspects, it is recommended that they go on to Chapters 9 and 10 and then return to this appendix.

We shall now discuss the four types of endogenous technical progress in turn.

1. Induced technical progress

Samuelson pointed out that the competitive solution of directing technical progress to minimize instantaneous unit cost is nonoptimal. Extended studies on this topic were conducted by Nordhaus [24]. He postulated a planning authority which aims at the maximization of the infinite discounted integral of per capita consumption. Both the saving/income ratio and the direction of technical progress are now control variables at the disposal of the state. The problem now takes the form:

$$\text{Max} \int_0^\infty e^{-\delta t} c(t)\, dt = \int_0^\infty e^{-\delta t} [1 - s(t)] A_2(t) f[k(t)]\, dt \tag{7.A.1}$$

subject to

$$\dot{k}(t) = s(t) A_1(t) f[k'(t)] - nk'(t) + \{\hat{A}_1(t) - g[\hat{A}_1(t)]\} k'(t) \tag{7.A.2}$$

$$\dot{A}_1(t) = \hat{A}_1(t) A_1(t) \qquad \dot{A}_2(t) = g[\hat{A}_1(t)] A_2(t) \tag{7.A.3}$$

where $c(t)$ is per capita consumption and δ is the social discount rate.

Invoking the Pontryagin format, Nordhaus derived certain implications from this model. These are summarized in the following:

(1) The first-order conditions (Euler equations) provide shadow price interpretations for the adjoint variables. Specifically, shadow prices should be assigned to technical progress. Since technical progress is not marketable, optimal growth can hardly be attained under a competitive market.

(2) If the optimal path exhibits steady-state growth, then, as we have seen in Section 7.1.1, only technical progress of the pure labor-augmenting type can prevail.

(3) Moreover, if the elasticity of factor substitution is greater than unity, no golden age path can be optimal. If the same elasticity is less than unity, then there is a golden age optimal path. In fact, in the former case, the growth rate of output becomes unbounded and the convergence of the maximand is in question.

Nordhaus did not examine the stability property of the optimal path. Nor did he compare the optimal solution with the competitive solution. But he questioned the usual literary discussion of induced technical progress where it is postulated that a *fixed* research budget may be used toward various possible innovations. He argued that the spreading of the fixed research budget over large outputs would lead to internal economies of scale and the breakdown of the competitive system.

2. Learning by doing

In his original contribution, Arrow postulates an optimal growth model that maximizes the infinite integral of discounted aggregate consumption flow. A study by Sheshinski [25] considered a model in which disembodied technical progress augments labor efficiency and capital and labor are smoothly substitutable for each other (this is similar to Levhari [26]). A fiscal policy is then devised to steer the actual growth to the social optimum.

We shall concentrate on the results of Levhari [21] and Arrow [10]. The problem can be considered assuming $m \neq 1$.

A.   THE OPTIMAL SAVING PROBLEM

$$\text{Max} \int_0^\infty e^{-\delta t}\{G(t) - G[h(t)] - \dot{G}(t)\}\, dt \qquad \text{(from (7.2.21) and the definition of consumption)} \qquad (7.A.4)$$

subject to:

$$G(t)^{1-m} - G^{1-m}[h(t)] = (1-m)L_0 e^{nt} \qquad \text{(from footnote 9)} \qquad (7.A.5)$$

$$0 \leq \dot{G}(t) \leq G(t) - G[h(t)] \qquad (7.A.6)$$

Substituting (7.A.5) into (7.A.4) we get

$$\text{Max} \int_0^\infty e^{-\delta t}\{G(t) - [G(t)^{1-m} - (1-m)L_0 e^{nt}]^{1/(1-m)} - \dot{G}(t)\}\, dt \qquad (7.A.7)$$

subject to (7.A.6).

Without considering (7.A.6), the Euler equation for this variational problem becomes

$$e^{-\delta t}\{1 - [1 - (1-m)L/G^{1-m}]^{m/(1-m)}\} = \delta e^{-\delta t} \qquad (7.A.8)$$

which implies

$$G(t) = \left[\frac{(1-m)L_0}{1 - (1-\delta)^{(1-m)/m}}\right]^{1/(1-m)} e^{nt/(1-m)} \qquad (7.A.9)$$

which is an exponential path. One can deduce from the work of Levhari [21] that

(1) If the initial condition $G(0)$ is on the exponential path of (7.A.9), then investment $\dot{G}(t)$ should follow what is dictated in (7.A.9); i.e., $\hat{G} = n/(1-m)$.
(2) If the initial condition $G(0)$ is under the exponential path (the right-hand side of (7.A.9)), investment should be stepped up to its maximum possible level. Since (7.A.6) abstracts from the minimum subsistence consumption, we should set $\dot{G}(t)$ equal to $Q(t) = G(t) - G[h(t)]$, until $G(t)$ reaches the said path. After that, (7.A.9) takes over.
(3) If the initial condition $G(0)$ is above the exponential path (the right-hand side of (7.A.9)), zero investment is warranted, i.e., $\dot{G} = 0$, until $G(t)$ reaches the said path. After that, (7.A.9) takes over.

If $\delta > n/(1-m)$, (7.A.7) converges and then the problem is an ordinary variational problem. Otherwise, the overtaking principle (Chapter 10) can then be applied.

B.   SOCIAL PRODUCT VS. PRIVATE PRODUCT OF INVESTMENT

We can calculate the marginal social product of investment, $\partial\phi/\partial G$, and the marginal private product of investment, the quasi-rent per machine. It can be shown that the former is equal to:[16]

$$\frac{\partial\phi}{\partial G} = 1 - \left\{\frac{G[h(t)]}{G(t)}\right\}^m \qquad (7.A.10)$$

---

[16] From footnote 12, $\phi = G - [G^{1-m} - (1-m)L]^{1/(1-m)}$. Thus $\partial\phi/\partial G = 1 - [1 - (1-m)LG^{m-1}]^{m/(1-m)}$; from footnote 9, $G[h(t)]/G(t) = [1 - (1-m)LG^{m-1}]^{1/(1-m)}$.

and the latter is:[17]

$$\frac{Q(v, t) - w(t)L(v, t)}{K(v, t)} = 1 - \left\{ \frac{G[h(t)]}{G(v)} \right\}^m \tag{7.A.11}$$

for a vintage-v machine at t. Obviously, since $G(v) < G(t)$, for $v < t$,

$$\frac{Q(v, t) - w(t)L(v, t)}{K(v, t)} < \frac{\partial \phi}{\partial G}$$

This spells out the divergence between the marginal social and private products of investment on all old machines.

Let r be that interest rate at which the investment in machines breaks even under a steady state.[18] Now, we know that labor receives its marginal social product:[19]

$$\frac{\partial \phi}{\partial L} = w(t)$$

As ϕ exhibits increasing returns (Section 7.2.2-B, 2(b)), capital must be receiving less than its social product under the steady state. Capital receives the private rate of return r. Hence,

$$r < \frac{\partial \phi}{\partial G}$$

One may contrast this result against the conclusion in Section 5.3 on this point.

Levhari showed that
(a) On the path (7.A.9), $\partial \phi / \partial G = \delta$; i.e., social product of investment equals social discount.
(b) Above the path (7.A.9), $\partial \phi / \partial G < \delta$, while under it, $\partial \phi / \partial G > \delta$.

3. Education

The complete Uzawa model postulates that social utility is identified with the infinite integral of discounted consumption per capita. Formally, this poses the problem:

$$\text{Max} \int_0^\infty [1 - s(t)]A(t)u(t)f[k(t)/A(t)u(t)]e^{-\delta t} dt \tag{7.A.12}$$

[17]$[Q(v, t) - w(t)L(v, t)]/K(v, t) = 1 - w(t)/A(v)$. Using (7.2.17) and (7.2.19), we obtain (7.A.11).

[18]That is,

$$1 = \int_0^{t - h(t)} \left\{ \frac{1 - w(\tau)}{A[h(t)]} \right\} e^{-r\tau} d\tau$$

where the integrand is the present value of quasi-rent at instant τ discounted to the instant $h(t)$, i.e., the moment when the machines just retired were first installed, and the unity on the left-hand side is the value of that machine.

[19]From footnote 17, we can derive

$$\frac{\partial \phi}{\partial L} = [G^{1-m} - (1-m)L]^{m/(1-m)}$$

$$= (G - Q)^m \qquad \text{(from footnote 17)}$$

$$= w \qquad \qquad \text{(from (7.2.23))}$$

subject to

$$\dot{k} = sAuf - nk \qquad (7.3.1)$$

$$\dot{A} = \phi(1-u)A \qquad (7.3.2)$$

$$0 \le u, s \le 1 \qquad (7.A.13)$$

Without going through the involved analysis of Uzawa, we may summarize his results below:

(1) There exists a "golden rule" path exhibiting exponential growth with the following steady-state conditions:

$$f'(z^*) = n + \delta \qquad (7.A.14)$$

where $z^* = k^*(t)/A^*(t)u^*$ is the effective capital/labor ratio; asterisks indicate optimal values.

$$u^*\phi'(1-u^*) = \delta - \phi(1-u^*) \qquad (7.A.15)$$

$$s^*f(z^*) = [n + \phi(1-u^*)]z^* \qquad (7.A.16)$$

$$f(z^*) - z^*f'(z^*) = \phi'(1-u^*)v^* \qquad (7.A.17)$$

where v^* is the marginal product of educational labor force.

The economic interpretations are:

(a) (7.A.14) restates the familiar golden rule: own-rate of interest for capital should exceed the biological interest rate (population growth rate) by the social discount.

(b) (7.A.15) states that the "marginal product of education" modified by the manpower "leakage" of education (since $1-u$ is the portion of "nonproductive" labor) should be equal to the social discount rate minus the labor-augmenting technical progress rate.

(c) (7.A.16) is a modified form of Solovian factor intensity balance: per capita investment should match the increases of labor force, both natural and technically augmented.

(d) (7.A.17) actually defines the shadow price for education effort, v^*.

(2) The optimal decision rule is as follows:

(a) If $z(0) = z^*$, follow the exponential path where $\hat{k} = \hat{A}$.

(b) If $z(0) > z^*$, consume everything ($s = 0$) until $z(t) = z^*$, then follow (a).

(c) If $z(0) < z^*$, save everything ($s = 1$) until $z(t) = z^*$, then follow (a).

The allocation role of labor force (i.e., the value of $u(t)$) during the transition phase in cases (b) and (c) is rather complicated, and we leave it out.

4. Research

Phelps generalized his golden rule analysis into the research model discussed in Section 7.3.2. He showed that to obtain the golden age path with the highest per capita consumption, exactly half of the labor force should be devoted to research. We shall sketch his derivation in two steps: the derivation of the golden age consumption path and the derivation of the golden rule consumption path.

A. THE GOLDEN AGE CONSUMPTION PATH

Let c be per capita consumption and z be the effective capital/labor ratio k/Au. Then from (7.3.2),

$$c = (1-s)\dot{K}/sL = Auf(z) - \dot{k} - nk$$

From (7.3.7), along a golden age path,

$$\hat{k} = \hat{K} - \hat{L} = \hat{L} = n = \hat{A}$$

Hence, the golden age consumption path must be

$$c(t) = \{A(0)u[f(z) - 2nz]\}e^{nt} \qquad \text{where } z = k/Au \qquad (7.A.18)$$

$$= c(0)e^{nt}$$

B. THE "GOLDEN RULE FOR RESEARCH"

Among all the golden age consumption paths of the form (7.A.18), Phelps then searches for the dominating path (or "commanding path"), where $c(0)$ is a maximum. $c(0)$ can be shown to be:[20]

$$\frac{L(0)e^{n\theta}}{\phi^{-1}(ne^{n\theta})}[u(1-u)][f(z)-2nz] = c_0(u, z) \qquad (7.A.19)$$

for some function $c_0(\cdot, \cdot)$.

Solving the problem,

$$\underset{u, z}{\text{Max }} c_0(u, z) = B[u(1-u)][f(z)-2nz]$$

where $B > 0$.

Since B is a positive constant and the rest of c_0 consists of two separable multiplicative terms, the first-order conditions are

$$\frac{d}{dz}[f(z)-2nz] = 0 \qquad (7.A.20)$$

$$\frac{d}{du}[u(1-u)] = 0 \qquad (7.A.21)$$

The first condition implies

$$f'(z^*) = 2n \qquad (z^* \text{ is the optimal value for } z)$$

which is the original golden rule requirement: marginal product of capital equals the growth rate of "efficiency labor."

The second condition implies

$$u^* = \tfrac{1}{2} \qquad (u^* \text{ is the optimal value for } u)$$

which dictates the allocation of *exactly half* (!) of the labor force into education activities. This holds irrespective of the value of n or the precise form of ϕ.

Phelps conceded that the conclusion of $u^* = \tfrac{1}{2}$ is unrealistically high. But he showed that when capital is required for research, the conclusion can be modified.

The main value of the whole exercise appears to be the demonstration of the significance of the specification of the ϕ function. Since empirical work is rather meager in this area, this exercise highlights the crying need for factual studies in economics today to match the sophisticated constructions of model builders.

---

[20]Dividing (7.3.6) by $A(t) = A(0)e^{nt}$ on both sides and noting that $\dot{A}(t) = nA(0)e^{nt}$ and $A(t-\theta) = A(0)e^{-n\theta}e^{nt}$, as well as that $\hat{A} = n$, we can obtain

$$n = e^{-n\theta}\phi\{(1-u)L_0e^{n\theta}/A(0)\}$$

Since $\phi' > 0$, ϕ^{-1} exists as an inverse function for ϕ. Hence,

$$\frac{(1-u)L_0e^{n\theta}}{A(0)} = \phi^{-1}(ne^{n\theta}) \text{ or } A(0) = \frac{L_0e^{n\theta}(1-u)}{\phi^{-1}(ne^{n\theta})}$$

Substituting back into (7.A.18), we obtain (7.A.19).

REFERENCES

[1] Rothbarth, E., "Causes of the Superior Efficiency of U.S.A. Industry as Compared with British Industry," *Economic Journal*, vol. LVI, Sept. 1946, pp. 383–90.

[2] Habbakuk, H. J., *American and British Technology in the Nineteenth Century*, Cambridge University Press, London, 1962.

[3] Kennedy, Charles, "Induced Bias in Innovation and the Theory of Distribution," *Economic Journal*, vol. LXXIV, Sept. 1964.

[4] Weizsäcker, C. C., "Tentative Notes on a Two-Sector Model with Induced Technical Progress," *Review of Economic Studies*, vol. XXXIII, July 1966, pp. 245–51.

[5] Samuelson, Paul A., "A Theory of Induced Innovation Along Kennedy-Weizsäcker Lines," *Review of Economics and Statistics*, vol. XLVII, Nov. 1965, pp. 343–56.

[6] Drandakis, Emanuel, and Edmund S. Phelps, "A Model of Induced Invention, Growth and Distribution," *Economic Journal*, vol. LXXVI, Dec. 1966, pp. 823–40.

[7] Chang, W. T., *Essays on the Theory of Induced Inventions and Economic Growth*, Doctoral Dissertation, University of Rochester, 1968.

[8] Alchian, A. A., "Reliability of Progress Curve in Airframe Production," *Econometrica*, vol. XXXI, Oct. 1963, pp. 679–93.

[9] Verdoorn, P. J., "Fattori che rigolano lo sviluppo della producttivita del lavoro," *L'Industria*, 1, 1949.

[10] Arrow, K. J., "The Economic Implications of Learning by Doing," *Review of Economic Studies*, vol. XXIX, June 1962, pp. 155–73.

[11] Schultz, T. W., "Capital Formation by Education," *Journal of Political Economy*, vol. LXVII, 1960, pp. 571–87.

[12] Uzawa, Hiorfumi, "Optimum Technical Change in an Aggregate Model of of Economic Growth," *International Economic Review*, vol. 6, Jan. 1965, pp. 18–31.

[13] Phelps, Edmund S., "Models of Technical Progress and the Golden Rule of Research," *Review of Economic Studies*, vol. XXXIII, April 1966, pp. 133–45.

[14] Solow, R. M., "A Skeptical Note on the Constancy of Relative Shares," *American Economic Review*, vol. XLVIII, Sept. 1958, pp. 618–31.

[15] Zarembka, Paul, "On the Empirical Relevance of the CES Production Function," *Review of Economics and Statistics*, vol. LII, Feb. 1970, pp. 47–53.

[16] Kennedy, Charles, "Samuelson on Induced Invention," *Review of Economics and Statistics*, vol. XLVIII, Dec. 1966, pp. 442–44.

[17] Samuelson, P. A., "Rejoinder: Agreements, Disagreements, Doubts and the Case of Induced Harrod Neutral Technical Change," *Review of Economics and Statistics*, vol. XLVIII, Dec. 1966, pp. 444–48.

[18] Tobin, James, in *The Theory and Empirical Analysis of Production*, M. Brown, Ed., National Bureau of Economic Research, 1967, p. 52.

[19] Shell, K., "Toward a Theory of Inventive Activity and Capital Accumulation," *American Economic Review Supplement*, vol. LVI, May 1966, pp. 62–68.

[20] Shell, K., "A Model of Inventive Activity and Capital Accumulation," in *Essays on the Theory of Optimal Economic Growth*, K. Shell, Ed., M.I.T. Press, Cambridge, Mass., 1967.

[21] Levhari, D., "Further Implications of Learning by Doing," *Review of Economic Studies*, vol. XXXIII, Jan. 1966, pp. 31–8.

[22] Park, S. Y., an unpublished paper.

[23] Adelman, Irma, "A Linear Programming Model of Education Planning," in *The Theory and Design of Economic Development*, Irma Adelman and Erik Thorbecke, Eds., Johns Hopkins Press, Baltimore, Md., 1966.

[24] Nordhaus, W. D., "The Optimal Rate and Direction of Technical Change," in *Essays on the Theory of Optimal Economic Growth*, K. Shell, Ed., M.I.T. Press, Cambridge, Mass., 1967.

[25] Sheshinski, E., "Optimal Accumulation with Learning-by-Doing," in *Essays on the Theory of Optimal Economic Growth*, K. Shell, Ed., M.I.T. Press, Cambridge, Mass., 1967.

[26] Levhari, D., "Extensions of Arrow's Learning by Doing," *Review of Economic Studies*, vol. XXXIII, April 1966, pp. 117–31.

[27] Atkinson, A. B., and J. E. Stiglitz, "A New View of Technical Change," *Economic Journal*, vol. LXXIX, Sept. 1969, pp. 73–78.

EXERCISES

7.1. Atkinson and Stiglitz [27] asserted that real-life technical progress affects only a portion of the production isoquant rather than the whole spectrum of techniques. Formulate a growth model with equations, under the following assumptions:

(1) There is only one final good serving both as investment and consumption good.

(2) Capital is malleable and nondepreciable.

(3) Labor grows exponentially at the constant rate n.

(4) The saving/income ratio is constant.

(5) At any point of time, there exists N available techniques of the fixed-proportions type. For the ith technique at time t, $a_i(t)$ units of capital stock combined with $b_i(t)$ units of labor service are required to produce one unit of output.

(6) If the output produced at t according to technique i is $Q_i(t)$, then $\hat{a}_i(t) = \hat{b}_i(t) = -g[Q_i(t)]$; $g' > 0$; $g(0) = 0$.

Why is it not possible to determine uniquely the growth path of this model? *Hint:* Is Q uniquely determined?

8

extensions of the neoclassical model: the inclusion of monetary assets

8.1 INTRODUCTION

The various growth models discussed so far are "barter" models. Money per se rarely appears in any of these works.[1] Our story so far is in a sense incomplete.

(1) The models examined are exclusively "real" models for developed economies. One of the hallmarks of economic development is the transformation of a subsistence economy into a "monetized" economy.[2] Does the presence of money affect the pattern of economic growth?

(2) The majority of economists who study the growth process of the free enterprise economies are not disinterested bystanders. An understanding of the workings of the economic system is a prelude to the prescription of policy measures for the attainment of better performance. But most of the models we have studied so far are "self-contained." There is no room left for control variables to carry out public policies.

(3) The predominant portion of the growth literature comes from the neoclassical school. In most such works the existence of Keynesian difficulties is neither denied nor explicitly considered. Solow considers the neoclassical and Keynesian aspects as two sides of the same coin. How can these two sides be synthesized into a comprehensive theory?

While elaborate theories to answer such questions do not exist, certain cornerstones for such theories have already been laid. These will be reviewed in the current chapter.

A year before the Solow-Swan papers appeared in 1956, Tobin constructed a neoclassical macro model [1] combining both the aggregate production

---

[1]In his 1956, paper, Solow sketched the possible inclusion of monetary assets in a growth model. In his critique to Solow, Eisner also mentioned the monetary aspects of growth.

[2]Roughly speaking, "monetization" means production is no longer aimed at direct consumption but at cash rewards.

function and the monetary sector. However, the dynamic mechanism was not specified in detail. Subsequently, in a series of papers appearing between 1965 and 1968 [2–4], Tobin cast his theory in terms of balanced growth models. The essence of his approach is that saving in a monetary economy may take the form of either physical capital or an expansion of the real balance of "outside money."[3] For this reason, the balanced growth capital/labor ratio (and therefore the output per worker, the wage and rent rates, etc.) depends upon the "portfolio balance," viz., the decision of the public to hold a particular portion of wealth in money assets and a particular portion in physical assets.

Tobin's work was modified and criticized by Levhari and Patinkin [5] regarding the omission of the use value of money, and by Sidrauski [6] because of the omission of short-run analysis. A deeper question is whether the saving behavior should be explained on the basis of intertemporal utility maximization on the part of the household—a line adopted by Sidrauski [7] and by Cass and Yaari [8]. Again, more emphasis can be placed on the labor market, as in the model of H. Rose [9] and the work of Phelps [10]. We omit the latter model because it is related to models with imperfect markets, a topic too involved and important to be dealt with in any haphazard manner, although full treatment is beyond the scope of this text.

Section 8.2 is devoted to Tobin's model and those of his main critics. Section 8.3 reviews the work of Sidrauski, Cass and Yaari, and Rose.

While different models disclose different facets of the economic reality, it seems that much more theoretical as well as empirical work is needed to develop a fully satisfactory theory.

8.2 TOBIN AND HIS CRITICS

8.2.1. The Tobin model

Both money and governmental expenditures enter the Tobin model. Since the fiscal aspect was never analyzed in full detail, we shall omit it for the sake of simplicity. Real balance held by the public is created by government transfer payments (e.g., national dividends). Also, Tobin usually considers the saving/income ratio a nondecreasing rate of the rate of interest. Three cases are possible: (a) the saving/income ratio s is a constant, i.e., assuming the Keynesian saving function; (b) s increases with a finite slope as interest rate rises (which appears rather plausible), or (c) s is zero or unity depending upon whether the interest rate is above or below a given threshold.[4] We shall follow Harry Johnson [11] and concentrate on case (a) only. In Section 8.2.1-A, the assumptions of the simplified Tobin model will be compared with the simple Solow model. In Section 8.2.1-B, the dynamic equations of the Tobin system

---

[3]"Outside" means that it is not the debt of "members" *of* the economy, e.g., commercial banks, but the debt of some organization *above* the economy, e.g., a central bank.

[4]At that magical interest rate, saving may occupy any portion of the income.

will be sketched. In Section 8.2.1-C, a graphic analysis compares the balanced growth positions of the Tobin and Solow models, followed by some simple comparative dynamic results. In Section 8.2.1-D, Tobin's general discussions of the role of money will be reviewed in the growth context.

A. ASSUMPTIONS

The general assumptions of the (simplified) Tobin model are: constant returns, diminishing but positive marginal product of capital, constant population growth rate, constant saving/income ratio, competitive markets, and full flexibility for wages and prices.

The special assumptions are:

(1) Nature of money.   All government debt constitutes legal tender and vice versa[5] with yield rate (if any) specified by the government.
(2) Definition of disposable income.   The private sector regards the sum of national output plus the increase of the real balance of money as disposable income. The inclusion of expansions of real balance into disposable income reflects a money illusion inherent in the existence of outside money.
(3) "Portfolio balance."   There are only two forms of wealth: physical capital and the real balance of money. The proportions (in value terms) of these two assets held by the public depend upon the difference between the rental rate and the "real yield of monetary assets," the latter being the excess of nominal yield over the rate of inflation.

Assumption (3) is again a simplified version of Tobin's theory where, besides "real yield," income and wealth[6] may affect the composition of the wealth held by the public.

A numerical example: The working of the model is exemplified below. Suppose the consumption propensity of an economy is 4/5, which is deemed too low by the government for either of two reasons:

(a) Under balanced growth, such a high saving ratio implies a high capital/labor ratio and a low rate of return on capital[7] such that the investor would not invest and effective demand lags behind output capacity.
(b) Under balanced growth, a high capital/labor ratio means that much output is diverted to supply the new labor force with required equipment so that the consumption flow is unduly reduced.[8]

Our current interest is how the government can steer the economy away from these undesirable states of affairs through monetary policy. Suppose that the government declares a "national dividend" and every household receives bond

---

[5]Bonds are the only money in Tobin's world.

[6]This more or less corresponds to the Keynesian trichotomy of demand for money: speculative, transactive, and precautionary.

[7]The comparative dynamics between s and $f'(k)$ has been analyzed in Section 2.3.

[8]The "dynamic inefficiency" due to oversaving will be discussed in Chapter 9.

currency of a certain amount. Suppose that the portfolio balance relation is such that as long as bonds and physical assets yield equal rates of return the public is willing to consider both objects as perfect substitutes. Also suppose that the value of bonds distributed is equal to 20% of the national output. Tobin's definition of disposable income then implies that the public feel that they are 120% as rich as their true output reflects. Out of this "augmented income" they spend four-fifths, which is 96% of the entire physical output. So, by such financial wizardry, the saving/income ratio is finally brought down to acceptable size.

B. THE MODEL FOR BALANCED GROWTH

Besides the usual definitions for the symbols $L, K, k, f(k)$, etc., as in the Solow model, let us define

M the quantity of money
p the price level
M/p the real balance
$m = M/L$ the per capita money holdings
y the per capita disposable income according to Tobin's definition (assumption (2))
ρ the portion of savings kept in monetary form

The above definitions and assumptions lead to the following identities:

(1) The monetary expansion and physical capital:

$$\frac{d(M/p)}{dt} = (M/p)(\hat{M} - \hat{p}) \qquad \text{(logarithmic differentiation)} \qquad (8.2.1$$

$$= [\rho/(1-\rho)](\hat{M} - \hat{p})K \qquad \text{(since } M/p = \rho[K + (M/p)])$$

(2) The monetary expansion and disposable income:

$$yL = Lf + \frac{d(M/p)}{dt} \qquad \text{(definition of } y) \qquad (8.2.2$$

$$= Lf + [\rho/(1-\rho)](\hat{M} - \hat{p})K$$

(3) Investment and monetary expansions:

$$\dot{K} = syL - \frac{d(M/p)}{dt} \qquad (8.2.3$$

$$= sLf + (s-1)[\rho/(1-\rho)](\hat{M} - \hat{p})K \qquad \text{(from (8.2.2))}$$

(4) Investment per capita:

$$\dot{K}/L = \dot{k} + nk \qquad (\dot{K} = \frac{d}{dt}(Lk) = L\dot{k} + \dot{L}k) \qquad (8.2.4$$

$$= sf + (s-1)[\rho/(1-\rho)](\hat{M} - \hat{p})k$$

These building blocks can be used for the dynamic equation depicting the evolution of the Tobin world.

From (8.2.1)–(8.2.4) one obtains:

$$\dot{k} = sf - \left[\frac{(1-s)\rho}{1-\rho}(\hat{M}-\hat{p})+n\right]k \tag{8.2.5}$$

To close the system, we have two governmental controls:

(a) The monetary supply:

$$m = M/L(0)e^{nt} \tag{8.2.6}$$

where M, the money supply, is controlled by the government.

(b) The yield of monetary assets η, which affects

$$\rho = \rho(x) \quad \text{with } \rho' \geq 0 \tag{8.2.7}$$

where $x = (\eta - \hat{p}) - f'(k)$ is the difference of real rates of return and η is the nominal yield of the money asset, specified by the government.

With known initial conditions $M(0)$, $k(0)$, and $L(0)$, and given governmental controls $M(t)$ and $\eta(t)$, the whole system is determined.

Three specimens of $\rho(x)$ are shown in Figure 8.1.

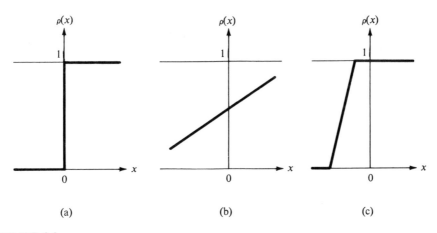

FIGURE 8.1

Equation (8.2.5) is somewhat comparable to (2.1.4), the fundamental dynamic equation in Chapter 2.

Equating $\dot{k}$ to zero, we have the balanced growth equation:

$$sf(k) = \left[\frac{(1-s)\rho(x)}{1-\rho(x)}(\hat{M}-\hat{p})+n\right]k \tag{8.2.8}$$

Since balanced growth also requires the per capita real balance M/pL to be constant, we have $\hat{M} - \hat{p} = n$. Thus (8.2.8) becomes

$$sf(k) = \left[\frac{(1-s)\rho(\eta - n + \hat{M} - f')}{1 - \rho(\eta - n + \hat{M} - f')} + 1\right]nk$$

$$= \frac{1 - s\rho(\eta - n + \hat{M} - f')}{1 - \rho(\eta - n + \hat{M} - f')} nk$$

(8.2.8)

C. THE COMPARATIVE BALANCED GROWTH STATES

Tobin focused his attention on the very long run, where the economy enters its dynamic equilibrium of balanced growth. We can deduce certain results from his model:

(1) Government can directly control the rate of growth of money, $\hat{M}$, but not the growth rate of the real balance,

$$\frac{(d/dt)(M/p)}{M/p}$$

which by the definition of balanced growth must be equal to n.

(2) Consequently, the rate of inflation $\hat{p}$ is equal to the excess of the growth rate of money over the growth rate of population, *under balanced growth*.

(3) Monetary expansion is equivalent to a reduction of the nominal yield. At the margin, a 1% increase in monetary expansion (implying a 1% increase in the rate of inflation) reduces the real yield by exactly 1%, just as a 1% reduction of nominal yield would.

(4) A monetary economy has a lower balanced growth capital/labor ratio than a barter economy, other things being equal. Therefore, from Table 2.7, the former also has a lower per capita output, a lower wage rate, a higher output/capital ratio, a higher rent rate, etc.

(5) Between two monetary economies, a lower nominal yield or a higher rate of monetary expansion, other things being equal, means a lower portion of saving in monetary assets, and hence a higher balanced growth capital/labor ratio, a higher output per worker, etc.

Points (1) and (2) follow the definition of balanced growth and hence

$$\frac{(d/dt)(M/p)}{M/p} = \hat{M} - \hat{p} = n$$

Point (3) is the consequence of (8.2.8'), as is the first part of point (5). Under balanced growth, $\dot{k} = 0$. Equation (8.2.8') can now be rewritten as

$$f(k)/k = A(k)$$

(8.2.8)

$$= [(1 - s\rho)/(1 - \rho)](n/s)$$

$$\geq n/s$$

where $A(k)$ is the average product of capital. The behavior of $(1 - s\rho)/(1 - \rho)$ is

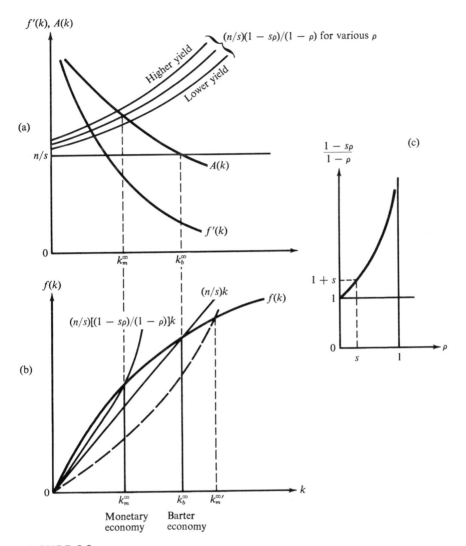

FIGURE 8.2

depicted in Figure 8.2c. Plotting (8.2.8″) in Figure 8.2a,[9] we have verified point (4) and the second part of point (5). Figure 8.2b facilitates the comparison between the Tobin model and the simple Solow model.

Tobin attributes the paradoxical result (4) (the monetary economy yields a lower per capita output than a barter economy) to the abstraction from "financial intermediations" in the above model. The real-life saving ratio depends upon institutional aspects. Availability of a full range of financial assets helps a society to mobilize its saving potential to its full capacity.

[9]Using the fact that $(d/d\rho)\left[(1-s\rho)/(1-\rho)\right] > 0$, $\rho' \geq 0$, and $dx/dk = -f''(k) > 0$.

D. DISCUSSIONS

Tobin's analysis of a variable saving/income ratio (dependent upon rent only) yields essentially similar results. He commented that the model we discussed above is unrealistic in two ways:

(1) No distinction is made between the functions of money as the storage of value and the means of payment.
(2) The effects of risk and uncertainty are not considered.

However, he did not present a fully developed analysis on either point. The second point presumably will be explored in the near future, judging by the research efforts devoted to a related topic: optimal saving under uncertainty (e.g., Phelps [10], Levhari and Srinivasan [12]).

Tobin further pointed out that money is not neutral in his model, since the rate of its expansion affects the long-run value of the capital/labor ratio. On the other hand, his model assumes full flexibility for prices of all goods and services, so that full employment is consistent with any rate of inflation or deflation.

8.2.2. Levhari and Patinkin

Levhari and Patinkin claimed that Tobin obtained his paradoxical result (4) (that introduction of money lowers long-run per capita output) only by ignoring two major functions of money: Money provides convenience to the daily life of consumers; it also facilitates the operation and management of business firms. Hence, two adaptations may be made:

(1) The national income figure should include a new item: the service of the cash balance kept.
(2) The real cash balance may be considered as a productive factor in its own right.

Tobin omitted both uses of money and hence understated the national income of a monetary economy and overstated the productive capacity of the barter economy[10] at the same time. We shall now consider the Levhari-Patinkin adaptations one at a time.

A. MONEY SERVICE AS A CONSUMPTION GOOD

Levhari and Patinkin proposed two modifications to Tobin's model:

(1) Not only should the increase of money holdings be included in the definition of disposable income, but the holding of money itself provides a service to its owner. Otherwise, if there were no advantage in owning *some* money, one could never feel richer (and consume more) by owning *more* money. This *service* can be evaluated at its opportunity cost: if the own-rate of interest of capital is $f'(k)$ and the real yield of money asset is $\eta - \hat{p}$, then $-x = f' + \hat{p} - \eta$

---

[10]In Tobin's formulation, an economy can produce the same amount of goods by abandoning the use of money.

is the rate of opportunity (interest) cost by keeping savings in money form. Therefore, disposable income should be

$$yL = Lf(k) + d(M/p)/dt - (M/p)x \qquad (8.2.9)$$

(2) The saving ratio is itself an increasing function of both $f'(k)$ and $-\hat{p}$. Higher yield of physical assets and higher rate of *de*flation both encourage savings.

We shall consider the consequences of either modification in turn. Modification (1) nullifies result (4) of Section 8.2.1-C (a monetary economy has a lower k^∞).

Proof.   Dividing (8.2.9) by L and using the new definition for y, we can proceed as in 8.2.1-B to get a result parallel to (8.2.8).

$$f(k^\infty) = \frac{(1-s\rho)n + s\rho x}{(1-\rho)s} k^\infty \begin{Bmatrix} > \\ = \\ < \end{Bmatrix} (n/s)k^\infty$$

Graphically, the dashed curve in Figure 8.2*b* shows the possibility of $[(1-s\rho)n + s\rho x]/(1-\rho)s$ being smaller than n/s; consequently, $k_m^{\infty\prime} > k_b^\infty$.

Modification (2) nullifies result (5) of Section 8.2.1-C. Levhari and Patinkin showed that when the saving ratio depends upon both the rental rate and the rate of deflation $-\hat{p}$, the following possibilities exist:

(a) The two curves in Figure 8.2*b* may intersect more than once, causing multiple balanced growth paths.

(b) Even at a stable balanced growth path, the parametric increase of the rate of monetary expansion has ambiguous effects on the long-run capital/ labor ratio.

It is the dependence of s on $-\hat{p}$ that opens up such possibilities.

B.   MONEY SERVICE AS A PRODUCTION GOOD

Levhari and Patinkin pointed out that without money, firms would have to divert resources to the search for bartering opportunities. A simple, approximate way to handle this problem is to regard money as another input in a linear homogeneous production function. Money services enter into production cost and hence automatically into disposable income. The balanced growth position can be characterized by a pair of conditions (8.2.10) and (8.2.11):

$$[g(k, m/p) + nm/p]s = [(m/p) + k]n \qquad (8.2.10)$$

where $g(k, m/p)$ is the per capita output

$nm/p = \dfrac{d(M/p)/dt}{L}$ is the per capita increase of the real balance

$(m/p) + k$ is the per capita wealth

$[(m/p) + k]n$ is the sum of physical investment and monetary expansion needed to keep those firms with novice workers well equipped and provided with liquid funds.

Equation (8.2.10) is similar to (8.2.8′).

$$\frac{\partial g}{\partial k} = \frac{\partial g}{\partial (m/p)} - \hat{p} \tag{8.2.1}$$

where the left-hand side is the own-rate of interest for physical investment and the right-hand side shows the "real yield" of investing in real balance. The inflation rate is subtracted from the marginal product of the real balance.

Equation (8.2.11) states that the marginal dollar used in the real balance should obtain a return comparable to that of the marginal dollar invested in the physical good. In the latter case, it is the sum of the rate of appreciation $\hat{p}$ plus the marginal product $\partial g/\partial k$ that reflects the total return.

Note that although the government supplies the money, it is the market forces that determine the price level and hence the size of the real balance. Under the usual assumptions,[11] the "invisible hand" chooses the mode of production that maximizes per capita output with labor (one unit, by definition) and capital (k units, historically given) taken as known data. Since $m/p = 0$ is a possibility, the existence of positive real balances indicates that the monetary economy affords the higher output/worker ratio vis-à-vis the barter economy. Therefore, Tobin's result (4) is contradicted in this case.

For the modified model all attempts to obtain comparative dynamics fail. No result holds unambiguously. Nor is it possible to deduce stability properties for the balanced growth paths.

Levhari and Patinkin observed that if the increments of real balance are used by the government for consumption or investment, the above analysis has to be modified again.

8.2.3. Sidrauski

A. THE ASSUMPTIONS AND THE MODEL

Sidrauski considers a model structurally similar to the simplified Tobin model we have discussed. The main difference is the role price expectations play in Sidrauski's world. To simplify matters, he assumed that money asset bears no interest, i.e., $\eta \equiv 0$.

In the Tobin model presented in Section 8.2.1 the *current* inflation rate $\hat{p}$ enters into both the calculation of current disposable income in (8.2.1)–(8.2.5) and the determination of the yield differential, $x = \eta - \hat{p} - f'$, in (8.2.7). It may be argued that people take action only on the expectations of concurrent events (i.e., contemporaneous inflation rate) because those events themselves cannot be observed with strict simultaneity.

The twin key assumptions of Sidrauski are:

(1) It is the *expected* inflation rate, π, rather than $\hat{p}$ that enters into (8.2.1)–(8.2.5) and (8.2.8). Hence, (8.2.5) becomes

$$\hat{k} = sA(k) - [(1-s)\rho/(1-\rho)](\hat{M} - \pi) - n \tag{8.2.12}$$

---

[11]Convex production set, etc.

Also, x is redefined as $x = -(f' + \pi)$ in (8.2.7), η being set to zero.

(2) Expectations are modified according to an "adaptive" behavior; i.e.,

$$\dot{\pi} = b[\hat{p} - \pi] \tag{8.2.13}$$

The economic assumptions behind (8.2.13) are that people base their actions upon their imperfect forecasts of the short-run rate of inflation (deflation), and these forecasts are often wrong. However, people also realize that market forces are capricious and that observations of the immediate past do not form the best forecast for the future either. Hence, forecasts of short-run inflation rate are adjusted at each time by a fraction of past errors, i.e., the divergence between the forecast and the observed values.

Differentiating logarithmically the portfolio balance identity, $M/p = [\rho/(1-\rho)]K$, and using the result to eliminate $\hat{p}$ from (8.2.13), we can obtain:[12]

$$\dot{\pi} = [b/(1 + \phi b)](\hat{m} - \pi - \psi \hat{k}) \tag{8.2.13'}$$

where $\phi = -(d/dx)\{\ln[\rho/(1-\rho)]\}$ with $x = -(f' + \pi)$ and $\psi = (1 + \phi f'' k)$.

B.   GRAPHIC ANALYSIS

Sidrauski addressed himself to three questions:

(1) The *existence* and *uniqueness* of the balanced growth path for (8.2.12)–(8.2.13') with $\dot{\pi} = 0$. This last condition calls for exact price forecasts, i.e., $\pi = \hat{p}$. Replacing π by $\hat{p}$, we are back at the Tobin system of Section 8.2.1. A graphic analysis similar to Figure 8.2*b* shows that there exists one and only one balanced growth.

(2) The *stability* property of the balanced growth path. After intricate but basically elementary calculations (which we do not reproduce here), Sidrauski proceeded to characterize two loci on the $k-\pi$ plane:

(a) $\hat{k} = \Lambda_1(k, \pi) = 0$ where $\Lambda_1(k, \pi_0)$ is negative for $k > k_0$ and positive for $k < k_0$ for $\Lambda_1(k_0, \pi_0) = 0$. In other words, the $\Lambda_1 = 0$ locus always exerts a vertical force of attraction.

(b) $\dot{\pi} = \Lambda_2(k, \pi) = 0$. Two cases are now possible:

　(i) If $1 + \phi b > 0$, then $\Lambda_2(k_0, \pi)$ is negative if $\pi > \pi_0$ and positive if $\pi < \pi_0$ where $\Lambda_2(k_0, \pi_0) = 0$.

　(ii) If $1 + \phi b < 0$, then $\Lambda_2(k_0, \pi)$ is positive if $\pi > \pi_0$ and negative if $\pi < \pi_0$ where $\Lambda_2(k_0, \pi_0) = 0$.

In other words, the $\Lambda_2 = 0$ locus exerts a horizontal force of attraction or rejection depending upon the sign of $1 + \phi b$.

Sidrauski found that both loci have positive slopes and that the $\Lambda_2 = 0$ locus is steeper at the point of intersection. Using the phase diagram analysis reproduced in Figure 8.3, it is shown that the steady-state solution is:

(a) Always stable if the speed of adjustment coefficient b is small so that $1 + \phi b > 0$. In that case, the rate of inflation and the capital/labor ratio

---

[12] $\hat{M} - \hat{p} = -(d/dx)\{\ln[\rho/(1-\rho)]\}(f''\hat{k} + \dot{\pi}) + \hat{K}$. Subtracting $\hat{L} = n$ from both sides, solving for $\hat{p}$, and substituting in (8.2.13), we obtain (8.2.13').

converge monotonically either at all times or after the capital/labor ratio wanders off in a wrong direction for a short interval.

(b) Almost always unstable (except the razor edge case when $k(0)$ and $\pi(0)$ fall on the dotted arrows in Figure 8.3b) if the speed of adjustment coefficient b is so large that $1 + \phi b < 0$. Either the inflation rate and the capital/labor ratio diverge monotonically or the capital/labor ratio (or sometimes both the capital/labor ratio and the inflation rate) makes a vain approach to the steady state, only to be deflected back forever.

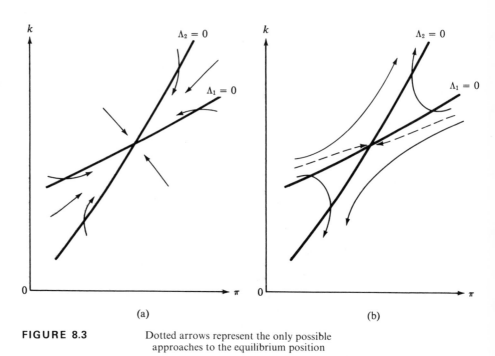

(a)   (b)

FIGURE 8.3   Dotted arrows represent the only possible
                            approaches to the equilibrium position

(3) The effect of *variations* of the rate of monetary expansion. In the stability analysis, the rate of monetary expansion is always held constant. Now suppose that in the stable case the value of $\hat{M}$ has been μ_1 up to $t = 0$ and that it is raised to $\mu_2 > \mu_1$ after that point in time. Sidrauski showed that a path such as the AA' arrow in Figure 8.3a may well occur, which implies that the long-run promise of an increased capital/labor ratio (hence output per worker) may be preceded by an immediate decline of the same ratio(s) for certain finite periods. But—without careful analysis—how long this contrary movement will last cannot be stated *a priori*. This shows the potential pitfalls of attempting to accomplish certain policy goals through manipulating the monetary supply.

8.2.4. Comment

Basically, the difference between Tobin and Levhari and Patinkin is a matter of realism. Without empirical tests, one cannot judge *a priori* whether saving is correlated more to the "disposable income" à la Tobin or à la Levhari and Patinkin. The role played by money in production is also something requiring factual study. Societies can get along amazingly well even when hyperinflation of an extreme form destroys money's roles either as a means of payment or as a storage of value. The difference between Tobin and Sidrauski is more a matter of methodology. By introducing an adaptive behavior, a rather reasonable concept, Sidrauski succeeded in avoiding pitfalls along the comparative balanced growth approach. The only question one may harbor is this: If unstable dynamic movements take place, is it likely or desirable for a government to maintain a fixed rate of monetary expansion? But this leads to many other problems perhaps only future research work can answer.

The noticeable fact is that none of the authors mentioned is entirely happy with his model. So the future presumably holds great promise in this area.

8.3 OTHER MONETARY MODELS

The models discussed in the last section neither explain the demand for money down to the level of individual preference nor include the whole paraphernalia of Keynesian monetary mechanisms, e.g., the implications on levels of employment. This section presents some more ambitious formulations.

8.3.1. Micro-oriented models

We shall briefly sketch a model by Sidrauski as well as the monetary version of the Cass-Yaari model introduced in Section 6.2.

A. THE SIDRAUSKI MODEL [7]

In the last section we saw that Tobin specified the demand for money without explicitly deriving it. Levhari and Patinkin took Tobin to task for this reason. But they themselves did not trace back to the household utility functions either. In the following model, Sidrauski explicitly inserted money into the "family utility function." We shall sketch his assumptions and set up the model.

1. Assumptions on individual families. The economy is made of representative families, each of which aims at the maximization of a discounted utility integral over the infinite horizon:

$$\text{Max } W = \int_0^\infty u\left[c(t), \frac{m(t)}{p(t)}\right] e^{-\delta t} \, dt \qquad (8.3.1)$$

where $c(t)$ is the consumption flow per capita at t

$m(t)$ is the money stock per capita at t

$p(t)$ is the price level

u is the instantaneous utility indicator which is concave in its arguments

δ is the social rate of discount

At each point in time, this family is subject to two constraints, one on the stock of wealth, the other on the flow of income, both stated on a per capita basis.

(a) The wealth constraint—which limits the size of the family portfolio at each instant:

$$a(t) = k(t) + \frac{m(t)}{p(t)} \tag{8.3.2}$$

where a is per capita wealth, k is per capita capital, and m/p is per capita real balance.

(b) The income constraint—which shows how the family portfolio changes over time due to the difference between receipts and expenditures, etc.

$$\dot{a}(t) = v(t) + f\left[k(t)\right] - nk(t) - \left[n + \pi(t)\right]\left[m(t)/p(t)\right] - c(t) \tag{8.3.3}$$

where $v(t)$ is the per capita transfer income

f is the concave per capita output function

$n[k + m/p]$ is the equipment and money needed to provide for the newborn generation (in the family)

$\pi(t)$ is the expected inflation rate

$c(t)$ is the per capita consumption

We may contrast (8.3.1) with Section 8.1.2-A. There money is a consumption good and the opportunity cost imputation hints at a utility maximizing behavior of some sort but saving decisions still come from some "simple decision rules."

2. The model.   By solving the variational maximization problem, it is possible to obtain the consumption per capita path, $c(t)$, the capital per capita path, $k(t)$, and the real balance per capita path, $m(t)/p(t)$, parametrically with respect to: (i) the initial asset holding $a(0)$, (ii) the given transfer income flow $v(t)$, and (iii) the expected rate of inflation path, $\pi(t)$. While $a(0)$ is historically given, $\pi(t)$ and $v(t)$ are determined through macroeconomic forces. It is noteworthy that a family can purchase capital by liquidating cash holdings through (8.3.2). Therefore, at the micro level, no family is concerned about the actual economy-wide capital/labor ratio.

Taking the economy as a whole, the government makes transfer payments to households and finances such payments by issuing money. For any policy-determined money stock M and history-determined population size L, the cash balance $m = M/L$ is thus decided. Since the demand for real balance m/p is decided by families at the micro level, the price p assumes whatever level is necessary to adjust the per capita cash balance to the "real balance." Everything now hinges upon the price expectation $\pi(t)$. This in turn depends upon an adaptive expectation formula, as we have seen in the other Sidrauski model discussed in Section 8.1.3.

3. Discussion.   Sidrauski derived from the above model certain conclusions parallel to those summarized in Section 8.1.3.

The main interest in this version of the Sidrauski model is its formulation— the derivation of the demand for real balance from the micro level. The above version comes from a highly condensed version of Sidrauski's doctoral dissertation. Hopefully, a coming book by Foley and Sidrauski will spell out more fully such points as:

(a) In the microeconomic problem, the entire π-path between 0 and ∞ is assumed to be given (see (8.3.3)). In other words, perfect foresight is presumed at the initial point $t = 0$, On the other hand, the postulation of an adaptive expectation (see (8.2.13)) shows that $\pi(t)$ is determined piecemeal as the future unfolds itself. How are these two views reconciled?

(b) Sidrauski remarked that at the micro level the demand for consumption as well as physical capital is completely determined once π, v, and $a(0)$ are known. He further pointed out that at the macro level

$$\dot{k} = f(k) - nk - c \qquad (8.3.4)$$

However, there seems to be no assurance that (8.3.4) will always hold. For example, households of a resource-rich (reflected by a "high" f-curve), capital-poor ($k(0)$ small) economy may decide upon a $k(t)$ path and a $c(t)$ path, consistent with (8.3.1)–(8.3.3) but implying that $\dot{k} > f(k) - nk - c$ over certain time intervals.[13] It seems (8.3.4) should also enter as a constraint in the variational problem.[14]

Jorgenson's discussion [13] of Sidrauski's paper lists further problems related to this model.

B. THE CASS-YAARI MODEL [8]

In Section 6.2 we discussed a model by Cass and Yaari. Their discussions of a monetary asset have been delayed to the present. For lack of space we shall not go into detail, except to contrast the broad outlines of their version against the Sidrauski model considered above. The Cass-Yaari version also derives the saving behavior from the micro level. But instead of Sidrauski's "eternal" families, Cass and Yaari deal with mortal individuals. In that respect they have captured more realism. On the other hand, Cass and Yaari neither include money as an object of desire (like Sidrauski) nor set up a demand function for real balance in any genuine sense. The real balance is simply a perfect substitute for physical capital as a storage of value; hence, the rate of interest in money terms modified by the inflation rate must be no more than the rental rate in nontrivial balanced growth. Otherwise capital will no longer exist! On the other hand, if the difference between the interest rate and the inflation rate is less than the rental rate, no one would hold money either. In their model, there are three

---

[13]This necessitates a foreign loan and is of course out of the question in a closed economy as discussed by Sidrauski.

[14]That is, after it is rewritten as an inequality: $\dot{k} \leq f(k) - nk - c$.

possibilities. In some cases, money cannot exist at any moment. In others it can exist in the short run but not in the balanced growth state. But in still other cases, money exists even in a steady-state situation. Cass and Yaari also specified a very special monetary policy: Money is created to pay interest only.

8.3.2. Macro-oriented models

The model developed by Hugh Rose [9] integrates Keynesian elements and the Phillips curve into the neoclassical framework. We have selected this model as representative of theories of similar persuasion, and we shall concentrate on the long-run version. For simplicity of comparison, all Rose's equations are re-formulated along neoclassical lines.

We shall first discuss his assumptions, most of which differ from the simple Solovian model. Next we shall synthesize a model, and finally we shall make some brief comments.

A. ASSUMPTIONS

(1) Production. There exists an aggregate production function showing constant returns, diminishing marginal products, and embodied Harrod-neutral technical progress.

(2) Technical progress. Labor efficiency increases at a rate that varies positively with the ratio of employed labor force to total labor force.

(3) Labor market. (a) The rate of increase of the money wage is positively associated with the employment ratio (ratio of employed labor force to total labor force), and inversely associated with the "effective" capital/employment ratio. Full employment leads to an infinite rate of wage increase. (b) The labor supply increases at a constant rate. (c) Labor is hired up to the point at which the value of the marginal product of labor is equated to the wage rate.

(4) Capital market. Both the investment and the saving schedules depend upon two factors: the interest rate and the effective capital/employment ratio. Both the investment/capital ratio and the saving/capital ratio decrease with the effective capital/employment ratio. (Equivalently, both ratios increase with the profit rate, i.e., the marginal product of capital.) The former decreases with high interest rate, the latter increases with it. The Keynesian identity between saving and investment imposes a restriction on the admissible pairs of these two variables.

(5) Money market. (a) The demand for the real balance per unit of output varies inversely with the interest rate. (b) The supply of the monetary stock is controlled by the government.

Certain special conditions to ensure the stability of the system will be discussed later.

The assumption on production is neoclassical. The assumption of endogenous labor-augmenting technical progress is akin to Kennedy's induced investment hypothesis discussed in Section 7.1.1. The remaining assumptions are largely Keynesian, with one important departure: the Phillips curve approach concerning wage increases (assumption (3a)). This element, rather than the deficiency of effective demand, forms the source of persistent unemployment in the model. In contrast with other simplified models discussed so far, this model appears to be directly applicable to policy issues of the day.

B. MODEL FORMULATION

Let $\qquad$ L be the labor force

$\qquad\qquad$ N be the employment

$\qquad$ $z = N/L$ be the employment ratio

$\qquad\qquad$ a be the Harrod-neutral technical progress index

$\qquad$ $k' = K/aN$ be the effective capital/employment ratio

$\qquad\qquad$ $f(k')$ be the output per unit of efficiency-labor (effective labor)

$\qquad\qquad$ $A(k')$ be the average product of capital

$\qquad\qquad$ s be the average saving/income ratio, which is now a variable

$\qquad\qquad$ p be the price level

$\qquad\qquad$ w be the wage rate

$\qquad\qquad$ w' be the wage rate per unit of "efficiency-labor"

$\qquad\qquad$ i be the interest rate

$\qquad$ $\Lambda = M/Qp$ be the ratio of money to income

1. Preliminary analysis. There are three basic relationships in the Rose model leading up to the dynamic equations depicting the evolution of the economy: (a) the warranted rate of growth relation, which relates the effective capital/employment ratio to the interest rate via the saving–investment identity;

(b) the labor productivity–wage relation, which specifies both the effective capital/employment ratio and the interest rate as functions of the "efficiency wage" rate whereby the employment ratio is determined; and (c) the technical progress relation, which stipulates the rate of labor-augmenting technical progress as a function of the employment ratio.

(a) The warranted rate of growth relation.[15]   Assumption (4) above becomes:

$$\hat{K} = \phi(k', i) \qquad\qquad\qquad (8.3.5)$$

$$\equiv \psi(k', i)$$

$$= sA(k') \qquad \text{(saving–investment identity divided by } K\text{)}$$

where ϕK and ψK stand for aggregate investment and saving, respectively, with

$\dfrac{\partial \phi}{\partial k'} < 0 \qquad \dfrac{\partial \phi}{\partial i} < 0 \qquad$ reflecting that investment is stimulated by high profit rates but hindered by high interest rates

$\dfrac{\partial \psi}{\partial k'} < 0 \qquad \dfrac{\partial \psi}{\partial i} > 0 \qquad$ reflecting that both high profit rates and high interest rates are conducive to saving

[5](Desired investment)/(capital) is the warranted rate.

Equation (8.3.5) resembles the well-known *IS* curve in intermediate macro theory. It allows us to solve *i* in terms of k'; that is,

$$i = i(k') \tag{8.3.6}$$

This expresses the market-clearing interest rate as a function of the effective capital/employment ratio.

(b) The relationship between the interest rate, the effective capital/employment ratio, and the wage rate. From assumption (5), the demand for the real balance can be written as

$$\Lambda(i) = \frac{M}{Qp} \qquad \text{(by definition)} \tag{8.3.7}$$

with $\Lambda'(i) < 0$.

Rose provisionally assumed that the government keeps the money supply (in money units) proportional to the output (in physical units).

From assumption (3c), entrepreneurs hire labor up to the point where

$$a(t)\left[f(k') - k'f'(k')\right] = w(t)/p(t) \tag{8.3.8}$$

where the left-hand side is the marginal product of labor and the right-hand side is the real wage, or

$$f(k') - k'f'(k') = w'(t)/p(t) \tag{8.3.8'}$$

if the wage rate is calculated for one unit of "efficiency-labor."

Eliminating *p* by combining (8.3.7) and (8.3.8'), we have

$$\frac{\Lambda(i)}{M/Q} = \frac{f - k'f'}{w'} \tag{8.3.9}$$

where the left-hand side is a decreasing function of the interest rate *i* and the right-hand side is an increasing function of the effective capital/employment ratio.[16]

This demand for labor relation plays a role here that is causally opposite to its role in the simple Solow model. There the wage rate is determined by the marginal product of the fully employed labor force; here the size of employment is determined by whatever wage rate rules in the labor market. As we see, for any given "efficiency wage" rate w', and with M/Q held constant, there is a second relation linking k' and *i* through (8.3.9). This relation is akin to the *LM* curve in traditional macro theory. In conjunction with (8.3.6), k' and *i* can be simultaneously determined, *granted there is no multiplicity of solutions*. This allows us to write

$$k' = g(w') \tag{8.3.10}$$

Rose imposed the further assumption that $dk'/dw' > 0$. This is possible if and only if the graphs of (8.3.6) and (8.3.9) intersect only once for all values of

[16] $(d/dk')\left[f - k'f'\right] > 0$.

w', and moreover the former locus cuts the latter locus from below if i is plotted against k', as in Figure 8.4a.

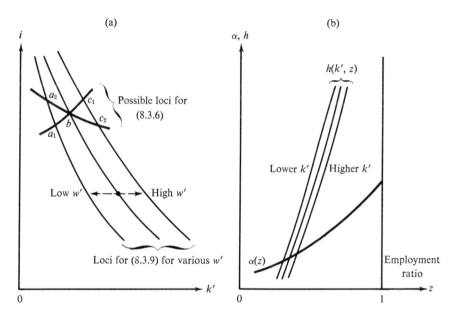

FIGURE 8.4

In Figure 8.4, the locus for (8.3.6) may have either a positive or a negative slope. We now turn to the slope of the other locus. In (8.3.9), we note that the larger the effective capital/employment ratio, the higher the marginal product of "efficiency-labor." Keeping the wage rate for "efficiency-labor" constant for the moment calls for a lower price level to maintain the wage and value of marginal product equivalence. A low price level raises the real balance represented by the same money stock. That situation is consistent only with a lower interest rate. Therefore, the locus for (8.3.9) must have a negative slope. Now if the efficiency wage rate were higher, corresponding to the same interest rate i (and price level p), it should be equated with a higher marginal product of labor. The latter would be consistent only with a higher effective capital/employment ratio, as shown by the dotted arrows in Figure 8.4a. Comparing the intersections between the (8.3.6) locus and the family of loci for (8.3.9), i.e., a_1, b, c_1 or a_2, b, c_2, we observe that a higher wage is associated with a higher effective capital/employment ratio.

(c) The technical progress relation. For simplicity, we define a new variable,

$$v = K/aL = k'z$$

which represents the ratio of capital to total effective labor force.

Assumption (3) states that

$$\hat{a} = \alpha(z) \tag{8.3.11}$$

$$= \alpha(v/k')$$

$$= \alpha[v/g(w')]$$

where $\alpha' > 0$.

2. The twin dynamic equations.   We are now ready to describe the dynamic movements of the Rose model. Since wage is determined in a manner not aimed at the clearance of labor markets, the ratio of capital to total effective labor is different from the effective capital/employment ratio. The interactions among population growth, the warranted rate of accumulation, and technical progress decide the movement of the former ratio. But it is the effective capital/employment ratio that decides the marginal product of labor, hence the employment ratio and the technical progress. Therefore, it takes a second dynamic equation to describe the operation of the labor market and close the system.

(a) The "capital intensity" equation governs the growth rate of the ratio of capital to *total* "effective labor." By definition, we have

$$\hat{v} = \hat{K} - \hat{a} - \hat{L} \tag{8.3.12}$$

$$= s(k', i)A(k') - \alpha(v/k') - n$$

If the saving/income ratio is constant and full employment is perpetually maintained so that $v = k'$, then we have the simple Solow model with Harrod-neutral technical progress, namely,

$$\hat{k}' = sA(k') - [\alpha(1) + n]$$

$$= (sf/k') - [\alpha(1) + n]$$

which is equivalent to what we had in Section 2.3.

(b) What makes all the difference is the labor market assumption which implies the wage equation that explains the growth rate for the wage rate:

$$\hat{w} = h(k', z)$$

where $\partial h/\partial k' < 0$ reflecting that lower profit rates ease pressure for wage increases

$\partial h/\partial z > 0$ reflecting that higher employment strengthens wage demands
$\lim_{z \uparrow 1} h(k', z) = \infty$ shows that explosive inflation is associated with full employment

Rose further assumed that $\partial h/\partial z > \alpha'(z)$ when $h = \alpha$ to ensure stability (i.e., under higher employment, wage rises no less rapidly than efficiency). This is seen in Figure 8.4*b*.

Comparing (8.3.8) and (8.3.8'), we have

$$\hat{w}' = h(k', z) - \alpha(z) \tag{8.3.13}$$

$$= h[g(w'), v/g(w')] - \alpha[v/g(w')]$$

Equation (8.3.12) can be rewritten as

$$\hat{v} = \phi\{g(w'),\, i[g(w')]\} - \alpha[v/g(w')] - n \tag{8.3.14}$$

Equations (8.3.13) and (8.3.14) constitute a complete system of differential equations characterizing the evolution of the economy.

3. Growth at the "natural rate." The steady-state solution for (8.3.13) and (8.3.14) entails the following:

(a) $\hat{K} = \hat{Q} = n + \alpha(z^{\infty})$; i.e., capital and output grow as fast as "efficiency labor."

(b) $\hat{w} = \alpha(z^{\infty})$; i.e., wage grows at the same rate as output per worker.

(c) $\hat{z} = \hat{i} = \hat{f}' = \hat{k}' = 0$; i.e., there exists a constant (un)employment ratio, interest rate, and rent rate, along with a constant effective capital/employment ratio.

(d) Any constant value of M/Q can satisfy a steady-state solution for (8.3.13) and (8.3.14). This has the following policy implication:

> *Policy implication* (*i*). The real magnitudes in a steady-state growth path cannot be affected by changes of the M/Q ratio. The effect of such changes on the real system is transient (since the steady-state path can be shown to be stable) and only the price level will be affected in the long run.

(e) An upward shift of the $h(k', i)$ function would lead to a lower value of z^{∞} and hence a smaller $\alpha(z^{\infty})$. This implies:

> *Policy implication* (*ii*). A more belligerent union policy on wages leads to a higher unemployment ratio and a slower rate of increase in productivity in the long run.

(f) On the other hand, the government may pursue a policy of inflation, so that $M(t)/Q(t) = [M(0)/Q(0)]e^{\mu t}$, for some $\mu > 0$. It can be seen from (8.3.9) that if the price level rises at μ, the money wage level rises at $[\mu + \alpha(z^{\infty})]$, and constant levels of i, k', z can be maintained. The only difference is, it amounts to a downward shift of the $h(k', z)$ function by the amount μ. Higher long-run employment ratio z^{∞} and thus higher rate of labor-augmenting technical progress rate $\alpha(z^{\infty})$ can be secured. The reason that inflation is beneficial is as follows: $h(k', z)$ reflects the militancy of unions to demand rises of *money* wages. Barring a cost-of-living escalator clause, organized labor can only bargain for the growth rates of money wages. By "diluting" money periodically at the rate μ, the government is literally cutting ground from under the working class. While the capitalists promise a rate of wage increase of $\mu + \alpha(z^{\infty})$, the government helps them get away with a real wage increase of no more than $\alpha(z^{\infty})$. They hire a higher portion of workers and, therefore, according to (8.3.11), automatically reap a high technical progress rate. In short, we have

> *Policy implication* (*iii*). Inflation can ameliorate relations with organized labor by giving less but promising more. This will raise both the employment ratio and the labor-augmenting technical progress rate.

Real "efficiency wage" will be lowered, but wage will increase faster in real terms in the long run.[17]

Due to space limitations, we shall not delve into Rose's discussion of fiscal policies and types of technical progress nor his proof of the local stability of his system.

C. DISCUSSIONS

The ingenuity of the Rose model and its apparent relevance to real-life economics are striking. Rose speculates that the higher employment ratio in England is due to the success of an inflationary policy stated above.

However, we must not overlook certain key assumptions, e.g., the technical progress function, which conditions the "anti-union" tone of the final results. As long as unemployed labor exists in the economy, the relevance of the employment ratio as a spur to labor-augmenting technical progress is not obvious. One may well argue that the size of the wage-share or the level of the efficiency wage w' can serve as a better stimulation for labor-saving inventions. The more dubious conclusion is about the beneficial effects of inflation. Unions learn and wage demands will soon anticipate price rises if the government plays Rose's game. Moreover, in the real-life world, inflation causes balance-of-payment crises, which in turn force tight credit policies on the government. It is usually the consequence of credit squeezes that impedes investment and retards technical progress. These aspects probably are too complicated to be included in one model. On the other hand, for those who intend to apply the Rose model directly to real-life policy issues, they are relevant points to be kept in mind.

8.3.3. Final remarks

The only consensus economists can reach today about monetary growth models is that much work remains to be done. It is not possible to select one *best* theory from among the existing ones, nor is it feasible to discuss all the existing models in this fast-growing area. Perhaps the least we should do after cataloguing a selected sample of such theories is to present a general review of this material.

Tobin's model is the simplest among those we cited. It offers definite results: (1) an economy with money has a lower output per labor level, etc., and (2) unambiguous comparative balanced state studies can be made. The Levhari-Patinkin modification offers a somewhat more sophisticated model, but almost anything can happen in their framework. Sidrauski's modification on Tobin leads to quite concrete results from an adaptive hypothesis on expectations. Both his stability analysis and his transient studies open up new ground. Worthy of note is the possibility that unbalanced growth and "overshooting" behavior apparently exist only in a monetary economy.

While the above models consider the demand for money and the saving

---

[17]All these can hold only if the union does not demand a cost-of-living clause.

behavior as results of simple decision rules, the models of Sidrauski and Cass and Yaari reported in this section regard both as consequences of intertemporal utility maximization. Certainly, models are much more complicated along the second approach, yet there is little ground to believe that the latter approach is methodologically superior in its present form. These models imply that individuals have perfect foresight and make irrevocable decisions over their life-times at the very beginning of their economic life. Empirical studies are badly needed to settle the relative merits of alternative hypotheses.

The model of H. Rose is in a class of its own. In spite of certain controversial features of his assumptions, it is an ingenious example of integration of the Keynesian and neoclassical elements.

REFERENCES

[1] Tobin, James, "A Dynamic Aggregative Model," *Journal of Political Economy*, vol. LXIII, April 1955, pp. 103–15.

[2] Tobin, James, "Money and Economic Growth," *Econometrica*, vol. XXXIII, Oct. 1965, pp. 671–84.

[3] Tobin, James, "The Neutrality of Money in Growth: A Comment," *Economica*, N.S. 34, Feb. 1967, pp. 69–72.

[4] Tobin, James, "Notes on Optimal Monetary Growth," *Journal of Political Economy*, vol. LXXVI, 1968, pp. 833–59.

[5] Levhari, David, and Donald Patinkin, "The Role of Money in a Monetary Economy," *American Economic Review*, vol. LXVIII, Sept. 1968, pp. 713–53.

[6] Sidrauski, Miguel, "Inflation and Economic Growth," *Journal of Political Economy*, vol. LXXV, Dec. 1967, pp. 796–810.

[7] Sidrauski, Miguel, "Rational Choice and Patterns of Growth in a Monetary Economy," *American Economic Review, Supplements*, vol. LXVII, May 1967,

pp. 534–44.

[8] Cass, D., and M. E. Yaari, "Individual Saving, Aggregate Capital Accumulation and Efficient Growth," in *Essays on the Theory of Optimal Growth*, K. Shell, Ed., M.I.T. Press, Cambridge, Mass., 1967.

[9] Rose, Hugh, "Unemployment in a Theory of Growth," *International Economic Review*, vol. 7, no. 3, September 1966, pp. 260–82.

[10] Phelps, Edmund S., "The Accumulation of Risky Capital," *Econometrica*, vol. 1962, pp. 729–43.

[11] Johnson, Harry G., *Essays in Monetary Economics*, Allen and Unwin, London, 1967.

[12] Levhari, D., and T. N. Srinivasan, "Optimal Savings Under Uncertainty." *Review of Economic Studies*, vol. XXXVI, April 1969, pp. 153–64.

[13] Jorgenson, Dale, "Discussion," *American Economic Review, Supplements*, vol. LXVII, May 1967.

EXERCISES

8.1. Suppose the economy is appropriately described by the simple Tobin model with one exception. As Tobin pointed out, the saving ratio is higher in a monetary economy than in a barter economy due to the existence of financial intermediaries. Let s_m and s_b be the ratios for the monetary and barter economies, respectively, and suppose that $\rho = s_m$.

(a) Prove that if s_b is 0.2, then s_m must be greater than 0.25 for the long-run output per worker to be higher in the monetary economy.

(b) Prove that in general, the monetary economy is more productive if $s_m > s_b/(1 - s_b)$.

8.2. (a) Rose recognized the variability of the term $s(k', i)$ in (8.3.12), whereas, in his simple model, Tobin postulated his saving/income ratio as a constant. Does this mean that the Rose model is more general in this respect?

(b) Tobin included the "portfolio balance" as an important element of his theory. How did Rose handle the same relationship between the relative yields and the relative weights of money and real assets in national wealth? (*Hint:* What constitutes the numerator and the denominator of the saving/income ratio in each model?)

9

optimal growth and intertemporal efficiency

9.1 PRELIMINARIES

The plethora of growth literature is a challenge to the uninitiated. Symptomatic of a fast growing field, there have been few efforts to classify this profusion of theories and models into a compact taxonomy. Table 9.1 attempts to provide a bird's-eye view of the entire field. Some of our nomenclature is borrowed from Hicks [1], although our framework is at variance with his.

TABLE 9.1

Growth literature	Examples	Static analogs
1. Positive theories	Solow model	Competitive equilibrium
2. Normative theories		
A. "Efficiency" conditions	Phelps-Koopmans theorem	Pareto optimality
B. Optimal growth programs	Ramsey model	Models with Bergsonian social utility index

Positive theories, which predict the evolution of an economy, have been the subject of Part I (Chapters 1–8). Normative theories, which prescribe patterns of growth for an economy, will be discussed in Part II.

According to the broad categories of objectives, literature on both the efficiency conditions and optimal growth programs can be classified into two types: that pertaining to optimal capital accumulation per se and that pertaining to optimal consumption streams. The first type considers the massing of capital goods at some target date as desirable in its own right. The second regards only consumption as the ultimate aim of economic activities. Moreover, optimal growth models can be classified into those studying the traversal path, those studying the steady state or golden age, and those studying asymptotic behavior. These are summarized in Table 9.2. These classifications are by no means exhaustive. For instance, the "inverse optimal problem" discussed by Kurz [2] and Goldman [3] examines the class of objective functions the maximization of which leads to a given growth path derived from a "positive" growth theory. It is therefore not neatly categorized as either a "positive theory" or a "normative theory."

TABLE 9.2

	Capital-oriented	Consumption-oriented
Efficiency conditions	DOSSO conditions	Malinvaud conditions Phelps-Koopmans theorem
Optimal growth programs Traversal problem	Samuelson's capital accumulation model	Ramsey problem
Golden-age problem	von Neumann balanced growth models	Golden rule theory

Asymptotic problem
  Finite horizon
  Infinite horizon
	Turnpike theorem
	Relative stability theorem for maximal growth
		Consumption turnpike theorem
		Ramsey-Koopmans problem

The rest of this section is devoted to three topics: the interrelations among and relative significance of the three main strands of growth literature presented in Table 9.1, the types of objective functions that underlie the classifications of Table 9.2, and the various alternative forms and comparative merits of the objective functions for the consumption-oriented optimal growth programs.

Section 9.2 is devoted to the study of efficiency conditions in general, and Section 9.3 discusses the impact of money and debt on the efficiency problem. The various optimal growth programs are covered in the ensuing chapters.

9.1.1. Comparison of positive and normative theories

A. DIFFERENCES IN PURPOSE AND STRUCTURE

"Positive" growth models contain enough behavioral and technical conditions to predict how the stylized world would evolve. "Normative" growth theories analyze what ought not to be or what ought to be; they include two subclasses of literature: studies on efficiency conditions and optimal growth programs.

Studies on efficiency conditions limit themselves to weeding out certain classes of growth programs that should not be followed. What is left over is still a broad class of candidate programs. In general, only one or a few in this candidate class would be truly optimal according to certain criteria. In fact, according to some criteria, some programs in the candidate class may be even less optimal than some members outside the candidate class. However, a criterion in the form of an objective function is a highly subjective matter. Economists may leave the selection of the objective function to certain political processes. In that case, they would hasten to point out what is noncontroversial: that programs outside the candidate class should never be chosen. There may be different sets of efficiency conditions, each based upon a distinct set of premises and implying a distinct class of candidate programs.

In contrast, *studies on optimal growth programs* start with an objective function and strive to decide the exact optimal growth path(s). Neither type of normative study, on the other hand, assumes an entirely determinate model. Certain behavioral relations are replaced by conditions involving control variables. Hence, the controllability and the existence of certain norms of performance set normative theories apart from positive theories. The specification of exact objective functions rather than general notions of efficiency differentiates optimal growth studies from efficiency condition studies.

Table 9.3 summarizes the examples in Table 9.1 in terms of the above discussion.

B. RELATIVE MERITS

One may question the usefulness of a growth model, once the optimal growth theory is in full bloom. Surely, growth theorists studying the dynamic economic processes do not have the same detachment as a biologist observing the population explosion of alewives. Since eventual control of the growth process is inherent in the motive of study, why should one stop short of the optimal growth framework? The answer probably should be twofold:

(1) *Knowledge* is the only rational basis for *action.* Thorough understanding of the positive aspects of economic growth is prerequisite to construction of operational models for optimal growth. The advances in neoclassical growth models in the late 1950s possibly contributed as much to the current development of optimal growth models as Pontryagin's Maximum Principle. Hence, further development of growth theory is desirable.

(2) Present optimal growth models often impute to the economy a controllability that no economic planner (in either the Communist or non-Communist world) enjoys. Moreover, it requires "tunnel vision" on the decision maker's part so that one national target may be pursued at the expense of all the rest. However, the real-life economic planner may well be a "satisficer" à la H. A. Simon rather than a maximizer. Granted that a maximand can be properly postulated, it may be a complicated function involving diverse measurements, such as the unemployment rate, the Gini index, the rate of change of the price level beside the old-fashioned per capita consumption. Since misspecification of the objective function may lead to unfortunate consequences, an easier and safer procedure for policy makers may be to simulate parametrically a moderate number of feasible paths and select the one that appears most satisfactory. In that respect, the positive growth models are definitely easier to handle.

TABLE 9.3

	Positive theory	Normative theory	
	The Solow model	Efficiency condition The Phelps-Koopmans theorem	Optimal program The Ramsey model (generalized)
Technical condition	$\dot{k}(t) = f[k(t)] - nk(t) - c(t)$	$\dot{k}(t) = f[k(t)] - nk(t) - c(t)$	$\dot{k}(t) = f[k(t)] - nk(t) - c(t)$
Behavioral condition:	$c(t) = (1-s)f[k(t)]$	—	—
Control variable	—	$\dot{k}(t)$	$\dot{k}(t)$
Notion of efficiency	—	$[k^1(\cdot), c^1(\cdot)]$ superior to $[k^0(\cdot), c^0(\cdot)]$ if and only if $c^1(t) \geq c^0(t)$ for all t and $c^1(t) > c^0(t)$ for some t	—
Objective function	—	—	$\text{Max} \int_0^\infty u[c(t)]dt$ where $u' > 0$
Results	Dynamic equation: $\dot{k}(t) = sf[k(t)] - nk(t)$	Candidate class: $\{[k(\cdot), c(\cdot)]\|\text{Lim Inf } k(t) \leq f'^{-1}(n)\}$ where f'^{-1} is the inverse of $f'(k)$	(a) Euler condition: $\dfrac{d}{dt}(\ln u') = f' - n$ (b) First integral rule: $\dot{k} = \dfrac{\bar{u} - u}{u'}$ where $\bar{u}$ is a constant (c) A definite optimal program

9.1.2. Comparison of various performance norms

A. CAPITAL–ORIENTED VERSUS CONSUMPTION–ORIENTED

Most optimal growth theories have an objective function that is a special case of

$$V\left[\mathop{C(\cdot)}\limits_{0}^{T}, \mathop{K(\cdot)}\limits_{0}^{T}\right] \tag{9.1.1}$$

$$V\left[\mathop{c(\cdot)}\limits_{0}^{T}, \mathop{k(\cdot)}\limits_{0}^{T}\right] \tag{9.1.2}$$

where $C_0^T(\cdot)$ and $K_0^T(\cdot)$ represent consumption and capital (vector) paths from time zero to the horizon T, which may be finite or infinite, c and k are their per capita counterparts, and V is a real-valued functional.

In fact, almost without exception, these models belong to either of two special cases (or their variants).

Case 1.   The capital-oriented case:

$$V = k(T) \qquad \text{with } k(T) = \mu k^*, \quad T < \infty \tag{9.1.3}$$

where k^* is a given vector.

Case 2.   The consumption-oriented case:

$$\int_0^T u[c(t), t]\, dt \qquad \text{where } T \le \infty \tag{9.1.4}$$

Case 1 maximizes the composite capital dosage cumulated up to T, where the proportional composition of that dosage is predetermined. This corresponds to the Kantorovich formulation [4].

Case 2 maximizes the time integral of a "felicity index" u that depends upon both the per capita consumption (pattern) at instant t and that instant. The Ramsey model [5] is a special case of this.

The different explicit forms of the objective function delineate different types of optimal growth models. Similarly, the different emphases (on capital stock or consumption flow) also call for correspondingly different efficiency conditions. These are classified in Table 9.2.

We may note further the following three points:

(1) The consumption-oriented model appears to be the more "basic" type, since terminal capital is required only because of its productivity in some post-horizon era. However, for reasons to be discussed in Section 9.1.3-D (terminal capital as bequest) and point (3) immediately below (cases where noneconomic forces require the *stock* of capital, e.g., fulfilling campaign promises prior to re-election day), (9.1.3) may be more appropriate than (9.1.4).

(2) In a capital-oriented model, a consumption good is either subsumed as an input for producing labor force or regarded as a given requirement (necessary evil!) to be fulfilled. In a consumption-oriented model, capital

is strictly an intermediate good. This fact becomes quite important in developing the efficiency conditions in the next section.

(3) The presence of the capital good may be desirable for prestige, preparedness, etc. Harry Johnson once surmised that the demand for large steel works, etc., in less-developed countries should be handled in this manner. In this case, however, capital remains an intermediary good, since we can postulate a hypothetical output (prestige, for example) automatically produced by the capital owned.

B. TIME PATTERNS AND OPTIMAL GROWTH PROBLEMS

Studies on both the capital-oriented and the consumption-oriented programs can be reclassified according to their time patterns. If we specify the initial position and determine the optimal path, this is called the traversal problem. If we do not specify the initial position, but insist upon a balanced growth (or at least a golden age growth) path, we obtain the "golden rule problem." Under certain conditions, the finite-horizon traversal problem has a solution path that "arcs" toward the solution of the golden rule problem; this is called the turnpike theorem or the consumption turnpike theorem. On the other hand, the extension of the DOSSO efficiency condition to the infinite horizon yields the relative stability problem (see Solow and Samuelson [6] and Furuya and Inada [7]). The study of the asymptotic behavior in the Ramsey model becomes the Ramsey-Koopmans problem. In both cases the golden rule solution serves as the asymptote.

We shall now comment upon the alternative forms of the objective function and their relative merits in Sections 9.1.3-A–C. More will be said when we cover the specific models in later chapters. A suggested alternative will be set forth in Section 9.1.3-D.

9.1.3. Forms of the objective function for a consumption-oriented program

As we have seen, the types of objective function distinguish the capital-oriented studies from those that are consumption-oriented. Likewise, the consumption-oriented models again can be classified according to certain issues pertaining to the forms of their maximands. In later chapters we shall select certain representative models and analyze them in detail. This necessarily slights models with alternative forms of maximands. We choose to comment on certain basic features of the objective functions at this early stage to provide a general perspective on the matter. The discussions are on a broad level, leaving concrete examples to later chapters. This arrangement can free later (more technical) chapters from "philosophical" arguments on the ground rules. It can also caution readers not to accept the subsequent mathematical developments without examining their economic foundations. If the reader so desires, he may skip this item on first reading.

A. FINITE VERSUS INFINITE HORIZONS

Most of the consumption-oriented models cover the entire time span from here to eternity. This fashionable assumption of an infinite horizon can be defended on the following grounds:

(1) Empirical evidence can never be conclusive *against* the immortality of the present society. In contrast, mathematical convenience persuades us that an infinite horizon is an expedient substitute for finite but very remote horizons. Unless we are convinced of an impending Doomsday, why not select the easiest approach to handle?

(2) A truncated, short, finite horizon (in which the society survives the planning interval) can scarcely be satisfactory. There must be some terminal capital stock, yet the size and composition of this stock depend upon post-horizon events. So a short finite horizon does not constitute an effective cut off point. (See Malinvaud ([8], p. 150).)

In contrast to this, one may equally argue that:

(1) The idealization of an infinite horizon is far from an unmixed blessing. Deep-seated mathematical difficulties arise as a consequence. (See Fisher [9].) The following partial list indicates the paradoxical results emerging from the assumption of an infinite horizon:

(a) Reasonable objective functions may lead to the nonexistence of an optimal solution. (See Koopmans [10, 11].) Hence, mathematical necessity may triumph over ethical convictions.

(b) The maximization of each identical individual's welfare may conflict with the maximization of every generation's welfare. (See Samuelson [12, 13].) Hence, conceptual dilemmas occur.

(c) Competitive equilibrium implies neither Pareto optimum nor even production efficiency. (See Malinvaud [14] and Koopmans [15].) Hence, familiar static theorems may fail.

(d) Efficiency prices suitable for intertemporal profit calculations need not agree with price systems suitable for present value calculations. Specifically, price systems that can yield finite present values may not have enough discriminatory power to separate optimal programs from non-optimal ones. Price systems with sufficient discriminatory power toward the various programs may lead to diverging present values for the optimal programs. (See Radner [16].) Hence, conceptual problems in choosing efficiency criteria emerge.

After reviewing all such cases, the wisdom of assuming an infinite horizon becomes dubious.

(2) On a more pedestrian level, one also questions the pragmatism of an infinite horizon. A planner rarely has adequate information about future resources and technology. Also, he cannot often commit his successors to his favorite policies. These qualify much of the operational relevance of very-long-period planning, be it infinite or finite.

B. INTERTEMPORAL INDEPENDENCE VERSUS DEPENDENCE IN PREFERENCE PATTERNS

Most of the objective functions used in optimal growth theory fulfill the independence postulate. This implies that the marginal rate of substitution between the consumption levels in any two periods should never be affected by the consumption level of any other period(s). As my colleague A. Brzeski puts it: "Were this applicable to any individual, the relative importance between his lunch and his supper would be entirely unaffected by what type of breakfasts, if any, he had that morning or he expects to have, the morning after." Hicks ([1], p. 252 ff.) first condemned the lack of realism of this postulate. However, once the independence assumption is relaxed, time-additive forms (integrals, sums) no longer suffice to characterize the objective function. This would force us to depart from the familiar mathematical tools, such as the calculus of variations (or Pontryagin's Maximum Principle) and dynamic programming. This author has done some explorative work on this topic [17]. More research along such lines is still needed.

C. WEIGHTING SCHEME FOR "INTERGENERATIONAL COMPARISONS"

When long planning horizons encompass the life spans of more than one generation, intergenerational welfare problems come to the fore. Often the expression $u[c(t), t]$ in (9.1.5) is written in the product form $A(t)u[c(t)]$, where $u[\cdot]$ is a function invariant with respect to t. The common economic interpretation is as follows:

(1) Each generation has an infinitely small life span and $u[\cdot]$ is the *identical, cardinal* utility indicator for the representative individual of any generation.
(2) Generation t is assigned a welfare weight $A(t)$, which usually takes the exponential form $e^{-\delta t}$ with δ as the "time preference" rate.
(3) $\int A(t)u[c(t)]\, dt$ is then a social welfare function formed as a weighted sum of the representative individual's utility.
(4) Sometimes it is argued that the *size* of each generation should also be taken into consideration. Suppose that generations increase at the rate n; then

$$\int A(t)u[c(t)]\, dt = \int e^{(n-\delta)t}u[c(t)]\, dt$$

Various views have been expressed in the past, concerning the form of $A(t)$. These are summarized below:

(1) Ramsey argued against a positive "time preference" rate δ [5]. He considered it unethical to regard one generation as more important than the other (perhaps because future generations have no recourse against *our* insistence to receive the heaviest welfare weight!).

(2) Koopmans proposed [10, 11] that our ethical convictions should be modified, if necessary, to accommodate the mathematical facts, e.g.:

(a) If $n - \delta > 0$, the infinite-horizon problem admits no optimal solution.
(b) With the presence of technical progress, the difference $n - \delta$ should be

no greater than some negative number. Otherwise, again no solution exists.

We should note that in this case substituting a finite horizon for an infinite horizon can only formally sidestep the difficulty. For then, a "corner solution" indicates that each generation should save to its utmost capacity—saving for the prodigal feast of the last generation. In view of the uncertainty about the timing and, in fact, the existence of a last generation, this formally valid solution is economically bizarre while politically suicidal. (The nonexistence of solutions for the inifinite-horizon cases is now understandable. Each postponement of the final feasting spree increases the social welfare. But pushed to the limit, a bitter irony emerges: The feast never occurs but the abstinence remains forever!)

(3) Phelps and Polak [18] emphasized the problem of intergenerational conflict. The present generation derives its utility from the consumption pattern of infinitely many nonoverlapping generations, yet it has no control over the activity of even the next generation. The optimal policy of the present generation will be contingent upon the saving policy of all subsequent generations. A game-theoretic equilibrium can then be derived, with each generation choosing a policy that is optimal whenever the policies of other generations are known and given.

D. A PROPOSAL

The discussions in subsections A–C above are illuminating. However, for real-life planners, it appears that we should seek a pragmatic alternative. This author believes that the following form may be operationally adequate:

$$V\left[\underset{0}{\overset{T}{c(\cdot)}}; k(T) \right] \tag{9.1.5}$$

where T is the expected life span of the present generation and V is a functional depending (in a nonadditive way) upon the consumption path during the life span of the contemporaries and the terminal capital bequeathed to the immediate next generation.

This device by-passes the mathematical complexity of infinite horizons and the conceptual dilemmas of deciding welfare weights. For the finite-horizon problem, the intertemporal dependence of preference can be recognized. The decision upon the size and composition of the bequeathed capital stock is no more difficult than the decision of a static consumer shopping for a present. It is not necessary to secure the full details of the recipient's preference pattern or capacity to consume. Nor does it even matter whether the recipient enjoys the present in a particular way. The gift enters into the giver's preference field and that alone counts.

9.2 EFFICIENCY CONDITIONS

In this section we will first review some static propositions and then consider three sets of dynamic efficiency conditions in turn.

9.2.1. Review of some static welfare propositions

Efficiency conditions refer to the production of desired goods. Starting from a given program with given initial endowments, if more of some desired goods can be produced without reducing the production of any others, then the original economic program is inefficient. Desired goods serve their purpose in their own right. Intermediary goods serve their purpose by being processed into desired goods. Therefore, if intermediary goods with positive opportunity cost (i.e., desired goods can be produced in their stead) are left unprocessed, then there is inefficiency. This holds true in both static and dynamic situations.

In the static context, a competitive equilibrium in an economy devoid of externalities and nonconvexities (roughly speaking, technical interaction of production and/or consumption processes and increasing marginal rates of productivity, transformation, and substitution) precludes production inefficiency. In other words, price-taking, profit-maximizing firms will collectively attain production efficiency under equilibrium prices. This need not hold in a dynamic context. There, profit maximization is a necessary but insufficient condition for efficiency under a competitive system.

The following is an example of static inefficiency. When compared with the example of dynamic inefficiency in Section 9.2.3-B it can be seen how the latter emerges.

Example of static inefficiency. An economy is composed of

(1) identical individuals, each with a utility function: $U(x_1, x_2) = \sqrt{x_1 x_2}$
(2) an aggregate production set: $(x_1^2 + x_2^2 + y^2) \leq 3$, and $x_1, x_2, y \geq 0$, where x_1 and x_2 are desired goods, while y is not a desired good

The solution $(1, 1, 1)$ equates every consumer's marginal rate of substitution between the desired goods to their marginal rate of transformation. Yet this is not an efficient program. *Some nondesired good (y) with positive opportunity cost is left over.*

A competitive market can rectify this inefficiency. The demand for y is lower than its supply at $(1, 1, 1)$. Hence, price-output adjustments would lead to the efficient production program: $(\sqrt{3/2}, \sqrt{3/2}, 0)$. *Profit-maximizing firms will not leave nondesired goods in stock if they can be transformed into desired goods.*

9.2.2. The Dorfman-Samuelson-Solow conditions for intertemporal efficiency[1]

In a capital accumulation model where all consumption levels enter as side constraints, only terminal capital goods are desired goods. The question is how to attain the highest satisfaction, starting from a given initial position. Dorfman, Samuelson, and Solow provided lucid explanations about how to derive efficient

---

[1]See Chapter 12 of [19].

conditions for optimal programs. Instead of reproducing their discussions with reference to a discrete time model, we shall follow closely Samuelson's continuous time version [20]. The final message is simple: *There should be an efficient price system that reflects the relative desirability of various capital goods at the terminal date. Profit maximizers partaking in the optimal accumulation program should exactly break even with reference to the efficient price system.* A corollary to this states: *All marginal rates of substitution, transformation, technical substitution, and productivity should be equal to the efficient price ratios.*

A formal presentation of the results follows.

A.   FORMULATION

$$\text{Max } V[K(T)] \tag{9.2.1}$$

subject to:

$$F[\bar{C}(t) + \dot{K}(t); K(t)] = 0 \qquad \frac{\partial F}{\partial \dot{K}_i} < 0 < \frac{\partial F}{\partial K_j} \quad \text{for } i, j = 1, \dots, n \tag{9.2.2}$$

where V is an objective function dependent only upon the terminal capital vector

F is the instanteneous production function (cf. equation (4.4.1) in Section 4·4)

K is the capital vector and $\dot{K}$ the investment vector

$\bar{C}$ is the consumption vector, assumed to be given

B.   DERIVATION

This is a Mayer type of variational problem [21]. Setting up the Lagrangian, we have

$$\Lambda = V - \int_0^T \lambda F \, dt \tag{9.2.3}$$

which yields the following first-order conditions:

$$\frac{\partial V}{\partial K_i(T)} = \lambda(T) \frac{\partial F}{\partial K_i(T)} \qquad i = 1, \dots, n$$

$$\lambda(t) \frac{\partial F}{\partial K_i} = \dot{\lambda}(t) \frac{\partial F}{\partial \dot{K}_i} + \lambda(t) \frac{d}{dt}\left(\frac{\partial F}{\partial \dot{K}_i}\right) \qquad i = 1, \dots, n \tag{9.2.4}$$

$$F = 0$$

Rearranging these conditions we obtain

$$\frac{\partial V / \partial K_i(T)}{\partial F / \partial K_i(T)} = \lambda(T) \qquad i = 1, \dots, n$$

$$\frac{d}{dt}\left[\ln\left(\frac{\partial F}{\partial \dot{K}_i}\right)\right] - \frac{\partial F / \partial K_i}{\partial F / \partial \dot{K}_i} = \frac{\dot{\lambda}}{\lambda} \qquad i = 1, \dots, n \tag{9.2.4'}$$

$$F = 0$$

C. INTERPRETATION

Eliminating $\lambda(T)$ from the first set of equations in (9.2.4′), we have

$$\frac{\partial V/\partial K_i(T)}{\partial V/\partial K_j(T)} = \frac{\partial F/\partial K_i(T)}{\partial F/\partial K_j(T)} \qquad \text{for } i,j = 1,\dots,n$$

which states that *the marginal rate of substitution between any two capital goods at the terminal date must be equal to the marginal rate of factor substitution between these two capital goods at that instant.*

Eliminating $\dot{\lambda}/\lambda$ from the second set of equations in (9.2.4′), we have

$$\frac{d}{dt}\left[\ln\left\{\frac{\partial F/\partial \dot{K}_i}{\partial F/\partial \dot{K}_j}\right\}\right] = -\frac{\partial F/\partial K_j}{\partial F/\partial \dot{K}_j} - \left(-\frac{\partial F/\partial K_i}{\partial F/\partial \dot{K}_i}\right) \qquad i,j = 1,\dots,n \qquad (9.2.5)$$

which states that the relative rate of change of the marginal rate of transformation between any two capital goods must be equal to the difference between the own-rates of interest for these two goods.

The economic meaning of this model can be seen as follows. Suppose we select the ith good as the numeraire. Hence, $\partial F/\partial \dot{K}_i = -1$. The rate of interest, by definition, now becomes

$$-\frac{\partial F/\partial K_i}{\partial F/\partial \dot{K}_i} = \frac{\partial F}{\partial K_i}$$

The price of good j is equivalent to its opportunity cost, $-\partial F/\partial \dot{K}_j$.

A person borrowing one dollar and investing in good j incurs two types of costs:

Interest cost: $-\dfrac{\partial F/\partial K_i}{\partial F/\partial \dot{K}_i} = \dfrac{\partial F}{\partial K_i}$

Capital loss (if any): $\dfrac{d}{dt}\ln\left\{\dfrac{\partial F/\partial \dot{K}_i}{\partial F/\partial \dot{K}_j}\right\}$

He also receives rental income: $-\dfrac{\partial F/\partial K_j}{\partial F/\partial \dot{K}_j}$

Comparing these terms, item by item, with (9.2.5), we see that the opportunity costs, the own-rate of interest, and the relative desirability of each capital good at T together constitute a dynamic equilibrium price path. All profit maximizers taking the price–interest system as given would exactly break even.

D. COMMENTS

The Dorfman-Samuelson-Solow conditions apply to finite-horizon models with all terminal capital goods as desired goods. Under such contexts, profit-maximizing, competitive firms collectively enforce the production efficiency just as in the static case of Section 9.2.1.

9.2.3. The Malinvaud conditions

Both the Malinvaud conditions and the Phelps-Koopmans theorem address themselves to consumption-oriented optimal growth problems with infinite horizons. The desired goods are consumption goods only. These set the Malinvaud and Phelps-Koopmans results apart from those of Dorfman, Samuelson, and Solow.

A. RESULTS

Malinvaud [14, 22] considered a discrete time model in which the growth program is characterized by three infinite sequences:

(1) The input sequence: $a = (a_1, a_2, \ldots)$
(2) The output sequence: $b = (b_1, b_2, \ldots)$
(3) The consumption sequence: $y = (y_1, y_2, \ldots)$

The relationships among these sequences is shown in the following schematic diagram:

$$a_t \!-\!\!\!<\!\!\text{Production}\!\!>\!\!\to b_{t+1} = \begin{cases} y_{t+1} \\ + \\ a_{t+1} \end{cases} \!\!-\!\!\!<\!\!\text{Production}\!\!>\!\!\to b_{t+2} = \begin{cases} y_{t+2} \\ + \\ a_{t+2} \end{cases}$$

An efficient program is one compared to which no other feasible program can provide more of some good in some periods without providing less of some other good in some period. This definition is an extension of the definition of production efficiency discussed earlier (Section 9.2.1). Obviously, efficient programs are generally nonunique.

Malinvaud proved, under proper conditions, that a program $\bar{a}, \bar{b}, \bar{y}$ is efficient if and only if there exists a fourth infinite sequence—the price sequence $\bar{p} = (p_1, p_2, \ldots)$—such that the following conditions are fulfilled:

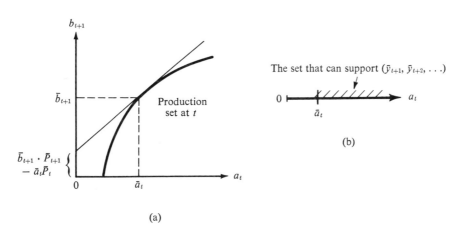

(a)

The set that can support $(\bar{y}_{t+1}, \bar{y}_{t+2}, \ldots)$

(b)

FIGURE 9.1

(a) Intertemporal profit maximization. For all feasible production pairs $\{(a_t, b_{t+1})\}$,

$$\bar{b}_{t+1} \cdot \bar{p}_{t+1} - \bar{a}_t \cdot \bar{p}_t \geq b_{t+1} \cdot \bar{p}_{t+1} - a_t \cdot \bar{p}_t \quad \text{for all } t$$

If there is only a single good, so that both a_t and b_{t+1} are numbers rather than vectors, this condition may be illustrated by Figure 9.1a.

(b) Terminal cost minimization. For all input vectors a_t, at instant t, that can support the subsequent consumption sequence $\bar{y}_{t+1}, \bar{y}_{t+2}, \ldots, \bar{a}_t \cdot \bar{p}_t \leq a_t \cdot p_t$. This is illustrated in Figure 9.1b.

The derivations of these results are discussed in Malinvaud [14, 22], Koopmans [15], and Radner [16].

B. INTERPRETATIONS AND COMMENTS

1. Relation to neoclassical models.   We shall now adapt the Malinvaud conditions to the neoclassical context. Writing period $(t+1)$ as $(t+\Delta t)$, we have

$$
\begin{aligned}
-\bar{a}(t)\bar{p}(t) + \bar{b}(t+\Delta t)\bar{p}(t+\Delta t) &= -\bar{a}(t)\bar{p}(t) + \bar{a}(t)\bar{p}(t+\Delta t) + [\bar{a}(t+\Delta t) - \bar{a}(t)] \\
&\qquad \bar{p}(t+\Delta t) + \bar{y}(t+\Delta t)\bar{p}(t+\Delta t) \\
&\geq -\bar{a}(t)\bar{p}(t) + a(t)\bar{p}(t+\Delta t) + [a(t+\Delta t) - a(t)]\bar{p}(t+\Delta t) \quad (9.2.6) \\
&\qquad + y(t+\Delta t)\bar{p}(t+\Delta t) \\
&= -\bar{a}(t)\bar{p}(t) + b(t+\Delta t)\bar{p}(t+\Delta t)
\end{aligned}
$$

for all feasible pairs $[a(t), b(t+\Delta t)]$.

Setting Δt to approach zero after dividing both sides of (9.2.6) by Δt, we have

$$\bar{a}\dot{\bar{p}} + (\dot{\bar{a}} + \bar{c})\bar{p} \geq a\dot{\bar{p}} + (\dot{a} + c)\bar{p} \tag{9.2.7}$$

where $\bar{c}$ and c are instantaneous rates of consumption such that:

$$\bar{y}(t) = \int_{t-\Delta t}^{t} \bar{c}(\tau)\, d\tau, \qquad y(t) = \int_{t-\Delta t}^{t} c(\tau)\, d\tau$$

hence

$$\operatorname*{Lim}_{\Delta t \downarrow 0} \frac{\bar{y}(t+\Delta t)}{\Delta t} = \bar{c}(t), \qquad \operatorname*{Lim}_{\Delta t \downarrow 0} \frac{y(t+\Delta t)}{\Delta t} = c(t)$$

Rewriting $\bar{a}$ as $\bar{k}$, $(\dot{\bar{a}} + \bar{c})$ as $f(k)$, a as $\bar{k} + h$, $(\dot{a} + c)$ as $f(\bar{k} + h)$, and $(\dot{\bar{p}}/\bar{p})$ as $\bar{r}$,

$$h\bar{r} + f(\bar{k} + h) - f(\bar{k}) \leq 0 \tag{9.2.8}$$

Setting h to approach zero after dividing both sides of (9.2.8) by h, one obtains the condition

$$f'(\bar{k}) - \bar{r} = 0 > f''(k) \qquad \text{(in (9.2.8), } h \text{ can be either positive or negative)} \tag{9.2.9}$$

This, of course, is the competitive condition in the neoclassical growth model. We work with per capita magnitudes here because in a neoclassical model the labor supply at a given time is fixed and we can normalize $L(t)$ to be unity.

Similar translation renders Malinvaud's terminal cost-minimization condition into $\overline{K}(t) \le K(t)$ for all $K(t)$ satisfying the following set of conditions:

$$\left.\begin{array}{ll} \dot{K}(\tau) = F[K(\tau), L(0)e^{n\tau}] - C(\tau) \\ C(\tau) \ge \overline{C}(\tau) & t \le \tau < \infty \\ K(t) \text{ is the initial condition} \end{array}\right\} \qquad (9.2.10)$$

The first two conditions in (9.2.10) can be converted to equivalent forms on a per capita basis:

$$\dot{k} = f(k) - nk - c; \qquad c \ge \bar{c} \qquad (9.2.10')$$

This is a condition absent in the neoclassical growth literature, where efficiency is not the center of attention.

2. Significance of the terminal cost-minimization condition.   The relevance of the terminal cost-minimization condition is seen from the following example.

Example of dynamic inefficiency.   Consider a Solow model with zero population growth, no possibility for production (i.e., $f(k) = 0$ for all k, and initial capital $k(0) = 1$. The dynamic relation can be expressed as

$$\dot{k}(t) \le -c(t)$$

showing that the only economic activity is consumption out of stock. A strict inequality would indicate the presence of waste.

Two feasible programs are as follows:

> *Plan 1.* $c^1(t) = e^{-t}$ with $k(t) = 1 - \int_0^t e^{-t}\,dt = e^{-t}$, where $k(\infty) \to 0$
> *Plan 2.* $c^2(t) = \frac{1}{2}e^{-t}$ with $k(t) = 1 - \frac{1}{2}\int_0^t e^{-t}\,dt = \frac{1}{2} + \frac{1}{2}e^{-t}$, where $k(\infty) \to \frac{1}{2}$

The fact that $\dot{k}(t) = -c(t)$ excludes any waste, in the ordinary sense. However, only plan 1 is efficient. This is seen from the fact that $c^1(t) > c^2(t)$ for all t, although they both start with the same initial capital stock. In fact, half a unit of capital stock will never be consumed under plan 2, which signifies waste of a more subtle type. This type of waste, however, can be ruled out by the terminal cost-minimization condition, since the flow $C^2(t) = \frac{1}{2}e^{-t}$ can be supported by an initial capital $\frac{1}{2} < 1 = k(0)$.

Comparing this example with the example in Section 9.2.1, the inefficiency in both cases originates from the same source: wasteful storage of economic resource in intermediary good. However, here the parallel ends. In the earlier example, the introduction of the competitive system can eradicate the inefficiency, as we commented upon before. In the example above, all depends upon whether we postulate a finite number of producers. If the number of individuals is finite, competitive equilibrium still can be shown to imply dynamic efficiency under an infinite horizon ([15], p. 110, footnote 2). But if one assumes, in addition, infinitely many generations, then *a competitive economy may collectively follow an inefficiency path* (as in plan 2 above). In fact, with a single good and zero interest rate (since $f'(k) \equiv 0$, for $f(k) \equiv 0$), competitive equilibrium requires only that capital decumulate as much as consumption, i.e., $\dot{k}(t) = -c(t)$ with no wastage allowed.

9.2.4. The Phelps-Koopmans theorem

The Malinvaud conditions extend the static theory of production efficiency into a multigood dynamic model. The Phelps-Koopmans theorem evaluates the efficiency of growth paths in a one-sector framework. The Malinvaud approach requires the construction of an efficiency price system, no mean task in itself. The Phelps-Koopmans criterion is readily applicable to the time path of the capital/labor ratio. Therefore, in spite of the fact that the Phelps-Koopmans theorem only establishes a sufficient condition for inefficiency, while the Malinvaud conditions are both sufficient and necessary for efficient programs, the Phelps-Koopmans theory constitutes a more convenient apparatus in the growth theorist's toolkit. Subsections A–C will present the main result along the lines of Phelps [23], and subsection D will provide some general commentary.

A. ASSUMPTIONS AND DEFINITIONS

(1) All the assumptions in the simple Solow model (Section 2.1) stand except the constancy of the saving/income ratio.

(2) The marginal product is a strictly decreasing function of the capital/labor ratio, and there exists a capital/labor ratio k^* at which the marginal product of capital is equal to the population growth rate n.

Definition. A *growth program* is the pair of time paths $k(t)$, $c(t)$, where

$$\dot{k}(t) \leq f[k(t)] - nk(t) - c(t)$$
$$k(0) = k_0 \text{ is given} \tag{9.2.11}$$

with $k(t)$ and $c(t)$ representing per capita capital stock and consumption flow at t.

Definition. Any program is *"dynamically inefficient"* if there exists another feasible program starting with the same initial capital/labor ratio but providing higher per capita consumption at some instant and lower per capita consumption at no instant compared with the program in question.

Obviously, this criterion for efficiency is relevant if and only if the performance index can be written as $U\left[\begin{matrix}\infty \\ c(t) \\ 0\end{matrix}\right]$, where U is an increasing functional of $c(t)$.

B. THEOREM AND PROOF

Theorem. A particular program $[k^0(t), c^0(t)]$ is dynamically inefficient if there exist T and $\delta > 0$, where $k^0(t) \geq k^* + \delta$ for all $t > T$.

In view of the assumptions, this theorem states that any program prescribing a time path of marginal physical product of capital forever lower than the population growth rate by at least a certain constant amount is dynamically inefficient.

Proof. We shall first note that any program in (9.2.11) is "dynamically inefficient" if the inequality in (9.2.11) holds in the strict sense over any interval. Consider now any program $[k^0, c^0]$, with

$$\dot{k}^0 = f[k^0(t)] - nk^0(t) - c^0(t)$$
$$k^0(T) = k^* + \delta, \quad k^0(t) \geq k^* + \delta \qquad \text{for all } t \geq T$$

We shall show that $[k^0, c^0]$ is dynamically inefficient by constructing $[k^1, c^1]$, which is itself inefficient but is superior to $[k^0, c^0]$.

Set

$$k^1(t) = \begin{cases} k^0(t) & \text{for } t < T \\ k^0(t) - \delta & \text{for } t \geq T \end{cases}$$

$$c^1(t) = \begin{cases} c^0(t) & \text{for } t < T \\ f[k^1(t)] - nk^1(t) - \dot{k}^1(t) & \text{for } t \geq T \end{cases}$$

In other words, at T, amount δL of capital is abandoned and subsequently the capital/labor ratio in $[k_1, c_1]$ is kept below the same ratio in $[k_0, c_0]$ by the amount δ at all times. The abandonment of asset at T makes $[k^1, c^1]$ inefficient. But for $t \geq T$

$$c^1(t) - c^0(t) = \{f[k^0(t) - \delta] - f[k^0(t)]\} - n[k^0(t) - \delta - k^0(t)] - [\dot{k}^1(t) - \dot{k}^0(t)]$$

$$= g[k^0(t) - \delta] - g[k^0(t)] \tag{9.2.12}$$

where

$$g(k) = f(k) - nk$$

$$\dot{k}^1(t) = (d/dt)[k^0(t) - \delta] = \dot{k}^0(t)$$

In Figure 9.2 we see that $g(k)$ reaches its peak at k^*. Since $k^0(t) > k^* + \delta$ for $t > T$, $k^0(t) > k^0(t) - \delta > k^*$. Thus $c^1(t) > c^0(t)$ for all $t > T$, showing that $[k^0, c^0]$ is inefficient.[2]

C. DISCUSSIONS

Certain implications may be derived from the Phelps-Koopmans theorem.

(1) It is a rather simple exercise to show that any "dynamically inefficient" program fails the second criterion of the Malinvaud condition. Converted into aggregate terms, the program $[k^0, c^0]$ above provides a consumption stream $C^0(t) = L_0 e^{nt} c^0(t)$ for $t > T$ by starting with an initial capital $K^0(T) = L_0 e^{nT} k^0(T)$. According to our proof above, with an initial capital $L_0 e^{nT}[k^0(T) - \delta] < K^0(T)$ it is possible to provide a consumption stream $C^1(t) = L_0 e^{nt} c^1(t) > L_0 e^{nt} c^0(t)$. Definitely, $[K^0(T) - \delta]$ can also support the stream $c^0(t)$. This completes the demonstration.

(2) One important consequence of the Phelps-Koopmans theorem is that a competitive growth economy can be "dynamically inefficient" (and hence can fail to meet the Pareto optimality conditions) when the horizon is infinite. This holds true whether the saving function is of the Keynesian type or is micro-economically determined. The former case is examined here, whereas the latter is left for the next section.

In Figure 9.2, the dotted locus $(n/s)k$ cuts $f(k)$ at Q to the right of q. This

---

[2]Analytically, $g'(k^*) = f'(k^*) - n = 0$ and $g''(k) = f''(k) < 0$. For $t > T$, $g'[k^0(t) - \theta\delta] < 0$ for all θ, $0 < \theta < 1$. Thus, $g[k^0(t) - \delta] = g[k^0(t)] - \delta g'[k^0(t) - \theta\delta] > g[k^0(t)]$. From (9.2.12), $c^1(t) > c^0(t)$.

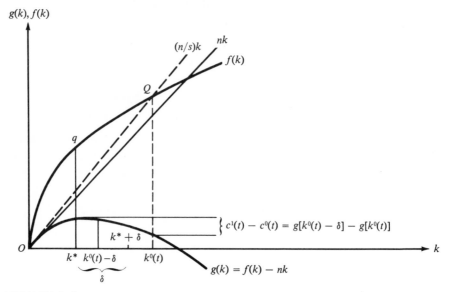

FIGURE 9.2

supplies one example of how a growth equilibrium can determine a capital/labor ratio located perpetually to the right of k^* and incur dynamic inefficiency. Resorting to the notation of Section 6.2, where $A(k) = f(k)/k$, we may derive a criterion for the saving/income ratio to preserve dynamic efficiency.

Since $k^\infty = A^{-1}(n/s)$, $k^* = f'^{-1}(n)$, the requirement for dynamic efficiency is

$$A^{-1}(n/s) = k^\infty \leq k^* = f'^{-1}(n) \tag{9.2.1}$$

Since A is a strictly decreasing function of k, we have the alternative form

$$n/s \geq A[f'^{-1}(n)]$$

or, equivalently,

$$s \leq n/A[f'^{-1}(n)] \tag{9.2.}$$

which marks the upper limit for the efficient range of s.

The theorem may be both sharpened and generalized.

1. Sharpening. Being a sufficient condition, the Phelps-Koopmans theorem may fail to detect some dynamically inefficient programs. Cass and Yaari proposed a modified criterion [24] which provides a test that is both sufficient and necessary: (k^1, c^1) is inefficient if there exists (k^2, c^2) starting from the same initial position with

$$\int_t^\infty [c^2(\tau) - c^1(\tau)] \exp\left[-\int_t^\tau [r^1(u) - n]\, du\right] d\tau > 0 \qquad \text{for any } t \tag{9.2.}$$

where $r^1(\tau) = f'[k(\tau)]$.

This criterion is easier to apply than the Malinvaud conditions. But the construction of $c^2(t)$ and the calculation of $r^1(t)$ are the "increment costs" (as compared to the Phelps-Koopmans theorem) for the necessity property.

2. Generalization. So far we have assumed that for a constant k^*, $f'(k^*) = n$. This need not hold when there is technical progress. Whenever there is technical progress, Phelps showed [25] that one can employ a "commanding growth path" (alias quasi-golden rule path) $k^*(t)$ for the same purpose where

$$f'[k^*(t), t] = n \qquad (9.2.16)$$

with $k^*(t)$ as the capital/*efficiency-labor* ratio and $f[k^*, t]$ as the shifting production function due to technical progress. Again, if after some instant T a growth program requires $k(t) > k^*(t)$ for all t, then that growth program is dynamically inefficient. $k^*(t)$ need not be a feasible path in itself. It is defined by (9.2.16).

Other extensions can also be found in Phelps [25].

Every tool has its proper (and limited) range of application. The Phelps-Koopmans theorem is no exception. While this is no reflection upon the theoretical apparatus, it is the responsibility of its potential users to beware of the inherent limitations of the tools in question. Both the Malinvaud terminal cost-minimization condition and the Phelps-Koompans theorem are relevant only in the infinite horizon case. In the latter case, overaccumulation forever stowed away is *the* source of inefficiency. Samuelson showed [13] that if the horizon is finite, an *efficient* program may have $k(t) > k^*(t)$ for most of the time *but* with an eventual decumulation of capital stock. Strictly speaking, the Phelps-Koopmans condition is not applicable in this case. Both the finite horizon and the eventual decumulation are at variance with the Phelps-Koopmans formulation. However, Samuelson's work shows how crucial is the infinite horizon assumption for the Phelps-Koopmans theorem.

9.3 MONEY, DEBT, AND INTERTEMPORAL EFFICIENCY

9.3.1. Introduction: Samuelson

In Chapter 8 we introduced various monetary growth models. However, in all these models, with the exception of that of Cass and Yaari, little consideration is given to the role money plays in the lifetime consumption plan of individuals. The part that Cass and Yaari played in this respect is postponed to this section, since their works followed the analysis of Samuelson [12, 13, 26, 27] and Diamond [29], while these latter studies involve the concept of "efficiency," which we have not discussed so far. We shall first introduce Samuelson's treatment of this topic.

A. SAMUELSON'S ASSUMPTIONS AND GENERAL RESULTS

Samuelson considered an extreme example in which every individual lives for three periods and works only in the first two, producing one unit of output in each. No durable capital input nor nonperishable consumption good exists with a positive market value. The land we use and the air we breathe are *free* goods in his parable. The growth rate of the size of the overlapping generations is a constant (positive, zero, or negative) and society is *immortal*. Samuelson further specified that each individual has the same utility function, which is symmetric with respect to the consumption of each period.

Samuelson showed that:

(1) If the population is stationary, zero interest rate maximizes the utility of each and every person. In fact, each person consumes two-thirds unit in each period.

(2) If the population grows at the rate *n*, then an interest rate equal to *n* is the optimal rate in the sense that the utility of each person is again at the maximum. In other words, the "biological" interest rate is the optimal rate.

(3) However, under competitive forces the biological interest rate is an unstable solution. Instead, under a competitive market, the interest rate converges to some other rate, which is negative under a loglinear utility function, whether population grows or contracts.

(4) The existence of money as a "social contrivance" that serves as a storage of value can set the interest rate at the biological rate and improve the well-being of each and every individual.

(5) The optimality of the biological interest rate as compared to the competitive equilibrium rate is due to the existence of infinitely many generations. If there were a terminal generation, that generation would be worse off than other generations under the biological rate. They save but can receive nothing out of their savings.

An intuitive explanation for the above results is as follows. In Samuelson's world there exists a strong urge to save, the alternative being starvation in retirement. But there is little alternative in a moneyless economy; neither investment nor stockpiling is feasible. The capital market is therefore a borrower's market and negative interest rates emerge in a competitive equilibrium. In fact, with a stationary population the competitive rate must be so negative that the middle-aged alone will save to compensate for the dis-saving of both the spendthrift youngsters and the idle oldsters. From the individual's point of view, each person "exports" his early earnings in exchange for the "imported" consumption of the last period. The negative, competitive interest rate is a less favorable "term of trade" than the biological interest rate. The introduction of money changes the situation entirely. Here is durable storage of value, available to all potential lenders as a last refuge for their savings. With a higher interest rate, everybody's welfare is improved. Since every generation has a successor generation, the increase in the interest rate means that each generation is supporting its preceding generation to a higher degree while receiving a higher compensation from the generation succeeding itself.

B. AN EXAMPLE

We may consider Samuelson's example. The problem faced by each individual under a balanced growth situation is

$$\text{Max } \tfrac{1}{3} (\ln c_1 + \ln c_2 + \ln c_3) \tag{9.3.1}$$

subject to the budgetary equation

$$c_1 + \frac{c_2}{1+r} + \frac{c_3}{(1+r)^2} \leq 1 + \frac{1}{1+r} \qquad c_1, c_2, c_3 \geq 0 \tag{9.3.2}$$

Since (9.3.1) implies that the desire for c_i, $i = 1, 2$, or 3 can never be satiated, (9.3.2) always takes the equality form under an optimal plan.

In period t, let the size of the three surviving generations be, respectively, $L(t-2, t)$, $L(t-1, t)$, and $L(t, t)$. Since the size of the population grows at the rate n, we have

$$L(t-2, t)(1+n)^2 = L(t-1, t)(1+n) = L(t, t) \tag{9.3.3}$$

The clearance of the commodity market then requires

$$L(t, t)c_1 + L(t-1, t)c_2 + L(t-2, t)c_3 - L(t, t) - L(t-1, t) \tag{9.3.4}$$

$$= L(t, t)\left[c_1 + \frac{c_2}{1+n} + \frac{c_3}{(1+n)^2} - 1 - \frac{1}{1+n} \right]$$

$$= 0$$

Comparing (9.3.2) and (9.3.4), obviously when the interest rate is equal to the population growth rate (i.e., $r = n$), the solution of (9.3.1) and (9.3.2) will automatically satisfy the market clearance equation (9.3.4), which represents the feasibility frontier for consumption at the macro level. To prove the optimality of the biological interest rate, one can refer to Figure 9.3, where the population growth is assumed to be zero for simplicity. Plotting the consumption level for the three periods on the three axes, we can construct two planes in Figure 9.3a.

(1) Plane ABC represents the macro feasibility frontier, (9.3.4), which now becomes

$$c_1 + c_2 + c_3 = 2 \tag{9.3.5}$$

This plane is "cross-generational" in nature. c_1, c_2, and c_3 stand for the representative consumption levels of a youngster, a middle-aged consumer, and an oldster, at the *same* period.

(2) Plane $\alpha\beta\gamma$ represents the micro budgetary constraint, (9.3.2). This plane is intertemporal in nature, showing the consumption levels of the *same* individual when he is young, middle-aged, and old, respectively.

The consumption point (c_1, c_2, c_3) must be on the plane $\alpha\beta\gamma$. This reflects the fact that all income is spent. It also has to be in the plane ABC. If (c_1, c_2, c_3) is located above that plane, aggregate demand will exceed aggregate supply,

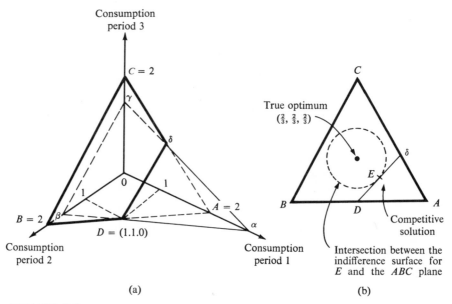

FIGURE 9.3

which is an impossibility. If it is under that plane, excess supply will again make the interest rate nonviable. Specifically, under competitive forces, the utility surface passing through (c_1, c_2, c_3) is tangential to the plane $\alpha\beta\gamma$ but usually cuts the plane ABC. For that surface to be tangential to the ABC plane it is necessary for the $\alpha\beta\gamma$ plane to coincide with the ABC plane, i.e., $r = n = 1$. Since the log-linear form in (9.3.1) implies equal discounted expenditures for all three periods, we have

$$c_i = (1+x)/3x^{i-1} \qquad i = 1, 2, 3 \quad \text{where } x = 1/(1+r)$$

Substituting into (9.3.5), we find that $(x-1)(x^2 - 3x - 1) = 0$; i.e.,

$$x = \begin{cases} 1 \\ (3+\sqrt{13})/2 \\ (3-\sqrt{13})/2 \end{cases} \quad \text{or } r = \begin{cases} 0 \\ -0.7 \text{ approx.} \\ -4.3 \end{cases}$$

The last solution is irrelevant, since the interest rate per period can never be less than -1.

C. LERNER'S COMMENT

Samuelson's view was questioned by Lerner [28]. Lerner measures social welfare by summing up the utility of all individuals at any one period; i.e.,

$$L(t, t) \left[\tfrac{1}{3} \ln c_1\right] + L(t-1, t) \left[\tfrac{1}{3} \ln c_2\right] + L(t-2, t) \left[\tfrac{1}{3} \ln c_3\right]$$
$$= \left[\tfrac{1}{3} L(t, t)\right] \left[\ln c_1 + (\ln c_2)/(1+n) + (\ln c_3)/(1+n)^2\right]$$

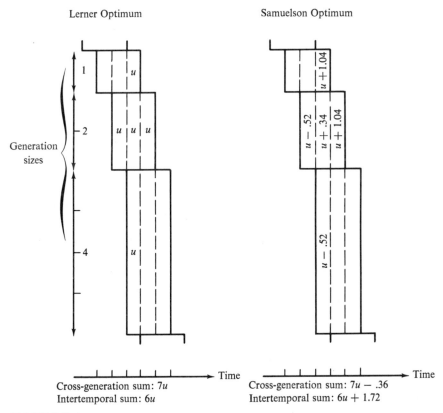

FIGURE 9.4

By this method, he showed that the optimal interest rate should be zero, regardless of the value of n.

With this Samuelson entirely agrees. But Samuelson believes that if every person is happier under the biological interest regime, then that scheme should be a more suitable public goal. He conceded, however, that if the society is going to reach Doomsday at some finite future date, the Lerner view would bring more welfare.

Schematically, we can compare the two optimal schemes in Figure 9.4. Each block in Figure 9.4 represents a generation. The height of the block stands for the population size, each generation being twice as numerous as its predecessor. The vertical dashed lines partition lives of each generation into three periods. The utility level obtained by a certain generation at a certain period is written inside the block. Under the Lerner optimum there is a uniform utility level for any person in any period which is designated u (actually, $u = -.15 < 0$, but such a negative utility level reflects an *improper* choice of the origin rather than disutility). We then calculate the corresponding utility levels under the Samuelson optimum as ($u \pm$ some value). In calculating the lifetime utility sum for a certain generation or the population utility sum for a certain period, the generation sizes are always considered as weights. It is immediately seen that the Samuelson optimum has a larger lifetime sum, while the Lerner optimum has a larger population sum. It is not obvious, though, how the population sum can be calculated if the utility index is no longer reducible to a time-additive form.

9.3.2. Diamond

Samuelson's parable casts the issue in its crystalline form. However, it was Diamond [29] who extended Samuelson's analysis into the traditional growth theory context. Besides the monetary asset (i.e., public bonds), there also exist durable capital goods. Output is no longer fixed but depends upon the capital/ labor ratio. Identical individuals, grouped into overlapping generations, maximize their utility levels over their two-period lives, working in the first period and retiring in the second. Part of the wage income is saved over the working life. The principal and interest of this saving are consumed during retirement. Out of the individual decisions, the saving volume of the economy is determined.

Following Samuelson, Diamond showed the optimal property of the biological interest rate in his model. This can be seen as follows:

Let c be per capita consumption and c_1 and c_2 be the per capita consumption for working and retired individuals, respectively. Under the assumption of a constant population growth rate and identical individuals, the twin relationships characterizing a balanced growth situation are:

(1) The micro relation:

$$\begin{cases} \text{Max } u(c_1, c_2) \\ c_1 + \dfrac{c_2}{1+r} = \text{Discounted income stream} \end{cases} \quad (9.3.6)$$

(2) The macro relation:

$$c = c_1 + \frac{c_2}{1+n} = f(k) - nk - \dot{k} \quad (9.3.7)$$

$$= f(k) - nk$$

(since $\dot{k} = 0$ along a balanced growth path)

Under the competitive forces, the consumption point (c^1, c^2) is determined at the position where the highest indifference curve becomes tangential to the budgetary constraint in (9.3.6) *and* meets (in general *cuts*) the macro feasibility frontier in (9.3.7). The optimal situation is achieved where the budgetary constraint coincides with the macro feasibility frontier, i.e., when the market rate of interest coincides with the "biological rate." But the market forces need not guarantee an optimal balanced growth.

Diamond then postulates that per capita asset holding depends upon both the wage rate and the rent rate. Internal debt affects the individual decisions in two ways: (a) interest payments over outstanding debts are taxed away out of the workers' earnings; (b) outstanding public bonds partially substitute for physical capital in individuals' portfolios, and thus the reduction of the capital/labor ratio raises the marginal product of capital which is equivalent to rent. He found that the flotation of government bonds may either increase or decrease the individual utility level.

9.3.3. Cass and Yaari

The structure of the Cass and Yaari [24] model has already been discussed in Sections 6.1 and 8.2. The introduction of monetary assets into their model is quite akin to Diamond's work. However, Diamond concentrates on comparative balanced growth paths. Cass and Yaari extend the analysis into the full dynamic framework. Moreover, they explicitly recognize capital gain, which is not considered in the Diamond model. The main contribution of the Cass and Yaari study is that if there exists a positive real cash balance in a balanced growth equilibrium, then such an equilibrium must fulfill the criterion of dynamic efficiency. The interested reader may refer to the original paper for its derivation.

REFERENCES

[1] Hicks, J. R., *Capital and Growth*, Oxford University Press, Oxford, 1965.

[2] Kurz, Mordecai, "The General Instability of a Class of Competitive Growth Processes," *Review of Economic Studies*, vol. XXXV, April 1968, pp. 155–74.

[3] Goldman, S., "Optimal Growth and Continual Planning Revisions," *Review of Economic Studies*, vol. XXXV, April 1968, pp. 145–54.

[4] Kantorovich, L. V., *The Best Use of Economic Resources*, English version edited by G. Morton, Harvard University Press, Cambridge, Mass., 1965.

[5] Ramsey, F. P., "A Mathematical Theory of Saving," *Economic Journal*, vol. XXXVIII, Dec. 1928, pp. 543–59.

[6] Solow, R. M., and P. A. Samuelson, "Balanced Growth Under Constant Returns to Scale," *Econometrica*, vol. XXI, July 1953, pp. 412–24.

[7] Furuya, H., and K. Inada, "Balanced Growth and Intertemporal Efficiency in

Capital Accumulation," *International Economic Review*, vol. XXVII, Jan. 1962, pp. 94–108.

[8] Malinvaud, Edmond, "The Analogy Between Atemporal and Intertemporal Theories of Resource Allocation," *Review of Economic Studies*, vol. XXVIII, June 1961, pp. 143–60.

[9] Fisher, F. M., "Discussions," in *Study Week on the Econometric Approach to Planning, Pontificiae Scientiarum Scripta Varia*, XXVIII, Rand McNally, Chicago, 1965.

[10] Koopmans, T. C., "On the Concept of Optimal Economic Growth," in *Study Week on the Econometric Approach to Planning, Pontificiae Scientiarum Scripta Varia*, XXVIII, Rand McNally, Chicago, 1965.

[11] Koopmans, T. C., "Objectives, Constraints and Outcomes in Optimal Growth Models," in *Econometrica*, vol. XXXV, Jan. 1967, pp. 1–15.

[12] Samuelson, P. A., "An Exact Consumption Loan Model of Interest with or Without the Social Contrivance of Money," *Journal of Political Economy*, vol. LXVI, Dec. 1958, pp. 467–82.

[13] Samuelson, P. A., "A Turnpike Refutation of the Golden Rule in a Welfare Maximization Many-Year Plan," in *Essays on the Theory of Optimal Economic Growth*, K. Shell, Ed., M.I.T. Press, Cambridge, Mass., 1967.

[14] Malinvaud, Edmond, "Capital Accumulation and Efficient Allocation of Resources," *Econometrica*, vol. XXI, April 1953, pp. 233–68.

[15] Koopmans, T. C., *Three Essays on the State of Economic Science*, McGraw-Hill, New York, 1957.

[16] Radner, Roy, "Efficiency Prices for Infinite Horizon Production Programs," *Review of Economic Studies*, vol. XXXIV, Jan. 1967, pp. 51–66.

[17] Wan, H. Y., Jr., "A Note on the Ramsey Model," summary of a paper presented at the First World Congress of the Econometric Society, *Econometrica*, vol. 34, Supplement, 1966.

[18] Phelps, E. S., and R. A. Polak, "On Second-Best National Saving and Game Equilibrium Growth," *Review of Economic Studies*, vol. XXXV, April 1968, pp. 185–200.

[19] Dorfman, Robert, P. A. Samuelson, and R. M. Solow, *Linear Programming and Economic Analysis*, McGraw-Hill, New York, 1958.

[20] Samuelson, P. A., "Efficient Paths of Capital Accumulation in Terms of Calculus of Variations," in *Mathematical Methods in the Social Sciences, 1959*, K. H. Arrow et al., Eds., Stanford University Press, Stanford, Calif., 1960.

[21] Bliss, G. A., *Lectures on the Calculus of Variations*, University of Chicago Press, Chicago, 1946.

[22] Malinvaud, E., "A Corrigendum," *Econometrica*, vol. XXX, 1962, pp. 570–73.

[23] Phelps, E. S., "A Second Essay on the Golden Rule of Accumulation," *American Economic Review*, vol. LV, Sept. 1965, pp. 783–814.

[24] Cass, D., and M. E. Yaari, "Individual Saving, Aggregate Capital Accumulation, and Efficient Growth," in *Essays on the Theory of Optimal Economic Growth*, K. Shell, Ed., M.I.T. Press, Cambridge, Mass., 1967.

[25] Phelps, E. S., *Golden Rules of Economic Growth; Studies in Efficient and Optimal Investment*, Norton, New York, 1966.

[26] Samuelson, P. A., "A Reply," *Journal of Political Economy*, vol. LXVII, Oct. 1959, pp. 518–22.

[27] Samuelson, P. A., "Infinity, Unanimity and Singularity: A Reply," *Journal of Political Economy*, vol. LXVII, Oct. 1960, pp. 76–83.

[28] Lerner, A. P., "Consumption Loan, Interest and Money," *Journal of Political Economy*, vol. LXVII, Oct. 1959, pp. 512–25.

[29] Diamond, P. A., "National Debt in a Neoclassical Model," *American Economic Review*, vol. LV, Dec. 1965, pp. 1126–50.

EXERCISES

9.1. (a) Consider an economy facing an aggregate production function:

$$Q = 10K^{1/4}L^{3/4}$$

Population grows at 2% per annum. Determine the range for the saving/income ratios which guarantee dynamically efficient growth.

(b) Suppose the aggregate production function is the same as in (a). The saving/income ratio is 25%. Find the range for population growth rates which guarantee dynamically efficient growth.

(c) Assume the aggregate production function takes the form

$$Q = 10e^{.01t}K^{1/4}L^{3/4}$$

Population grows at 2%. Deduce the *commanding path* for $k(t)$. Is that path feasible?

9.2. If the aggregate production function takes the form

$$Q = nK + \frac{KL}{k+L}$$

Population grows at the rate n. Find the range for the saving/income ratios which guarantee dynamically efficient growth.

9.3. Consider the following optimal growth problem:

$$\text{Max} \sum_{i=1}^{5} x_i - \frac{1}{2} \sum_{i,j=1}^{5} \left(\frac{1}{2}\right)^{|i-j|} a_{ij}x_i x_j$$

subject to:

$$\sum_{j=1}^{5} \left(\frac{1}{3}\right)^{j} x_j \le k_1 \qquad x_j \text{ non-negative}$$

where k_1 is some small value, say, 0.2. Compare the optimal solutions obtained under the alternative hypotheses:

(a) $a_{ij} \equiv 1$ (intertemporally dependent preference)

(b) $a_{ij} = \begin{cases} 1 & \text{for } i = j \\ 0 & \text{for } i \ne j \end{cases}$ (intertemporally independent preference)

10

consumption-oriented optimal growth models

10.1 INTRODUCTION—THE MODIFIED RAMSEY MODEL

Most optimal growth models belong to the "consumption-oriented" variety. The pioneering work of Ramsey [1] was more or less ignored during the rise of modern macroeconomics, when unemployment and inflation were much more pressing issues than speculative and utopian studies on optimal growth. Tinbergen [2, 3] and Samuelson and Solow [4] provided the main contributions prior to 1962. Since then, the works of Chakravarty [5] and Weizsäcker [6] have formulated and answered the existence problem, an issue heuristically dealt with by Ramsey. Samuelson [7], Cass [8], and Koopmans [9] solved the question of asymptotic behavior and thus provided a theory unifying the golden rule studies of Phelps [10], Swan [11], Mrs. Robinson [12], and others on the one hand and the Ramsey model on the other. These topics will form the subject matter of the present section. Our discussion follows rather closely the excellent analyses of Samuelson [7] and Koopmans [9].

For lack of space, the rest of the chapter will be devoted to the Uzawa two-sector optimal growth model as representative of the disaggregations of the Ramsey model.

10.1.1. The general framework

We shall first introduce and discuss the general assumptions and then turn to a device that can handle certain "divergent maximands," a problem that underlies the existence of an optimal path.

A. ASSUMPTIONS AND FORMULATION

Ramsey assumed a constant population and an instantaneous utility function that is the difference between the utility of consumption and the disutility of work. Samuelson and Solow [4] simplified this model and assumed a constant labor supply. Samuelson [7], Cass [8], and Koopmans [9] adopted a framework close to the simple Solow model. Our main analysis follows the model of Koopmans and adopts the following assumptions:

(1) All the Solovian assumptions except the constancy of the saving/income ratio (see Section 2.1).

(2) Part of the Inada derivative conditions:

(a) The marginal product of capital is strictly decreasing with zero as its asymptotic limit.

(b) The average product of labor is zero without any capital input.

(3) The objective function of the planner is the discounted infinite utility integral with the instantaneous utility function possessing the following properties:

(a) It depends upon the per capita consumption alone and is an increasing function of the latter. Ramsey assumed a constant population, so his model is a special case of this.

(b) The marginal utility is strictly decreasing, with zero as its asymptotic limit.

(c) The instantaneous utility of zero consumption is negative infinity.

(4) The population growth rate is smaller than the limit of the marginal product of capital as capital goes to zero. *Symbolically*, these assumptions imply the following *tentative* formulation:

$$\text{Max } U[c(\cdot)] = \int_0^\infty u(c)e^{-\delta t}\, dt \tag{10.1.1}$$

subject to:

$$\dot{k} = f(k) - nk - c \qquad \begin{array}{l} k \geq 0, \quad c \geq 0 \\ k(0) = k_0 \text{ is given} \end{array} \tag{10.1.2}$$

with

$$\begin{array}{ll} f(0) = 0 & u(0) = -\infty \\ f'(\infty) = 0 & \\ f'(0) > n & u'(c) > 0 \\ f''(k) < 0 & u''(c) < 0 \end{array} \tag{10.1.3}$$

where c and k stand for per capita consumption and capital, respectively, n and δ represent population growth rate and time preference rate, respectively, and $u(\cdot)$ and $f(\cdot)$ denote the instantaneous utility function and per capita product function.

Unless explicitly stated to the contrary, we shall stick to the above assumptions.

B. DISCUSSIONS

1. Production. The assumptions on f are somewhat weaker than the Inada conditions. Specifically, $f'(0)$ and $f(k)$ may be bounded above. Equation

(10.1.2) can be rewritten as

$$\dot{k} = g(k) - c \tag{10.1.2'}$$

where $g(k)$ is defined as $f(k) - nk$ with

$$
\begin{array}{ll}
g(0) = 0 & \\
g'(0) > 0 & g'(\infty) = -n \\
g''(k) < 0 &
\end{array}
\tag{10.1.3'}
$$

We observe that in (10.1.2′) if $\dot{k} = 0$, then

$$c = g(k)$$

If $c = 0$, then

$$\dot{k} = g(k)$$

Therefore, $g(k)$ represents either the balanced growth consumption per capita or the maximum rate of capital deepening (since $c \geq 0$). This function can be graphically depicted as in Figure 10.1a.

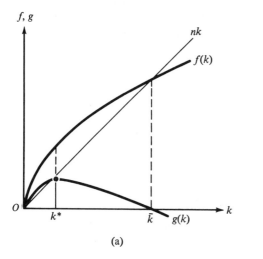

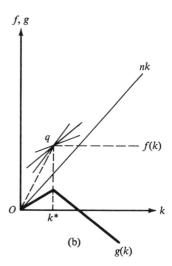

FIGURE 10.1

Two observations can be made:

(1) $g(k)$ has a unique maximum at k^*, where $0 < k^* < \bar{k}$ with $g(\bar{k}) = 0$. This follows from the fact that $g'(k^*) = 0$ for some k^* and g is concave (i.e., $g'' < 0$). Interested readers can verify that the conditions $g(0) = 0$ and $g'(0) > 0 > -n = g'(\infty)$ in (10.1.3′) are necessary to ensure the *existence* of a peak for g at some positive k^*.

This assertion can be graphically verified by means of the following examples, where the above-mentioned conditions are violated.

Example 1. $f(k) = nk - k^2$
Example 2. $f(k) = nk + 1 - (1+k)^{-1}$

Figure 10.1b depicts a case where a maximum for $g(k)$ exists although g is not differentiable.

(2) Regardless of the initial value $k(0)$, along any optimal path there must exist an instant T when

$$0 \le k(t) \le \bar{k} \quad \text{for all } t \ge T$$

That $k(t)$ must be non-negative is self-evident; that $k(t) \le \bar{k}$ eventually, for all large values of t, can be seen from the following facts:

(a) Suppose $k(0) \le \bar{k}$. There is no way to have $k(t) > \bar{k}$ for any t. Note that consumption is non-negative. Granted that $c = 0$ when $k(\tau) = \bar{k}$ for some τ, (10.1.2') states that $\dot{k}(\tau) = g(\bar{k}) - c = 0 - 0 = 0$. Thus we can set T equal to zero.

(b) Suppose $k(0) > \bar{k}$. We then observe that as long as $k > \bar{k}$, $\dot{k} = g(k) - c \le g(k) < 0$. Were $c(t) \equiv 0$, $k(t)$ would have a stationary position at $\bar{k}$, which would be approached asymptotically. We shall see from the discussions on utility that follow that any reasonable consumption path will not only be strictly positive (hence the optimal one must be so as well) but will also be kept above some positive level.[1] Then, the $k(t)$ path must be decreasing over time throughout the period when $k(t) \ge \bar{k}$.[2] Therefore, at some finite future instant T, $k(T) = \bar{k}$.

For convenience, we follow Koopmans and assume that the initial value $k(0)$ is between 0 and $\bar{k}$.

2. Utility.   The assumption on $u(c)$ implies the situation depicted in Figure 10.2. We observe that $\text{Lim}_{c \downarrow 0} \, u(c) = -\infty$ implies that any reasonable consumption path should avoid $c(t) = 0$ for any t. Starvation should be avoided at all cost. Now if $k(t) = 0$, $f[k(t)] = 0$ and one cannot keep $c(t)$ positive for any subsequent interval, which implies that an optimal program must try to keep both $k(t)$ and $c(t)$ positive for all t. Another way to visualize this situation is to observe that $u'(c)$ is strictly decreasing according to assumption (3) (see Section 10.1.1-A) and (10.1.3). Now $u'(c)$ cannot be bounded above, since

$$u(0) = u(c_0) - \int_0^{c_0} u'(x) \, dx = -\infty$$

with $u(c_0) > 0$ for some c_0. Hence, $\text{Lim}_{c \downarrow 0} \, u'(c) = +\infty$. This says that with infinitely large marginal utility at zero consumption level, one would consume some positive amount at all times, whatever the opportunity cost.

3. Maximand.   The infinite horizon, the independence assumption (triperiod noncomplementarity à la Koopmans), and the welfare weights have been discussed in Section 9.1. The assumptions (a) that the instantaneous felicity func-

---

[1] If $c(t) = 0$ or $c(t) \downarrow 0$, the utility integral becomes minus infinity. If $k(0) > \bar{k}$, definitely one can do better, e.g., by setting $c(t) = \text{Max}_{0 \le k \le \bar{k}} g(k)$.

[2] With a speed no less than the minimum consumption level.

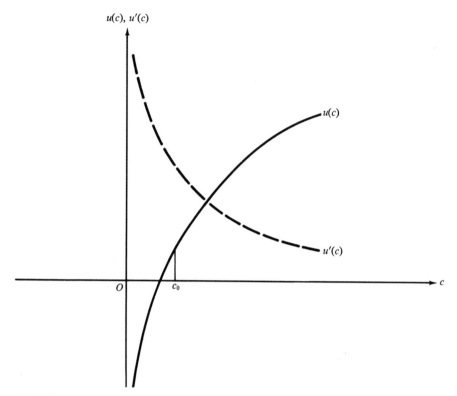

FIGURE 10.2

tion does not depend upon time and (b) that the welfare weighting takes an exponential form are embodied in (10.1.1). These imply the "stationarity" property of Koopmans [13] and Koopmans, Diamond, and Williamson [14], which means that if one infinite consumption stream is superior to another and we construct another two infinite consumption streams by postponing the first pair of infinite streams for a finite interval and substituting over that interval a common finite stream, then the new stream containing the better old stream is superior to the new stream containing the worse old stream. See Figure 10.3.[3]

The sophisticated analysis of Koopmans et al. showed that if $\delta = 0$ (time neutrality), then the objective function cannot fulfill both the following require-

---

[3]Obviously, if $\int_0^\infty e^{-\delta t}u[c^1(t)]\,dt > \int_0^\infty e^{-\delta t}u[c^2(t)]\,dt$, then, by multiplying both sides by $e^{-\delta T}$, we have $\int_0^\infty e^{-\delta(t+T)}u\,[c^1(t)]\,dt > \int_0^\infty e^{-\delta(t+T)}u[c^2(t)]\,dt$. On changing origin of the variable of integration, we have

$$\int_T^\infty e^{-\delta t}u[c^1(\tau - T)]\,d\tau > \int_T^\infty e^{-\delta t}u[c^2(\tau - T)]\,d\tau \qquad (\tau = t + T)$$

Adding to both sides the term $\int_0^T e^{-\delta t}u[c^0(\tau)]\,d\tau$, we prove stationarity.

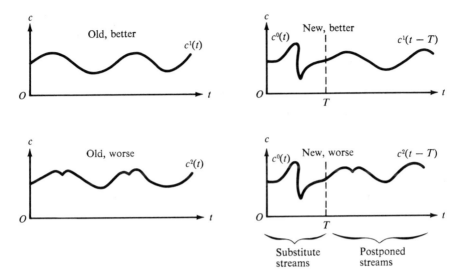

FIGURE 10.3

ments : (i) to be sensitive to any local consumption variation and (ii) to assign to each program a real number as a preference index. For instance, the functional

$$V_1[c(\cdot)] = \text{Lim Inf}_{t \to \infty} \{u[c(t)]\}$$

can assign to each stream an "extended real number" ($-\infty$, $+\infty$ included), but it may ignore any variations in the consumption stream for the first zillion years. An index

$$V_2[c(\cdot)] = \int_0^\infty u[c(t)]\, dt$$

encounters an even more fundamental problem : The integral *often indiscriminately* diverges to infinity. For instance, suppose $u(c) = \sqrt{c}$ and there are two alternative consumption streams, c^1, $c^2 : c^2(t) = 4c^1(t)$; hence,

$$\int_0^T u[c^2(t)]\, dt = 2\int_0^T u[c^1(t)]\, dt \qquad \text{for all } T < \infty$$

By all reasonable standards, one would expect $V_2[c^2(\cdot)] = 2V_1[c^1(\cdot)]$. But mathematically, $V_2[c^2(\cdot)] = \infty$, and $V_1[c^1(\cdot)] = \infty$. This utter lack of discriminating power rules out $V_2[c(\cdot)]$ as a useful formulation.

It is now seen that whether the expression (10.1.1) converges or not is in question (hence we stressed the words "symbolically" and "tentative" in introducing (10.1.1)). We shall see now that for $\delta \leq 0$, (10.1.1) diverges. It will be seen later that (10.1.1) converges for $\delta > 0$.

Let us pursue a policy that $k(t) \equiv k(0)$ if $0 < k(0) < \bar{k}$. If $k(0) = \bar{k}$, we set

$c(t) = 1$, say, for a small interval until t_0 where $0 < k(t_0) < \bar{k}$ and then set $\bar{k}(t) \equiv k(t_0)$ for $t > t_0$. The utility integral in (10.1.1) can be now written as

$$u\{g[k(0)]\} \int_0^\infty e^{-\delta t}\, dt$$

or,

$$u(1) \int_0^t e^{-\delta t}\, dt + u\{g[k(t_0)]\} \int_{t_0}^\infty e^{-\delta t}\, dt$$

which both diverge for $\delta < 0$. The divergence of the integral may be verified graphically as well as algebraically.

We shall see in Section 10.1.6 that for $\delta < 0$ no optimal program can be defined.

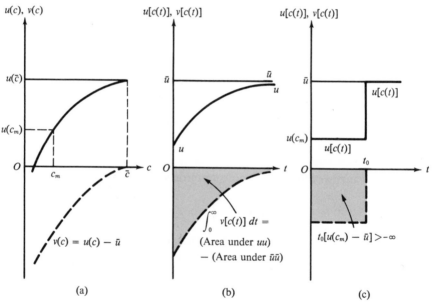

FIGURE 10.4

C. THE RAMSEY-WEIZSÄCKER DEVICE

For the boundary case where zero time preference prevails, Ramsey proposed a method to sidestep the difficulty, which requires either production saturation with finite capital or utility saturation with finite consumption. Chakravarty [5] showed that if such requirements are not met, a meaningful ranking of infinite programs often becomes impossible. Weizsäcker [6], Gale [15], and McFadden [16] subsequently discussed an approach to generalize the Ramsey device.

1. The Ramsey device. Ramsey attempted essentially to change the origin of the instantaneous utility index. Granted that this index reaches a maximum at some finite consumption level, $\bar{c}$, then we can redefine an instantaneous utility index, $v(c) = u(c) - u(\bar{c})$; evidently, $v(c) \leq 0$ for all c. This is shown in Figure 10.4a. Obviously the most desirable program will provide $c(t) \equiv \bar{c}$, and hence the divergent expression $\int_0^\infty u[c(t)] \, dt$ can be geometrically represented by the area of the infinite half-strip with "area" $[u(\bar{c})](+\infty)$. Usually, the optimal (feasible) program falls short of this. Let the optimal $u[c(t)]$ path be represented by the curve uu in Figure 10.4b. The difference between the uu curve and the $\overline{uu}$ line is the "utility deficiency" represented by the shaded area under the axis: $\int_0^\infty v[c(t)] \, dt$. The crucial question is whether this area will be finite.

The answer is "It depends." However, if there is a "nonempty" class of feasible paths with finite utility deficiencies (the "eligible class"),[4] then all that is required is to minimize this deficiency; i.e.,

$$\text{Min} \int_0^\infty \{u(\bar{c}) - u[c(t)]\} \, dt = \text{Max} - \int_0^\infty \{u(\bar{c}) - u[c(t)]\} \, dt \qquad (10.1.4)$$

$$= \text{Max} \int_0^\infty v[c(t)] \, dt$$

This is a well-defined problem, solvable by variational methods.

To prove that there is at least one path in the "eligible class," we observe that by setting $c(t)$ at a low level, say $c_m > 0$, we can obtain a continuous increase of $k(t)$ up to t_0, when $f[k(t_0)] = \bar{c}$.

From t_0 on, due to Ramsey's assumption of a constant population (i.e., $n = 0$), we can stop accumulation and consume at the constant level $\bar{c}$. Hence, $\bar{c} = f[k(t_0)] - 0 = f[k(t_0)]$. The resultant utility path becomes

$$u[c(t)] = \begin{cases} u(c_m) & 0 \leq t < t_0 \\ u(\bar{c}) & t_0 \leq t < \infty \end{cases} \qquad (10.1.5)$$

Obviously, the "deficiency" is $t_0[u(\bar{c}) - u(c_m)] < \infty$, as depicted in Figure 10.4c.

When there is no utility saturation but there is production saturation, the argument is somewhat more complicated. Without going into detail we may mention that : (a) Here v is defined as $u[c(t)] - u[f(k\dagger)]$, where $k\dagger$ is the saturating level of capital. (b) For $k(0) > k\dagger$, $\int_0^\infty v[c(t)] \, dt$ may have a finite positive value.

2. Generalizations. In the Ramsey device, the existence of a comparison path $u(\bar{c})$, where $\int_0^\infty \{u[c(t)] - u(\bar{c})\} \, dt > -\infty$, is essential. Weiszäcker generalized this device by introducing the *overtaking principle*. We shall first introduce some definitions to facilitate the discussion of this principle.

Definition. Suppose $u[c^1(t), t]$ and $u[c^2(t), t]$ are the two instantaneous utility streams corresponding to the alternative consumption streams, $c^1(t)$ and $c^2(t)$. If there exists T such that

$$\int_0^t \{u[c^2(\tau), \tau] - u[c^1(\tau), \tau]\} \, d\tau \geq 0 \quad \text{for all } t \geq T \qquad (10.1.6)$$

then c^2 *overtakes* c^1.

---

[4]That is, if there is at least one eligible path.

If both $\int_0^\infty u[c^1(\tau), \tau] \, dt$ and $\int_0^\infty u[c^2(\tau), \tau] \, dt$ are convergent, then (10.1.6) implies that $\int_0^\infty u[c^2(\tau), \tau] \, dt \geq \int_0^\infty u[c^1(\tau), \tau] \, d\tau$. This is shown in Figure 10.5.

Utility integral

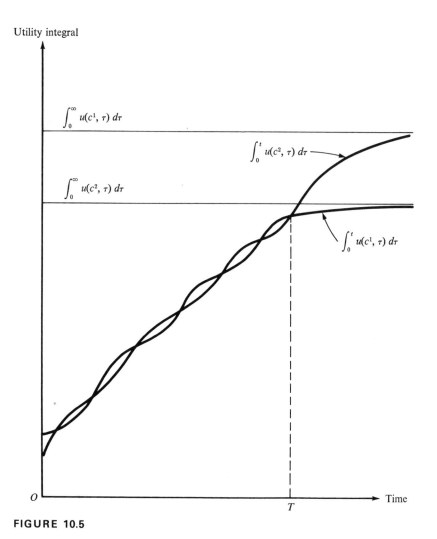

FIGURE 10.5

Definition. $c^*(\cdot)$ is *strongly optimal* if it *overtakes* all alternative consumption streams $c(\cdot)$ derived from the same $k(0)$.

We observe that the overtaking principle is a generalization of the ordinary maximization process and that if we adopt the Ramsey device of minimizing the utility deficit, the resultant optimal program must overtake all the alternative feasible paths (derived from the same $k(0)$).

On the other hand, it is possible that no path overtakes all the other feasible paths:

Case a: Every feasible path is overtaken by some other path. We shall observe such an example in Section 10.1.6.

Case b: Two feasible paths each fail to overtake the other. This can be seen from Example 1.

Example 1. $u[c^1, \tau] = 1$; $u[c^2, \tau] = 1 + \sin \tau/(1 + \tau)$.

Case b gives rise to a tie. To resolve the dilemma, we may broaden the definition of optimality. One way is to introduce the concept of "catching up."

Definition.   If $\text{Lim}_{T \to \infty} \text{Inf}_{t \geq T} \int_0^t [u(c^2, \tau) - u(c^1, \tau)] \, d\tau \geq 0$, then $c^2(\cdot)$ *catches up* with $c^1(\cdot)$.

Definition.   A feasible program is *optimal* if it *catches up* with all alternative feasible programs.

It is seen that in Example 1, each program catches up with the other in the sense that the "least favorable partial difference" of utility streams since T diminishes to zero as T grows large. The upshot is: the tie is broken by declaring both contending parties to be winners! However, sometimes even such a procedure is not sufficient. Sometimes neither program catches up with the other, as in

Example 2. $u[c^1, \tau] = 1$; $u[c^2, \tau] = 1 + \sin \tau$

We note that it can be proved that the assumptions made in Section 10.1.1-A imply the existence of a comparison path when $\delta = 0$ and that there exists a unique, strongly optimal path (from now on, we call it "the optimal path" for short). However, the above review indicates that once we relax the special assumptions, matters may become very difficult indeed. Interested readers should refer to Gale [15] and McFadden [16].

10.1.2. The steady-state solution: the golden rule

We shall now discuss the "golden rule" of accumulation, which (1) singles out those balanced growth paths that provide the maximum per capita consumption, (2) helps to screen out dynamic paths that fail the Phelps-Koopmans criterion for efficiency, and (3) forms the asymptotic path for certain optimal growth paths. The theorem will be stated and interpreted and finally generalized in several directions.

A. THE THEOREM

In 1960, Phelps [10] proposed the following problem: In the framework of the simple Solow model, among all the alternative balanced growth paths, which path yields the highest per capita consumption?

This problem can be formulated as

$$\underset{k}{\text{Max}} \; c = g(k) - \dot{k} \qquad \text{(from (10.1.2'))}$$

$$= g(k) \qquad \text{(since balanced growth implies } \dot{k} = 0)$$

(10.1.7)

Under the assumptions in (10.1.3) and the definition of $g(\cdot)$, there exists a unique solution, k^*, as shown in Figure 10.1a.

The assumption $f'' < 0$ also implies the differentiability of f and hence of g. Therefore, the first-order condition for the maximization of (10.1.7) leads to the so-called golden rule, which has two alternative forms:

(1) The "biological interest rate" condition.

$$g'(k) = 0 = f'(k) - n \qquad (10.1.8)$$

That is to say, the own-rate of interest should be equated with the growth rate of population.

(2) The saving–capital share equality. From (10.1.8) we obtain its equivalent

$$
\begin{aligned}
kf'(k)/f(k) &= nk/f(k) \\
&= nK/[Lf(k)] \\
&= \dot{K}/Q \\
&= s
\end{aligned}
\qquad (10.1.9)
$$

where kf'/f is the capital share and s is the saving/income ratio.

B. INTERPRETATION AND SIGNIFICANCE

1. Interpretation.   Phelps [10] and Swan [11] independently arrived at the "golden rule" in the form of (10.1.8) and (10.1.9). Mrs. Robinson [12] also discovered the same result, but her version regards the golden rule conditions as a theorem relating to income distribution. This Samuelson regarded as incorrect [17]. In Figure 10.1b there is only one technique at q ("Harrod-Domar" case), but f and g are still defined (although conditions in (10.1.3) are not entirely met). The interest rate is "indeterminate" at q. It is determined by market forces, etc., not represented in the model. Interest rate can vary anywhere from zero to the average product of capital. The three lines through q show this indeterminacy. However, to maximize c, the saving ratio s, for instance, should be equated to $nk^*/f(k^*)$, regardless of the value of the interest rate. Similarly, in general, k^* should always be chosen so that the left-hand derivative of f is greater than or equal to n, which is greater than or equal to the right-hand derivative of f regardless of the existence of $f'(k^*)$.

In the example in Figure 10.1b, this inequality is in the form $f(k^*)/k^* \geq n \geq 0$.

Thus, (10.1.8) and (10.1.9) are production theorems rather than distribution theorems.

2. Significance.   The golden rule applies only to comparisons among balanced growth paths for which the capital/labor ratio remains forever constant. However, in reality the historically given capital/labor ratio $k(0)$ need not agree with the "optimal" capital/labor ratio k^*. Moreover, there is no evidence that balanced growth is more desirable than other growth patterns. This leads to Pearce's [18] query about the usefulness of the golden rule. In his reply [19], Phelps admitted that the golden rule is only "*quasi*-optimal." However, more recent studies acknowledge the true importance of the golden rule in two aspects:

(a) It provides a commanding path, $k(t) \equiv \bar{k}$, for the Phelps-Koopmans theorem. As shown in Section 9.2, any program with a capital path eventually surpassing $\bar{k}$ all the time by at least some finite constant must be nonoptimal.

(b) If one subscribes to a Ramsey type of model, then the optimal path can be shown to approach the golden rule path monotonically. This will be analyzed below.

C. GENERALIZATIONS

(1) In all models permitting golden age growth, one can search for the golden age path that permits maximum consumption per unit of efficiency labor. In other words, among all the golden age paths, each providing a per capita consumption path rising at the labor-augmenting technical progress rate, one aims to attain the path of highest consumption per capita. Phelps' model on research [20] discussed in Chapter 7, Solow's putty–clay model [21], and the multisector model by Kemp and Thanh mentioned in Section 5.2 [22] are examples of this. The general condition is the equality between the own-rate of capital and the rate of increase of "efficiency labor."[5]

(2) Figure 10.1*b* illustrates that in the single-sector model the differentiability of f is not essential for the existence of golden rule growth. We shall further consider a model that is a variant of the "golden rule of procreation" of Phelps (social utility is independent of n in our case):

Let n be an increasing function of k. Every other assumption stands as before. We now wish to maximize per capita consumption under balanced growth. This can be done graphically by shifting the $[n(k)]k$ curve upward until the curve $[n(k)]k + \bar{c}$ barely touches the $f(k)$ curve, as shown in Figure 10.6*a*. The equilibrium condition at k^* implies that

$$f'(k^*) = n(k^*) + n'(k^*)k^*$$

$$> n(k^*) \qquad \text{(since } n' > 0\text{)}$$

This indicates that if the population growth rate increases with per capita capital, the modified golden rule should set the own-rate of interest greater than the biological interest n.

Alternatively, one can assume that n is an increasing function of c and that the curves $[n(c)]k + c$ become nonparallel straight lines. The same analysis applies.

Figure 10.6*b* considers a special form of $f(k)$ where the marginal product of capital is undefined at one golden rule technique, k_m^*. Also there exists a whole series of golden rule techniques, ranging from k_m^* to k_M^*.

(3) The golden rule problem actually extends to models where aggregate production functions fail to exist. Consider Example 1 in Section 4.2.3-B, which concerns the reswitching problem. It can be proved that in order to obtain maximum consumption per capita under balanced growth, one should choose the technique into whose efficient interest range n falls. Hence, in Example 1,

---

[5]The sum of the population growth rate and the labor-augmenting technical progress rate.

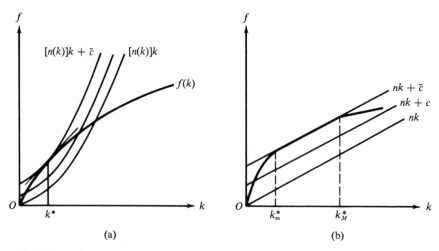

FIGURE 10.6

for the birth rate to fall between 0.1 and 3.1 per period, technique 2 is preferred. Otherwise, technique 1 should be chosen.

The relation of such extensions to the general theory of optimal growth has not been completely explored.

10.1.3. The transient solution—existence and uniqueness

Returning to the Ramsey-Koopmans problem, we wish to determine whether there may be zero, one, or more optimal programs when time neutrality is assumed.

A. THE UNIQUENESS PROBLEM

We shall show that due to the concavity of the $f(\cdot)$ and $u(\cdot)$ functions,[6] i.e., $f'', u'' < 0$, *there can be at most one optimal program.*

Proof of uniqueness.   Suppose there are two optimal feasible programs (c^1, k^1) and (c^0, k^0), both sharing the same initial capital/labor ratio k_0. We can construct another feasible program $(c^{1/2}, k^{1/2})$ which is superior to at least one of the two supposedly optimal programs. This contradiction will complete the proof.

Set $(k^{1/2}, c^{1/2}) = [\frac{1}{2}(k^0 + k^1), g(k^{1/2}) - \dot{k}^{1/2}]$. We shall first show that $(k^{1/2}, c^{1/2})$ is feasible and then prove that it provides more utility than either (k^0, c^0) or (k^1, c^1), or both.

1. Test for feasibility.

$$k^{1/2} = \tfrac{1}{2}(k^0 + k^1) > 0 \quad \text{for all } t \qquad (\text{since } k^0, k^1 > 0)$$

$$c^{1/2} = g(k^{1/2}) - \dot{k}^{1/2}$$

[6]That is, the laws of variable proportions and diminishing marginal utility hold.

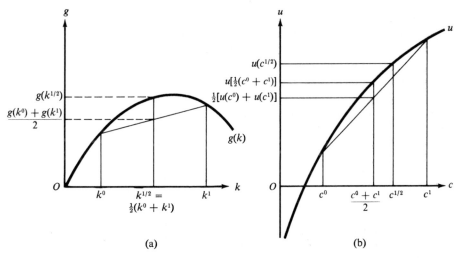

FIGURE 10.7

Since $g(k)$ is concave (see Figure 10.7a),

$$g(k^{1/2}) = g[(k^0+k^1)/2] > [g(k^0)+g(k^1)]/2$$
$$\dot{k}^{1/2} = \dot{k}^0/2+\dot{k}^1/2$$

Thus,

$$c^{1/2} > [g(k^0)-\dot{k}^0]/2+[g(k^1)-\dot{k}^1]/2$$
$$= (c^0+c^1)/2 \tag{10.1.10}$$
$$> 0 \quad \text{for all } t \qquad (\text{since } c^0, c^1 > 0)$$

2. Test for superiority.   The monotonicity and concavity of u imply that (see Figure 10.7b):

$$u(c^{1/2}) > u[(c^0+c^1)/2] \qquad (\text{monotonicity, i.e., } u' > 0)$$
$$\geq [u(c^0)+u(c^1)]/2 \qquad (\text{concavity, i.e., } u'' < 0) \tag{10.1.11}$$

Hence, integrating from 0 to T,

$$\int_0^T u[c^{1/2}(t)]\, dt > \tfrac{1}{2}\int_0^T [c^1(t)]\, dt + \tfrac{1}{2}\int_0^T [c^2(t)]\, dt \tag{10.1.12}$$

$$\geq \operatorname*{Min}_{1,2}\left\{\int_0^T u[c^1(t)]\, dt, \int_0^T u[c^2(t)]\, dt\right\} \quad \text{for all } T$$

Obviously, (c^0, k^0) and (c^1, k^1) cannot both catch up with $(c^{1/2}, k^{1/2})$. Since this contradicts the claim of at least one of the candidates to be optimal, the proof for uniqueness is complete.

B.   THE EXISTENCE PROBLEM

Some models do not admit an optimal growth path even though the first-order conditions for an optimum are met. Such paths may even be pessima for all we know. To avoid misleading results, the existence problem cannot be dismissed as an issue of no consequence.

1. Conceptual framework.   The Ramsey-Koopmans proof of the existence of an optimal program centers upon a comparison utility stream: $u[c(t)] \equiv u(\bar{c}) \equiv \bar{u}$, say. An easy grasp of the relevant concepts may be obtained from Chart 10.1.

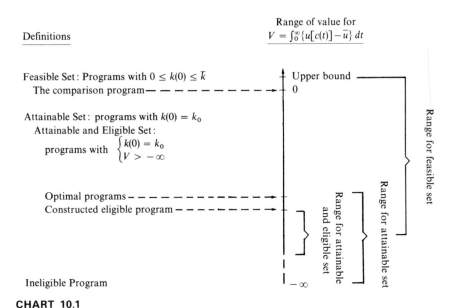

CHART 10.1

The purpose of a comparison stream is to convert the study of divergent utility integrals into the study of incremental utility integrals of the form $V = \int_0^\infty \{u[c(t)] - \bar{u}\} \, dt$. It is then hoped that among the attainable programs (with $k(0) = k_0$) we can find a program maximizing V. To ensure the existence of an optimal program, two facts must be ascertained.

(a) There must be an upper bound for V over the "attainable set." Its existence can be demonstrated by showing that V is bounded from above over the entire feasible set. Since the attainable set is a subset of the feasible set, V must be bounded above over the attainable set also.

(b) There must be some attainable programs with V not infinitely worse than the comparison stream. This may be proved by constructing one "eligible program."

Failure of (a) would lead to the prospect that two attainable programs, one dominating the other according to all criteria (e.g., overtaking or catching up), both have $+\infty$ as their V value. Failure of (b) would allow the possibility that all attainable programs have $-\infty$ as their V value. These would contravene the value of V as a basis for selection of an optimal program.

2. The analytic derivations.   (a) Proof that there exists an upper bound for V over the feasible set: For any T, we have

$$\int_0^T \{u[c(t)] - u(\bar{c})\} \, dt \leq u'(\bar{c}) \int_0^T [c(t) - \bar{c}] \, dt \qquad \text{(due to the concavity of } u(\cdot); \\ \text{see Figure 10.8)} \qquad (10.1.13)$$

$$= u'(\bar{c}) \int_0^T \{g[k(t)] - \dot{k}(t) - g(k^*)\} \, dt \qquad \text{(from (10.1.2'))}$$

$$\leq -u'(\bar{c}) \int_0^T \dot{k}(t) \, dt \qquad \text{(since } g[k(t)] \leq g(k^*); \\ \text{see Figure 10.1}a)$$

$$= u'(\bar{c}) \, [k(0) - k(T)]$$

$$\leq u'(\bar{c})\bar{k} \qquad \text{(since } 0 \leq k(t) \leq \bar{k} \text{ for all } t, \text{ the bracketed} \\ \text{term is maximized for } k(0) = \bar{k}, k(T) = 0)$$

Setting T equal to $+\infty$, we find that

$$V \leq u'(\bar{c})\bar{k} \qquad (10.1.14)$$

This means that, regardless of the initial value $k(0)$ and regardless of the growth pattern, *no feasible program can be infinitely better than the comparison stream.*

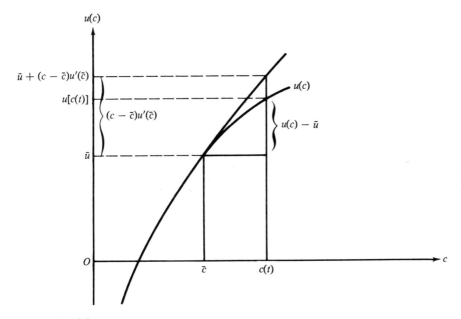

FIGURE 10.8

(b) Proof that there exists an attainable program that is not infinitely worse than the comparison stream (in other words, the attainable and eligible set is non-empty):

Case (i) : If $k(0) \geq k^*$, then set $c(t) \equiv \bar{c}$ for $t \geq 0$. We immediately obtain a program $(\bar{c}, k^*)$ such that $V = 0$.

Case (ii): If $k(0) < k^*$, then set

$$c(t) = \tfrac{1}{2}g[k(t)] \qquad \text{for } 0 \leq t < T \quad \text{where } k(T) = k^*$$
$$c(t) = g(k^*) \qquad \text{for } t \geq T$$

In this case, $V = \int_0^T (u\{\tfrac{1}{2}g[k(t)]\} - \bar{u})\, dt = V_0$, say, which is a finite negative number.

(c) We shall now show that there actually is an optimal program. The results in (a) and (b) establish the fact that *if* an optimal program exists, the associated V value will be in the finite range $[V_0, 0]$. This enables us to employ the calculus of variations technique, which is convenient in deriving *necessary conditions* but notoriously inconvenient in reaching *existence proofs*. One of the first-order *necessary* conditions (Section 10.1.4) states that in an optimal infinite-horizon program (if one exists), the per capita capital and per capita consumption must either both be strictly increasing functions of time or both be strictly decreasing functions of time from $[k(0), c(0)]$ to $[k^*, \bar{c}]$. Or in the knife-edge case, if $[k(0), c(0)] = (k^*, \bar{c})$, then we have seen in Section 10.1.2 that (k, c) should always take that value; hence,

(i) $V = \int_0^T \{u[c(t)] - \bar{u}\}\, dt$, where $k(T) = k^*$, since from T on, $u[c(t)] = \bar{u}$

(ii) $\dot{k}(t) \neq 0$ from 0 to T

Therefore, the optimal capital/labor path $k(t)$ is an invertible function. For each number z between $k(0)$ and $k^* = k(T)$, there is a unique time $t(z)$ such that $\dot{k}[t(z)] = z$ (i.e., $t(\cdot) = k^{-1}(z)$).[7]

Now this permits us to express the utility deficit as a function of k, namely,

$$u[c(t)] - \bar{u} = u\{c[t(k)]\} - \bar{u}$$

Since

$$dt = \frac{dk}{dk/dt} = \frac{dk}{\dot{k}} \quad \text{and} \quad \begin{cases} k = k(0) = k_0 & \text{when } t = 0 \\ k = k(t) = k^* & \text{when } t = T \end{cases}$$

we may follow Ramsey and rewrite the maximization problem:

$$\underset{c,\,k}{\text{Max}} \int_{k_0}^{k^*} \frac{u\{c[t(k)]\} - \bar{u}}{\dot{k}}\, dk = \underset{c}{\text{Max}} \int_{k_0}^{k^*} \frac{u\{c[t(k)]\} - \bar{u}}{g(k) - c[t(k)]}\, dk \qquad (10.1.$$

As Koopmans commented, the beauty of (10.1.15) is that k is the variable of integration (like the running variable i in $\Sigma_i A_i$, say), and $c[t(k)]$ is the "control variable," the instrument to be employed for maximization. Since no $\dot{c}$ is involved, this is not a variational problem but a simple calculus problem. Using a combination of diagrammatic and analytic arguments, we can prove the existence of an optimal program.

---

[7] Readers less convinced of the necessity of this argument may plot a parabolic k path to visualize the fact that corresponding to each z there may be two values of t such that $k(t) = z$.

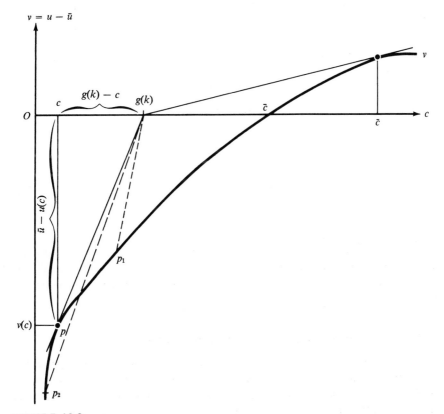

FIGURE 10.9

First we shift the origin (Figure 10.8) to $\bar{u}$ to obtain Figure 10.9. In the case $k(0) < k^*$, we know that $c(t) < \tilde{c}$ at all times between 0 and T; hence, $u(c) < \bar{u}$. Therefore,

$$\text{Max} \frac{u(c)-\bar{u}}{g(k)-c} \quad \text{is equivalent to} \quad \text{Min} \frac{\bar{u}-u(c)}{g(k)-c}$$

The ratio $[\bar{u}-u(c)]/[g(k)-c]$ is the slope of any chord linking $[g(k), 0]$ to $[c, v(c)]$ on the $v(c) = u(c)-\bar{u}$ curve, like $g(k)p_1$ and $g(k)p_2$ in Figure 10.9. Obviously, the slope reaches its minimum at the tangency position.

The interested reader can work out the case where $k(0) > k^*$ ($\tilde{c}$ turns out to be the optimal consumption level).[8]

---

[8] Note that:

$$\int_{k_0}^{k^*} \frac{u-\bar{u}}{g-c}\, dk = -\int_{k^*}^{k_0} \frac{u-\bar{u}}{g-c}\, dk$$

This diagram can also form the basis of comparative dynamic studies of variations of the production function and the utility function. Koopmans [23] showed that the smaller the marginal product of capital or the more "curved" the utility function, then the higher the initial consumption.

We shall now see that we can find that unique pair of optimal paths: $[k(t), c(t)]$.

Figure 10.9 shows that for each k, and therefore $g(k)$, there corresponds a unique $c = c[t(k)]$. Hence, we can substitute this function $c[t(k)]$ into (10.1.2) to obtain

$$\dot{k} = g(k) - c[t(k)]$$
$$= h(k), \text{ say} \tag{10.1.}$$

or

$$\frac{dk}{h(k)} = dt$$

Integrating on both sides from 0 to t we obtain

$$\int_{k_0}^{k(t)} \frac{dk}{h(k)} = t - 0 = t \tag{10.1.}$$

which lets us derive $k(t)$ as a function of t. This is because the area under the known curve $1/h(k)$ from the fixed k_0 to this yet undetermined $k(t)$ should be t. Once $k(t)$ is known, $c[t(k)]$ follows by way of Figure 10.9. This completes the proof of existence.

10.1.4. The transient solutions—first-order conditions

In Section 10.1.3-B we discussed the existence problem for an optimal program. One of the arguments used (that $\dot{k}$ and $\dot{c}$ must have the same sign, which never changes over time) depends upon the necessary conditions to be discussed here. The proof of the necessity of these conditions does not rely upon the existence theorem. The necessary conditions enable us to characterize the optimal paths satisfactorily *if they exist*. The prior use of the existence theorem assures us that we are not characterizing some imaginary constructions. Consider now the variational problem:

$$\text{Max} \int_0^\infty \{u[c(t)] - \bar{u}\} \, dt$$

subject to

$$\dot{k}(t) = g[k(t)] - c(t)$$
$$k(0) = k_0 > 0$$

We can rewrite it as

$$\text{Max}_k \int_0^\infty (u\{g[k(t)] - \dot{k}(t)\} - \bar{u}) \, dt \tag{10.1.}$$

In the following pages we shall consider in turn: (a) the Euler equation, its interpretations, and the Ramsey rule; and (b) phase diagram analysis and the transversality condition.

A. THE EULER EQUATION

1. The mathematical condition. From the theory of the calculus of variations, we have the first-order necessary condition for (10.1.18):

$$\frac{\partial}{\partial k}(u-\bar{u}) = \frac{d}{dt}\left[\frac{\partial}{\partial k}(u-\bar{u})\right] \qquad \text{(the Euler equation)}$$

Carrying out the computations, we have

$$u'(c)g'(k) = -\frac{d}{dt}[u'(c)] \tag{10.1.19}$$

$$= -u''(c)\dot{c}$$

This is a second-order differential equation in k after writing $c = g(k) - \dot{k}$. We can also write

$$\dot{c} = -u'g'/u'' \tag{10.1.19'}$$

For simplicity we set p equal to $u'(c)$, where p is the "shadow price" of consumption good in "utils," i.e., the marginal utility. We can then rearrange (10.1.19) to yield

$$\hat{p}(t) = -[f'(k)-n] \qquad \text{where } \hat{p} = \dot{p}/p \tag{10.1.20}$$

which is equivalent to[9]

$$p(t) = p(0)\exp\left\{-\int_0^t \{f'[k(\tau)]-n\}\,d\tau\right\} \tag{10.1.21}$$

This is a form with interesting economic interpretations.

2. The economic interpretation. Equation (10.1.21) represents a basic marginal equivalence relation; one unit of resource at time zero should yield equal marginal benefits no matter how we use it.

Through direct consumption, one unit of resource per capita at $t = 0$ yields the marginal utility of $p(0)$.

By a continual reinvestment process, this dosage of resource at $t = 0$ can compound itself to $\{\exp(\int_0^t f'[k(\tau)]\,d\tau)\}$ units by instant t. But by then the population will be increased e^{nt}-fold. Therefore, sacrificing one unit of consumption per capita at instant 0 can result in an incremental per capita consumption of

$$\exp\left\{\int_0^t f'[k(\tau)]\,d\tau - nt\right\} = \exp\left\{\int_0^t (f'[k(\tau)]-n)\,d\tau\right\}$$

units. Each unit of per capita consumption gives rise to a marginal utility of $p(t)$. Therefore, the fruit of a t-interval abstinence, in "util" terms, is

$$p(t)\exp\left\{\int_0^t \{f'[k(\tau)]-n\}\,d\tau\right\}$$

Equating this expression with $p(0)$, we obtain an equivalent form of (10.1.21).

[9]On integration,

$$\ln p(t) - \ln p(0) = -\int_0^t \{f'[k(\tau)]-n\}\,d\tau \qquad (\text{since } \hat{p} = d/dt\,\ln p)$$

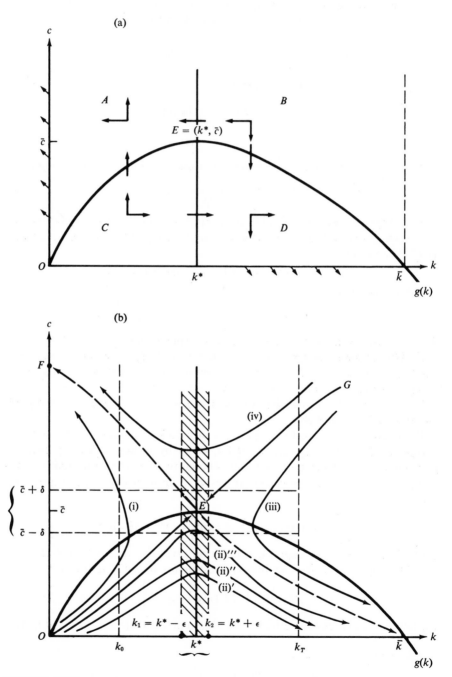

FIGURE 10.10

3. The first integral rule.   Since the time variable is absent in the integrand, the calculus of variations provides an alternative form of (10.1.19), namely,

$$u(c) - \bar{u} = k \frac{\partial}{\partial k} [u(c) - \bar{u}] + M = -k u'(c) + M \tag{10.1.22}$$

where M is a constant of integration.

Now, we observe from (10.1.19) that if $k(0) = k^*$, then $g'(k^*) = 0$ and $\dot{c} = 0 = k$ (since $u''(\bar{c}) < 0$). This is consistent with the golden rule program $[k^*, \bar{c}]$. But then,

$$M = [u(c) - \bar{u}] + k u'(c) = 0 + 0 = 0$$

Hence, we have the Keynes-Ramsey rule:

$$\dot{k} = \frac{\bar{u} - u(c)}{u'(c)} \tag{10.1.22'}$$

which may be stated as follows: The rate of increase of the capital/labor ratio equals the utility deficit divided by the marginal utility. This is the analytic translation of the tangency condition in Figure 10.9.

B. PHASE DIAGRAM ANALYSIS

1. Analysis.   Plotting c against k in Figure 10.10 and observing the twin differential equations.

$$\dot{k} = g(k) - c \tag{10.1.2'}$$

$$\dot{c} = -u'g'/u'' \tag{10.1.19'}$$

where

$$\frac{(-u')}{(u'')} > 0 \quad \text{and} \quad g' \begin{Bmatrix} > \\ = \\ < \end{Bmatrix} 0 \quad \text{for } k \begin{Bmatrix} < \\ = \\ > \end{Bmatrix} k^*$$

we can partition the non-negative half-strip $\{(k, c)| 0 \le k \le \bar{k}, c \ge 0\}$ into four regions by means of $g(k)$ and $k = k^*$.

Results in (10.1.2') and (10.1.19') can be tabulated as in Table 10.1.

TABLE 10.1

	$c < g(k)$	$c = g(k)$	$c > g(k)$
$k < k^*$	$\dot{k}, \dot{c} > 0$	$\dot{k} = 0 < \dot{c}$	$\dot{k} < 0 < \dot{c}$
$k = k^*$	$\dot{k} > 0 = \dot{c}$	$\dot{k} = 0 = \dot{c}$	$\dot{k} < 0 = \dot{c}$
$k > k^*$	$\dot{k} > 0 > \dot{c}$	$\dot{k} = 0 > \dot{c}$	$\dot{k}, \dot{c} < 0$

In Figure 10.10a, the arrows show the directions of movement for (k, c) from a given location. From that diagram a series of results can be deduced:

(a) The optimal path cannot pass through regions A and D:

(i) Any point in A leads to a path that inexorably drifts toward the c axis and beyond. This violates the restriction of $k \ge 0$.

(ii) Any point in D leads to a path pressing toward the k axis. This implies that $c(t)$ will be less than $\bar{c}$ by an ever-increasing margin. So will the magnitude of "utility deficit," $\bar{u} - u(c)$. Therefore, the path will be ineligible. Since eligible paths do exist (Section 10.1.3-B–3(b), case (i)), such an ineligible path cannot be optimal.

(b) The optimal path cannot cross the boundaries between any two regions,

(i) Starting from C, if the path reaches the $k = k^*$ line, it will be in D. with the possible exception of the point $(k^*, \bar{c})$ (see c(ii) below).

(ii) Starting from C, if the path reaches the $g(k)$ curve, it will be in A.

(iii) Starting from B, if the path reaches the $k = k^*$ line, it will be in A.

(iv) Starting from B, if the path reaches the $g(k)$ curve, it will be in D.

(c) If the optimal path is at $(k^*, \bar{c})$, it will stay there forever and it must have been there since the beginning of time.

(i) From Table 10.1 we observe if $[k(t), c(t)] = (k^*, \bar{c})$, $\dot{k} = 0 = \dot{c}$, so extrapolating forward, it will always be there.

(ii) Similarly, extrapolating backwards, it must have always been there. This rules out that an optimal path from B or C can actually reach $(k^*, \bar{c})$ at any finite future instant.

(d) Throughout B or C, k and c both increase or both decrease, respectively, in a strictly monotonic way.

2. Conclusions. From the above, we can partition all possible situations into three cases:

Case 1. $k_0 = k^*$. Optimal policy—golden rule: $c(t) \equiv g(k^*)$ and $k(t) \equiv k^*$ for all t.

Case 2. $k_0 < k^*$. Optimal policy: $c(t)$ and $k(t)$ both maintain a strictly monotonic, increasing, asymptotic approach to $\bar{c}$ and k^*, respectively. This is represented by the OE curve in Figure 10.10b.

Case 3. $k_0 > k^*$. Optimal policy: $c(t)$ and $k(t)$ both maintain a strictly monotonic, decreasing, asymptotic approach to $\bar{c}$ and (k), respectively. This is represented by the GE curve in Figure 10.10b.

3. "Transversality condition." Consider the Euler equation in (10.1.19) as a second-order differential equation in k. This requires two boundary conditions to determine any particular path. Usually in a finite-horizon program the beginning value k_0 is given and the end value $k(T)$ is prescribed. In an infinite-horizon program, the substitute for the given end value is the statement

$$\lim_{t \to \infty} k(t) = k^* \tag{10.1.}$$

which is sometimes called the transversality condition. However, for further discussion of this term, one may refer to Shell [24].

10.1.5. The asymptotic problem

The justification of the infinite-horizon formulation is partly due to the fact that long-period finite-horizon problems yield optimal growth paths that can be approximated adequately by policies determined in the infinite-horizon problem. We shall not attempt a rigorous proof here. Instead we shall make a plausible argument. For a detailed but different type of derivation, one may read Samuelson [7].

A. GENERAL RESULTS FOR A FINITE–HORIZON PROBLEM

A finite-horizon problem differs from an infinite-horizon problem in having an end capital in lieu of a transversality condition. In the present context we can summarize the basic results below:

(1) The Euler equation in (10.1.19) still holds. So do its equivalent forms.
(2) The first integral rule (10.1.22) remains valid.
(3) Either by dividing (10.1.19) into (10.1.2′) or by dividing (10.1.2′) into (10.1.19) we can obtain differential equations relating c and k, viz.,

$$\frac{dk}{dc} = \frac{(u'')[c-g(k)]}{u'g'} \quad \text{or} \quad \frac{dc}{dk} = \frac{u'g'}{(u'')[c-g(k)]} \tag{10.1.24}$$

These differential equations have solution curves that are drawn in Figure 10.10*b*.

Depending upon the values of k_0 and $k_T = k(T)$, we have four types of curves, (see Table 10.2). The peak and trough of the k path occur when $g(k) = c$; the peak and trough of the c path occur when $k = k^*$. Moreover, the peak for the k path always occurs at a value less than k^* and the trough at a value greater than k^*. Similarly, the peak for the c path occurs always below $\bar{c}$ and the trough below $\bar{c}$. These curves are governed by the rules indicated by the arrows in Figure 10.10*a*.

TABLE 10.2

Types	Characteristics	Time paths for k	Time paths for c	Specimen in Figure 10.10*b*
1	$k_0, k_T \leq k^*$	First increase, then decrease	Monotonically increasing	(i)
2	$k_0 \leq k^* \leq k_T$	Monotonically increasing	First increase, then decrease	(ii)′, (ii)″, (ii)‴
3	$k^* \leq k_0, k_T$	First decrease, then increase	Monotonically decreasing	(iii)
4	$k_T \leq k^* \leq k_0$	Monotonically decreasing	First decrease, then increase	(iv)

B. THE TURNPIKE THEOREM

1. A review of Figure 10.10b. The curves EF and $E\bar{k}$ in broken lines are the only curves arriving at the c axis or the vicinity of $\bar{k}$ without crossing either the $k = k^*$ line or the $c = g(k)$ curve at any instant in the past. Tracing back through time, they point backward asymptotically to the point $E = (k^*, \bar{c})$. These two curves together with OE and GE constitute the limiting loci for curves of the families (i) through (iv).

Further analysis provides more information. For instance, consider the family (ii) curves. All members of family (ii) pass through first the vertical dotted line at k_0 and then the vertical dotted line at k_T. The sojourn period in between is:

$$\int_{k_0}^{k_T} \frac{dk}{g(k) - c(k; c_0)} = T \tag{10.1}$$

which is a variant of (10.1.17). Here c_0 denotes the c value as the particular curve cuts the $k = k_0$ dotted line and $c(k; c_0)$ signifies any particular curve with $c(0) = c_0$.

From the fact that all the curves in family (ii) are solutions to the same differential equation (10.1.24) we know that they may never meet each other at any regular point. This implies that for any k, $c(k; c_0^2) > c(k; c_0^1)$ if and only if $c_0^2 > c_0^1$. In view of (10.1.25), we conclude that

(a) For given k_0 and k_T, $\partial c(k)/\partial T > 0$, where $c(k)$ denotes per capita consumption allowed when per capita capital is k.

(b) The higher c_0 is, the more time it takes for k to move between any particular pair of levels. In particular, let

$$T_1 = \int_{k_0}^{k_1} \frac{dk}{g(k) - c(k; c_0)} \quad \text{and} \quad T_2 = \int_{k_2}^{k_T} \frac{dk}{g(k) - c(k; c_0)} \qquad k_0 < k_1 < k_2 < k_T$$

then

$$\frac{\partial T_i}{\partial c_0} > 0 \qquad i = 1, 2$$

2. A demonstration of the theorem. For a finite-horizon problem with initial and final k values equal to k_0 and k_T, $k_0 < k^* < k_T$, and with a planning horizon equal to T, we may ask how much of the time $k(t)$ is outside the zone

$$k^* - \varepsilon \le k(t) \le k^* + \varepsilon \quad \text{for some } \varepsilon > 0 \tag{10.1}$$

The consumption turnpike theorem asserts that we can

(a) make an upper estimate for the outside sojourn time

(b) prove that this estimate is independent of T; hence, the larger T is, the more is the proportion of time over which (10.1.26) is fulfilled

(c) verify that violation of (10.1.26) occurs (if it occurs at all) only in the beginning or the end.

Graphically, we shall assume that curve (ii)''' in Figure 10.10b corresponds to the finite-horizon optimal program. We now introduce four symbols: T_1^∞, T_2^∞, T_1^T, T_2^T.

Sojourn time	Along (ii)'''	Along OE	Along $E\bar{k}$
From k_0 to $(k^* - \varepsilon)$	T_1^T	T_1^∞	
From $(k^* + \varepsilon)$ to k_T	T_2^T		T_2^∞

From result (b) in subsection 1, above, we realize that $T_1^T < T_1^\infty$, $T_2^T < T_2^\infty$. Hence, time spent outside the zone implied by (10.1.26) must be

$$T_0 = T_1^T + T_2^T < T_1^\infty + T_2^\infty$$

where T_1^∞ and T_2^∞ are independent of T, proving assertions (a) and (b). Hence,

$$\underset{T \to \infty}{\text{Lim}} \left[(T - T_1^\infty - T_2^\infty)/T \right] = 1$$

Figure 10.10*b* illustrates that assertion (c) is fulfilled as well.

We can prove that $k(t)$ for members of family (iv) has similar properties in an entirely symmetric manner. Likewise the $c(t)$ paths corresponding to members of families (i) and (iii) can be shown to have similar "catenary" properties toward $\bar{c}$.

We now ask whether the $c(t)$ path in families (ii) and (iv) would stay inside a zone $(\bar{c} - \delta) \leq c \leq (\bar{c} + \delta)$ for most of the time when T becomes large. Similar questions can be asked about the $k(t)$ path for families (i) and (iii), *mutatis mutandis*.

By scanning Figure 10.10*b*, we conclude that by choosing an ε small enough relative to δ, for a curve with some T, say, $\overline{T}$, the portion inside the $(k^* - \varepsilon) \leq k \leq (k^* + \varepsilon)$ bracket entirely falls within the $(\bar{c} - \delta) \leq c \leq (\bar{c} + \delta)$ bracket. For all curves with $T \geq \overline{T}$, the corresponding curves will be even higher. Hence, they will be inside the δ bracket. Let $T^* = \text{Max} [\overline{T}, T_1^\infty + T_2^\infty]$; then T^* is the upper bound for the periods in which the $c(t)$ path lies outside the δ bracket. The above proof relies upon the uniform convergence of the solution curves for the differential equation in (10.1.24′).

The proof for the catenary properties of $k(t)$ for families (i) and (iii) is entirely similar.

10.1.6. Time preference

A. POSITIVE TIME PREFERENCE

We shall first review the above results under the case of positive time preference ($\delta > 0$ in (10.1.1)). Most of them stand with minor modifications. Next, we shall consider the price relations in the modified Ramsey model. Without elaboration, we note that:

(1) The uniqueness of optimal solution remains valid. The Ramsey-Weizsäcker device becomes unnecessary as long as $c(t)$ is always larger than some finite constant[10] because even the best program will entail a convergent discounted utility integral.

(2) The steady-state solution has to be modified somewhat. The best balanced growth path should equate the marginal utilities of devoting one unit of present per capita resource to direct consumption or to investment. Used in consump-

---

[10]Otherwise, u may diverge to negative infinity.

tion, this yields a marginal benefit of the order $u'[c(0)]$. In investment, for a t interval it would give rise to $\exp \int_0^t f'[k(\tau)] \, d\tau$ units of goods to be divided by a population e^{nt} times as large. Hence, this will provide $\exp \int_0^t (f'-n) \, d\tau$ units of per capita consumption, each unit yielding a marginal welfare of $u'[c(t)]e^{-\delta t}$ units. Equating the two marginal benefits, we obtain

$$u'[c(0)] = \left\{ \exp \int_0^t [f' - (n+\delta)] \, d\tau \right\} u'[c(t)] \tag{10.1.}$$

By the definition of balanced growth, $u'[c(0)] = u'[c(t)]$ since $c(0) = c(t)$ for all t. Moreover, $f'[k(\tau)]$ is a constant, since $k(\tau)$ is a constant for all τ. In order for (10.1.27) to hold, the exponent must be zero; i.e.,

$$f'(k) = n + \delta \tag{10.1.}$$

A more formal derivation can be obtained by substituting $e^{-\delta t}u'$ for u' in (10.1.19) to obtain

$$(u'g' + u''\dot{c} - \delta u')e^{-\delta t} = 0 \tag{10.1.}$$

Setting $\dot{c}$ equal to zero in view of the balanced growth assumption, we again obtain (10.1.28).

(3) The Euler condition stands as before, although its form becomes (10.1.29) above. The Keynes-Ramsey rule disappears because the first integral rule is valid only when t does not enter explicitly into the integration.

(4) The phase diagram analysis and the asymptotic properties remain valid although the equilibrium point is now (k^δ, c^δ), where $k^\delta = f'^{-1}(n+\delta)$ and $c^\delta = g(k^\delta)$. Interested readers may refer to Koopmans [9].

Turning to the price relations, we follow Koopmans and introduce $p(t) = e^{-\delta t}u[c(t)]$ as the shadow price associated with a consumption stream $c(t)$, in terms of "utils." The results he obtained are somewhat generalized in what follows.

1. Price associated with an eligible program. Let c^e be the consumption stream of an eligible program that may or may not be optimal or feasible, p^e the associated price path, and c an alternative consumption stream that may or may not be feasible.

Due to the concavity of $u(\cdot)$ and using the argument shown in Figure 10.8,

$$\int_0^T [e^{-\delta t}u(c) - e^{-\delta t}u(c^e)] \, dt \leq \int_0^T p^e(c - c^e) \, dt \tag{10.1.}$$

This relation is relevant for both finite-horizon and infinite-horizon problems if both integrals converge when $T \to \infty$.

Two interpretations are possible, depending upon where one inserts a zero in (10.1.30):

(a) Among all c yielding the same welfare as c^e or more (which includes c^e itself), c^e minimizes the expenditure. That is,

$$\int_0^T p^e(c-c^e)\,dt \geq \int_0^T e^{-\delta t}[u(c)-u(c^e)]\,dt \qquad \text{(from (10.1.30))}$$

$$\geq 0 \qquad \text{(by assumption)}$$

$$= \int_0^T p^e(c^e-c^e)\,dt$$

(b) Among all c incurring the same expenditure as c^e or less (again, c^e itself is one of these), c^e maximizes the benefit. That is,

$$\int_0^T e^{-\delta t}[u(c^e)-u(c^e)]\,dt = 0$$

$$\geq \int_0^T p^e(c-c^e)\,dt \qquad \text{(by assumption)}$$

$$\geq \int_0^T e^{-\delta t}[u(c)-u(c^e)]\,dt \qquad \text{(from (10.1.30))}$$

The finite-dimensional analog to (10.1.30) is the relation between one particular consumption ensemble c^e and other ensembles c with a plane $p^e(c-c^e)=0$ drawn at that particular ensemble and tangential to the indifference locus $u(c)=u(c^e)$. Here the word "eligible" is used in its weak sense. It may be neither attainable nor optimal. The ensemble c^e may be in the interior or exterior of the production frontier, or else it is located at a point where the indifference loci cut the production frontier. p^e only signifies the "directional cosines" for the tangential plane; it is not a true budget plane.

2. Price associated with a feasible and eligible consumption stream. Consider two feasible and eligible programs, the first identified with the superscript f, as is its price:

$$\int_0^T p^f[g(k)-g(k^f)]\,dt \leq \int_0^T [p^f g'(k^f)]\,(k-k^f)\,dt \qquad (10.1.31)$$

Again this is due to the concavity of $g(\cdot)$, derivable in a manner analogous to Figure 10.8. Interpreting $[p^f g'(k^f)]$ as implied rent, (10.1.31) is analogous to the finite-dimensional case, where any movement along the production frontier should not yield an increase of output surpassing the incremental (implied) rent.

3. Price associated with an optimal program. Let c^o, k^o, and p^o be the quantities associated with an optimal program, finite or infinite. Equation (10.1.20) still holds; i.e.,

$$\dot{p}^o = -g'(k^o)p^o \qquad (10.1.20')$$

Consider an optimal program and another attainable program. The left-hand side of (10.1.31) can be written as[11]

$$\int_0^T [p^o(c-c^o)+p^o(\dot{k}-\dot{k}^o)]\,dt = \int_0^T [p^o(c-c^o)-\dot{p}^o(k-k^o)]\,dt + p^o(T)[k(T)-k^o(T)]$$

---

[11] After integrating by parts, note that $k(0)=k^o(0)=k_0$, since both are attainable.

Substituting back into (10.1.31), rearranging, and using (10.1.20'), we have

$$\int_0^T p^o(c-c^o)\,dt + p^o(T)[k(T)-k^o(T)] \leq 0 \tag{10.1.32}$$

This states that the optimal program maximizes the present value of the consumption stream plus terminal capital over the attainable set.

4. Price associated with an infinite optimal program. Let c^i, k^i, and p^i be the relevant quantities. We then have

$$\operatorname*{Lim}_{t\to\infty} p^i(t) = \operatorname*{Lim}_{t\to\infty}\{e^{-\delta t}u'[c^i(t)]\}$$

$$= u'(\bar{c})\operatorname*{Lim}_{t\to\infty} e^{-\delta t} = 0 \tag{10.1.33}$$

We now note that

$$-\bar{k} \leq k(T)-k^i(T) \leq \bar{k} \qquad \text{(at any time, the } k \text{ value of an attainable}$$
$$\text{program is between 0 and } \bar{k}\text{)}$$

Hence,

$$\operatorname*{Lim}_{T\to\infty}\{p^i(T)[k(T)-k^i(T)]\} = 0 \qquad \text{(from (10.1.33))}$$

Setting T to approach $+\infty$ in (10.1.32) and using the above result, we have

$$\int_0^\infty p^i(c-c^i)\,dt \leq 0$$

which shows that the optimal infinite program yields the maximum value of consumption stream.

We may also note that since u' is a monotonic function of c, the consumption turnpike theorem also has its dual version in terms of price p.

B. NEGATIVE TIME PREFERENCE

1. General discussion.   A negative time preference rate ($\delta < 0$) may appear rather bizarre to the average economist at first glance. However, our prejudice against such an assumption may be due to the writings of the Austrian school, who tried hard to justify the positive interest rate observed. The adoption of a negative time preference rate may be quite appropriate in the context of the Ramsey model. Individuals need not undervalue their old age compared with their earlier years. This corresponds to a negative time preference, which means a heavier weight for the more distant future than for the near future. A society may behave in precisely the same way, assuming that the present generation is not entirely selfish toward their young. Moreover, if population size increases over time, the instantaneous utility function may not be dependent upon the per capita consumption alone: The per capita consumption today may affect only half as much population as the per capita consumption fifty years from now. The economic consequence of a negative time preference rate is an encouragement to invest. Under zero time preference, the difference between the marginal

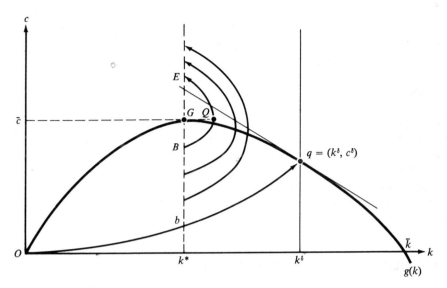

FIGURE 10.11

product of capital and the growth rate for population ($g' = f' - n$) approaches zero. Under a negative time preference, the same difference presumably can go to some negative value, meaning that further capital accumulation is permissible. However, from the mathematical point of view, a negative time preference rate leads to difficulties.

This forms the basis of Koopmans' view: Moral conviction ought to be *corrected* (!) to conform to logical (mathematical) necessity. We should be aware of the fact that such mathematical difficulties become inevitable only if we interpret the assumptions of infinite horizon, infinitely growing population, constant technology $f(\cdot)$, and constant preference $u(\cdot)$ in a literal manner. Of course, the relaxation of any of these hypotheses may not improve matters. Koopmans [30] has shown cases where the avoidance of mathematical difficulties in such generalizations may actually require a sufficiently large positive discount rate (the Inagaki results [26]) rather than non-negative discount rates.

2. Demonstration.   We shall not reiterate Koopmans' proof that every attainable program can be *bettered* when $\delta < 0$ (hence, there is no *best* program to be spoken of). Instead, a phase diagram analysis seems to demonstrate the point quite well.

We now modify the phase diagram in Figure 10.10b to obtain Figure 10.11. For any finite-horizon problem, the discussion in Section 10.1.5 is valid with only minor modifications; for example, the equilibrium point is now (k^δ, c^δ), where $g'(k^\delta) = \delta$ and $c^\delta = g(k^\delta)$. The Euler equation remains valid and the initial and final capital helps to decide which solution curve in the phase diagram corresponds to the particular T.

Consider a finite-horizon problem with $k_0 = k_T = k^*$. The curve prescribes an increase of k in the first phase until the $g(k)$ curve is crossed, then the decumulation begins. Along the arc BQ, per capita consumption is below the golden-rule consumption $\bar{c}$, which the planner might well have chosen, throughout the T interval (this would imply a "degenerate path" at the single point G in the kc plane). The detour to Q is fully compensated by a per capita consumption higher than $\bar{c}$ over the QE arc. The longer the horizon, the lower the initial consumption and the more to the right the solution curves, as shown in Figure 10.11 by the two loci enveloping the BQE path. But when T approaches infinity the path becomes bq. The whole path lies below the $c = \bar{c}$ line. Constant abstinence is never rewarded by eventual compensation. Hence, the bq path cannot be optimal. Yet if there were any optimal path, the necessary conditions for optimality would exclude any path different from the bq path. This is similar to what we analyzed in Section 10.1.4. This completes both the demonstration and the interpretation of the nonexistence of an optimal path.

10.2 THE UZAWA TWO-SECTOR MODEL

One of the major misgivings applied economists entertain about most optimal growth models is their high degree of aggregation. Applied economists confronting binary choices in screening investment projects usually complain that theoretical development is agonizingly slow in coming to their rescue. In this respect, it appears that two-sector models are at least a step in the right direction.

In (positive) growth theory, the two-sector model does not differ very much from the one-sector model. The variability of the opportunity cost of investment is practically the only novelty (notwithstanding the weighty studies on indeterminacies). The Hahn-Samuelson discovery of underdeterminacy in heterogeneous capital goods models indicates difficulties in further degrees of disaggregation. The situation is somewhat different with optimal growth. On the one hand, two-sector optimal growth models provide useful prescriptions for intersectoral resource allocations. On the other, the Hahn-Samuelson dilemma evaporates (as Samuelson noted) once an explicit social objective appears on the scene.

Before we become too elated, we must note that a two-sector model is still a far cry from what the practitioners demand. Detailed disaggregation still escapes us. Nor do the present two-sector models necessarily lead to the millenium. Though the Pontryagin formulation is fully general in scope, present works rely heavily upon phase diagrams, a tool hopelessly incapable of generalization when there are more than three relevant variables.

On the other hand, as empirical studies proceed, economists may be able to resort to more specific formulations—e.g., specifying types of production functions and the value ranges of their parameters. If so, numerical analysis may be used for more disaggregated models. It is perhaps reasonable to speculate that in such futuristic model building, economic insight gained from simpler models would be a valuable asset. Accordingly, we believe that studies of presently available models are fruitful for both the theoretically and the practically inclined.

There exist a number of two-sector optimal growth models, notably those of Shell [24], Srinivasan [25], Stoleru [27], Uzawa [28], and Kurz [29]. We shall confine our discussion to that of Uzawa and encourage the interested reader to consult the literature for the rest.

10.2.1. Assumptions

The two-sector *optimal growth* model of Uzawa is essentially an extension of his two-sector *growth* model. Most of the technical assumptions in the latter model are carried over, while assumptions on social preferences take the place of assumptions on market and household behavior. Basically, his assumptions are of two types:

(1) Preferential:
(a) The planner maximizes a discounted integral of the infinite-horizon per capita consumption stream.
(b) There exists a minimum (subsistence) level of consumption per capita below which the economy cannot survive.
(2) Technical:
(a) The sectoral production functions are linear homogeneous and obey the six Inada conditions. (This is the same as assumption (3) in Section 4.3.)
(b) Labor input is homogeneous and its supply grows at a constant exponential rate n. Capital input is homogeneous and perfectly malleable. It depreciates at the relative rate μ. (These are the same as assumptions (4) and (6) in Section 4.3.)
(c) The consumption good sector is more capital intensive than the investment good sector. (This is assumption (9) in Section 4.3.)

Assumption (2c) is dispensed with in Uzawa's generalizations. Deeper insights may be gained by comparing this model with both the two-sector growth models of Uzawa and Inada and the one-sector Ramsey model in Section 10.1.

(1) Comparison with the model in Section 4.3:
(a) The assumptions on market behavior (assumptions (1) and (2) on foresight and adjustments) and household behavior (assumptions (5) and (7) on savings) in Section 4.3 are dropped in the optimal growth version. As normative economics goes, *what will be* gives way to *what should be*.
(b) In the model of Section 4.3, as long as s_w and s_r are not both 0 or both 1, the overall saving/income ratio lies somewhere between zero and unity. Let s be the value of such an overall ratio; one can find the output point by maximizing a Mill-Graham surrogate utility function: $[(\dot{K} + \mu K)^s C^{1-s}]$ over the production frontier (where μ is the depreciation rate). Obviously the outputs of both sectors must be positive. In an optimal growth model, no such assurance is present. Special assumptions on negative output or

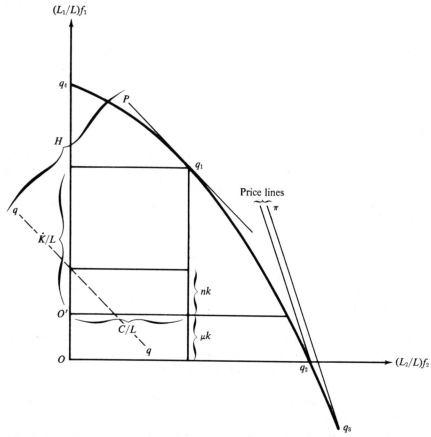

FIGURE 10.12

minimum consumption per capita must be made so that we will not end up with any one output negative. In Figure 10.12, for instance, the production frontier is $q_2 q_4$. Suppose the shadow price ratio is such as that reflected by the price line πq_3. If there is no output constraint, mathematical analysis will lead us to a point such as q_3, which lies on the *extension* of the relevant production frontier, implying a *negative* rate of *gross* investment!

(2) Comparison with the Ramsey model:

(a) The Uzawa model assumes that the instantaneous felicity index is the "identity function":[12] Plotting total utility at any moment against per capita consumption, one obtains a 45° ray. This of course is a special case of the Ramsey u function.

(b) Koopmans assumed that $u(0) = -\infty$ to rule out zero consumption in an optimal program. For Uzawa, $u(0) = 0$. Therefore, some special lower

---

[12] If $F(x) = x$ for all x, then F is an identity function.

bound must be specified. However, when the subsistence requirement is positive, sometimes no feasible path exists. This will be discussed below.

Despite such differences, a large portion of the results in the last section remain valid. For instance, Uzawa showed that the value of the objective function is bounded from above for all feasible paths. He also proved that if an optimal path exists, it must be unique. Other similarities will be discussed later.

10.2.2. The formulation

(1) We shall first review the notations we are going to use in our discussion. They are practically the same as those used in Section 4.3.

c consumption per capita
$f_i(\cdot)$ output per *worker* in sector i as a function of k_i
k overall capital labor ratio
k_i capital per *worker* in sector i
$L(t)$ total labor force at t
$L_i(t)$ labor force in sector i at t
n population growth rate
μ depreciation rate
δ time preference rate
Subscripts: $i = 1$ investment sector
               $i = 2$ consumption sector

(2) We now introduce some useful yet self-evident preliminary results:
(a) By definition:

$$L_1 + L_2 = L \quad \text{and} \quad L_1 k_1 + L_2 k_2 = K$$

(b) Applying Cramer's rule to the above relations[13] or using Figure 10.13,[14]

$$\frac{L_1}{L} = \frac{k_2 - k}{k_2 - k_1} \qquad \frac{L_2}{L} = \frac{k - k_1}{k_2 - k_1} \qquad (4.3.10)$$

[13] First dividing the twin equations in (a) by L.

[14] In Figure 10.13, construct aI parallel to CQ and extend IQ to b. Then,

$$\overline{aI} = k_2$$
$$\overline{cI} = k$$
$$\overline{bI} = k_1$$
$$\overline{Id}/\overline{dI} = \overline{IQ}/\overline{Qb}$$
$$= \overline{aC}/\overline{Cb}$$
$$= (k_2 - k)/(k - k_1)$$

Therefore,

$$\frac{L_1}{L} = \overline{Id} = \frac{\overline{Id}}{\overline{Id} + \overline{dI}} = \frac{k_2 - k}{(k_2 - k) + (k - k_1)} = \frac{k_2 - k}{k_2 - k_1}$$

and

$$\frac{L_2}{L} = \overline{dI} = \frac{\overline{dI}}{\overline{Id} + \overline{dI}} = \frac{k - k_1}{(k_2 - k) + (k - k_1)} = \frac{k - k_1}{k_2 - k_1}$$

(c) Using the definitions in (1) above, we then obtain:

Per capita consumption, c:	$L_2 f_2/L = [(k-k_1)/(k_2-k_1)] f_2$
Per capita gross investment:	$L_1 f_1/L = [(k_2-k)/(k_2-k_1)] f_1$
Per capita net investment, $\dot{K}/L$:	$(L_1 f_1 - \mu K)/L$
	$= [(k_2-k)/(k_2-k_1)] f_1 - \mu k$

(d) We now have the dynamic equation for k:[15]

$$\dot{k} = (\dot{K}/L) - nk = [(k_2-k)/(k_2-k_1)] f_1 - (n+\mu)k$$

(3) The formulation of the Uzawa model can now be completed. Uzawa seeks the feasible consumption path that maximizes the discounted integral of per capita consumption. Algebraically, this means

$$\text{Max} \int_0^\infty e^{-\delta t} c(t)\, dt = \int_0^\infty e^{-\delta t} \left[\frac{(k-k_1) f_2}{k_2-k_1} \right] dt \tag{10.2.1}$$

subject to:

$$\dot{k} = [(k_2-k) f_1/(k_2-k_1)] - (n+\mu)k \qquad \text{with } k(0) \text{ given} \tag{10.2.2}$$

$$(k-k_1) f_2/(k_2-k_1) \geq w_{\min} \qquad (w_{\min} \geq \text{the subsistence level of } c) \tag{10.2.3}$$

$$(k_2-k)/(k_2-k_1) \leq 1 \tag{10.2.4}$$

k, k_1, and k_2 are all control variables subject to the restrictions (10.2.2)–(10.2.4). Equation (10.2.2) is more transparent; it depicts the forms any $k(t)$ path can take. Equation (10.2.3) limits L_2/L from below, so that the proportion of labor allocated to the consumption sector must be adequate to produce the minimal required consumption goods. Equation (10.2.4) shows the logical restriction: the labor force allocated to the consumption sector can never exceed the total labor supply.

(4) Further transformation is needed to simplify the analysis. We follow Uzawa and provisionally assume $w_{\min} = 0$ in (10.2.3). When f_2 and $k_2 - k_1$ are greater than zero, we can reduce (10.2.3) to

$$k - k_1 \geq 0 \tag{10.2.3'}$$

Multiplying (10.2.4) through by $(k_2 - k_1)$ and rearranging, we have

$$k_2 - k \geq 0 \tag{10.2.4'}$$

Substituting in $[1 - (k-k_1)/(k_2-k_1)]$ for $(k_2-k)/(k_2-k_1)$ in (10.2.2), we have

$$\dot{k} = \left[1 - \frac{k-k_1}{k_2-k_1} \right] f_1 - (n+\mu)k \tag{10.2.2'}$$

10.2.3. The Pontryagin format

Due to the presence of inequality constraints, the Pontryagin maximum principle is much more convenient for the Uzawa problem than the classical variational methods of Euler and Lagrange. Hence, we shall follow the Pontry-

[15] $\dot{k} = \hat{k}k = (\hat{K} - \hat{L})k$ but $\hat{K}k = \dot{K}/L$ and $\hat{L} = n$.

agin approach. We shall first set up the Hamiltonian and state the necessary conditions. Our presentation differs slightly from Uzawa's since we employ fewer constraints and variables. Next, we shall attempt to provide economic interpretations for the Hamiltonian as well as all the necessary conditions.

A. THE FORMAT

The Hamiltonian form corresponding to the problem of (10.2.1) and (10.2.2')–(10.2.4') is

$$H = \left\{ e^{-\delta t}\left[\frac{k-k_1}{k_2-k_1}\, f_2 \right] + \psi_k\left[\left(1 - \frac{k-k_1}{k_2-k_1} \right) f_1 \right] \right\} - \psi_k(n+\mu)k$$

$$+ \psi_2(k_2 - k) + \psi_1(k - k_1)$$

(10.2.5)

Regrouping, we have

$$H = (e^{-\delta t}f_2 = \psi_k f_1)\left(\frac{k-k_1}{k_2-k_1} \right) + \psi_k[f_1 - (n+\mu)k] + \psi_2(k_2 - k) + \psi_1(k - k_1) \quad (10.2.5')$$

ψ_k, ψ_1, and ψ_2 take non-negative values only. They are the adjoint variables corresponding to (10.2.2')–(10.2.4'), respectively, and represent shadow prices, to be discussed below. k is the state variable, indicating the position of an economy. k_1 and k_2 are control variables, serving as policy instruments.

According to the Pontryagin theory there are six necessary conditions for an optimum. These are:

(a) The primal-dual dynamic equations:

$$\dot{k} = \frac{\partial H}{\partial \psi_k} = \left[1 - \frac{k-k_1}{k_2-k_1} \right] f_1 - (n+\mu)k \tag{10.2.6}$$

$$\dot{\psi}_k = -\frac{\partial H}{\partial k} = \left[\frac{\psi_k f_1 - e^{-\delta t}f_2}{k_2-k_1} \right] + (n+\mu)\psi_k - (\psi_1 - \psi_2) \tag{10.2.7}$$

(b) The maximum conditions:

$$0 = \frac{\partial H}{\partial k_1} = [e^{-\delta t}f_2 - \psi_k f_1]\frac{k-k_1}{(k_2-k_1)^2} + \left[1 - \frac{k-k_1}{k_2-k_1} \right]\psi_k f_1' - \frac{e^{-\delta t}f_2 - \psi_k f_1}{k_2-k_1} - \psi_1 \tag{10.2.8}$$

$$0 = \frac{\partial H}{\partial k_2} = -[e^{-\delta t}f_2 - \psi_k f_1]\frac{k-k_1}{(k_2-k_1)^2} + \frac{k-k_1}{k_2-k_1}e^{-\delta t}f_2' + \psi_2 \tag{10.2.9}$$

(c) The complementary slackness conditions:

$$k_2 - k \geq 0; \quad \psi_2 \geq 0; \quad \psi_2(k_2 - k) = 0 \tag{10.2.10}$$

$$k - k_1 \geq 0; \quad \psi_1 \geq 0; \quad \psi_1(k - k_1) = 0 \tag{10.2.11}$$

B. ECONOMIC INTERPRETATIONS

Most of the economic literature on optimal growth emphasizes the phase diagram analysis, for which the Pontryagin format serves as building blocks. This topic we shall turn to in Section D, which follows. Presently we shall attempt to provide economic interpretations to (10.2.5)–(10.2.11). This will be done both literally and graphically.

1. Preliminaries. (a) Meanings of adjoint variables. ψ_k represents the shadow value of one unit of capital per capita in social welfare terms. ψ_1 "reflects" the desirability of producing capital goods alone. ψ_2 "reflects" the desirability of producing consumption goods alone. The loose wording for ψ_1 and ψ_2 indicates that we shall explain the signs of ψ_1 and ψ_2 rather than their magnitudes at this moment.

(b) Complementary slackness conditions. In Uzawa's model, the speed of accumulation reaches its ceiling when all resources are devoted to the investment sector; hence, the overall capital/labor ratio coincides with the sectoral capital/labor ratio of the first (investment) sector. Therefore,

$$\psi_1 > 0 \text{ implies } k = k_1 \tag{10.2.1}$$

On the other hand, if there is some consumption good produced, then,

$$k > k_1 \text{ implies } \psi_1 = 0 \tag{10.2.1}$$

These twin implications together with the non-negativity of ψ_1 and (10.2.4) are equivalent to (10.2.11).

Moreover, the speed of decumulation is limited by the force of depreciation. In other words, no equipment can be directly consumed, and the most a planner can do to boost consumption is to shift all resources to the second (consumption) sector, so that $k = k_2$. By an analysis parallel to the foregoing paragraphs, we can justify (10.2.10).

The last two equalities in (10.2.10) and (10.2.11), respectively, imply that the last two terms of (10.2.5) or (10.2.5′) are zero under an optimal policy.

2. Interpretation of the Hamiltonian. The maximand in (10.2.5′) can also be seen to be the difference between (a) the "value" of net product per capita, and (b) imputed capital cost per capita. This will be verified as follows:

(a) The valuation of net product per capita is illustrated by Table 10.3.

(b) Imputation of capital cost per capita. Each unit of capital per capita involves an implicit cost. To maintain the (economic) system at the same state, i.e., to keep the per capita capital at the same level in the face of a growing population requires that capital grow at the same rate as population. Putting it another way, if nothing is done beyond replacing the depreciated equipments, capital per capita will shrink at the relative rate n or at the absolute level of nk units per capita. Valued at ψ_k, the "shrinkage cost" or "the imputed interest at the biological rate" is $\psi_k nk$.

Combining (a) and (b) we have verified our interpretation of (10.2.5′).

3. The dynamic equations. Equation (10.2.6) is a repetition of (10.2.2′). Its economic meaning is already shown in its derivations. We shall concentrate on (10.2.7). Dividing by $-\psi_k$ we have

$$\frac{1}{\psi_k}\frac{\partial H}{\partial k} = -\hat{\psi}_k = -\frac{\psi_k f_1 - e^{-\delta t}f_2}{\psi_k(k_2 - k_1)} - n - \mu + \frac{\psi_1 - \psi_2}{\psi_k} \tag{10.2.7}$$

TABLE 10.3

	Per capita output	"Unit value" in social welfare terms	Value
Consumption good	$c = \dfrac{(k-k_1)f_2}{k_2-k_1}$	$e^{-\delta t}$	$\dfrac{e^{-\delta t}(k-k_1)f_2}{k_2-k_1}$
Investment good, gross	$\dfrac{(k_2-k)f_1}{k_2-k_1}$		
Minus depreciation	μk		
Net	$\dfrac{(k_2-k)f_1}{k_2-k_1}-\mu k$	ψ_k	$\psi_k\left[\dfrac{(k_2-k)f_1}{k_2-k_1}-\mu k\right]$
Value of net product			$\dfrac{e^{-\delta t}(k-k_1)f_2+\psi_k(k_2-k)f_1}{k_2-k_1}$

which states that the "marginal net yield" $(\partial H/\partial k)/\psi_k$ must be balanced out by the rate of devaluation $-\hat{\psi}_k$, ψ_k being the value of one unit of capital per capita in social welfare terms.

We now turn to the evaluation of the "marginal net yield." From (10.2.7), $(\partial H/\partial k)/\psi_k$ may be valued higher than the "net own-rate of interest" $[(\psi_k f_1 - e^{-\delta t}f_2)/\psi_k(k_2-k_1)]-n-\mu$ if all resources are devoted to the investment good sector, i.e., $\psi_1 > 0$. Alternatively, $(\partial H/\partial k)/\psi_k$ may be valued lower than the above term if all resources are devoted to the consumption good sector, i.e., $\psi_2 > 0$. But if both goods are produced, then the "marginal net yield" equals the "net own-rate of interest."

The interpretation of the latter term is

$$\text{Net own-rate of interest} = \begin{cases} \text{Gross own-rate of interest} \\ \qquad\qquad \text{minus} \\ \text{Rate of depreciation } \mu \\ \qquad\qquad \text{minus} \\ \text{Rate of shrinkage } n \end{cases}$$

TABLE 10.4

Increase of per capita consumption:	$\dfrac{f_2}{k_2-k_1}\cdot e^{-\delta t} = \dfrac{f_2 e^{-\delta t}}{k_2-k_1}$
Decrease of per capita gross investment:	$\dfrac{-f_1}{k_2-k_1}\cdot \psi_k = -\dfrac{f_1\psi_k}{k_2-k_1}$
Difference, per *unit* of k	$\dfrac{f_2 e^{-\delta t}-f_1\psi_k}{k_2-k_1}$
Difference, per *unit value* of k	$\dfrac{f_2 e^{-\delta t}-f_1\psi_k}{(k_2-k_1)\psi_k}$

The concept of a shrinkage rate has been explained above. The depreciation rate is self-evident.

The calculation of the gross own-rate of interest follows Table 10.4. By differentiating the first two per capita levels in Section 10.2.2, 2(c), with respect to k, we obtain, for one marginal unit of k, the values given in Table 10.4.[16] Later, in (10.2.12), we shall see that $(f_2 e^{-\delta t} - f_1 \psi_k)/\psi_k(k_2 - k_1) = f_1'$.

4. The meaning of the maximum conditions. H can be regarded as a function of k_1 and k_2 only, subject to $k_1 \leq k \leq k_2$ with values of k, ψ_k, and t given. The partial derivative of the value of net product $e^{-\delta t}c + \psi_k(\dot{k} + nk)$ with respect to k_1 is seen from (10.2.8) to be

$$\frac{\partial H}{\partial k_1} + \psi_1 = \psi_1 \geq 0$$

Strict positiveness occurs only when $\psi_1 > 0$; i.e., all resources have shifted to the investment good sector and no further increase of k_1 is possible through resource reallocations.

Similarly, the partial derivative of the value of net product with respect to k_2 is seen from (10.2.9) to be

$$\frac{\partial H}{\partial k_2} - \psi_2 = -\psi_2 \leq 0$$

Strict negativity holds when all resources have already been shifted to the consumption sector and no further lowering of k_2 can be achieved through resource reallocations.

5. A graphical summary.   (a) The interpretation of H.   In Figure 10.13, for given $k(t)$, we can construct a per capita Edgeworth box of size $k \times 1$. The efficient input combinations along the contract curve IQC are in one-to-one correspondence with the output combinations along the production frontier $q_2 q_4$ in Figure 10.12. The relative efficient price ratio $\psi_k e^{\delta t}$ implies a price line Pq_1 with $e^{-\delta t}/\psi_k$ as its slope. Under such a price ratio, point q_1 represents the output point that maximizes the gross output per capita. Subtracting depreciation μk, we obtain the net product per capita vector, $O'q_1$. Subtracting nk from $O'q_1$ and

---

[16]One may use graphic methods to verify entries in this table. For instance, the expression $-f_1/(k_2 - k_1)$ can be derived from Figure 10.14 as follows: In the figure,

$$\frac{\Delta \text{ gross investment per capita}}{\Delta \text{ capital per capita}} = -\overline{QQ'}/\overline{CC'}$$

$k \to k + \Delta k$ leads to changes in:

Consumption: $\overline{CQ} \uparrow \overline{CQ'}$
Gross investment: $\overline{IQ} \downarrow \overline{IQ'}$ } (on a per capita basis)

$$\overline{QQ'}/\overline{IQ} = \overline{CC'}/\overline{aC}$$

$$-\overline{QQ'}/\overline{CC'} = -\overline{IQ}/\overline{aC}$$

$$\overline{IQ} = L_1 f_1/L = [(k_2 - k)/(k_2 - k_1)]f_1 \qquad \text{(see Figure 10.13)}$$

Therefore, from $\overline{aC} = k_2 - k$

$$-\overline{QQ'}/\overline{CC'} = -f_1/(k_2 - k_1)$$

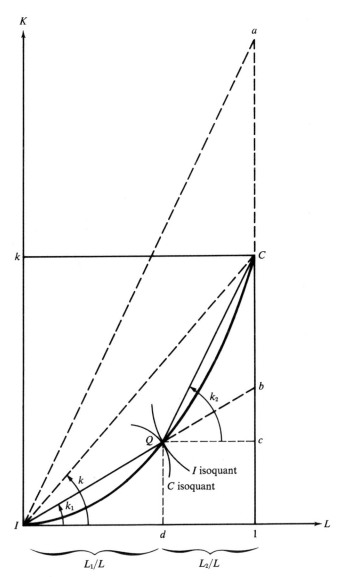

FIGURE 10.13

applying the shadow prices ψ_k and $e^{-\delta t}$ to the two vector components, we obtain H, which is the distance between Pq_1 and qq.

(b) Evaluation of $\partial H/\partial k$. The computation in Table 10.4 can be derived from Figure 10.14 as illustrated in footnote 16.

(c) $\partial H/\partial k_i = 0$.   From Figures 10.12 and 10.13 we realize that H is represented parametrically with respect to k_1 and k_2, since the point Q in Figure 10.13 corresponds to the point q_1 in a one-to-one manner. The maximization of H,

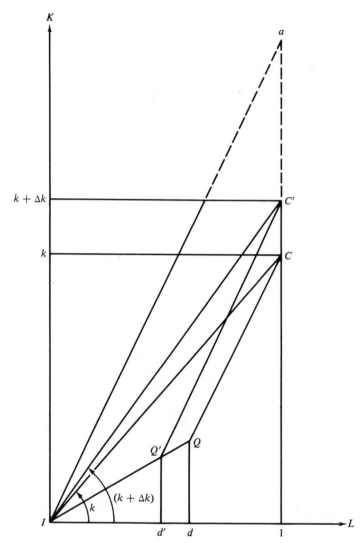

FIGURE 10.14

taking $k(t)$ as given, implies (10.2.8) and (10.2.9), where for interior solutions

$$\frac{\partial H}{\partial k_i} = 0 \qquad i = 1, 2$$

For corner solutions, ψ_1 and ψ_2 make up the difference.

(d) $\psi_1(k - k_1) = 0$, $\psi_2(k_2 - k) = 0$. We shall consider here one corner solution case. When k_2 reaches its lower limit k, the production point in the Edgeworth box reaches the point I and the production point in the production frontier diagram reaches q_2. By then the limiting tangent at q_2 may differ with the price ratio and ψ_2 makes up the difference. The other corner solution is symmetrical to this.

10.2.4. Transformation and analysis

The formulation represented by (10.2.5)–(10.2.11) is only the first step toward solving the problem. It is not easily analyzable because ψ_k depends on both k and t. Equations (10.2.8) and (10.2.9) have to be reduced to more familiar terms. Also, the optimal values for k_1 and k_2 have to be expressed in a more clear-cut manner.

We shall first consider the case where $k_2 > k > k_1$, and therefore $\psi_1 = 0 = \psi_2$.

1. Derivation of the shadow input price ratio, ω. Dropping ψ_1 and ψ_2 and rearranging, we obtain from (10.2.8) and (10.2.9)[17]

$$e^{-\delta t} f_2' = \psi_k f_1' = (e^{-\delta t} f_2 - \psi_k f_1)/(k_2 - k_1) \tag{10.2.12}$$

$$e^{-\delta t}(f_2 - k_2 f_2') = \psi_k(f_1 - k_1 f_1') \tag{10.2.13}$$

Equation (10.2.12) states that the value of marginal products of capital should be the same in the two sectors under an optimal policy. Equation (10.2.13) states the equal value of marginal products condition for labor.

Dividing (10.2.12) by (10.2.13), we have

$$(f_i/f_i') - k_i = \omega \qquad i = 1, 2 \tag{10.2.14}$$

where ω is the common wage/rent ratio under the optimal policy. Here "wage," "rent," and "wage/rent ratio" are all shadow values of the respective concepts. Graphically, (10.2.14) is the tangency condition for the isoquants of the two sectors in the Edgeworth diagram in Figure 10.13.

From the Inada conditions, (10.2.14) implies

$$\frac{d\omega}{dk_i} = -\frac{f_i f_i''}{f_i'^2} > 0 \qquad i = 1, 2 \tag{10.2.15}$$

ω and k_1 as well as k_2 go from zero to infinity together, and ω and k_i are strictly increasing functions of each other, as shown in Section 4.3 and Appendix 4.3.

2. Transforming the dual system from ψ_k to ω. By transforming the adjoint variable to ω, Uzawa succeeded in achieving two goals:

(i) To directly write out the optimal choices for the input quantity ratios k_i as $k_i(\omega)$, corresponding to the input price ratio, ω.

(ii) To construct a simple phase diagram in ω–k space with a limiting state $\dot{k} = 0 = \dot{\omega}$.

---

[17] After dropping ψ_1 and ψ_2 (since they vanish) and solving for $e^{-\delta t} f_2'$ and $\psi_k f_1'$ in (10.2.8) and (10.2.9), respectively, we obtain (10.2.12). Again dropping ψ_1 and ψ_2 and summing (10.2.8) and (10.2.9), interchanging the equal expressions $e^{-\delta t} f_2'$ and $\psi_k f_1'$, and canceling terms involving k, we obtain (10.2.13).

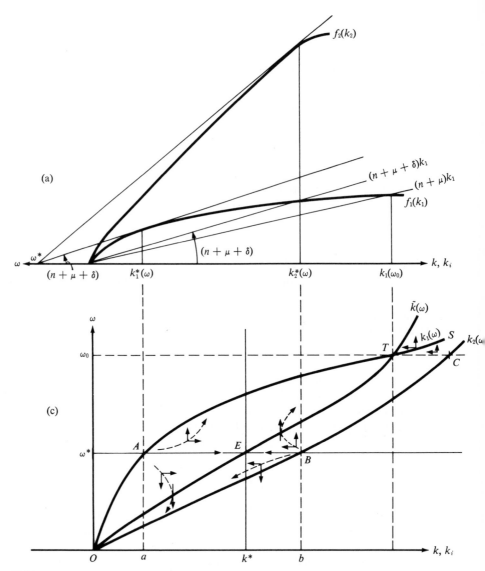

FIGURE 10.15

Uzawa made the transformation in two steps:

(a) Transformation into $(f_1'/f_2') = e^{-\delta t}/\psi_k$.[18] $e^{-\delta t}/\psi_k$ is the commodity price ratio, capital good being the numeraire. Taking the logarithmic derivative of this term with respect to time and comparing with (10.2.7') and (10.2.12), we have

$$\hat{f}_1' - \hat{f}_2' = f_1' - (n + \mu + \delta) \tag{10.2.}$$

[18] From (10.2.12).

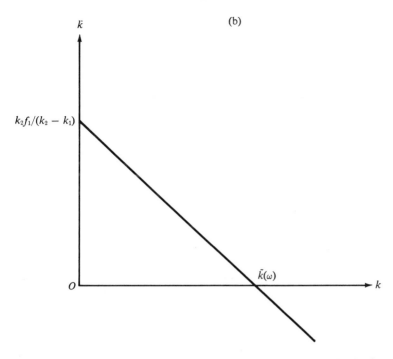

showing that as long as both goods are produced, the rate of price increase of the consumption good relative to the capital good *should be* equal to the gross own-rate of interest for capital minus the depreciation rate, the biological interest rate, and the social rate of discount.

Although (10.2.16) has clear economic interpretations, for analytical convenience another transformation is necessary.

(b) Transformation into ω. Using (10.2.14) and (10.2.15) we see that:[19]

$$\hat{f_i'} = -\dot{\omega}/(\omega + k_i) \tag{10.2.17}$$

Noting that any k_i is a function of ω and f_i' is a function of k_i, we can rewrite (10.2.16) and (10.2.2) as follows.

3. The twin dynamic equations. From (10.2.16) and (10.2.17) we get

$$\dot{\omega} = \frac{(\omega + k_1)(\omega + k_2)}{k_2 - k_1} \{(n + \mu + \delta) - f_1'[k_1(\omega)]\} \tag{10.2.18}$$

Now (10.2.2) can be rewritten as

$$\dot{k} = \frac{k_2(\omega)f_1[k_1(\omega)]}{k_2(\omega) - k_1(\omega)} - \left\{n + \mu + \frac{f_1[k_1(\omega)]}{k_2(\omega) - k_1(\omega)}\right\}k \tag{10.2.19}$$

These twin equations form the basis of the subsequent analysis.

[19]Equation (10.2.15) implies that $\dot{\omega} = -(f_i/f_i')\hat{f_i'}$ or $\hat{f_i'} = -\dot{\omega}/(f_i/f_i')$. Comparing (10.2.14), we obtain (10.2.17).

4. Phase diagram analysis. Define

$$\omega^* = k_1^{-1}[f_1'^{-1}(n+\mu+\delta)]$$

$$\tilde{k}(\omega) = \left[\frac{k_2 f_1}{(n+\mu)(k_2-k_1)+f_1}\right]$$

These are shown in Figure 10.15a and b.
Inspection of (10.2.18) shows that[20]

$$\dot{\omega} \left\{\begin{matrix}>\\=\\<\end{matrix}\right\} 0 \quad \text{if and only if} \quad \omega \left\{\begin{matrix}>\\=\\<\end{matrix}\right\} \omega^* \qquad (10.2.)$$

Inspection of (10.2.19) shows that[21]

$$\dot{k} \left\{\begin{matrix}>\\=\\<\end{matrix}\right\} 0 \quad \text{if and only if} \quad k \left\{\begin{matrix}<\\=\\>\end{matrix}\right\} \tilde{k}(\omega) \qquad (10.2.)$$

We now plot $k_1(\omega)$, $k_2(\omega)$, $\tilde{k}(\omega)$ and the $\omega = \omega^*$ line in the k–ω plane in Figure 10.15c.[22,23] The intersection of $\tilde{k}(\omega)$ and $\omega = \omega^*$ determines $k^* = \tilde{k}(\omega^*)$. Based upon (10.2.20) and (10.2.21), arrow signs can be plotted showing how a solution curve of (10.2.18) and (10.2.19) will move in the k–ω plane, given the initial point $[k(0), \omega(0)]$. The optimal path is that solution curve with $\omega(0)$ correctly chosen. As in Section 10.1, all the solution curves fulfill a first-order

[20] $f_1'' < 0$, $k_1' > 0$; therefore, $f_1'[k_1(\omega)]$ is negatively associated with ω.

[21] $n+\mu+f_1/(k_2-k_1) > 0$.

[22] The construction of the $k_1(\omega)$ and $k_2(\omega)$ curves is shown in Figure 10.13a. From any point, say ω^*, on the ω axis of Figure 10.15a draw two tangent lines to f_1 and f_2. These help to determine $k_1(\omega^*)$ and $k_2(\omega^*)$ where these are the abscissas of the tangent points. By assumption, $k_2(\omega) > k_1(\omega)$ for all ω.

[23] The relative position of $\tilde{k}$ with respect to k_1 and k_2 can be deduced as follows:

$$\tilde{k}(\omega) = \{1+[(n+\mu)(k_2-k_1)/f_1]\}^{-1}k_2(\omega) < k_2(\omega) \quad \text{for all } \omega.$$

Also,

$$\tilde{k}(\omega) = k_1\Big/\left\{(k_1/k_2)(1)+(1-k_1/k_2)\frac{(n+\mu)k_1}{f_1}\right\} \left\{\begin{matrix}>\\=\\<\end{matrix}\right\} k_1(\omega)$$

if and only if

$$\frac{(n+\mu)k_1}{f_1} \left\{\begin{matrix}<\\=\\>\end{matrix}\right\} 1$$

Let ω_0 be such that $f_1[k_1(\omega_0)] = (n+\mu)k_1(\omega_0)$; then

$$\tilde{k}(\omega) \left\{\begin{matrix}\geq\\=\\<\end{matrix}\right\} k_1(\omega) \quad \text{if and only if} \quad \omega \left\{\begin{matrix}\leq\\=\\>\end{matrix}\right\} \omega_0.$$

The determination of ω_0 is shown in Figure 10.15a.

necessary condition (Euler equation). But it is the fulfillment of a transversality condition that distinguishes the optimal path from other solution curves.

We shall approach the problem by steps.

(1) In Figure 10.15c, for given $k(0)$ one must choose a $\omega(0)$ such that

$$k_2[\omega(0)] \geq k(0) \geq k_1[\omega(0)]$$

that is, the initial point $[k(0), \omega(0)]$ must be between the $k_1(\omega)$ and $k_2(\omega)$ curves. For the case which is presently discussed, the choice must strictly be between these two curves.

(2) The five regions in Figure 10.15c may be analyzed one by one. Following the arrows, we obtain the information for Table 10.5.

TABLE 10.5[a]

Between k_1 and k_2	On $k_1(\omega)$	On $k_2(\omega)$
(k, ω) in OAE $\downarrow$ (k, ω) in $OBE \rightarrow (k, \omega)$ on OB arc	$\longrightarrow$	toward 0
(k, ω) in $ATE \rightarrow (k, \omega)$ on AT arc $\uparrow$ (k, ω) in $BETC$ (k, ω) in $CTS \rightarrow (k, \omega)$ on TS arc	toward T	

[a] $\omega(0) \neq \omega^*$.

For all five regions, the system ends up with $k = k_1$ or $k = k_2$, as the case may be, with one very important exception. When $A = k_1(\omega^*) < k(0) < k_2(\omega^*) = B$, and if we set $\omega(0) = \omega^*$, then $\omega(t) \equiv \omega^*$ and k approaches k^* monotonically.

We now turn to two other cases: $k(0) = k_1$ or $k(0) = k_2$. If $k(0) = k_1, \psi_1 \geq 0$, and if $k(0) = k_2, \psi_2 \geq 0$. The effect of positive ψ_1 or ψ_2 is to prevent the solution curve to pass outside the $k_1(\omega), k_2(\omega)$ lines. However, we may simply note that (10.2.2) is not affected by the signs of ψ_1 and ψ_2. This helps us to determine in which direction the solution curve will be deflected along the boundary. This substantiates our entries about the OB, AT, and TS arcs in Table 10.5. Moreover, it also shows that along the OA and CB arcs, one can select (k, ω) patterns converging to points A or B without violating the necessary conditions for optimality.

We now note that points O and T are not optimal. Near O, output per capita dwindles with capital per capita toward zero; hence, consumption per capita will always be much lower than at E. Similarly, a top-heavy capital/labor ratio near T will necessitate a high investment per capita, so that the consumption per capita will again be extremely low.

The optimal policy can be summarized as

If $k_2(\omega^*) \geq k(0) \geq k_1(\omega^*)$, then set $\omega(0)$ to ω^*.

If $k_2(\omega^*) < k(0)$, set $\omega(0) = k_2^{-1}[k(0)]$ and follow the OA arc to A.

If $k_1(\omega^*) > k(0)$, set $\omega(0) = k_1^{-1}[k(0)]$ and follow the CB arc to B.

10.2.5. A second graphical summary

In Figure 10.15a the condition $f_1'[k_1(\omega^*)] = (n+\mu+\delta)$ determines both $k_1(\omega^*)$ and ω^*. A tangent line to $f_2(k_2)$ from ω^* determines $k_2(\omega^*)$. Referring to the definition of $k(\omega)$, $k^* = \tilde{k}(\omega^*)$ can also be found. We can now summarize all the information in Figure 10.16.

(1) If the initial endowment point falls in the specialization cone for investment good, all labor force (and capital) will be devoted to the investment good sector. The initial wage/interest ratio (represented by the slope of

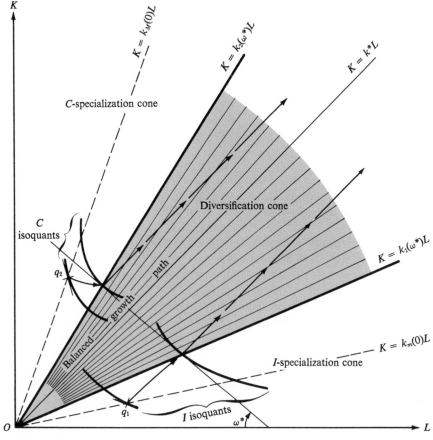

FIGURE 10.16

isoquant at q_1) is lower than ω^*. Massive investment builds up the capital/labor ratio until it enters the diversification cone.

(2) If the initial endowment point falls in the specialization cone for consumption good, all labor force (and capital) will be devoted to the consumption good sector. Natural labor growth as well as depreciation of capital will reduce the capital/labor ratio, with a concomitant fall of the wage/interest ratio (from the slope of isoquant at q_2) toward ω^*, until the diversification cone is reached.

(3) If the endowment point falls inside the diversification cone, there will be no change of the factor price ratio ω. Both goods will be produced according to the standard techniques (represented by the factor ratios $k_1(\omega^*)$ and $k_2(\omega^*)$ while the capital/labor ratio approaches monotonically the k^* ratio.

10.2.6. The general case

Uzawa introduced a positive minimum consumption per capita and found that the limiting line in Figure 10.15c has to shift from OAT to another curve roughly parallel to it at its right. On that line, consumption per capita is at the minimum. This new line (not drawn) cuts the $\tilde{k}(\omega)$ line from below at some point, say (k^{**}, ω^{**}). He showed that if $k(0)$ is less than that value k^{**}, then every path would lead to an impasse—the minimum consumption per capita cannot be maintained forever. Otherwise, the earlier analysis carries over, except that the new limiting line takes the place of the OAT line.

Uzawa further considered cases where the capital good industry may be more capital intensive all the time or some of the time. In such cases, the approach of (k, ω) to its ultimate limit (k^*, ω^*) remains monotonic. However, ω may not reach ω^* at any finite future instant (as in the above case).

It remains to say a few words about the limiting position (k^*, ω^*). At this position, the investment sector produces just enough capital good to replace depreciated equipment and meet the demand for new equipment due to labor growth, for both sectors. The gross own-rate of interest in that sector is exactly the sum of the population growth rate, the depreciation rate, and the discount rate. The latter condition determines ω^* and $k_2(\omega^*)$. The production function of the consumption sector determines $k_2(\omega^*)$. The relative sizes of the "extra output" per worker of the capital good sector $\{f_1[k_1(\omega^*)] - (n+\mu)k_1(\omega^*)\}$ and the requirement for investment in the consumption good sector per worker $(n+\mu)k_2(\omega^*)$ determine the labor allocation ratio and hence k^*.

REFERENCES

[1] Ramsey, Frank P., "A Mathematical Model of Saving," *Economic Journal*, Dec. 1928, pp. 543–59.

[2] Tinbergen, Jan, "The Optimal Rate of Saving," *Economic Journal*, vol. LXVI, Dec. 1956, pp. 603–09.

[3] Tinbergen, Jan, "Optimal Savings and Utility Maximization over Time," *Econometrica*, vol. XXVIII, April 1960, pp. 481–89.

[4] Samuelson, P. A., and R. M. Solow, "A Complete Capital Good Model Involving Heterogeneous Capital Goods," *Quarterly Journal of Economics*, vol. LXX, Nov. 1956, pp. 537–62.

[5] Chakravarty, S., "The Existence of an Optimal Saving Program," *Econometrica*, vol. XXX, Jan. 1962, pp. 178–87.

[6] von Weizsäcker, C. C., "Existence of Optimal Programmes of Accumulation for an Infinite Time Horizon," *Review of Economic Studies*, vol. XXXII, April 1965, pp. 85–104.

[7] Samuelson, P. A., "A Catenary Turnpike Theorem Involving Consumption and the Golden Rule," *American Economic Review*, vol. LV, June 1965, pp. 486–96.

[8] Cass, D., "Optimum Growth in an Aggregative Model of Capital Accumulation," *Review of Economic Studies*, vol. XXXII, July 1965, pp. 233–40.

[9] Koopmans, T. C., "On the Concept of Optimal Economic Growth," in *Study Week on the Econometric Approach to Planning, Pontificiae Scientiarum Scripta Varia* XXVIII, Rand McNally, Chicago, 1965.

[10] Phelps, Edmund S., "The Golden Rule of Accumulation," *American Economic Review*, vol. LV, Sept. 1965, pp. 783–814.

[11] Swan, Trevor W., "Growth Models of Golden Ages and Production Functions," in *Economic Development with Special Reference to East Asia*, K. E. Berrill, Ed., Macmillan, London, 1963.

[12] Robinson, Joan, "A Neo-classical Theorem," *Review of Economic Studies*, vol. XXIX, June 1962, pp. 219–326.

[13] Koopmans, T. C., "Stationary Ordinal Utility and Impatience," *Econometrica*, vol. XXVIII, April 1960, pp. 287–309.

[14] Koopmans, T. C., P. A. Diamond, and R. E. Williamson, "Stationary Utility and Time Perspective," *Econometrica*, vol. XXXII, Jan.–April 1964, pp. 82–100.

[15] Gale, David, "On Optimal Development in a Multi-Sector Economy," *Review of Economic Studies*, vol. XXXIV, Jan. 1967, pp. 1–18.

[16] McFadden, Daniel, "The Evaluation of Development Programmes," *Review of Economic Studies*, vol. XXXIV, Jan. 1967.

[17] Samuelson, P. A., "Comments," *Review of Economic Studies*, vol. XXIX, June 1962, pp. 251–54.

[18] Pearce, I. F., "The End of the Golden Age in Solovia: A Further Fable for Growthmen Hoping to be 'One up' on Oiko," *American Economic Review*, vol. LII, Dec. 1962, pp. 1088–97.

[19] Phelps, E. S., "Reply," *American Economic Review*, vol. LII, Dec. 1962, pp. 1097–99.

[20] Phelps, E. S., "Substitution, Fixed Proportions, Growth and Distribution," *International Economic Review*, vol. IV, Sept. 1963, pp. 265–88.

[21] Solow, R. M., "Substitution and Fixed Proportions in the Theory of Capital," *Review of Economic Studies*, vol. XXIX, June 1962, pp. 207–18.

[22] Kemp, M. C., and P. C. Thanh, "On a Class of Growth Models," *Econometrica*, vol. XXXIV, April 1966, pp. 257–82.

[23] Koopmans, T. C., "Intertemporal Distribution and Optimal Aggregative Economic Growth," in *Ten Economic Studies in the Tradition of Irving Fisher*, W. Fellner, et al., Eds., Wiley, New York, 1967.

[24] Shell, K., "Applications of Pontryagin's Maximum Principle to Economics," in *Proceedings of the Varenna Summer School on Mathematical Systems, Theory and Economics*, G. P. Szegö and H. W. Kuhn, Eds., Springer-Verlag, New York, 1969.

[25] Srinivasan, T. N., "Optimal Savings in a Two Sector Model of Growth," *Econometrica*, vol. XXXII, July 1964, pp. 358–73.

[26] Inagaki, M., *Optimal Economic Growth*, North-Holland, Amsterdam, 1969.

[27] Stoleru, L. G., "An Optimal Policy for

Economic Growth," *Econometrica,* vol. XXXIII, April 1965, pp. 321–48.

[28] Uzawa, H., "Optimal Saving in a Two Sector Model of Growth," *Review of Economic Studies,* vol. XXXI, Jan. 1964, pp. 1–24.

[29] Kurz, M., "Optimal Paths of Capital

Accumulation Under the Minimum Time Objective," *Econometrica,* vol. XXXIII, April 1960, pp. 42–66.

[30] Koopmans, T. C., "Objectives, Constraints and Outcomes in Optimal Growth Models," *Econometrica,* vol. 35, no. 1, Jan. 1967, pp. 1–15.

EXERCISE

10.1. Consider the problem:

$$\text{Max} \int_0^1 u(c)\, dt$$

subject to:

$$\dot{k} = f(k) - c$$
$$k(0) = 1$$
$$k(1) = 0$$
$$u(c) = \sqrt{c}$$
$$f(c) = k$$

(a) Solve for the optimal paths of c and k.

(b) Compare the rate of growth for c and the marginal product of capital (the own rate of interest for capital); why is one rate higher than the other?

(c) If $k(1) = w$, a non-negative number, $u(c) = c^x$, x being a positive fraction, and $f(k) \equiv yk$, y being a positive number. The horizon is z rather than 1. Discuss the comparative dynamics of the model with respect to w, x, y, and z.

(d) In the above problem, no solution exists if $x = 1$. Why?
   (This is the problem of Tinbergen and Chakravarty.)

11

accumulation-oriented optimal growth models

11.1 CLOSED PRODUCTION MODELS; VON NEUMANN BALANCED GROWTH

A brief survey will be given of the vast growth literature concerning what has been called "the closed production model" (defined below). Three topics can be outlined in this area:

(1) Balanced growth paths and their dual prices.

(2) Balanced growth paths and efficient capital accumulation—the turnpike problem.

(3) Balanced growth paths and efficient capital accumulation—the relative stability problem.

The first item was examined by von Neumann [1], followed by Georgescu-Roegen [2], Gale [3], and Karlin [4]. The next two items were first studied by Dorfman, Samuelson, and Solow [5–7]. Subsequently, Morishima [8,9], Radner [10], Nikaido [11], McKenzie [12–14], Furuya and Inada [15], and Inada [16] restated the Dorfman-Samuelson-Solow theorems and refined their proofs to rule out certain exceptional cases. Koopmans [17] provided an ingenious summary of the literature for both the von Neumann model and the turnpike problem. Further work has been done by Winter [18, 19].

In this section we shall examine the basic assumptions of the model as well as the von Neumann results. The next two sections are devoted to the turnpike problem and the relative stability problem.

11.1.1. Closed production models

Like the closed input–output analysis, closed production models contain neither final (consumption) goods nor a household sector providing labor and other "nonproducible" inputs. If the household sector is included in the model, it will be considered as another production sector using consumption goods as inputs to produce labor services. Such a strictly technocratic view may be appropriate under state-directed economies either in wartime or during certain "crash programs" for industrialization. On the other hand, McKenzie showed [20] that, by setting up "pseudo" commodities, consumption-oriented models can be subsumed under the closed production model. This will be discussed later in this section (11.1.1-D).

A. ASSUMPTIONS

The literature in this area usually postulates that time is divided into discrete units and that the economy contains a finite number of sectors (say, n). The assumption of discrete time units has certain advantages, which we will illustrate with one example. The simplest continuous time model assumes lagless production. But when a given process uses a certain input without producing the same commodity as an output, and an economy operates that process alone, that particular input must disappear altogether. This implies a growth rate of $-\infty$, an analytically awkward concept. On the other hand, in a discrete time model, output lags behind input for one period and the same process would give a finite negative growth rate, -1. No mathematical inconvenience is involved. To conform to the greater portion of the literature, we shall adopt the following convention: *Time is discrete; output lags behind input for one period.*

The choice of time unit is seldom mentioned in the literature. For convenience it should be long enough to eliminate the need to postulate work in progress as separate goods. One may even conceive the time interval to be so long that all capital equipment would expire during its course. However, the present literature usually operates on a high level of abstraction so that concerns over such pragmatic details are usually disregarded.

We shall first spell out the usual assumptions and then introduce symbols to interpret their meanings. The commonly adopted assumptions are:

(1) The technology is linear, convex, and closed.
(2) Costless disposal is possible.
(3) Finite inputs can only produce finite outputs ("facts of life").
(4) All commodities are producible.

Let (x, y) stand for the "process" of using an input vector x now to produce an output vector y one period later, where both x and y are non-negative, n-dimensional vectors. Let T be the set of feasible production plans; then "(x, y) belongs to T" means that "y is producible from x (one period later)." Consider the neoclassical production process:

$$x = \begin{bmatrix} K \\ L \end{bmatrix} \qquad y = \begin{bmatrix} F(K, L) \\ 0 \end{bmatrix}$$

We may depict T as the points on the production surface.[1] T is called the *technology.*

---

[1] Here we have sidestepped the issue of labor growth or capital durability.

Assumption (1) includes three subassumptions:

(1a) "Linearity": If (x, y) is a feasible plan, $(\lambda x, \lambda y)$ must be feasible for all non-negative λ. This is the familiar assumption of constant returns.

(1b) Convexity: If (x^1, y^1) and (x^2, y^2) are both feasible plans, any weighted average of the input vector can produce the weighted average of the output vector. This shows that the production surface is concave.

(1c) "Closedness": If there is a sequence of feasible production plans (x^j, y^j) with the input and output sequences approaching x^∞ and y^∞ as their respective limits, then (x^∞, y^∞) belongs to T; i.e., the limiting output vector is producible from the limiting input vector. One common-sense implication says that there is no "taboo" input ratio, approaching which, output makes a *discontinuous* drop.

Symbolically,

If $(x, y) \in T$, then $(\lambda x, \lambda y) \in T$ for all $\lambda \geq 0$

If $(x^1, y^1), (x^2, y^2) \in T$, then $[\lambda x^1 + (1 - \lambda)x^2, \lambda y^1 + (1 - \lambda)y^2] \in T$ for all λ, $0 \leq \lambda \leq 1$

If $(x^j, y^j) \in T$, for $j = 1, 2, \ldots$, $\operatorname{Lim} x^j = x^\infty$, $\operatorname{Lim} y^j = y^\infty$, then $(x^\infty, y^\infty) \in T$

Together, these imply that T is a closed, convex cone in a $2n$-dimensional space.

Assumption (2) implies that if (x, y) is a feasible plan, any plan involving no more output *and* no less input must also be feasible. Symbolically,

If $0 \leq x_i^1 \leq x_i^2$, $y_i^1 \geq y_i^2 \geq 0$, $i = 1, 2, \ldots, n$, $(x^1, y^1) \in T$, then $(x^2, y^2) \in T$

The title "costless disposal" cogently capitulates the economic content of the assumption.

Assumption (3) rules out any unbounded increase of value through production, as we shall see later. Symbolically,

If $x_i < \infty$, $i = 1, 2, \ldots, n$, then $y_i < \infty$, $i = 1, 2, \ldots, n$

Assumption (4) rules out the case where any commodity may appear only in the initial period. This prevents the uninteresting case where any proportional growth means zero output for all commodities (since at least one commodity is not producible). Symbolically,

There exists $(x^i, y^i) \in T$ such that $y_i^i > 0$ for all $i = 1, \ldots, n$

In other words, there is at least one process that can produce each of the n outputs.

Using assumptions (1c) and (3), we can deduce that "no output is producible from zero inputs" (see Koopmans [17]). Using assumptions (1b) and (4), it is possible to deduce that there exists (x^0, y^0) such that $y_i^0 > 0$ for all i (see Karlin [4]).[2]

---

[2] That is, there is one process that can simultaneously produce all the n outputs.

TABLE 11.1

Assumptions	Neoclassical analogs	
	$\bar{F}$-form	F-form
(1a) Linearity (1b) Convexity (1c) Closedness	First-order homogeneous Concave Continuous	First-order homogeneous Concave Continuous
(2) Costless disposal	$\dfrac{\partial \bar{F}}{\partial y_i} < 0 < \dfrac{\partial \bar{F}}{\partial x_j}$	$\dfrac{\partial F}{\partial y_i} < 0 < \dfrac{\partial F}{\partial x_j}$
(3) Facts of life	$\bar{F}$ is bounded for any given x, $_2y$	$F(y;x) = 0$ is bounded in y space for any given x
(4) Positive output	$\bar{F}(_2y;x) > 0$ for some x and some $_2y$ with $y_i > 0$; $i = 2, \ldots, n$	$F(y;x) = 0$ for some x and y with $y_i > 0$ for $i = 1, \ldots, n$

B. A NEOCLASSICAL SPECIAL CASE

In this text we have mainly followed a neoclassical formulation. It is perhaps also fair to presume that a sizable group of our readers are more at home with differentiable transformation (production) functions than with set-theoretical formulations. To facilitate our grasp of the present material, we shall follow Dorfman, Samuelson, and Solow [5] and McKenzie [12] to provide a neo-classical formulation more or less parallel to the above statements.

Let $\bar{F}(_2y;x) = y_1$ be the transformation function showing the amounts of y_1 producible with the input vector $x = (x_1, x_2, \ldots, x_n)$ and the subvector for alternative outputs $_2y = (y_2, \ldots, y_n)$. A more symmetrical (and Hicksian) formulation is to postulate a function:

$$F(y;x) \equiv \bar{F}(_2y;x) - y_1$$

The various assumptions listed above have their analogs in this neoclassical version. These are listed in Table 11.1. On the other hand, this neoclassical version is not as general as the set-theoretical version specified before. For instance, the original von Neumann case where there are only a finite number of "basic" processes (while all the rest are derived from them by averaging or disposal of certain commodities) cannot be expressed in the neoclassical manner. In fact, $\partial \bar{F}/\partial y_i$ or $\partial F/\partial y_i$ need not be nonzero everywhere. Therefore, we shall emphasize the set-theoretical version from now on.

11.1.2. The von Neumann results

We shall now introduce certain basic definitions and concepts and then sum-marize the von Neumann results. After that, the derivation of these results will be presented and the relevance of the von Neumann model will be considered.

A. DEFINITIONS AND CONCEPTS

(1) The expansion ratio $\mu(x, y)$. Since the numbering of commodities is arbitrary, we shall assume that $x_i > 0$ for $i = 1, 2, \ldots, n'$ and $x_i = 0$ for $i = n' + 1, \ldots, n$. Then

$$\mu(x, y) = \operatorname*{Min}_{1 \le i \le n'} \left[y_i / x_i \right]$$

$\mu(x, y)$ is well defined for all pairs of (x, y) with the exception of $(0, 0)$. Equivalently, we may define $\mu(x, y) = \operatorname{Max} \lambda$ such that $y_i \ge \lambda x_i$ for all i. The exclusion of $\left[y_i / x_i \right]$ for $n' < i \le n$ is to rule out the ambiguity of $[0/0]$ if $x_i = 0 = y_i$.

Example.

$$x = (3, 2) \qquad y = (4, 4) \qquad \text{(Here, } n' = n = 2\text{)}$$

$$\frac{y_1}{x_1} = \frac{4}{3} < 2 = \frac{4}{2} = \frac{y_2}{x_2}$$

Hence,

$$\mu(x, y) = \frac{4}{3}$$

This is also shown graphically in Figure 11.1, where x and y are shown. This process (x, y) can be represented by an arrow from x to y. To indicate the calculation of μ, we extend the Ox ray to intersect the rectangle Oy_1yy_2 at $w = (4, \frac{8}{3})$. Note that any point on the Ox ray represents a scale expansion of the input ensemble x. The largest balanced expansion that can be provided out of the output ensemble y is w. The ratio of such a balanced expansion is measured by the quotient $\overline{Ow}/\overline{Ox} = \mu$.

(2) The von Neumann growth factor.   Consider all the non-null, feasible processes (x, y) and calculate the associated expansion ratios. The maximum growth factor,

$$\mu^* = \operatorname*{Max}_{(x,y) \in T} \mu(x, y)$$

is defined as the von Neumann growth factor. Noting that for $\lambda > 0$ the two processes (x, y) and $(\lambda x, \lambda y)$ share the same expansion ratio, we may select one pair as representative. Since the null process $(x, y) = (0, 0)$ is a maverick of no interest, we can consider only those processes with some positive inputs (following the first conclusion in the final paragraph of Section 11.1.1-A, only $(0, 0)$ is ruled out). Since we do not want to preclude any process just because a given input is absent, the ordinary procedure of choosing a numeraire is unsatisfactory. For instance. if labor is the numeraire in any automation process, the capital/labor ratio for any specific capital is $+\infty$, ruling out the possibility of distinguishing one automation process from another. Instead, we consider only the set S of those processes for which the sum of all their input units is equal to unity (i.e., x belongs to the simplex S').

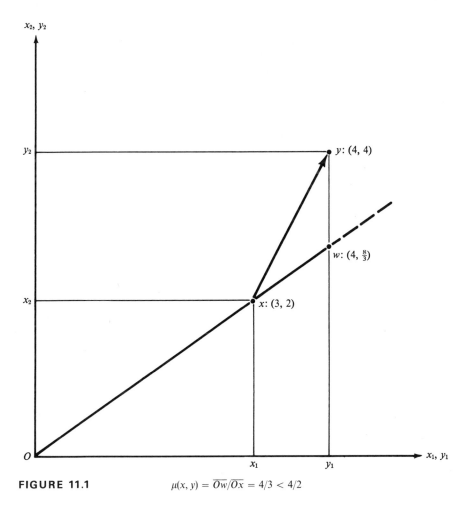

FIGURE 11.1 $\mu(x, y) = \overline{Ow}/\overline{Ox} = 4/3 < 4/2$

Example.   In the two-goods world, the simplex S' is represented by the set of vectors:[3]

$$S' = \{(\theta, 1 - \theta)|0 \leq \theta \leq 1\}$$

Graphically, this is shown as the line segment S' in Figure 11.2 that links the two unit vectors $(0, 1)$ and $(1, 0)$ and forms a $-45°$ angle with the horizontal axis.

Any process with a non-null input vector can be "normalized" so that its input vector belongs to S'. This is done by dividing all the vector components in x and y by the factor $\Sigma_{i=1}^{n} x_i$.

---

[3]A "simplex" is the set of non-negative vectors that are either unit vectors or their (positively) weighted averages. In three-dimensional space, this is a triangle. In two-dimensional space, it is a line segment.

Example.   The process $[(3, 2); (4, 4)]$ can be normalized into $[(.6, .4); (.8, .8)]$. This is depicted in Figure 11.2 where the original vector is shown as the arrow $\vec{xy}$. By constructing the Ox ray, we obtain its intersection with S' at ξ. By constructing the ray Oy to intersect the line through ξ parallel to xy, we obtain η. The $\vec{\xi\eta}$ arrow is the "representative" of $\vec{xy}$ in the set S. It is a scaled-down similitude of the latter.

(3) Balanced growth process.   This means a process (x, y) where $y = \lambda x$. Such a process has both x and y lying on the same ray from the origin. One specimen $(z, \lambda z)$ is shown in Figure 11.2, where z is in S' and hence the process $\overrightarrow{z(\lambda z)}$ is in S.

(4) Von Neumann processes.   Those activities (x, y) that give rise to the maximal expansion ratio are called *von Neumann processes*. Formally, (x^*, y^*) is a von Neumann process if $\mu(x^*, y^*) = \mu^*$. A von Neumann process may or may not be a balanced growth process.

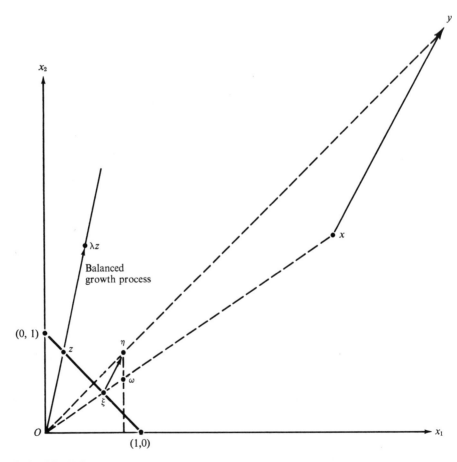

FIGURE 11.2

TABLE 11.2 [a]

	Process 1 : (x^1, y^1)	Process 2 : (x^2, y^2)
First good	$y_1^1/x_1^1 = 2$	$y_1^2/x_1^2 = 3.5$
Second good	$y_2^1/x_2^1 = 2$	$y_2^2/x_2^2 = 3$
Expansion ratio	2	3
Is it a balanced growth process?	Yes	No
Is it a von Neumann process?	No	Yes

[a]Superscripts refer to processes; subscripts refer to goods.

Example.   In the two-goods world, there are two processes in the technology:

$$(x^1, y^1) = [(1, 2); (2, 4)]$$

$$(x^2, y^2) = [(2, 1); (7, 3)]$$

The growth rate of each good in each process can be presented as in Table 11.2.

(5) Von Neumann prices. This is a "semipositive" (i.e., non-negative and not all components are zero) n-dimensional price vector, p^* such that the profit function

$$\Pi(x, y) = p^* \cdot (y - \mu^* x)$$

is nonpositive for all processes and breaks even for a given von Neumann process (x^*, y^*). The von Neumann price vector p^* is said to be associated with the von Neumann process (x^*, y^*). The economic interpretations are:

$$p^* \cdot y \quad \text{is the revenue}$$
$$p^* \cdot \mu^* x \quad \text{is the cost (interest included)}$$
$$(\mu^* - 1) \quad \text{is the von Neumann interest rate}$$

The gist is that no process can be profitable; a von Neumann process breaks even but no non–von Neumann process can outbid a von Neumann process under the von Neumann price–interest system.

Example 1. The "normalized" technology set[4] takes the following form:

$$S = \left\{ [x(\theta), y(\theta)] \middle| x_1(\theta) = \frac{\cos \theta}{\sin \theta + \cos \theta}; x_2(\theta) = \frac{\sin \theta}{\sin \theta + \cos \theta}; \right.$$

$$\left. y_1(\theta) = \cos \theta; y_2(\theta) = \sin \theta; \quad 0 \le \theta \le \frac{\pi}{4} \right\}$$

Here, all processes are "balanced," the expansion ratio being $(\sin \theta + \cos \theta) \ge 1$. This case is analyzed in Figure 11.3. Each $x(\theta)$ is located on the simplex S', since $x_1(\theta) + x_2(\theta) = 1$ for all θ. Moreover, each $y(\theta)$ is located on the quarter-circle, since $y_1^2(\theta) + y_2^2(\theta) = 1$ for all θ. Each process is then represented by an arrow starting from S' and ending on the unit circle while lying in a ray from the origin. The rate of expansion can be directly read off the diagram, once we have

[4]Strictly speaking, this includes only "basic" processes. "Derived" processes can be obtained through disposal of outputs.

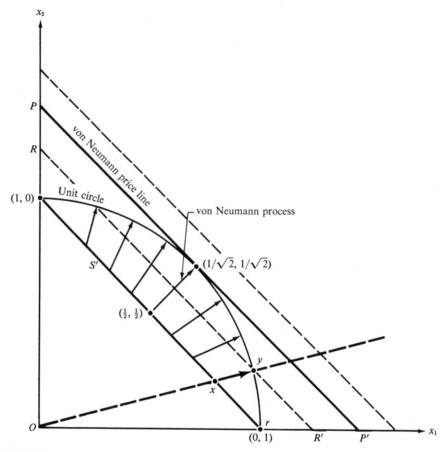

FIGURE 11.3

constructed the dotted iso-μ loci parallel to S'. Consider a process $\vec{xy}$ that lies in the Oxy ray. y is on the intersection of the unit circle and the RR' line. Since RR' is parallel to S', $\overline{Oy}/\overline{Ox} = \overline{OR'}/\overline{Or} = \overline{OR'}$ (since $\overline{Or} = 1$). Hence, $\overline{OR'} = \mu(x, y)$. The highest iso-$\mu$ locus contacting the unit circle is PP'. The point of contact is $1/\sqrt{2}, 1/\sqrt{2}$. Hence, we know

The von Neumann process (x, y) is $[(1/2, 1/2); (1/\sqrt{2}, 1/\sqrt{2})]$

The von Neumann growth factor μ^* is $\dfrac{1/\sqrt{2}}{1/2} = \sqrt{2}$

Finally, the PP' line can also serve as the von Neumann price line, implying a 1:1 price ratio between the two goods. This can be shown as follows. Any input vector is located on S'. If PP' is the price line, then since S' is parallel to PP', all processes must start with identical *initial* cost. After the inclusion of the von Neumann interest rate, $\mu^* - 1$, the *current* cost for any process must be on the line PP'. Since no process in S has a y vector lying to the northeast of PP', all processes are profitless. Since the process (x^*, y^*) has the output vector y^* on PP', (x^*, y^*) breaks even. This concludes the demonstration that the PP' line does represent the von Neumann price line.

Example 2. Suppose that the "normalized" technology set contains one single "basic" process, $[(.6, .4); (.8, .8)]$; i.e., the (ξ, η) pair shown in Figure 11.2. By constructing a vertical (dotted) line through η to intersect the $O\xi$ ray at ω, we obtain a balanced von Neumann process: $(\xi, \omega) = [(.6, .4); (.8, .5\dot{3})]$. This is obtained from (ξ, η) by disposing of $\overline{\eta\omega} = .2\dot{6}$ units of the second output, y_2.

Actually, there exist infinitely many von Neumann processes (ξ, ρ) where $\rho = \theta\eta + (1-\theta)\omega$ $(0 \le \theta \le 1)$. They all share the same balanced growth factor: $\mu^* = \frac{4}{3}$.

The von Neumann price vector associated with the von Neumann process (ξ, ω) must take the form $(p_1, 0)$. If the second good y_2 was of any positive value, then the von Neumann process (ξ, η) would show a positive profit $.26 \, p_2 > 0$, which is against the definition of a von Neumann price vector.

B. RESULTS

The well-known results of the von Neumann model under the above-listed assumptions can be summarized as follows:

(1) There exists at least one von Neumann process with semipositive inputs (i.e., non-negative and not all zero) for each technology.

(2) The set of von Neumann processes is convex; i.e., any weighted average of von Neumann processes is a von Neumann process.

(3) There exists at least one von Neumann price vector with semipositive components for all von Neumann processes.

(4) The set of von Neumann price vectors (associated with a given von Neumann process) is convex; i.e., any weighted average of von Neumann price vectors is a von Neumann price vector.

(5) For any von Neumann process (x^*, y^*) where $y_i^* > \mu^* x_i^*$, $p_i = 0$ in all the associated von Neumann price vectors.

(6) The von Neumann interest rate $(\mu^* - 1)$ is unique, with $\mu^* > 0$.

C. DERIVATIONS[5]

The original von Neumann proof relies on the fixed point theorem. For a simple analytical proof, one may refer to Karlin. Koopmans constructed an extremely ingenious geometric proof for the two-commodity case. However, even with the Koopmans device, the reader is required to reorient himself for a novel diagram. Since one of our purposes in this volume is to acquaint readers with the most results requiring the least action on their part, we shall attempt a proof for the two-goods case with a sequence of traditional diagrams. Except for result (3), the proofs are extremely simple. The order of the proofs is arranged according to analytical convenience.

[5]This item can be skipped by a reader pressed for time.

Proof of (6). Since for any given technology there can be at most one maximum expansion ratio, uniqueness of μ^* is self-evident. From the last result in Section 11.1.1-A, there exists a process (x^0, y^0) with $y^0 > 0, \mu(x^0, y^0) > 0$. Therefore, $\mu^* \geq \mu(x^0, y^0) > 0$. So μ^* is positive as required.

Proof of (2). If for all i, $y_i^{*1} \geq \mu^* x_i^{*1}$, $y_i^{*2} \geq \mu^* x_i^{*2}$, obviously, for all i, $[\lambda y_i^{*1} + (1-\lambda)y_i^{*2}] \geq \lambda\mu^* x_i^{*1} + (1-\lambda)\mu^* x_i^{*2} = \mu^*[\lambda x_i^{*1} + (1-\lambda)x_i^{*2}]$ for all λ, $0 \leq \lambda \leq 1$. Since $y_i^* \geq \mu^* x_i^*$ for all i defines a von Neumann process, the weighted average for the von Neumann processes (x^1, y^1) and (x^2, y^2) must also be a von Neumann process.

Proof of (4). If $p^1 \cdot (y - \mu^* x)$ and $p^2 \cdot (y - \mu^* x)$ are either nonpositive or zero,[6] then $[\lambda p^1 + (1-\lambda)p^2] \cdot (y - \mu^* x) = \lambda[p^1 \cdot (y - \mu^* x)] + (1-\lambda)[p^2 \cdot (y - \mu^* x)]$ must be either nonpositive or zero for all λ, $0 \leq \lambda \leq 1$. Also, the weighted average of semipositive price vectors must remain semipositive. According to the definition of the von Neumann price, the weighted average vector of von Neumann price vectors qualifies as a von Neumann price vector.

Proof of (5). From any unbalanced von Neumann process, one may derive a balanced von Neumann activity. Let an unbalanced von Neumann activity be $(x^*, \mu^* x^* + \eta)$, where η is a semipositive vector with some zero components.[7] Since the von Neumann process breaks even under the von Neumann price p^*,

$$0 = p^* \cdot (y^* - \mu^* x^*) = p^* \cdot \eta$$

$$= \sum_{i=1}^{n'} p_i^* \eta_i + \sum_{i=n'+1}^{n} p_i^* \eta_i$$

(assuming $\eta_i > 0$, for $n' < i \leq n$)

$$= 0 + \sum_{i=n'+1}^{n} p_i^* \eta_i$$

Obviously, $p_i^* = 0$ for $n' < i \leq n$. This completes the proof.

Proof of (1). Out of each process in S, we can obtain a balanced process out of the unbalanced. This is illustrated by the derivation of (ξ, ω) from (ξ, η) in Figure 11.2. The resulting set of processes, together with those derivable by the disposal of outputs, can be represented by n-dimensional arrows *starting from* (*simplex*) S' and lying in rays from the origin. The arrow heads form a closed bounded convex set, σ, similar to that shown in Figure 11.3. Construct hyperplanes[8] parallel to S'. The farther the hyperplane on which the arrow head lies is from S', the greater is the expansion ratio μ. Obviously there exists a highest

---

[6] $p \cdot (y - \mu^* x)$ is the profit for the process (x, y).

[7] Otherwise, if η has no zero component, $[y - (\mu^* + \Delta\mu)x]$ is a vector with all positive components, for some $\Delta\mu > 0$, μ^* would no longer be maximal.

[8] In n-dimensional space, the set of points x satisfying $p \cdot x = $ constant for given p is called a *hyperplane*. If $n = 3$, it is simply a plane. For $n = 2$, it is a line. If H is the hyperplane, geometrically, the ray containing vector p is perpendicular to H and p is sometimes called the *normal* of H.

iso-μ locus that shares a point in common with σ. Here the von Neumann growth factor and the von Neumann processes are jointly determined. This proves the existence of the von Neumann process.

Proof of (3).   We shall now define the set Z of net output vector:

$$Z = \{z | z = (y - \mu^* x)\}$$

for each process (x, y) in S. The economic meaning is as follows. Since each commodity can grow at the ratio μ^* per period, inputs of all commodities one period before should be compounded by the factor μ^* to reach their current worth. Subtracting these from the outputs, we obtain the net output vector. The interested reader can confirm that the resultant set of vectors is closed, bounded, and convex (in the n-dimensional space), following the properties of the set S of (x, y) (in the $2n$-dimensional space). Moreover, the origin that corresponds to the balanced von Neumann processes $(x^*, \mu^* x^*)$ (since $\mu^* x^* - \mu^* x^* = 0$) is also in Z.

In Figure 11.4 we illustrate how we can derive z from x and y. Noting that $z = y - \mu^* x$, we rearrange to obtain

$$z + \mu^* x = y$$

We first locate $\mu^* x$ by constructing the Ox ray to intersect the line joining $(\mu^*, 0)$ and $(0, \mu^*)$. We then construct a parallelogram with 0, $\mu^* x$, and y as the three known vertices. The fourth vertex is z. We can easily check that $z + \mu^* x = y$ is fulfilled in this construction.

Applying the above procedure for all (x, y) in S, we obtain Z.

Obviously, no vector in Z can have all its components positive. Were this false, there must exist a vector, $v = \bar{y} - \mu^* \bar{x}$ in Z, all of whose components are positive. In other words, $v_i > 0$ for $i = 1, \ldots, n$. By selecting a small enough positive value of ε, it must be true that

$$v_i \geq \varepsilon \bar{x}_i \quad \text{for all } i = 1, \ldots, n$$

But then,

$$\bar{y}_i = v_i + \mu^* \bar{x}_i$$
$$\geq (\varepsilon + \mu^*) \bar{x}_i$$

Hence,

$$\mu(\bar{x}, \bar{y}) \geq \mu^* + \varepsilon > \mu^*$$

which contradicts the definition of μ^* as the maximal expansion ratio. This leads to the conclusion that the convex set Z and the convex set P, which is the positive orthant[9] (containing vectors with all components strictly positive), have no point in common, the origin is both in Z and in the boundary of P.

---

[9]In two-dimensional space, the set of x with all components strictly positive is the "positive quadrant." In three-dimensional space, such a set is the "positive octant;" in n-dimensional space, the "positive orthant."

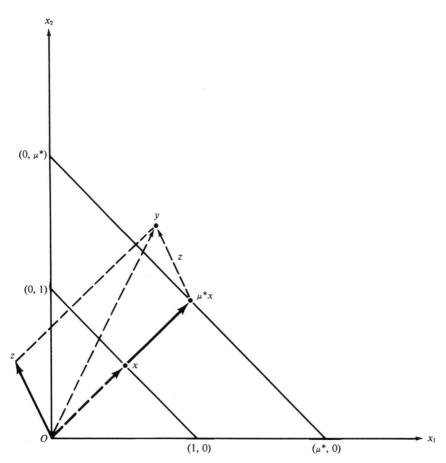

FIGURE 11.4

Hence, we may construct a hyperplane, $H = \{v | p \cdot v = p \cdot 0 = 0\}$, separating Z on one side and P on the other,[10] such that

$$p \cdot v > 0 \quad \text{for all } v \text{ in } P \tag{11.1.1}$$

$$p \cdot v \leq 0 \quad \text{for all } v \text{ in } Z \tag{11.1.2}$$

Here not all the components of p are zero. This is the standard separation theorem for convex sets. Now, suppose that $p_i < 0$ for $i = 1, \ldots, n'$, and $p_i \geq 0$ for $i = n' + 1, \ldots, n$; then we can select a vector q in P, such that

---

[10]One may refer to Hadley [21] or Karlin [4] for the separation of convex sets. Koopmans [22] also mentions it.

$$q_i = \begin{cases} -\dfrac{2}{\displaystyle\sum_{j=1}^{n'} p_j} > 0 \quad \text{for } i = 1, 2, \ldots, n' \\[4ex] \dfrac{1}{\displaystyle\sum_{j=n'+1}^{n} p_j} > 0 \quad \text{for } i = n'+1, \ldots, n \end{cases}$$

Then we have

$$p \cdot q = -2 + 1 = -1$$

which shows that the vector q of P lies on the same side of H as Z. This contradicts the fact that H separates P and Z (it violates (11.1.1)). Therefore, we know that the vector p, the *normal* of H, is semipositive.

Interpreting p as a semipositive price vector, we conclude that under p and μ^*,

(1) No process makes a profit (from (11.1.2)).
(2) All balanced von Neumann processes break even (since their associated vector z is the origin).
(3) From (1) and (2), the commodities produced in an unbalanced von Neumann process in excess of $(\mu^* x_i^*)$ command zero price. Figure 11.1 shows that any unbalanced von Neumann process cannot have a lower profit figure than its derived balanced von Neumann process. Hence, all von Neumann processes break even. Therefore, p qualifies as a von Neumann price vector p^*, according to the definition given in Section 11.1.2-A. The proof is now complete.

Figure 11.5 illustrates the relationship among P, Z, and H in a two-commodity world. Lines parallel to H are drawn, and these are iso-profit lines in the neoclassical framework. The fact that H goes through the origin shows that any point on H breaks even. The fact that Z shares the origin with H but never includes points on both sides of H signifies that all processes are profitless, but some (especially the von Neumann process) break even. The fact that P lies on the other side of Z helps us to decide that the prices forming H are non-negative, as discussed in the formal proof above.

The northeastern boundary of the net-output set Z (in heavy line) resembles the Marshall-Meade offer curve in international trade appearing in the writings of Samuelson, Bardhan, and others. The only difference is that in our construction of Z we have telescoped a two-period production process into one period, by using the von Neumann growth factor μ^*. Only by multiplying by μ^* are we able to subtract past input (x_i) from present output (y_i). Hence, the northeast frontier of Z is a *value*-transformation locus, rather than a *physical*-transformation locus.

Actually, the problem of depicting the two-commodity von Neumann model is due to our common inability to visualize four-dimensional diagrams, even

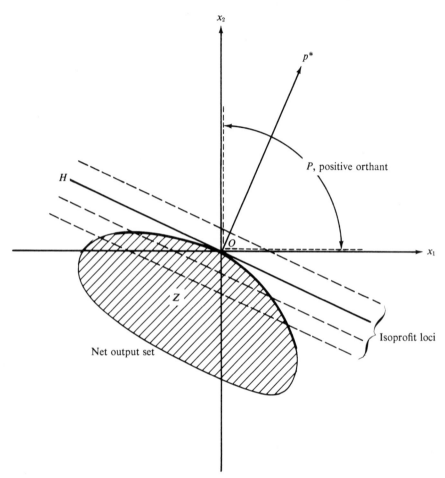

FIGURE 11.5

though we do live in a four-dimensional space–time system. Otherwise, we can depict T as a four-dimensional closed convex cone. Separating this cone from the cone of process rays with faster-than-feasible expansion ratios lies a hyperplane whose normal $(p_1^* \mu^*, p_2^* \mu^*, p_1^*, p_2^*)$ provides the information we need. The rays lying both in this hyperplane and in T represent the breaking-even processes, and this set includes the subset of von Neumann process rays, of which the balanced von Neumann rays form a subset.

D.   COMMENTARY

As Koopmans noted, the von Neumann model is at once a path-breaking analytic achievement and a piece of rather poor economics. On the plus side, it is the first rigorous model in the modern theory of competitive equilibrium, and it deals with heterogeneous capital goods. On the minus side, an economy may neither desire to pursue balanced growth nor have the appropriate initial capital structure to conduct von Neumann activities. Moreover, the abstraction from technical progress and the exclusion of consumption goods from the model also make it useless in practical applications.

However, the turnpike theorems indicate that under certain conditions, long-duration optimal growth paths should be "near" the von Neumann activities. The straight-down-the-turnpike theorem shows that, under even broader assumptions, one may obtain a "nearly" optimal long-duration policy by actually carrying out von Neumann activities. Both of these models apply for finite-horizon problems of efficient capital accumulation. For the infinite-horizon case, it can also be shown that under certain conditions, infinite-growth programs satisfying intertemporal efficiency conditions should also stay "near" the von Neumann activities. These will be discussed below.

We now turn to a model by McKenzie [20]. Space does not allow us to discuss this paper in detail, but we shall report the main framework, summarized in Table 11.3.

"Utility stock" at the terminal instant is the only desired good in the economy. The interesting point is that in the framework of capital-accumulating models, McKenzie achieved the same goal as the "consumption-oriented" models in maximizing the discounted sum of utility. He then proceeded to derive a turnpike theorem under such a framework.

μ^* serves as the time preference rate (discount rate). Actual population growth rate is a variable in his model.

11.2 THE TURNPIKE PROBLEM

11.2.1. Formulation and general background

The general framework of the turnpike problem is as follows: Under assumptions (1)–(4) of Section 4.1, we solve for the efficient capital accumulation problem:

$$\text{Max } \lambda \tag{11.2.1}$$

subject to:

$$y^N = \lambda \tilde{y} \tag{11.2.2}$$

$$(x^j, y^j) \text{ in } T \qquad \text{for } j = 1, 2, \ldots, N \tag{11.2.3}$$

$$y_i^j \geq x_i^{j+1} \qquad \text{for } i = 1, 2, \ldots, n, \quad j = 1, 2, \ldots, N-1 \tag{11.2.4}$$

$$x^1 \text{ given} \tag{11.2.5}$$

In other words, starting from the given initial vector x^1, we seek to arrive at the "largest" terminal vector y^N that is proportional to a given vector $\tilde{y}$ by a sequence of feasible activities. Alternatively, as Radner [10] pointed out, we

TABLE 11.3

Types of inputs and outputs	Remarks
Commodities Population Utility flow Utility stock	As in usual models. Novelty; variable population growth. Novelty; serving as a transition to utility stock. Novelty; past utility stock "grows" at the von Neumann rate μ^*.[a]

[a]Let $U(t)$ be the stock of utility at period t and $u(t)$ be the flow of utility at period t. McKenzie maximizes

$$U(N) = \sum_{t=1}^{N} u(t)\,(\mu^*)^{N-t} = (\mu^*)^N \sum_{t=1}^{N} (\mu^*)^{-t} u(t)$$

may specify an objective function $U(\cdot)$, defined only over y^N. The formulation of (11.2.1) and (11.2.2), from this point of view, can be written as

$$U(y^N) = \operatorname*{Min}_{1 \le i \le n} \frac{y_i^N}{\tilde{y}_i}$$

These basic concepts are shown in Figure 11.6, where x^1 is the initial input vector and the y ray stands for the desired terminal capital proportions. The optimal path $x^1(\lambda^* \tilde{y})$ is said to exhibit the turnpike property because it arcs toward the von Neumann ray Ox^*, and for most of the time it is within a cone containing the latter. The von Neumann ray is thus said to be a turnpike. All long-duration (long-distance) optimal paths must go close to it. On the other hand, the straight-down-the-turnpike theorem says, supposing that we take an alternative path by staying actually on the von Neumann ray between x^{*b} and x^{*f}, we can get back to the desired ray, $O\tilde{y}$, at the horizon N. The comparative loss compared to the truly optimal path decreases as the time horizon increases until the percentage loss is negligible. This nearly optimal path is $x_1 x^{*b} x^{*f} \tilde{y}$, shown also in Figure 11.6.

11.2.2. Some useful concepts and additional assumptions

The model specified in (11.2.1)–(11.2.5) does not in general exhibit turnpike properties. To rule out different exceptional cases, there exist different types of turnpike theorems based upon their respective, special assumptions. Using weaker assumptions, Winter [19] developed a straight-down-the-turnpike theorem. The situation is not unlike the two-sector growth model, where different sets of sufficient assumption sets give rise to different (determinant) models.

We shall first introduce a set of useful concepts and then present a list of commonly adopted assumptions so that in the next section we can state that the combination of certain conditions may lead to particular types of results.

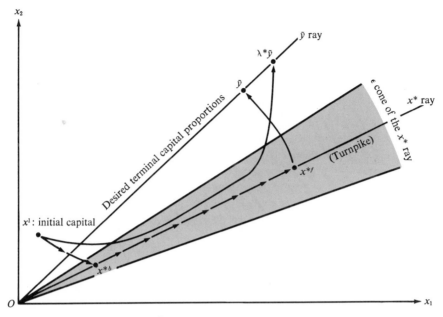

FIGURE 11.6 Optimal path: $x^1 \to \lambda^*\tilde{y}$
Straight-down-the-turnpike path: $x^1 \to \to x^{*b} \to \to x^{*f} \to \to \tilde{y}$

A. SOME USEFUL CONCEPTS

1. "Value-preserving." This is an adjective applicable to:

(a) A *process* that breaks even under p^* and μ^*: $p^* \cdot (y - \mu^* x) = 0$. Obviously, the von Neumann process is value-preserving by the definition of p^*. Also, the total abandonment of input vectors that are free under the von Neumann prices is value-preserving!

(b) A *path* that consists of a chain of value-preserving processes

$$[(x^1, y^1), (x^2, y^2), \ldots] \text{ with } x^{t+1} = y^t$$

Again, growth right down the von Neumann (balanced process) ray is value-preserving.

2. "Angular distance" between two non-null vectors. Due to constant returns to scale, the Euclidean distance[11] between two input vectors does not reflect their "qualitative" or "compositional" differences. Two input vectors along the same ray from the origin may be quite distant by the Euclidean measure. Yet they are "qualitatively" identical, save for their magnitudes. Radner [10] and McKenzie [13] hence measure the "distance" of two nonzero vectors by the Euclidean distances between their radial projections upon the unit sphere. This is seen from Figure 11.7. The projection of x^i on the unit sphere

---

[11]That is, the common definition for distance. For vectors x and y, the Euclidean distance is $[(x - y) \cdot (x - y)]^{1/2}$.

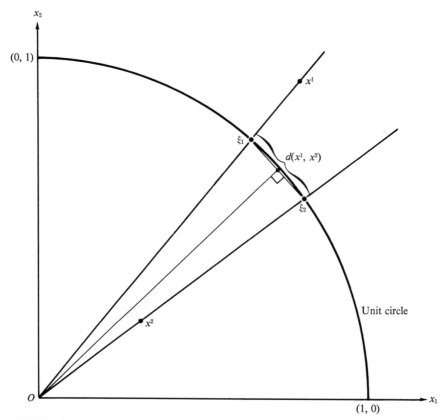

FIGURE 11.7

is ξ_i, $i = 1, 2$. The (Euclidean) distance between ξ_1 and ξ_2 is denoted as

$$d(x_1, x_2) = \overline{\xi_1 \xi_2}$$

Since $d(x^1, x^2)/2 = \sin(\theta/2)$, where θ is the angle between the Ox^1 and Ox^2 rays, this distance measure is called *angular distance*.

3. Instantaneous efficiency; intertemporal efficiency and the efficiency envelope. We duplicate a diagram of Dorfman, Samuelson, and Solow in Figure 11.8 to explain the above concepts. Starting from initial input vector x^1, we can reach any point on the y^1 locus. Starting from $\overline{y}^1$, we can reach any point on the y^2 locus. But if we intend to go for $\overline{y}^2$ at the end of period 2, we could not afford to stop over at any point on the y^1 locus other than the point $\overline{y}^1$, at the end of period 1. The attainment of the one-period y^t loci is called *instantaneous efficiency*. The coordination of various processes, one for each period, is called *intertemporal efficiency*. Specifically, if the minimal locus of inputs for producing $\overline{y}^2$ is depicted by the dotted line, the tangency of that line and the y^1 locus assures intertemporal efficiency; i.e., the point $\overline{y}^2$ does locate on the efficiency envelope (highest output locus) attainable by an *efficient two-period* program from x^1.

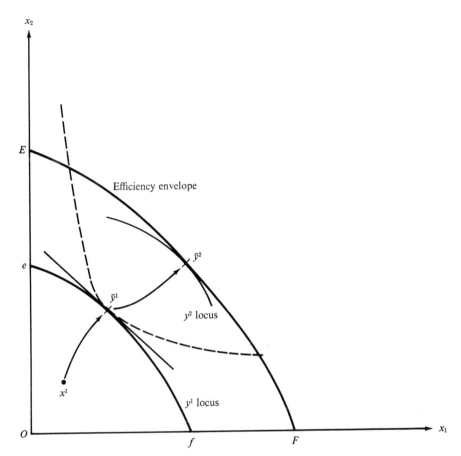

FIGURE 11.8

Since EF is tangent to the y^2 locus from $\bar{y}^1$, as well as other one-period loci starting from alternative positions on ef, it is called an *envelope*. The above general concepts, the assumption of constant returns to scale, and the unchanged technology enable us to telescope multiperiod growth patterns into a single diagram. In fact, this is what Winter did, after introducing certain concepts discussed below.

4. Present-value technology. For any technology T there corresponds a von Neumann growth factor μ^* (results (1) and (6) of Section 11.1.2). One can then consider a fictitious technology T' that contains a process $(x, y/\mu^*)$ for each process (x, y) in T. The correspondences between these two are listed in Table 11.4. T' is called the *present-value technology*.

5. Infinite period production set; m-period production set. Starting from any input vector x, the set of all vectors producible in m periods under T' is called the m-period production set, $A_m(x)$; the set of all vectors producible by a chain of processes of any positive length under T' or the limit of such producible vectors

TABLE 11.4

	Actual	Present value
Technology	T	T'
Process	(x, y)	$(x, y/\mu^*)$
Balanced von Neumann process	$(x^*, \mu^* x^*)$	(x^*, x^*)
von Neumann growth factor	μ^*	1
von Neumann price	p^*	p^*
Breaking even (value-preserving)	$p^* \cdot (y - \mu^* x) = 0$	$p^* \cdot (y - x) = 0$

(when m approaches infinity) is called the *infinite-period set*,[12] $\overline{A}(x)$. Due to constant returns to scale, if y is in $A_m(x)$ or $\overline{A}(x)$, then λy is in $A_m(\lambda x)$ or $\overline{A}(\lambda x)$ for all $\lambda > 0$. Obviously, x^* is in $A_m(x^*)$ for all m and it is in $\overline{A}(x^*)$ as well.[13] The concepts $\overline{A}(x)$ and $\overline{A}(x^*)$ are shown in Figure 11.9. $\overline{A}(x)$ is obviously related to an infinite-period efficiency envelope (which cannot be depicted graphically).

6. The $\phi(x)$, $\pi(x)$, and $\mu(x)$ functions. Winter introduced the following three concepts:

$$\phi(x) = \text{Inf } \lambda \quad \text{such that } x \text{ is in } \overline{A}(\lambda x^*)$$
$$\pi(x) = \text{Sup } \lambda \quad \text{such that } \lambda x^* \text{ is in } \overline{A}(x)$$
$$\mu(x) = \text{Sup } \lambda \quad \text{such that } \lambda x \text{ is in } \overline{A}(x)$$

x will be barely lying inside the infinite production set of $\phi(x)x^*$, showing how little of a von Neumann input vector it takes to eventually produce the vector x. $\pi(x)x^*$ indicates how much of the von Neumann output mix is eventually producible from an initial input vector x. $\mu(x)x$ represents the most output along the same ray of x that can be produced from the initial input x.

All these can be seen from Figure 11.9. Obviously, $\phi(x)$ and $\pi(x)$ are first-order homogeneous functions and $\mu(x)$ is zero-order homogeneous. Since at worst, from x, one can reach $\pi(x)x^*$ and from $\pi(x)x^*$ one can then reach $[\pi(x)/\phi(x)]x$, we have $\mu(x) \geq [\pi(x)/\phi(x)]$.

With the above preparation, we are in a position to discuss the following additional assumptions, besides the four in Section 11.1.1-A, required for the various turnpike theories.

B. ADDITIONAL ASSUMPTIONS

(5) Accessibility.

(a) $\pi(x^1) > 0$. In other words, from the initial input vector one can reach the von Neumann ray.

(b) $\phi(\tilde{y}) < \infty$. In other words, from the von Neumann ray it is possible to reach the ray of the terminal stock vector.

(6) "von Neumann-free" inputs yield sub-μ^* expansion ratios. Starting from an input vector x such that $p^* \cdot x = 0$, $\mu(x, y) < \mu^*$ in T or $\mu(x, y) < 1$ in T' for all y.

---

[12] $\overline{A}(x)$ is the closure of the union of all sets $A_m(x)$, over all m.

[13] Following the definition of the balanced von Neumann process, x^* begets x^*.

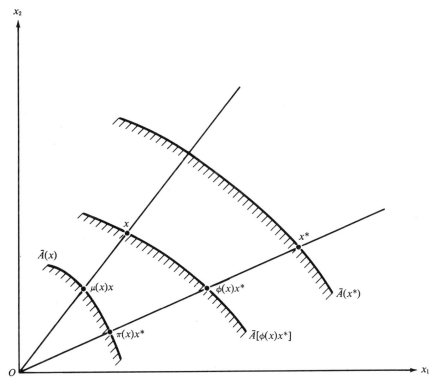

x_2

$\bar{A}(x)$

x

x^*

$\mu(x)x$

$\phi(x)x^*$

$\bar{A}(x^*)$

$\pi(x)x^*$

$\bar{A}[\phi(x)x^*]$

O

x_1

FIGURE 11.9

(7) Any possible value-preserving return is always attainable via the von Neumann ray. If $\mu(x) = 1$, then $\pi(x) = \phi(x)$.

(8) Unique breaking-even process. There is only one value-preserving process: (x^*, x^*).

(9) x^* has all positive components.

(10) $T' = \{x, y| Ay \leq x\}$ where A is an $n \times n$ matrix satisfying these conditions:

(a) All entries are non-negative.

(b) All columns sum up to unity.

(c) Indecomposable. This means that A cannot be rearranged through renumbering of rows and columns into a "block triangular" form.[14]

(d) Primitive. This means that the unique, positive characteristic root of A (which exists due to a theorem of Debreu and Herstein [23]) is larger than the modulus (absolute value) of any other characteristic root.

(11) $\tilde{y}$ has all positive components.

[14] That is, some form like:

$$\begin{bmatrix} * & * & * \\ 0 & * & * \\ 0 & 0 & * \end{bmatrix}$$

Nonzero elements may occur only in starred submatrices.

The economic meaning is: Every input is needed to produce any one output.

The above seven assumptions are not equally fundamental. Certain assumptions imply the others. On the other hand, different theories assume different subsets of these seven. Table 11.5 presents a summary of the relations between theories and assumptions.

For lack of space, we will not discuss certain types of turnpike theorems—for example, the Dorfman-Samuelson-Solow (DOSSO)-McKenzie version—in spite of their generality. We shall only sketch the Morishima version without presenting proofs. Interested readers should refer to the source articles.

A few observations can be made here.[15]

(a) Assumption (5) (accessibility) is the foundation of all these alternative models. Without accessibility, we cannot take the straight-down-the-turnpike path, which also serves as the "comparison path" (see below) for the proof of all turnpike theorems. In Figure 11.6, the accessibility assumption guarantees the existence of the $x^1 x^{*b}$ and x^{*f} $\tilde{y}$ arcs.

(b) Assumption (8) implies that in p^* all prices are positive. Otherwise, the process of totally abandoning a free input vector is a break-even process, as well as the process (x^*, x^*). This contradicts assumption (8). Since no input is free, assumption (6) holds by default. On the other hand, unless a process is on that von Neumann ray, i.e., (x^*, x^*), each period must incur some value loss. Also by definition, no value gain can ever be attained. Therefore, starting from $x \neq x^*$, $\mu(x)x$ must be less worthy than x. In other words, $p^* \cdot x > p^* \cdot [\mu(x)x]$. Hence, $\mu(x) < 1$ for all $x \neq x^*$. For x^*, $\mu(x^*) = 1 = 1/1 = [\pi(x^*)/\phi(x^*)]$. Therefore, assumption (7) is also satisfied.[16] This means that if the Radner-Nikaido turnpike theorem is valid, the Winter theorem must be also.

(c) Assumption (10) implies (with the help of results in Debreu and Herstein [23]) that (i) the A matrix has a unique positive characteristic root, unity, larger in modulus than other roots;[17] (ii) the A matrix has a strictly positive characteristic vector x^*, such that $Ax^* = 1 \cdot x^* = x^*$; and (iii) the A matrix can be associated with a vector $p^* = (1, 1, \ldots, 1)$ such that for all (x, y) where $x = Ay$:

$$
\begin{aligned}
p^* \cdot x &= p^* \cdot (Ay) \\
&= (p^{*\prime} A) \cdot y \\
&= p^* \cdot y \qquad (p^{*\prime} A = p^{*\prime}, \text{ since all column sums } = 1)
\end{aligned}
$$

Therefore, the positivity of p^* is assured $[p^* = (1, 1, \ldots, 1)$ makes all non-disposal processes break even] and hence assumption (6) is again satisfied. It can also be shown that for this Morishima case, any value-preserving path cannot lie beyond an angular distance δ away from x^* for more than $M(\delta)$ periods. This is true for all $\delta > 0$ and $M(\delta)$ is independent of the duration or initial point of the path (see Inada [16]). Winter proved that this property and

---

[15]Points (b) and (c) are technical notes, not crucial to the general understanding of subsequent material.

[16]The only "value-preserving return" that is possible is from x^* to x^*.

[17]From (iii) below, $p^{*\prime} A = p^{*\prime}$; therefore, that unique positive characteristic root is unity.

TABLE 11.5

	Assumptions						
	(5)	(6)	(7)	(8)	(9)	(10)	(11)
Turnpike theorem—Joint product version (Radner)	✓			✓			
Extension (Nikaido)	✓			✓	✓		
Turnpike theorem—No joint product version (Morishima)	✓					✓	✓
Straight-down-the-turnpike theorem (Winter)	✓	✓	✓				

assumptions (1)–(6) jointly imply assumption (7). Hence, the Morishima assumptions are also sufficient for the Winter theorem. Furthermore, the fact that x^* has all positive components implies that assumption (9) also holds.

(d) On the other hand, neither the Radner case nor the Morishima case is a special case of the other. For the Radner case, there may be infinitely many basic processes, none a weighted average of the other. This contrasts with the Morishima case, where there are only n basic processes, one for each good (i.e., y is a unit vector). All the rest are weighted sums of these n processes. On the other hand, under the Morishima case, all nondisposal processes break even. This contrasts with assumption (8), according to which only the von Neumann process breaks even.

11.2.3. The theorems

A. THE STRAIGHT-DOWN-THE-TURNPIKE THEOREM

We shall state without proof two interesting results of Winter.

Result a. For any ε, $0 < \varepsilon \le 1$, if assumptions (1)–(7) are satisfied, then there exists $M(\varepsilon)$ such that for all $N > M(\varepsilon)$.

$$\overline{A}\big[\pi\{(1-\varepsilon)x^1\}x^*\big] \subset A_N(x^1) \subset \overline{A}\big[\pi\{(1+\varepsilon)x^1\}x^*\big]$$

This result is depicted in Figure 11.10. Loosely speaking, the N-period production frontier can be approximated with increasing accuracy for long programs by "restricted-path" infinite-period production frontiers. The "restricted-path" frontier is obtained by going from the initial position to the von Neumann ray in the first period before branching in other directions.

We now introduce the definitions:

$U(y^N)$ is a utility function continuous and nondecreasing in the final state vector y^N and strictly increasing in at least one component of y^N

$V_N(x^1)$ is the maximum attainable value of $U(y^N)$ through a feasible N-period chain starting from x^1

Result b. Winter proved that for any $\varepsilon > 0$, $\delta > 0$, there exists $M(\varepsilon, \delta) > 0$ such that for all $N \ge M(\varepsilon, \delta)$ there exists a feasible path that (i) coincides with the turnpike for more than $(1-\delta)(N+1)$ periods, and (ii) attains a utility level that is no less than $V_N[(1-\varepsilon)x^1]$. This result promises that for a long enough horizon there exists a feasible path that rides the turnpike for any high fraction

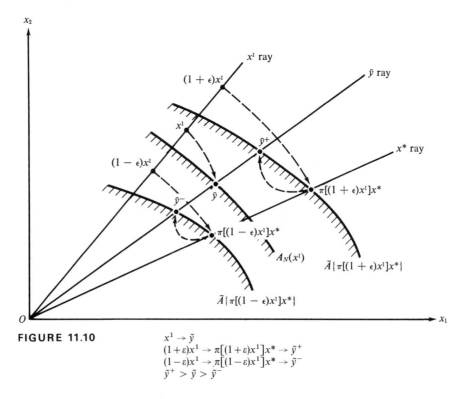

FIGURE 11.10

$x^1 \to \tilde{y}$
$(1+\varepsilon)x^1 \to \pi[(1+\varepsilon)x^1]x^* \to \tilde{y}^+$
$(1-\varepsilon)x^1 \to \pi[(1-\varepsilon)x^1]x^* \to \tilde{y}^-$
$\tilde{y}^+ > \tilde{y} > \tilde{y}^-$

of the time and reduces the utility level by a degree no more than the effect of an arbitrarily small reduction of the initial endowment.

Winter maintained that the attractiveness of his results is due to two facts: They are based upon very general assumptions, and they point out an easily defined feasible path (*riding* the turnpike) with predictable upper bounds on efficiency losses that decrease in importance with the lengthening of the horizon.

B.   THE RADNER-NIKAIDO THEORY

Result of Radner.   For any $\delta > 0$, if assumptions (1)–(5) and (8) are fulfilled, there exists $M(\delta, x^1)$ such that the optimal path for the problem in (11.2.1)–(11.2.5) cannot stay away from the x^* ray by more than an angular distance of δ for more than $M(\delta, x^1)$ periods. $M(\delta, x^1)$ is independent of N.

Proof.   The accessibility assumption implies that in an n-commodity world it takes at most n periods to reach the von Neumann ray, and it takes at most n periods to reach the proportion $\tilde{y}$ from the von Neumann ray. Difficulties in attaining a certain output proportion can only arise from the shortage of a particular input.[18] Such a difficulty is either insurmountable (ruled out by assuming accessibility) or it can be overcome within n steps. In each step, one

---

[18]Otherwise, one can accomplish the access by "costless" disposal of suitable amounts of inputs.

new input can be produced. Interested readers may refer to Koopmans [17] for a two-goods example.

Define:

$$\pi_n(x^1) = \text{Max } \lambda \quad \text{such that } (\lambda x^*) \text{ is in } A_n(x^1)$$
$$\phi_n(\tilde{y}) = \text{Min } \lambda \quad \text{such that } \tilde{y} \text{ is in } A_n(\lambda x^*)$$

One straight-down-the-turnpike path can be described as follows:

$$\overbrace{x^1 \to \pi_n(x^1)x^*}^{\text{first } n \text{ periods}} : \overbrace{\pi_n(x^1)x^* \to \pi_n(x^1)x^*}^{(N-2n) \text{ periods}} : \overbrace{\pi_n(x^1)x^* \to [\pi_n(x^1)/\phi_n(\tilde{y})]\tilde{y}}^{\text{last } n \text{ periods}}$$

$$\text{Value loss} = \{p^* \cdot x^1 - p^* \cdot [\pi_n(x^1)/\phi_n(\tilde{y})]\tilde{y}\}$$

The optimal path starting from x^1 and ending at $\lambda^* \tilde{y}$ cannot do worse.

Now since the breaking-even process is unique, let us consider the minimal value loss ratio for processes starting from an input with an angular distance no less than δ from x^*. Define:

$$\theta(\delta) = \mathop{\text{Min}}_{\substack{(x,\, y)\, \in\, T \\ d(x,\, x^*)\, \geq\, \delta}} \left[1 - \frac{p^* \cdot y}{p^* \cdot x} \right]$$

$$> 0$$

Suppose the optimal path involves N' periods more than an angular distance of δ from the x^* ray. Then the value loss must be at least

$$\{1 - [1 - \theta(\delta)]^{N'}\}p^* \cdot x^1 \leq p^* \cdot x^1 - p^* \cdot \lambda^* \tilde{y} \qquad \text{(since inside } \delta \text{ there may still} \quad (11.2.6)$$
$$\text{be loss)}$$
$$\leq p^* \cdot x^1 - p^* \cdot [\pi_n(x^1)/\phi_n(\tilde{y})]\tilde{y}$$

Dividing all numbers by $p^* \cdot x^1$ and rearranging the first and third members, we get

$$[1 - \theta(\delta)]^{N'} \geq \frac{\pi_n(x^1)}{\phi_n(\tilde{y})} \frac{p^* \cdot \tilde{y}}{p^* \cdot x^1} \qquad (11.2.7)$$

$$\equiv C(x^1)$$

where $C(x^1)$ is dependent only on x^1.

Taking logarithms on both sides,

$$N' \ln [1 - \theta(\delta)] \geq \ln C(x^1) \qquad (11.2.8)$$

Recognizing that both sides of (11.2.7) and $[1 - \theta(\delta)]$ are positive fractions whose logarithmic values are negative, we obtain, by division,

$$N' \leq M(\delta, x^1) \equiv \text{Int} \left[\frac{\ln C(x^1)}{\ln \{1 - \theta(\delta)\}} \right] + 1$$

where Int $[z]$ stands for the largest integer no greater than z. This completes the proof.

Obviously, when $N \to \infty$, $N'/N \downarrow 0$. Hence, the longer the horizon, the higher

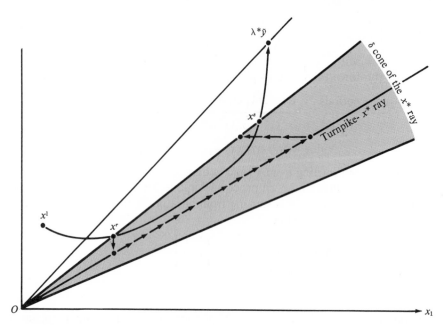

FIGURE 11.11 The comparison path is the arrow-signed path straight down the turnpike.

the proportion of time that the optimal path stays inside the ε cone of the von Neumann ray.

Note that the fact that p^* has all positive components guarantees that $(p^* \cdot \bar{y})/(p^* \cdot x^1) < \infty$.

Result of Nikaido. With the addition of assumption (9) to those underlying Radner's result, it can be shown that all periods in which the optimal path is more than an angular distance of δ from the x^* ray are located either in the first M periods or in the last M periods (M independent of N).

The proof is omitted because it is almost a duplication of the Radner proof. One seeks the first period when the optimal path enters the δ cone and the last period emerging from it, say, at x^r and x^s. Then a comparison subpath is obtained through disposal activities. And then the entire reasoning process is repeated (one may refer to Koopmans [17]). The graphic depiction is in Figure 11.11.

In the simplest special case of the Radner-Nikaido model, the technological cone is strictly convex. Except for disposal processes, no process is a weighted average of other processes. The unique von Neumann process, except in some unrealistic cases, must produce more than one commodity. Hence this case of strictly convex technology is called the joint *product case*. To visualize this, we can consider the two-commodity world where any input vector allows a strictly concave production frontier.

C. THE MORISHIMA THEORY

In contrast to the Radner theory where a joint product is usually present, Morishima postulates that for each "basic" process, there is one and only one output. Also, for each output, there is only a finite number of "basic" processes producing it. Morishima seeks to characterize the optimal solution for the following problem:

$$\text{Max } \lambda$$

subject to

$$\lambda \tilde{y} \le y^N$$

$$\left.\begin{matrix} (y^t, y^{t+1}) \in T \\ (x^1, y^1) \in T \end{matrix}\right\} t = 1, \ldots, N-1$$

Morishima proved that starting from a given x^1 and aiming at the "maximal" vector on the $O\tilde{y}$ ray, the optimum path must lie within an angular distance δ from the von Neumann process ray Ox^*, save for at most M periods, where M depends upon x^1, $\tilde{y}$, and δ, but not upon N, the length of the horizon.

Specifically, there exists a sequence of price vectors associated with the optimal path such that in each period no process earns a positive profit and the optimal process breaks even. It can be proved that as time goes by, the price vector approaches closer and closer to a certain price vector, with all components positive. This is called the *price turnpike theorem*. Now, for the subinterval where the price vector is sufficiently close to the price turnpike, the output vector approaches retrogressively to the von Neumann process ray, i.e., within this subinterval, the earlier the time, the closer the output vector to the Ox^* ray. This is called the *quantity turnpike theorem*.

D. FINAL REMARKS

The turnpike theorem of Dorfman, Samuelson, and Solow was of deep interest to economists. Subsequent discoveries of exceptional cases stimulated further research. In retrospect, the development of the turnpike theorem subsequent to Dorfman, Samuelson, and Solow, is of crucial importance logically but of marginal importance economically. From the logical point of view, unless one has a watertight set of assumptions, one can never gauge the range of validity of the proposition. On the other hand, all the counterexamples constructed so far fall into two very special categories; neither appears to be plausible in the real world. We shall now discuss two counterexamples and examine their economic content.

1. The cyclical counterexample (Kuhn-Morishima). Assume the A matrix takes the form:

$$\begin{pmatrix} 0 & 1 \\ 1 & 0 \end{pmatrix}$$

with $+1$ and -1 as characteristic values and $(1, 1), (1, -1)$ as row characteristic vectors or column characteristic vectors. This means that the A matrix is imprimitive or cyclical. In this case,

$$p^t = \begin{pmatrix} c_1 + (-1)^t c_2 \\ c_1 - (-1)^t c_2 \end{pmatrix} \qquad y^{N+1-t} = \begin{pmatrix} C_1 + (-1)^t C_2 \\ C_1 - (-1)^t C_2 \end{pmatrix}$$

where p^t and y^t are the price and output vectors for period t, and c_1, c_2, C_1, and C_2 are constants. Neither p^t nor y^t approaches the steady-state values (c_1, c_1) or (C_1, C_1).

One can always set ε to be so small, e.g., $\varepsilon = |C_2|/2$, that the optimal y path invariably falls out of the ε neighborhood of $x^* = (C_1, C_1)$. Hence the optimal path is never near the turnpike. The following tables show these points.

Example 1. $c_1 = 1 = c_2$

t	1	2	3	4...
p^t	$(0, 2)$	$(2, 0)$	$(0, 2)$	$(2, 0)$...

For all t, p^t is never near the price turnpike $(1, 1)$.

Example 2. $C_1 = 2, C_2 = 1$

t	1	2	3	4...
z^t	$(1, 3)$	$(3, 1)$	$(1, 3)$	$(3, 1)$...

For all t, z^t is away from $x^* = (2, 2)$ by a distance more than $\frac{1}{2}$.

The economic interpretation of a cyclical input matrix is that all industries can be partitioned into a number of groups $k = 1, 2, \ldots, K$, say. The intergroup relation is such that the kth group needs only the product of the $(k-1)$st group as inputs, $k = 2, \ldots, K$, while the first group needs only the product of the Kth group. Obviously, such a technical setup is seldom, if ever, encountered in the real world.

2. The "inaccessible" counterexamples. Assume the A matrix takes the form:

$$\begin{pmatrix} 1 & .2 \\ 0 & 5 \end{pmatrix}$$

In this case the von Neumann process is $(1, 0)$ and the von Neumann growth factor is unity. However, if the terminal capital ray is along the axis of the second good, then obviously the optimal path will not be close to the von Neumann process, regardless of the duration of the time horizon. This is due to the fact that there is no route leading from the von Neumann ray to the terminal ray. Sheer accumulation of the first commodity does not facilitate the economy to realize its community aspiration—to attain the highest number of the second commodity at a predestined date. This example seems to warn economic planners not to concentrate on production indices that produce commodities of low social preference. Overall, it still represents a rather artificial situation, since in the real world every sector depends upon all the other sectors to some degree.

11.3 RELATIVE STABILITY THEOREM FOR INTERTEMPORALLY EFFICIENT INFINITE PATHS

In consumption-oriented models, current interest seems to concentrate on infinite-horizon models. In accumulation-oriented models, the focus is on finite horizons. Turnpike theorems occupy the center of stage, while their infinite-horizon counterpart, the relative stability theorem, is usually neglected. In the following we shall discuss the concept, the formulation, and the significance of the "relative stability" theorem. Notes on the derivation of results are included in Appendix 11.1.

11.3.1. Conceptual notions

The paper and comment by Solow and Samuelson [7, 24] first introduced the concept of relative stability. Furuya and Inada [15] formulated the problem in the way we shall adopt here. Fisher [25] corrected certain errors in the Furuya-Inada article. Before a full-scale discussion can be presented, we shall introduce the following definitions:

(1) *Intertemporal efficiency of order N.*   Starting from a given input vector x^1, if we follow a given time path and in N periods arrive at an output vector y^N such that no alternative path can yield an alternative output vector η^N at N, where $\eta^N > y^N$, then the first path is intertemporally efficient of order N.

(2) *Intertemporal efficiency of the infinite order.*   An infinite path $x^1 y^1 y^2 \ldots$ $y^N \ldots$ such that for all N the subpath from x^1 to y^N is intertemporally efficient of order N is said to be intertemporally efficient of the infinite order.

(3) *Relative stability.*   If

$$\lim_{N \to \infty} \frac{y_i^N}{(y^N \cdot y^N)^{1/2}} = \bar{y}_i^\infty \quad \text{for } i = 1, \ldots, n$$

then y is relatively stable. The factor $(y^N \cdot y^N)^{1/2}$ is the vector length. The dividing out of such a factor makes all resultant vectors of equal unit length and hence facilitates comparison. Literally, it means that the ray through a given variable point approaches asymptotically a given ray (a von Neumann ray in our case).

The relative stability theorem states that under proper conditions, any intertemporally efficient path of infinite order is relatively stable; in fact, it approaches a von Neumann ray; from each initial position, there exists a unique intertemporally efficient infinite path.

11.3.2. Formulation

A. ASSUMPTIONS

The Furuya-Inada formulation starts with a set of assumptions somewhat weaker than the assumptions about the von Neumann model we quoted earlier. Specifically, T is still assumed to be a closed, convex (superadditive in their terminology) cone. The "no output is producible from zero output" assumption is adopted instead of assumption (3) above. Costless disposal (assumption (2) above) is replaced by "any non-negative inputs can produce some non-negative inputs." Assumption (4) above (every good is producible) is skipped, but something stronger is introduced later. All these slight weakenings of assumptions do not lead to much significant generalization. For all practical purposes, we discuss the Furuya-Inada theory on the foundation of assumptions (1)–(4) of Section 11.1.

The important results of Furuya and Inada are obtained from two further assumptions:

(12) An output vector with all positive components can be produced from any semipositive input vectors in a finite number of periods. Symbolically, there exists $n' \leq n$ such that starting from any semipositive x^1 one can initiate an n'-period path to reach a vector η with all components positive.

Assumption (12) implies both assumptions (4) and (5) above. Its full strength will be seen later.

(13) The technology T is "strongly superadditive" in the terminology of Furuya and Inada. When two input vectors are not proportional to each other,[19] the weighted average of the inputs can produce more than the weighted average of the outputs.

Assumption (13) implies assumption (8), where there exists only one value-preserving process.

B. RESULTS

(1) Under assumptions (1)–(4) and (12), it is possible to show that
(a) Every von Neumann process exhibits balanced growth.
(b) Every von Neumann process can be associated with a price vector with all prices positive.

Roughly speaking, assumption (12) implies that every output has a positive opportunity cost in terms of any other alternative output. Therefore, if for a von Neumann process (x^*, y^*), $y^* = \mu^* x^* + \eta$, where η contains some positive and some zero components, it is always possible to find another process that curtails the growth factor of those commodities in (x^*, y^*) in excess of the von Neumann growth factor μ^* in favor of others. This entails an expansion ratio higher than μ^*, which is impossible. Therefore, η must be a null vector.

Also we note that a certain good is destined to be a free good under the von

[19]The proviso is needed to retain constant returns.

Neumann prices if that good grows at a rate faster than μ^* in the von Neumann process. When any unbalanced von Neumann process is ruled out, it is then always possible to select a positive price system.

(2) Under assumptions (1)–(4), (12), and (13), it can be proved that:

(a) Paths that are intertemporally efficient of the infinite order approach asymptotically the von Neumann ray.

(b) From each initial input vector there exists a unique intertemporally efficient path of infinite order.

The heuristic basis of result (2a) is almost self-evident. The same assumptions would validate the Radner version of the turnpike theorem. Every optimal path under the turnpike formulation has to arc toward the von Neumann path until the penultimate stage before branching out. If the penultimate stage is indefinitely postponed, the efficient paths approach ever more closely to the von Neumann ray and we obtain the relative stability theorem.

The reasons behind result (2b) are only slightly subtler. In the turnpike problem, the efficient path that starts from a given position and ends on a particular ray at a particular instant T must be unique, under "strong superadditivity." Otherwise, an intermediary path will do better than either. Replacing the terminal ray by the von Neumann ray and postponing the terminal condition at N into a transversality condition asymptotically attained at infinity, we obtain the uniqueness theorem for the intertemporally efficient infinite path.

11.3.3. Significance

Over the years, few applications have been made of the relative stability theorem in optimal growth theory. However, the future may well hold greater promise for this theorem. The turnpike theorem is a theorem about definite future requirements. In period N, one should have as much as possible of certain capital stocks in proportion to the $\tilde{y}$ ray. The relative stability theorem is applicable for a world with uncertain requirements at an unspecified time. Preparedness dictates that capital cumulation paths should go close to the von Neumann ray, in anticipation of any contingent needs of whatever form and at whatever moment. As more and more economic research is devoted to the implications of uncertainty, we venture to guess that the relative stability theorem will gain more and more attention relative to theorems of the turnpike family.

APPENDIX 11.1

Outline of the proofs for the results in Section 11.3.2–B

Proof of result (1a). Suppose the result were false. There exists, then, a von Neumann process (x^*, y^*) and the von Neumann growth factor μ^* such that

$$y^* = \mu^* x^* + \eta \qquad \text{with } \eta \text{ semipositive}$$

From assumption (12), there exists an n'-period path leading from η to ξ, the latter having all components positive. By costless disposal, there exists an n'-period path from η to ψx^* for some $\psi > 0$. By the same token, from $\mu^* x^*$, we can obtain $(\mu^*)^2 x^*$ in the next period, ..., up to $(\mu^*)^{n'+1} x^*$ in the n' periods. By convexity and linearity, from $\mu^* x^* + \eta = y^*$ we can obtain $[(\mu^*)^{n'+1} + \psi] x^*$ in n' periods. Hence, starting from x^* we can reach $[(\mu^*)^{n'+1} + \psi] x^*$ in $(n'+1)$ periods, or $(\bar{\mu})^{n'+1} x^*$ in $(n'+1)$ periods, where

$$\bar{\mu} = [(\mu^*)^{n'+1} + \psi]^{1/(n'+1)}$$

and, hence, $\bar{\mu} > \mu^*$.

This implies that there exist $(n'+1)$ processes $(x^1, y^1), \ldots, (x^{n'+1}, y^{n'+1})$ in T where $x^1 = x^*$, $y^t \geq x^{t+1}, t = 2, \ldots, n'$ and $y^{n'+1} = (\bar{\mu})^{n'+1} x^*$.

Due to the fact that T is a convex cone, the weighted sum of input vectors can produce the weighted sum of output vectors. Now multiplying the tth input and output by the factor $(\bar{\mu})^{1-t}$ and summing up, we obtain

$$(x^0, y^0) = \left\{ \bar{\mu}\left(\frac{x^1}{\bar{\mu}} + \frac{x^2}{(\bar{\mu})^2} + \cdots + \frac{x^{n'+1}}{(\bar{\mu})^{n'+1}} \right), \bar{\mu}\left(\frac{y^1}{\bar{\mu}} + \frac{y^2}{(\bar{\mu})^2} + \cdots + \frac{y^{n'+1}}{(\bar{\mu})^{n'+1}} \right) \right\} \text{ is in } T$$

Now,

$$y^0 \geq \bar{\mu}\left(\frac{x^2}{\bar{\mu}} + \frac{x^3}{(\bar{\mu})^2} + \cdots + \frac{x^{n'+1}}{(\bar{\mu})^{n'}} + \frac{(\bar{\mu})^{n'+1} x^*}{(\bar{\mu})^{n'+1}} \right) \qquad \text{(since } y^t \geq x^{t+1})$$

$$= \bar{\mu}\left(x^1 + \frac{x^2}{\bar{\mu}} + \frac{x^3}{(\bar{\mu})^2} + \cdots + \frac{x^{n'+1}}{(\bar{\mu})^{n'}} \right) \qquad \text{(since } x^* = x^1)$$

$$= \bar{\mu} x^0$$

Hence,

$$\mu(x^0, y^0) \geq \bar{\mu} > \mu^*$$

which contradicts the definition of μ^*. This completes the proof.

Proof of result (1b). Applying result (1a) to the proof of result (3) in Section 11.1.2-B, we note that the only point of intersection between Z and P is the origin. Now, we may consider all points $z = y - \mu^* x$ such that (x, y) is in T, regardless of whether x is in the simplex S'. The resultant set $\tilde{Z}$ is clearly a cone containing Z. Yet it still contains no point of P other than the origin. We now invoke a separation theorem of Koopmans [22, pp. 91–92]: "If two closed cones intersect only at their common vertex, and one cone (P) does not contain an entire line, a separating hyperplane H exists that intersects the particular cone mentioned only at its origin."

Hence, all the unit vectors in P have strictly positive values according to the price system. This implies that all prices are positive in that price vector normal to H. The proof is now complete.

Proof of result (2a). The whole proof is largely parallel to our proof of the Radner turnpike theorem in Section 11.2.3-B. We shall show that for any $\delta > 0$ there exists N_δ such that no intertemporally efficient path of infinite order can afford to be outside a δ cone of the von Neumann ray for more than N_δ periods.

We shall first prove that any process outside a δ cone from the unique von Neumann ray incurs a periodic loss. Under the assumption of a strictly convex cone T [assumption (13)], only the von Neumann process can break even. Suppose the contrary; then both (x^*, y^*) and (x^0, y^0) in T break even with (x^0, y^0) not proportional to (x^*, y^*). Strong superadditivity then implies that for any λ, $0 < \lambda < 1$, there exists (x^λ, y^λ) in T such that $x^\lambda = \lambda x^* + (1 - \lambda) x^0$ and $y^\lambda - [\lambda y^* + (1 - \lambda) y^0]$ has all components positive. Since p has all positive elements from result (1b) above,

$$p^* \cdot (y^\lambda - \mu^* x^\lambda) > \lambda p^* \cdot (y^* - \mu^* \cdot x^*) + (1 - \lambda) \cdot p^* (y^0 - \mu^* \cdot x^0) = 0$$

But this contradicts the definition of p^*. In fact, in the above derivation, we have also ruled out the possibility of multiple von Neumann processes. Hence, we have deduced assumption (8)—the uniqueness of the "value-preserving" process.

Let us revert back to the present-value technology of Section 11.2.2-A. As in the proof of the Radner version of the turnpike theorem, we may again use the concept $\theta(\delta)$, which is the minimum loss ratio per period for processes outside the δ cone of the von Neumann ray.

We next note that due to assumption (12), starting from any non-null input vector one can reach the von Neumann ray in at most n periods. Also starting from the von Neumann ray, one can reach any other ray in at most n periods. The maximum value loss ratio in the path starting from any arbitrary input x^1 and ending on an arbitrary ray $\tilde{y}$ via the von Neumann turnpike can be calculated.

We note that the straight-down-the-turnpike path mentioned above can be written as

$$\underbrace{x^1 \to \pi_n(x^1)x^*}_{n \text{ periods}} : \underbrace{\pi_n(x^1)x^* \to \pi_n(x^1)x^*}_{\substack{\text{certain number of} \\ \text{periods, say } (N-2n)}} : \underbrace{\pi_n(x^1)x^* \to [\pi_n(x^1)/\phi_n(\tilde{y})]\tilde{y}}_{n \text{ periods}}$$

No value loss can occur in the middle arc along the x^* ray, so the value loss ratio is simply

$$\left(1 - \frac{\pi_n(x^1)}{\phi_n(\tilde{y})} \frac{p^* \cdot \tilde{y}}{p^* \cdot x^1}\right) = 1 - C(x^1, \tilde{y}) < 1 \qquad \text{for } x^1, \tilde{y} \text{ in } S'$$

The universal accessibility postulated under assumption (12) implies that $\phi_n < \infty$ and $\pi_n > 0$ for all x^1 and $\tilde{y}$. Since all prices are positive, $p^* \cdot \tilde{y} > 0$ and $p^* \cdot x^1 > 0$. Hence, $C > 0$. Due to the closedness of T, we can calculate

$$\bar{C} = \underset{x^1, \tilde{y} \in S}{\text{Min }} C(x^1, \tilde{y})$$

We now define

$$N_\delta = \text{Int}\left[\ln \bar{C}/\ln \{1 - \theta(\delta)\}\right] + 1$$

which is a positive, finite number, dependent only on δ.

We can then show that any infinite path cannot stay outside the δ cone from x^* for N_δ or more periods and still be intertemporally efficient of infinite order.

Suppose that this is not true and that the N_δth time the path strays outside the δ cone happens in the $(N-1)$ period. Define $y^N = \lambda \tilde{y}$. Then we should not be able to construct an N-period path from x^1 and attain $\bar{\lambda}\tilde{y}$ with $\bar{\lambda} > \lambda$. However, following the N-period straight-down-the-turnpike path alluded to before to reach $\bar{\lambda}\tilde{y}$, we find that the value loss is

$$1 - \frac{\bar{\lambda}p^* \cdot \tilde{y}}{p^* \cdot x^1} = 1 - C(x^1, \tilde{y}) \le 1 - \bar{C}$$

The value loss following the infinite path is

$$1 - \frac{\lambda p^* \cdot \tilde{y}}{p^* \cdot x^1} \ge 1 - \{1 - \theta(\delta)\}^{N_\delta}$$

$$> 1 - \{1 - \theta(\delta)\}^{\ln \bar{C}/\ln \{1 - \theta(\delta)\}}$$

But $\bar{C} = \{1 - \theta(\delta)\}^{\ln \bar{C}/\ln\{1 - \theta(\delta)\}}$, as one can easily prove by taking logarithms. Hence,

$$1 - \frac{\bar{\lambda}p^* \cdot \tilde{y}}{p^* \cdot x^1} < 1 - \frac{\lambda p^* \cdot \tilde{y}}{p^* \cdot x^1}$$

indicating that $\bar{\lambda} > \lambda$, which is a contradiction. This completes the proof. Since there can be only a finite number of periods for which the infinite path is outside the δ cone about x^*, eventually, after those exceptional periods, the path must be within every δ cone about x^*.

Proof of result (2b).   This proof can be divided into two parts:
(1) Were there two intertemporally efficient infinite paths starting from the same x^1, both would approach the same limit $\pi(x^1)x^*$.
(2) It then would be possible to construct a third path that would approach a limit $\bar{\pi}x^*$ with $\bar{\pi} > \pi(x^1)$.

The proofs of these will be illustrated with diagrams so that the rigorous proof can be grasped even by the less analytically inclined reader. First we shall concentrate on the present-value technology T', where the maximal balanced growth rate is normalized to $\mu^* = 1$.

Proof of (1). Suppose that there exist two distinct (intertemporally) efficient (infinite) paths starting at period $m+1$. We can always set m equal to 1, and $x^m = x^1$ would represent the last common point of the two paths. Call the two paths $(x^1, u^2, u^3, \ldots)$ and $(x^1, v^2, v^3, \ldots)$. By result (2a), both approach the unique von Neumann path. In the present-value technology, let us denote the limits as $\pi_u x^*$ and $\pi_v x^*$, respectively. We shall show that $\pi_u = \pi_v$. Otherwise, one must be larger, and without losing generality we may assume that $\pi_u < \pi_v$. For any $\varepsilon > 0$, no matter how small ε is, eventually the u sequence will be inside the ε sphere about $\pi_u x^*$ and the v sequence will be inside the ε sphere about $\pi_v x^*$. Let us suppose that by period $N - n$ both sequences have entered forever

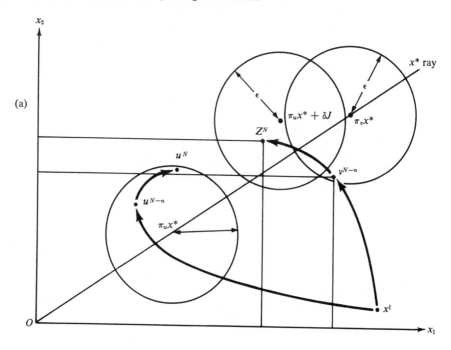

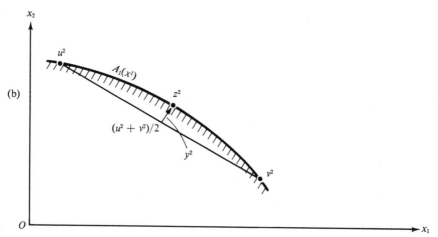

FIGURE 11.12 (a) v^{N-n} provides more of x_1 but less of x_2 than u^N. But the $x^1-v^{N-n}-z^N$ sequence ends up with more of both x_1 and x_2 than any point in the ε sphere about $\pi_u x^*$ and hence dominates u^N.

(b) "Strong superadditivity" of T' implies strict convexity of the $A_1(x^1)$ frontier (one-period production frontier). Hence, one can use the same input x^1 and get more than the average output: $(u^2 + v^2)/2$. The excess, z^2, can then be used to produce δx^* in at most n steps due to assumption (12).

their respective ε spheres.[20] The smaller the value of ε, the larger N must be. The values of N and ε will be decided later. One may now define three new subsequences:

$$w^t = \frac{\pi_u}{\pi_v} v^t \qquad t = N-n, N-n+1, \ldots, N$$

$$y^t = \left(1 - \frac{\pi_u}{\pi_v}\right) v^t, \quad (y^t, y^{t+1}) \text{ in } T', \quad t = N-n, N-n+1, \ldots, N-1, y^N = \delta J$$
$$\text{where } J = (1, 1, \ldots, 1)$$

$$z^t = w^t + y^t \qquad t = N-n, N-n+1, \ldots, N$$

From the fact that T' is a cone, the w^t sequence, being a scaling down of the v sequence, is a feasible sequence approaching $\pi_u x^*$. From assumption (12), the n-period sequence from y^{N-n} to δJ is also feasible. From the convexity of T', $(z^t, z^{t+1}, \ldots)$ is also feasible since the sum of feasible input vectors can support the sum of the corresponding output vectors. The z sequence approaches $\pi_u x^* + \delta J$ as a limit, and z^N is within the ε sphere about the latter point. Selecting $\varepsilon = \delta/2$, we now know that z^N must provide more of every good than u^N. Hence, the u sequence is inefficient. This contradicts our premises that the u sequence is efficient. So π_u must be equal to π_v.

All these are illustrated in Figure 11.12a.

Proof of (2). Suppose that both the u sequence and the v sequence are efficient and (due to (1)) approach the common limit $\pi(x^1) x^*$. Because of strong superadditivity there exists a point z^2 such that (x^1, z^2) is in T' and $z^2 = \frac{1}{2}(u^2 + v^2) + y^2$ where y^2 contains some positive components. (This is shown in Figure 11.12b.) We again define three new sequences:

$$w^t = \frac{1}{2}(u^t + v^t) \qquad t = 2, \ldots$$

$$y^t \text{ such that } (y^t, y^{t+1}) \text{ is in } T', \quad t = 2, \ldots, n+1, \quad \text{and} \quad y^{n+2} = y^{n+3} = \ldots = \delta x^* \text{ for some } \delta > 0 \cdot$$

$$z^t = w^t + y^t, t = 2, \ldots, n+2, n+3 \ldots$$

Due to the fact that T' is a convex cone, all these are feasible. Now,

$$\underset{t \to \infty}{\text{Lim}} z^t = \underset{t \to \infty}{\text{Lim}} w^t + \underset{t \to \infty}{\text{Lim}} y^t$$

$$= \frac{1}{2}[\pi(x^1)x^* + \pi(x^1)x^*] + \delta x^*$$

$$= [\pi(x^1) + \delta]x^*$$

$$= \bar{\pi} x^*$$

with $\bar{\pi} > \pi(x^1)$

Noting that $(x^1, z^2, z^3, \ldots)$ is a feasible sequence, we conclude that $\bar{\pi} > \pi(x^1)$ contradicts the definition of $\pi(x^1)$. Hence, there cannot be two intertemporally efficient infinite paths emanating from a common initial point x^1. This completes the proof.

REFERENCES

[1] von Neumann, John, "A Model of General Economic Equilibrium," *Review of Economic Studies*, vol. XIII, 1945–46, pp. 1–9.

[2] Georgescu-Roegen, Nicholas, "The Aggregate Linear Production Function and Its Applications to von Neumann's Economic Model," in *Activity Analysis of Production and Allocation*, T. C. Koopmans, Ed., Wiley, New York, 1951.

[3] Gale, David, "The Closed Linear Model of Production," in *Linear Inequalities and Related Systems*, H. Kuhn and A. W. Tucker, Eds., Princeton University Press, Princeton, N.J., 1956.

[4] Karlin, Samuel, *Mathematical Methods and Theory in Games, Programming and Economics*, Addison-Wesley, Reading, Mass., 1959.

[5] Dorfman, Robert, P. A. Samuelson, and R. M. Solow, *Linear Programming and Economic Analysis*, McGraw-Hill, New York, 1958.

[20] By selecting an arbitrarily large N, one can make ε arbitrarily small.

[6] Samuelson, P. A., "Efficient Paths of Capital Accumulation in Terms of the Calculus of Variations," in *Mathematical Methods in the Social Sciences, 1959*, K. J. Arrow, S. Karlin, and P. Suppes, Eds., Stanford University Press, Stanford, Calif., 1960.

[7] Solow, R. M., and P. A. Samuelson, "Balanced Growth Under Constant Return to Scale," *Econometrica*, vol. XXI, July 1954, pp. 412–24.

[8] Morishima, M., "Prices and the Turnpike. II. Proof of a Turnpike Theorem: the No Joint Product Case," *Review of Economic Studies*, vol. XXVIII, Feb. 1961, pp. 89–97.

[9] Morishima, M., *Equilibrium, Stability and Growth*, Oxford University Press, Oxford, 1965.

[10] Radner, Roy, "Paths of Economic Growth That Are Optimal with Regard Only to Final States: A Turnpike Theorem," *Review of Economic Studies*, vol. XXVIII, Feb. 1961, pp. 98–104.

[11] Nikaido, H., "Persistence of Continual Growth near the von Neumann Ray: A Strong Version of the Radner Turnpike Theorem," *Econometrica*, vol. XXXII, Jan.–April 1964, pp. 151–62.

[12] McKenzie, L. W., "The Dorfman-Samuelson-Solow Turnpike Theorem," *International Economic Review*, vol. IV, Jan. 1963, pp. 29–43.

[13] McKenzie, L. W., "Turnpike Theorems for a Generalized Leontief Model," *Econometrica*, vol. XXXI, Jan.–April 1963, pp. 165–80.

[14] McKenzie, L. W., "The Turnpike Theorem of Morishima," *Review of Economic Studies*, vol. XXX, Oct. 1963, pp. 169–76.

[15] Furuya, H., and K. Inada, "Balanced Growth and Intertemporal Efficiency in Capital Accumulation," *International Economic Review*, vol. III, Jan. 1962, pp. 94–101.

[16] Inada, K., "Some Structural Characteristics of Turnpike Theorems," *Review of Economic Studies*, vol. XXXI, Jan. 1964, pp. 43–58.

[17] Koopmans, T. C., "Economic Growth at a Maximal Rate," *Quarterly Journal of Economics*, vol. LXXVIII, Aug. 1964, pp. 239–94.

[18] Winter, S. G., Jr., "Some Properties of the Closed Linear Model of Production," *International Economic Review*, vol. VI, May 1965, pp. 199–210.

[19] Winter, S. G., Jr., "The Norm of a Closed Technology and the Straight-Down-the-Turnpike Theorem," *Review of Economic Studies*, vol. XXXIV, Jan. 1967, pp.

[20] McKenzie, L. W., "Accumulation Programs of Maximal Utility," in *Value, Capital and Growth*, J. N. Wolfe, Ed., Aldine, Chicago, 1968.

[21] Hadley, George, *Linear Algebra*, Addison-Wesley, Reading, Mass., 1961.

[22] Koopmans, T. C., *Three Essays on the State of Economic Science*, McGraw-Hill, New York, 1957.

[23] Debreu, G., and I. N. Herstein, "Nonnegative Square Matrices," *Econometrica*, vol. XXI, Oct. 1953, pp. 597–607.

[24] Solow, R. M., and P. A. Samuelson, "A Brief Comment," *Econometrica*, vol. XXII, Oct. 1954, p. 504.

[25] Fisher, F. M., "A Comment," *International Economic Review*, vol. IV, May 1963, pp. 232–34.

Appendix

a mathematical review

The bulk of our text relies primarily on the Solow version of the fundamental dynamic equation, a broad understanding of which requires only elementary calculus and the *total product of capital* curve of undergraduate micro theory. We have taken pains to reduce and transform the dynamic relations in other models back to the fundamental equation. Hence, a large portion of Chapters 4 through 10 can be understood on the strength of one's familiarity with the total product of capital diagram alone.

However, this appendix is intended as a useful reference for those readers interested in more details of certain topics in the text. For those specializing in growth theory it represents a rather self-contained tool kit to be used toward a more exhaustive comprehension of the text. Every result presented here is directly useful at one point or another.

No attempt is made to present material rigorously, and certain results are stated without proof. In these cases, however, the reader is directed to suitable references. Some results are justified graphically rather than by analytical proof. Exercises are provided to help in the development of operational skills.

A.1 PRELIMINARY AND MISCELLANEOUS TOPICS

A.1.1. Differentiating an integral with respect to a parameter

1. **Problem.** Evaluate $\partial I/\partial r$ where $I = \int_{T_1(r)}^{T_2(r)} F(r, t)dt$, with T_1, T_2, and F possessing continuous derivatives.

2. **Formula.**

$$\frac{\partial I}{\partial r} = -\frac{dT_1}{dr} F[r, T_1(r)] + \frac{dT_2}{dr} F[r, T_2(r)] + \int_{T_1(r)}^{T_2(r)} \frac{\partial F(r, t)}{\partial r} dt \qquad (A.1)$$

3. **Justification.** The quantity I can be graphically represented in Figure A.1 as the area under the F curve between $T_1(r)$ and $T_2(r)$. A change of value of r, to $(r+h)$, say, will exert three types of influence on I: (i) the movement of the lower limit (of integration) from $T_1(r)$ to $T_1(r+h)$, (ii) a movement of the upper limit from $T_2(r)$ to $T_2(r+h)$, and (iii) a shift of the height of the entire curve from $F(r, t)$ to $F(r+h, t)$ at each t. Any increase in T_2 or $F(r, t)$ increases I and any increase in T_1 decreases I. Hence for h taking small values, ΔI is approximately:

$$-\Delta T_1 F[r, T_1(r)] + \Delta T_2 F[r, T_2(r)] + \int_{T_1(r)}^{T_2(r)} \Delta F(r, t)dt$$

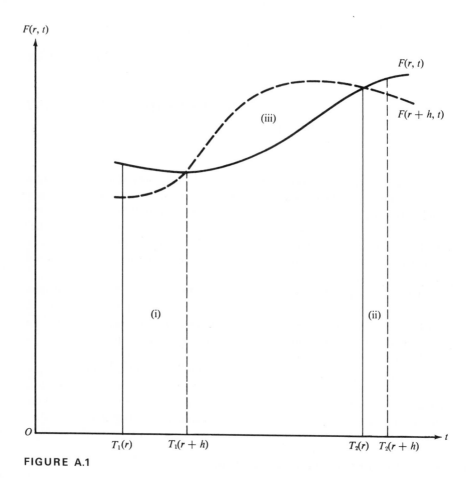

FIGURE A.1

with the three terms represented by the areas marked (i), (ii), and (iii), respectively. Thus, $\Delta I = $ (ii) + (iii) − (i). Dividing by h and letting h approach zero, one obtains the formula.

4. Comment. This formula is very useful in computing the present worth of an investment or lifetime income stream in Chapters 5 and 6.

A.1.2. Constrained maximization: Lagrange multiplier: equality case

PROBLEM I

1. Statement of the problem.

$$\text{Max } c(v, k_2) \tag{A.2}$$

subject to

$$F(v, k_1, k_2) = 0$$

Determine the necessary conditions for a maximum.

2. Formula. Setting $\Lambda = c(v, k_2) - \lambda F(v, k_1, k_2)$ where Λ is called the Lagrangian function and λ is called the Lagrange multiplier, the necessary conditions are:

$$0 = \left\{ \begin{array}{c} \dfrac{\partial \Lambda}{\partial v} \\[2mm] \dfrac{\partial \Lambda}{\partial k_1} \\[2mm] \dfrac{\partial \Lambda}{\partial k_2} \\[2mm] \dfrac{\partial \Lambda}{\partial \lambda} \end{array} \right\} = \left\{ \begin{array}{c} \dfrac{\partial c}{\partial v} - \lambda \dfrac{\partial F}{\partial v} \\[2mm] -\lambda \dfrac{\partial F}{\partial k_1} \\[2mm] \dfrac{\partial c}{\partial k_2} - \lambda \dfrac{\partial F}{\partial k_2} \\[2mm] F(v, k_1, k_2) \end{array} \right\} \tag{A.3}$$

3. Justification. In the three-dimensional space for v, k_1, and k_2, the constraint $F = 0$ is represented by a bulging surface, S, while the iso-value contour loci can be represented by concentric cylinders. Only the highest attainable member is shown in Figure A.2. The optimal point at (v^*, k_1^*, k_2^*) is characterized by three necessary conditions:
  (1) The vertical line VV' through the optimal point is tangential to S (i.e., $\partial F/\partial k_1 = 0$).
  (2) There is a tangent line TT' common to S and the locus $c(v, k_2) = $ Max and perpendicular to VV' [i.e., $(\partial F/\partial v)/(\partial F/\partial k_2) = (\partial c/\partial v)/(\partial c/\partial k_2)$].
  (3) The optimal point is on S [i.e., $F(v^*, k_1^*, k_2^*) = 0$].
Conditions (1) and (3) correspond to the second and fourth conditions in (A.3). Solving for λ from the first and third conditions in (A.3) and equating the two, we get result (2) above.

4. Comment. The problem posed is actually the determination of a two-sector golden rule path (Section 10.2) in disguise. The fact that the number of variables in the constraint may be unequal to the number of variables in the optimand makes our version slightly more general than those in ordinary texts. The formula applies with any number of variables and constraints, *mutatis mutandis*.

PROBLEM II

1. Statement of the problem.

$$\text{Max} \int_0^T u[c(t)] \, dt \tag{A.4}$$

subject to

$$\int_0^T E[c(t), w, r, t] \, dt = 0$$

2. Formula. Setting $\Lambda = \int_0^T \{u[c(t)] - \lambda E[c(t), w, r, t]\} dt$, we obtain the necessary conditions:

$$0 = \frac{du[c(t)]}{dc(t)} - \lambda \left\{ \frac{\partial E[c(t), w, r, t]}{\partial c(t)} \right\} \quad \text{for all } t \text{ between 0 and } T \tag{A.5}$$

$$0 = \int_0^T E[c(t), w, r, t] \, dt$$

3. Comment. This is the optimal lifetime consumption stream problem (Section 6.1) in disguise, where the constraint is the generalized budget condition. Infinitely many variables are involved here. The first equation can be formally deduced from differentiating Λ partially by $c(t)$. More rigorously, we can treat this as a degenerate calculus of variations problem. From (A.5), we can deduce $c(t)$ as a function dependent not only on t but also on parameters w and r.

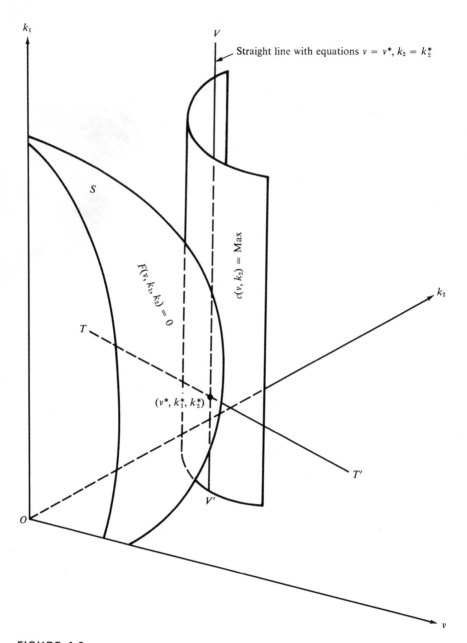

FIGURE A.2

A.1.3. Constrained maximization; duality; complementary slackness—inequality case

1. Statement of the problem.

$$\text{Max } G(k_1) \quad \text{where } G \text{ is differentiable} \tag{A.6}$$

subject to:

$$0 \le k_1 \le k \qquad k \text{ being given}$$

2. Transformation of the problem. We shall first consider a generalized problem with a and b as the parametric values for the lower and upper limits of the range of k_1. Later we shall set a equal to 0 and b equal to k.

We shall now take a different point of view. Define:

$$M(a, b) = \text{Max } G(k_1) \qquad \text{with } a \le k_1 \le b \text{ and } G \text{ continuous in } k_1$$

Here we regard the highest attainable value of G as potentially dependent upon the range of choice: interval $[a, b]$.[1] In Figure A.3e, for instance, an increase of b to $b + h$ enables an increase of M by ΔM. Define also,

$$\lambda_a = \frac{\partial M(a, b)}{\partial a} \quad \text{and} \quad \lambda_b = \frac{\partial M(a, b)}{\partial b} \tag{A.7}$$

Obviously, an increase in a decreases the range of choice for k_1 and an increase in b increases it. The attainable maximum cannot be increased (decreased) if the range of choice narrows (broadens). Hence, we have:

$$\lambda_a \le 0 \le \lambda_b$$

This is illustrated by the five cases in Figure A.3. For cases (a) and (e) the optimum value k_1 falls on the boundary and the shifting of a or b does affect the highest attainable level of $G(M)$. For case (c), an interior maximum for G occurs and small changes of a and b are irrelevant for the determination of M. Note, however, even when we have boundary maxima as in cases (b) and (d), an infinitesimal change of a or b has no effect on $M(a, b)$.[2]

We may also note the position of the optimal k_1, i.e., k_1^*, in the five cases. The G function is depicted as concave ("diminishing returns" in economic terms). However, if G is nonconcave, the only novelty is that the optimal values of k_1 may be non-unique. When G is strictly concave, the above quinchotomy is both mutually exclusive and exhaustive for all nontrivial cases (i.e., $a < b$).

We shall now form the generalized Lagrangian function (along the lines of Kuhn-Tucker):

$$\Lambda = G(k_1) - \lambda_a(k_1 - a) + \lambda_b(b - k_1) \tag{A.8}$$

$$= G(k_1) - \lambda_a y_a + \lambda_b y_b$$

where $y_a = k_1 - a$ and $y_b = b - k_1$. y_a^*, y_b^* will denote these variables evaluated at $k_1 = k_1^*$.

3. Duality, complementary slackness condition, and necessary conditions for constrained maximization. We have from (A.6) and (A.8):

(1) The duality relations:

$$\frac{\partial \Lambda}{\partial \lambda_a} = -y_a \le 0 \qquad \frac{\partial \Lambda}{\partial y_a} = -\lambda_a \ge 0$$

$$\frac{\partial \Lambda}{\partial \lambda_b} = y_b \ge 0 \qquad \frac{\partial \Lambda}{\partial y_b} = \lambda_b \ge 0 \tag{A.9}$$

These are true by the definitions of Λ, y_a, and y_b. A certain symmetry (explained below) between y_a

[1] In defining G as the highest attainable magnitude, k_1 takes an optimal value. Hence M is no longer a function of k_1.

[2] Strictly speaking, the effect is of second-order smallness.

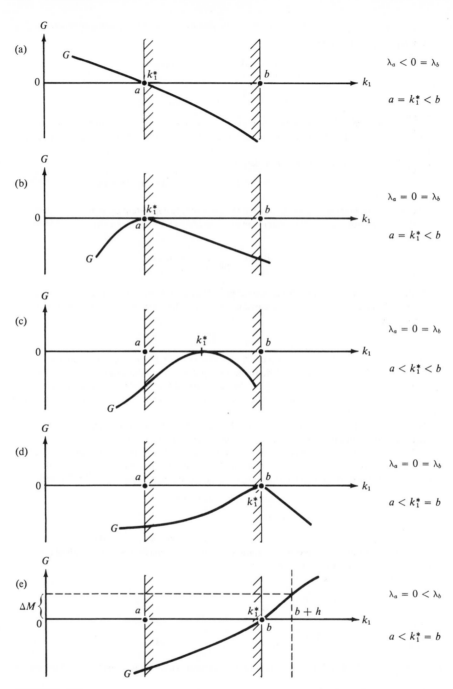

FIGURE A.3

and λ_a (and y_b and λ_b) gives rise to the appelation of duality. In consequence, λ_a and λ_b are also called dual (adjoint) variables.

(2) The complementary slackness conditions:

$$\lambda_a \neq 0, \text{ then } y_a^* = 0; \qquad y_a^* \neq 0, \text{ then } \lambda_a = 0$$
$$\lambda_b \neq 0, \text{ then } y_b^* = 0; \qquad y_b^* \neq 0, \text{ then } \lambda_b = 0 \qquad \text{(A.10)}$$

These are seen from Figure A.3 and the definitions of y_a^*, y_b^*.

Hence,

$$\lambda_a y_a^* = 0 = \lambda_b y_b^*$$

But beware that the fact that y_a^* (or y_b^*) = 0 never entitles us to deduce that λ_a (or λ_b) $\neq$ 0. Similarly, the vanishing of the adjoint variable(s) λ_a, λ_b does not imply the nonvanishing of the corresponding slack variables. See Figure A.3b and d, where $\lambda_a = 0 = y_a^*$ and $\lambda_b = 0 = y_b^*$, respectively.

The best aid to memorization is: Plotting the absolute value of a dual variable ($|\lambda|$) against the absolute value of its corresponding slack variable ($|y|$), the graph is an L-shaped locus coinciding with the axes. In other words, at least one of the two is zero and both cannot be nonzero.

(3) $\partial \Lambda / \partial k_1 = 0$ at the optimal position. This is actually a back-handed way to define λ_a and λ_b when they are nonzero. They take such values as make the equation valid. This equation and the complementary slackness conditions together form the necessary conditions for an optimum. When G is concave they are also sufficient.

4. Comment.   The above concepts are related to both linear programming and Pontryagin's maximum principle, which follow. These latter are important tools in Appendix 7.1 and Sections 10.2 and 11.2. We assumed that the so-called constraint qualification condition is met. Otherwise, the aforementioned conditions may not be necessary (see (2) in Section A.6).

A.2 DIFFERENCE EQUATIONS

A.2.1. Basic concepts and classifications

BASIC CONCEPTS

Consider a sequence of numbers or vectors: $Q(\cdot) = \{Q(0), Q(1), \ldots\}$. If there exists a function relating any term $Q(t)$ to its n preceding terms and the index t—for example,

$$Q(t) = \bar{F}[Q(t-1), Q(t-2), \ldots, Q(t-n), t] \qquad \text{for all } t \qquad \text{(A.11)}$$

then Equation (A.11) is said to be a *difference equation characterizing the sequence* $Q(\cdot)$.

Starting from the other end, if by empirical observation or theoretical deduction we have obtained (A.11), and there exists a sequence $Q(\cdot)$ such that for *any* $(n+1)$ *successive terms* in $Q(\cdot)$, Equation (A.11) is satisfied, then this *sequence* is a *solution for the difference equation* (A.11). For an algebraic equation, the solution is a number. For a difference equation, the solution is a sequence.

The maximum number of successive preceding terms required to predict $Q(t)$ is called the *order* of the equation. Equation (A.11) is of the nth order.

There may be more than one sequence satisfying a difference equation. Usually we are interested in a given solution which assumes certain assigned values: $Q(m_1), \ldots, Q(m_p)$ at periods $m_1, m_2, \ldots, m_p$. These p values are *boundary values*. If the periods $m_1, m_2, \ldots, m_p$ are simply the p succeeding periods starting at period 0 (i.e., $m_1 = 1$, etc.), then these values are called *initial values*. For an nth-order equation, n initial values will characterize uniquely one specific solution. If $p < n$, then we obtain a class of specific solutions but cannot discriminate among them.

CLASSIFICATIONS AND EXAMPLES

We may introduce our discussion with Chart A.1. We can now describe each distinction in turn with examples related to applications appearing in this volume.

1. Vector equations.   Each term in (A.11) (except t) is a vector. The solution is a vector sequence.

CHART A.1

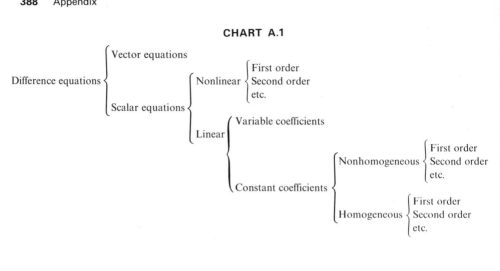

Example:

$$x(t) = Ax(t-1) \qquad \text{say,} \quad x(t) \text{ is } 2 \times 1, \qquad A = \begin{pmatrix} 0.1 & 0.7 \\ 0.9 & 0.3 \end{pmatrix}$$

This appears in the Morishima version of the turnpike theorem mentioned in Chapter 11.

2. Scalar equations. Each term in (A.11) is a number.

3. Nonlinear equations. In this case (A.11) *cannot* take the special form:

$$Q(t) - \left[\sum_{i=1}^{n} a_i(t)Q(t-i) + a_0(t) \right] = 0 \tag{A.12}$$

Example:

$$Z(t) = q \frac{Z(t-1)-1}{Z(t-2)-1} Z(t-2)$$

where q may be a fraction, say, .95. This appeared in Section 1.3.

4. Linear equation. F takes the form of (A.12). Note that only the dependent variable Q has to enter linearly, not the independent variable t. Thus, $Q(t) - .9Q(t-1) = t^2$ is consistent with (A.12).

5. Variable-coefficient linear equation. In this case, not all the terms $a_i(t)$, $i = 1, ..., n$, in (A.12) are constants.

Example:

$$x(t) - tx(t-1) = 0$$

No such equations appear in this volume.

6. Constant-coefficient, nonhomogeneous linear equation. In (A.12), all the $a_i(t)$ terms are constants for $i = 1, ..., n$, except that $a_0(t)$ is not constant.

Example:

$$Q(t) - C_1 Q(t-1) = C_2 C_3{}^t$$

This type of equation appeared both in Section 1.2 concerning the stability of the Harrod model and in Section 5.2 concerning the existence of an equilibrium path in a putty–clay model.

7. Constant-coefficient, homogeneous, linear difference equation.[3] Not only are all $a_i(t)$ constant, but also $a_0 = 0$.

Example:

$$Q(t) = CQ(t-1)$$

This appears in Chapter 1 concerning the Harrod-Domar equilibrium path.

A.2.2. Solutions of difference equations

There exists no standard method for solving nonlinear difference equations. Sometimes problems are solved by using graphical methods. At other times an analytical approach yields the needed insight. Either way, the mode of analysis depends upon the equation we face as well as the questions we want to answer. These analyses usually do not provide a compact formula for the standard term of the solution sequence. But then our economic problems may well be solved without requiring a "closed form" solution.

We shall consider only the constant-coefficient, linear difference equations involving a scalar, which are used in Chapters 1 and 5.

THE SCALER EQUATION

Consider the equation

$$Q(t) - \sum_{i=1}^{n} a_i Q(t-i) = a_0(t)$$

$$= F[Q(t), Q(t-1), ..., Q(t-n)] \tag{A.13}$$

In growth theory, we encounter either the homogeneous case (i.e., $a_0 = 0$) or special subcases of the nonhomogeneous case (i.e., $a_0 \neq 0$) with $a_0(t)$ equal to a or ac^t. We shall consider these in turn.

1. Homogeneous case, where $a_0(t) = 0$.   First let us consider an algebraic equation called an auxiliary equation:

$$F[\lambda^n, \lambda^{n-1}, ..., 1] = \lambda^n - \sum_{i=1}^{n} a_i \lambda^{n-i} \tag{A.14}$$

$$= f(\lambda)$$

$$= 0$$

Equation (A.14) is obtained by replacing $Q(t-i)$ with λ^{n-i} in (A.13) for $i = 0, 1, ..., n$. It has n roots,

---

[3]Readers familiar with the term "homogeneity" in the theory of production functions may wonder how that word is applicable here. This we shall presently examine. Consider a linear difference equation of the form (A.13), where the coefficients may be either constants or functions of the independent variable. We observe that if $Q(t)$ is one of its solution sequences, for arbitrary $m \neq 0$ $mQ(t)$ is also a solution sequence if and only if $a_0(t) = 0$. Rewrite (A.13) to obtain:

$$0 = [Q(t) - \sum_{i=1}^{n} a_i(t)Q(t-i) - a_0(t)] = L$$

where L is of zeroth-order homogeneity in terms of $Q(t), Q(t-1), ..., Q(t-n)$ (in the sense of Euler) if and only if $a_0(t) = 0$. One may also say that F in Equation (A.11) is a *linear homogeneous* function (here, linear means a function homogeneous in the first order) of $Q(t-1), ..., Q(t-n)$, if the difference equation is both linear and homogeneous. But the reverse need not hold. If $\bar{F}$ is a homogeneous function of the first order of $Q(t-1), ..., Q(t-n)$, the difference equation need not be *linear*. For example,

$$Q(t) = \sqrt{Q(t-1)Q(t-2)}$$

say, $\lambda_1, \lambda_2, ..., \lambda_n$. Some of these may be real, some may be complex, some may be repeated, some distinct.

Conclusions:

(a) If λ_j is a root for (A.14), i.e., $f(\lambda_j) = 0$, then the sequence $Q(\cdot) = \{(\lambda_j)^t|t = 0, 1, 2, ...\}$ is a solution for (A.13) with $a_0(t) = 0$.

Proof.

$$F[Q(t), ..., Q(t-n)] = F[\lambda_j^t, ..., \lambda_j^{t-n}]$$

$$= \lambda_j^{t-n}\{\lambda_j^n - \sum_{i=1}^{n} a_i\lambda_j^{n-i}\}$$

$$= \lambda_j^{t-n}f(\lambda_j)$$

$$= (\lambda_j^{t-n})(0)$$

$$= 0 \qquad \text{for all } t$$

(b) If λ_j and λ_k are roots of (A.14), then $Q(t) = (b_j\lambda_j^t + b_k\lambda_k^t)$ is a solution to (A.13).

Proof. Let $Q(\cdot) = \{b_j\lambda_j^t + b_k\lambda_k^t|t = 0, 1, 2, ...\}$.

$$F[Q(t), ..., Q(t-n)] = (b_j\lambda_j^t + b_k\lambda_k^t) - \sum_{i=1}^{n} a_i(b_j\lambda_j^{t-i} + b_k\lambda_k^{t-i})$$

$$= b_j(\lambda_j^t - \sum_{i=1}^{n} a_i\lambda_j^{t-i}) + b_k(\lambda_k^t - \sum_{i=1}^{n} a_i\lambda_k^{t-i})$$

$$= b_j(0) + b_k(0) = 0$$

(c) If f has no repeated root, then the general solution to (A.13) is:

$$Q(t) = \sum_{j=1}^{n} b_j\lambda_j^t \qquad (A.15)$$

Proof. That (A.15) is a solution follows from the procedure proving (b). That all solutions must be of this form follows from the two observations below:

(i) Any nth-order difference equation is uniquely determined by n *initial conditions*. Given the latter, we can generate the whole sequence period by period from the equation.

(ii) For any particular solution with initial conditions $Q(0), ..., Q(n-1)$, we can represent that solution with a sequence of the form (A.15) by solving the b_j's from:

$$\begin{pmatrix} 1 & 1 & ... & 1 \\ \lambda_1 & \lambda_2 & ... & \lambda_n \\ \lambda_1^2 & \lambda_2^2 & ... & \lambda_n^2 \\ \vdots & \vdots & & \vdots \\ \lambda_1^{n-1} & \lambda_2^{n-1} & ... & \lambda_n^{n-1} \end{pmatrix} \begin{pmatrix} b_1 \\ b_2 \\ \vdots \\ b_n \end{pmatrix} = \begin{pmatrix} Q(0) \\ Q(1) \\ Q(2) \\ \vdots \\ Q(n-1) \end{pmatrix} \qquad (A.16)$$

This is possible, since distinct λ_j's imply a nonsingular square matrix.

(d) If the root λ_1 is repeated m times for (A.14), then $(t^{i-1}\lambda_1^t)$ is a solution for (A.13) for $i = 1, ..., m$. The proof is omitted here. This result is not used in this volume, but it does appear in Hick's review article [1] on Harrod's *Toward a Dynamic Economics*.

(e) To determine the specific solution, we have only to set $t = 0, 1, ..., n-1$ and solve the co-efficients b_j by equating the general solution in those periods to the n initial values. The procedure is similar to (A.16).

2. Nonhomogeneous case, where $a_0(t) \neq 0$. (a) *General procedure.* The general solution can be written as: $Q(\cdot) = Q^c(\cdot) + Q^p(\cdot)$, where $Q^c(\cdot)$ the *complementary solution*, satisfies the derived homogeneous equation

$$Q^c(t) - \sum_{i=1}^{n} a_i Q^c(t-i) = 0$$

and $Q^P(\cdot)$, the *particular integral*, satisfies the nonhomogeneous equation

$$Q^P(t) - \sum_{i=1}^{n} a_i Q^P(t-i) = a_0(t)$$

Hence there are three steps in solving the nonhomogeneous equation:
   (1) Obtain any one particular integral (which need not be unique).
   (2) Determine the complementary solution as for the homogeneous case.
   (3) Determine the specific solution we need by solving for the undetermined coefficients in $Q^c(\cdot)$ with the initial conditions.
The basis for this procedure is seen in what follows.

   Let $Q(\cdot)$ be the specific sequence we look for and $Q^P(\cdot)$ be the "particular integral" sequence we obtained. By definition:

$$Q(t) - \sum_{i=1}^{n} a_i Q(t-i) = a_0(t)$$

$$Q^P(t) - \sum_{i=1}^{n} a_i Q^P(t-i) = a_0(t)$$

Subtracting the second from the first, we see that the difference must satisfy the derived homogeneous equation.

   The only new task here is to find the particular integral. We shall only consider the two cases: $a_0(t) = a$ and $a_0(t) = ac^t$.

   (b) *Two useful special cases.*   We can write out the particular integral sequences for the two cases we mentioned:

$a_0(t)$	$Q^P(t)$
a	$a\left(1 - \displaystyle\sum_{i=1}^{n} a_i\right)^{-1}$
ac^t	$a\left(1 - \displaystyle\sum_{i=1}^{n} a_i c^{-i}\right)^{-1} c^t$

The interested reader may verify these by substitution.

   For the special case of first-order difference equations of the form:

$$Q(t) = (1+g)Q(t-1) + ac^t$$

we often try an alternative method in the main text. We write down a sequence of equations:

$$Q(t) \quad - \quad (1+g)Q(t-1) = ac^t$$
$$(1+g)Q(t-1) - (1+g)^2 Q(t-2) = (1+g)ac^{t-1}$$
$$(1+g)^2 Q(t-2) - (1+g)^3 Q(t-3) = (1+g)^2 ac^{t-2}$$
$$\vdots \qquad\qquad \vdots$$
$$(1+g)^{t-1} Q(1) \quad - \quad (1+g)^t Q(0) \quad = (1+g)^{t-1} ac$$

Summing up, we obtain:

$$Q(t) = (1+g)^t Q(0) + a(1+g)^t \left[\frac{c}{1+g} + \left(\frac{c}{1+g}\right)^2 + \ldots \left(\frac{c}{1+g}\right)^t \right]$$

$$= (1+g)^t Q(0) + a(1+g)^t \left(\frac{c}{1+g}\right) \frac{1 - [c/(1+g)]^t}{1 - c/(1+g)}$$

$$= (1+g)^t \left[Q(0) + \frac{ac}{1+g-c} \right] - \frac{ac}{1+g-c} c^t$$

A.2.3. Relative stability

BASIC CONCEPTS

The single most important concept in difference equations as applied to the theory of growth is the *relative stability* concept introduced by Solow and Samuelson.

Consider a solution to a difference equation:

$$Q(t) = Q^e(t) + R(t) \tag{A.17}$$

$$= Q^e(0)\lambda_1^t + R(t)$$

where $Q^e(0)$ has all positive components, $\lambda_1 > 0$, $Q^e(t)$ is the "equilibrium growth" component growing at rate $(\lambda_1 - 1) > -1$, and $R(t)$ is the residual term.

Equilibrium is defined according to some criterion. In the context of a von Neumann model with a unique balanced growth path, the definition of $Q^e(t)$ is natural. In the context of Harrod's model, Jorgenson defined $Q^e(t)$ as the growth path at the warranted rate.

The Solow-Samuelson definition for relative stability is:

$$\text{Lim}_{t \to \infty} [Q_i(t)/Q_i^e(t)] = \text{constant for all } i \tag{A.18}$$

where the subscript i denotes the ith vector component in a vector equation.

AN EXAMPLE

To appreciate the importance of this definition, we may consider the example:

$$Q(t) = (2)^t \binom{1}{1} - (1)^t \binom{0}{1} \qquad \text{with } Q^e(t) = (2)^t \binom{1}{1}$$

The succeeding points in the sequences $Q(\cdot)$ and $Q^e(\cdot)$ are:

t	0	1	2	3	4	...
$Q(t)$	(1, 0)	(2, 1)	(4, 3)	(8, 7)	(16, 15)	...
$Q^e(t)$	(1, 1)	(2, 2)	(4, 4)	(8, 8)	(16, 16)	...

In the traditional sense, $Q(t)$ never approaches $Q^e(t)$. The distance in two-dimensional space is always unity. However, this "distance" definitely loses its relative importance as time goes on. The relative stability definition reflects this fact well because

$$\text{Lim}_{t \to \infty} \frac{Q_2(t)}{Q_2^e(t)} = 1 = \frac{Q_1(t)}{Q_1^e(t)}$$

$Q(t)$ is relatively stable with respect to $Q^e(t)$.

Actually, the angular convergence to the equilibrium path (due to Radner) and the convergence to the equilibrium point in a "present-value" economy (due to Inada) are generalizations of the Solow-Samuelson condition. If Q^e has all nonzero components, then the relative stability condition can apply and all three criteria are equivalent.

A SUFFICIENT CONDITION FOR LINEAR DIFFERENCE EQUATIONS

We shall state a sufficient condition here:

If $\lambda_1 > |\lambda_i|$ for $i > 1$ where $|\lambda_i|$ is the modulus (or absolute value) of a complex (or real) root λ_i and there exists a particular integral to the equation which exhibits a growth rate for any component eventually slower than λ_1, then the solution of the vector difference equation, $\sum_{j=1}^{n} (c_j \lambda_j^t) \xi_j$ is relatively stable. ξ_j is an n-dimensional vector $j = 1, ..., n$.

Proof.

$$\frac{Q_i(t)}{Q_i^e(0)\lambda_1^t} = 1 + \left[\frac{\sum_{j=2}^{n} c_j \lambda_1^t \xi_{ij} + Q_i^P(t)}{Q_i^e(0)\lambda_1^t} \right] \tag{A.19}$$

where ξ_{ij} is the ith component of ξ_j. This ratio approaches unity as t goes to infinity. Hence (A.18) is satisfied with the constant equal to unity.

If λ_j is real for all j, the convergence of the bracketed terms to zero is obvious. If λ_j is complex, the situation may not be self-evident for some readers not familiar with complex numbers. Therefore, we shall digress into such matters.

REVIEW OF COMPLEX NUMBERS

Facts about the complex numbers:

(1) If $f(\lambda) = 0$ has all real coefficients (as is the case in our context), complex roots come in conjugate pairs, i.e., $f(\alpha + i\beta) = 0$ implies $f(\alpha - i\beta) = 0$ (where $\iota = \sqrt{-1}$).

(2) A complex number $\alpha + i\beta$ can be written as $|\lambda|\,(\cos\theta + i\sin\theta)$ where $|\lambda| = \sqrt{\alpha^2 + \beta^2}$ and θ = arc tan (β/α). ($|\lambda|$ is the "modulus" of λ.) This is seen in Figure A.4.

(3) Using Taylor's expansion at 0,

$$f(x) = f(0) + \frac{f'(0)x}{1!} + \frac{f''(0)x^2}{2!} + \cdots$$

we have:

$$\sin x = 0 + x + 0 - \frac{x^3}{3!} + 0 + \frac{x^5}{5!}\cdots \xrightarrow{\text{setting } x = \theta}\ i\sin\theta = 0 + i\theta + 0 - \frac{i\theta^3}{3!} + 0 + \frac{i\theta^5}{5!}\cdots$$

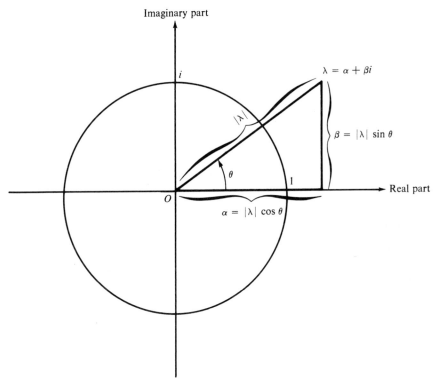

FIGURE A.4

$$|\lambda| = \sqrt{\alpha^2 + \beta^2}$$
$$\theta = \text{arc tan } (\beta/\alpha)$$

$$\cos x = 1 + 0 - \frac{x^2}{2!} + 0 + \frac{x^4}{4!} + 0 \ldots \xrightarrow{\text{setting } x = \theta} \cos \theta = 1 + 0 - \frac{\theta^2}{2!} + 0 + \frac{\theta^4}{4!} + 0 \ldots$$

$$e^x = 1 + x + \frac{x^2}{2!} + \frac{x^3}{3!} + \frac{x^4}{4!} + \frac{x^5}{5!} + \ldots \xrightarrow{\text{setting } x = i\theta} e^{i\theta} = 1 + i\theta - \frac{\theta^2}{2!} - \frac{i\theta^3}{3!} + \frac{\theta^4}{4!} + \frac{i\theta^5}{5!} \ldots$$

Hence, $\lambda = |\lambda|(\cos \theta + i \sin \theta) = |\lambda|e^{i\theta}$, and its conjugate is

$$\bar{\lambda} = |\lambda|(\cos \theta - i \sin \theta) = |\lambda|[\cos (-\theta) + i \sin (-\theta)]$$
$$= |\lambda|e^{-i\theta}$$

(since $\cos (-\theta) = \cos \theta$, $\sin (-\theta) = -\sin \theta$).

(4) $(\lambda)^t$ and $(\bar{\lambda})^t$ will then take the forms $|\lambda|^t e^{i\theta t}$ and $|\lambda|^t e^{-i\theta t}$, respectively.

In $R(t)$ of (A.17), the corresponding terms will appear as $c\lambda^t \xi + \bar{c}(\bar{\lambda})^t \bar{\xi}$, say, with the ith component assuming the form $(c\xi_i)(\lambda)^t + (\overline{c\xi_i})(\bar{\lambda})^t$. $c\xi_i$ and $\overline{c\xi_i}$ again will be conjugate complex numbers: $ae^{i\psi\theta}/2$ and $ae^{-i\psi\theta}/2$, say, respectively, so that the ith component becomes:

$$\frac{a}{2}|\lambda|^t[e^{i(t+\psi)\theta} + e^{-i(t+\psi)\theta}] = \frac{a}{2}|\lambda|^t\{[\cos (t+\psi)\theta + i \sin (t+\psi)\theta] + [\cos (t+\psi)\theta - i \sin (t+\psi)\theta]\}$$
$$= a|\lambda|^t \cos (t+\psi)\theta$$

This is the "harmonic" (sinusoidal) term, prominent in trade cycle theory. In the growth context, this is a disturbance term, with an absolute value less than or equal to $a|\lambda|^t$. Hence if $\lambda_1 > |\lambda|$, their effect in (A.19) must damp toward zero.

A.3 DIFFERENTIAL EQUATIONS

A.3.1. Basic concepts and classifications

BASIC CONCEPTS

Consider an unknown function $k(t)$, with derivatives dk/dt, d^2k/dt^2, etc. An equation of the form:

$$F\left[\frac{d^n k}{dt^n}, \frac{d^{n-1}k}{dt^{n-1}}, \ldots, \frac{dk}{dt}, k, t\right] = 0 \qquad \text{(A.20)}$$

valid for all t is called a *differential equation*. On the other hand, given (A.20), any $k(\cdot)$ satisfying (A.20) for all t is said to be the *solution* of the latter.

If the highest order of derivative appearing in (A.20) is n, then it is an *nth-order* differential equation.

As in difference equations, usually there are infinitely many solutions corresponding to one differential equation. It takes n *initial* (or *boundary*) *conditions* of the form $k(0) = k_0$, $dk(0)/dt = \dot{k}_0$, etc. to completely determine a specific solution.

CLASSIFICATIONS AND EXAMPLES

Differential equations are classified as *partial* or *ordinary* differential equations depending upon whether or not partial derivatives of an unknown function appear. Most differential equations used in growth theory are ordinary differential equations, the independent variable being time. The only partial differential equations that do emerge are those characterizing aggregate production functions, such as the Cobb-Douglas case, where

$$\frac{\partial Q}{\partial K} = \frac{\alpha Q}{K}; \qquad \frac{\partial Q}{\partial L} = \frac{(1-\alpha)Q}{L}$$

We now turn to ordinary differential equations. Rather than repeating the definitions we shall compare the usage of such terms in difference equations and differential equations and provide examples. See Table A.1.

Again we do not encounter any linear differential equation with variable coefficients in growth

TABLE A.1

Term	Difference equation	Differential equation	Example	Where used
Vector equation	Q is a vector in (A.11)	Q is a vector in (A.20)	$\dot{Q} = AQ; A$ is $n \times n$	Chapter 7
Scalar equation	Q is a scalar in (A.11)	Q is a scalar in (A.20)	$\dot{Q} = \frac{s}{a} Q$	Chapter 1
Linear equation	$Q(t) - \sum_{i=1}^{n} a_i(t)Q(t-i) - a_0(t) = 0$	$Q(t) - \sum_{i=1}^{n} a_i(t) \frac{d^n}{dt^n} Q(t) - a_0(t) = 0$		
Nonhomogeneous	$a_0(t) \neq 0$	$a_0(t) \neq 0$	$K - \dfrac{\dot{K}}{\beta} = \dfrac{C_0}{\beta} e^{\gamma t}$	Exercise
Homogeneous	$a_0(t) = 0$	$a_0(t) = 0$	$\dot{\kappa} - \gamma\kappa = 0$	Later in this appendix
Nonlinear equation	(A.11) cannot be put in the above form	(A.20) cannot be put in the above form	$\dot{k} = sf(k) - nk = g(k)$ $\dfrac{\ddot{Q}}{\dot{Q}} = \dfrac{1\dot{Q}}{q Q}$	Chapters 2, 5, 10 Chapter 1 Exercise

theory *per se*. Their applications to the maximum principle will be sidestepped by a heuristic argument.

We may note that a first-order nonlinear differential equation plays a role in Part I, whereas second-order nonlinear differential equations arising from calculus of variations problems also occupy our attention in Chapter 10, Part II.

A.3.2. Quantative Solutions

In growth theory, economists rarely attempt an explicit solution of a specific differential equation. More likely, it is the stability property of a broad class of differential equations which is sought after. However, in providing examples, in conducting local stability analysis, and in cases where special forms (usually Cobb-Douglas) of production functions are assumed, now and then one solves explicitly a differential equation. We shall consider a sequence of special cases (not mutually exclusive) which we shall encounter.

1. First-order, constant coefficient, homogeneous linear equation.

$$\dot{\kappa} = \gamma\kappa \qquad \text{with } \kappa(0) = \kappa_0 \text{ as the initial value} \tag{A.21}$$

Solution.   Dividing both sides by κ one obtains

$$\hat{\kappa} = \frac{d \ln \kappa}{dt} \qquad \left(\text{where } \hat{x} = \frac{\dot{x}}{x} = \frac{dx/dt}{x} \text{ for any } x\right)$$

$$= \gamma$$

Integrating between 0 and t, we obtain

$$\ln \kappa(t) - \ln \kappa_0 = \ln \left[\kappa(t)/\kappa_0\right]$$

$$= \gamma t$$

Taking the antilogarithm and multiplying both sides by κ_0, we obtain

$$\kappa(t) = \kappa_0 e^{\gamma t} \tag{A.21s}$$

Equation (A.21s) is the solution for (A.21). This result is useful later in stability analysis.

2. First-order, constant coefficient, nonhomogeneous linear equation:

$$\beta\kappa - \dot{\kappa} = C_0 e^{\gamma t} \qquad \text{with } \kappa(0) = \kappa_0 \text{ and } \kappa(1) = \kappa_1 \tag{A.22}$$

(C_0 is an unknown).

This equation has a "two-point boundary value" at $t = 0$ and $t = 1$. The value $\dot{\kappa}(0)$ is not known.

Solution.   Any "particular integral" $\kappa^P(t)$ satisfying (A.22), must fulfill the relation:

$$\beta\kappa^P - \dot{\kappa}^P = C_0 e^{\gamma t}$$

Substracting this from (A.22), we obtain:

$$\beta\kappa^C - \dot{\kappa}^C = 0 \qquad \text{where } \kappa^C = \kappa - \kappa^P \text{ is the complementary solution}$$

Using the result (A.21s), we know that $\kappa^C = \kappa_0^C e^{\beta t}$ for some yet undetermined parameter κ_0^C. In order to solve for κ^P, we observe that if $\kappa^P = \alpha e^{\gamma t}$, then $\dot{\kappa}^P = \alpha\gamma e^{\gamma t}$. Substituting in (A.22), we have:

$$\alpha(\beta - \gamma)e^{\gamma t} = C_0 e^{\gamma t}$$

or

$$\alpha = \frac{C_0}{\beta - \gamma} \quad \text{and} \quad \kappa^P = \frac{C_0 e^{\gamma t}}{\beta - \gamma}$$

Hence, $\kappa(t)$ has the general form:

$$\kappa = \kappa^C + \kappa^P = \kappa_0^C e^{\beta t} + \frac{C_0 e^{\gamma t}}{\beta - \gamma}$$

Setting t equal to 0 and 1, we have:

$$\kappa_0^C + \frac{C_0}{\beta - \gamma} = \kappa_0$$

$$\kappa_0^C e^\beta + \frac{C_0 e^\gamma}{\beta - \gamma} = \kappa_1$$

which yields:

$$\kappa_0^C = \frac{\kappa_0 e^\gamma - \kappa_1}{e^\gamma - e^\beta}; \quad C_0 = \frac{(\kappa_1 - \kappa_0 e^\beta)(\beta - \gamma)}{e^\gamma - e^\beta}$$

Hence, we have the solution:

$$\kappa(t) = \frac{(\kappa_0 e^\gamma - \kappa_1)e^{\beta t} + (\kappa_1 - \kappa_0 e^\beta)e^{\gamma t}}{e^\gamma - e^\beta} \tag{A.22s}$$

3. First-order, constant coefficient, linear differential equation system. We now analyze the vector equation:

$$\dot{x} = Ax \tag{A.23}$$

Before doing so, a digression into matrix algebra is necessary.

(a) *Matrix definitions.* Consider an $n \times n$ square matrix A, a complex number λ (which may be real), a pair of nonzero vectors π and ξ, each consisting of n complex elements (which may be real). In the equations:

$$A\xi = \lambda\xi$$
$$\pi'A = \lambda\pi' \tag{A.24}$$

λ is called the characteristic (eigen, latent) value (root), ξ is called the characteristic (eigen) column vector corresponding to λ, and π' is called the characteristic (eigen) row vector corresponding to λ. Equation (A.22) can be written as

$$(A - \lambda I)\xi = 0$$
$$\pi'(A - \lambda I) = 0 \qquad \text{where } I = \begin{bmatrix} 1 & & 0 \\ & \ddots & \\ 0 & & 1 \end{bmatrix} \text{ is the identity matrix} \tag{A.24'}$$

From algebra, the so-called characteristic (latent) equation

$$|A - \lambda I| = f(\lambda) = 0$$

has n roots, some of which may be real, some complex, some repeated, some distinct. For any root λ, the matrix $(A - \lambda I)$ is singular, meaning that both its rows and its columns are linearly dependent. In other words, (A.24) admits solution vectors ξ and π which are not null vectors.

(b) *Some basic results.* (1) If $\xi(\pi')$ is a characteristic vector corresponding to λ so is $\mu\xi(\mu\pi')$, μ being any real number not equal to zero. (ii) If all n roots of the characteristic equation are distinct, then[4] we can scale up (or down) the $2n$ characteristic vectors in such a way that after defining

$$\Xi = \begin{bmatrix} \xi_1 & \vdots & \xi_2 & \vdots & \cdots & \vdots & \xi_n \end{bmatrix}$$

$$\Pi = \begin{bmatrix} \cdots \pi_1' \cdots \\ \cdots \pi_2' \cdots \\ \pi_n' \end{bmatrix}$$

$$\Lambda = \begin{bmatrix} \lambda_1 & & & 0 \\ & \lambda_2 & & \\ & & \ddots & \\ 0 & & & \lambda_n \end{bmatrix}$$

[4]See ref. 2, pp. 249–251.

the following relations hold:

$$\Pi\Xi = I = \Xi\Pi \qquad \text{(biorthogonality)} \tag{A.25}$$

$$\Pi A\Xi = \Lambda \qquad \text{(diagonalizability)} \tag{A.26}$$

Hence:

$$A = \Pi^{-1}\Lambda\Xi^{-1} \tag{A.27}$$

$$= \Xi\Lambda\Pi \qquad \text{(from (A.25) and (A.26))}$$

and (A.23) now becomes

$$\dot{x} = \Xi\Lambda\Pi x$$

Ξ, Λ, and Π are all $n \times n$; $|A - \lambda_j I| = 0$, for all j or $\Pi\dot{x} = \Lambda(\Pi x)$.

Since $(d/dt)(\Pi x) = \Pi\dot{x}$, each component of the above vector equation is of the type we considered in subsection 1, homogeneous linear equations. Hence, solving these n equations, we have:

$$\pi_i' x(t) = \pi_i' x(0)e^{\lambda_i t}$$

Together, we have:

$$\Pi x(t) = \begin{bmatrix} e^{\lambda_1 t} & & 0 \\ & \ddots & \\ 0 & & e^{\lambda_n t} \end{bmatrix} \Pi x(0)$$

or,

$$x(t) = \Xi \begin{bmatrix} e^{\lambda_1 t} & & 0 \\ & \ddots & \\ 0 & & e^{\lambda_n t} \end{bmatrix} \Pi x(0) \tag{A.23s}$$

Note that we have not discussed high-order, linear, constant-coefficient, single differential equations. By setting $x_1 = x$, $x_2 = dx/dt$, ..., we can transform any such nth-order single equation into a first-order vector differential equation like (A.23).

4. Nonlinear differential equations. As we noted earlier, most of the differential equations in growth theory belong to the nonlinear category. No standard method exists for solving them. However, for certain special types, solution is comparatively simple.

(1) *Variable separable type.* In principle, most differential equations in growth theory are of this type, i.e.,

$$\dot{k} = g(k)$$

which can be readily rewritten as

$$\frac{dk}{g(k)} = dt$$

However, in most cases, the left-hand side is not easily integrable. Unless we wish to attain numerical solutions, the above approach may not be fruitful. The following example is given to show how the solution can be obtained when such a procedure works.

$$\dot{\kappa} = s\kappa^\alpha L_0^{1-\alpha} e^{(1-\alpha)nt} \tag{A.28}$$

This can be transformed into

$$\frac{d\kappa}{\kappa^\alpha} = (sL_0^{1-\alpha})e^{n(1-\alpha)t} dt$$

Integrating between 0 and t, we obtain

$$\int_{\tau=0}^{\tau=t} \kappa^{-\alpha}d\kappa = \int_{\tau=0}^{\tau=t} e^{n(1-\alpha)t}dt(sL_0^{1-\alpha})$$

or

$$\frac{\kappa^{1-\alpha}(t)-\kappa^{1-\alpha}(0)}{1-\alpha} = \frac{sL_0^{1-\alpha}(e^{n(1-\alpha)t}-1)}{n(1-\alpha)}$$

which gives us

$$\kappa(t) = \{\kappa^{1-\alpha}(0)+(sL_0^{1-\alpha}/n)\left[e^{n(1-\alpha)t}-1\right]\}^{1/(1-\alpha)} \qquad (A.28s)$$

(2) *The use of an "integration factor."* This can be illustrated by the following example.

$$\dot{k} = sk^\alpha - nk \qquad (A.29)$$

By multiplying both sides by the strictly positive factor e^{nt} and rearranging, we obtain:

$$(\dot{k}+nk)e^{nt} = sk^\alpha e^{nt}$$

or

$$\frac{d}{dt}(ke^{nt}) = se^{n(1-\alpha)t}(ke^{nt})^\alpha$$

This is almost a repetition of case (1) above. Hence:

$$ke^{nt} = \{k(0)^{1-\alpha}+(s/n)\left[e^{n(1-\alpha)t}-1\right]\}^{1/(1-\alpha)}$$

$$k(t) = e^{-nt}\{k(0)^{1-\alpha}+(s/n)\left[e^{n(1-\alpha)t}-1\right]\}^{1/(1-\alpha)} \qquad (A.29s)$$

There are, of course, other types of nonlinear differential equations used in growth theory which may not be solved in this manner. For instance, partial fraction expansion is needed to solve Jorgenson's differential equation in his two-sector model. Since this lies outside our volume, we shall not discuss it here.

We shall now wind up this topic by discussing one particular partial differential equation. The Cobb-Douglas production function can be derived from the following system:

$$\frac{\partial Q}{\partial K} = \alpha\frac{Q}{K} \qquad \frac{\partial Q}{\partial L} = (1-\alpha)\frac{Q}{L} \qquad (A.30)$$

Both equations can be rewritten to obtain the variable separable forms:

$$\left.\frac{dQ}{Q}\right|_{\bar{L}} = \alpha\frac{dK}{K} \qquad \text{where } L \text{ is held at } \bar{L} \text{ for any } \bar{L} > 0$$

$$\left.\frac{dQ}{Q}\right|_{\bar{K}} = (1-\alpha)\frac{dL}{L} \qquad \text{where } K \text{ is held at } \bar{K} \text{ for any } \bar{K} > 0$$

or

$$\left.\begin{array}{l} \ln Q = \ln K^\alpha + C_1(L) \\ \ln Q = \ln L^{1-\alpha} + C_2(K) \end{array}\right\} \quad \begin{array}{l} \text{where } C_1 \text{ and } C_2 \text{ are "constants of integration"} \\ \text{depending upon } L \text{ and } K, \text{ respectively.} \end{array}$$

Taking antilogs:

$$Q = C_1(L)K^\alpha$$

$$= C_2(K)L^{1-\alpha}$$

Hence, dividing by $K^\alpha L^{1-\alpha}$, we obtain:

$$\frac{Q}{K^\alpha L^{1-\alpha}} = \frac{C_1(L)}{L^{1-\alpha}} = \frac{C_2(K)}{K^\alpha} = A$$

where A is a positive constant.

Therefore, we have the solution to the partial differential equation:

$$Q = AK^\alpha L^{1-\alpha} \tag{A.30s}$$

A.3.3. Qualitative analysis—application to the stability problem of an equilibrium

BASIC CONCEPTS

Economists are interested in stability analysis for two reasons:

(1) To predict the ultimate state of the economy: whether or not the economy will eventually approach a given position or a given class of positions.

(2) To predict whether or not an economy perturbated from a certain self-perpetuating position will return to that position.

The first point concerns the problem of global stability, the second concerns the problem of local stability. These concepts will be developed below.

1. The causal system. Assuming that we have a "causal" system (rather than a "historical" system) in Samuelson's parlance [3], we can write:

$$\dot{k} = g(k) \tag{A.31}$$

where k is the vector of "state variables," $\dot{k}$ shows the direction of change, and time does not enter explicitly.

In growth theory, the economic system is rarely truly causal. Population growth is usually regarded as an exogenously determined element. However, by virtue of the assumption of constant population growth rate, the system can be transformed into the form (A.31). Technical progress is another "historical" (time-dependent) factor. Either by considering it as purely labor augmenting in nature (i.e., equivalent to a higher rate of growth for labor supply) or by considering the degree of labor augmentation vs. capital augmentation as endogenously decided (Section 7.1), economists can still obtain a system in the form of (A.31). In passing we may note that both happy assumptions (constant population growth rate and labor-augmenting technical progress) were initiated by Harrod. One may pause to contemplate how complicated the life of growth theorists would be, were such assumptions not adopted (see Vanek [4]).

2. Equilibrium and stability. Suppose $g(k) = 0$ has a root at k^*, and suppose $k(t^*) = k^*$; obviously from (A.31), $\dot{k}(t^*) = 0$. k^* is considered an equilibrium position, since such a position is self-perpetuating.

Now suppose the value of $k(0)$ is different from k^*; the question then is whether or not $k(t)$ will approach k^*.

If $k(t) \to k^*$ for k close to k^*, then k^* is a (locally) stable equilibrium.

If $k(t)$ becomes farther and farther from k^* for $k \neq k^*$, k^* is an unstable equilibrium.

If $k(t)$ becomes neither closer to nor farther from k^*, for all k close to k^*, then k^* is a neutral equilibrium.

If $k(t) \to k^*$ for k close to k^* for $k > k^*$ *and $k(t)$ gets farther from k^* if $k < k^*$*, then k^* is a stable–unstable equilibrium. Interchanging the inequalities, also results in a stable–unstable equilibrium.

If $k(t) \to k^*$ for all k, then k^* is a *globally* stable equilibrium.

PHASE DIAGRAM ANALYSIS

Plotting (A.31) in a diagram, we obtain a "phase diagram" like Figure A.5.

The points shared by the locus of (A.31) and the k axis are equilibrium positions. Moreover, for that portion of the locus lying above the k axis, the direction of change for k is positive, hence an arrow can be drawn toward the right along the locus; similarly for that portion below the k axis,

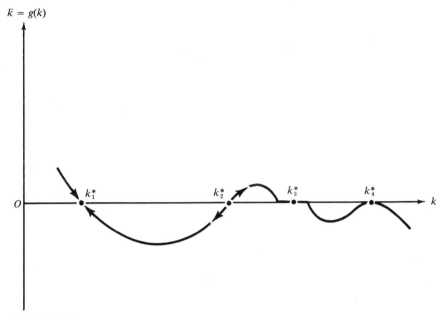

$\dot{k} = g(k)$

O k_1^* k_2^* k_3^* k_4^* k

FIGURE A.5

the direction of change for k is negative and the arrow points to the left. By considering the directions of the arrows along the locus on both sides of an equilibrium position, the stability of that equilibrium can be determined.

In the particular configuration shown in Figure A.5, we observe that positions k_1^*, k_2^*, k_3^*, and k_4^* are, in turn, a local stable equilibrium, an unstable equilibrium, a neutral equilibrium, and a stable–unstable equilibrium. None of these is a global equilibrium.

While the above example concerns a scalar differential equation, the same technique can be applied to a two-variable equation system. We shall now consider two examples:

Example 1.

$$\dot{k} = sf(k) - nk \qquad\qquad\qquad \text{(A.32)}$$

$$= G(k)$$

where we postulate: (a) $G(0) = 0$; (b) $G'(0) > 0$; (c) $G''(k) < 0$; and (d) $G(\infty) < 0$.

In Figure A.6a, condition (a) rules out a curve like G^1, so G must start from the k axis. Condition (b) rules out a curve like G^2, so starting at the origin with a positive slope, G must be positive for some small k. Condition (d) specifies that G is negative for large k, ruling out G^4, so that with G continuous (since G' exists), G must cut the k axis. Condition (c) rules out any increase of the G curve after falling though the k axis, ruling out G^3. Hence, there must be one unique, finite k at which $0 = G(k^\infty) = \dot{k}$. We call that k value, k^∞. For k near k^∞ (in fact, any $k > 0$) we can read off $\dot{k} = G(k)$ and draw the arrow, so k^∞ is stable.

Example 2.

$$\dot{k} = [f(k) - nk] - c$$

$$= g(k) - c \qquad \text{where the properties of } g(k) \text{ are the same as those of } G(k) \text{ in Example 1} \qquad \text{(A.33)}$$

$$\dot{c} = h(k) \qquad \text{where sgn } h(k) = \text{sgn } (k^\infty - k) \text{ for some } k^\infty > 0$$

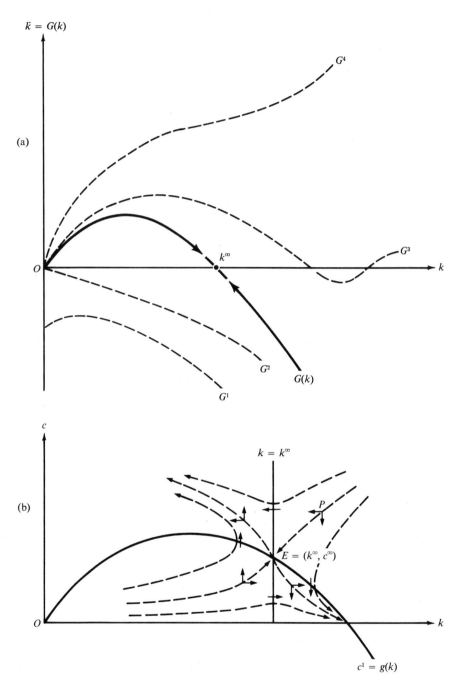

FIGURE A.6

Now by plotting in the c–k space the two "boundary" lines:

$$\dot{k} = 0 \qquad \text{i.e., } c = g(k)$$

and

$$\dot{c} = 0 \qquad \text{i.e., } k = k^{\infty}$$

we can partition the positive quadrant into four sectors as in Figure A.6b. At each point (k, c) where both coordinates are positive, we can evaluate the direction of change according to the differential equation system outlined above. Taking any point, P located to the right of $k = k^{\infty}$ and above the $c = g(k)$ curve, we observe from (A.34) that $\dot{k} < 0$ and $\dot{c} < 0$. Hence, the so-called state vector $[k(t), c(t)]$ tends to move downward and to the left. This is depicted by the small arrow emanating from P. Similarly we can draw arrows for typical points in all four regions of the diagram and on all branches of the boundary loci.

We note that for all positive (k, c) pairs, there is only one unique equilibrium, at $E = (k^{\infty}, c^{\infty})$. This is called a "saddle point" in terms of its stability behavior. Unless the economic system has an initial vector located on (or a displacement sets the economy upon) one of the two dashed arrow lines leading to E, then the system will not approach (return to) E asymptotically. This can be seen by considering the various "solution curves" traced out by the solutions to (A.33), given arbitrary initial conditions. The formula for the solution curves can be obtained by dividing the first equation by the second in (A.33) or vice versa, to obtain a differential equation relating c and k only. The existence of a "saddle point" is only possible when there is more than one differential equation in the system.

Example 1 relates to the basic Solow model, whereas Example 2 is based upon the work of Koopmans.

In growth theory, the phase diagram can be used to study the existence, uniqueness, and stability of a system. In optimal growth theory, after determining the asymptotic behavior of an optimal system (e.g., $[k(t), c(t)] \rightarrow (k^{\infty}, c^{\infty})$ in Example 2), we deduce that under optimal control an economic system should always be located on one of the two dashed arrow lines to E. Given current value $k(t)$, we can read the optimal current consumption level, $c(t)$, off one of these two arrow lines.

Unlike the method of linearization to be discussed below, a phase diagram may study the *global* as well as the *local* stability properties of a system. On the other hand, if we have an equation system involving three equations the phase diagram is very cumbersome. Should the number of equations exceed three, the phase diagram approach is obviously inapplicable.

There are occasions where the method of linearization is more potent than the phase diagram approach. Section 7.1 contains one such example. On the other hand, there are also instances where the phase diagram approach may succeed where the method of linearization fails. We shall see that the case in Figure A.7 is one of these.

METHOD OF LINEARIZATION

Consider the dynamic system $\dot{k} = G(k)$, where $G(k^{\infty}) = 0$ and $J_G(k^{\infty})$ is a finite, non-null, $n \times n$ Jacobian matrix evaluated at k^{∞}, where the (i, j)th element is $\partial G_i / \partial k_j$ and G_i and k_j are the ith and jth components of $G(k)$ and k.

Defining $\kappa = k - k^{\infty}$ for some k close to k^{∞}, we have a linearized system by Taylor's expansion at k^{∞}:

$$\dot{\kappa} = \dot{k} - 0$$

$$= G(k)$$

$$= G(k^{\infty}) + J_G(k^{\infty})\kappa + o(\kappa)$$

$$\doteq J_G(k^{\infty})\kappa$$

$$= A\kappa$$

where $o(\kappa)$ denotes terms of the order of the cross products or squares of the components of κ and A is an $n \times n$ matrix. $o(\kappa)$ can be ignored when all components of κ are very small. Two cases can now be considered.

(1) If all the characteristic roots of A are distinct, our discussion of (A.23) and (A.23s) indicates that:

$$\kappa(t) = \Xi \begin{bmatrix} e^{\lambda_1 t} & & 0 \\ & \ddots & \\ 0 & & e^{\lambda_n t} \end{bmatrix} \Pi \kappa(0)$$

$$= \Xi \begin{bmatrix} e^{\alpha_1 t} & & 0 \\ & \ddots & \\ 0 & & e^{\alpha_n t} \end{bmatrix} \begin{bmatrix} e^{i\beta_1 t} & & 0 \\ & \ddots & \\ 0 & & e^{i\beta_n t} \end{bmatrix} \Pi \kappa(0)$$

where[5] $\alpha_j = R(\lambda_j)$ is the real part of λ_j and $\beta_j = I(\lambda_j)$ is the imaginary part of λ_j (i.e., $\lambda_j = \alpha_j + i\beta_j$).

As we have seen before, in our digressions on complex numbers in Section A.2.3, the term $e^{i\beta_j t}$ corresponds to sinusoidal movements of an absolute magnitude less than or equal to unity. Therefore, we conclude:

If $\alpha_j < 0$ for all j, then $\lim_{t \to \infty} \kappa(t) \to 0$.

(2) If λ_j is repeated m times, we now state without proof that terms like $t^i e^{\lambda_j t}$, $i = 0, ..., m-1$, will appear. Since

$$\left| t^i e^{\lambda_j t} \right| = \left| \frac{t^i}{e^{-\alpha_j t}} \right| \left| e^{i\beta_j t} \right| \leqq \left| \frac{t^i}{e^{-\alpha_j t}} \right|$$

If $\alpha_j < 0$,

$$\lim_{t \to \infty} \left| \frac{t^i}{e^{-\alpha_j t}} \right| = 0 \quad \text{for any finite } i.$$

Hence the criterion in case (1) also applies here.

Therefore, if all the characteristic roots of $J_G(k^\infty)$ have negative real parts, $\lim_{t \to \infty} \kappa(t) = 0$ and the equilibrium at k^∞ is *locally* stable.

For a single-equation case ($n = 1$), the linearized system becomes $\dot{\kappa}(t) = \gamma \kappa(t)$, where $\gamma = G'(k^\infty)$. This is usually not used in economics because

(a) A phase diagram analysis as in Figure A.6a is just as simple and can yield both global and local results.

(b) The range of applicability is narrower than the phase diagram analysis. For Figure A.7, global stability is clearly shown at the origin with a phase diagram, yet even the local stability cannot be established through linearization because of the vanishing of γ. This example also demonstrates the rationale for assuming a non-vanishing J_G.

We now give an example from Section 7.1 where the linearization approach succeeds while the phase diagram analysis fails. The linearized system is:

$$D\alpha = C_2 \kappa; \qquad D\kappa = C_3 \alpha + C_1 \kappa$$

where D stands for the d/dt operator and $C_1, C_2 < 0 < C_3$.

The "operational calculus" approach used in that section follows the above equations with:

$$\begin{bmatrix} D & -C_2 \\ -C_3 & D - C_1 \end{bmatrix} \begin{bmatrix} \alpha \\ \kappa \end{bmatrix} = \begin{bmatrix} 0 \\ 0 \end{bmatrix}$$

Hence, in analogy with an algebraic equation, we may also expect a condition[6]

$$\begin{vmatrix} D & -C_2 \\ -C_3 & D - C_1 \end{vmatrix} = 0$$

defined in some way. Replacing D by λ, we obtain a characteristic equation.

----

[5] If a given λ_j is real, then $\beta_j = 0$.

[6] If the determinant is nonzero, then

$$\begin{bmatrix} \alpha \\ \kappa \end{bmatrix} = \begin{bmatrix} D & -C_2 \\ -C_3 & D - C_1 \end{bmatrix}^{-1} \begin{bmatrix} 0 \\ 0 \end{bmatrix} = \begin{bmatrix} 0 \\ 0 \end{bmatrix}$$

which contradicts the fact that $\begin{bmatrix} \alpha \\ \kappa \end{bmatrix}$ is any arbitrary small vector.

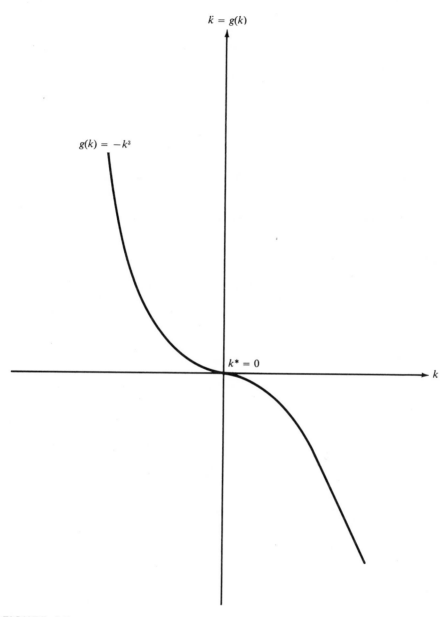

FIGURE A.7

This approach is intuitively appealing. However, its rigorous justification requires the theory of operators, which lies beyond the scope of our volume.

With the tools built up in the preceding sections, we may proceed now in a somewhat different manner. First, the linearized system can be written as:

$$\begin{bmatrix} \dot{\alpha} \\ \dot{\kappa} \end{bmatrix} = \begin{pmatrix} 0 & C_2 \\ C_3 & C_1 \end{pmatrix} \begin{bmatrix} \alpha \\ \kappa \end{bmatrix}$$

where $\begin{pmatrix} 0 & C_2 \\ C_3 & C_1 \end{pmatrix}$ is the value of the J_G matrix at the equilibrium.

Then we can find the characteristic roots for J_G through the equation $|J_G - \lambda I| = \lambda^2 - C_1\lambda - C_2C_3$. Thus,

$$\lambda_1, \lambda_2 = \tfrac{1}{2}\left[C_1 \pm \sqrt{C_1^2 + 4C_2C_3}\right]$$

If the "discriminant" $C_1^2 + 4C_2C_3$ is greater than or equal to zero, then due to the fact that $4C_2C_3$ is less than zero ($C_2 < 0 < C_3$), $|C_1| > \sqrt{C_1^2 + 4C_2C_3}$. Since $C_1 < 0$, both roots are negative.

If the "discriminant" $C_1^2 + 4C_2C_3$ is less than zero, then both roots are complex, but since $C_1 < 0$, the real parts of both roots are negative.

Therefore, under any case, the equilibrium is locally stable.

A.4 CALCULUS OF VARIATIONS

The calculus of variations is essential to the understanding of Chapter 10, parts of Appendix 7.1 and Section 9.2. It also improves our grasp of Section 6.1 concerning optimal life cycle earnings as well as Section 1.2 regarding Harrod's "Second Law."

A.4.1. Basic concepts

The standard form of the problem is as follows:

$$\underset{k(t)}{\text{Max}} \; V = \int_0^T F(t, k, \dot{k}) \, dt \quad \text{with } k(0), k(T) \text{ given}, k(\cdot) \text{ differentiable} \tag{A.34}$$

where F is continuously twice differentiable.

Figure A.8a shows that V is the area under the integrand curve. The height of that curve, F, at any point t depends upon t, the level $k(t)$, and the slope $\dot{k}(t)$ of the *variable curve* $k(\cdot)$ in Figure A.8b.

In Figure A.8c, four specimens of admissible $k(\cdot)$'s are given.

For any t, obviously $k(t)$ can take various values as long as $0 < t < T$. Hence, for each t there corresponds one degree of freedom. Since there are infinitely many points between 0 and T, the problem is infinitely dimensional and the entire $k(\cdot)$ path is the variable to be controlled.

Our purpose is to characterize the first-order condition necessary for a maximum. In other words, we try to characterize the optimal path, $k^*(\cdot)$.

A.4.2. Necessary conditions for optimum

Suppose $k^*(\cdot)$ is found; then, by definition,

$$\int_0^T F[t, k^*(t), \dot{k}^*(t)] \, dt \geq \int_0^T F[t, k(t), \dot{k}(t)] \, dt \quad \text{for all admissible } k \tag{A.35}$$

Equation (A.35) holds true for any admissible k. In particular, it holds if $k = k^* + \varepsilon(k^0 - k^*)$, where k^0 is a particular admissible curve and ε is a real number.

F: "Performance curve"

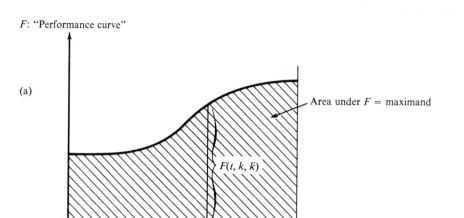

(a)

Area under F = maximand

$F(t, k, \dot{k})$

0   t T t

k: "Variable curve"

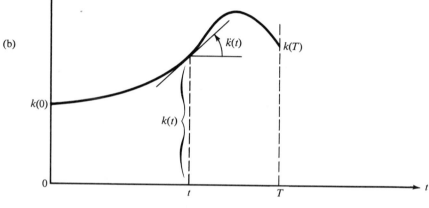

(b)

$\dot{k}(t)$ $k(T)$

$k(0)$

$k(t)$

0   t T t

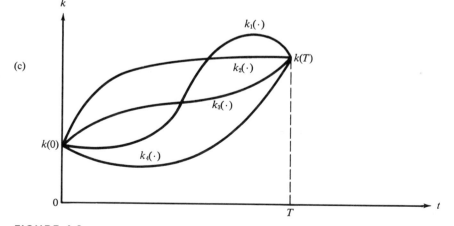

k

(c)

$k_1(\cdot)$

$k(T)$

$k_2(\cdot)$

$k_3(\cdot)$

$k(0)$

$k_4(\cdot)$

0   T t

FIGURE A.8

In Figure A.9a, the relationship among k^*, k^0, and k is illustrated. This is contrasted with the two-dimensional maximization problem in Figure A.9b.

In the two-dimensional analog, by considering the set of points $S = \{k|k = k^* + \varepsilon(k^0 - k^*)\}$ we are restricting our attention to the points on the AB line. Since k^* is the maximum *at large*, k^* must not give rise to a value less than that implied by any other k in set S.

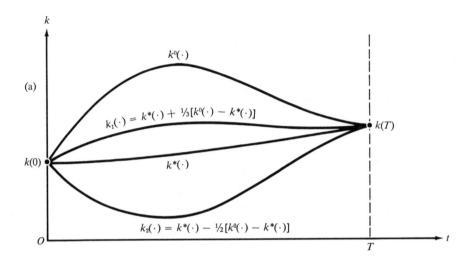

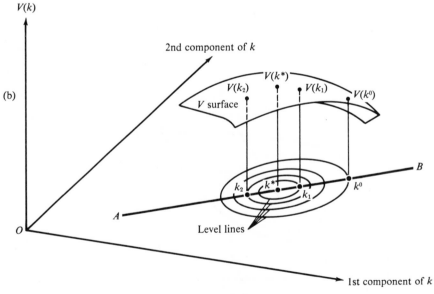

FIGURE A.9

In (b), $k_1 = k^* + \frac{1}{3}(k^0 - k^*)$
$k_2 = k^* - \frac{1}{2}(k^0 - k^*)$

Analogously, in our infinite-dimensional problem, we can also conclude that as a special case of (A.35) we have:

$$\int_0^T F[t, k^* + (0)(k^0 - k^*), \dot{k}^* + (0)(\dot{k}^0 - \dot{k}^*)]\, dt = I(0)$$

$$\geq I(\varepsilon)$$

$$= \int_0^T F[t, k^* + \varepsilon(k^0 - k^*), \dot{k}^* + \varepsilon(\dot{k}^0 - \dot{k}^*)]\, dt$$

(A.36)

where $I(\varepsilon)$ is the value of V with k^0 fixed and $k = k^* + \varepsilon(k^0 - k^*)$. Hence, this is a function of ε only.

In the two-dimensional analog, if we make a vertical cross section of the V surface along the AB line, we have Figure A.10.

If we plot the "right-hand" members of (A.36) with respect to ε, we obtain exactly the same type of diagram. The "equilibrium" (or "optimality") condition is:

$$0 = I'(0)$$

$$= \left(\frac{d}{d\varepsilon}\int_0^T F[t, k^* + \varepsilon(k^0 - k^*), \dot{k}^* + \varepsilon(\dot{k}^0 - \dot{k}^*)]\, dt\right)_{\varepsilon = 0}$$

$$= \int_0^T \left(\frac{d}{d\varepsilon} F\right)_{\varepsilon = 0} dt$$

$$= \int_0^T \left[\frac{\partial F(t, k^*, \dot{k}^*)}{\partial k}(k^0 - k^*) + \frac{\partial F(t, k^*, \dot{k}^*)}{\partial \dot{k}}(\dot{k}^0 - \dot{k}^*)\right] dt$$

(A.37)

where the partials are evaluated for $\varepsilon = 0$, i.e., $k = k^*$, $\dot{k} = \dot{k}^*$,

$$0 = \int_0^T (F_k \kappa + F_{\dot{k}} \dot{\kappa})\, dt \quad \text{where } \kappa = k^0 - k^*$$

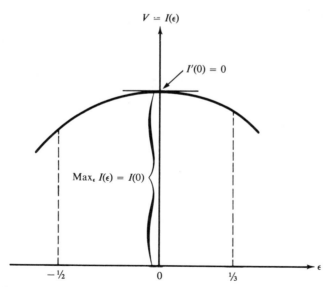

FIGURE A.10

Integrating by parts,

$$\int_0^T F_k(\dot{\kappa}\,dt) = \int_0^T F_k\,d\kappa$$

$$= \left(\kappa F_k\right)_{t=0}^{t=T} - \int_0^T \left[\left(\frac{d}{dt}F_k\right)\kappa\right]dt$$

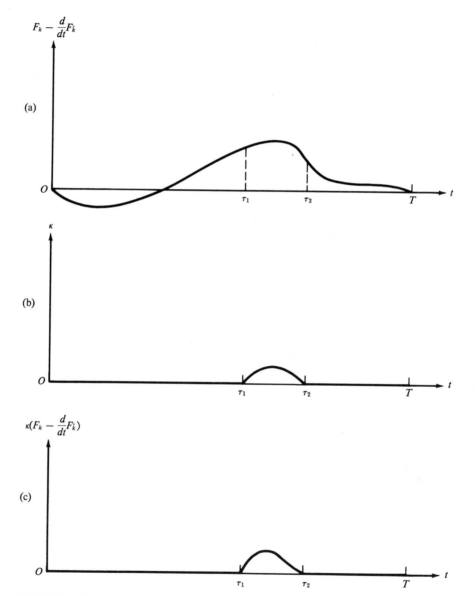

FIGURE A.11

Since F is twice differentiable, $F_k \equiv \partial F/\partial \dot{k} \neq \infty$ at $t = 0$, T. But $\kappa(0) = k^0(0) - k^*(0) = 0 = k^0(T) - k^*(T) = \kappa(T)$ since the admissibility of k^0 implies that $k^0(0) = k^*(0) =$ the fixed initial value and $k^0(T) = k^*(T) =$ the fixed terminal value. Thus

$$\int_0^T F_k \dot{\kappa}\, dt = -\int_0^T \left[\left(\frac{d}{dt} F_k \right) \kappa \right] dt$$

Hence, substituting back into (A.36), we have:

$$0 = \int_0^T \left(F_k - \frac{d}{dt} F_k \right) \kappa\, dt = \int_0^T J(t)\, dt \tag{A.38}$$

Now $F_k - (d/dt)F_k$ is independent of the choice of k^0. Suppose $F_k - (d/dt)F_k > 0$ at $t = \tau_0$. Then, because of the continuity of F_k and $(d/dt)F_k$, $F_k - (d/dt)F_k > 0$ over an entire open interval (τ_1, τ_2) which contains τ_0. We can still choose k^0 at will. Hence we may set:

$$k^0(t) = \begin{cases} k^*(t) & \text{for } t \leq \tau_1 \\ k^*(t) + (t - \tau_1)(\tau_2 - t) & \text{for } \tau_1 < t < \tau_2 \\ k^*(t) & \text{for } t \geq \tau_2 \end{cases}$$

Hence,

$$\kappa(t) = \begin{cases} 0 & t \leq \tau_1 \\ (t - \tau_1)(\tau_2 - t) > 0 & \tau_1 < t < \tau_2 \\ 0 & t \geq \tau_2 \end{cases}$$

We then have the situation shown diagramatically in Figure A.11. Hence,

$$\int_0^T \left(F_k - \frac{d}{dt} F_k \right) \kappa\, dt = \int_0^{\tau_1} \left(F_k - \frac{d}{dt} F_k \right)(0)\, dt + \int_{\tau_1}^{\tau_2} \left(F_k - \frac{d}{dt} F_k \right)(t - \tau_1)(\tau_2 - t)\, dt$$

$$+ \int_{\tau_2}^T \left(F_k - \frac{d}{dt} F_k \right)(0)\, dt > 0$$

which contradicts (A.38). Similarly, if $F_k - (d/dt)F_k < 0$ at τ_0, we can get a contradiction. This is true for all τ_0, $0 < \tau_0 < T$. Thus we have

$$F_k = \frac{d}{dt} F_k \qquad \text{(the Euler equation)} \tag{A.39}$$

We must realize that the Euler equation is exactly like the vanishing of the first derivatives. It is only a necessary condition for an *interior* optimum. It is unnecessary for boundary optima and it is not sufficient to rule out an interior *pessimum*, or a local but not global maximum.

A.4.3. Specializations and extensions

MISSING VARIABLES

(1) Suppose $F = F(k, t)$ so that $\partial F/\partial \dot{k} = 0$ (since $\dot{k}$ is absent in F); then (A.39) becomes $F_k = 0$. This verifies the procedure we used in Section A.1.

(2) Suppose $F = F(k, \dot{k})$ so that $\partial F/\partial t = 0$. We now have:

$$\frac{dF}{dt} = F_k \dot{k} + F_{\dot{k}} \ddot{k}$$

$$= \left(\frac{d}{dt} F_{\dot{k}} \right) \dot{k} + F_{\dot{k}} \ddot{k} \qquad \text{(using (A.39))} \tag{A.40}$$

$$= \frac{d}{dt}(\dot{k} F_{\dot{k}})$$

Thus, by integrating (A.40), we get

$$F - \dot{k}F_{\dot{k}} = \text{constant} \qquad \text{(first integral rule)} \tag{A.41}$$

Intuitively, if two functions have the same slopes at each instant, they can differ from each other, at most, by a constant, as shown in Figure A.12. This result is very useful in Section 10.1. We shall consider an example:

$$\text{Max} \int_0^1 (\beta k - \dot{k})^{1/2} dt \qquad k(0) = 1, \, k(1) = 0$$

Noting:

$$F = (\beta k - \dot{k})^{1/2}, \quad F_k = \tfrac{1}{2}\beta(\beta k - \dot{k})^{-1/2}, \quad F_{\dot{k}} = -\tfrac{1}{2}(\beta k - \dot{k})^{-1/2}, \quad \frac{d}{dt} F_{\dot{k}} = \tfrac{1}{4}(\beta k - \dot{k})^{-3/2}(\beta \dot{k} - \ddot{k})$$

we obtain the Euler equation:

$$\tfrac{1}{2}\beta(\beta k - \dot{k})^{-1/2} = \tfrac{1}{4}(\beta k - \dot{k})^{-3/2}(\beta \dot{k} - \ddot{k})$$

or

$$\ddot{k} - \beta \dot{k} = 2\beta(\dot{k} - \beta k)$$

or

$$\ddot{k} - 3\beta \dot{k} + 2\beta^2 k = 0$$

Alternatively, following the first integral rule,

$$F - \dot{k}F_{\dot{k}} = (\beta k - \dot{k})^{1/2} + \tfrac{1}{2}\dot{k}(\beta k - \dot{k})^{-1/2}$$

$$= \text{constant}$$

These two equations and the endpoint conditions $k(0) = 1$ and $k(1) = 0$ can be used to solve for $k(t)$. These results were used in the Ramsey-Chakravarty problem mentioned in the exercise problem of Chapter 10.

LAGRANGE MULTIPLIERS AND THE MAYER PROBLEM

1. Many dependent variables. Suppose the variational problem contains more than one dependent variable; the above problem remains the same except that k should be regarded as a vector.

2. Side conditions. Suppose the aforementioned variational problem is further associated with the following constraints:

$$\int_0^T G(k, \dot{k}, t) \, dt = 0$$

and

$$H(k, \dot{k}, t) = 0 \quad \text{for each } t, 0 \leq t \leq T$$

We shall state without proof that in this case we must formulate the Lagrangian:

$$\int_0^T \Lambda \, dt = \int_0^T [F + \lambda G + \mu(t)H] \, dt \tag{A.42}$$

where λ is a scalar and μ is a function both serving as Lagrange multipliers. The first-order necessary conditions now become:[7]

[7]The first equation stands for a vector of n equations of the form:

$$\frac{\partial \Lambda}{\partial k_j} - \frac{d}{dt}\left[\frac{\partial \Lambda}{\partial \dot{k}_j}\right] = 0$$

$$\frac{\partial \Lambda}{\partial k} - \frac{d}{dt}\left[\frac{\partial \Lambda}{\partial \dot{k}}\right] = 0$$

$$\int_0^T G\, dt = 0$$

$$H = 0 \quad \text{for all } t$$

We note that in the first (vector) equation, Λ takes the place of F.

3. The Mayer problem.   One form of the Mayer problem which appears in Chapter 9 takes the form:

$$\text{Max } V[k(T)]$$

subject to:

$$H(k, \dot{k}, t) = 0 \quad \text{for all } t,\, 0 \le t \le T$$

We now have a modified form of (A.42):

$$V + \int_0^T \mu(t)H\, dt \tag{A.43}$$

with the necessary conditions

$$\mu(t)\frac{\partial H}{dk} - \frac{d}{dt}\left[\mu(t)\frac{\partial H}{\partial \dot{k}}\right] = 0$$

$$H = 0 \quad \text{for all } t$$

$$\frac{\partial V}{\partial k(T)} = \mu(T)\frac{\partial H}{\partial k(T)}$$

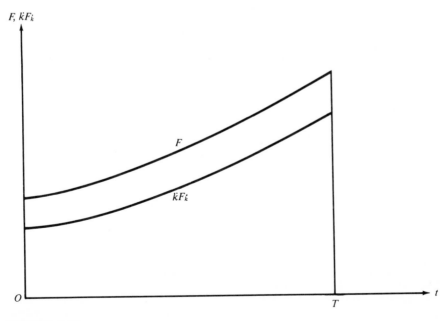

$F,\, kF_k$

F

kF_k

O

T

t

FIGURE A.12

The last (vector) equation is something new. Intuitively, it states that at the end of the interval $[0, T]$, the impact of an increase of k is felt directly through $\partial V/\partial k$. This is the set of conditions corresponding to the intertemporal efficiency conditions of Dorfman, Samuelson, and Solow.

A.5 THE MAXIMUM PRINCIPLE (OPTIMAL CONTROL THEORY)

Pontryagin's maximum principle is a method to solve variational problems both of the classical types (like those in Section A.4) and the nonclassical types. It is relatively simple to state the necessary conditions derived through such an approach. However, proving the underlying results involves mathematical concepts beyond the scope of this volume. We shall follow the work of Leitmann [5] and provide certain geometrical rationales for the central results.

A.5.1. Basic concepts

Define:

$\bar{x}$ as the n-dimensional *state vector*, characterizing the state of the system.
u as the m-dimensional *control vector*, taking values within a set U.
$\dot{\bar{x}} = \bar{f}(\bar{x}, u)$ as the *dynamic equation*, showing the rate of transformation of $\bar{x}$.
$\dot{x}_0 = f_0(\bar{x}, u)$ as the instantaneous *cost function*.
$\bar{x}^0$ as the initial state $\Big\}$
$\bar{x}^T$ as the final state $\Big\}$ both taken as given

and let

$$x_0(T) - x_0(0) = \int_0^T f_0(\bar{x}, u)\, dt$$

be the performance index to be minimized with $\bar{x}(0) = \bar{x}^0$ and $\bar{x}(T) = \bar{x}^T$.

$\bar{f}$ and f_0 possess continuous first partial derivatives with respect to all their arguments.

Note that we are now considering a simple problem with fixed endpoints $\bar{x}^0$ and $\bar{x}^T$, but with an undetermined time span from 0 to T and a time-independent cost function. Specifically, 0 and T are defined as those values of t where $\bar{x}(t)$ takes values of $\bar{x}^0$ and $\bar{x}^T$, respectively.

The problem we have can be written as:

$$\operatorname*{Min}_{u(t)\varepsilon U} \int_0^T f_0(\bar{x}, u)\, dt \tag{A.44}$$

subject to:

$$\dot{\bar{x}} = \bar{f}(\bar{x}, u) \tag{A.45}$$

and

$$\bar{x}(0) = \bar{x}^0; \qquad \bar{x}(T) = \bar{x}^T \tag{A.46}$$

We observe that for any admissible control, i.e., a u function with $u(t)$ belonging to U for $0 \le t \le T$, (A.45) becomes:

$$\dot{\bar{x}} = g(\bar{x}, t) \quad \text{where } g(\bar{x}, t) = \bar{f}[\bar{x}, u(t)]$$

which can be solved for $\bar{x}(t)$ in conjunction with $\bar{x}(0) = \bar{x}^0$. The resultant path, $\bar{x}(t)$, when substituted into (A.44), implies a given performance level.

For any given $u(t)$, the $(n+1)$-dimensional vector function $x(t) = [x_0(t), \bar{x}(t)]$ is called a trajectory. The trajectory which yields the minimum performance index among all trajectories under admissible controls and transforms the state vector from $\bar{x}^0$ to $\bar{x}^T$ is the optimal trajectory.

A.5.2. Primary results

Under the assumed conditions, the existence of an optimal trajectory $x^*(t)$ implies:
  (1) There exists a continuous vector function $\psi^*(t) \neq 0$ and $H = \psi^* \cdot f(x, u)$ such that:

$$\dot{x}_j^* = \frac{\partial H}{\partial \psi_j} \quad \text{and} \quad \dot{\psi}_j^* = -\frac{\partial H}{\partial x_j} \qquad j = 0, 1, ..., n \tag{A.47}$$

$$\underset{u \ in \ U}{\text{Max}} \ H(x^*, \psi^*, u) = H(x^*, \psi^*, u^*) \tag{A.48}$$

$$= 0$$

  (2) $\dot{\psi}_0^* = 0$ (since $\partial f_j/\partial x_0 = 0$ for $j = 0, 1, ..., n$). Usually we can set $\psi_0 = -1$.
  The H function is called a "Hamiltonian," while the ψ_j's are called adjoint (dual) variables. From (A.47), we have $2(n+1)$ differential equations. Since $\bar{x}(0)$ and $\bar{x}(T)$ are known quantities, while ψ_0 is a constant function presumably with value (-1), we then have $2(n+1)$ boundary conditions for all these $2(n+1)$ equations. The control vector $u(t)$ is determined by (A.48).

  However, proper understanding of the Pontryagin theory can best be gained through comparisons among this theory, the classical variational theory, and the "static" Lagrangian formulation.

A.5.3. Relations to the calculus of variations and the static Langrangian formulation

COMPARISON WITH CALCULUS OF VARIATIONS

Most problems solvable with the maximum principle can be solved by means of the classical calculus of variations.

  However, there are two principal differences, one concerned with the point of view and the other with convenience. Theoretically, the end product of optimal control analysis is "synthesis," which expresses the optimal value of the control vector u as a policy function of the state vector x. The block diagram of Figure A.13 depicts the working of such a policy function.

  The optimal control theory offers a "closed loop" control because the optimal control u is related to the present state, while the closed loop control modifies the state $(x \to u \to \dot{x} \to x$, closing the loop). In contrast, traditional variational analysis relates the optimal control to the historical time t, after specifying the initial state $x(0)$ one is concerned with. In this case, $x(0)$ is called the "open-loop" control. Traditional variational analysis has to solve the problem each time for a different initial state. Optimal control analysis solves a family of infinitely many problems all at once, because it tells us what to do wherever we are, by means of the policy function. In practice, synthesis is often difficult to achieve. Therefore, the difference in viewpoints (closed vs. open loops) is often of only academic interest.

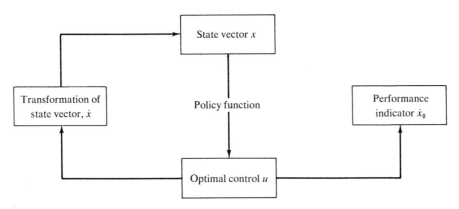

FIGURE A.13

On the more pragmatic level, when the control variable is restricted to take values in a given set (e.g., the educational labor force must be a non-negative fraction of the total labor force), the maximum principle provides a method of solution both convenient and illuminating. Moreover, the adjoint variables serving as shadow prices in economics come as a by-product. Thus, the maximum principle sometimes also provides a convenient way to obtain the phase diagram, as we shall see in application to Section 10.2.

At the present, we shall transform the variational problem in Section A.4 into the maximum principle format. The problem in (A.34) is:

$$\underset{k(t)}{\text{Max }} V = \int_0^T F(t, k, \dot{k})\, dt \qquad k(0) = k_0 \text{ and } k(T) = k_T$$

We now first prepare a table of comparative notations:

Variational problem	Maximum principle format
V	$x_0(T)$ ($x_0(0)$ being 0)
F	$-f_0$
k	x_1
t (in F)	x_2
t (in dt)	t
$\dot{k}$	u

Next, we can set up the problem:

$$\text{Min} \int_0^T f_0(x_1, x_2, u)\, dt$$

subject to:

$$\dot{x}_1 = u \qquad \dot{x}_2 = 1$$

$$\bar{x}(0) = (k_0, 0) \qquad \bar{x}(T) = (k_T, T)$$

The Hamiltonian takes the forms:

$$H = \psi_0 f_0(x_1, x_2, u) + \psi_1 u + \psi_2$$

$$= F(x_1, x_2, u) + \psi_1 u + \psi_2 \qquad \text{(assuming } \psi_0 \neq 0, \text{ hence setting it equal to } -1)$$

The optimal trajectory is associated with (x^*, ψ^*), such that

$$\dot{x}_1 = \frac{\partial H}{\partial \psi_1} = u$$

$$\dot{x}_2 = \frac{\partial H}{\partial \psi_2} = 1$$

$$\dot{\psi}_1 = -\frac{\partial H}{\partial x_1} = -\frac{\partial F}{\partial x_1} \tag{A.49}$$

$$\dot{\psi}_2 = -\frac{\partial H}{\partial x_2} = -\frac{\partial F}{\partial x_2}$$

$$0 = \frac{\partial H}{\partial u} = \frac{\partial F}{\partial u} + \psi_1$$

$$0 = H$$

From the first condition in (A.49), we can substitute $\dot{x}_1$ for u in the fifth condition. Taking the time derivative of the resultant equation and eliminating $\dot{\psi}_1$ from the third condition, we get the Euler equation:

$$\frac{\partial F}{\partial x_1} = \frac{d}{dt}\left(\frac{\partial F}{\partial \dot{x}_1}\right) \qquad (A.39)$$

If t does not enter into F, then from the fourth condition ψ_2 is a constant. Writing out the expression of H in the sixth condition, and rearranging, we get the "first integral rule":

$$0 = F + \psi_1\dot{x}_1 + \psi_2 \qquad \text{(using the first condition of (A.49))}$$

$$= F - \left(\frac{\partial F}{\partial u}\right)\dot{x}_1 + \psi_2 \qquad \text{(using the fifth condition of (A.49))} \qquad (A41')$$

$$= F - \dot{x}_1\left(\frac{\partial F}{\partial \dot{x}_1}\right) - \text{constant} \qquad \text{(again using the first condition)}$$

In the above demonstration, while the maximum principle arrives at the Euler equation (and if $\partial F/\partial t = 0$, also the first integral rule) along a slightly more roundabout route than the classical method, we can obtain the $\psi_1(t)$ function from the fifth condition in (A.49). $-\psi_1(0)$ and $-\psi_1(T)$ denote the rate of change of the attainable utility sum if k_0 and k_T were slightly different. On the other hand, $-\psi_2(t) = F - \dot{k}F_k$ (from the sixth condition in (A.49)). $-\psi_2(T)$ measures the effect on the utility sum by a longer planning horizon T. $-[\psi_2(0)-\psi_2(T)]$, on the other hand, measures the effect of "postponing the T-year plan" for a short interval. All four effects are worthy by-products of the maximum principle.

RELATION WITH THE STATIC LAGRANGIAN FORMULATION

An intuitive interpretation of the maximum principle is possible by comparison with the static Lagrangian problem:

$$\text{Max } U(x) \text{ subject to } p \cdot x = I$$

This problem, where both p and x are n-dimensional vectors, has the Lagrangian:

$$\Lambda = U(x) - \lambda[(p \cdot x) - I]$$
$$= x \cdot \{(\text{grad } U - \lambda p)\} + [(U - x \cdot \text{grad } U) + \lambda I]$$

where grad $U = (\partial U/\partial x_1, ..., \partial U/\partial x_n)$. Term by term, the composition of Λ is:

Utility gain (loss) in trading: $x \cdot (\text{grad } U - \lambda p)$
(Marshallian) consumer's surplus: $U - x \cdot \text{grad } U$
Marginally imputed utility on income: λI

Taking p as given, the *maximum attainable* utility is represented by the last two terms and is determined by the preference pattern (U) and the income level. Since the sum of these two is defined as the potential optimal level, trading can never increase utility. At best, trading realizes what is potentially one's due. Nonoptimal trading, on the other hand, can lead to losses.

In the Pontryagin case, let us assume that $\psi_0 = -1$ and $f_0(x, u, t) = -F(x, u, t)$; the Lagrangian formulation will then be:

$$\Lambda = \int_0^T \{F(x, u, t) + \bar{\psi} \cdot [\dot{\bar{x}} - \bar{f}(x, u, t)]\}\, dt$$

$$= \int_0^T [F(x, u, t) - \bar{\psi} \cdot \bar{f}]\, dt + \left\{[\bar{\psi}(T) \cdot \bar{x}(T) - \bar{\psi}(0) \cdot \bar{x}(0)] - \int_0^T \dot{\bar{\psi}}(t)x(t)dt\right\}$$

$$= -\int_0^T H\, dt + \left\{[\bar{\phi}(0)\bar{x}(0) - \bar{\phi}(T)\bar{x}(T)] + \int_0^T \dot{\bar{\phi}}(t)x(t)dt\right\}$$

where $\bar{\phi} = -\bar{\psi}$.

The term $[\bar{\phi}(0)\bar{x}(0) - \bar{\phi}(T)\bar{x}(T)]$ represents the "using up" of the imputed value of resources ($\bar{\phi}$ standing for the shadow price vector). The integral $\int \dot{\bar{\phi}} x$ designates the appreciation of imputed value of stocks on hand over the entire period. These terms correspond to the term $[(U - x \cdot \text{grad } U) + \lambda I]$ in the static analog.[8] The Hamiltonian part can never be positive at any point of time under any feasible policy. On the other hand, any nonoptimal policy may incur a negative Hamiltonian and result in utility losses. The optimal plan here maximizes the Hamiltonian to zero, just as the best trading policy in the static case maximizes $\{x \cdot (\text{grad } U - \lambda p)\}$ to zero.[9]

The above intuitive interpretation lays the foundation for our discussion of a graphical justification of the results in Section A.5.2. The tools are due to Leitmann [5].

A.5.4. Graphical justifications

PRELIMINARIES

We now give a simple economic example to illustrate Leitmann's graphic derivation of the maximal principle.

Suppose the total cumulative cost is to be minimized in stockpiling certain capital stock, $\bar{x}^T$. At the present moment, certain (initial) stocks $\bar{x}^0$ have been cumulated at a given (initial) cost: x_0^0. The total cumulative cost may be expressed as

$$x_0(T) = x_0^0 + \int_0^T f_0 \, dt \tag{A.50}$$

Following an optimal policy, the minimal total cumulative cost can be written as a function:

$$\Phi(x_0^0, \bar{x}^0) = x_0^*(T) \tag{A.50a}$$

where various combinations of x_0^0 and $\bar{x}^0$ corresponding to the same level of $x_0^*(T)$ form a hypersurface.

For the sake of convenience in graphical depiction, we shall first assume that there is only one type of capital goods being stockpiled, i.e., $\bar{x}^0 = x_1^0$. Later we assume that there are two types of capital goods. Our discussion actually holds for any arbitrarily large (but finite) number of goods.

The S curve in Figure A.14a is a specimen of this iso-minimal cost accumulation locus (IMCAL, for short). For definiteness we assume the algebraic form:

$$x_0^0 - \sqrt{x_1^0} + \sqrt{x_1(T)} = x_0^*(T) \tag{A.50b}$$

with $x_1(T) = 4$, the desired terminal capital and $x_0^*(T) = 2$, the minimum cost of accumulation.

The vertical line $x_1(T) = 4$ is a "finishing line" all trajectories must reach. The problem is how to reach that line at the lowest cumulate cost.

For $x_0^*(T) = 2$, the suitable "initial conditions" include:
(a) Initial capital: 1 unit; initial cumulate cost: 1
(b) Initial capital: $2\frac{1}{4}$ units; initial cumulate cost: 1.5,
    etc.
These combinations are shown in Figure A.14a.

The concavity of the IMCAL may reflect the existence of learning phenomena. One may double the stock without doubling the cumulate cost. Hence, this IMCAL is not the total cost curve we know in micro theory.

By varying the value of $x_0^*(T)$, we get a whole family of IMCAL, three of which are shown in Figure A.14a. From the additive nature of x_0^0 in the Φ function, the whole family of IMCAL can be

---

[8]Strictly speaking, the term $\int \dot{\bar{\phi}} x$ can hardly appear in the static version. Stock can gain value (in utils) due to nothing else but the passing of time. It bears a relation to $[\bar{\phi}(0) \cdot \bar{x}(0) - \bar{\phi}(T) \cdot \bar{x}(T)]$ akin to the one relating interest income to principal.

[9]There is, of course, another difference between the two models. p is given by market forces in the static analog, while ψ appears as a shadow price vector implied by the optimization operations.

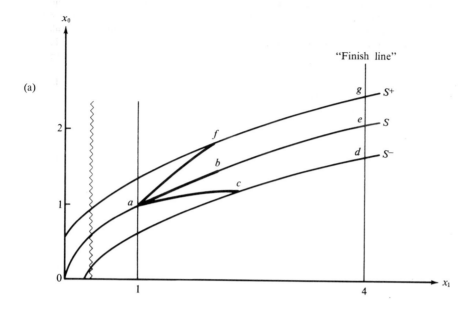

(a)

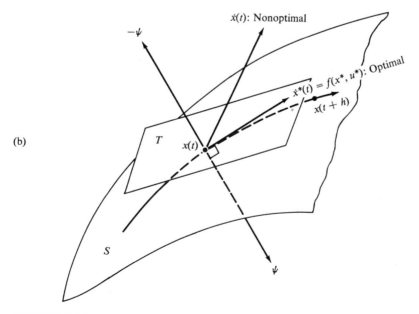

(b)

FIGURE A.14

obtained by a vertical "translation" (displacement) of any member of the family. S^- shows that if it were possible to accumulate one unit of initial stock at an initial cumulate cost of $\frac{1}{2}$, then the accumulation of 4 units can be accomplished at a cumulate cost of $1\frac{1}{2}$. S^+ shows if (out of previous mistakes, for example) 1 unit of initial capital is accumulated at an initial cost of 1.5, then the minimal cumulate cost, starting from that position, is 2.5.

The significance of the above analysis is that:

(1) No feasible trajectory can cross under any IMCAL.

(2) Any optimal feasible trajectory must *lie along* one IMCAL.

These two preliminary results are shown in Figure A.14a.

If ac is a feasible trajectory (i.e., it crosses under the IMCAL S and reaches S^- at c), then the trajectory acd is also. At d, it accomplishes a desired capital accumulation at a lower total cumulate cost than at e. This contradicts the definition that S is an IMCAL (since the cost it incurs is not minimal). Since S^- is any IMCAL below S, result (1) is proved.

Suppose af is an arc of an optimal feasible trajectory. Since f is on S^+, result (1) states that the said trajectory cannot go under S^+ again. Therefore the cumulate total cost must at least be what is represented by g on the finishing line, which is higher than what can be attained at e along the S surface. This contradicts the claim that af is an arc of an optimal trajectory, proving result (2).

Following Leitmann, we shall only consider the case where along the optimal trajectory the gradient of $\Phi = (1, \partial\Phi/\partial x_{01}, ..., \partial\Phi/\partial x_{0n})$ exists. Geometrically, this implies that the surface does not have a "vertical" tangent plane (in Figure A.14) along the optimal trajectory. Alternatively speaking, this rules out a surface S whose tangent plane contains some lines parallel to the x_0 axis. In Figure A.14a, this restriction means that the portion of the IMCALs S, S^+, S^- near the origin must be ruled out as inappropriate. This is shown by the saw-tooth line of the graph. The reason is that the tangents of these IMCALs at the origin have a vertical slope.

DERIVATION OF THE MAIN RESULTS

1. $H[x^*, \psi, u^*] = 0$.   After making the assumption that grad Φ exists (i.e., it is finite), we define $\psi(t) = [\psi_0(t), \bar{\psi}(t)]$ as the vector perpendicular to S at the point $x^*(t) = [x_0^*(t), \bar{x}^*(t)]$ and $\psi_0(t) < 0$. Since the optimal trajectory $x^*(t)$ is entirely in S (preliminary result (2)), $\dot{x}^*(t)$ at $x^*(t)$ is contained in the tangent plane of S at $x^*(t)$. Since $\psi(t)$ is perpendicular to the tangent plane of S at $x^*(t)$, it must be perpendicular to $\dot{x}^*(t)$ in S.

We note that the analytical definition of an inner product $\psi \cdot f$ is:

$$\psi \cdot f \equiv (\psi \cdot \psi)^{1/2}(f \cdot f)^{1/2} \cos \theta$$

where θ is the angle between ψ and f. Since $\cos(\pi/2) = 0$, and since this holds true for all t, we have:

$$\psi(t) \cdot \dot{x}^*(t) \equiv \psi(t) \cdot f[x^*(t), u^*(t)]$$

$$\equiv 0 \qquad\qquad\qquad\qquad \text{(A.48a)}$$

$$\equiv H[x^*(t), \psi(t), u^*(t)]$$

This proves part of (A.48), namely, that the Hamiltonian along the optimal trajectory has zero value.

Before we go on, we present a two-capital-goods version of Figure A.14a in Figure A.14b. When S is a curve, the optimal trajectory coincides with S. When S is of a higher dimension, then the optimal trajectory $x(t)$ lies in S. Two points $x^*(t)$ and $x^*(t+h)$ are shown in Figure A.14b. $\dot{x}^*(t) =$ Lim $h \to 0 [x^*(t+h) - x^*(t)]/h$ is shown as an arrow contained in the tangent plane T of S at $x^*(t)$. ψ is perpendicular to S at $x^*(t)$, and hence it is automatically perpendicular to T as well as to any line in T through $x^*(t)$, which includes $\dot{x}^*(t)$. Now, at $x^*(t)$ we set $\psi_0 < 0$ so that $\psi(t)$ points downward rather than upward. Actually, this is a matter of convention.

We now note that for θ obtuse, i.e., $\pi > \theta > \pi/2$, $\cos \theta < 0$. This result is useful to prove the following.

2. Max $H[x^*, \psi^*, u] = H[x^*, \psi^*, u^*]$.   Preliminary result (1) states that $x^*(t)$ can never cross under S. Hence the angle θ is always obtuse or rectangular (from Figure A.14b), which means that $H = \psi \cdot f \leqq 0$ along all *feasible* trajectories.

Along the optimal trajectory, $H = 0$, proving the other part of (A.48).

In the maximization of H with respect to u in U, we take ψ^* as given. Because u^* regulates the evolution of the state variables through $\dot{x} = f$, when x^* moves along S, the normal to S, i.e., ψ^*, also shifts in time. We now proceed to prove that:

3. $\psi^* = -\partial H/\partial x$.   Our proof is constructive. We consider:

(a) The evolution of the tangent plane T as characterized by a given set of linearly independent vectors, $v_1, \ldots, v_n$, which uniquely determines T.

(b) The evolution of a system of equations:

$$\psi(0) = -\,\text{grad } \Phi \quad \text{at } t = 0 \tag{A.51}$$

$$\dot{\psi}(t) = -\frac{\partial H}{\partial x} = -J'\psi$$

where

$$J' = \begin{bmatrix} \dfrac{\partial f_0}{\partial x_0} & \dfrac{\partial f_1}{\partial x_0} & \cdots & \dfrac{\partial f_n}{\partial x_0} \\[2ex] \dfrac{\partial f_0}{\partial x_1} & \dfrac{\partial f_1}{\partial x_1} & \cdots & \dfrac{\partial f_n}{\partial x_1} \\[2ex] \vdots & \vdots & & \vdots \\[2ex] \dfrac{\partial f_0}{\partial x_n} & \dfrac{\partial f_1}{\partial x_n} & \cdots & \dfrac{\partial f_n}{\partial x_n} \end{bmatrix}$$

We shall show that $\psi(t)$ is perpendicular to all v, hence it is perpendicular to S corresponding to the qualification for $\psi^*(t)$. So $\psi = \psi^*$.

(1) We observe that the optimal trajectory $x^*(t)$ "carries along" a tangent plane to S at $x^*(t)$. Since S is in $(n+1)$-dimensional space, the tangent plane must be $(n+1)-1 = n$-dimensional, spanned by n linearly independent vectors: $v_1(t), \ldots, v_n(t)$, as shown in Figure A.15. Since any point on a tangent plane is a sum of the tangent point and a vector in the tangent plane, we have, by Taylor expansion,

$$\frac{d}{dt}(x^* + v_j) = \dot{x}^* + \dot{v}_j = f[(\dot{x}^* + v_j), u]$$

$$= f[x^*(t), u(t)] + Jv_j(t) \qquad j = 1, \ldots, n$$

where

$$J = \begin{bmatrix} \dfrac{\partial f_0}{\partial x_0} & \dfrac{\partial f_0}{\partial x_1} & \cdots & \dfrac{\partial f_0}{\partial x_n} \\[2ex] \dfrac{\partial f_1}{\partial x_0} & \dfrac{\partial f_1}{\partial x_1} & \cdots & \dfrac{\partial f_1}{\partial x_n} \\[2ex] \vdots & \vdots & & \vdots \\[2ex] \dfrac{\partial f_n}{\partial x_0} & \dfrac{\partial f_n}{\partial x_1} & \cdots & \dfrac{\partial f_n}{\partial x_n} \end{bmatrix}$$

But $\dot{x}^* = f$; hence:

$$\dot{v}_j = Jv_j \tag{A.52}$$

(2) $\psi(0) \cdot v_j(0) = 0$ for all j by the definition of $\psi(0)$ as a normal to S. Moreover,

$$\frac{d}{dt}[\psi(t) \cdot v_j(t)] = \psi \cdot \dot{v}_j + \dot{\psi} \cdot v_j$$

$$= \psi' J v_j - v_j' J' \psi \qquad \text{(by (A.51) and (A.52))}$$

$$= 0$$

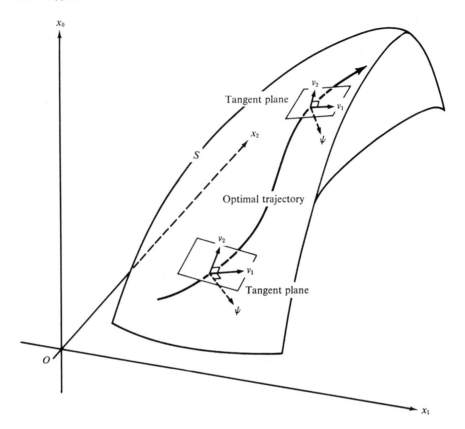

FIGURE A.15

Therefore:

$$\psi(t)\cdot v_j(t) = \psi(0)\cdot v_j(0) + \int_0^t \frac{d}{ds}\left[\psi(s)\cdot v_j(s)\right] ds \tag{A.53}$$

$$= 0 + \int_0^t (0)\, ds = 0$$

At any $x(t)$ on S, $\psi(t)$ is a normal to S satisfying the requirement for the optimal adjoint vector $\psi^*(t)$ discussed in **2**. We can hence set $\psi^*(t) = \psi(t)$. Thus $\psi^*(t)$ satisfies the second equation of (A.47).

A.5.5. Generalization and extensions

1. $\phi_0 = 0$. In this case, the geometric treatment does not hold, yet (A.47) and (A.48) remain valid. We rarely encounter such a case in economics.

2. Initial and terminal transversality conditions. If the endpoints $\bar{x}^0$ and $\bar{x}^T$ are not determined and the only conditions are $\theta^0(\bar{x}^0) = 0$ and $\theta^T(\bar{x}^T) = 0$, both θ^0 and θ^T may be vector conditions of dimensions lower than N. These are called transversality conditions. It can be shown that the results in Section A.5.3 remain valid. Moreover, $\psi^*(0)$ ($\psi^*(T)$) should be perpendicular to the plane containing the locus $\theta^0(\bar{x}^0) = 0$ [$\theta^T(\bar{x}^T) = 0$].

3. f_j **contains the time variable** t. After setting $x_{N+1} = t$, the conclusions above remain valid.

4. A fixed time interval. In this case, after considering t as an extra state variable as in 3, above, we can further specify the initial and terminal points of time as transversality conditions.

5. Time optimality. The function f_0 may take the special form $f_0 \equiv 1$. In this case, it is the sojourn time that is to be minimized. Problems of this type are called time-optimal problems.

6. The restriction on state variables. This leads to rather complicated analysis. The reader is referred to Leitmann [5].

A.6 BACKGROUND READINGS

For readers intending to do research work in various topics of growth theory, the material presented in this appendix is obviously inadequate. The references listed below may be helpful for those who wish additional analytical tools.

(1) Differentiation of integrals with respect to a parameter. The derivation of this rather simple formula can be found in:

Apostol, T. M., *Mathematical Analysis, A Modern Approach to Advanced Calculus*, Addison-Wesley, Reading, Mass., 1957, p. 220.

(2) Constrained maximization. An excellent treatise can be found in:

Hadley, George, *Nonlinear and Dynamic Programming*, Addison-Wesley, Reading, Mass., 1964. Chapters 3 and 6, pp. 53–103 and 185–211.

Deeper mathematical insight can be obtained from:

Gamkrelidze, R. V., "Extremal Problems in Finite Dimensional Spaces," *in Journal of Optimization, Theory and Applications*, Vol. 1, 1967, pp. 173–189.

(3) Difference equations. A useful reference is:

Allen, R. G. D., *Mathematical Economics*, Macmillan, London, 1957, Ch. 6, pp. 176–208.

A more fundamental point of view was taken by Samuelson in:

Samuelson, P. A., *Foundations of Economic Analysis*, Harvard University Press, Cambridge, Mass., 1947, Appendix B, pp. 380–439.

An old but encyclopedic treatise of the subject is:

Jordán, K., *Calculus of Finite Differences*, Chelsea, New York, 1947.

(4) Differential equations. Most "mathematics for economists" books emphasize linear differential equations, which have very little use in the growth literature. A very good source dealing with existence and stability of solutions as well as the phase diagram is:

Pontryagin, L. S., *Ordinary Differential Equations*, Addison-Wesley, Reading, Mass., 1962.

On vectorial differential equations, one may also refer to:

Bellman, R., *Matrix Analysis*, McGraw-Hill, New York, 1960, Ch. 10, pp. 159–182.

(5) Calculus of variations. A good book on this topic is:

Gel'fand, I. M. and Fomin, S. V., *Calculus of Variations*, Prentice-Hall, Englewood Cliffs, N.J., 1963.

A deeper book is:

Akhiezer, I. N., *The Calculus of Variations* (translated by Alice H. Frink), Blaisdell, Waltham, Mass., 1962.

(6) Maximum principle. Our discussion follows the following source:

Leitmann, George, *An Introduction to Optimal Control*, McGraw-Hill, New York, 1966.

(7) "Mathematics for Economists." Areas (5) and (6) are covered by two books to appear soon:

Hadley, George, and Kemp, M. C., *Economic Applications of Variational Methods*, North-Holland Pub. Co., Amsterdam (forthcoming).

Intriligator, M. D., *Mathematical Optimization and Economic Theory*, Prentice-Hall, Englewood Cliffs, N.J., 1971.

REFERENCES

[1] Hicks, J. R., "Mr. Harrod's Dynamic Theory," *Economica*, N.S., 16, May, 1949.

[2] Hadley, George, *Linear Algebra*, Addison-Wesley, Reading, Mass., 1961.

[3] Samuelson, P. A., *Foundation of Economic Analysis*, Harvard University Press, Cambridge, Mass., 1947.

[4] Vanek, J., "Toward a More General Theory of Growth with Technological Change,"

Economic Journal, Vol. LXXVI, 1966, pp. 841–854.

[5] Leitmann, George, *Optimal Control Theory*, McGraw-Hill, New York, 1966.

EXERCISES

A.1. Consider the problem:

$$\text{Max } \int_0^T (1 - w_0 e^{\lambda t} b) \frac{e^{-rt}}{a} \, dt \qquad \text{for non-negative } T$$

Show that the first-order necessary conditions are:

$$T \geq 0$$
$$1 \geq w_0 e^{\lambda t} b$$
$$T(1 - w_0 e^{\lambda t} b) = 0$$

A.2. Consider the problem:

$$\text{Max } \int_0^T u[c(t)] \, dt$$

subject to:

$$\int_0^T [c(t) - w(t)] e^{-rt} \, dt = 0 \qquad c(t) \geq 0$$

Prove that for an interior optimum [$c(t) > 0$ for all t], $u'[c(t)]/u'[c(0)] = e^{-rt}$.

A.3. (a) Solve the difference equations:

  (i) $Q(t) - 1.05Q(t-1) = 0$
  (ii) $Q(t) - 1.05Q(t-1) = (1.02)^t$

(b) Prove that the solution of (a)-(i) is relatively stable with respect to the 5% growth path.

A.4. (a) Solve analytically the differential equation:

$$\dot{P} = P(1 - P)$$

This can be done by first making the partial fraction expansion:

$$\frac{1}{P(1-P)} = \frac{1}{P} + \frac{1}{1-P}$$

and then following the "variable separable" approach.

Verify that the solution is the well-known "growth curve"

$$P(t) = \frac{1}{1 + (1/P(0) - 1)e^t}$$

which was used by Samuelson in his population model and by Jorgenson in his dual economy model.

(b) Analyze the stability property of this equation through a phase diagram.

A.5. In Figure A.6a, replace the k-axis by a Δk-axis (where $\Delta k = k_{t+1} - k_t$). From any point (k, o) on the k-axis plot a vertical line to determine the point $(k_t, \Delta k)$ where $\Delta k = G(k_t)$. Draw a 45° line from $(k_t, \Delta k)$ to determine k_{t+1}. By iteration show that the dynamic system is stable.

A.6. (a) Solve the following problem by both the traditional calculus of variations method and the maximum principle:

$$\text{Max } \int_0^T e^{-rt} \left[\dot{x} - \frac{\dot{x}^2}{2} + \dot{x}x \right] dt$$

(b) Assuming that $r = 4$, solve the Euler differential equation to find the general form of $x(t)$.

index